SUBSCRIBE

and receive 1 year (26 issues) of Antique Trader print or digital version.

Antique Trader is a magazine in which your interest and passion for antiques and collectibles is encouraged, celebrated and expanded. Every issue contains exclusive content from industry-leading authors and experts in bottles, fine art, dolls, furniture, antiques business, and lamps, among others. Plus, you'll also find current antique market trends and values, profiles of fellow collectors and their treasures, expert appraisals, as well as in-depth insights on niche collectibles.

Our Pledge to You

100% SATISFACTION GUARANTEE!

You can cancel anytime, for any reason, no questions asked, and receive

COLLECTING ROCKS, GEMS & MINERALS

10 things you didn't know

1 Collectors of rocks, gems and minerals (rockhounds) are an organized and active community with two magazines serving the community for a minimum of 40 years. In fact, Rocks & Minerals magazine has been in publication since 1926, while Rocks & Gems magazine is 41 years young.

2 A large rose and smoky quartz (pictured at right), measuring 15½ inches by 8 inches, sold for $662,500 during Heritage Auctions' Nature & Science Signature Auction June 2, 2013 – part of the largest fine mineral collection ever to appear at auction. The quartz, which was discovered in a small mine in Brazil sometime between 1959 and 1972, is referred to as the "La Madona Rosa," for what some believe is an uncanny resemblance to modern day images of the Virgin Mary.

A lattice of elongated Copper crystals discovered in the Keweenaw Peninsula, Mich. sold for $22,500 at Heritage Auctions' June 2 Nature & Science Auction.

3 There are several hundred rock, gem and mineral shows held each year in the U.S. Show information can be found at www.rockngems.com and www.rocksandminerals.com.

4 The Smithsonian Museum of Natural History houses approximately 350,000 mineral specimens

and 10,000 gems – one of the largest collections in the world.

5 A Linarite specimen (shown above right), a rarely seen copper mineral – discovered during a dig in New Mexico in 1979, sold for $158,500 during Heritage Auctions' June 2, 2013 auction.

6 There are more than 80 museums that contain significant gems and minerals exhibit/collections around the world. More than half of all those are located in North America.

7 Examples of metallurgy (definition: *Art and science of extracting metals from their ores and modifying the metals for use*) date back more than 7,000 years, based on discovery of jewelry made from forged copper.

8 Rock and mineral collecting expeditions are growing in popularity. Companies like Geology Adventures lead tours stateside and abroad.

9 A sample of ore, from the famous Cripple Creek mining region of Colorado, sold for $2,375 in June 2013. The high-grade sample is a gray wall rock, which sandwiches a ribbon of purple Flurite that cuts through brassy, bladed crystals of Calaverite: Gold Telluride.

10 A great portal to locating collecting clubs in your area is www.gemandmineral.com/states.html.

Compiled by Antoinette Rahn

Sources: "Collecting Rocks, Gems and Minerals," by Patti Polk, Webster's Dictionary, Smithsonian National Museum of Natural History, Heritage Auctions, American Geoscience Institute, The Gem and Mineral Exploration Company

All photos courtesy Heritage Auctions

Above, Linarite mineral sample, fetched $158,500, while the rose and smoky quartz specimen at right claimed top lot, selling for $662,500, during a June 2 auction at Heritage Auctions.

ANTIQUES&COLLECTIBLES

2014 PRICE GUIDE • Eric Bradley

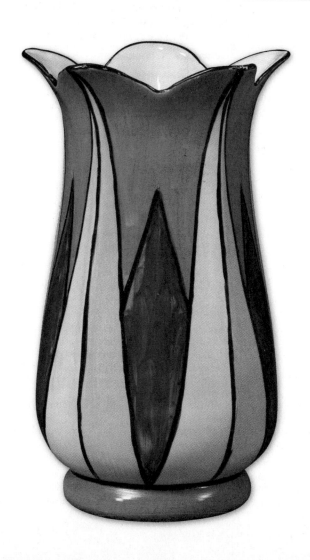

Copyright ©2013 F+W Media, Inc.

Published by

Krause Publications, a division of F+W Media, Inc.
700 East State Street • Iola, WI 54990-0001
715-445-2214 • 888-457-2873
www.krausebooks.com

To order books or other products call toll-free 1-800-258-0929
or visit us online at www.krausebooks.com

ISSN: 1536-2884

ISBN-13: 978-1-4402-3664-8
ISBN-10: 1-4402-3664-X

Cover Design by Sharon Bartsch
Designed by Jana Tappa
Edited by Eric Bradley

Printed in the United States of America

Front cover, clockwise from top:
Tiffany Studios Poppy table lamp, leaded shade with orange poppies against a butterscotch background, four-legged urn base with three-light cluster, $35,000 (James D. Julia, Inc.)
Art Nouveau diamond, demantoid garnet, plique à jour enamel, platinum-topped gold brooch, August Wilhelm Holström, Fabergé Workmaster, Russian hallmarks, 1-3/4" x 1-1/2", $5,975 (Heritage Auctions)
Clarice Cliff Bizarre ware vase, England, 20th century, Newport Pottery Co., tulip-form, polychrome geometric pattern, shape 361, backstamp, 8-1/4" h., $652 (Skinner, Inc.)
"Superman" (Columbia, 1948), three sheet (41" x 81"), large format poster featuring ultimate superhero in action, $8,963 (Heritage Auctions)
Pennsylvania painted pine spice chest, 19th century, smoke decoration on red ground, 16-1/2" h. x 17" w., $1,778 (Pook & Pook, Inc.)

Back cover:
Herringbone water pitcher, blue opalescent, translucent blue applied handle, outstanding color depth and opalescence, fourth quarter 19th century, 9" h., $1,495 (Jeffrey S. Evans & Associates)
Sony TR-510 transistor radio, five-transistor version of Sony's famous 610, Japan, 1959, $70-$100 (Michael Jack and Steve Lock)

Contents

LISTINGS

Introduction

Eric Bradley

Thirty years ago, this price guide you are holding was as thin as your average magazine. Back then, the easiest way to trade antiques was through classified ads. Antiques were purchased sight unseen and the first check to reach the seller by "snail mail" sealed the deal. Auctioneers were primarily in the estate liquidation service and rarely reached an audience outside their own counties. No one imagined an i-anything.

During the last three decades technology boomed, tastes changed and this – the 30th edition of the *Antique Trader Antiques & Collectibles Price Guide* – now tips the scales with a hefty 800+ pages and gives you a comprehensive survey of the world's most popular fine art and collectibles.

This book is overflowing with color photographs to help you focus your collecting instincts or teach you something you didn't know about the things you already own. You'll find advice and lessons from experts in the field and collectors themselves. Categories cover a broad range of items being collected today. The values for most entries are actual prices paid at auction at established and trustworthy auction houses.

The items collectors are interested in changes each year. These trends can be affected by popular culture, the growing number of antiques reality television shows, and even the greater economy as a whole.

Here's a look at some markets that are currently hot or on the rise:

- Sports memorabilia
- World and ancient coins
- Western art
- Historical Americana
- Vintage advertising
- Mid-century modern decorative arts
- Vintage firearms
- Superb examples of fine minerals and natural history
- Celebrity or entertainment memorabilia
- Space memorabilia (especially items from NASA's Apollo lunar exploration missions)
- High-grade comic books across all eras
- Jewelry (especially large colored diamonds and gemstones)
- Books (signed first editions, Americana, science fiction, and fantasy)
- Illustration art
- Comic art

The Amazing Spider-Man #19 (Marvel, 1964), CGC NM+ 9.6, cream to off-white pages, Steve Ditko cover and art. **$1,673**

Eric Bradley is public relations associate at Heritage Auctions, ha.com, the world's third largest auction house and the world's largest collectibles auctioneer, and is editor of the Antique Trader Antiques & Collectibles Price Guide, *America's No. 1 selling reference book on collectibles. He is the former editor of* Antique Trader *magazine and is an award-winning investigative journalist with a degree in economics. Bradley's work has received press from* The New York Times *and* The Wall Street Journal. *He also served as a featured guest speaker on investing with antiques. He lives in Dallas with his wife, Kelly, and their three children, Patrick, Olivia and Megan.*

Collecting trends are influenced by a number of factors:

1. The average American collector is still very much feeling the effects of The Great Recession and its weak recovery. This could explain why mid-range antiques and collectibles have seen little to no increase in value, however, flea markets are booming nationwide as collectors satisfy the urge to hunt for new finds.

2. Many financial advisors are instructing high net worth individuals to allocate as much as 20 percent of their wealth in non-traditional assets such as fine art and collectibles. This protects the purchase price from tax increases and offering better returns than what can be found in the unpredictable stock market and low-yield bond market. This explains why the very best examples in every category continue to set new records each year.

3. A rapidly growing middle class in Brazil, India, China, and Russia is fueling demand for jewelry, art, wine, and gold. No wonder, since all four easily hold up as a reliable store of wealth, can cross between borders, and can become fairly liquid on short notice.

4. We are in the midst of the greatest transfer of assets in human history. Baby Boomers (generally referred to people born between 1946 and 1964) stand to inherit an estimated $12 trillion during the next few decades. One study estimates their median inheritance to be about $64,000. However, Baby Boomers themselves are expected to bequeath or transfer a staggering $30 trillion to their heirs during the next 30 to 40 years. According to a 2010 MetLife study, roughly 10 percent of the total wealth in the United States will change hands every five years between 2030 and 2045.

It's hard to make predictions about what the future will bring, but it's safe to say this veritable tsunami of fine art, antiques and collectibles will circulate faster in the next few decades than it did in its entire existence. We fully expect these demographic changes to push the market for collectibles to new heights as well as introduce or reinvigorate some collecting categories. Another key factor to keep in mind as you build a collection or prepare to sell one: People in their 30s, 40s and 50s tend to buy the toys of their youth. It's easy to dial back the clock on your target and see what's going to be popular in the next few years.

We are already seeing strength returning to two venerable hobbies. Popular in the 1970s – and some would say responsible for inspiring a whole generation of collectors – vintage bottle collecting has seen a renaissance during the last three years. A number of world record prices have been set at auction and experts say attendance at expos and events is at an all-time high. Still, most of the record prices occur at the high end of the market and haven't yet filtered down through the entire category.

The world of collecting fine rocks, gems and minerals is seeing new investment by auction houses that are working to bring the category into the arena. This has led, in part, to a number of large collections coming to market and heavy investment from wealthy collectors.

However, buying for a profit is often limited to those who study these markets day in and day out. Our advice to you is this: Find the things you're most passionate about, then learn about them, then collect them – in this order. Collecting is a highly personal pursuit – you don't have to justify it to anyone but yourself. In order to maximize your enjoyment and the impact of the money you invest in your new passion you must first take the time to learn about what it is you're setting out to pursue. The Internet is an easy choice (and as you'll see, we offer you a number of resources to get started). Reference guides are crucial as are the relationships you develop with fellow collectors, auction house specialists, and dealers.

In fact, it is this social fabric that is at the essence of collecting. Collecting would not be fun if it weren't for the cozy shops nestled along rural roads or tucked in downtown buildings. Auctions aren't very enjoyable when you're the only person in the room (or in a grassy field) and not surrounded by like-minded people who are passionate about the things you're also passionate about. Much of the enjoyment of an antiques show is marveling at how so many people have cultivated their knowledge over decades to show you stunning treasures you didn't even know you wanted.

In this year's edition we've expanded and updated the most popular sections and added new ones, too. You'll notice special attention is drawn to the very best items pursued by collectors as Top Lots.

A book of this magnitude is a team project and many thanks are owed to editor Mary Sieber; *Antique Trader* magazine Editor and Online Editor and Content Manager Antoinette Rahn; *Antique Trader* magazine Print Editor Karen Knapstein; designer Jana Tappa; editorial director Paul Kennedy; and several specialists and contributors. Ever the professionals, they work year round to make this book the best it can be. Their patience, hard work, and great ideas are always focused on one goal: selecting the topics, images and features our readers will find the most fascinating. We hope you enjoy the results. As always, we welcome your thoughts and comments on this and future editions. Feel free to reach out at ATpriceguide@fwmedia.com.

— Eric Bradley

Antique Trader.

About AntiqueTrader.com

We think you'll be impressed with the new layout, sections and information in this year's annual. Because the antiques world (like everything else) is constantly changing, I invite you to visit AntiqueTrader.com and make it your main portal into the world of antiques.

Like our magazine, AntiqueTrader.com's team of collectors, dealers and bloggers share information daily on events, auctions, new discoveries and tips on how to buy more for less. Here's what's you'll find at AntiqueTrader.com:

- **Free eNewsletters:** Get a recap of the world of antiques sent to your inbox every week.
- **Free Classified Ads:** Discover inventory (great and small) from around the world offered to buy, sell or trade.
- **Expert Q&A columns:** Learn how to value and sell your collections online and for the best prices.
- **The Internet's largest free antiques library:** Dig into thousands of articles on research, prices, show reports, auction results and more.
- **Blogs:** Get vital how-to information about topics that include selling online, buying more for less, restoring pieces, spotting fakes and reproductions, displaying your collections and finding hidden gems in your town!
- **Show Guides:** Check out the Internet's most visited antiques events calendar for links to more than 1,000 auctions, fleas, conventions and antiques shows worldwide.

Advertising

Thousands of advertising items made in various materials, some intended as gifts with purchases, others used for display or given away for publicity, are actively collected.

Before the days of mass media, advertisers relied on colorful product labels and advertising giveaways to promote their products. Containers were made to appeal to the buyer through the use of stylish lithographs and bright colors. Many of the illustrations used the product in the advertisement so that even an illiterate buyer could identify a product.

Advertisements were put on almost every household object imaginable and became constant reminders to use the product or visit a certain establishment.

W.H. Elliott clock maker's trade sign, painted zinc, inscribed company name on face, 19th century, 38" h. **$1,422**

Pook & Pook, Inc.

Coca-Cola school zone steel sign, cast iron base, some wear and scratches, wear is more extensive on reverse, 63" x 30" **$1,300**

Matthews Auctions

"John M. Cleckner Book and Job Printing" trade sign, painted tin, circa 1900, 40" x 29"........**$889**

Pook & Pook, Inc.

Krispy Kreme Doughnuts porcelain sign, rarity due to sign being porcelain instead of normal steel, red KK logo started appearing on signs and Krispy Kreme trucks in the 1940s, 23" x 36"....................**$425**

Matthews Auctions

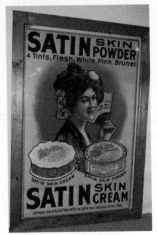

Satin Skin Powder paper ad, displayed in wood frame, some tears and slight discoloration, 44" x 31" **$150**

Matthews Auctions

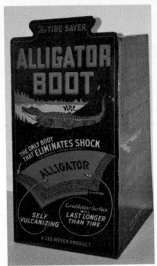

Alligator Boot "The Tire Saver" metal countertop display, good color and shine, smaller version, 24" x 12" x 13" **$2,800**

Matthews Auctions

Arden Milk die-cut sign, advertisement for Arden Farm Co., a small California dairy company formed in the 1930s and still operating today as Arden Group, Inc., minor wear, 48" x 24" **$800**

Matthews Auctions

Sand painted Masonic hall lodge sign, 19th century, 49-1/4" x 72". **$770**

Pook & Pook, Inc.

Philip Morris clock advertising "Now's the Time to Call for Philip Morris," made of wood, in working condition, 38" h. **$240**

Morphy Auctions

"Preserve Your (car) With Blue Ribbon Polishes" stainless steel sign, good color and some shine, marked "American Art Works Inc Coshocton, Ohio," crease in field and along bottom edge and some wear **$1,900**

Matthews Auctions

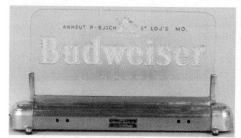

Glass Budweiser advertising sign, shown lit up and inactive, 10-3/4" x 19-1/2", made by Anheuser-Busch, mild paint loss to "Anheuser-Busch Saint Louis" on glass, some oxidation to chrome base, chip to bottom corner of glass, not visible when sign in metal base...**$180**

Morphy Auctions

Classic paper advertising sign for Winchester arms and ammunition with artwork by H.R. Poore, particular item was discovered at a yard sale and sold at auction. **$4,025**

James D. Julia

Michelin Man "bibendum" small air compressor, cast iron, fair condition, heavy paint wear, missing top cover over gauge, no breaks in cast iron, rarity lies in the fact that it is made of cast iron as most were made of celluloid, 11" x 12" x 7"..**$1,300**

Matthews Auctions

"Pirelli Tyres Made in England" large tin sign with blue lettering and yellow background, 36" x 84". **$360**

Woodbury Auction LLC

Winchester Flashlights window display, five-piece light cardboard poster, features man working on an early roadster automobile using a Winchester flashlight, very little wear, 40" x 90".....................................**$1,900**

Matthew Auctions

Tin embossed Dog 'n Suds sign, circa-1950s, promoting the Dogs 'n Suds drive-in restaurant chain founded in 1953 by two music teachers who opened a hot dog and root beer stand in Champaign, Ill., a franchise still operating in cities throughout the Midwest, 64" x 64"..........**$1,200**

Zurko Promotions

Buddy Lee Phillips 66 advertising doll, hard plastic, marked "Buddy Lee" in high-relief letters on back, dressed in original gas station attendant uniform with orange patch, minus hat, rich painted facial features and side-glancing eyes, some wear rubs on head, 13" h. **$141**

McMasters Harris Apple Tree Auctions

Celluloid-over-cardboard Murine Eye Tonic sign, early 20th century, features an image commonly seen in Murine Eye Remedy Co. ads at the time, 9" x 6-1/2" **$3,600**

Morphy Auctions

BUFFALO BRAND SALTED PEANUTS

"Buffalo Brand Salted Peanuts" two-sided outdoor wood sand sign, minimal number produced, excellent condition, 10-1/2' x 11" **$26,400**

Showtime Auction Service

"Super Chevrolet Service" DSP die-cut sign, bowtie logo image introduced by Chevy company founder Charles Durant in 1913, marked "Walker and Company," chipping at top of mounting holes and minor stains, 42" x 48" **$2,800**

Matthews Auctions

Goodrich Shoes "Shoes that make the athlete" cardboard countertop display, 23" x 16" x 4" **$175**

Matthews Auctions

Wrigley Chewing Gum countertop display, metal rack holds four different kinds of gum, green paint has wear and chipping, plastic face has a crack, 14" x 14" x 7".............................. **$240**

Matthews Auctions

ADVERTISING

Eagle Bird Cigarettes porcelain sign, rare, 10 layers of porcelain and good color, some chipping around edges and at mounting holes **$3,000**

Matthews Auctions

"Pontiac Authorized Dealer Klinger Motors Inc." lighted clock, marked "Pam Clock NY," clock operates but unit does not light up, 18" x 15" x 4" **$300**

Matthews Auctions

"It's Easy to Dye With Diamond Dyes" stainless steel embossed sign on wooden countertop display cabinet with sliding back for access, sign in excellent condition, wood cabinet in good condition, minor wear, 30" x 21" x 10" **$1,400**

Matthews Auctions

Coca-Cola "At Ease...for Refreshment" U.S. Army Nurse Corps cardboard sign in wood frame, 29" x 59" **$325**

Matthews Auctions

Aunt Jemima pancake flour wooden crate, early 19th century, minor wear, features Aunt Jemima character logo, marked "Aunt Jemima Mills Company, St. Joseph, Mo.," renamed in 1913 from the original Davis Milling Co., 10" x 22" x 13" **$100**

Matthews Auctions

"H.P. Hood & Sons Ice Cream" porcelain sign, rarity of sign lies in promotion of ice cream and not traditional H.P. Hood & Sons Milk messaging, includes two-inch scar above cow's head, nickel-size repair on forehead, 30" dia **$9,350**

Showtime Auction Service

Polar Bear Tobacco store bin, tin, tobacco produced by Luhrman & Wilbern Tobacco Co. of Ohio, early 20th century, rarity is inclusion of the word "SCRAP" on the cover **$4,200**

Showtime Auctions

Asian Arts & Artifacts

Asian art (aka Eastern art) is highly prized by collectors. They are attracted by its fine workmanship and exquisite attention to detail, plus the undeniable lure of the exotic.

Often lumped under the generic header "Oriental," Asian art actually embraces a wide variety of cultures. Among the many countries falling under the Asian/Eastern art umbrella: Bali, Bhutan, Cambodia, China, India, Indonesia, Japan, Korea, Laos, Thailand, Tibet, Vietnam, and the Pacific Islands. Also in the mix: art forms indigenous to the native cultures of Australia and New Zealand, and works of art celebrating the traditions of such Eastern-based religions as Buddhism and Hinduism.

The influence of Eastern art on Western art is strong. As Western artisans absorbed the cultural traditions of the East, stylistic similarities crept into their work, whether subconsciously or deliberately. (The soft matte glazes popularized by Van Briggle Pottery, for example, resulted from founder Artus Van Briggle's ongoing quest to replicate the "dead" glazes of the Chinese Ming Dynasty.)

Chinese porcelain was one of the first representations of Asian art to entice buyers in the United States; export of the ware began in the 1780s.

Japanese porcelain, originally billed as "Nippon," began to make its way to U.S. shores near the end of the 19th century. Early Chinese porcelain was often distinguished by a liberal use of blue and white; Japanese porcelain, by a similar reliance on floral and landscape motifs. Consumers found the products of both countries desirable, not only because of their delicacy, but also because pieces of comparable quality were not yet available domestically.

Porcelain was not the only outlet for Eastern creativity. Among the many other materials utilized: ivory, jade, bone, hardstone, marble, bronze, brass, gold, silver, wood, and fabric (primarily silk). Decorative treatments ranged from cloisonné (enamel sections in a pattern of metal strips) to intricate hand carving to the elaborate use of embroidery, gilt, and lacquer.

Asian art in any form offers a unique blend of the decorative and the functional. The richness of the materials and treatments utilized transforms even everyday objects into dazzling works of art. Among myriad items receiving this Cinderella treatment: bowls, vases, planters, chess sets, snuff bottles, rugs,

Famille rose enameled porcelain stick-neck vase, Qianlong mark, Republic period, long neck issuing from a body of compressed ovoid form and painted with magpies resting on seasonal flowering branches rendered in a combination of opaque and translucent enamels, recessed base bearing six-character mark in black regular script on a ground of turquoise enamel that also appears on interior of neck, 21" h..............**$43,750**

Bonhams

robes, tapestries, tables, trays, jars, screens, incense burners, cabinets, and tea caddies. Even a simple item such as an oil lamp could be reborn through imaginative artistry: A Chinese version from the 1920s, its exterior worked in cloisonné, emerged as a colorful, ferocious dragon.

This multitude of products makes Asian art an ideal cross-collectible. Some may be interested only in the output of a specific country or region. Others may be drawn to a specific type of collectible (kimonos, snuff boxes, depictions of Buddha). There will even be those attracted solely to pieces created from a specific material, such as jade, ivory, or porcelain. Aficionados of any of these categories have a lifetime of collecting pleasure in store.

The timeline of Asian art is a long one, with value often determined by antiquity. Due to age and rarity, minor flaws (jade nicks, porcelain cracks, and chips) are not generally a detriment to purchase. Any restoration should only be done by a professional, and only after careful analysis as to whether or not restoration will affect value.

Asian art continues to be produced and imported today at an overwhelming rate (and often of "souvenir-only" quality). Collectors seeking museum-quality pieces are strongly advised to purchase only from reputable dealers, and to insist on proof of provenance. A Chinese gilt bronze figure of Vajrasattva, with an incised "Xuande" mark, sold for more than $1.5 million at auction. Modern replicas fetch considerably less.

Large cast bronze seated figure of the Amitabha Buddha, Ming dynasty, imposing figure with serene expression and downcast eyes, plump face and neck, head surmounted with a prominent ushnisha and tight conical curls with a small urna at the front, his hands held in bhumisparsa mudra calling the earth to witness and commemorate his victory over temptation, seated in dhyanasana with chakra incised on upward-facing feet below the domed chest centered with a raised svastika and framed by a loosely draped robe with embellished hem containing decoration of lotus and peony blossoms, interior garments tied with a bow at waist, all raised atop a separately cast multi-tiered lotus-form base, 28-1/4" h. overall $314,500

Bonhams

Hu Zaobin (1897-1942), "Two Tigers" hanging scroll, ink and color on paper, signed Zaobin with two seals of the artist reading Hushi zhizhang and Zaobin xiehu, 57-3/4" x 26-1/4" $3,750

Bonhams

▶ Anonymous (Qing dynasty) group of seven Imperial edicts and edict fragments, ink and color on silk brocade, mounted as hand scrolls; one dated Shunzhi ba nian (1651), one dated Kangxi liu nian (1667), one dated Jiaqing shishi nian (1809), one dated Daoguang er nian (1822), one with three dates of Tongzhi si nian, Tongzhi shi er nian and Guangxu shi liu nian (1865, 1873, and 1890), together with one bearing a date reading Kangxi shi shi nian (1675) and one bearing a date reading Yongzheng shi san nian (1735), each with text reading from left to right in Manchu characters and repeated from right to left in Chinese characters, the Chinese text opening with the woven characters Fengtian Gaomin (by command of Heaven) flanked by two dragons, followed by text in black or colored ink, with two large seal impressions containing Manchu and Chinese characters; 12" x 134" one edict...**$98,500**

Bonhams

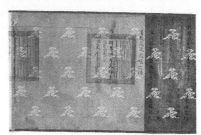

Huang Huanwu (1906-1985), "Welcoming Pine on Huangshan," ink and color on paper, now laid down, mounted and framed; titled Huangshan ying ke song and signed Huang Han Huanwu with two seals of the artist reading Huangwu xiesheng and feng jing zhe bian du hao, 17-7/8" x 25".............................. **$20,000**

Bonhams

Terracotta head of a deity, Java, Majapahit period, 14th-16th century, modeled with full lips, broad nose below heavy lidded eyes and raised arching brows, slightly raised coiffure smooth above ear with distended lobes, 6-1/2" h **$4,000**

Bonhams

Fernando Amorsolo Y Cueto (1892-1972), "The Tinikling Dance," oil on canvas, framed, signed at the lower right F. Amorsolo and dated 1951, 23-1/2" x 33-3/8" sight. **$62,500**

Bonhams

Jianyao stoneware tea bowl, 11th/12th century, conical section, interior and exterior surfaces below brown mouth rim covered in thick black glaze of "hare's fur" markings that pools unevenly in welts around the exterior to expose the russet hue of unglazed walls, low foot and recessed base, 4-3/4" dia.....................................**$2,000-$3,000**

Bonhams

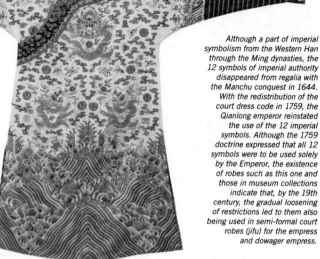

Silk embroidered 12-symbol empress's informal robe, mid-to-late 19th century, body and upper sleeves decorated with a celestial landscape featuring nine dragons in seed stitch on an ivory colored ground amid clouds and bats carrying the eight treasures and eight precious things, shou medallions, 12 symbols of imperial authority in orthodox placement, lishui border in hurricane wave pattern, blue silk lining and gilt metal buttons, 56" l $52,500

Bonhams

Although a part of imperial symbolism from the Western Han through the Ming dynasties, the 12 symbols of imperial authority disappeared from regalia with the Manchu conquest in 1644. With the redistribution of the court dress code in 1759, the Qianlong emperor reinstated the use of the 12 imperial symbols. Although the 1759 doctrine expressed that all 12 symbols were to be used solely by the Emperor, the existence of robes such as this one and those in museum collections indicate that, by the 19th century, the gradual loosening of restrictions led to them also being used in semi-formal court robes (jifu) for the empress and dowager empress.

Monumental andesite seated figure of Ganesha, Java, Classical period, 9th-10th century, seated on platform encircled by gallery of skulls, plump feet pressed together in yogic posture, four arms bear axe, rosary, jar of sweets, and tusk, headdress of matted locks surmounted by a skull and adorned by anklets, foliate armlets, necklaces, and serpent swagged from shoulder to waist, 48" h.......$31,250

Bonhams

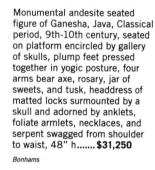

Tuff standing female, Java, Majapahit period, 14th-16th century, squat proportions, thick sarong, she holds loose end with right hand and left on her thigh securing the hem, bare torso and broad shoulders, loop earrings, coiffure curving back behind left ear, 11" h.......................$4,000-$6,000

Bonhams

Two Tibetan gilt metal repoussé plaques, 16th/17th century, fragments from a large pedestal, each worked in high relief with an animated temple lion standing guard with a cintamani ornament on its head, long curly mane frames defined facial features, one with traces of red pigment on open mouth, each accented with tufts of curls and other features retaining the darker hue of the metal and with partial border with floral motifs to one side, 7-1/2" x 10-1/4" and 7-7/8" x 10-1/4" ....$3,000-$5,000

Bonhams

Embroidered silk rank badge, Kangxi period, made for a civil official of the third rank, embroidered almost entirely in seed stitch with a central peacock facing a red sun, the bird with long wings and flowing tail with one leg raised on a rocky outcropping amid waves, on a blue ground with ruyi clouds, individual elements of the scene surrounded by couched gold-wrapped threads, framed by a thin border of stylized scrolls also in seed stitch, badge currently framed and glazed, 11-3/4" x 11-1/2" $15,000-20,000

Bonhams

Embroidered silk rank badge, late Ming/early Qing dynasty, of the military fifth rank and depicting a white bear amid cloud scrolls above precious items floating on stylized waves, executed in colored silk satin-stitch on a ground of couched metallic wrapped thread, 13-1/4" x 13-1/2" $25,000

Bonhams

Pu Quan (1913-1991), two paintings of horses and grooms, pair of hanging scrolls, each ink and color on silk; the first dated renxu zhi dong (winter of 1982) and signed Aixin Jueluo Pu Quan with three seals of the artist reading Songchuang and Aixin Jueluo Pu Quan zi Songchuan shuhua yin; the second inscribed with a two-line poem and signed Pu Songchuang with three seals of the artist reading Pu Songchuang yin, Xuexi, and Aixin Jueluo Pu Quan zi Songchuan shuhua yin, 12-1/2" x 15-1/2" each ....$2,000-$3,000

Bonhams

TOP LOT!

Blue and white porcelain vase, tianqiuping, Yongzheng Mark and period, resting on a band of stiff lappets under a main body of interlocking lotus, pomegranate, peony, camellia, and seasonal flowers drawn with tendrils under a shaded cloud collar and xiangcai band enclosing a frieze of waves setting off the tapered cylindrical neck rendered with further lotus blossoms and scrolling foliate tendrils under a cloud and dart border suspended from a classic wave band at the rim, six-character mark in seal script on the recessed base, 21" h $5,906,500

Bonhams

▲ Tibetan chest of rectangular section surmounted by a fitted lid affixed by unusual metal hasps, top and three sides covered in red ground of scrolling lotus vines and mongoose, metonymically recalling Kubera, the dharmapala of wealth, 24" h **$2,500**

Bonhams

Bronze figure of Radha, Bengal, India, 19th century, standing on a plain dome base in a flexed pose with her right hand extended offering a bud and her left to the side providing balance, modeled with full rounded limbs and narrow waist, well-defined face with blank almond eyes, 21-1/2" h **$3,750**

Bonhams

Powder blue ground porcelain covered jar with famille verte and gilt enamel decoration, Late Qing/Republic period, potted globular form, traditional palette with figures set in four cusped reserves bordered by underglaze blue ground for butterflies and flowers drawn in gilt, flattened globular cover painted en suite, recessed base centered with a double ring, 16-1/2" h......**$2,000-$3,000**

Bonhams

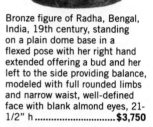

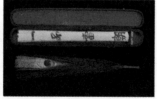

Tuff seated male, Java, Majapahit period, 14th-16th century, his legs tucked to the side while seated on a dome platform, portly figure hides a cylindrical object behind his back, stern expression on his well-modeled face, coiffure arranged with a bud-like top knot, 8-1/2" h **$1,250**

Bonhams

First rank peacock feather plume, late Qing dynasty, single-eyed peacock feather plume with its original silk wrapper and a fabric-lined box, wrapper with four applied cut characters, reading "Yi pin dang chao" (rising to the first rank and dominate the court), 14-3/4" length of plume... **$2,750**

Bonhams

Black stone stele of Buddha, Northeast India, Pala period, circa 10th century, Buddha stands within domed shrine, fringed with lotus blossoms and raised stupas flanking his shoulders, with right hand Buddha makes gesture of charity, varada mudra, and his left holds pleated robe end, body draped in a sheer robe that falls in pleats by his ankles, 26-1/2" h...........**$20,000**

Bonhams

Large cloisonné enameled metal vase, 19th century, with tall cylindrical neck above a globular body and decorated in brightly colored enamels with flowering peony bushes issuing from ornamental rockwork encircling base, all silhouetted against a dark red ground with an overall key-fret pattern in gilt cloisons, further gilt accenting the rim and foot, bearing a Qianlong mark framed by dragons on the base, 17-1/8" h......................................$9,375

Bonhams

Hardwood scroll pot constructed from a thickly walled segment displaying naturalistically carved nodules throughout the exterior, polished to a soft luster with a deep orange hue, 9-7/8" h...................$3,000-$5,000

Bonhams

Blue and white porcelain plaque, 17th century, circular plaque painted with a scholar seated on a river bank shaded by a pine bough with his attendant standing nearby, mountain peak in distance, scene enclosed by a narrow key fret band, 9" dia................... $4,000-$6,000

Bonhams

Unusual lapis lazuli conjoined double vase rendered as two full-shouldered vases conjoined at sides, decorated with a wide band filled with taotie masks and abstract archaistic images carved in relief against a key-fret patterned ground, both mouth and foot rims encircled with borders of further key-fret decoration, conforming domed cover with raised leaf petal design surrounding two globular form finials, large boulder dominated by deep blue with variegated stripes and scattered with numerous gold flecks, 11" h..$20,000

Bonhams

Burlwood brush pot, 19th century, naturalistic form with dense swirling grain of honey brown hue, applied hardwood mouth rim and base of conforming shape, 9" h ... $1,000-$1,500

Bonhams

Lee Man Fong (Indonesian-Chinese, 1913-1988), "Young Fisherwoman," oil on canvas, framed, depicting in foreground a young woman wearing a large woven hat and showing across her chest the crossed ties of a bundle carried on her back, with sails of a few junk boats visible in the distance, signed L. Fong at the lower left, 23-1/2" x 17-1/2" sight **$31,250**

Bonhams

Cast bronze censer in the form of a three-legged toad, 18th/19th century, animal raised on three claw feet with open mouth issuing scrolling plumes at sides continuing back to knees, lid with raised warts and bulging eyes opening to interior lid with conical opening, figure attached to a fitted reticulated wood base of naturalistic form centered on a lingzhi fungus, 6-1/2" l. **$4,375**

Bonhams

Red sandstone relief panel of Mithuna (Loving Couple), North India, 2nd century A.D., standing frontally wearing sheer lower garments with left hands on their hips, female holds a drooping lotus and is adorned with large circular earrings and a link belt across her hips, male holds a small lotus blossom in right hand and is adorned with a thick necklace, 25-3/4" h.............................**$20,000**

Bonhams

Holy man, Eastern Java, Majapahit, 13th-14th century, seated in meditation with hands folded, wearing a skirt cinched at waist by elaborate flowing knot, sash draped from shoulder to waist terminating in a pleated swag at the shoulder, hair arranged in elegant coiffure with ornamental wave-like pattern above his forehead, 7-1/2" h .... **$4,000-$5,000**

Bonhams

Copper alloy figure of Raktalokeshvara, Srivijaya, Peninsular Thailand, 8th-9th century, deity enshrined on double-lotus over square base, cushion supporting his posture of meditation, left hand holds stem of lotus while he opens its petals with his right, long jatas are piled above his head with escaping locks spilling over his shoulders, torso modeled and adorned with a long necklace and utapala cord, shrine decorated with a ring of lotus buds with two symmetrically arching larger buds flanking a central projection that likely held a parasol, 7-1/2" h..........**$20,000**

Bonhams

A gilt copper alloy figure of Syamatara, 16th century, bodhisattva exhibiting a penetrating expression enhanced by recent ritual application of "cold gold" to her face and neck, elaborately attired in bejeweled raiment inlaid with numerous turquoise cabochons (some possibly replaced), and seated in the lalitasana posture of royal ease with her right arm held in varadamudra while her left is held in vitarkamudra clasping the stem of a stylized lotus suspended at her left shoulder, all supported by a crisply cast lotus petal plinth, base unsealed revealing an interior with tightly curled holy writings, 7-1/4" h $32,500

Bonhams

Terracotta panel of a Yakshi, North or Eastern India, Sunga period, ca. 200-50 B.C., rectangular panel modeled with a yakshi with an ovoid face and elaborate coiffure, narrow shoulders, heavy breast, wide hips and attenuated limbs, she stands on a domed platform surrounded by four attendants within an architectural frame, 20" h ....$3,000-$5,000

Bonhams

Limestone of Shiva and Parvati, Northwest India, circa 8th century, Shiva wears animal skin dhoti, serpent across his torso and beaded necklace, and holds a mala in his right hand and a waterpot in left, thick coiffure supporting a crescent; Parvati with similar adornments holds a flower blossom and chauri in her hands, Nandi's head flanks Shiva's right knee, diminutive figure stands between devine couple on flat platform, 12" h ......$12,000-$16,000

Bonhams

Tuff kneeling woman, Majapahit period, 14th-16th century, left arm drawn across bare torso, ovoid face with well-defined features and thick coiffure flowing down her back in a ponytail, 9" h..............$2,000-$3,000

Bonhams

Tuff figure of a boy, Java, Majapahit period, 14th-16th century, plump figure seated with large feet beneath his swollen belly and chest adorned with jeweled belt and necklace, rounded face with well-defined features, flowing coiffure and elaborate ear ornaments, 8-3/8" h.... $2,000-$3,000

Bonhams

Mottled red sandstone relief of a Bacchanalian scene, India, Mathura, Kushan period, 2nd century, central female figure supported in intoxicated state by tall male and smaller female attendant, who is trying to restore her dhoti, another female at upper right with elaborate coiffure looks on, each adorned with beaded earrings and thick necklaces and disc belts, 27-1/2" h.... $12,500

Bonhams

Netsukes

Netsukes – the miniature buttonlike carvings used in Japan to suspend articles from the sash of a kimono and as ornamental fasteners on boxes – have been a high-end niche collectible in the United States for decades. Intricately detailed netsukes have won the favor of a number of distinguished collectors, including the late diplomat Jack A. Mang and his wife, Helen Randall Mang, whose 1,100-piece collection, assembled over the last 60 years, was auctioned at Quinn's Auction Galleries of Falls Church, Va., on Dec. 7, 2012.

The top earner in the Mang collection is an 18th-century Kyoto school ivory netsuke of a crouching baku, a mythical beast whose name means "eater of bad dreams." The carving incorporates all of the baku's distinctive physical characteristics: a long snout, two tusks, clawed feet, and the body of a horse with flaming posterior. Measuring 2-3/4" long, it sold for $45,000, far surpassing its presale estimate of $15,000 to $20,000.

The Mangs were longtime residents of the nation's capital and founding members of the Washington, D.C. chapter of the International Netsuke Society (www.netsuke.org), which is the largest international organization of netsuke collectors with members in 31 different countries.

Ivory netsuke of Lunar Hare, attributed to Shigemasa No. 3, Osaka, second half of 19th century. Provenance: Sotheby's, London, Dec. 20, 1967 .... **$1,300**
Quinn's Auction Galleries

Wood netsuke of turtle group, carved by Hoju, mid-19th century. **$6,500**
Quinn's Auction Galleries

Wood netsuke of roaring dragon holding ball, carved by Kaigyokudo, Osaka, circa 1833-1843, signed by artist **$7,000**
Quinn's Auction Galleries

TOP LOT!

Ivory netsuke of a baku, Kyoto School, 18th century, crouching figure with eyes inlaid in black, design is unique for this "eater of bad dreams" and incorporates all of the characteristics of the mythical beast, long snout, two tusks, body of a horse, clawed feet, and flames, good color and well-patinated on the back, unsigned. 2-3/4". **$45,000**

Quinn's Auction Galleries

Ivory netsuke of dragon emerging in vapor cloud from alms vessel, Kyoto, late 18th century. Provenance: Purchased from Joseph U. Seo, 1955. .... **$13,000**

Quinn's Auction Galleries

Ivory netsuke of Dutchman with karako seated on right shoulder, carved by Yoshinaga Miura Kanjuken, mid-19th century. Provenance: Purchased from R. Koscherak, 1951. ..... **$1,400**

Quinn's Auction Galleries

Bone netsuke depicting a sennin grasping a mokugyo, Kyoto, mid-18th century. Provenance: F. Meinertzhagen. **$23,000**

Quinn's Auction Galleries

Autographs

In *The Meaning and Beauty of Autographs*, first published in 1935 and translated from the German by David H. Lowenherz of Lion Heart Autographs, Inc. in 1995, Stefan Zweig explained that to love a manuscript, we must first love the human being "whose characteristics are immortalized in them." When we do, then "a single page with a few lines can contain the highest expression of human happiness, and... the expression of deepest human sadness. To those who have eyes to look at such pages correctly, eyes not only in the head, but also in the soul, they will not receive less of an impression from these plain signs than from the obvious beauty of pictures and books."

John M. Reznikoff, founder and president of University Archives, has been a leading dealer and authority on historical letters and artifacts for 32 years. He described the current market for autographs as "very, very strong on many fronts. Possibly because of people being afraid to invest in the market and in real estate, we are seeing investment in autographs that seems to parallel gold and silver."

Reznikoff suspects that Civil War items peaked after Ken Burns' series but that Revolutionary War documents, included those by signers of the Declaration of Independence and the Constitution are still undervalued and can be purchased for under$500.

Currrently, space is in high demand, especially Apollo 11. Pop culture, previously looked at as secondary by people who dealt in Washingtons and Lincolns, has come into its own. Reznikoff anticipates continued growth in memorabilia that includes music, television, movies and sports. Babe Ruth, Lou Gehrig, Ty Cobb and Tiger Woods are still good investments but Reznikoff warns that authentication is much more of a concern in sports than in any other field.

The Internet allows for a lot of disinformation and this is a significant issue with autographs.

There are two widely accepted authentication services: Professional Sports Authenticator (PSA/DNA) and James Spence Authentication (JSA). A dealer's reliability can be evaluated by seeing whether he is a member of one or more of the major organizations in the field: the Antique Booksellers Association of America, UACC Registered Dealers Program and the National Professional Autograph Dealers Association (NPADA), which Reznikoff founded.

There is an additional caveat to remember and it is true for all collectibles: rarity. The value of an autograph is often determined less by the prominence of the signer than by the number of autographs he signed.

— *Zac Bissonnette*

Michael Jordan autographed Spalding NBA official game basketball, large black felt tip pen autograph graded 9-10 out of 10 in Upper Deck Authentication..**$1,138**

SCP Auctions

AUTOGRAPHS

Yogi Berra and Mickey Mantle full color, framed photographs, each signed by that National Baseball Hall of Fame inductee, framed and matted Berra photo 21-1/2" x 25-1/2", Mantle photo 20" x 24", pre-certified by PSA/DNA. Provenance: From the personal collection of Ozzie Smith $756

SCP Auctions

Dwight D. Eisenhower signed letter with original envelope, also signed, dated Sept. 27, 1943 to his wife, Mamie. Single page letter on Allied Force Headquarters/Office of the Commander-in-Chief stationery, includes comments about receiving a letter from their son, a student at West Point, and Eisenhower's own sentiments about politics and war, and concludes with "Loads of love – Always/Ike"; slight creasing, 8" x 10-1/2" $3,493

Nate D. Sanders, Inc.

One-of-a-kind Bugs Bunny hand-drawn sketch signed by animator Chuck Jones, on reverse side of a Chuck Jones Enterprises business card, minor creasing, 2" x 3-1/2". $425

Nate D. Sanders, Inc.

Patsy Cline pocket-sized country souvenir photo album with signature by Cline and four other singers including Johnny Cash, George Jones, and Carl Perkins, vintage front and back covers and red comb-bound spine, 31 pages and photographs of 28 other country stars in addition to Cline and Cash, very good condition, 3-1/4" x 5" $686

Nate D. Sanders, Inc.

King of the Ring Muhammad Ali and the king of rock and roll, Elvis Presley, 8" x 10" photo signed by Ali in a dark blue felt tip pen, pre-certified by PSA/DNA, framed, 14-1/4" x 17-1/4".......**$1,138**

SCP Auctions

Autographed postcard signed "Olga et Picasso" with small ink drawing illustrating the New Year's greetings famed artist Pablo Picasso wrote to conductor Henri Defosse in French, translated to "As my friends are served at this table, we send you our best wishes," dated Dec. 2, 1919, minor scattered soiling $23,000

Swann Galleries

TOP LOT!

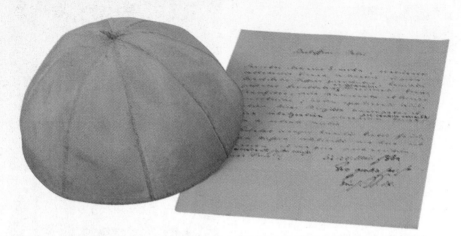

Pope Pius IX (1792-1878) white solideo accompanied by ink endorsement related to the doctrine of papal infallibility and a letter penned by a priest asking permission to use holy relics and other religious mementos; 7-1/2" dia., good condition, has retained its shape by resting on a wood and padded mold over the centuries. Provenance: From the collection of Lord St. John of Fawsley. Solideos are seldom offered for sale to the public because white solideos are reserved for the pope (the rest of the clergy wear black solideos) **$2,716**

RR Auctions

John Lennon autograph letter, circa 1968, response to fan mail with suggestion that the reader consider transcendental meditation. The letter, with provenance from Christie's, is signed "With love/John Lennon/jai garden," written on stationery from the Spiritual Regeneration Movement Foundation of India, 7-1/2" x 10-1/4", toning, separation to fold lines and chipping to edges.................................**$17,365**

Nate D. Sanders, Inc.

Photo of NASA's Apollo 11 crew signed in black felt tip by Neil Armstrong, Michael Collins, and Buzz Aldrin, date of Aug. 16, 1969 appears on mount, authenticated by Zarelli; trimmed edges and a few surface impressions as well as a vertical crease from top edge down, said to have been the result of Neil Armstrong's son sitting on the photo during the official ceremony for the Apollo 11 crew at the Houston Astrodome; photo 9-1/4" x 7", 13-1/2" x 11" with mount and frame **$3,076**

RR Auctions

Moe Howard, leader of the Three Stooges, autographed letter, signed "Moe" on rarely seen Three Stooges stationery, note is a response to a letter from a fan, circa 1969, with comments about the Three Stooges filming a pilot in color called "Kook's Tour"; 5" x 8", light toning, creasing, and small chip to bottom edge.............................. **$349**

Nate D. Sanders, Inc.

Signed and dated Theodore Roosevelt cabinet card bust portrait, signature and date "Feb 18th 1909" on mount below image, 5-1/2" x 4"............**$1,600**

Swann Galleries

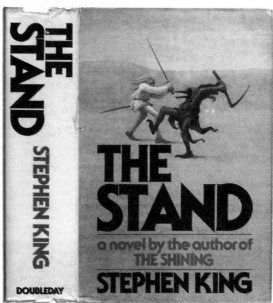

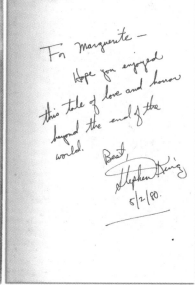

Stephen King signed copy of his book, *The Stand,* autograph inscription in blue felt tip to front free endpaper, dated 5/2/80, book club edition, 6" x 8-1/2", foxing to top edge, mild toning to leaves, dust jacket in very good condition **$916**

Nate D. Sanders, Inc.

Banks

Most collectible banks are designed for one purpose: to encourage children to save money. How well the bank accomplished this task makes all the difference in making it collectible by later generations.

Manufactured from the late 1800s to the mid-1900s, mechanical, still, and register banks (which indicate the value of the coins deposited) are marvels of ingenuity made of tin, lead or cast iron. Although banks come in all makes and functions, the most desirable banks employ a novelty or mechanical action when a coin is placed inside. Banks are sought after because they so efficiently represent the popular culture at the time they were made. This is evident in the wartime registering banks sporting tin lithographic decorations of superheroes or animation characters or the cast iron figures that propagated racial stereotypes common from 1880 to 1930. Many early cast iron bank models have been reproduced during the years, especially in the 1950s and 1960s. A key indicator of a reproduction is fresh, glossy paint or dull details in the casting.

According to 10 years of sales data on LiveAuctioneers.com, most mechanical banks sell at auction for between $500 and $1,000. Morphy Auctions is the world leader in selling mechanical banks, offering more than 5,800 at auction during the last 11 years alone. The most important collection sold at auction so far is the Stephen and Marilyn Steckbeck Collection offered in October 2007. The top lot of the collection was an exceptional "Jonah and the Whale"

Cast iron "Boy Stealing Watermelons" mechanical bank, Kyser & Rex, 6-1/2" h................................... **$6,600**

Morphy Auctions

Cast iron pelican mechanical bank, J&E Stevens Co., rabbit variation, 7-1/2" h............ **$10,200**

Morphy Auctions

Cast iron "Tommy" mechanical bank, Harper Manufacturing Co. of London, 12" l. **$7,800**

Morphy Auctions

mechanical bank, which realized $414,000. The $7.7 million collection still holds records for the most valuable banks ever sold, and they continue to dominate headlines whenever a piece from the Steckbeck Collection is resold. In September 2012, Morphy's auctioned an early Freedman's mechanical bank of a seated figure, measuring 10-1/2" tall, with Steckbeck provenance, for $117,500.

A collection as fine and complete as the Steckbeck Collection hasn't come to auction since, but that doesn't mean fine examples are not coming to market. "There are a dozen or so collections that I know of that would bring over $1 million," said Dan Morphy, owner and founder of Morphy Auctions. "There are dozens of other bank collections that would fall in the six figure ranges."

However, it is apparent that collectors are holding out for those special examples. The number of fine banks offered at auction does not appear to be increasing. In fact, many auctioneers have taken to grouping banks together in order to push lot values over several hundred dollars, although this is only true with lesser quality or common banks.

Morphy says condition – like all other categories of collecting – is king. "Banks in top condition seem to be the trend these days," he said.

So, on the basis of affordability, now is the time to start a collection. "I always tell new collectors that they should buy what they like," Morphy said. "Even if you pay a little more than you should for a bank, the value in the enjoyment of owning it will more than offset the high price one may pay."

Cast iron hen mechanical bank, J&E Stevens Co., 9-3/4" l. **$6,000**

Morphy Auctions

Cast iron "Picture Gallery" mechanical bank, Shepherd Hardware Co., with original trap, 8-1/4" h. **$4,500**

Morphy Auctions

A top on Morphy's list to offer at auction is a "Darkey & the Watermelon" mechanical bank. Otherwise known as the Football Bank, it was designed and patented by Charles A. Bailey, June 26, 1888. Known as the leader in mechanical bank design, Bailey's "Darkey & the Watermelon" bank incorporated all of his imagination and design talents: When the right leg of a figure is pulled back into position, a coin is then placed in a small football; a lever in the figure's coattails is pressed and the football with coin is kicked over into a large watermelon. Only one or two of these banks are known to exist.

"That would be my dream bank," Morphy said, "in that I would also want to buy it!"

Like their predecessors crafted nearly 150 years ago, contemporary banks blur the line between tool and toy. Some modern banks that may make interesting collectibles in the future include digital registering banks that tabulate coin and paper money deposits or those licensed by famous designers. But beware, antique-looking banks are still being reproduced and can be found very cheaply at lesser-quality flea markets or sold online.

For more information on banks, see *The Official Price Guide to Mechanical Banks* by Dan Morphy, 2007, morphyauction.com.

Cast iron "Trick Pony" mechanical bank, Shepherd Hardware Co., 7-1/2" l. **$6,000**

Morphy Auctions

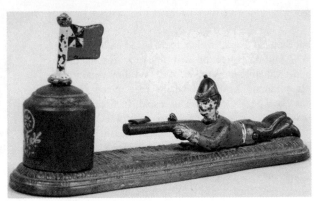

Cast iron "Wimbledon" mechanical bank, Harper Manufacturing Co. of London, flag may be an early replacement, 12" l. **$6,000**

Morphy Auctions

Cast iron "Afghanistan" mechanical bank, maker unknown, 3-1/2" h. **$5,100**

Morphy Auctions

Cast iron "Globe Savings Fund" mechanical bank, original drawer, 7-1/4" h. **$3,900**

Morphy Auctions

Cast iron "Darktown Battery" mechanical bank, J&E Stevens Co., late 19th century, pitcher features a slot to insert coin and batter is in place next to catcher, swinging mechanism allows batter to lift his arms and avoid a direct hit, 10" l. **$3,600**

Morphy Auctions

Cast iron "Multiplying" mechanical bank, J&E Stevens Co., 6-1/2" h. **$5,100**

Morphy Auctions

Cast iron "Paddy & The Pig" mechanical bank, J&E Stevens Co., blue/grey jacket variation, 8-1/4" h. **$3,600**

Morphy Auctions

Cast iron "Darktown Battery" reproduction mechanical bank, circa 1950s, not a vintage 1890s or early 1900s relic. **$250**

Cast iron "Monkey & Coconut" mechanical bank, J&E Stevens Co., brown base variation, 8-1/2" h.................................... **$2,700**

Morphy Auctions

Cast iron "Clown on Globe" mechanical bank, J & E Stevens Co., designed by James H. Bowen, patented 5/20/1890, when globe is brought into position and lever is released, globe and clown whirl around; pressing knob makes clown stand on his head. ... **$5,310**

Bertoia Auctions

Cast iron "Stump Speaker" mechanical bank, Shepherd Hardware Co., green jacket and brown face variation, 10" h. **$2,400**

Morphy Auctions

Cast iron "Elephant & Three Clowns" mechanical bank, J & E Stevens Co., designed by James H. Bowen, patented 8/28/1883, tan base, place coin between rings held by acrobat, move ball on feet of other acrobat, and elephant will strike coin with his trunk, which will cause it to fall into receptacle........................ **$1,416**

Bertoia Auctions

Chalkware ballooning bank, American, circa 1876, rare, 7" h. **$500**

Heritage Auctions

Cast iron "Boy Acrobat on Trapeze" mechanical bank, Barton and Smith Co., 9-1/2" h.... **$1,800**

Morphy Auctions

Cast iron "Jonah & the Whale" mechanical bank, Shepherd Manufacturing Co., original trap, 10-1/4" l. **$2,280**

Morphy Auctions

Cast iron "Smyth X-Ray" mechanical bank, Henry C. Hart Mfg. Co., Detroit, circa 1898, set coin in holder and look into eyepiece to see through coin – a series of four angled mirrors create the optical illusion that the coin is transparent; rare. **$5,900**

Bertoia Auctions

Cast iron "Bad Accident" mechanical bank, J&E Stevens Co., 10" l. **$2,400**

Morphy Auctions

Cast iron "Eagle & Eaglets" mechanical bank, J&E Stevens Co., working bellows, 8" l................. **$2,280**

Morphy Auctions

Cast iron "Professor Pug Frog's Great Bicycle Feat" mechanical bank, J & E Stevens Co., Cromwell, Connecticut, designed by Charles A. Bailey, circa 1886, red and yellow version, when crank is turned and lever pressed, Professor Pug Frog performs his bicycle feat and coin placed on bicycle is deposited in bank. **$5,015**

Bertoia Auctions

Glass "Jumbo Peanut Butter" elephant container/bank, depicts circus elephant with "Jumbo Peanut Butter" blanket on back, circa 1930s, The Frank Tea & Spice Co., original tin screw-on lid at bottom, coin slot on lid, 3-1/2" h...... **$417**

Hake's Americana & Collectibles

Cast iron beehive mechanical bank with rare key, nickel plated cast iron designed by Arthur Golton, 1892, formed with "ECONOMY ACCUMULATES WEALTH" relief text and scrollwork, store sold version, accompanied by 7-1/8" long rod with rectangular opening on one end for use as key, interior contains original cardboard containers to hold coins, 6-3/4" x 6-3/4" x 6-3/4" h. **$560**

Hake's Americana & Collectibles

Cast iron hall clock still bank, Hubley, retaining original paper face, painted in gold overall, with red filigree grille at front panel, 5-7/8" h. **$560**

Bertoia Auctions

Cast iron "Pineapple Hawaiian" mechanical bank, maker unknown, dated July 4, 1960, 9" h. **$300**

Morphy Auctions

Cast iron "Golden Possum" still bank, A.C. Williams, 4-1/2" l. **$420**

Morphy Auctions

Tin "Africa" flywheel bank, made by Lehmann, circa early 1900s, flywheel allows cart to roll and ostrich to step forward, coin slot located behind rider (not shown), 7" l. x 5" h. **$411**

Hake's Americana & Collectibles

Tin World War II "Keep 'Em Rolling" dime register bank, tin litho, made in United States, from the Carl Lobel Collection, 2-1/2" x 2-1/2" x 3/4". **$312**

Hake's Americana & Collectibles

Pressed steel Donald Duck toy telephone bank, rare, N.N. Hill Brass Co., circa mid-1930s, thick die-cut cardboard Donald figure attachment, rotary dial, designated coin slots for pennies (1), nickels (5) and dimes (10), rare, 4-3/4" h. **$575**

Hake's Americana & Collectibles

Cast iron cabin bank, mechanical, J & E Stevens Co., Cromwell, Connecticut, patent date of June 2, 1885, 80% paint remains, 2-3/4" x 4-1/4" x 3-1/2" h. .. **$305**

Hake's Americana & Collectibles

Cast iron U.S.S. Maine commemorative still bank, 4-1/2" x 5"... **$1,495**

Heritage Auctions

Ceramic Batman and Robin bank set, Lego of Japan, 1966, from the Ben Novack, Jr. Estate Collection, 6-3/4" h. **$388**

Heritage Auctions

Cast iron McKinley & Roosevelt jugate elephant still bank, raised portraits of the 1900 Republican nominees on one side, inscribed "Prosperity McKinley Teddy," 3-1/2" x 2-1/2". **$866**

Heritage Auctions

Cast iron "Santa at Chimney" mechanical bank, Shepherd Hardware Co., original trap, 6" h. **$3,000**

Morphy Auctions

Cast iron sandpiper still bank, Germany, hand-painted lead example, slot on back of head, key lock on lifting head, 4-1/2" h. **$1,180**

Bertoia Auctions

Composition "Muttley" character bank, maker unknown, circa late 1960s, 7-1/4" h.; Muttley first appeared in "Wacky Races" in 1968 and in various later Hanna-Barbera animated series. **$232**

Hake's Americana & Collectibles

Plastic Bugs Bunny Talking bank, Sears, 1977, original box, battery-operated twin coin bank featuring Elmer Fudd and Bugs Bunny, requires one "D" battery, from the Jack and Julie Juka Collection. **$18**

Heritage Auctions

Plaster "Dick Tracy's God-Daughter bank," Jayess Co. with Chicago Tribune copyright, circa 1940s, relief portrait of Dick Tracy along with incised text "Sparkle Plenty Savings Bank - Dick Tracy - God-Father" and relief portrait of Gravel Gertie and incised text "Mother - Gravel Gertie," 5-1/2" d. x 8-3/4" w. x 12" h. **$115**

Hake's Americana & Collectibles

Cardboard Communist Party election bank, Communist Party ticket was headed by Earl Browder and James W. Ford, 1940, serial number 0449 on paper wrapper, wrapper largely covers an earlier wrapper, "Chicago Committee To Aid Victims Of German Fascism," 1940 outer wrapper includes text such as "Contribute To The Campaign Fund Of The Communist Party Of Illinois - The Working Class Against The Capitalist Class," 2-1/4" d. x 5" h. **$118**

Hake's Americana & Collectibles

BANKS

Cast iron "Diamond Safe" bank, hinged locking door and coin slot in top, logo on door reads, "DIAMOND SAFE."..............**$184**

Heritage Auctions

Cast iron "Cat/Dog/Monkey Organ Bank," mechanical, Kyser & Rex Co., Frankford, Pennsylvania, patent # D-259,403, June13, 1882, 80% of paint remains, 4" x 5-1/4" x 7-1/4" h. **$420**

Hake's Americana & Collectibles

Ceramic Mickey Mouse still bank by Faiencerie d' Onnaing, circa 1930s, stamped with company name and "Made In France" on underside, coin slot on back of head, 6" h. **$575**

Hake's Americana & Collectibles

Celluloid, "Al Smith Contributor" donation bank, two-sided celluloid and metal coin back, issued by Democratic State Central Committee of Rhode Island, top reads: "Do Your Bit To Elect Al Smith And Our Democratic State Ticket. Every Dime Will Help," 2" dia. **$239**

Heritage Auctions

Papier-mâché "Bobbing-Head Slave Child" mechanical bank, circa 19th century, on top of base is a "hill" atop which 5-1/2" composition figure sits, coins deposited through a slit in front of figure, drawer opens from back of wood base in order to retrieve coins, 5" x 6-3/4" x 10-3/4" h. **$1,553**

Heritage Auctions

Cast iron "Chief Big Moon" bank, J. & E. Stevens Co., Cromwell, Connecticut, circa 1899, spring-loaded platform from which a frog emerges, 9" l. x 6" h. **$750**

Heritage Auctions

Barbie

At the time of the Barbie doll's introduction in 1959, no one could have guessed that this statuesque doll would become a national phenomenon and eventually the most famous girl's plaything ever produced.

Over the years, Barbie and her growing range of family and friends have evolved with the times, serving as an excellent mirror of the fashion and social changes taking place in American society. Today, after nearly 55 years of continuous production, Barbie's popularity remains unabated among both young girls and older collectors. Early and rare Barbie dolls can sell for remarkable prices, and it is every collector's hope to find a mint condition #1 Barbie.

Collection of individually packaged vintage Barbie accessories, includes Barbie "Ponytail" case, outfits #911 Golden Girl, #912 Cotton Casual, Peachy Fleecy Coat #915, Cruise Stripes #918, Fashion Undergarments #919, and Barbie-Q #962, some missing components of each **$1,600**
Ivey-Selkirk Auctioneers

Fabergé™ Imperial Elegance™ Barbie, porcelain bisque, blue satin gown with embroidery and hand-sewn Swarovski crystals, matching jeweled tiara, earrings and choker **$180**
Morphy Auctions

#3 Blonde Ponytail Barbie in Solo in the Spotlight #982, circa 1960s, earlier box, has "BLOND" printed on it, and "T.M." after logo, two-part stand, original bathing suit and open-toe Japan shoes **$500**
McMasters Harris Apple Tree Doll Auctions

Skipper, "Barbie's Little Sister," circa 1963, dressed in original red and white swimsuit, marked with Skipper 1963 Mattel, Inc. and the number 5 on her bottom, accompanied by original vinyl Skipper carrying case with approximately a dozen outfits, including ballet outfit, dress coat, masquerade costume, case 10-1/2" x 7" x 5-1/2" **$120**

Scheerer McCulloch Auctioneers

Brunette Ponytail Barbie, circa 1959, original box, stand, booklet, and "Genuine Barbie by Mattel" wrist tag, painted features including blue eyes, red lips, nails and toenails, pearl green earrings, dressed in original black and white striped bathing suit, black pumps and white sunglasses with blue lenses, some discoloration to arms and legs, streaking from earring color **$190**

D.G.W. Auctioneers

Barbie clothing sets: Peachy Fleecy Coat #915, Registered Nurse #991, and Orange Blossom #987. .... **$425**

D.G.W. Auctioneers

Barbie cases, circa 1961 and 1963, featuring several Barbie wardrobe items and accessories, with 1965 Barbie and 1958 Midge **$35**

GWS Auctions LLC

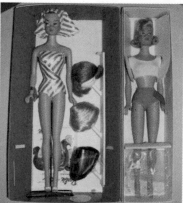

"Fashion Queen" Barbie, circa 1963, with brown molded hair and accompanying wigs in red flip, blonde bubble-cut, and brunette pageboy, dressed in bronze and white swimsuit and hair covering; includes original Midge doll, circa 1963, sans freckles, which appeared on later versions of Midge, dressed in beach attire of teal top and shorts, original Mattel arm tag, stand, shoes, and original box **$350**

D.G.W. Auctioneers

"Barbie and Midge" vinyl dome lunch box, King-Seeley Thermos Co., circa 1965, fold-down space to eat lunch, minor light scuffing on back of box...................... **$140**

SeriousToyz

Blonde #1 Barbie, circa 1959, in original box (cardboard insert and sunglasses missing) with original stand, booklet, bathing suit, metal hoop earrings and shoes, soft blonde ponytail in original set with curly bangs, rubber band holding bottom of pony tail partially disintegrated, some fading to color, original face paint and nail polish................................... **$4,000-$6,000**

Morphy Auctions

#4 Ponytail Barbie in original box, circa 1960, with Barbie Pigtail doll case, extra dresses, original stand, two pairs of sunglasses, shoes, and several outfits **$325**

Kennedy Auctions Service

Barbie in Gold 'N Glamour #1647, circa 1963, highlighted bubble-cut coiffure and pale pink lips, sleeveless sheath dress with turquoise chiffon bodice, golden tweed jacket with short full sleeves and attached scarf, golden tweed skirt, matching hat with fur edging, elbow-length brown tricot gloves, brown pumps, gold clutch, excellent condition, 11".......**$450**

Theriault's

Barbie in Resort Set #963, tan complexion and red lips, summer resort attire of blue and white striped jersey top, white shorts, red cotton jacket with white striping, white open-top cap, cork-heeled wedge shoes with white vinyl tops, gilt bracelet and three gear-shaped charms, 11".....**$500**

Theriault's

Barbie in Career Girl #954, circa 1961, bubble-cut hairstyle and coral-colored lips, two-piece black and white tweed suit with fitted short jacket and wide collar, red knit body blouse, matching tweed hat with black velvet ribbon and red satin rose, elbow-length black tricot gloves, black open-toe shoes, 11"............................. **$150**

Theriault's

◀ Barbie in Fashion Luncheon #1656 with short, page-boy hairstyle, two-piece pink jacket dress with silk bodice and textured skirt, matching jacket with pink satin collar, border and front tie with rhinestone pin, pink satin hat, pink pumps and elbow-length pink gloves, excellent condition, 11"...**$500**

Theriault's

▶ Blonde side-swirl ponytail Barbie in Benefit Performance #1667, circa 1966, red velvet tunic with fitted bodice, rhinestone accents, wide flared skirt over white tulle skirt with red ribbons, red open-toe shoes and white gloves, 11"......... **$350**

Theriault's

Blonde painted-hair Ken in Play Ball #792, circa 1963, two-piece striped baseball uniform with red piping and felt letter "M," red vinyl baseball cap, red socks, black studded shoes, baseball bat, ball and glove; and blonde painted-hair Ken in Touchdown #799, red jersey sweater with number 7 in white felt, red cotton pants, black and red socks, black shoes, vinyl football helmet, shoulder pads, carrying a football, both in excellent condition, both 12".....................................**$50**

Theriault's

Barbie in Plantation Belle #966, circa 1960, whitened complexion with orange eyeliner, pale pink dotted nylon dress with tiers of lace trim and ruffles, white nylon petticoat with tulle ruffles, white open-toe shoes, white tricot gloves, pink pearl necklace and bracelet, wide-brimmed hat and matching straw purse with sequins and beads, 11"............................**$650**

Theriault's

Barbie in Open Road #985 and Ken in Rally Day #788, circa early 1960s, side-swirl blonde ponytail Barbie in striped slacks, beige knit short-sleeved sweater, khaki car coat with toggle buttons, straw hat with red chiffon scarf, cork wedge shoes with red vinyl tops, red sun glasses, and road map tucked in coat pocket, reddish/brown-haired Ken in khaki slacks, yellow boat-neck jersey, khaki car coat, red cap, argyle socks, brown and white saddle shoes... **$350**

Theriault's

Empress Bride® Barbie®, circa 1992, fifth in the series of Barbie versions created by designer Bob Mackie, ivory bridal gown with gold embroidery and pleated tulle skirt, matching tiara and choker, original box........**$150**

Morphy Auctions

Twist N' Turn Barbies: light brunette Barbie in Suede 'n Fur #3491, brown faux-suede skirt and coat, dark brown, white and black fur, brown calf-high boots; and Fiery Felt #1789 ensemble with bright orange felt coat with orange fringe trim, matching hat, light orange flexible rain boots, and gold bead buttons, excellent condition, 11"...**$550**

Theriault's

Barbie Dream Carriage with Two Horses, Mattel... **$120**

Quinn Auction Galleries

"Barbie Queen of the Prom" board game, circa 1960, object of game is to buy a formal dress, start dating a boy, be elected club president, then win the game by becoming queen of the prom...................................**$44**

SeriousToyz

Barbie superheroes: Catwoman, Supergirl, Spider-Man's Mary Jane in bridal fare, Batgirl, Wonder Woman (two versions), and Fantastic Four, near mint condition, largest box 13-1/2" x 9" **$125**

Morphy Auctions

Barbie #3, brunette ponytail, painted blue eyes, ruby lips, dressed in Orange Blossom #987, yellow sheath dress, lace nylon over dress, hat with yellow tulle, bouquet of flowers, short white gloves and open-toe heels, original box and booklet, black carrying case, additional clothing and accessories from early 1960s, Barbie in near mint condition, clothing and case in very good condition **$300**

Frasher's Doll Auctions

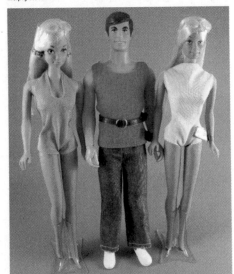

Malibu Barbie, Busy Ken, Malibu PJ, circa 1972, Ken in original outfit with wrist tag, PJ has original sunglasses and hair ties, Barbie has original wrist tag, bathing suit and sunglasses.......................**$80**

McMasters Harris Apple Tree Doll Auctions

Two pieces from Barbie Designers' Salute to Hollywood Collection™, both by designer Vera Wang, both in original boxes, both circa 1998: strapless satin lavender gown with stole and lavender evening bag, matching earrings, necklace and brooch; ivory satin wedding gown with sheer arms, black velvet-like piping and matching velvet bow at crown of tulle veil **$90**

Morphy Auctions

Barbie pedal car, metal body, pink paint, official Barbie logo and floral design, circa 1970s $172

Bob's Gas Pumps

Barbie summer clothing sets with accessories, mint in package, includes set of striped top and yellow shorts; set of striped skirt, sunglasses, and red heels; set of summer hat, green heels, and striped purse; and set of three handbags **$450**

Quinn's Auction Galleries

1963 Barbie Ge-tar with crank, plays "Bicycle Built for Two."........**$125**

Photo by Steve Evans

Brunette Ponytail Barbie #3 in Apple Print Sheath Dress #917, hair in original setting, fragile bottom elastic and thinning spot on top of hair............**$325**

McMasters Harris Apple Tree Doll Auctions

American Girl Barbie dressed in midnight blue with blue open-toe Japanese shoes and silver clutch purse...................................**$175**

McMasters Harris Apple Tree Doll Auctions

Barbie Pan American Airways Stewardess #1678 hard-to-find ensemble, original blue twill jacket, white short sleeve blouse, blue twill skirt, black shoulder bag, black closed toe pumps, blue hat with Pan American emblem, white gloves (non-original).................................**$950**

McMasters Harris Apple Tree Doll Auctions

Blonde molded hair Ken and Titian Bubble Cut Barbie, Ken in Army and Air Force #797 partial outfit, Barbie in Dinner at Eight #946. .... **$125**

McMasters Harris Apple Tree Doll Auctions

Barbie in Debutante Ball #1666, full hair, face and nail paint, original shoes and replaced gloves. **$325**

McMasters Harris Apple Tree Doll Auctions)

Golden Legacy Barbie, Bob Mackie dress, produced in celebration of Barbie's 50th anniversary, 2009.......................... **$125**

McMasters Harris Apple Tree Doll Auctions

Barbie Silkstones, Spa Getaway and The French Maid versions, never removed from box, hard vinyl to resemble porcelain, circa early 2000s. **$175**

McMasters Harris Apple Tree Doll Auctions

Molded head Miss Barbie, painted brown hair with orange painted headband, bendable left leg, open and close eyes, dressed in Golden Glory #1645, circa 1964............................**$200**

Quinn's Auction Galleries

Titian Bubble Cut Barbie, circa 1963, rare side-part hair, painted nails, faded lips, knit dress, fur-lined collar on winter coat with hat, gold-colored clutch **$325**

McMasters Harris Apple Tree Doll Auctions

Baskets

The American Indians were the first basket weavers on this continent and, of necessity, the early Colonial settlers and their descendants pursued this artistic handicraft to provide essential containers for berries, eggs, and endless other items to be carried or stored.

Rye straw, split willow and reeds are but a few of the wide variety of materials used. Nantucket baskets, plainly and sturdily constructed, along with those made by specialized groups, draw the greatest attention to this area of collecting.

Paint-decorated woven-splint basket, probably Eastern Woodland Indian tribe, late 19th century, rectangular basket with two carved hardwood handles, upright splints with natural and blue-painted surfaces, horizontal weavers painted red, blue, and yellow, split on one handle, 6-1/2" h. x 10-3/8" w. x 11-5/8" l. overall. **$600**

Skinner, Inc., www.skinnerinc.com

Cherokee rib-type woven splint double-lidded basket, white oak, melon form with wrapped rim and opposing demilune-form lids hinged through arched handle, whole raised on applied circular foot, $3.00 penciled on top of handle, probably western North Carolina, first half 20th century, 14" h. overall, 6-3/4" h. to rim, 11-1/2" dia. rim..................**$184**

Jeffrey S. Evans & Associates

Indian-made painted woven-splint basket, Northeastern American Indian tribe, late 19th/early 20th century, oblong basket, exterior splints painted red, blue, and black, minor losses and breaks, 5-1/8" h x 12" w. x 15" l. **$480**

Skinner, Inc., www.skinnerinc.com

Two woven baskets and painted firkin **$178**

Pook & Pook, Inc.

Woven rattan Nantucket basket, late 19th/early 20th century, deep round basket with carved ash handles, 12" h. x 14-1/2" dia. **$1,200**

Skinner, Inc., www.skinnerinc.com

Group of four splint baskets, 19th century, tallest 9-1/2" h...**$213**

Pook & Pook, Inc.

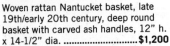

Woodlands painted basket, 6" h. x 13-1/2" w., and gathering basket, 12" h. x 13-1/4" w. **$237**

Pook & Pook, Inc.

Small Nantucket basket, late 19th/early 20th century, deep round basket with carved ash swing handle fastened with brass ears, 5" h. to top of upright handle, 3-1/8" h. to rim, rim 3-3/8" dia..................................... **$600**

Skinner, Inc., www.skinnerinc.com

Indian-made woven-splint sewing basket, Northeastern Woodland Indian tribe, late 19th/early 20th century, round basket tapering to square bottom, two carved bentwood handles, exterior with woven curlicues, interior sides mounted with four small oval open hexagonal-weave baskets, 5" h., 11" dia.. **$185**

Skinner, Inc., www.skinnerinc.com

Nantucket basket, R. Folger, Nantucket, Massachusetts, late 19th century, round basket with carved hardwood swing handle and faceted ear, interior turned wooden base stenciled "R. FOLGER/ MAKER/NANTUCKET/MASS.," losses, 3-3/4" h. to rim, 7-1/4" h. to top of upright handle, 6" dia..................................**$360**

Skinner, Inc., www.skinnerinc.com

Nantucket basket made by Ferdinand Sylvaro (1869-1952), Nantucket, Massachusetts, early to mid-20th century, round form with swing handle, decorated with three bands of darker caning, inscribed paper maker's label on base, 12-1/4" h. to top of upright handle, 13" dia.........**$1,440**

Skinner, Inc., www.skinnerinc.com

Six woven baskets, largest 3-1/2" h. x 17" w **$237**
Pook & Pook, Inc.

Splint oak melon basket, God's-eye handle,
8-1/2" h. x 12" w. **$533**
Pook & Pook, Inc.

New England Woodlands painted basket, late 19th
century, 7" h. x 13-3/4" w....................................**$563**
Pook & Pook, Inc.

Massive Pennsylvania rye straw basket
with lid, late 19th century, 12" h. x
21-1/2" w...**$267**
Pook & Pook, Inc.

TOP LOT!

Charles II beadwork basket, late 17th century, initialed
EG, 5-1/2" h. x 24" w. x 18" dia.................. **$24,885**
Pook & Pook, Inc.

Three splint gathering baskets, 19th century, largest 21" dia. **$207**

Pook & Pook, Inc.

Two Pennsylvania rye straw baskets, 19th century, 4-1/2" h. x 12-1/4" w. and 6-1/2" h. x 20-1/2" w. **$119**

Pook & Pook, Inc.

Two Shenandoah Valley of Virginia woven splint egg baskets, white oak, each of circular form with X-wrap rim, high arched handle and slight kick-up bottom, first half 20th century, 11" h. overall, 11-1/2" dia., 12" dia. **$104**

Jeffrey S. Evans & Associates

Splint oak basket, 19th century, retaining old red surface, 9" h...**$486**

Pook & Pook, Inc.

Contemporary Nantucket lightship basket with bone whale appliqué, 6-1/2" h...........................**$59**

Pook & Pook, Inc.

Bookends

Once a staple in many homes, bookends serve both functional and decorative purposes. They not only keep a person's books in order, they look good while they're doing it.

Bookends are commonly made of a variety of metals – bronze, brass, pewter, or silver plate – as well as marble, wood, ceramic, and other natural or manmade materials. The art they feature represents many subjects, with wildlife, domesticated animals and pets, sports figures or items, nautical themes, and fantasy themes as favorites.

The value of an antique bookend is determined by its age, the material it is made from, what it represents, the company that created it, and how scarce it is.

Tiffany Studios grapevine adjustable bookends, gold patina, backed with caramel slag glass, signed on underside "Tiffany Studios New York 1027," very good to excellent condition with some minor discoloration to patina, 6" h., expands from 14" to 22-3/4"......................................**$1,500-$2,500**

James D. Julia, Inc.

Pair of cast figural Coca-Cola bottle bookends, circa 1963, cast bronze with gold wash finish, good to very good condition with some wear, scuffs and scratches to the finish, 5-1/4" w. x 8-1/4" h.................. **$58**

James D. Julia, Inc.

Tiffany Studios grapevine bookends, gold grapevine overlay design set against caramel slag glass ground, signed "Tiffany Studios New York 1024," very good to excellent condition with minor wear, 6" h. x 5-1/2" w. with tongue measuring 5-1/2". **$1,438**

James D. Julia, Inc.

Russel Wright rodeo circus bookends, Russel Wright, Inc., American, circa 1930, chrome-plated brass, 8-1/2" w. x 2-1/2" d. x 3-3/4" h. **$21,000**

Russel Wright, Inc.

Small Rook bookends, Rookwood, designed by William McDonald, cast in 1920, mottled brown mat glaze, impressed with Rookwood symbol, date and shape 2275, no crazing, excellent original condition, 4-5/8" h. **$425**

Mark Mussio, Humler & Nolan

Horse Head bookends, Rookwood, designed by William P. McDonald, cast in 1928, Nubian Black Glaze, impressed on bottom with Rookwood symbol, date and shape 6014, impressed "W.P. McDonald" on side near base, excellent original condition, 6" h. **$550**

Mark Mussio, Humler & Nolan

Single Owl bookends, Rookwood, designed by William McDonald, cast in 1929, dark blue mat crystalline glaze, impressed with Rookwood symbol, date, shape 2655 and designer's monogram, excellent, original condition, fine glaze, 5-5/8" h. **$275**

Mark Mussio, Humler & Nolan

Colonial woman bookends, Rookwood, designed by William McDonald, cast in 1915, version of Nacreous Glaze, impressed with Rookwood logo, date, shape 2185, and upside down P, indicative of luster glaze, wheel ground X, restoration on rear corner of one figure, 5-1/2" h. **$170**

Mark Mussio, Humler & Nolan

Rookwood Egyptian bookends in tan mat glaze, 1924, designed by William P. McDonald whose initials appear on plinth of each, marks include company logo, date and shape number 2510, few minor scuffs, head of one maiden knocked off and reattached, 5-3/8" h. **$300**

Mark Mussio, Humler & Nolan

Frankart patinated metal horse head bookends, Frankart, Inc., New York, circa 1935, marks: FRANKART INC., PAT. APPL'D FOR, 5-1/8" h. **$75**

Heritage Auctions

Art Deco marbleized orange and green Bakelite bookends, maker unknown, American, circa 1930, unmarked, 6-1/4" h. **$406**

Heritage Auctions

Large Rook bookends, Rookwood, designed by William McDonald, cast in 1920, dark blue mat glaze, impressed on base with Rookwood logo, date and shape 2274, excellent original condition, 6-3/8" h..**$400**

Mark Mussio, Humler & Nolan

Seal bookends, Rookwood, designed by Kataro Shirayamadani, mat green crystalline glaze, impressed with Rookwood symbol, date and shape 2642, wheel ground X to base, professional restoration to flipper, 6-3/8" h. x 7-1/2" l. ...**$2,100**

Mark Mussio, Humler & Nolan

Blackbird bookends, Rookwood, Shirayamadani design, cast in 1929, light brown mat glaze, impressed with Rookwood symbol, date and shape 2658, one with tiny grinding nick at base, 5-1/2" h. x 5-3/8" w. **$425**

Mark Mussio, Humler & Nolan

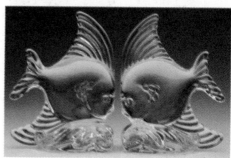

Heisey figural fish bookends, colorless, each with polished base, Heisey Glass Co., mid-20th century, undamaged, 6-1/2" h. **$92**

Jeffrey S. Evans & Associates

Bakelite and chrome bookends, red Bakelite base with triangulated chrome and Bakelite elements, maker unknown, American, circa 1930, 5-3/8" h. **$563**

Heritage Auctions

The Sphynx bookends, Rookwood, Louise Abel design, cast in 1929, "Frogskin" glaze, mottled green over blue mat glazes, each impressed with Rookwood symbol, date and shape 2503, one has small nick to rear edge, 7" h. ea. **$650**

Mark Mussio, Humler & Nolan

Armor patinated bronze figural bookends depicting Pandora opening box, New York, circa 1922, marks: ARMOR BRONZE, 19 © 22, 7-1/8" h. **$106**

Heritage Auctions

Cast brass or bronze Native American Indian head bookends, circa 1920, small areas of oxidation, 5-1/4" h. x 5" w. **$50**

Woodbury Auctions

Roycroft hammered copper pair of bookends, each with hanging bail, stamped mark and original patina, first quarter 20th century, 5-1/4" h. x 4" x 3-1/4"..$100-$150

Jeffrey S. Evans & Associates

Pirate bookends, Littco, circa 1928, cast iron, painted, good condition, paint loss throughout, corner chipped on back of base approximately 1/4" x 1/4", 7" h. x 4" l. x 2-7/8" d. Littlestown Hardware and Foundry Co., Inc. began as a gray iron foundry on May 24, 1916. They are still in operation today in Littlestown, Pennsylvania, producing commercial aluminum castings. Between the world wars, they began producing a line of heavy solid cast iron decorative items for the home, including doorstops and bookends, from 1920 to 1932. Their catalog featured over 40 designs, some of which were sculpted by a local artist living in nearby Wrightstown. In 1941, the price of the company's most expensive bookend was 80 cents per pair. During World War II, raw materials for bookends were not "essential," so bookend production ceased, and LITTCO began manufacturing products for the war effort. **$50**

Louis J. Dianni, LLC

Bookends, patinated bronze, circa 1925, Snead & Co., vessel at full sail on ocean, top right marked 1925, very good condition, 5-1/8" h. x 4-1/4" l. x 2" d.. **$40**

Louis J. Dianni, LLC

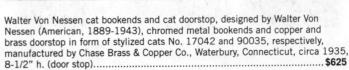

Art Deco bookends, woman sitting on book, marked Nuart NYC, 8-1/2" h. **$150**

Martin Auction Co.

Walter Von Nessen cat bookends and cat doorstop, designed by Walter Von Nessen (American, 1889-1943), chromed metal bookends and copper and brass doorstop in form of stylized cats No. 17042 and 90035, respectively, manufactured by Chase Brass & Copper Co., Waterbury, Connecticut, circa 1935, 8-1/2" h. (door stop)..**$625**

Heritage Auctions

Art Deco cast bookends, marked on back "DES PAT APFL FOR". **$50**

Arus Auctions

Red and black enameled metal elephant-form bookends, maker unknown, American, circa 1935, 4-1/8" h. **$313**

Heritage Auctions

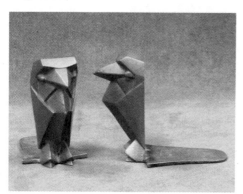

Art Deco brass raven bookends, signed Art Brass Co. NY., 4" h. **$125**

William J. Jenack Auctioneers

Southern Belle bookends, Rookwood, William McDonald design, cast in 1934, mat glazes of pink, brown, ivory and yellow, each impressed with Rookwood logo, date and shape 6252, one has pinhead size nick to rear, 6-1/2" x 5-1/2".......**$200**

Mark Mussio, Humler & Nolan

Cast Indian head bookends, 4-3/4" h. x 5-1/2" w. **$200**

Greater London Auctions

Bookends, boy and girl looking at each other, colorful traditional outfits, each 5-1/2" h. **$275**

Morphy Auctions

Assembled gilt bronze figural bookends, Isadore Konti (American/Austrian, 1862-1938), depicting two opposing athletes in pushing pose, raised on rectangular base, one signed I. Konti, each inscribed Copyright 1908, by R Holstein, 6-3/8" h........................ **$1,600**

Leslie Hindman Auctioneers

Chelsea ship's bell, clock, and barometer bookends. $700

Susanin's Auctions

Bronze-over-plaster ram bookends, signed J. Krupka, dated 1914, 8" x 8-1/2" x 5".......................$190

Stephenson's Auction

Bookends with brass sailboats on iron bases, 5-1/2" h. $80

Saco River Auction

Bradley & Hubbard bookends, 6-1/2" h. $130

Martin Auction Co.

Bookends, frosted glass, shape of hands holding bottles, 19th century, 9-1/2"h. $125

Kaminski Auctions

Roseville white rose ceramic bookends, 5" l. x 4-1/2" h. $90

Vero Beach Auction

Batchelder bookends, tile and brass, circa 1925, stamped POTTER STUDIO E102, 5-1/4" sq. x 7" d. $250

Kaminski Auctions

Books

With an excess of 100 million books in existence, there are plenty of opportunities and avenues for bibliophiles to feed their enthusiasm and build a satisfying collection of noteworthy tomes without taking out a second mortgage or sacrificing their children's college funds. With so many to choose from, the true challenge is limiting a collection to a manageable size and scale, adding only volumes that meet the requirements of bringing the collector pleasure and holding their values.

What collectors are really searching for when they refer to "first editions" are the first printings of first editions. Every book has a first edition, each of which is special in its own right. As Matthew Budman points out in *Collecting Books* (House of Collectibles, 2004): "A first represents the launching of a work into the world, with or without fanfare, to have a great impact, or no impact, immediately or decades later.... Holding a first edition puts you directly in contact with that moment of impact."

Devon Gray, director of Fine Books and Manuscripts at Skinner, Inc., explains the fascination with collectible books. "Collectors are always interested in landmarks of human thought and culture, and important moments in the history of printing."

What makes a first edition special enough to be considered collectible is rarity and demand; the number of people who want a book has to be greater than the number of books available. So, even if there are relatively few in existence, there has to be a demand for any particular first edition to be monetarily valuable.

Author Richard Russell has been collecting and selling books since 1973; in his book, *Antique Trader Book Collector's Price Guide*, he explains that innovative (or perhaps even unpopular) books that are initially released in small printings "will eventually become some of the most sought after and expensive books in the collector's market." He gives as an example John Grisham's *A Time to Kill* (Wynwood Press, 1989), which had an initial print run of just 5,000 hardcover copies. The author bought 1,000 himself at wholesale with the plan to sell at retail and turn a bit of profit. When Grisham couldn't sell them at $10 apiece, he was giving them away out of his law office.[1] The book is valued at about $4,000 today.

Learning how to recognize first editions is a key to protecting yourself as a collector; a book collector can't take it for granted that the person you are buying from (especially if they are not a professional bookseller) has identified the book properly. Entire volumes have been written on identifying first editions; different publishing houses use different means of identification, many utilizing differing methods and codes. However, according to *Antique Trader Book Collector's Price Guide*, there are several details that will identify a first edition:

- The date on the title page matches the copyright date with no other printings listed on the copyright page (verso)

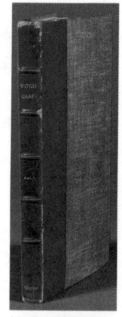

John Hale (1636-1700), *A Modest Enquiry into the Nature of Witchcraft*, Boston: Kneeland and Adams, 1771, second edition, 158 pages, lacking the final blank. Octavo in fours; bottom portion of title, with imprint, trimmed away and replaced with a photostatic facsimile, untrimmed throughout, title page faded, toning and spotting to contents, rebound in half red morocco and buckram boards, rubbed. The "Epistle to the Reader" is rather chilling as it was written in March 1697/8 by John Higginson, pastor of the church in Salem. This critique of the Salem trials, first published posthumously in 1702, is a detailed and thoughtful refutation of the modes and methods of that disastrous escapade. **$2,400**

Skinner, Inc., www.skinnerinc.com

Maurice Sendak, *Where the Wild Things Are*, New York: Harper & Row, 1963. First edition in dust jacket, inscribed with a drawing, color illustrations by Sendak, oblong octavo, green cloth-backed pictorial boards, very slight toning along edges; pictorial endpapers, bottom final binding thread loose at hinge; first issue dust jacket, lower outer margin clipped; custom blue leather and cloth clamshell case gilt-lettered along spine. **$18,000**

Swann Galleries

- "First Edition," "First Printing," "First Issue," or something similar is listed on the copyright page
- A publisher's seal or logo (colophon) is printed on the title page, copyright page, or at the end of the text block
- The printer's code on the copyright page shows a "1" or an "A" at one end or the other (example: "9 8 7 6 5 4 3 2 1" would indicate first edition; "9 8 7 6 5 4 3 2" would indicate second edition).

As is the case with so many collectibles, condition is paramount. If a book was published with a dust jacket, it must be present and in great condition to assess the book's maximum value. Gray uses an example to illustrate the importance of condition: "A book with a very large value basically has further to fall before it loses it all. A great example is the first edition of the printed account of the Lewis and Clarke expedition. In bad condition its value is in the four-figure range; in better condition, it gets up to five figures; and in excellent condition, six figures."

She continues, "Another example: The 1920 first American edition of T.S. Eliot's *Poems* sells for around $300 in poor condition, with no dust jacket; and $1,200 to $1,500 in good condition, in a good dust jacket; the copy that Eliot gave to Virginia Woolf sold for 90,000 British pounds [approximately $136,000]; all the same edition."

Signatures enhance book values because it often places the book into the author's hands. Cut signatures add slightly to a book's value because the author didn't actually sign the book – they may have never even held the book with the added cut signature. When the book itself is signed, even if with a brief inscription, it holds a slightly higher value. If the author is known for making regular appearances and accommodating all signature requests, the signature adds little to the value of the book because the supply for signed examples is plentiful.

"Real value potential comes into play with association material," Gray explains. "For example, a famous novelist's Nobel-winning story is based on a tumultuous affair he had with a famous starlet under his heiress-wife's nose, and you have the copy he presented to his wife, with her 'notes.'"

Even a title that has been labeled as "great," "important," or "essential" doesn't mean a particular edition — even a first edition — is collectible or monetarily valuable. After all, if a much-anticipated book is released with an initial print run of 350,000, chances are there will be hundreds of thousands of "firsts" to choose from — even decades after publication. Supply far outweighs demand, diminishing value.

The overly abundant supply of book club editions (which can be reprinted indefinitely) is just one of the reasons they're not valued by collectors. Some vintage book club editions were also made from inferior materials, such as high-acid paper using lower quality manufacturing processes.

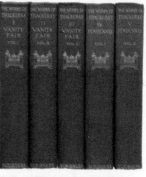

H.G. Wells, *Things to Come*, Cresset Press, 1935. First edition, first printing, signed by author; faint rubbing to cloth with staining to lower corner of front board, affecting pastedown; minor rubbing to dust jacket with a few small chips and tears. From the John McLaughlin/Book Sail Collection. **$925**

Heritage Auction Galleries

Edgar Rice Burroughs, *Land of Terror*, 1944. First edition, first printing; mild bumping to boards, owner's name stamped on front pastedown, minor toning and light rubbing to dust jacket. From the John McLaughlin/Book Sail Collection. **$259**

Heritage Auctions

William Makepeace Thackeray, *The Works of William Makepeace Thackeray*, Kensington Edition, New York: Charles Scribner's Sons, 1903-1904. Complete in 32 octavo volumes, frontispieces, plates, and text illustrations, after the originals; bound in original publisher's full green cloth, gilt, spines uniformly sunned, some rubbing to bindings, one tissue guard torn............................**$15**

Heritage Auctions

Determining if a book is a book club edition is easier than determining if it is a first edition. Some of the giveaways that Matthew Budman lists in *Collecting Books* include:

• No price on dust jacket

• Blind stamp on back cover (small impression on the back board under the dust jacket); can be as small as a pinprick hole

• "Book Club Edition" (or similar notation) on dust jacket

• Books published by the Literary Guild after World War II are smaller format, thinner and printed on cheap paper.

Fledgling book collectors should also be aware of companies that built a burgeoning business of publishing a copious number of "classic" and best-seller reprints; just a few of the long list are Grosset & Dunlap, Reader's Digest, Modern Library, A.L. Burt, Collier, Tower and Triangle. Many of these companies' editions are valued only as reading copies, not as collectibles worthy of investment.

Proper care should be implemented early on when building a collection to assure the books retain their condition and value. Books should be stored upright on shelves in a climate-controlled environment out of direct (or even bright indirect) sunlight. Too much humidity will warp covers; high temperatures will break down glues. Arrange them so similar-sized books are side-by-side for maximum support, and use bookends so the books don't lean, which will eventually cause the spines to shift and cause permanent damage.

A bookplate usually will reduce a book's value, so keep that in mind when you're thinking of adding a book with bookplate to your collection, and avoid adding bookplates to your own volumes. Also, don't pack your volumes with high-acid paper such as newspaper clippings, and always be careful when placing or removing them from the shelf so you don't tear the spine.

Building a book collection — or any collection, for that matter — on a budget involves knowing more about the subject than the seller. Learning everything possible about proper identification of coveted books and significant authors involves diligence and dedication, but the reward is maximum enjoyment of collecting at any level.

—*Karen Knapstein, Print Editor,* Antique Trader *magazine*

1 John Grisham's Favorite Mistake: Giving Away First Editions, http://www.thedailybeast.com/newsweek/2012/04/01/john-grisham-s-favorite-mistake-giving-away-first-editions.html

Ian Fleming, *Diamonds Are Forever*, London: Jonathan Cape, 1956. First edition, first printing, inscribed and signed by author, "To Lionel from Ian with affection" on front free endpaper. Octavo, 257 pages, publisher's black cloth binding with silver titles, original pictorial dust jacket priced "12s. 6d. net." Slight bowing, light soiling and rubbing to boards, minor fading to spine titles, small bump to spine head, mild bumping to corners, some foxing to first and last few leaves and along text edges, minimal foxing within body of text, minor overall wear and rubbing to jacket, some tiny tape reinforcements to verso of jacket at spine and flap fold ends, miniscule puncture to rear flap fold, minimal loss to extremities, purple ink mark, mostly unobtrusive, through jacket price.................................**$21,250**

Heritage Auctions

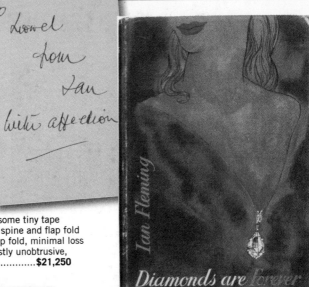

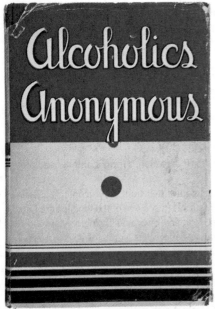

Bill Wilson, *Alcoholics Anonymous: The Story of How Many Thousands of Men and Women Have Recovered from Alcoholism*, New York City: Works Publishing, Inc., 1939. Rare first edition, first printing of Alcoholics Anonymous' famous "Big Red Book." Octavo, [x], 400 pages, publisher's binding of full red cloth, front cover lettered in gilt, spine lettered in gilt, rare original dust jacket, jacket spine a bit toned, some foxing, damp staining at corners and thumb soiling to jacket, jacket chipped at front panel near headcap and lower corner, several tears with corresponding tape repairs to verso; binding rubbed, gilt in binding oxidized, gutters before title page and between second and third blank leaves starting. It is believed that only 4,760 copies of the ordered run of 5,000 were printed due to paper shortages. **$15,000**

Heritage Auctions

Group of four first edition books, Zane Grey, various publishers, good or better condition..................**$325**

Heritage Auctions

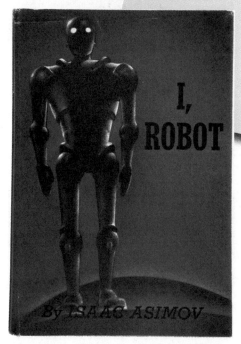

Isaac Asimov, *I, Robot*, New York: Gnome Press, Inc., 1950. First edition, presentation copy, inscribed by Asimov on front free endpaper, "For: Martin Greenberg who actually got this book out, by God / Love! Isaac Asimov 12/2/50." Also inscribed by Greenberg on front pastedown, "Gnome Press File Copy Martin Greenberg." Octavo, 253 pages, publisher's full red cloth, front cover and spine stamped in black, dust jacket, minor rubbing to jacket and binding extremities, minor soiling to rear jacket panel. **$8,125**

Heritage Auctions

Maurice Sendak, *Where the Wild Things Are*, New York: Harper & Row, 1963. True first printing, color illustrations by Sendak, oblong octavo, green cloth-backed pictorial boards, mild soiling, mostly to turn-ins; scattered light soiling on a few pages; original first issue dust jacket, moderately toned with minor creasing to edges, lower inside corner of front flap clipped; custom box of 1/4 gilt-lettered burgundy morocco over blue cloth. **$6,240**

Swann Galleries

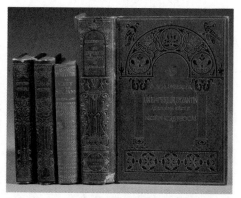

Byzantine Empire and Constantinople, 11 volumes: *Finlay's History of the Byzantine Empire*, London, 1853, in publisher's cloth, two volumes; Davey's The Sultan and His Subjects, New York, 1897, in publisher's cloth, two volumes; Clement's Constantinople the City of the Sultans, Boston, 1895, in gilt-stamped publisher's cloth; Edmondo de Amicis' Constantinople, New York and London, 1896, in publisher's cloth, two volumes; Grosvenor's Constantinople, Boston, 1895, in gilt publisher's cloth, two volumes; Schlumberger's Un Empereur Byzantin au Dixieme Siecle Nicephore Phocas, Paris, 1890, in decorated publisher's cloth, and one other. **$450**

Skinner, Inc., www.skinnerinc.com

Stendhal, Balzac, Hugo, et al., contributors, Edmund Gosse, ed., *A Century of French Romance*, Versailles Edition, one of 250 numbered sets, New York: Appleton, 1901-1902. Set number 119, 20 octavo volumes, illustrated with original plates in colors (frontispieces hand-colored), photogravure portraits, and text portraits; publisher's contemporary half burgundy crushed levant morocco over marbled boards, spines tooled in floral motif and lettered in gilt in compartments, four raised bands, top edge gilt, others uncut, marbled endleaves; spines slightly darkened, some rubbing and mild wear to spines, a few joints just starting, bookplates. **$44**

Heritage Auctions

Aubrey Beardsley (1872-1898), three volumes: *Malory's Morte D'Arthur*, New York: Dutton, 1927, limited to 1,600 copies, publisher's gilt cloth, t.e.g.; *Fifty Drawings by Aubrey Beardsley*, New York, 1920, numbered 233 of 500 and signed by the publisher, ornately stamped gilt publisher's cloth; *A Second Book of Fifty Drawings*, London, 1899, limited to 1,000 copies, red publisher's cloth, pictorial gilt stamped, spine worn and faded, all titles illustrated throughout.................. **$431**

Skinner, Inc., www.skinnerinc.com

Nathaniel Hawthorne (1804-1864), *The Scarlet Letter, a Romance*, Boston: Ticknor, Reed, and Fields, 1850. Octavo, first edition, first issue, with the word "reduplicate" on page 21, four pages of ads; small mark on title and three spots in text, contents otherwise good; modern scarlet morocco, a.e.g., inner gilt dentelles and spine very good; 4-1/2" x 7"..................**$1,200**

Skinner, Inc., www.skinnerinc.com

Albert Deane Richardson (1833-1869), *Beyond the Mississippi*, Hartford: American Publishing Co., 1867. Octavo, publisher's gilt cloth, engraved title pages and folding maps, one corner torn with slight loss, illustrated throughout, bindings, worn, torn and shaken, brown endleaves, 6" x 9". Deane was an acclaimed journalist and Union spy whose life ended in a scandalous murder when he was only 36. ... **$49**

Skinner, Inc., www.skinnerinc.com

Henry George Bohn, *A Catalogue of Books*, London, 1841. Very thick octavo (4.75 in.), half red sheepskin, quite rubbed, back board detached, ex library copy with release stamp inside front board; Bohn's famous "Guinea" catalog prepared by William Lowndes with the assistance of Bernard Quaritch, includes descriptions of more than 23,000 titles. Together with: Thomas Thorpe's Catalogue of the Most Extensive, Valuable and Truly Interesting Collection of Curious Books, 1842; Catalogue of the Greater Part of the Library of Thomas Crofton Croker, 1854; and Catalogue of the Singularly Curious, Very Interesting and Valuable Library of Edward Skegg, Esq., 1842. .... **$480**

Skinner, Inc., www.skinnerinc.com

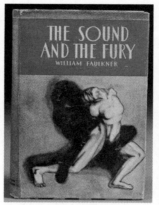

William Faulkner (1897-1962), *The Sound and the Fury*, New York: Jonathan Cape and Harrison Smith, 1929. First edition, in publisher's white cloth and black and white patterned boards and end papers, Kollwitz dust jacket with an advertisement for Lot Houses by Elizabeth Manning for $2.50 on back flap, dust jacket with small chip at head of spine in margin before red band, spine somewhat sunned, top board edges and head of spine slightly darkened. **$7,380**

Skinner, Inc., www.skinnerinc.com

Gilbert Burnat (fl. circa 1649), *Ethicae Dissertationes*, Leiden: Maire, 1649. First edition, octavo, in a contemporary speckled calfskin binding with the arms of Jacques Auguste de Thou in gilt on front and back boards, leather split at front joint. Confusion could easily arise between the two Scottish Gilberts, Burnet and Burnat. The more famous Burnet was six years old when this book was published. Further confusion may ensue because de Thou, the French book collector, died in 1617................................. **$215**

Skinner, Inc., www.skinnerinc.com

First edition, Hugh Lofting, *Doctor Dolittle's Caravan*, with a Dec. 19, 1946, one-page autograph letter signed by Lofting, New York: Frederick A. Stokes, 1926; 342 pages, including 75 full-page black-and-white illustrations reckoned in the pagination, with color frontispiece and tissue guard, pictorial endpapers, minor wear to extremities................ **$56**

Heritage Auctions

Jules Verne (1828-1905), *The Castle of the Carpathians*, New York: The Merriam Co., 1894. First American edition, octavo, illustrated with wood engravings, bound in maroon publisher's cloth, titular castle and dragon-like nyctalop on front board, binding shaken, preliminaries starting, head chipped, contents good.................... **$1,000-$1,200**

Skinner, Inc., www.skinnerinc.com

Theodore Roosevelt (1858-1919), *The Wilderness Hunter*, inscribed to Jacob Riis (1849-1914), New York: Putnam's Sons, 1893. "To my beloved friend, Jacob A. Riis; may you enjoy the north woods as much as I enjoyed the great plains of the Rockies! Theodore Roosevelt, July 1901." Illustrated throughout, in worn publisher's binding. Riis, the Danish-American photographer, journalist, and social reformer, and Roosevelt were best friends. **$3,198**

Skinner, Inc., www.skinnerinc.com

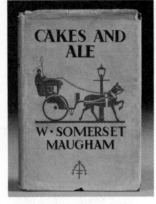

W. Somerset Maugham (1874-1965), *Cakes and Ale*, London: William Heinemann Ltd., 1930. First edition, first state, with "won'" instead of "won't" on page 147, line 14, blue publisher's cloth, edge-worn, chipped dust jacket, spine panel darkened........... **$390**

Skinner, Inc., www.skinnerinc.com

Ernest Hemingway (1899-1961), *A Farewell to Arms*, New York: Charles Scribner's Sons, 1929. First trade edition, first printing, without legal disclaimer on page [x], publisher's black cloth with gold paper labels, in first issue dust jacket, with "Katharine Barclay" uncorrected on front flap, cloth intact, corners slightly soft, dust jacket faded and somewhat darkened, with a 2" piece missing from dust jacket at foot of spine. **$1,200**

Skinner, Inc., www.skinnerinc.com

Basil of Caesarea (330-379), *Opera Omnia*, Paris: Cramoisy, 1638. Three folio volumes, all title pages printed in red and black, engraved frontispiece of Basil facing the title in volume one, text printed in parallel columns of Greek and Latin throughout, bound in uniform contemporary calf, decorated in blind with roll tools, spines with gilt lettering and tooling. **$390**

Skinner, Inc., www.skinnerinc.com

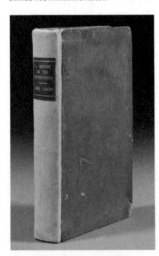

First edition, John Adams (1735-1826), *A Defence of the Constitutions of Government of the United States of America*, London: for C. Dilly, 1787. Octavo; published as a complete work, Adams later added two other volumes; contemporary speckled calf boards, corners bumped, amateurishly rebacked, pulling on first and last signatures, new endleaves, original fly leaf at rear with marginal stains, marginal stain on title and last leaf from turn-ins, some spotting to contents, 5-1/4" x 9-1/2". **$5,228**

Skinner, Inc., www.skinnerinc.com

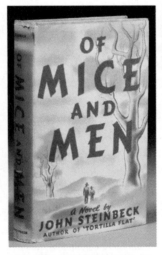

John Steinbeck (1902-1968), *Of Mice and Men*, New York: Covici-Friede, 1937. First edition, first issue, with the words, "and only moved because the heavy hands were pendula" on page nine, dot between the two eights on page 88, beige publisher's cloth with labels printed in orange and black, dust jacket with "$2.00" on front flap, spine of dust jacket tanned from sun exposure, colors on front of dust cover are bright. **$840**

Skinner, Inc., www.skinnerinc.com

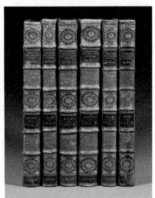

Bernard Picart (1673-1733), *The Ceremonies and Religious Customs of the World*, London: William Jackson for Claude du Bosc, 1733-1739. First English edition, seven volumes bound in six, 223 full-paged engraved plates, 31 of which are double-paged or folding, contemporary boards, rebacked, some hinges starting, labels chipped, volume two with intermittent water stains, corners bumped, boards abraded, ex libris Thomas Western, 11-1/2" x 18". The most exhaustive study of comparative religion composed to date with stunningly detailed accounts and illustrations of the rituals and practices of religions major and minor from North, South and Central America, the Caribbean, Europe, Britain, Asia, including the Indian subcontinent, Africa, and the Pacific Islands................. **$4,200**

LITTLE GOLDEN BOOKS

Western Publishing Co., Inc., one of the largest printers of children's books in the world, began in Racine, Wisconsin when Edward Henry Wadewitz purchased the West Side Printing Co. in 1907. In 1910, the name was changed to Western Printing and Lithographing Co.

By its seventh year, sales had topped $127,000. Wadewitz was approached by the Hamming-Whitman Publishing Co. of Chicago to print its line of children's books. Unable to pay its bills, Hamming-Whitman left Western with thousands of books in its warehouse and in production. Trying to cut its losses, Wadewitz entered Western into the retail book market for the first time. It proved so successful that the remaining Hamming-Whitman books were liquidated.

After acquiring Hamming-Whitman on Feb. 9, 1916, Western formed a subsidiary corporation called Whitman Publishing Co. Whitman grossed more than $43,500 in children's book sales in its first year. Sam Lowe joined the Western team in 1916. Lowe sold Western and Whitman on the idea of bringing out a 10-cent children's book in 1918.

By 1928, sales were more than $2.4 million. Western was able to keep its plant operational during the Depression years (1929-1933) by introducing a jigsaw puzzle and a new series of books called Big Little Books.

Western formed the Artists and Writers Guild Inc. in the 1930s to handle the development of new children's books. This company, located on Fifth Avenue in New York City, had an immense hand in the conception of Little Golden Books.

In 1940, Sam Lowe left the company and George Duplaix replaced him as head of the Artists and Writers Guild. Duplaix came up with the concept of a colorful children's book that would be durable and affordable to more American families than those being printed at that time. The group decided on 12 titles to be released at the same time. These books were to be called Little Golden Books. The books sold for 25 cents each. In September 1942, the first 12 titles were printed and released to stores in October.

Within five months, 1.5 million copies of the books had been printed and they were in their third printing. They became so popular with children that by the end of 1945, most of the first 12 books had been printed seven times. When the books were first released, they were sold mainly in book and department stores. From there, they moved into variety, toy, and drug stores, and finally in the late 1940s, to something new called the supermarket.

The First 12 Little Golden Books

1 Three Little Kittens
2 Bedtime Stories
3 The Alphabet A-Z
4 Mother Goose
5 Prayers for Children
6 The Little Red Hen
7 Nursery Songs
8 The Poky Little Puppy
9 The Golden Book of Fairy Tales
10 Baby's Book
11 The Animals of Farmer Jones
12 This Little Piggy

Sales of Little Golden Books were doing so well that in 1944, Simon & Schuster decided to create a new division headed by George Duplaix, called Sandpiper Press. Duplaix hired Dorothy Bennett as the general editor. She was responsible for many of the subjects used in Little Golden Books through the mid-1950s.

In 1952, on the tenth anniversary of Little Golden Books, approximately 182,615,000 Little Golden Books had been sold. In their eleventh year, almost 300 million Little Golden Books had been sold. More than half of the titles printed by 1954 had sold more than a million copies each.

Little Golden Books have been printed in more than 42 countries. In 1982, Little Golden Books were 40 years old and more than 800 million books had been sold. On Nov. 20, 1986, the one billionth Little Golden Book was printed in the United States, *The Poky Little Puppy*.

Little Golden Books are still published today.

For more information on Little Golden Books, see *Warman's Little Golden Books Identification and Price Guide* by Steve Santi.

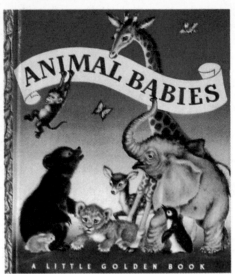

Alphabet From A-Z, The
Illustrator: Blake, Vivienne
Book No. 3   1942   42 pgs.   1st ed.   **$50**
Four-color and black and white,
blue spine with dust jacket.   **$50-$200**
Book No. 3   1942 (1950) 42 pgs.   18th ed.   **$16**
Four-color and black and white, golden
paper spine, song added to last page.

Animal Babies
Illustrator: Werber, Adele
Author: Jackson, Kathryn & Byron
Book No. 39   1947   42 pgs.   1st ed.   **$16**
Four-color and black and white, golden paper spine.
Book No. 39 1947 (1949) 28 pgs.   3rd ed.   **$12**
Four-color.

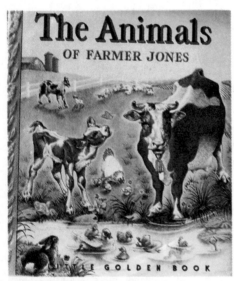

Animals of Farmer Jones, The
Illustrator: Freund, Rudolf
Author: Gale, Leah
Book No. 11   1942   42 pgs.   1st ed.   **$50**
Four-color and black and white.
Blue spine with dust jacket.   **$50-$200**
Book No. 11 1942 (1943) 24 pgs.   1st ed.   **$22**
Four-color and black and white, blue spine.
Blue spine with dust jacket.   **$40-$100**
Book No. 11 1942 (1947) 42 pgs.   10th ed.   **$15**
Four-color and black and white, golden paper spine.

Baby's Book
Illustrator: Smith, Bob
Author: Smith, Bob
Book No. 10   1942   42 pgs.   1st ed.   **$50**
Four-color and black and white.
Blue spine with dust jacket.   **$75-$300**

Baby's House
Illustrator: Blair, Mary
Author: Mchough, Gelolo
Book No. 80   1950   28 pgs.   1st ed.   **$20**
Four-color, golden paper spine.
"B" edition with complete puzzle   **$150**

Big Brown Bear, The
Illustrator: Tenggren, Gustaf
Author: Duplaix, Georges
Book No. 89   1947   42 pgs.   1st ed.   **$25**
Four-color, golden paper spine.
Book No. 89 1947 (1952) 28 pgs.   2nd ed.   **$15**
Four-color, golden paper spine.

Bedtime Stories
Illustrator: Tenggren, Gustaf
Author: Miscellaneous authors
Book No. 2   1942   42 pgs.   1st ed.   **$50**
Four-color and black and white.
Blue spine with dust jacket.   **$50-$150**
Five Stories: Chicken Little, The Three Bears, The
Three Little Pigs, Little Red Riding Hood, The
Gingerbread Man
Book No. 2   1942 (1955) 28 pgs.   21st ed.   **$12**
Four-color, foil spine.
Three Stories: The Gingerbread Man, Chicken Little,
Little Red Riding Hood

Brave Cowboy Bill
Puzzle Edition
Illustrator: Scarry, Richard
Author: Jackson, Kathryn & Byron
Book No. 93   1950   42 pgs.   1st ed.   **$125**
Without puzzle   **$20**

Bugs Bunny
Illustrator: Warner Bros.
Author: McKimson, Tom
Book No. 72   1949   42 pgs.   1st ed.   **$15**
Four-color and black and white, golden paper spine.
Book No. 72 1949 (1952) 28 pgs.   7th ed.   **$10**
Four-color and three-color, foil spine.

Christmas Carols
Illustrator: Malvern, Corinne
Author: Wyckoff, Marjorie
Book No. 26   1946   42 pgs.   1st ed.   **$20**
Four-color and black and white.
Blue spine with dust jacket.   **$50-$125**
First edition is unstated and lists to book #34 on
back cover and #36 on dust jacket.
Book No. 26 1946 (1949) 42 pgs.   5th ed.   **$15**
Four-color and three-color, golden paper spine.

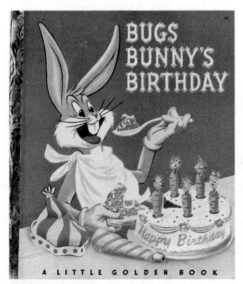

Bugs Bunny's Birthday
Illustrator: Warner Bros.
Author: Warner Bros.
Book No. 98   1950   28 pgs.   1st ed.   **$14**

Christmas in the Country
Illustrator: Worcester, Retta
Author: Collyer, Barbaba; Foley, John R.
Book No. 95   1950   28 pgs.   1st ed.   **$25**

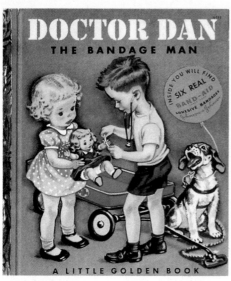

Doctor Dan, the Bandage Man
Illustrator: Malvern, Corinne
Author: Gaspard, Helen
Book No. 111 1950   28 pgs.   1st ed.   **$100**
Without Band-Aids   **$18**

Duck and His Friends
Illustrator: Scarry, Richard
Author: Jackson, Kathryn & Bryon
Book No. 81   1949   28 pgs.   1st ed.   **$14**
Four-color, golden paper spine.
Book No. 81   1949 (1951) 28 pgs.   2nd ed.   **$150**
Four-color, foil spine.
Book No. 81   1949 (1954) 24 pgs.   4th ed.   **$10**
Four-color, foil spine.

First Little Golden Book of Fairy Tales, The
Illustrator: Elliott, Gertrude
Book No. 9   1946   24 pgs.   1st ed.   **$20**
Four-color and black and white.
Blue spine with dust jacket.   **$50-$100**
Three stories: Jack and the Beanstalk, Puss in Boots,
Sleeping Beauty
Book No. 9   1946 (1947) 42 pgs. 2nd ed.   **$16**
Four-color and black and white, golden paper spine.

Fix It, Please
Illustrator: Wilkin, Eloise
Author: Mitchell, Lucy Sprague
Book No. 32   1947   42 pgs.   1st ed.   **$35**
Four-color and black and white, golden paper spine

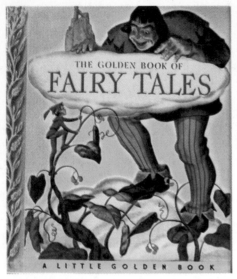

Golden Book of Fairy Tales, The
Illustrator: Hoskins, Winfield
Book No. 9   1942   42 pgs.   1st ed.   **$50**
Four-color and black and white.
Blue spine with dust jacket.   **$50-$200**
Four stories: Jack and the Beanstalk, Cinderella,
Puss in Boots, Sleeping Beauty
Book No. 9 1942 (1943) 24 pgs. 1st ed. **$22**
Four-color and black and white, blue spine.
Three stories: Jack and the Beanstalk, Puss in Boots,
Cinderella
Blue spine with dust jacket.   **$40-$100**
Four-color and black and white.

Happy Family, The
Illustrator: Elliott, Gertrude
Author: Nicole
Book No. 35   1947   42 pgs.   1st ed.   **$40**
Four-color and black and white.
Blue spine with dust jacket.   **$50-$175**
Last title with a dust jacket.

I Can Fly
Illustrator: Blair, Mary
Author: Krauss, Ruth
Book No. 92   1950   42 pgs. 1st ed.   **$25**

Let's Go Shopping
Ilustrator: Combes, Lenora
Author: Combes, Lenora
Book No. 33   1948   42 pgs. 1st ed.   **$17**
Four-color and black and white, golden paper spine.
Book No. 33 1948 (1949) 42 pgs. 5th ed. **$15**
Four-color and three-color, golden paper spine.
Book No. 33 1948 (1950) 42 pgs. 6th ed. **$15**
Four-color and three-color, golden paper spine.
Song added to last page.

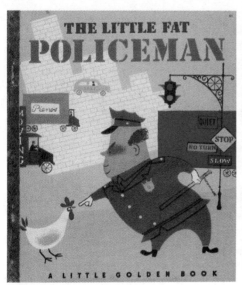

Little Fat Policeman, The
Illustrator: Provenson, Alice & Martin
Author: Brown, Margaret Wise
Book No. 91   1950   42 pgs.   1st ed.   **$12**
Book No. 91 1950 (1951) 28 pgs.   2nd ed.   **$14**

Little Golden Book of Hymns, The
Illustrator: Malvern, Corinne
Author: Werner, Elsa Jane
Book No. 34   1947   42 pgs.   1st ed.   **$16**
Four-color and black and white, golden paper spine.
Book No. 34 1947 (1949) 28 pgs.   4th ed.   **$8**
Four-color, golden paper spine.
Book No. 34 1947 (1950) 42 pgs.   8th ed.   **$12**
Four-color, golden paper spine.

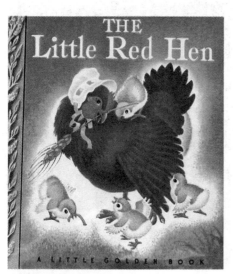

Little Red Hen, The
Illustrator: Freund, Rudolf
Author: Potter, Marion
Book No. 6   1942   42 pgs.   1st ed.   **$50**
Four-color and black and white.
Blue spine with dust jacket.   **$50-$200**
Book No. 6   1942 (1949) 42 pgs.   12th ed.   **$15**
Four-color and three-color.

Little Golden Book of Poetry, The
Illustrator: Malvern, Corinne
Book No. 38   1947   42 pgs.   1st ed.   **$16**
Four-color and black and white, golden paper spine.
Book No. 38 1947 (1948) 28 pgs.   2nd ed.   **$12**
Four-color, golden paper spine.

Mother Goose
Illustrator: Elliott, Gertrude
Author: Fraser, Phyllis
Book No. 4   1942   42 pgs.   1st ed.   **$50**
Four-color and black and white.
Blue spine with dust jacket.   **$50-$200**
Book No. 4   1942 (1943) 24 pgs.   4th ed.   **$20**
Four-color and black and white, blue spine, abridged
for World War II.
Blue spine with dust jacket.   **$40-$100**
Book No. 4   1942 (1953) 28 pgs.   22nd ed. **$12**
Four-color and three-color, foil spine.

Nursery Songs
Illustrator: Malvern, Corinne
Author: Gale, Leah
Book No. 7   1942   42 pgs.   1st ed.   **$40**
Four-color and black and white.
Blue spine with dust jacket.   **$50-$200**

My First Book
Illustrator: Smith, Bob
Author: Smith, Bob
Book No. 10 1942 (1943) 42 pgs.   4th ed.   **$40**
Four-color and black and white.
Blue spine with dust jacket.   **$60-$150**

Pets for Peter
Puzzle Edition
Illustrator: Battaglia, Aurelius
Author: Werner, Jane
Book No. 82   1950   42 pgs.   1st ed. **$125**
Four-color, foil spine.
Missing puzzle.   **$10**

Poky Little Puppy, The
Illustrator: Tenggren, Gustaf
Author: Lowrey, Janet Sebring
Book No. 8   1942   42 pgs.   1st ed.   **$50**
Four-color and black and white.
Blue spine with dust jacket.   **$50-$200**
Book No. 8   1942 (1950) 42 pgs.   21st ed.   **$15**
Four-color, golden paper spine.
Book No. 8   1942 (1950) 28 pgs.   22nd ed.   **$10**
Four-color, foil spine.

Prayers for Children
Illustrator: Dixon, Rachel Taft
Book No. 5   1942   42 pgs. 1st ed.   **$40**
Four-color and black and white.
Blue spine with dust jacket.   **$50-$200**
Book No. 5   1942 (1948) 42 pgs.   12th ed.   **$15**
Four-color and black and white, golden paper spine.
Prayer "Till the victory is ours" changed to "Good
Night."
Book No. 5   1942 (1950) 42 pgs.   18th ed.   **$12**
Four-color and three-color, golden paper spine, song
added to last page.
Book No. 5   1942 (1950) 42 pgs.   19th ed.   **$10**
Four-color and three-color, golden paper spine, song
on last page given solid background.

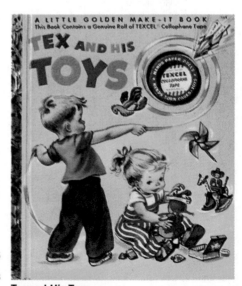

Saggy Baggy Elephant, The
Illustrator: Tenggren, Gustaf
Author: Jackson, Kathryn & Byron
Book No. 36   1947   42 pgs.   1st ed.   **$25**
Four-color and black and white, golden paper spine.
Book No. 36 1947 (1949) 28 pgs.   4th ed.   **$18**
Four-color, golden paper spine.
Book No. 36 1947 (1955) 28 pgs.   11th ed.   **$8**
Four-color, foil spine.
Book No. 36 1947 (1955) 24 pgs.   11th ed.   **$5**
Four-color, foil spine.
11th ed. published with 28 and 24 pgs.

Tex and His Toys
Illustrator: Malvern, Corinne
Author: Nast, Elsa Ruth
Book No. 129 1952   28 pgs.   1st ed.   **$90**
Without tape and activities.   **$3**

Three Little Kittens
Illustrator: Masha
Book No. 1   1942   42 pgs.   1st ed.   **$50**
Four-color and black and white.
Blue spine with dust jacket.   **$50-$200**
Book No. 1   1942 (1946) 24 pgs.   9th ed.   **$30**
Four-color and black and white, blue spine, "To
Albert" no longer written above clothsline.
Blue spine with dust jacket.   **$40-$100**
Book No. 1   1942 (1951) 42 pgs.   17th ed.   **$20**
Four-color and three-color, golden paper spine, song
added to last page.
Book No. 1   1942 (1952) 28 pgs.   19th ed.   **$12**
Four-color and three-color, foil spine, song on page 4.

Toys
Illustrator: Masha
Author: Oswald, Edith
Book No. 22   1945   42 pgs.   1st ed.   **$25**
Four-color and black and white.
Blue spine with dust jacket.   **$50-$150**
Book No. 22 1945 (1949) 42 pgs.   9th ed.   **$16**
Four-color and three-color, golden paper spine.

Ukelele and Her New Doll
Puzzle Edition
Illustrator: Grant, Campbell
Author: Grant, Clara Louise
Book No. 102 1951   28 pgs.   1st ed.   **$125**
Without puzzle.   **$25**

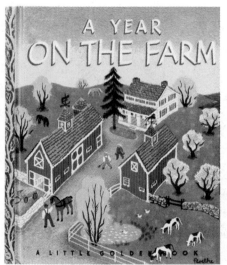

Year on the Farm, A
Illustrator: Floethe, Richard
Author: Mitchell, Lucy Sprague
Book No. 37   1948   42 pgs.   1st ed.   **$20**
Four-color and black and white, golden paper spine.
Book No. 37 1948 (1949) 42 pgs.   4th ed.   **$15**
Four-color and three-color, golden paper spine.

COOKBOOKS

Whether you're just starting a collection or are a seasoned connoisseur of culinary literature, this section is a valuable resource for identifying, pricing and learning about 20th-century American cookbooks published from the late 1800s up to about the 1970s—a large slice of publishing history filled with rich examples of culinary art, culture, trends, humor and, of course, recipes for some great food.

The best advice for collecting cookbooks is probably true for collecting anything—collect what you find interesting, meaningful, fun or important. Let your collection be an expression of your interest, not just the value the marketplace puts on your books.

Try to buy books with dust jackets whenever possible. A dust jacket not only protects the book, but it often provides hard-to-find information about the author or the cookbook itself. Dust jackets are often missing from older cookbooks and, when intact, instantly add value.

Buy the best condition you can afford. Buying a book in "cooking copy" condition is a good idea only if you intend to use it in the kitchen, or consider it a "placeholder" in your collection.

Store your cookbooks out of the kitchen, out of the basement, and out of the attic. Even the cleanest kitchens tend to be a challenging environment for a book (grease, smoke, moisture, humidity, etc.) A lot of great old books have been ruined by insects, moisture, heat, and other effects of improper storage.

If you intend to use the cookbooks you purchase, consider buying the best copy you can afford and buying another one in marginal shape for the kitchen.

Buy from reputable dealers who know cookbooks, know how to describe them, and offer a money-back satisfaction guarantee.

Focus your collection on a particular sub-category or passion. This might be anything from a collection of cookbooks from your region to a collection about confections, cakes, or cocktails. From a buyer's point of view, focused and complete collections are more desirable than a disparate gaggle of books. From a collector's perspective, it will make your treasure hunting more manageable.

For more information on cookbooks, see *Antique Trader Collectible Cookbooks Price Guide* by Patricia Edwards and Peter Peckham.

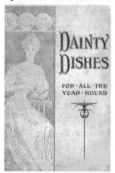

Dainty Dishes For All the Year Round
1914
Rorer, Mrs. S. T.
North Brothers Mfg.
Stapled booklet
64 pages
Extensive directions for using a rotary crank freezer. Black-and-white photos of mother and daughter making ice cream.
$25-$44

Sunset Cook Book of Favorite Recipes
1949, 1952, 1957
Chase, Emily (editor)
Lane Publishing Co.
Hardcover, wire bound
415 pages
Finest recipes that appeared in Sunset Magazine over 20 years. Cover colors vary but contents identical. Shown is the 1949 green cover.
$25-$44

Joy of Cooking, The
1943
Rombauer, Irma S.
Bobbs-Merrill
Hardcover
1943 printing of the blue diamond cover—one of the most desirable editions. The 1946 printing with the same cover has slightly different contents.
$55-$98

Cosmopolitan Seattle
1935, 1936
Penny, Prudence
Post-Intelligencer, Seattle
Stapled Booklet
48 pages
Recipes from local Seattle Restaurants, circa 1936. Many black and white photos of local chefs. Presented to the Founder Members of the Seattle Post-Intelligencer Homemakers' Club.
$39-$69

Good Housekeeping Cook Book, The
1943
Marsh, Dorothy B. (editor)
International Readers League or Stamford House
Hardcover
950 pages
This cover is used for two versions. 1943: contains 950 pages plus a 32-page wartime supplement. The preface to the 3rd Edition states that the book includes a wartime supplement after page 694. However, the 32-page supplement is actually between pages 582 and 583 and does not affect the pagination of the book. 1944: completely revised edition contains a preface to the 7th Edition, 981 pages and no wartime supplement.
$31-$66

Elsie's Cook Book
1952
Botsford, Harry and Elsie the Cow
Bond Wheelwright
Hardcover
374 pages
Illustrations by Keith Ward
$25-$44

Kenmore Binding of the American Woman's Cook Book and the United States Regional Cook Book
1947 & 1952
Berolzheimer, Ruth (editor)
Culinary Arts Institute
Hardcover
846 pages and 752 pages
The two-volume set, in slipcase, is a promotional set of the American Woman's Cook Book and the United States Regional Cook Book bound for Sears Roebuck.
Color and black and white photos
Thumb-indexed
$88-$156

Hawaiian and Pacific Foods
1967
Bazore, Katherine
Gramercy
Hardcover
290 pages
Recipes and customs of the Hawaiian, Samoan, Chinese, Japanese and Filipino
$13-$23

Duncan Hines Dessert Book, The
1955
Hines, Duncan
Pocket
Paperback
362 pages
Recipes attributed to contributors, including chefs from around the country.
$11-$19

Domestic Arts Edition of the American Woman's Cook Book, The
1939
Berolzheimer, Ruth (editor)
Consolidated Book Publishers
Hardcover
815 pages plus an unpaginated chapter titled "Cooking for Fifty." The American Woman's Cook Book, a thick and thorough domestic bible, was printed with many different covers and titles, most with identical contents.
Thumb-indexed
Speckled edge decoration. Black-and-white and color photos.
$88-$157

Piggly Wiggly All Over the World Cook Book
Circa 1925
Piggly Wiggly
Soft cover
224 pages
A collection of recipes "by the finest chefs and cooking kitchens in the United States," prepared for The Piggly Wiggly shopper.
Ads from food manufacturers throughout. Not dated. Appears to be published in the 1920s.
$41-$73

Modern Method of Preparing Delightful Foods, The
1927
Allen, Ida Bailey
Corn Products Refining Co.
Hardcover
109 pages plus index
Compelling writings on historical American cooking in colonial times. Includes a photo of Mrs. Allen. Promotes cooking with Karo Syrup, Kingsford Cornstarch and Mazola Oil.
$19-$34

General Foods Kitchens Cookbook, The
1959
The Women of General Foods Kitchens
Random House
Hardcover, also available in soft cover
436 pages
Available in two cover designs, identical contents.
Illustrated by Mary Ronin. Photos by George Lazarnick.
$13-$23

Betty Crocker's Good and Easy Cook Book
1954
Crocker, Betty
Simon and Schuster
Hardcover
256 pages
Appealingly small, spiral-bound cookbook with "1,000 time-saving, table-tempting recipes and hints for busy modern homemakers."
Illustrated with spot illustrations and color photos
$12-$22

Woman's Home Companion Cook Book
1946
Kirk, Dorothy (editor)
Garden City Publishing
Hardcover
952 pages
$60-$106

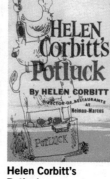

Helen Corbitt's Potluck
1962
Corbitt, Helen
Houghton Mifflin
Hardcover
181 pages
$12-$21

Mastering the Art of French Cooking, Volume Two
1970
Child, Julia; Beck, Simone
Alfred A. Knopf
Hardcover
555 pages plus index
Original editions measure 7.5" x 10.25". Book club reprints are slightly smaller. Both editions are high-quality printings and desirable. Volume II is a bit harder to find.
$49-$87

Watkins Hearthside Cook Book
1952
Robbins, Ruth
J. R. Watkins Co.
Hardcover
256 pages
Dust jacket folds out to become illustrated kitchen poster with a psalm quote.
$34-$61

Betty Crocker's Cooky Book
1963
Crocker, Betty
Golden Press
Hardcover, wire bound
Illustrations by Eric Mulvany
$22-$39

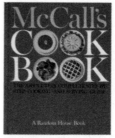

McCall's Cook Book
1963
Random House
Hardcover
786 pages
Same contents available in green, yellow, red or blue cover.
$36-$64

Good Housekeeping Everyday Cook Book
1903
Curtis, Isabel Gordon (editor)
Good Housekeeping
Hardcover
314 pages plus index
The first Good Housekeeping cookbook.
$25-$44

Cross Creek Cookery
1942
Rawlings, Marjorie
Kinnan
Charles Scribner's and
Sons
Hardcover
230 pages
$39-$69

**Favorite Recipes From
Famous Eating Places**
1950
Kennedy, Nancy (editor)
Simon and Schuster
Soft cover, wire bound
252 pages plus map
$20-$36

**My Better Homes &
Gardens Cook Book**
1938
Editors of Better Homes
and Gardens
Better Homes and
Gardens
Hardcover binder
$25-$44

**Boston Cooking-School
Cook Book, The**
1918-1922
Farmer, Fannie Merritt
Little, Brown and Co.
Hardcover
656 pages
3rd edition. The 1918
Revised Edition of the
Fannie Farmer classic
with additional chapters
on the cold pack method
of canning, on the drying
of fruits and vegetables,
and on food values
Edited by Mary Farmer
Only the 1918 printing
includes wartime recipe
supplement.
122 half-tone illustrations
$53-$94

**Lily Wallace New
American Cook Book,
The**
1946
Wallace, Lily Haxworth
Books, Inc.
Hardcover
931 pages
Cover colors vary but
contents are identical.
Sequel to the 1941
edition.
Color and black-and-
white photos and
illustrations
$41-$73

**New England Butt'ry
Shelf Cookbook, The**
1968
Campbell, Mary Mason
The World Publishing
Co.
Hardcover
192 pages
Illustrations by Tasha
Tudor **$37-$66**

Paris Cuisine
1952
Beard, James; Watt, Alexander
Little, Brown & Co.
Hardcover
272 pages
Endpapers show French restaurant menus.
Design and illustrations by Vladimir Bobri.
$46-$81

**Pillsbury Family Cook
Book, The**
1963
Pillsbury
Hardcover or binder
576 pages
Available in binder and
hardcover formats. Same
contents as blue and
yellow cover but not quite
as popular.
Color and black-and-white
photos and illustrations.
$25-$44

Boys' Cook Book, The
1959
Brown, Helen Evans
Doubleday
Hardcover
285 pages
Shown is a less
desirable 1970s reprint.
Illustrations by Harry O.
Diamond.
$13-$23

Bottles

Interest in bottle collecting, and high interest in extremely rare bottles, continues to grow, with new bottle clubs forming throughout the United States and Europe. More collectors are spending their free time digging through old dumps and foraging through ghost towns, digging out old outhouses (that's right), exploring abandoned mine shafts, and searching their favorite bottle or antique shows, swap meets, flea markets, and garage sales. In addition, the Internet has greatly expanded, offering collectors numerous opportunities and resources to buy and sell bottles with many new auction websites, without even leaving the house. Many bottle clubs now have websites providing even more information for the collector. These new technologies and resources have helped bottle collecting to continue to grow and gain interest.

Most collectors, however, still look beyond the type and value of a bottle to its origin and history. Researching the history of a bottle is almost as interesting as finding the bottle itself.

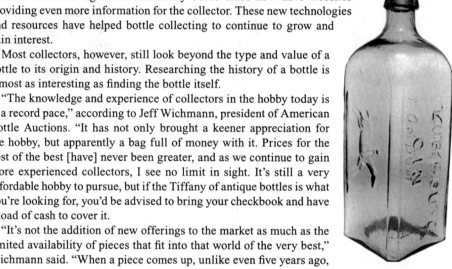

London Club House Gin, embossed horse and rider, teal blue, applied top, graphite pontil, 9-3/8", American 1855-1865...... **$2,000-$2,200**

"The knowledge and experience of collectors in the hobby today is at a record pace," according to Jeff Wichmann, president of American Bottle Auctions. "It has not only brought a keener appreciation for the hobby, but apparently a bag full of money with it. Prices for the best of the best [have] never been greater, and as we continue to gain more experienced collectors, I see no limit in sight. It's still a very affordable hobby to pursue, but if the Tiffany of antique bottles is what you're looking for, you'd be advised to bring your checkbook and have a load of cash to cover it.

"It's not the addition of new offerings to the market as much as the limited availability of pieces that fit into that world of the very best," Wichmann said. "When a piece comes up, unlike even five years ago, it's now every [person] for himself. There has always been the average example and there always will be, but it's the one-known bitters or odd-colored historical flask that is finally getting its due respect."

For more information on bottles, see *Antique Trader Bottles: Identification & Price Guide*, 7th edition, by Michael Polak.

Bottle Resources

- Bottles & Extras Magazine, the official publication of the Federation of Historical Bottle Collectors, 816-318-0160
- Antique Bottle & Glass Collector, Jim Hagenbuch, editor, 215-679-5849
- Norman C. Heckler & Co., 79 Bradford Corner Rd., Woodstock Valley, CT 06282, 860-974-1634, www.hecklerauction.com
- Glass Works Auctions, PO Box 187, East Greenville, PA 18041, 215-679-5849 glswrk@enter.net
- American Bottle Auctions, 2523 J St., Suite 203, Sacramento, CA 95816, 800-806-7722, www.americanbottle.com
- International Perfume Bottle Association, www.perfumebottles.org, IPBA_membership@verizon.net
- Colonial Williamsburg's DeWitt Wallace Decorative Arts Museum, Williamsburg, Va., 800-447-8679

D.T. Sweeny – Philadelphia / XX / Porter & Ale, medium cobalt blue, 6-7/8", smooth base, applied tapered double collar top, American 1855-1865.........**$1,500-$2,000**

Barber bottle, 8-3/8", fiery opalescent cranberry, Spanish lace pattern, square shape, polished pontil, tooled top, American 1885-1920...............**$200-$225**

Barber bottle, 8-1/8", medium emerald green, rib-pattern, white and orange enamel floral decoration, bell shape, pontil-scarred base, tooled top, American 1885-1920 .....**$200-$250**

Beer bottle, Anheuser-Busch Brwg Assn. – Norfolk VA. Branch, aqua, pint, crown tooled top, 1910-1920...................**$60-$70**

Beer bottle, Bay View – Brewing Co. – Seattle, Wash, mint green, quart, applied top, 1890-1905 ....**$200-$250**

Bitters bottle, Dr. A.W. Coleman's – Antidyspeptic and Tonic Bitters, dark blue green, 9-1/8", open pontil, applied tapered collar top, 1845-1860 .....**$850-$900**

Bitters bottle, John Moffat Phoenix Bitters – New York – Price, $2.00, deep yellow olive green, 7", pontil-scarred base, applied tapered collar top, 1840-1860.........**$4,600-$4,800**

Black glass magnum shape wine bottle (id seal "21"), "PS" script letters, dark olive green, 12-1/4", English or American 1790-1810 ....**$850-$900**

Blown bottle, early apothecary freeblown bottle (label reads: This was my grandmother's Buchu Alter's compound bottle-Aunt Mary Wilson), light green, 5", open pontil, folded over lip, 1820-1830 .....**$300-$350**

Blown three-mold toilet water bottle, light sapphire blue, 5-1/4", 15-rib-pattern, pontil-scarred base, rolled and flared lip, 1815-1835 ....**$300-$325**

Cobalt blue medicine bottle, USA Hospital, medium cobalt blue, 9", applied square collar, 1865-1870 ....**$1,600-$1,800**

Cobalt blue medicine bottle, Hall's Balsam For The Lungs – 8 & 9 Cottage Place N.Y. – J.F. Henry & Curran & Co., medium cobalt blue, 7-3/4", tooled top, 1880-1900 .....**$600-$650**

Whiskey nip figural revolver, amber, 8-1/2"
l, ground lip, original metal screw-on cap,
American 1890-1910.....................**$70-$80**

Casper's Whiskey
– Made By Honest
– North – Carolina
People, cobalt blue,
11-7/8", American
1890-1900
..........**$450-$500**

Whiskey cylinder,
deep blue green,
10-1/2", American
1865-1875
...........**$180-$190**

Two strapside whiskey flasks, "John Coyne – Cor.
Fayette & Seneca Sts. – Utica, N.Y.," yellow green,
pint, applied top, and "D.F. Flagg & Co. – 165
Blackstone St – Boston," tooled double collar top,
American 1880-1900............................ **$250-$300**

Fire grenade, "Spong & Cos Hand Fire Extinguishing Tube & Grenade – London," yellow olive,
12-3/4" long, tooled lip, English 1880-1900...**$400-$475**

Fire grenade, "Magic – Fire – Extinguisher Co.," golden yellow amber, 6-1/4", sheared and ground lip, American 1875-1895 ....**$600-$700**

W.K.L. & Co. Peppersauce, 10", medium green, open pontil, double rolled top, American 1840-1860. ....**$275-$300**

Hair restorer bottle, Mrs. S.A. Allen – Worlds Hair – Restorer – 355 Broome St. – New York, 7-3/8", dark amethyst, flared lip,1865-1875 ....**$700-$800**

Fruit jar, A. Stone & Co. – Philada, aqua, quart, pressed down groove wax sealer, American 1860-1870 ....**$250-$300**

Label under glass whiskey flask, white silhouette of Victorian women with embossed eagle on back, clear glass, 5-1/4", screw top lid, American 1895-1920 ....**$100-$125**

◀ Hawaiian bottle, H & H – Honolulu, 1868 ....\$1,800-\$2,500

▶ Hutchinson bottle, Phil Daniels – Anaconda – Mont., aqua green, 6-3/4", tooled top, American 1885-1895 ....\$150-\$200

Hutchinson bottle, Pittsburgh Bottling – J & D Miller – House, medium cobalt blue, 7-1/8", tooled top, American 1885-1900 ....\$350-\$400

Cone inkwell, emerald green, 2-1/2", pontil base, rolled lip, American 1850-1855 ....\$350-\$400

Ink bottle, A.M. Bertinguiot, cobalt blue, 2-3/8", open pontil, inward rolled lip, American 1840-1860 ....\$650-\$700

Fruit jar, Fridley & Cornman's
– Patent – Oct. 25th 1859 –
Ladies Choice, deep blue aqua,
quart, ground lip, original iron
closure, American 1859-1865
................**$1,800-$2,000**

Hawaiian bottle,
Macfarlane & Co.
(monogram "M"),
Honolulu, 1910
.... **$175-$225**

◀ Medicine bottle,
Hufeland's Life Cordial,
medium yellow green,
7-1/8", open pontil,
American 1840-1860
.... **$750-$800**

▶ Medicine bottle,
Rohrer's Expectoral
Wild Cherry Tonic –
Lancaster, PA, amber,
10-3/8", iron pontil,
American 1850-1860
...... **$450-$475**

◀ Ten-diamond pattern
chestnut flask,
blue aqua, 5-1/2",
American 1815-1835
.... **$900-$1,000**

Milk bottle, Santa Monica –
Dairy Co. – Santa Monica, Cal.,
medium amber, quart, American
1910-1920 .... **$200-$225**

Rib pattern chestnut flask,
deep red amber, 5-1/8", 24-rib
pattern swirled to left, American
1815-1835 .... **$225-$250**

Milk bottle, Seward – Dairy
– Seward, Alaska, clear
glass, quart, American
1910-1930 ....**$100-$130**

◄ Sandwich type
cologne, medium
pink amethyst,
11-1/8", American
1850-1880
.... **$300-$325**

Mineral water bottle,
Middletown Healing Spring
– Grays & Clark – Middleton
VT, golden yellow amber,
quart, smooth base,
American 1865-1875
................$1,200-$1,300

Mineral water bottle, Geyser
Spring – Saratoga Springs
– New York-Avery N. Lord –
66 Broad St. – Utica. N.Y.,
aqua, quart, smooth base,
American 1865-1875
.... **$800-$900**

► Large cologne
bottle, fiery
opalescent
turquoise blue,
10-1/2", English
1850-1870
.... **$125-$150**

Figural baseball bottle, deep cobalt blue, 2-3/4"
diameter, smooth base, ground lip, American
1885-1915, very rare ....$300-$350

Pair of poison bottles, emerald green, 5-1/2",
American 1890-1920................$140-$160

Soda bottle, Louis
Weber – Louisville – KY,
medium amber, 7-1/8",
American 1860-1870
...............$100-$125

Soda bottle, I. Sutton –
Cincinnati, deep cobalt
blue, 7-3/8", American
1840-1860
...............$250-$300

Target ball, bright
yellow, 2-1/2" diameter,
Czechoslovakian
1890-1910
............$100-$125

Target ball, N.B. Glassworks
Perth – N.B. Glass Works
Perth, light sapphire blue,
2-5/8" diameter, English
1880-1900 .....$100-$125

"Poison (motif of skull and crossbones)
– DP – Poison," cobalt blue, 2-7/8",
American 1890-1910.......$600-$650

Boxes

Boxes come in all shapes, sizes, and degree of antiquity—good news for the collector seeking a lifelong passion. Once early mankind reached the point where accumulation began, the next step was the introduction of containers designed especially to preserve those treasures.

Boxes have been created from every source material imaginable: wood, stone, precious metals, papier maché, porcelain, horn, and even shell. Among the most collectible:

- **Snuff boxes.** These small, lidded boxes first came to favor in the 1700s. Although originally intended as "for use" items, snuff boxes are now prized for the elegant miniatures often painted on both the box exterior and interior.

- **Pillboxes.** Like the snuffbox, these tiny boxes were as much in demand for their design as for their usefulness. Among the most desirable are 18th century pillboxes with enameled or repoussé (metal relief) decoration.

- **Match safes.** In the days before safety matches, metal boxes with a striker on the base kept matches from inadvertently bursting into flame. Match safe material ranged from base metal to sterling silver. Although flat, hinged safes were the most common, novelty shapes, such as animal heads, also proved popular.

- **Lacquered boxes.** Often classified as "Oriental" due to the 19th century fondness for decorating them with Asian motifs, lacquered boxes are actually found in almost every culture. Ranging anywhere from trinket- to trunk-sized, the common denominator is a highly polished, lacquered surface.

- **Folk art boxes.** The diversity of available folk art boxes accounts for their modern collectibility. Folk art boxes were often the work of untrained artisans, created solely for their own needs from materials readily at hand. Among the many choices: wallpaper boxes, decoupage boxes, and "tramp art" boxes. Fueled by the imagination and ingenuity of their makers, the selection is both fascinating and limitless.

Miniature Russian silver plique-a-jour enamel and filigree box in turquoise, amber and orange, flower heads and intricate scrollwork, impressed on cover with assayers right-facing Kokoshnik with 84 standards mark and silversmith HX initials in a square, possibly for Ivan Petrovich Khlebnikov, excellent condition, 1" x 1-3/4" x 2". $400

Mark Mussio, Humler & Nolan

Floral paint-decorated wooden box, probably northern Europe, early 17th century, rectangular beechwood box with pintle hinge on lid, wrought iron latch, decorated on top and sides with polychrome stylized flowers and leaves, with date "1613" inscribed on lower front panel, 6-3/8" h. x 13-3/4" w. x 9-5/8" d. **$1,080**

Skinner, Inc., www.skinnerinc.com

Grain-painted spice box, America, 19th century, crenellated crest and sides with two deep short drawers and two long drawers with applied molding, white porcelain drawer knobs and ornament, 18-1/8" h. x 17-3/4" w. x 7-1/2" d. **$923**

Skinner, Inc., www.skinnerinc.com

Trinket box with two drawers, America, early 19th century, rectangular dovetail-constructed box, painted white with pink and green budding flowers and leafy vine decoration, brass knobs on drawers, 6" h. x 10-7/8" w. x 8-1/4" d. **$840**

Skinner, Inc., www.skinnerinc.com

Two Pennsylvania painted pine boxes, 19th century, both retaining original grain decoration, 8-3/4" h. x 19" w. x 10" d. and 9-1/2" h. x 18" w. x 9-3/4" d. **$668**

Pook & Pook, Inc.

Inlaid mahogany slide-lid box, 19th century, probably sailor-made, rectangular dovetail-constructed box with shaped gallery, lid with heart-shaped pull tab, two inlaid bone heart plaques, incised geometric border, sides ornamented with incised compass-drawn medallions and lozenges, pintle-hinged compartment on bottom, 4-3/4" h. x 4-1/2" w. x 8-1/4" l. **$840**

Skinner, Inc., www.skinnerinc.com

Relief-carved mahogany document box, Continental, late 18th/early 19th century, dovetail-constructed rectangular box with snipe-hinged lid, top and sides with all-over relief-carved surface with roundels with five-point stars, pinwheels, quarterfans, geometric and undulating foliate medallions with foliate and sawtooth borders, top carved with initials "LKT" and "MLT," one side slides up to reveal drawer with six compartments, imperfections, 4-3/4" h. x 10-1/2" w. x 6" d. **$400**

Skinner, Inc., www.skinnerinc.com

Pennsylvania tin wrigglework lidded box, 19th century, with bird and floral decoration, 2-1/2" h. x 8" w. x 4" d.......................**$1,094**

Pook & Pook, Inc.

Painted pine dome lid box, southeastern Pennsylvania, probably Lancaster County, ca. 1810, original tulip decoration on ochre ground, 4" h. x 8-1/4" w. **$2,370**

Pook & Pook, Inc.

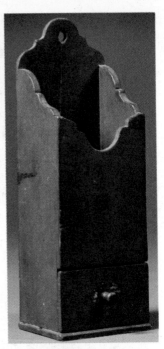

Green-painted wooden hanging pipe box, America, late 18th/early 19th century, shaped crest and sides, pierced back, single drawer, shrinkage crack, 15-1/2" h. x 5-1/4" w. x 4-3/4" d........**$1,920**

Skinner, Inc., www.skinnerinc.com

Inlaid mahogany veneer glove box, America or England, early 19th century, rectangular box with hinged lid centered with inlaid cornucopia and stringing, interior lined with black velvet, minor veneer loss, 2-7/8" h. x 11" w. x 5" d. **$150**

Skinner, Inc., www.skinnerinc.com

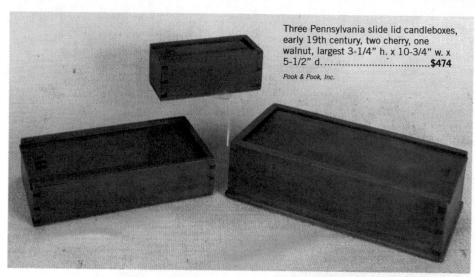

Three Pennsylvania slide lid candleboxes, early 19th century, two cherry, one walnut, largest 3-1/4" h. x 10-3/4" w. x 5-1/2" d. **$474**

Pook & Pook, Inc.

Pennsylvania walnut dome top box, ca. 1800, line inlay, 6-3/4" h. x 12-1/2" w. **$1,304**

Pook & Pook, Inc.

Pennsylvania painted and decoupage dresser box, 19th century, 4-1/2" h. x 9-1/2" w.................................**$119**

Pook & Pook, Inc.

Pennsylvania cherry hanging spice box, mid-19th century, 9-1/2" h. x 6-1/4" w. **$326**

Pook & Pook, Inc.

Pennsylvania painted poplar wall box, 19th century, original red surface, 14" h. x 11-1/2" w. x 11-1/4" d. **$1,422**

Pook & Pook, Inc.

York County, Pennsylvania painted pine slide lid candlebox, 19th century, 9-1/2" h. x 17-3/4" w. x 10" d............. **$593**

Pook & Pook, Inc.

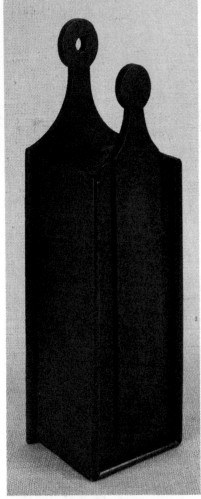

New England mahogany slide lid hanging candlebox, late 18th century, lollipop hanger, 18-1/4" h. x 4-3/4" w. **$652**

Pook & Pook, Inc.

Carved oak slide lid box, late 18th century, initialed "IB" and decorated with pinwheels, stars, etc., 4-3/4" h. x 9" w. x 5-1/2" d..**$593**

Pook & Pook, Inc.

Pennsylvania Federal cherry dresser box, circa 1810, eagle inlaid lid, 4-3/4" h. x 12-1/2" w. x 8" d... **$474**

Pook & Pook, Inc.

New England painted basswood dresser box, 19th century, original grained surface, 3-1/2" h. x 12" w. **$770**

Pook & Pook, Inc.

Pennsylvania walnut valuables box, 19th century, brass handles and fitted interior, 6-1/4" h. x 20-1/2" w. x 16-1/4" d. **$237**

Pook & Pook, Inc.

Lancaster County, Pennsylvania compass artist painted trinket box, ca. 1800, typical stylized flowers on blue-green ground, 6" h. x 7-1/4" w. **$8,295**

Pook & Pook, Inc.

Pennsylvania painted hard pine slide lid candle-box, early 19th century, original grain decorated surface, 5-3/4" h. x 13" w. x 8-3/4" d....**$1,126**

Pook & Pook, Inc.

Shaker grain painted bentwood box, mid-19th century, 4" h. x 10-1/2" w.......................**$972**

Pook & Pook, Inc.

Chester County, Pennsylvania Queen Anne walnut bible box, ca. 1760, 7" h. x 16" w. x 14-1/2" d. **$3,792**

Pook & Pook, Inc.

Presentation lap desk, brass inlay, fitted interior and leather writing surface, complete with inkwells, plaque reads "To R.G. Miller Esq., 1902", 8" x 9-3/4" x 10-1/2"....**$438**

Rago Arts and Auction Center

Lancaster or Berks County, Pennsylvania painted pine sewing box, late 18th century, slant lid with attached pincushion, old blue surface with green stippled panels and strap hinges, 6-3/4" h. x 14-1/2" w. x 12-3/4" d.................**$2,133**

Pook & Pook, Inc.

Rare papier-mâché painted cigar case, mid-19th century, decorated with a view of the Capitol in Washington, 3" h. x 5-3/4" w.......................**$3,159**

Pook & Pook, Inc.

Rare papier-mâché painted cigar case, mid-19th century, decorated with a view of Baltimore, 2-3/4" h. x 5-1/2" w...**$2,673**

Pook & Pook, Inc.

Battersea enamel pill box, oval form with original mirror to lid interior, inscribed "A Token of Esteem" on top of lid, first half 19th century, fine condition with minute flake to base edge, light crazing, mirror with losses to silvering, 7/8" h. x 1" x 1-3/4"....**$287**

Jeffrey S. Evans & Associates

American tramp art sewing box, heart-form with applied hearts, diamond-band inlays, pincushion top, single drawer, made partially from cigar boxes, late 19th/early 20th century, one foot detached but complete, small losses to drawer front, wear to fabric, 5-1/2" h. x 13" x 10-1/2"..............................**$115**

Jeffrey S. Evans & Associates

Ceramics

AMPHORA

The Amphora Co. began in the country village of Turn, in the Teplitz region of Bohemia. The Teplitz region supported the highest concentration of ceramic production, not only in Bohemia, but throughout all of the Austro-Hungarian Empire.

Amphora's aim was always to produce richly ornamented porcelain luxury items. In addition to the American exports, there were sales to European dealers. Through world exhibitions and international trade shows, Amphora's collections received many significant awards and certificates.

By 1900 Amphora was at the pinnacle of its success. After World War I, in 1918, Czechoslovakia was established. The company continued production until the end of the 1930s.

For more information on Amphora pottery, see *Antique Trader Pottery & Porcelain Ceramics Price Guide*, 6th edition.

— *Phil & Arlene Larke*

◄ Porcelain bust, "Sappho," early 20th century, marked RSTK Amphora, 17" x 11-1/2" x 7". **$344**

Rago Arts and Auction Center

Vase, two-tone blue and gold iridescent tones with pinched twist design, marked, 7" h.........**$275**

Woody Auction, LLC

Vase with maiden and swan by Ernst Wahliss, base stamped, 9" h. **$350**

Kaminski Auctions

Vase, Reissner, Stellmacher & Kessler, female bust beside conch shell, raised on tree form base, 25-3/4" h......**$375**

Leslie Hindman Auctioneers

Grape vine vase, basket woven form with gilt handles at top, green grape vine pattern with clusters of blue grapes, signed Amphora on bottom, very good condition, 13" h.....**$300**

Fontaines Auction Gallery

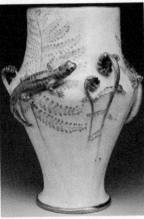

Stellmacher vase, two applied salamanders and fiddlehead ferns, Stellmacher mark, mint condition, 16" h. **$8,500**

Morphy Auctions

TOP LOT!

Daughter of the Rhine vase, applied jewels and enameled flowers, marked on underside, mint condition, 18-1/2" h. **$15,000**

Morphy Auctions

Iridescent glazed vase, early 20th century, Secessionist, urn-form with horizontal ribbing and raised stylized flowers, impressed Amphora within oval and number 3773, 12-1/2" h. **$1,100**

DuMouchelles

Art Nouveau double-handle vase with grapes in relief, signed, 13-1/2" h. **$300**

William J. Jenack Auctioneers

Vase with portraiture of "Maiden in the Woods," pink and blue flowers enameled in her hair, burnished gold highlights trees, rim and base, impressed Amphora, maroon logo Turn Teplitz Bohemia, RS+K for Reissner, Stellmacher & Kessel beneath, perfect condition, 4-1/2" h.....................................**$1,000**

Mark Mussio, Humler & Nolan

Terra cotta bust of fancy woman, 20" h. **$550**

Don Presley Auctions

Double vase with applied leaves and flower clusters, marked on bottom with crown above Austria Amphora, 10-3/4" h. **$475**

Quinn & Farmer Auctions

Dragon vase, baluster form, applied dragon with spread wings in bronzed iridescent finish, head on lip with open mouth, jagged teeth and spiral horns, bottom impress marked Amphora with written 52, very good to excellent condition, 14" h.............**$10,350**

James D. Julia, Inc.

CERAMICS

BELLEEK

The name Belleek refers to an industrious village in County Fermanagh, Northern Ireland, on the banks of the River Erne, and to the lustrous porcelain wares produced there.

In 1849, John Caldwell Bloomfield inherited a large estate near Belleek. Interested in ceramics and having discovered rich deposits of feldspar and kaolin (china clay) on his lands, he soon envisioned a pottery that would make use of these materials, local craftspeople and water power of the River Erne. He was also anxious to enhance Ireland's prestige with superior porcelain products.

Bloomfield had a chance meeting with Robert Williams Armstrong, who had established a substantial architectural business building potteries. Keenly interested in the manufacturing process, he agreed to design, build, and manage the new factory for Bloomfield. The factory was to be located on Rose Isle on a bend in the River Erne.

Bloomfield and Armstrong then approached David McBirney, a highly successful merchant and director of railway companies, and enticed him to provide financing. Impressed by the plans, he agreed to raise funds for the enterprise. As agreed, the factory was named McBirney and Armstrong, then later D. McBirney and Co.

Although 1857 is given as the founding date of the pottery, it is recorded that the pottery's foundation stone was laid by Mrs. J.C. Bloomfield on Nov. 18, 1858. Although not completed until 1860, the pottery was producing earthenware from its inception.

With the arrival of ceramic experts from the (William Henry) Goss Pottery in England, principally William Bromley, Sr. and William Wood Gallimore, Parian ware was perfected and, by 1863, the wares we associate with Belleek today were in production.

With Belleek Pottery workers and others emigrating to the United States in the late 1800s and early 1900s, Belleek-style china manufacture, known as American Belleek, commenced at several American firms, including Ceramic Art Company, Colombian Art Pottery, Lenox Inc., Ott & Brewer, and Willets Manufacturing Co.

Throughout its Parian production, Belleek Pottery marked its items with an Irish harp and wolfhound and the Devenish Tower. Its second period began with the advent of the McKinley Tariff Act of 1891 and the (revised) British Merchandise Act as Belleek added the ribbon "Co. FERMANAGH IRELAND" beneath its mark in 1891. Both the first and second period marks were black, although they occasionally

Rare porcelain vase with triple fish motif, 15-1/2" h. x 7" x 7". **$450**

International Auction Gallery

Three pieces, green mark dish, 7-1/4" dia.; green mark jug, 4-1/4" h.; green mark bowl, 4-1/2" dia. **$60**

Kaminski Auctions

Three-piece painted set, pot, sugar and creamer, third period black mark, 1926-1946, together with two marked steins, one Belleek piece cracked...........**$100**

Kaminski Auctions

CERAMICS

appeared in burnt orange, green, blue or brown, especially on earthenware items. Its third period began in 1926, when it added a Celtic emblem under the second period mark as well as the government trademark "Reg No 0857," which was granted in 1884. The Celtic emblem was registered by the Irish Industrial Development Association in 1906 and reads "Deanta in Eirinn," and means "Made in Ireland." The pottery is now utilizing its 13th mark, following a succession of three black marks, three green marks, a gold mark, two blue marks and three green. The final green mark was used only a single year, in 2007, to commemorate its 150th anniversary. In 2008, Belleek changed its mark to brown. Early earthenware was often marked in the same color as the majority of its surface decoration. Early basketware has Parian strips applied to its base with the impressed verbiage "BELLEEK" and later on, additionally "Co FERMANAGH" with or without "IRELAND." Current basketware carries the same mark as its Parian counterpart.

The identification scheme that follows is in the works by Richard K. Degenhardt: *Belleek The Complete Collector's Guide and Illustrated Reference* (both first and second editions). Additional information, as well as a thorough discussion of the early marks, is located in these works as well as on the Internet at Del E. Domke's website: http://home.comcast.net/~belleek_website.

Ceramic pitcher with silver overlay, Willets Manufacturing Co., circa 1890, marks to ceramic: (W on plinth), BELLEEK, WILLETS; marks to silver: STERLING, minor rubbing to silver overlay, 9-1/4" h.**$1,000**

Heritage Auctions

Porcelain figure, "Meditation," 1891-1926, standing, classically robed female in contemplative pose, second period black mark, 14-3/4" h. **$1,000**

Leslie Hindman Auctioneers

MARKS:

- American Art China Works - R&E, 1891-1895
- AAC (superimposed), 1891-1895
- American Belleek Co. - Company name, banner & globe
- Ceramic Art Co. - CAC palette, 1889-1906
- Colombian Art Pottery - CAP, 1893-1902
- Cook Pottery - Three feathers with "CHC," 1894-1904
- Coxon Belleek Pottery - "Coxon Belleek" in a shield, 1926-1930
- Gordon Belleek - "Gordon Belleek," 1920-1928
- Knowles, Taylor & Knowles - "Lotusware" in a circle w/a crown, 1891-1896
- Lenox China - Palette mark, 1906-1924
- Ott & Brewer - crown and shield, 1883-1893
- Perlee - "P" in a wreath, 1925-1930
- Willets Manufacturing Co. - Serpent mark, 1880-1909
- Cook Pottery - Three feathers with "CHC"

Vase, 1891-1926, second period black mark, modeled as two entwined fish supporting coral-form stem beneath nautilus shell, rocky stepped base applied with shells and coral, 12-1/4" h. x 6" w. x 5" d. **$700**

John Moran Auctioneers, Inc.

Finely decorated, large Willets (American) bowl, circa 1900, hand-painted band of flowers including peonies around body with geometric border and low circular foot, marked Belleek Willets on base with serpent mark and hand-painted inscription MIDDLETON, 3-3/4" h., 9-3/4" dia.................. **$300**

Case Antiques, Inc. Auctions & Appraisals

Eight saucers, each with second period black mark, in two patterns, together with a Belleek Collectors Society plaque, issued 1979, diameter of largest 7".. **$150**

Leslie Hindman Auctioneers

Sugar bowl and cream jug, 1863-1890, sugar bowl with first period black mark and impressed mark, inscribed in blue M0072203, modeled as conch shell supported on pierced coral-form base, ivory luster glaze; cream jug with partially rubbed mark (apparently first period black), impressed Belleek Fermanagh, impressed with symbol, modeled as nautilus shell with applied coral-form handle extending to base molded with shells, matte ivory glaze; sugar bowl 4" h. x 6-1/2" w. x 6-1/4" d.; cream jug 4-3/4" h. x 6-3/4" w. x 3-1/4" d. **$850**

John Moran Auctioneers, Inc.

Porcelain vase, painted all-around scene after "The Birth of Venus" by Casper-Philipp, good condition, 16-1/4" h. x 5-1/4" dia.............................**$1,100**

Ames Auctioneers

Partial tea service, most pieces dated 1863-1890, platter with first period black mark (17-3/4" w. x 14-1/4" d.), cream jug with first period black mark (3-1/2" h. x 4-1/2" w. x 3-1/2" d.), sugar bowl with first period black mark and impressed Belleek (3" h. x 3-3/4" dia.), three teacups with first period black mark and one teacup with first period red mark (2" h. x 3-1/2" dia.), three saucers with first period black mark and one saucer with first period red mark (5-1/4" dia.), kettle, unmarked (6" h. x 8" w. x 6" d.), various ivory-colored glazes, 12 pieces.....**$700**

John Moran Auctioneers, Inc.

Willets dragon vase, good condition, 7" h., 8" dia.......................**$90**

Royka's

Basket, 19th century, rim decorated with flowers and shamrocks, marked "Belleek Co. Ireland." **$50**

Louis J. Dianni, LLC

CERAMICS

BENNINGTON POTTERY

Bennington wares, which ranged from stoneware to parian and porcelain, were made in Bennington, Vermont, primarily in two potteries, one in which Captain John Norton and his descendants were principals, and the other in which Christopher Webber Fenton (also once associated with the Nortons) was a principal. Various marks are found on the wares made in the two major potteries, including J. & E. Norton, E. & L. P. Norton, L. Norton & Co., Norton & Fenton, Edward Norton, Lyman Fenton & Co., Fenton's Works, United States Pottery Co., U.S.P. and others.

The popular pottery with the mottled brown on yellowware glaze was also produced in Bennington, but such wares should be referred to as "Rockingham" or "Bennington-type" unless they can be specifically attributed to a Bennington, Vermont factory.

Bennington pottery pitcher, 19th century, Rockingham glaze with classical profiles in relief, 9" h. x 8" w. x 6-1/4" d. **$50**

Woodbury Auction LLC/Thomas Schwenke, Inc.

Four Bennington marbles, 19th century, one with blue and brown glaze over white ground, two with brown glaze, one with yellowish glaze, all in excellent condition, diameter of largest 1-1/2". ... **$125**

Crocker Farm

Bennington spittoon, good condition, 4" h., 8" dia. **$45**

Stevens Auction Co.

Three Bennington Pottery and flint enamel book bottles, attributed to Lyman & Fenton, Bennington, Vermont, circa 1849, larger flask embossed "BENNINGTON COMPANION," smaller two embossed "DEPARTED SPIRITS," largest 8" h. x 6" w. x 3" d., smaller two 5-3/4" h. x 4" w. x 2" d. **$800**

Keno Auctions

▼ Bennington, Vermont flint enamel lion, circa 1850, impressed Lyman Fenton & Co., standing figure with coleslaw mane, front paw resting atop globe on stepped plinth, 9-1/2" h., 11" l. **$10,073**

Pook & Pook, Inc.

TOP! LOT!

Bennington Pottery bottle, figure of man, by David Gil, circa 1970, 10" h. **$75**

Ahlers & Ogletree Auction Gallery

CLARICE CLIFF

Clarice Cliff was a designer for A.J. Wilinson, Ltd., Royal Staffordshire Pottery, Burslem, England, when it acquired the adjoining Newport Pottery Co., whose warehouses were filled with undecorated bowls and vases. In about 1925, Cliff's flair with the Art Deco style was incorporated into designs appropriately named "Bizarre" and "Fantasque," and the warehouse stockpile was decorated in vivid colors. These hand-painted earthenwares, all bearing the printed signature of designer Clarice Cliff, were produced until World War II and find enormous favor with collectors.

Note: Reproductions of the Clarice Cliff "Bizarre" marking appear on the market occasionally.

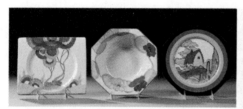

Three Bizarre ware dishes, England, 20th century, Newport and Wilkinson potteries, octagonal Nasturtium pattern center bowl, 9"; octagonal Orange Roof Cottage plate also stamped "Fantasque," 9-3/8"; Rhodanthe pattern Biarritz-form plate, also stamped "The Biarritz Royal Staffordshire Great Britain Regd. No. 784849," 9"; each with backstamp. **$563**

Skinner, Inc., www.skinnerinc.com

Four Forest Glen pattern items, England, 20th century, Newport and Wilkinson potteries, three-piece tea service: teapot, 3-1/4" h., sugar and creamer, jam pot with red base and patterned lid, 4-1/8" dia. **$516**

Skinner, Inc., www.skinnerinc.com

Five Bizarre ware conical sugar sifters, England, 20th century, Newport and Wilkinson potteries, one each Autumn Crocus, Rhodanthe, Aurea, and Gibraltar patterns, one with applied blue flowers to base on white ground, each with backstamp, 5-1/2" h. **$2,844**

Skinner, Inc., www.skinnerinc.com

Five items, England, 20th century, Newport and Wilkinson potteries, Bizarre ware vase with orange-leaf tree with black branches on yellow and white ground with cloud outlines and a band stylized green shrubbery, 8" h.; "Indian Summer" vase with flared black-lined rim, body with flared middle decorated with blue and black floral band, 7-5/8" h.; Bizarre ware Athens jug in Forest Glen pattern, 6" h; pair of Bizarre ware vases in Applique pattern, each incised "265," 6" h; each with backstamp.............**$5,629**

Skinner, Inc., www.skinnerinc.com

Eight-piece Fantasque Bizarre ware partial tea set, England, 20th century, Newport Pottery Co., Gibraltar pattern, teapot, creamer, open sugar, two coffee cups, two teacups and saucers, one dish, each with backstamp, teapot 5-3/4"............................ **$2,963**

Skinner, Inc., www.skinnerinc.com

Three Bizarre ware items, England, 20th century, Newport Pottery Co., pitcher in Secrets pattern with additional "Fantasque" label to stamp, 7-1/2" h.; bowl in Cafe-au-Lait pattern, 10" dia.; miniature clog in Gayday pattern, 6"; each with backstamp. **$889**

Skinner, Inc., www.skinnerinc.com

Seven Bizarre ware spice shakers, England, 20th century, Newport and Wilkinson potteries, two pairs of conical sugar sifters, one with partially etched design of flowers and fields, the other with thatched roof, height to 3-1/8"; small set of salt and pepper shakers and jam pot in bright hues, height to 1-7/8"................................ **$911**

Skinner, Inc., www.skinnerinc.com

Four Bizarre ware items, England, 20th century, Newport and Wilkinson potteries, Athens jug in Delecia pattern with backstamps for both firms and indistinct raised numbers, 7-1/4" h.; bowl with painted scene of tree and patch of flowers repeated on each side, 8" dia.; two tapered vases in My Garden pattern, one with orange ground, the other blue, 7-5/8" h.; each with backstamp. **$425**

Skinner, Inc., www.skinnerinc.com

Five tableware items, England, 20th century, Newport and Wilkinson potteries, Delecia Citrus pattern oblong dish, 11-5/8" l.; Rhodanthe pattern sugar sifter, 5" h.; My Garden cylindrical covered sugar with floriform finial, 3-1/8" h.; jam pot with yellow rose set against fuchsia spiral, 4" h.; toast rack with polychrome decoration of flowers and etched fields, 6" l. **$711**

Skinner, Inc., www.skinnerinc.com

Five-piece Bizarre ware partial tea set, England, 20th century, Wilkinson Ltd., each in Cabbage Flower pattern and Lynton-form, coffeepot, milk jug, creamer, open sugar, and cup and saucer, each with backstamp, coffeepot 7 1/8" high. **$521**

Skinner, Inc., www.skinnerinc.com

Fours pairs of Bizarre ware salt and pepper shakers, England, 20th century, Newport Pottery Co., two pairs Alpine and Berries patterns, one pair with brown flowers and green leaves and the other with thatched roof, 3-1/4".......... **$668**

Skinner, Inc., www.skinnerinc.com

Six Bizarre ware tableware items, England, 20th century, Newport and Wilkinson potteries, ovoid sugar sifter with design of thatched roof, 4-3/4" h.; two spice shakers with tapered ribbed bodies, one Aurea pattern, the other a geometric diamond design, 4-3/4" h.; Melon pattern jam pot with fruit finials, 3" h.; pair of cube-form Aurea pattern candlesticks, 2-1/4" h. **$830**

Skinner, Inc., www.skinnerinc.com

Five-piece Bizarre ware partial tea set, England, 20th century, Newport Pottery Co., Sungay pattern, teapot, creamer, open sugar, teacup and saucer, dish, each with backstamp, teapot 5-3/4". **$1,067**

Skinner, Inc., www.skinnerinc.com

Five-piece Bizarre ware partial tea set, England, 20th century, Newport Pottery Co., Windbells pattern, teapot, creamer, open sugar, and two cups and saucers, each with backstamp, teapot 5" h. **$1,007**

Skinner, Inc., www.skinnerinc.com

CERAMICS

!

COWEN

R. Guy Cowan opened his first pottery studio in 1912 in Lakewood, Ohio. The pottery operated almost continuously, with the exception of a break during World War I, at various locations in the Cleveland area until it was forced to close in 1931 due to financial difficulties.

Many of the 20th century's finest artists began with Cowan and its associate, the Cleveland School of Art. This fine art pottery, particularly the designer pieces, is highly sought after by collectors.

Many people are unaware that it was due to R. Guy Cowan's perseverance and tireless work that art pottery is today considered an art form and found in many art museums.

For more information on Cowan pottery, see *Antique Trader Pottery & Porcelain Ceramics Price Guide*, 6th edition.

Vessel, signed COWAN in block letters with Cowan logo, 5-3/4" x 9-1/4" x 5-1/4"....................**$15**

Dirk Soulis Auctions

Vase with volcanic-like glaze, black over April green flambé, marked with Cowan die impressed logo, excellent original condition, 7" x 11"............................**$190**

Mark Mussio, Humler & Nolan

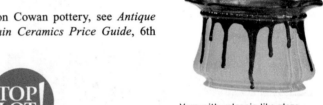

Jazz Bowl, rare smaller form, melon green glaze, designed and signed by Viktor Schreckengost, 8-1/4" h. and 13-5/8" dia. Known as shape X-42, the small Jazz Bowl is thought to be much less common than its larger counterpart. **$22,000**

Mark Mussio, Humler & Nolan

TOP LOT!

Swirl Dancer flower figure, original ivory, die impressed logo, 10-1/4" h.......................................**$270**

Rachel Davis Fine Arts

Chinese bird vase, marked (die impressed) Cowan seal, excellent condition, 11-1/4" h............**$110**

Belhorn Auctions

Two-handled vase, green glaze, impressed Cowan mark, 8" x 7"................................**$25**

Dirk Soulis Auctions

CERAMICS

DELFT

In the early 17th century, Italian potters settled in Holland and began producing tin-glazed earthenwares, often decorated with pseudo-Oriental designs based on Chinese porcelain wares. The city of Delft became the center of this pottery production and several firms produced the wares throughout the 17th and early 18th century. A majority of the pieces featured blue on white designs, but polychrome wares were also made. The Dutch Delftwares were also shipped to England, where eventually the English copied them at potteries in such cities as Bristol, Lambeth, and Liverpool. Although still produced today, Delft peaked in popularity by the mid-18th century.

Dutch Delft tobacco jar, 19th century, ovoid form with blue decoration depicting Indian smoking pipe, seated on plinth set with large jar labeled "STRASSBUR[G]" and other tobacco-related material with distant ships, domed brass cover, minor chips, 14" h. **$3,120**

Skinner, Inc., www.skinnerinc.com

Large Dutch Delft tobacco jar, 18th century, ovoid form with blue decoration, labeled "STRAATS/BURGER" within rococo cartouche surrounded by scrolling foliage topped by flower-filled vase, brass cover, minor glaze loss, 16" h. **$1,140**

Skinner, Inc., www.skinnerinc.com

Dutch Delft floral-decorated barber bowl, 18th century, oval, center decorated with cobalt animal and bird figures and flowers, wide fluted floral-decorated rim, table foot pierced for hanging, hairline, minor rim chips, 3" h., 10-7/8" dia. **$750**

Skinner, Inc., www.skinnerinc.com

Large chinoiserie-decorated Delft bowl, England or Continental, 18th century, piecrust rim, waterway scene with fishermen, chips, hairline, 4" h., 12-1/4" dia. .. **$840**

Skinner, Inc., www.skinnerinc.com

Dutch Delft charger with lion and gate decoration, 18th century, circular form with dark cobalt designs of standing lion before curved gate with two columns, flanked by trees and foliage, rim decorated with three repeating panels of flowers, chinoiserie figure in a landscape, rim chips, 13-7/8" dia......................... **$720**

Skinner, Inc., www.skinnerinc.com

Delftware vase, Continental (Dutch), 17th century, tin-glazed earthenware two-handled vase with Baroque decoration, marine landscape on one side and man with tricornered hat in hand on the other, blue and white and marked in blue AKQ for Q. Kleynoven, (1680) and numbered, 337/14, 6-1/4" h. **$300**

Cowan's Auctions, Inc.

CERAMICS

William & Mary figural-decorated Dutch Delft charger, 18th century, rim decorated with flowers and birds, table foot pierced for hanging, imperfections, 13-1/2" dia. **$1,920**

Skinner, Inc., www.skinnerinc.com

Large Delftware bowl, Britain, late 18th century, ornamented with polychrome bird in a garden in center, floral rim, rim chips, crazing, 2-1/2" h., 13-1/2" dia. **$360**

Skinner, Inc., www.skinnerinc.com

Delft charger with cobalt flower basket decoration, 18th century, minor rim chips, 13-3/4" dia. **$360**

Skinner, Inc., www.skinnerinc.com

Dutch Delft tobacco jar, 19th century, ovoid form with blue decoration depicting Indian smoking pipe, seated on plinth set with large jar labeled "ST. DOMINGO," with a tobacco plant, barrels, and distant ships, domed brass cover, minor glaze loss and chips, 12" h. **$3,000**

Skinner, Inc., www.skinnerinc.com

Two polychrome floral-decorated Delft plates and charger, 18th century, plates with similar floral central and rim decoration, imperfections, 7-7/8" dia., 8-7/8" dia., 13-3/4" dia. **$960**

Skinner, Inc., www.skinnerinc.com

Delft plate decorated with a woman holding a cornucopia and a flower stem, late 18th century, rim repair, glaze wear on rim, 8-7/8" dia. **$180**

Skinner, Inc., www.skinnerinc.com

Polychrome floral-decorated Delftware bowl, England, 18th century, round footed bowl, center with blue inscription "Success to Trade," exterior decorated with spray of blossoms and leaves, repaired, glaze wear, 4-3/8" h., 10-3/4" dia..................... **$1,020**

Skinner, Inc., www.skinnerinc.com

Dutch Delft tobacco jar, 18th century, ovoid form with blue decoration, labeled "ST. OMER" within rococo cartouche surrounded by scrolling foliage topped by flower-filled vase, domed brass cover, minor glaze loss, 15-1/2" h. **$960**

Skinner, Inc., www.skinnerinc.com

Dutch Delft tobacco jar, 18th century, ovoid form with blue decoration, labeled "MARTENIEK" within rococo cartouche surrounded by scrolling foliage topped by flower-filled vase, domed brass cover, minor glaze loss, 15-1/4" h.................... **$960**

Skinner, Inc., www.skinnerinc.com

DOULTON AND ROYAL DOULTON

Doulton & Co., Ltd., was founded in Lambeth, London, in about 1858. It operated there until 1956 and often incorporated the words "Doulton" and "Lambeth" in its marks. Pinder, Bourne & Co. Burslem was purchased by the Doultons in 1878 and in 1882 became Doulton & Co., Ltd. It added porcelain to its earthenware production in 1884. The "Royal Doulton" mark has been used since 1902 by this factory, which is still in operation. Character jugs and figurines (see "Figurines" section for more information) are commanding great attention from collectors at the present time.

John Doulton, the founder, was born in 1793. He became an apprentice at the age of 12 to a potter in south London. Five years later he was employed in another small pottery near Lambeth. His two sons, John and Henry, subsequently joined their father in 1830 in a partnership he had formed with the name of Doulton & Watts. Watts retired in 1864 and the partnership was dissolved. Henry formed a new company that traded as Doulton and Co.

In the early 1870s the proprietor of the Pinder Bourne Co., located in Burslem, Staffordshire, offered Henry a partnership. The Pinder Bourne Co. was purchased by Henry in 1878 and became part of Doulton & Co. in 1882.

With the passage of time, the demand for the Lambeth industrial and decorative stoneware declined whereas demand for the Burslem manufactured and decorated bone china wares increased.

Doulton & Co. was incorporated as a limited liability company in 1899. In 1901 the company was allowed to use the word "Royal" on its trademarks by Royal Charter. The

Early Lambeth vase decorated in 1878 with white daisies on blue ground, wrapped with dragon, impressed Doulton logo, date and incised monogram of artist (appears to be JWT), chip at base in area with prior restoration, two short minor firing separations to bottom, slight lean to vase, 14" h. **$1,500**

Mark Mussio, Humler & Nolan

well known "lion on crown" logo came into use in 1902. In 2000 the logo was changed on the company's advertising literature to one showing a more stylized lion's head in profile.

Today Royal Doulton is one of the world's leading manufacturers and distributors of premium grade ceramic tabletop wares and collectibles. The Doulton Group comprises Minton, Royal Albert, Caithness Glass, Holland Studio Craft and Royal Doulton. Royal Crown Derby was part of the group from 1971 until 2000 when it became an independent company. These companies market collectibles using their own brand names.

Character Jugs

Aramis, large, D 6441,
7-1/4" h. **$90**

Anne of Cleves, large, D 6653,
7-1/4" h. **$240**

Anne Boleyn, large, D 6644,
7-1/4" h. **$85**

Bacchus, large, D 6499,
7" h. **$100**

'Ard of 'Earing, large, D 6588,
7-1/2" h. **$1,250**

'Arriet, large, D 6208,
6-1/2" h. **$65**

Capt Hook, large, D 6597,
7-1/4" h. **$500**

Capt. Henry Morgan, large,
6-3/4" h. **$100**

Blacksmith, D 6571, large,
7" h. **$100**

Clown with white hair (The), large,
D 6322, 7-1/2" h. **$1,000**

Catherine Howard, large, D 6645,
7" h. **$115**

Catherine of Aragon, large, D
6643, 7" h. **$100**

Beefeater, large, D 6206,
6-1/2" h. **$125**

Catherine Parr, large, D 6664,
6-3/4" h. **$220**

Don Quixote, large, D 6455,
7-1/4" h. **$60**

Fortune Teller (The), large, D
6497, 6-3/4" h. **$200**

Cliff Cornell, large, variation No. 1, light brown suit, brown and cream
striped tie, 9" h. left). **$450**
Cliff Cornell, large, variation No. 3, dark brown suit, green, black and
blue designed tie, 9" h. right). **$750**

Gardener (The), large, D 6630,
7-3/4" h. **$150**

Groucho Marx, large, D 6710,
7" h. **$155**

George Washington and George III,
large, D 6749, 7-1/4" h. **$125**

Gladiator, large, D 6650,
7-3/4" h. **$600**

CERAMICS

Robinson Crusoe, large, D 6532, 7-1/2" h. **$175**

Hamlet, large, D 6672, 7-1/4" h. **$150**

Jane Seymour, large, D 6646, 7-1/4" h. **$100**

Gulliver, large, D 6560, 7-1/2" h. **$675**

Henry VIII, large, D 6642, 6-1/2" h. **$125**

Guardsman (The), large, D 6568, 6-3/4" h. **$95**

John Peel, large, D 5612, 6-1/2" h. **$100**

Johnny Appleseed, large, D 6372, 6" h. **$350**

Izaac Walton, large, D 6404, 7" h. **$85**

Paddy, large, D 5753, 6" h. .. **$120**

Old King Cole, large, D 6036, 5-3/4" h. **$230**

Mr. Pickwick, large, D 6060, 5-1/2" h. **$150**

Lumberjack, large, D 6610,
7-1/4" h. $100

Lawyer (The), large, D6498,
7" h. $90

Merlin, large, D 6529,
7-1/4" h. $100

Louis Armstrong, large, D 6707,
7-1/2" h. $185

Parson Brown "A," large, D 5486,
6-1/2" h. $125

Mad Hatter, large, D 6598,
7-1/4" h. $185

Ringmaster (The), large, D 6863,
7-1/2" h. $150

Robin Hood,
2nd version,
large, D 6527,
7-1/2" h. $65

Robin Hood,
2nd version,
small, D 6234,
3-1/4" h. $20

Sairey Gamp, large, No. 5451,
6-1/4" h. $65

Tony Weller, large, D 5531,
6-1/2" h. $230

Simple Simon, large, D 6374,
7" h. $500

CERAMICS

Scaramouche, large, first version, D 6558, 7" h. **$775**

Sleuth (The), large, D 6631, 7" h. **$100**

Sir Thomas More, large, D 6792, 6-3/4" h. **$210**

Santa Claus, doll and drum handle, large, D 6668, 7-1/2" h. **$185**

St. George, large, D 6618, 7-1/2" h. **$175**

Ugly Duchess, large, D 6599, 6-3/4" h. **$675**

Falstaff, large, D 6287, 6" h. ...**$100**

Walrus & Carpenter (The), large, D 6600, 7-1/4" h. **$130**

Veteran Motorist, large, D 6633, 7-1/2" h. **$125**

Yachtsman, large, D 6626, 8" h. **$150**

William Shakespeare, large, D 6689, 7-3/4" h. **$125**

Three Series Ware items, "Pottery in the Past" loving cup, No. D6696, hatpin holder, possibly "Henry VIII at Hampton Court," No. D3858, and "Thomas Touchy" tankard from "Sir Roger de Coverly" series, No. D3618, 1920s and later, loving cup undamaged, hatpin with minor crazing and kiln-splitting to base, tankard cracked at rim, glaze crazing, loving cup 6-1/8" h., hatpin 5" h., tankard 5-1/2" h. **$92**

Jeffrey S. Evans & Associates

Four Series Ware pitchers, "Woolsey" mid-sized jug, "Katherine" small-sized jug, small "Queens and Ladies" creamer, No. D3159, and small "Bluebell Gatherers" jug; "Woolsey" and "Queens" pitchers with dark green line rims, remaining two with brown line rims, each with printed marks, 1930s and later, 3-7/8" to 6-7/8" h. overall....................**$92**

Jeffrey S. Evans & Associates

Four Series Ware items, "Night Watchman" candlestick, No. D2002, "Bird Feeder & Flowers" child's mug, "Juliet" double-handled covered sugar bowl, No. D3696, and creamer, No. D1404, 1920s and later, glaze crazing, various sizes...............................
$115

Jeffrey S. Evans & Associates

Pair of Lambeth whiskey jugs, salt glaze stoneware, registry #4818, marked Doulton Lambeth, late 19th century, 8"....................**$30**

Kaminski Auctions

Dickensware items, "The Artful Dodger" candlestick, "Bill Sykes" cream jug, "Old Peggoty" pitcher, "Little Nell" pitcher, each with deep green line rims, ombre burnt orange grounds to rims and black outlines over-enameled in colors, 20th century, excellent condition, 4" to 5-3/4" h. overall. **$127**

Jeffrey S. Evans & Associates

Flambé scenic vase of landscape showing thatch-roofed houses along road with flowers in foreground, "woodcut" style, marked with Royal Doulton insignia, excellent original condition with a few short scratches, 11-3/8" h............................**$130**

Mark Mussio, Humler & Nolan

Four Series Ware items, "Coaching" pitcher with rope-twist handle, No. D2416, and three others with house in rustic scenery, all with dark green line rims, printed marks, 1920s and later, smallest pitcher undamaged, remaining with light to moderate glaze crazing, 4-1/2" to 6-1/8" h. overall............................ **$92**

Jeffrey S. Evans & Associates

Four Series Ware items, "Queen Elizabeth at Old Moreton" double-handled dish with black line rims, "Henry VIII at Hampton Court" quatrefoil-form dish with brown line rim, "Romeo" with brown-line rim, and "Bluebell Gatherers" cereal bowl with light green line rim, each with printed marks, 1920s and later, very good overall condition, various sizes. **$69**

Jeffrey S. Evans & Associates

Flambé landscape vase with scene of thatch-roofed house along road with flowers in foreground, "woodcut" style, bearing Royal Doulton inkstamp insignia, paper label attached to bottom, excellent original condition with short minor scratch, 9" h. **$160**

Mark Mussio, Humler & Nolan

FIESTA

The Homer Laughlin China Co. originated with a two-kiln pottery on the banks of the Ohio River in East Liverpool, Ohio. Built in 1873-'74 by Homer Laughlin and his brother, Shakespeare, the firm was first known as the Ohio Valley Pottery, and later Laughlin Bros. Pottery. It was one of the first white-ware plants in the country.

After a tentative beginning, the company was awarded a prize for having the best white-ware at the 1876 Centennial Exposition in Philadelphia.

Three years later, Shakespeare sold his interest in the business to Homer, who continued on until 1897. At that time, Homer sold his interest in the newly incorporated firm to a group of investors, including Charles, Louis, and Marcus Aaron and the company bookkeeper, William E. Wells.

Under new ownership in 1907, the headquarters and a new 30-kiln plant were built across the Ohio River in Newell, West Virginia, the present manufacturing and headquarters location.

In the 1920s, two additions to the Homer Laughlin staff set the stage for the company's greatest success: the Fiesta line. Dr. Albert V. Bleininger was hired in 1920. A scientist, author, and educator, he oversaw the conversion from bottle kilns to the more efficient tunnel kilns.

In 1927, the company hired designer Frederick Hurten Rhead, a member of a distinguished family of English ceramists. Having previously worked at Weller Pottery and Roseville Pottery, Rhead began to develop the artistic quality of the company's wares, and to experiment with shapes and glazes. In 1935, this work culminated in his designs for the Fiesta line.

For more information on Fiesta, see *Warman's Fiesta Identification and Price Guide* by Glen Victorey.

Fiesta Colors

From 1936 to 1972, Fiesta was produced in 14 colors (other than special promotions). These colors are usually divided into the "original colors" of cobalt blue, light green, ivory, red, turquoise, and yellow; the "1950s colors" of chartreuse, forest green, gray, and rose (introduced in 1951); medium green (introduced in 1959); plus the later additions of Casuals, Amberstone, Fiesta Ironstone, and Casualstone ("Coventry") in antique gold, mango red, and turf green; and the striped, decal, and Lustre pieces. No Fiesta was produced from 1973 to 1985. The colors that make up the "original" and "1950s" groups are sometimes referred to as "the standard 11." Fiesta is still produced today in a variety of contemporary colors.

In many pieces, medium green is the hardest to find and the most expensive Fiesta color.

Fiesta Colors and Years of Production to 1972

Antique Gold 1969-1972	Ivory 1936-1951
Chartreuse 1951-1959	Mango Red (same as original red) ..1970-1972
Cobalt Blue 1936-1951	Medium Green 1959-1969
Forest Green 1951-1959	Red .... 1936-1944 and 1959-1972
Gray 1951-1959	Rose 1951-1959
Green 1936-1951	Turf Green 1969-1972
(often called light green when comparing it	Turquoise 1937-1969
to other green glazes; also called "original" green)	Yellow 1936-1969

CERAMICS

Bottom Marks

Notice the different bottoms of two ashtrays. The top one has a set of rings with no room for a logo. The bottom ashtray has rings along the outer edge, opposite of the ring pattern on the ashtray above. The red example is an older example. The yellow ashtray with the logo can be dated to a time period after 1940.

An ink stamp on the bottom of a piece of Fiesta.

Bottom of 6" bread plate in turquoise, showing "Genuine Fiesta" stamp.

Bottom of a teacup saucer in turquoise, showing sagger pin marks and the "Genuine Fiesta" stamp.

Two different impressed marks on the bottoms of relish tray inserts.

Bottom of No. 1 mixing bowl in green, showing sagger pin marks, the "Fiesta/HLCo. USA" impressed mark, and the faint "1" size indicator. The impressed size mark on the bottom of the No. 2 mixing bowl in yellow is too faint to be seen in this image.

Examples of impressed Fiesta bottom marks.

Fiesta pieces were glazed on the underside, so before being fired, each piece was placed on a stilt to keep it off the floor of the kiln. The stilt was made up of three sagger pins positioned an equal distance from each other to form three points of a triangle. If you inspect the underside of any piece of Fiesta, which has a completely glazed bottom, you will notice three small blemishes in a triangular pattern. Later in Fiesta's production run, the undersides of pieces were glazed and then wiped, creating a dry foot, before going into the kiln to be fired.

A 9" cobalt blue plate rests on a stilt with sagger pins to show the basic idea of how it worked. Please note that this stilt is not the exact one that would have been used by Homer Laughlin China Co., but rather an updated style in use today by many ceramic studios.

Stack of four ashtrays in red, cobalt blue, ivory and yellow..... **$95, $95, $95, and $85, respectively**

5-1/2" fruit bowl in red. **$45**

#1 mixing bowl in red with an ivory lid. .... **$300 bowl, $1,250-$2,000 lid**

#3 mixing bowl with a yellow lid. ...... **$150 bowl, $1,250-$2,000 lid**

Dessert bowl in yellow. **$60**

4-3/4" fruit bowl in cobalt blue. **$35**

#4 mixing bowl in ivory. **$175**

#2 mixing bowl in turquoise with a cobalt blue lid. .... **$150 bowl, $1,250-$2,000 lid**

Covered onion soup bowl in ivory. **$775**

Cream soup cup in gray. **$75**

Footed salad bowl in ivory.... **$550**

11-3/4" fruit bowl in light green................................. **$395**

Individual salad bowl in yellow. **$145**

CERAMICS

Carafe in red. **$395**

Coffeepot in cobalt blue. **$325**

Eggcup in red....................... **$80**

#7 mixing bowl in ivory. **$650**

#6 mixing bowl in cobalt blue. **$400**

Demitasse coffeepot in light green.................................. **$600**

Demitasse cup and saucer in cobalt blue..................... **$115/set**

Three Tom & Jerry mugs in yellow, light green, and red..... **$75, $75, and $95, respectively**

10" plate in cobalt blue. **$50**

Covered sugar bowl and stick-handle creamer in red................. **$95 and $75, respectively**

Ring-handle creamer in turquoise................... **$35**

Sauceboat in yellow. **$75**

Stick-handle creamer in yellow....................... **$65**

8-1/2" nappy in red. **$70**

Two mustards in red and ivory. ....**$350 and $450, respectively**

Shakers in turquoise (note color variation)....**$35/pair**

Marmalades in red and ivory, including glass spoons with colored tips......... **$425 and $400, respectively**

Sweets comport in cobalt blue. **$150**

Ice pitcher in light green. $185

DripCut syrup pitcher in ivory. **$525**

Two-pint jug in red. **$175**

9" plate in yellow. **$25**

Disk water pitcher in turquoise. **$185**

13" chop plate in yellow. **$65**

10-1/2" compartment plate in red................. **$85**

Medium teapot in ivory.................................**$295**

Teacup and saucer in yellow...................... **$39/set**

12" compartment plate in light green............**$125**

Deep plate in rose.. **$65**

Oval platter in cobalt blue. **$65**

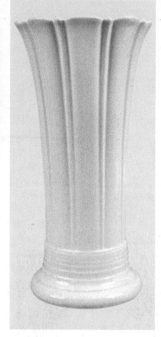

10" vase in ivory............. **$1,150**

Utility tray in red. **$65**

6" and 7" plates in medium green. ....**$35 each**

8" vase in yellow. **$785**

Bud vase in red. **$155**

Water tumbler in light green. . **$90**

FRANKOMA

John Frank started his pottery company in 1933 in Norman, Oklahoma. However, when he moved the business to Sapulpa, Oklahoma, in 1938, he felt he was home. Still, Mr. Frank could not know the horrendous storms and trials that would follow him. Just after his move, on Nov. 11, 1938, a fire destroyed the entire operation, which included the pot and leopard mark he had created in 1935. Then, in 1942, the war effort needed men and materials, so Frankoma could not survive. In 1943, John and Grace Lee Frank bought the plant as junk salvage and began again.

The time in Norman had produced some of the finest art ware that John would ever create and most of the items were marked either "Frank Potteries," "Frank Pottery," or to a lesser degree, the "pot and leopard" mark. Today these marks are avidly and enthusiastically sought by collectors. Another elusive mark wanted by collectors shows "Firsts Kiln Sapulpa 6-7-38." The mark was used for one day only and denotes the first firing in Sapulpa. It has been estimated that perhaps 50 to 75 pieces were fired on that day.

The clay Frankoma used is helpful to collectors in determining when an item was made. Creamy beige clay known as "Ada" clay was in use until 1953. Then a red brick shale was found in Sapulpa and used until about 1985 when, with the addition of an additive, the clay became a reddish pink.

Rutile glazes were used early in Frankoma's history. Glazes with rutile have caused more confusion among collectors than any other glazes. For example, a Prairie Green piece shows a lot of green but it also has some brown. The same is true for the Desert Gold glaze; the piece shows a sandy-beige glaze with some brown. Generally speaking, Prairie Green, Desert Gold, White Sand, and Woodland Moss are the most puzzling to collectors.

Carafe and cover, footed bulbous body tapering to short cylindrical neck, domed cover with rounded tab handle, made from No. 93 pitcher mold created in 1940 and discontinued in 1964, made for an organization, below five-point colored star is the name "Ted Witt," reverse incised with sailboat on water and dates 1946-47, turquoise glaze, marked "Frankoma," 6-1/2" h...........**$90**

In 1970 the government closed the rutile mines in America, and Frankoma had to buy it from Australia. It was not the same, so the results were different. Values are higher for the glazes with rutile. Also, the pre-Australian Woodland Moss glaze is more desirable than that created after 1970.

After John Frank died in 1973, his daughter Joniece Frank, a ceramic designer at the pottery, became president of the company. In 1983 another fire destroyed everything Frankoma had worked so hard to create. They rebuilt, but in 1990, after the IRS shut the doors for nonpayment, Joniece, true to the Frank legacy, filed for Chapter 11 (instead of bankruptcy) so she could reopen and continue the work she loved.

In 1991 Richard Bernstein purchased the pottery, and the name was changed to Frankoma Industries. The company was sold again in 2005 to Det and Crystal Merryman. Yet another owner, Joe Ragosta, purchased the pottery in 2008.

Frankoma Pottery was closed for good in 2010 with a factory closeout auction in Oklahoma in 2011.

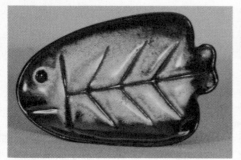

Christmas card in form of figural fish tray, marked "1960 the Franks, Frankoma Christmas Frankoma," Woodland Moss glaze, 4" l............................. **$95**

Flower holder, model of miniature hobby horse, marked "Frankoma," 1942, Ada clay, Prairie Green glaze, rare, 3-1/2" h. **$340**

Trivet, eagle sitting on branch, large wings fill up most of space, Peach Glow glaze, Model No. 2tr, 6" sq. **$76**

Vase, miniature spherical ringed shape, marked "Frankoma 500," Desert Gold glaze, Ada clay, 2-3/4" h..**$190**

Bucking Bronco bookends, Model No. 423, Prairie Green glaze, 5-1/2" h. .... **$560 pr.**

Bowl, deep round shape with three full-figure Tiki gods around sides, incised "Club Trade Winds, Tulsa, Okla. 6," Prairie Green, Sapulpa clay, early 1960s, 6-1/4" dia., 3-1/2" h. **$195**

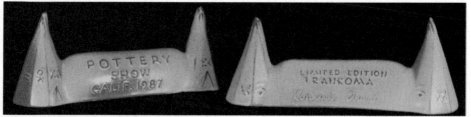

Sign advertising "Pottery Show – Calif. 1987," Prairie Green glaze, 9" l. **$115**

Wall plaque, figural, modeled as head of Peter Pan, designed by Joseph Taylor, made 1936-38 and 1972-75, Ada clay, Prairie Green glaze, 6" h. **$148**

Figure of Indian chief, No. 142, Desert Gold glaze, Ada clay, 7" h. **$190**

Model of Pekinese dog standing on hind legs, designed by Joseph Taylor, 1934-38, marked "Frankoma," glossy black glaze, 7-1/2" h. **$590**

Wall pocket, figural, Billiken, marked "Tulsa Court, No. 47, R.O.J.," Prairie Green glaze, Ada clay, 7" h. **$178**

Salt and pepper shakers in form of bull heads, Ada clay, matte yellow glaze, 1-3/4" h. .... **$165 pr.**

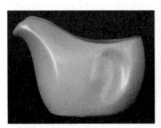

Christmas card in form of creamer, Model No. 560, "Xmas – The Franks – 1948" incised into Ada clay, Prairie Green glaze, rare, 2-1/4" h. **$125**

Vase, stovepipe, marked "Frankoma," Prairie Green glaze with silver overlay, 1940s, 8-3/4" h. **$645**

Stein, footed, advertising-type, for John Frank Memorial Charity Golf Tournament, blue, 150 created, 1973 .... **$30**

CERAMICS

FULPER POTTERY

From the "Germ-Proof Filter" to enduring Arts & Crafts acclaim – that's the unlikely journey of Fulper Pottery, maker of the early 20th-century uniquely glazed artware that's become a favorite with today's collectors.

Fulper began life in 1814 as the Samuel Hill Pottery, named after its founder, a New Jersey potter. In its early years, the pottery specialized in useful items such as storage crocks and drain pipes fashioned from the area's red clay. Abraham Fulper, a worker at the pottery, eventually became Hill's partner, purchasing the company in 1860. Renamed after its new owner, Fulper Pottery continued to produce a variety of utilitarian tile and crockery. By the turn of the 20th century, the firm, now led by Abraham's sons, introduced a line of fire-proof cookware and the hugely successful "Germ-Proof Filter." An ancestor of today's water cooler, the filter provided sanitary drinking water in less-than-sanitary public places, such as offices and railway stations.

In the early 1900s, Fulper's master potter, John Kunsman, began creating various solid-glaze vessels, such as jugs and vases, which were offered for sale outside the pottery. On a whim, William H. Fulper II (Abraham's grandson, who'd become the company's secretary/treasurer) took an assortment of these items for exhibit at the 1904 Louisiana Purchase Exposition—along with, of course, the Germ-Proof Filter. Kunsman's artware took home an honorable mention.

Since Chinese art pottery was then attracting national attention, Fulper saw an opening to produce similarly styled modern ware. Dr. Cullen Parmelee, who headed up the ceramics department at Rutgers, was recruited to create a contemporary series of glazes patterned after those of ancient China. The Fulper Vasekraft line of art pottery incorporating these glazes made its debut in 1909. Unfortunately, Parmelee's glazes did not lend themselves well to mass production; they did not result in reliable coloration. Even more to their detriment, they were expensive to produce.

In 1910, most of Parmelee's glazes disappeared from the line. A new ceramic engineer, Martin Stangl, was given the assignment of revitalizing Vasekraft. His most notable innovation: steering designs and glazes away from reinterpretations of ornate Chinese classics and toward the simplicity of the burgeoning Arts & Crafts movement. Among his many Vasekraft successes: candleholders, bookends, perfume lamps, desk accessories, tobacco jars, and even Vasekraft lamps. Here, both the lamp base and shade were of pottery; stained glass inserts in the shades allowed light to shine through.

Always attuned to the mood of the times, William Fulper realized that by World War I the heavy Vasekraft stylings were fading in popularity. A new and lighter line of Fulper Pottery Artware, featuring Spanish Revival and English themes, was introduced. Among the most admired Fulper releases following the war were Fulper Porcelaines: dresser boxes, powder jars, ashtrays, lamps, and other accessories designed to complement the fashionable boudoir.

Fulper Fayence, the popular line of solid-color, open-stock dinnerware eventually known as Stangl Pottery, was introduced in the 1920s. In 1928, following William Fulper's death, Martin Stangl was named company president. The artware that continued into the 1930s embraced Art Deco as well as Classical and Primitive stylistic themes. From 1935 onward, Stangl Pottery became the sole Fulper output. In 1978, the Stangl assets came under the ownership of Pfaltzgraff.

Unlike wheel-thrown pottery, Fulper was made in molds; the true artistry came in the use of exceptionally rich, color-blended glazes. Each Fulper piece is one-of-a-kind. Because of glaze divergence, two Fulper objects from the same mold can show a great variance. While once a drawback for retailers seeking consistency, that uniqueness is now a boon to collectors: Each Fulper piece possesses its own singular visual appeal.

4" cream pitcher and 4-5/8" lidded bowl, mat brown glaze, marked with early rectangular mark, mark on sugar cannot be read because glaze has covered it, each in excellent original condition............................ **$140**

Mark Mussio, Humler & Nolan

Handled pitcher, Oriental form hybridized with addition of handle, 1916-1922, Copper Dust crystalline glaze, marked with die-stamped "incised" mark, three flat chips to foot ring, 11-3/8" h. **$1,800**

Mark Mussio, Humler & Nolan

Two vases with Wisteria glaze, 8-1/8" vase with green applied at rim, 7-3/4" vase impressed with pottery logo, other has oval inkstamp, some roughness at rim of smaller vase, both in original condition. **$150**

Mark Mussio, Humler & Nolan

Vase, shape 537, black and yellow flambé glaze with blue highlights, marked with die-stamped "incised" logo, excellent original condition, 7-3/8"................ **$120**

Mark Mussio, Humler & Nolan

Vase, shape 17, textured brown glaze over blue high glaze, marked with Fulper rectangular ink stamp, small chip at base, 3-5/8"... **$110**

Mark Mussio, Humler & Nolan

Vase, shape 567, blue, green and purple glazes in both mat and glossy, raised Fulper logo, excellent original condition with some minor glaze bubbles, 6-5/8" h.. **$375**

Mark Mussio, Humler & Nolan

Vase, shape 523, mat maroon glaze over blue, marked with vertical ink stamp logo, excellent original condition, 10" h. **$300**

Mark Mussio, Humler & Nolan

Vase with oatmeal glaze over Mirrored Black, impressed with die-stamped "incised" mark, shape 536, small grinding chips at base, 13-1/2" h............... **$700**

Mark Mussio, Humler & Nolan

Vase with Chinese Blue glaze over Wisteria, marked with vertical "racetrack" logo, some glaze pulls to bottom of vase, some small glaze bubbles, 8" h. **$130**

Mark Mussio, Humler & Nolan

Two-handled vase, green glaze with large snowflake crystals, die-stamped with "incised" logo, excellent original condition, 8-3/4" h............................ **$225**

Mark Mussio, Humler & Nolan

Vase with two squared handles, dark blue glaze dripped over Wisteria glaze, marked with larger rectangular ink mark, excellent original condition, 11" h. **$250**

Mark Mussio, Humler & Nolan

Tall vase, Leopard Skin crystalline glaze, Flemington, N.J., 1910s, incised vertical racetrack mark, 12-1/2" x 7-1/2"................ **$875**

Rago Arts and Auction Center

Lamp vase in Mirrored Black glaze over Copper Dust glaze, vase has 14 ribs, Mirrored Black has many small silver crystals, Copper Dust is totally crystallized; marked with vertical ink stamp logo offset to accommodate cast wiring hole, excellent original condition, 13" h.. **$600**

Mark Mussio, Humler & Nolan

Vase, shape TP57 with three color glazes, beige, fawn and brown, marked with company's earlier squatty ink logo, excellent condition, 7-3/4" h............. **$250**

Mark Mussio, Humler & Nolan

Leopard Skin three-handled vase with black and white crystals, marked with vertical ink stamp logo, 6-3/8" h. **$1,600**

Mark Mussio, Humler & Nolan

Tall vase, Cucumber mat glaze, Flemington, N.J., 1910s, vertical racetrack stamp, 12-1/2" x 7-1/2"............................. **$1,250**

Rago Arts and Auction Center

Vase, shape 581, Cucumber Crystalline glaze or variant, snowflake crystals, vertical ink stamp symbol and incised D 581, excellent original condition with flat chip or pull to interior edge of foot ring, 9-1/2" h. **$200**

Mark Mussio, Humler & Nolan

Vase with flambé glazes of green, brown and blue covering exterior of vessel and running into interior, rectangular "Prang" ink stamp, excellent original condition, 7-5/8" h. **$325**

Mark Mussio, Humler & Nolan

Large urn-shape vase with two handles, blue green glaze with blue crystals, marked with large rectangular ink mark, professional restoration at base, 12" h.... **$200**

Mark Mussio, Humler & Nolan

Large early vase, 1909-1916 era, green dripped over Wisteria glazes, marked with rectangular Fulper ink stamp, excellent factory condition, 10-3/8" h. **$200**

Mark Mussio, Humler & Nolan

Vase with four buttresses, shape 47, blue, gold and red high glaze, die-stamped with "incised" logo, excellent original condition, 8" h. **$200**

Mark Mussio, Humler & Nolan

Large vase with Ivory over Mahogany to Mirrored Black glazes with some blue accents, impressed with Fulper "incised" mark, excellent original condition with some grinding nicks at base, 12-1/4" h. **$450**

Mark Mussio, Humler & Nolan

CERAMICS

Vase with spouted rim and gloss green glaze, marked with early Fulper rectangular logo, few minor glaze bubbles, excellent condition, 7-1/4" h. **$100**

Mark Mussio, Humler & Nolan

Six-sided vase covered with mahogany flambé glaze in yellow, blue and brown, impressed with "incised" mark, excellent original condition, 10-3/4" h. **$250**

Mark Mussio, Humler & Nolan

Vase, shape 537, blue, green and tan crystalline glaze, die-stamped "incised" logo, excellent original condition, 7-1/2" h. **$200**

Mark Mussio, Humler & Nolan

Three-handled "Bullet" vase with glossy green glazes applied over Wisteria mat glaze, vertical "racetrack" ink stamp, excellent factory condition, 6-1/4" h. **$250**

Mark Mussio, Humler & Nolan

Vase, 1916-1922 era, textured mat green glaze, die-stamped "incised" mark, excellent original condition, 7" h. **$250**

Mark Mussio, Humler & Nolan

Compote with blue crystalline glaze, marked with early rectangular ink stamp, small grinding nicks at base, 6" x 10-3/4". **$140**

Mark Mussio, Humler & Nolan

Bud vase with stovetop neck, variegated blue mat glaze, large rectangular ink mark dating vase to 1909-1916 era, excellent original condition, 5-1/2" h. **$80**

Mark Mussio, Humler & Nolan

Early corseted vase, gray and mahogany glazes, marked with rectangular ink stamp, excellent original condition, 7-1/8". **$325**

Mark Mussio, Humler & Nolan

Cylinder vase, shape 57, dark blue glaze applied over Famille Rose, marked with "h," trial mark, and Fulper's earliest mark, excellent original condition, 8" h. **$180**

Mark Mussio, Humler & Nolan

Two seven-sided vases, shape 445, each covered with drip glazes; 8-3/4" version with green and black flambé glaze and marked with Fulper paper sticker; 8-7/8" version in brown and blue glazes dripped over yellow, marked with early rectangular ink stamp, excellent original condition. **$550**

Mark Mussio, Humler & Nolan

GOUDA

Gouda is one of the decorative art world's strong and silent types, not withstanding its beautifully bright colors and rich floral and abstract designs – considered by many to be its calling card. While its place in today's market is less robust than some of its contemporaries, such as Weller and Rookwood, its pairing of subtle strength of identity and eye-catching design is what attracts people to it and makes it a collecting category to watch.

One of the indicators that Dutch pottery shouldn't be counted out is that higher-end pieces continue to attract attention, not unlike many other categories of antiques today.

"There appears to be a line in the sand with Gouda right now," said Stuart Slavid, vice president and director of Fine Ceramics, Fine Silver, European Furniture & Decorative Arts at Skinner, Inc. "Spectacular pieces are still doing very well, but there is very little or no movement at all for lower-end pieces."

The reasons for that vary, but some contributing factors appear to be advanced collectors looking for advanced pieces rather than more basic items; and the way in which people collect overall has changed some, Slavid explained.

"It used to be more people would start with good pieces, move to better pieces and then to great. Now more people with available discretionary income are starting with the very best pieces," he said.

Riley Humler, auction director and art pottery expert at Humler & Nolan, echoed Slavid's sentiments, adding that high-end pieces in every collecting arena are doing far better than the rest.

"I think the reason is serious collectors are looking for better pieces and avoiding lesser items," Humler said. "Quality has finally taken over for quantity. Part of that may be that serious collectors are generally older and have money. There are not enough young collectors to buy the more reasonable pieces, so one end of the market is doing fairly well and the other, not so well."

As with many situations, there are exceptions to the status quo, and that's also true in today's Gouda pottery market. While the most common Gouda pieces are seen in matte finishes, which are more modern and also more plentiful, early pieces, especially those with birds or butterflies under their gloss finishes, may be somewhat hard to find and tend to be more interesting, according to Humler.

Another example of an exception to the overall slowdown of interest in Gouda is white ground ware, which remains popular, according to experts at Rago Arts. At an unreserved auction on Jan. 12-13, 2013, at Rago Arts, the highlight of the 33 available lots of Gouda pottery was a pair of high-glaze white Zuid-Holland vases, circa 1905, featuring a floral motif, which sold for $3,375 – more than three times the lot's high estimate. Of the Gouda pieces featured at this sale, 22 commanded more than their low estimate, and of those 22 lots, eight fetched more than their high estimate.

Looking at the history of Gouda pottery, it's possible the founders of the earliest factories would be surprised to see what has become of their pottery — especially since many of the first companies to produce Gouda pottery did so to diversify their primary operation of

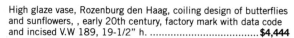

High glaze vase, Rozenburg den Haag, coiling design of butterflies and sunflowers, , early 20th century, factory mark with data code and incised V.W 189, 19-1/2" h. **$4,444**

Skinner, Inc., www.skinnerinc.com

CERAMICS

Numbered Zuid-Holland Gouda matte glaze charger, circa 1925, Rosalie pattern, bird on branch centering blossoming branches, PZH factory mark, 14-1/4" dia............**$830**

Skinner, Inc., www.skinnerinc.com

Rozenburg den Haag Gouda high glaze charger from the Netherlands, early 20th century, decorated with a bouquet of flowers on pale yellow, deep green, and deep blue ground, painted factory mark, 17-1/2" dia.........**$1,007**

Skinner, Inc., www.skinnerinc.com

Seven pieces, 20th century Zuid-Holland Gouda: charger, footed bowl, bottle-shaped vase, lantern, Crocus chambersticks, Blaren bowl. **$563**

Rago Arts and Auction Center

clay pipe production. With an abundance of clay in the Gouda region of the Netherlands, it made good sense for the companies to expand into pottery; and the public demand confirmed it, according to information on the MuseumgoudA website, www.museumgouda.nl.

It was 1898 when Plateelbakkerij Zuid-Holland, often referred to as PZH or Zuid-Holland, produced its first piece of Gouda pottery. Named for the region in the Netherlands, Gouda encompasses the pottery produced by several factories located there. While the earliest examples of Gouda were not the same as the brightly colored, matte glaze pieces collected today, they were often sought after for the same reason as today: décor for the home.

However, like many types of pottery, it didn't necessarily start out that way, said Joe Altare, founder of the Regina Pottery Collectors site (www.reginapottery.com). "One of the key points to remember about these wares is that some were designed as giftware and others for day-to-day use," Altare said. "Both were marketed to the middle class who finally had discretionary income to purchase decorative, rather than utilitarian wares."

People, then and now, are drawn in by the remarkable colors and designs.

"I stumbled across my first piece, a Regina compote, on eBay about 10 years ago. I knew nothing about Gouda pottery or the Regina factory, but the design captivated me and I had to have it," said Altare. "The design, variety and quality of execution captured my attention, and the many untold secrets of the [Regina] factory have fueled my passion these many years."

Although many of the companies that produced Gouda pottery remained in operation through the mid-1960s and 1970s, many consider the heyday of Gouda to have lasted through the first three decades of the 20th century. In fact, in the 1920s, a quarter of the workforce in the Gouda region was employed in the pottery industry, according to MuseumgoudA.

While Gouda pieces may not be setting high-profile auction records today, it remains a strong and serious representative of the ingenuity of decorative pottery. Plus, as more people are shopping at places like IKEA and Crate & Barrel for modern décor and furnishings, decorative pottery like Gouda lends itself nicely to that scene.

"I think Gouda fits very well in that space. It just hasn't caught on yet," said Slavid.

In addition to fitting into society's modern décor and design interests, another advantage for Gouda is that it is more affordable, according to Humler. "Even the best pieces are in most people's price range," he said.

With a history steeped in innovation primed by practicality and fans across the globe, a renewal and widespread rediscovery of Gouda pottery isn't out of the question.

— Antoinette Rahn, editor, Antique Trader *magazine*

Three-piece clock garniture, Zuid-Holland Gouda pottery, Netherlands, circa 1910, clock 20-1/2"... **$1,750**

Rago Arts and Auction Center

Fourteen pieces: Chambersticks, candlesticks, basket, inkwell, vases, tray, bowl, lidded jar, all from the 1920s, Netherlands. **$813**

Rago Arts and Auction Center

Nine pieces: 20th century Goedewaagen/Distel bowl, Ivora plaque, Schoonhoven lidded Isis box, PZH Helene bud vase, salt and four pieces featuring windmill and sailboat paintings........................ **$156**

Rago Arts and Auction Center

Four pieces: Zuid-Holland Gouda, 20th century Goes tray, Goedewaagen Orchidee charger, Sabany, lidded dresser boxes, Netherlands, all marked. **$344**

Rago Arts and Auction Center

Pairing of early 20th century PZH modern Gouda vase with Rembrandt inkwell.. **$219**

Rago Arts and Auction Center

Experimental floor vase, Zuid-Holland Gouda pottery, 20th century, matte glaze, baluster-form with spreading foot and intricate decoration of three owls interspersed with Rorschachesque designs, cream-colored ground, painted Gouda Zuid Holland and incised 226 A, short hairline crack on lip of rim, 25-3/4" h. **$4,444**

Skinner, Inc., www.skinnerinc.com

High-glazed rectangular-form vase, circa 1930, elongated stork designed in blue with Art Deco-influenced geometric floral accents, cream ground, marked 217, hairline crack near base, 12" h. **$338**

Skinner, Inc., www.skinnerinc.com

Seven pieces: 20th century Zuid-Holland Gouda vases, bowl, gourd-form vase, framed watercolor. **$438**

Rago Arts and Auction Center

Six pieces, early 20th century, Netherlands, all marked, Ponseav bud vase (back left), squat bowl (middle back), bottle-shaped vase with portrait (right middle and tallest piece measuring 11"), cup with tulips (back far right), double-handled bowl with irises (front left), bowl with tulips (front right). .. **$563**

Rago Arts and Auction Center

Mat jug and vase painted with florals and birds, Netherlands, circa 1910. .... **$563**

Rago Arts and Auction Center

Nine pieces: two Unique Metalique vases, Muvlee bowl and pitcher, Deco bulbous vase, Unicum vase, pitcher in raspberry glaze, and two plates by Leendert Muller, all marked, 1930-1950s, Netherlands... **$313**

Rago Arts and Auction Center

16-piece Ispahan tea set: teapot, creamer, sugar, tall pitcher, and set of six cups and saucers, Netherlands. **$88**

Rago Arts and Auction Center

Five pieces of Gouda pottery, early 20th century, Netherlands, all marked, Violette jug with stopper (far left and tallest at 9-1/4"), Maas creamer (front left), double-handled bud vase (center), Rozenburg gourd-shape vase (back right), and bowl (far right). **$438**

Rago Arts and Auction Center

Four pieces: footed Gouda bowl and jug in Clareth pattern, Clara vase and Barbara low bowl, all signed with pattern name. **$344**

Rago Arts and Auction Center

Two high glaze Zuid-Holland Gouda vases, painted with florals, Netherlands, circa 1905, tallest 12" h..**$3,375**

Rago Arts and Auction Center

Four pieces: Arnhem Gouda, Purdah bowl, lidded box, Olivia tray, Creta bowl, Netherlands. **$406**

Rago Arts and Auction Center

Four pieces: jug, pair of mini vases and chamberstick, Netherlands, circa 1910. .... **$125**

Rago Arts and Auction Center

Five piece grouping: Zenith Clematis jardinière (center back, 10" x 15-1/2" x 13" dia.) and fire bottle (far right), three Ed Antheunis vases (starting at far left): Rola, Bagdhad and Rolf, all pieces circa 1920... **$219**

Rago Arts and Auction Center

Eight-piece grouping of marked pottery from Gouda and Arnhem, Netherlands, early 20th century, Francis and Feo tazzas (far left and far right front), footed Yannis bowl, 1926 (second from left front), Abo flaring low bowl, 1931 (front center), a tray and three vases (back row, left to right). **$500**

Rago Arts and Auction Center

CERAMICS

GRUEBY

Some fine art pottery was produced by the Grueby Faience and Tile Co., established in Boston in 1891. Choice pieces were created with molded designs on a semi-porcelain body. The ware is marked and often bears the initials of the decorators. The pottery closed in 1907.

GRUEBY

Vessel with leaves, matte-green glaze, Boston, circa 1905, circular stamp, 4-1/2" x 5-1/2".... **$2,875**

Rago Arts and Auction Center

Early large vase with light green irises, Boston, circa 1900, circular faience stamp EWR 161, 13" x 8-1/4"............................**$28,750**

Rago Arts and Auction Center

Early tall vase with yellow buds, Boston, circa 1900, circular faience stamp, 23, 11-1/2" x 5-1/4"............................ **$6,875**

Rago Arts and Auction Center

Early squat vessel with two rows of leaves, Boston, circa 1900, circular faience mark, M.S., 5" x 7"............................**$5,938**

Rago Arts and Auction Center

Large bulbous vase with yellow trefoils and rounded leaves, Boston, circa 1905, circular stamp WP, 13" x 8"......... **$6,875**

Rago Arts and Auction Center

Vase, tall slender gently tapering cylindrical body molded with full-length pointed leaves alternating with flower buds around slightly flaring and scalloped rim, thick suspended green matte glaze, by Annie Lingley, impressed mark, minor grinding to foot chip, minor chip repair at rim, 9" h. ... **$2,880**

Vase, footed bulbous ovoid body tapering to a molded mouth, sides molded with full-length tapering pointed leaves, fine matte green glaze, modeled by Wilhelmina Post, few minor high point nicks, impressed company mark and artist logo, 6-5/8" h. **$3,565**

TOP LOT!

George Kendrick designed rare seven-handled vase, Boston, circa 1900, circular Grueby pottery stamp/5, 10-3/4" x 8-1/2"....................**$37,500**

Rago Arts and Auction Center

Squat vessel with leaves and buds, Boston, circa 1905, circular pottery stamp, 7" x 7-1/2".**$6,875**

Rago Arts and Auction Center

Two architectural tiles with geometric pattern, Boson, circa 1915, green tile stamped BOSTON 5635?, 1" x 8" sq.................................**$1,000**

Rago Arts and Auction Center

Vase, lower portion with ribbed design, signature mat green glaze, impressed pottery logo, incised with a conjoined RE possibly for Ruth Erikson, excellent, original condition, 8-3/4" h. x 9-1/4" w. **$2,500**

Mark Mussio, Humler & Nolan

Three water lily tiles, Boston, 1910s, all stamped BOSTON, 6" sq. ea. **$938**

Rago Arts and Auction Center

Vase, wide ovoid body with short rolled neck, thick medium brown matte glaze, impressed mark, glaze pucker near base, 6-1/8" h. **$1,150**

Large rare tile with forest decoration, Boston, 1910s, unmarked, 12" sq. x 2". .. **$9,375**

Rago Arts and Auction Center

Bowl-vase, wide flat mouth above swelled tapering sides, overall blue matte glaze, impressed mark, 6" dia., 5" h. **$575**

Vase, wide ovoid body tapering to a short molded neck, sides incised with wide, tall pointed leaves, thick green matte glaze, Grueby sticker on bottom and impressed initials, 5" h. **$1,495**

Vase, wide ovoid lower body molded with arched overlapping leaves issuing slender stems and flowers to wide angled shoulder tapering to short cylindrical neck, fine green matte glaze, designed by Lillian Newman, paper company label with "1623" and paper "tulip" label and symbol, 9-3/4" h. **$3,450**

"Kendrick" design, tall ovoid body below wide squatting incurved neck, sides and neck carved with wide pointed veined leaves, green glaze, dark brown interior glaze, unmarked but remnant of original paper label, drilled hole in bottom, small filled-in base chip, original quality oil font, 12-5/8" h. **$10,449**

Vase, wide squatty bulbous body molded with repeating design of wide rounded overlapping leaves, wide shoulder to wide, short rolled neck, dark green matte glaze, signed "W.P.," restored rim chips, 5-1/2" dia.......................... **$960**

Vase, tall swelled cylindrical body tapering to short flaring neck, fine slightly streaked matte green glaze, some pinhead-sized burst bubbles, area of think glaze on side, impressed round mark, 12-1/2" h. **$2,760**

Cuenca tile, oak, unusual size, Boston, ca. 1905, initialed G.A., 6" x 6-3/4". **$2,125**

Rago Arts and Auction Center

HAEGER

Sleek. Sinuous. Colorful and cutting edge. Timeless, trim of line, and, above all, thoroughly modern. That's the hallmark of Haeger Potteries. Since its 1871 founding in Dundee, Illinois, the firm has successfully moved from the utilitarian to the decorative. Whether freshly minted or vintage, Haeger creations continue to provide what advertisements called "a galaxy of exquisite designs. . . visual achievements symbolizing expert craftsmanship and pottery-making knowledge."

Today's collectors are particularly captivated by the modernistic Haeger output of the 1940s and '50s – from "panther" TV lamps and figurines of exotic Oriental maidens to chomping-at-the-bit statuary of rearing wild horses and snorting bulls. But the Haeger story began long before then, with the Great Chicago Fire of 1871.

Founder David Haeger had recently purchased a budding brickyard on the

Royal Haeger Earthwrap vase, marked Royal Haeger USA on base, 10-3/4" h. x 4" dia. **$30**

Quinn & Farmer Auctions

Royal Haeger pottery vase, stamped at underside, 12" h. x 8" w. **$15**

DuMouchelle's

banks of Dundee's Fox River. Following the fire, his firm produced bricks to replace obliterated Chicagoland structures. For the next 30 years, industrial production remained the primary emphasis of the Haeger Brick and Tile Co. It wasn't until 1914 that the company, now under the guidance of Edmund Haeger, noted the growing popularity of the Arts & Crafts movement and turned its attention to artware.

From the very beginning, Haeger was distinguished by its starry roster of designers. The first: J. Martin Stangl, former glaze wizard for Fulper. The design emphasis of Stangl and his early Haeger successors was on classically simple, uncluttered Arts & Crafts stylings. Haeger's roster of pots, jugs, vases, bowls, and candleholders all proved big hits with buyers.

An early zenith was reached with a pavilion at the 1934 Chicago World's Fair. In addition to home environment settings accented with Haeger, there was an actual working factory. Once fair-goers had viewed the step-by-step pottery production process, they could purchase a piece of Haeger on the way out. The World's Fair brought Haeger to America's attention – but its grandest days of glory were still ahead.

The year 1938 saw the promotion of Edmund Haeger's forward-thinking son-in-law, Joseph Estes, to general manager, the arrival of equally forward-thinking designer Royal Arden Hickman, and the introduction of the popular "Royal Haeger" line.

The multi-talented Hickman, snapped up by Haeger after stays at J.H Vernon, Kosta Crystal, and his own Ra Art, quickly made his mark. Earlier Haeger figurals were generally of animals and humans at rest. Under the guidance of Hickman, and the soon-to-follow Eric Olsen, *motion* was key: leaping fish, birds taking wing, and a ubiquitous snarling black panther. The energetic air of underlying excitement in these designs was ideally suited to the action-packed atmosphere of World War II, and the postwar new day that followed.

In 1944, Hickman left Haeger following a dispute over lamp production, returning only for

CERAMICS

occasional free-lance assignments. The 1947 arrival of his successor, Eric Olsen, coincided with the official celebration of Haeger's "Diamond Jubilee"; that's when much of the Olsen line made its debut. From towering abstract figural lamps to long-legged colts, self-absorbed stalking lions, and mystic pre-Columbian priests, his designs were ideal for the soon-to-be-ultra-current "1950s modern" décor.

"A work of art," Olsen stated, "is not only based on the 'beautiful' but also on such ingredients as interest, character, craftsmanship, and imagination."

Today, "The Haeger Potteries" continues as a family affair under the leadership of Joseph Estes' daughter, Alexandra Haeger Estes. And whether collectors favor the early Arts & Crafts pieces, the modernistic designs of the 1940s and '50s, or examples of today's output, one constant remains: This is artware collectors are eager to own. Retailer Marshall Field & Co. said it best in 1929: "Haeger Pottery will become an indispensible charm in your home!"

Pair of Royal Haeger leopard bookends with mat black and burnt orange glaze, both marked Royal Haeger, one marked R617 USA 1903-30D, the other marked R618 USA 1904-30D, mint condition, 11" and 8" h......**$325**

Belhorn Auction Services, LLC

Two vases, each in handled baluster form with modeled textured glaze, larger vase 10" h. x 14" dia. **$30**

Leslie Hindman Auctioneers

Royal Haeger Earthwrap vase, marked on base Royal Haeger USA, 11" h. x 5-1/2" dia. **$30**

Quinn & Farmer Auctions

Deer figure with original label, 14" h. **$60**

Echoes Antiques & Auction Gallery, Inc.

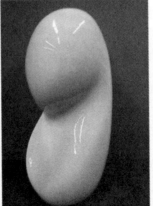

Royal Haeger pottery "Haeger Award 1947" head form sculpture designed by R. Rush, very good condition with kiln imperfection marks on base, 12-1/4" h. **$30**

B.S. Slosberg, Inc. Auctioneers

Royal Haeger large blue frothy bottle vase on stand, partial foil label at neck, vase affixed to stand, 16" h. x 8" dia...........**$20**

Quinn & Farmer Auctions

CERAMICS

HALL CHINA

From toilet seats to teapots, Hall China has, quite literally, produced it all. One of the most recognizable names in American pottery manufacture, Hall owes it longevity to a unique combination of product reliability and an uncanny ability to adapt to the particular needs of the times.

Founded in 1903 by Robert Hall, the firm was a restructuring of the defunct East Liverpool (Ohio) Pottery Co., a conglomeration of five smaller Ohio potteries. Hall's plans for his new company ended abruptly with his death in 1904; it fell to his son, Robert Taggart Hall, to carry out his father's ambitious agenda.

First up: Cutting production costs by finding a white china compound requiring only single-firing that would not craze. During 10 years of experimentation, the company sustained itself by producing such utilitarian whiteware as jugs, mugs, and, yes, even toilet seats. In 1911, new production manager Jackson Moore successfully developed a leadless glaze that met the single-fire, non-crazing, cost-effective requirements Hall had been seeking. That new formula proved to be the formula for Hall China's enduring success.

The company's earliest sales boom was due, in large part, to the onset of World War I. Since European imports were curtailed, it fell to domestic manufacturers, such as Hall, to produce the sort of heavy-duty china cookware required by large-scale entities, ranging from restaurants and hospitals, to the United States government.

Cooks exposed to Hall china were impressed by its durability, and, at war's end, the company made a seamless expansion into production of retail consumer ware. Promoting itself as the "World's Largest Manufacturer of Fireproof Cooking China," Hall became particularly known for its extensive line of brightly colored and gilded, imaginatively shaped teapots.

Hall's association with teapot production proved particularly fortunate. In an effort to boost sales (particularly during the Depression years of the 1930s), Hall produced specific lines of china that other manufacturers offered as premiums to their customers. Among the tie-in clients: Standard Coffee, General Electric, Hotpoint, and Jewel Tea. Hall's exclusive

Cameo Rose pattern teapot, covered, on E-shape dinnerware body. **$75**

Radiance shape drip jar, covered................... **$60**

Zephyr shape Fantasy pattern leftover container, covered... **$225**

Autumn Leaf pattern for Jewel Tea was both affordable and attractive, attracting consumers then and collectors now. Autumn Leaf quickly expanded its borders beyond teapots, covering a full range of dinnerware and decorative accessories, from cookie jars and canister sets to salt-and-peppers and serving dishes.

The seemingly endless array of Autumn Leaf pieces keeps collectors hopping. Its ubiquitous presence is rivaled only by that of another Hall pattern, Red Poppy, a premium for Grand Union. Like Autumn Leaf, Red Poppy was produced in a dizzying array of shapes and for a multitude of uses. The simple, homespun designs of both patterns, the general usefulness of the ware, as well as remarkable durability, have kept them favorites throughout the decades.

Hall kept abreast of changing tastes in the mid-20th century by releasing patterns by such "name" designers as Eva Zeisel. Among her most notable lines for Hall are 1949's Tomorrow's Classic and the 1956 release, Century. In later years, Donald Schreckengost contributed a line of whimsical Hall pieces, ranging from owl-shaped cookie jars to figural teapots, immortalizing in china such notables as Ronald Reagan.

Other sought-after Hall patterns include Wildfire, Meadow Flower, Blue Blossom, and Rose Parade. Some collections consist solely of Hall teapots; best-selling shapes were available in a rainbow of colors. Among the most instantly recognizable Hall teapots is the Arabian Nights-influenced Aladdin shape.

A 2010 merger with Homer Laughlin China Co. (the manufacturer of the equally well-known Fiesta line) brought two of America's best-loved and longest-lived potteries under one roof. As the ongoing proliferation of Hall China collectors and clubs attests, good style never goes out of style.

Coffeepot, covered, Tricolator, Coffee Queen, yellow. **$35**

Birch shape Victorian line teapot, covered, blue with gold decoration.. **$175**

Donut shape jug-type pitcher, large, Chinese red. **$135**

Centennial shape teapot, covered, forest green with gold decoration...**$125**

Bowling ball shape turquoise
teapot, covered................... **$500**

Cube shape teapot, covered,
in green, marked "The Cube"
with listing of design and patent
numbers, licensed by Cube
Teapots, Ltd., Leicester, England,
circa 1930s, East Liverpool,
Ohio. **$50**

Donut shape Autumn Leaf
pattern teapot, covered, 1993
reissue.............................. **$150**

Special Birdcage shape Jewel
Tea Autumn Leaf pattern teapot,
covered, specially produced for the
Autumn Leaf Club in 1995.. **$150**

Zephyr shape Chinese red water
bottle, covered, refrigerator ware
line. **$650**

Commemorative Donut shape
teapot, covered, part of a limited
edition produced for the East Liverpool High School Alumni Association, No. 2 of 16, 1997.. **$100**

Zephyr shape Blue Garden pattern
water bottle, covered, refrigerator
ware line............................. **$650**

Irish coffee mug, footed, pale
yellow, 6". **$15**

Basket shape Chinese red teapot,
covered.............................. **$250**

Bellevue shape Orange Poppy
pattern teapot, covered. ... **$1,800**

Kadota shape Crocus pattern
coffeepot, covered, drip-type, all-
china.................................. **$350**

Ball shape pitcher, No. 3, orchid......................... **$85**

McCormick Teahouse design teapot, covered, upright rectangular cottage-form with color transfer-printed design of an earlier English teahouse, 1985.... **$75**

Los Angeles shape teapot, covered, cobalt blue with standard gold trim. **$75**

Automobile shape Chinese red teapot, covered. . **$650**

Miniature Aladdin shape teapot, covered, light blue glaze, unmarked, overall 7" l., 5" h............... **$15**

Teapot, covered, Globe No-Drip pattern, dark pink with standard gold decoration. **$90**

Moderne shape marine blue teapot, covered.... **$85**

Ansel shape Tricolator coffeepot, covered, yellow art glaze. **$75**

HAVILAND

Over 60,000 chinaware patterns: Since its founding in 1840, that's the number totaled by the Haviland China Co. The company's story is a unique one. Although based in the United States, Haviland China produced its wares in the French porcelain capital of Limoges, exporting those products for sale domestically. Over the years, Haviland has become so closely identified with Limoges that many have used the terms interchangeably, or assumed Haviland was yet another of the numerous French firms that made Limoges their manufacturing base.

The Haviland company was actually the result of its founder's quest for the "ideal" china. New York importer David Haviland was dissatisfied with the china then available for his clientele. Its varying coloration (never consistently white) and grainy, porous texture made it not only visually unappealing, but also unsuitable for long-term use.

Twelve French Haviland porcelain gilt violet plates, circa 1900, signed A McM on reverse, designs are similar, not identical, one with edge chip, 8-1/2" dia. **$100**

Woodbury Auctions, The Schwenke Group

Haviland's search led him to Limoges, already a busy hub of porcelain production, and home to more than 40 manufacturing firms. The reason? The 1765 discovery of rare kaolin deposits in the Limoges vicinity. Kaolin was a necessary component of fine, hard paste porcelain. Blessed with abundant supplies of other necessities for porcelain manufacture (wood, water, and a willing work force), Limoges quickly gained renown for its superb products.

Impressed by the area's output—the porcelain had a pristine whiteness, as well as a smooth, non-porous finish—Haviland set up shop. The firm's dinnerware exports found immediate success, thanks to the delicate translucence of the ware and its exquisitely detailed decoration.

In the mid-19th century, at Haviland's peak of popularity, "fine dining" was a term taken seriously. Specific foods required specific serving dishes, and each course of a meal mandated its own type of tableware. Substituting a luncheon plate for a bread-and-butter plate was not only unthinkable, but in the worst possible taste. China cabinets in affluent homes were filled to overflowing, and much of that overflow was thanks to Haviland. Just a sampling from its vast dinnerware inventory includes: fish plates, bone plates, salad plates, chop plates, bon bon plates, and underplates; chocolate pots and coffee pots; bouillon cups, eggcups, and teacups; lemonade pitchers and milk pitchers; honey dishes and vegetable dishes; toast trays and celery trays; pudding sets and dessert sets; sauceboats and sauce tureens; broth bowls, soup bowls, and punch bowls. Imagine any conceivable fine dining need, and Haviland dinnerware was there to meet it.

Although dinnerware was its mainstay, Haviland also produced a multitude of other decorative yet useful porcelain housewares. Among them were dresser trays, hair receivers, ashtrays, and decorative baskets. A limited line of art pottery was also released from 1885 into the 1890s, utilizing the underglaze slip decoration technique known as "Barbotine." Developer Ernest Chaplet supervised this series for Haviland, in which pigments were combined with heavy white clay slip. The mixture, applied to the clay body of a piece, had the consistency of oil paint; the resulting finish had the texture of an oil painting.

Because various Haviland family members eventually branched out on their own, the porcelain markings are many. "H & Co." was the earliest, succeeded by such variations as "Haviland, France" and "Decorated by Haviland & Co." Theodore Haviland achieved much acclaim after forming his own firm in 1892, and those pieces are often marked "Theodore Haviland" or other variants of his name. (In 1941, the Theodore Haviland facility relocated to the United States.)

Haviland's overwhelming variety of available product, a necessity when first introduced, is a boon to today's avid porcelain collectors. Hunting down and accumulating a complete set of Haviland—even in a single dinnerware pattern—can (quite enjoyably) occupy a lifetime.

Haviland set of four five-well porcelain oyster plates, pinwheel type mold, each with different background color and heavy gold decoration, 9". **$375**

Strawser Auctions

Six French Haviland Limoges hand-painted game decorated plates with floral and gilt borders, marked Haviland & Co. Limoges on base, 8-3/4" sq. **$150**

Burchard Galleries

"Old Paris" porcelain, early Limoges pair of large two-handled, pink-ground mantel garniture vases, circa 1855-1865, attributed to atelier of Haviland & Co., flattened ovate baluster form, handles formed as gilt large grape leaves, clusters and vines in high relief down sides, knotted vines under everted gilt rims, bodies enameled with gilt vermiculi, brocade, rocaille and other patterns to shoulders, faces painted in polychrome enamels with a queen seated in throne, gilt scrolls down vase backs, both incised 39, various other incised marks, possibly 4561, very good to good condition, 28" h. **$950**

Jeffrey S. Evans & Associates

Thirteen-piece porcelain game set, each with different decoration, 12 7-1/2" plates, 18" x 11" platter, marked CFH / GDM................... **$130**

William H. Bunch Auctions

HULL POTTERY

The A.E. Hull Pottery Co. grew from the clay soil of Perry County, Ohio, in 1905. By the 1930s, its unpretentious line of wares could be found in shops and, more importantly, homes from coast to coast, making it one of the nation's largest potteries. Leveled by flood and ensuing fire in 1950, like a phoenix, Hull rose from the ashes and reestablished its position in the marketplace. Less than four decades later, however, the firm succumbed after eight bitter strikes by workers, leaving behind empty buildings, memories and the pottery shown in this volume.

Addis Emmet Hull founded A.E. Hull Pottery in July 1905. By the time the company was formed, the Crooksville/Roseville/Zanesville area was already well established as a pottery center. Hull constructed an all-new pottery, featuring six kilns, four of them large natural gas-fired beehive kilns.

The early years were good to Hull. In fact, after only two years of operation, Hull augmented the new plant by taking over the former facilities of the Acme pottery. By 1910, Hull was claiming to be the largest manufacturer of blue-banded kitchenware in the United States. By 1925 production reached three million pieces annually.

This early ware included spice and cereal jars and salt boxes. Some of these items were lavishly decorated with decals, high-gloss glazes or bands. This evolved into some early art ware pieces including vases and flowerpots.

T1 Blossom Flite honey jug, 6".............**$20-$70**

However, Hull could not keep up with the demand, especially the growing demand for artwares, which could be sold in five and dime stores. Hence, Addis Hull visited Europe and made arrangements to import decorative items from Czechoslovakia, England, France, Germany and Italy. To accommodate the influx of these items, Hull opened a facility in Jersey City, N.J. This arrangement continued until 1929, when import operations were discontinued.

No. 310 Orchid jardinière, 6". . **$45-$100**

In 1926 Plant 1 was converted to manufacture decorative floor and wall tiles, which were popular at the time. But by the time of Addis Hull's death in 1930, the company bearing his name was exiting the tile business. Plant 1, Hull's original, which had been converted to the now-discontinued line of tile production as well as being elderly, was closed in 1933.

When Addis Hull, Sr. died in 1930, management of the works was passed to his son, Addis Hull, Jr., who was involved in the formation of the Shawnee Pottery Co. By the late 1930s, Addis Junior left the family business and assumed the presidency of Shawnee.

World War II affected the entire nation, and Hull was no exception. This time period saw the production of some of Hull's most famous lines, including Orchid, Iris, Tulip and Poppy. Their airbrushed matte hues of pink, blue, green and yellow became synonymous with the Hull name. Sales of such wares through chain and dime stores soared.

The close of the decade saw the emergence of high-gloss glazed art pottery as the growing trend in decorative ceramics. Hull responded initially by merely changing the glaze applied to some of its earlier lines. Another significant development of the time was the growing influence of designer Louise Bauer on Hull's lines. First and most notable was her 1943 Red Riding Hood design, but also significant were her Bow-Knot and Woodland lines.

While the late 1940s and early 1950s saw the demise of long-time rivals Weller and Roseville, business at Hull flourished. This is particularly surprising given that on June 16, 1950, the pottery was completely destroyed by a flood, which in turn caused the kiln to explode, and the ensuing fire finished off the venerable plant.

A new plant officially opened on Jan. 1, 1952. With the new plant came a new company name – Hull Pottery Co.

Hull entered into dinnerware manufacture in the early 1960s at the behest of one of its largest customers, the J.C. Penney Co. Penney, whose offers to purchase Pfaltzgraff dinnerware were declined by the manufacturer, turned to Hull to create a competitive line. Hull's response to this was the new House 'n Garden line, which would remain in production until 1967 and would grow to 100 items.

During the 1970s and 1980s, the pottery was closed by no fewer than eight strikes, one of which lasted for seven weeks. The eighth and final strike by workers sounded the death knell for the pottery. In 1986, the Hull Pottery Co. ceased business operations.

For more information on Hull pottery, see *Warman's Hull Pottery Identification and Price Guide* by David Doyle.

O-6 Debonair pitcher, 5" tall x 6-1/2"......................... **$30-$40**

No. 132 Camellia/Open Rose hanging basket, 7". ......**$40-$120**

S15 Serenade fruit bowl, 7".............................. **$45-$80**

W15 Woodland double bud vase, 8-1/2".........................**$30-$120**

L-4 Water Lily vase, 6-1/2"......................... **$25-$35**

W24 Woodland Hi-Gloss ewer, 13-1/2"......................**$70-$180**

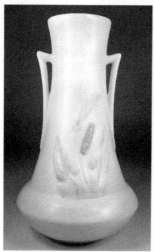

Calla Lily 560/33 mold vase, 10".............................**$50-$150**

The No. 410 Iris bud vase was produced in two color schemes, with different decorations front and rear, 7-1/2". .... **$40-$70**

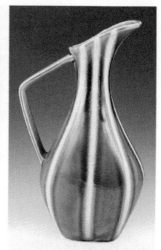

C56 Continental ewer, 12-1/2"........................ **$40-$80**

No. 218 Granada vase, 9".................................. **$10-$20**

No. 32 Early Artware vase, 8"................................. **$20-$40**

No. 520 Dogwood ewer, 4-3/4"........................... **$20-$45**

No. 79 Fantasy bowl, 6-1/2" x 5-1/2"........................... **$10-$15**

No. 425 Jubilee embossed jardinière, 5-1/2". .... **$5-$15**

No. 85 Mayfair bass viol planter or wall pocket, 7-1/4"........ **$25-$40**

E-13 Ebb Tide candleholders, 2-3/4". .... **$40-$80 each**

B-26 Bow-Knot pitcher-shaped wall pocket, 6"............. **$60-$200**

C314 Capri flying duck planter............................ **$15-$30**

B-1 Crescent bowls, 5-1/2"................... **$10-$15 each**

B5 Butterfly jardinière, 5"................................. **$20-$30**

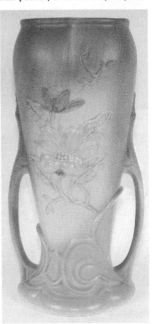

No. 20 Magnolia vase, 15"............................**$175-$250**

No. 53 Thistle vase, 6-1/2".......................... **$40-$70**

S23 Serenade ashtray, 13"................................. **$35-$45**

W-17 Wildflower vase, 12-1/2"......................**$70-$150**

No. 612 Poppy vase, 6-1/2".......................... **$35-$100**

F433 Imperial pedestal ivy vase,
10".............................. **$20-$25**

No. 91 novelty pigeon planter,
6-1/2" x 5-1/2"............. **$45-$70**

W9 Royal basket, 8-3/4"....**$45-$60**

No. 72 novelty flowered vase,
8-1/4" x 5-7/8"............. **$35-$45**

S-4 Parchment and Pine vase,
10-1/2"......................... **$35-$50**

W-4 Wildflower handled vase
marked "Hull Art USA W-4-6-
1/2"," 6-1/2". .... **$35-$45**

No. 113 Tulip flowerpot.. **$60-$80**

No. 527 House 'n Garden French
casserole with cover. .... **$6-$7**

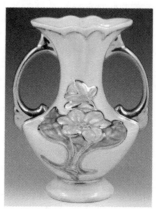

H-2 New Magnolia vase,
5-1/2".......................... **$25-$40**

No. 1 Tokay cornucopia,
6-1/2"......................... **$20-$30**

CERAMICS

IRONSTONE

Durability: When introduced in the early 1800s, that was ironstone china's major selling point. Durability also accounts for the still-ready availability of vintage ironstone china centuries after it first captivated consumers. Unlike its fragile porcelain contemporaries, this utilitarian earthenware was intended to withstand the ravages of time—and it has.

Ironstone owes its innate sturdiness to a formula incorporating iron slag with the clay. Cobalt, added to the mix, eliminated the yellowish tinge that plagued earlier attempts at white china. The earliest form of this opaque dinnerware made its debut in 1800 England, patented by potters William and John Turner. However, by 1806 the Turner firm was bankrupt. Ironstone achieved its first real popularity in 1813, when Charles Mason first offered for sale his "Patent Ironstone China." Mason's white ironstone was an immediate hit, offering vessels for a wide variety of household uses, from teapots and tureens to washbowls and pitchers.

Classic Gothic Octagon shape master waste jar, all white, Jacob Jurnival. .....**$950-$1,050**

Although the inexpensive simplicity of white ironstone proved popular with frugal householders, by the 1830s in-mold and transfer patterns were providing a dose of visual variety. Among the decorative favorites: Oriental motifs and homey images such as grains, fruits, and flowers.

Mason's patented formula for white ironstone lasted for 14 years. Upon its expiration, numerous other potteries jumped into the fray. By the 1840s, white ironstone found its way across the ocean, enjoying the same success in the United States and Canada as it had in England. By the 1880s, however, the appeal of white ware began to fade. Its successor, soon overtaking the original, was ironstone's most enduring incarnation, Tea Leaf.

First marketed as Lustre Band and Sprig, the Tea Leaf Lustreware motif is attributed to Anthony Shaw of Burslem; his ironstone pieces of the 1880s featured hand-painted copper lustre bands and leaves. Tea Leaf was, however, a decorative style rather than a specific product line. Since the design was not patented, potteries throughout England and the United States soon introduced their own versions. Design modifications were minor; today, collectors can assemble entire sets of ironstone in the Tea Leaf pattern from the output of different manufacturers. Although independently produced, the pieces easily complement each other.

During the late 1800s, ironstone tea sets were so ubiquitous that ornamenting them with a tea leaf was a logical choice. Buyers were intrigued with this simple, nature-themed visual on a field of white. Their interest quickly translated into a bumper crop of tea leaf-themed ironstone pieces. Soon, the tea leaf adorned objects with absolutely no relation whatsoever to tea. Among them: gravy boats, salt and peppers shakers, ladles, and even toothbrush holders and soap dishes.

There were, of course, more romantic rationales given for the introduction of the tea leaf motif. One holds that this decoration was the modern manifestation of an ancient legend. Finding an open tea leaf at the bottom of a teacup would bring good luck to the fortunate tea drinker. In this scenario, the tea leaf motif becomes a harbinger of happy times ahead, whether emblazoned on a cake plate, a candlestick, or a chamber pot.

For makers of Tea Leaf, the good fortune continued into the early 1900s. Eventually, however, Tea Leaf pieces became so prevalent that the novelty wore off. By mid-century, the pattern had drifted into obscurity; its appeal was briefly resuscitated with lesser-quality reproductions, in vogue from 1950 to 1980. Marked "Red Cliff" (the name of the Chicago-based distributor), these reproductions generally used blanks supplied by Hall China.

For today's collectors, the most desirable Tea Leaf pieces are those created during the pattern's late-Victorian heyday. Like ironstone itself, the Tea Leaf pattern remains remarkably durable.

Figural hen-on-nest covered dish, all white. **$225**

Alternate Panels ironstone compote, all white. **$225**

Rare Paneled Grape shape jam server, covered, by J.F. ....**$110-$140**

Eagle shape white ironstone gravy boat, Davenport, circa 1859s. **$110**

Rare Ceres shape ironstone eggcup, Elsmore & Forster, all white. **$225**

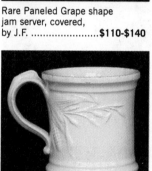

Chinese shape white ironstone mug, Anthony Shaw, circa 1858.................................... **$90**

Corn & Oats shape white ironstone mug, Davenport. ....**$90-$110**

Alternate Panels shape white ironstone teapot, unknown pottery, England, mid-19th century. ....**$125-$150**

Classic Gothic Octagon shape white ironstone soup tureen, cover, undertray and ladle, Samuel Alcock & Co., circa 1847.......................... **$1,200 set**

Olympic shape white ironstone sugar bowl, covered, Elsmore & Forster, 1864........................**$90**

Scalloped Decagon/Cambridge shape white ironstone sugar bowl, Wedgwood & Co..................**$100**

Sydenham shape white ironstone teapot, covered, copy of Victorian ironstone original design produced by Hall China for Red Cliff, circa 1960s. **$95**

Pond Lily Pad shape white ironstone relish dish, James Edwards.....................**$115-$130**

Divided Gothic shape white ironstone washbowl and pitcher set, John Alcock, circa 1848....................**$400-$450 set**

Inverted Diamond shape white ironstone teapot, covered, T.J. & J. Mayer, England, circa 1840s. **$250-300**

Tulip shape white ironstone teapot, covered, trimmed in blue, Elsmore & Forster, England, circa 1855..........................**$290-$320**

Cable shape Tea Leaf ironstone butter dish, cover and insert, Anthony Shaw. **$60**

Imari-style soup bowls, English, 19th century, unmarked, 10 in. dia...**$150**

Tobacco Leaf pattern, Fanfare shape covered toothbrush box, Elsmore & Forster, rare. **$675**

Ginger Jar shape Tea Leaf ironstone master waste jar, covered, Elsmore & Forster, rare. **$1,300**

New York shape teapot, luster band trim, Clementson. **$60**

Grape Octagon shape washbowl and pitcher set, luster band trim, unmarked. **$225**

Empress shape Tea Leaf ironstone two-handled cream soup bowl, Micratex by Adams, circa 1960s. **$35**

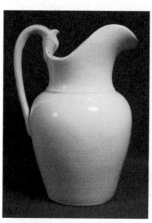

Dolphin-handled shape white ironstone wine pitcher, unmarked, circa 1850s. ....**$110-$130**

Berlin Swirl shape white ironstone covered vegetable tureen, T.J. & J. Mayer. **$190**

Favorite shape Tea Leaf ironstone coffeepot, covered, Grindley.
.... **$170**

Ceres shape dinner plate, dessert plate and handle less cup and saucer, green and copper luster trim........................ **$30-$50 set**

Lily of the Valley shape Tea Leaf ironstone chamber pot, Anthony Shaw. **$175**

MAJOLICA

In 1851, an English potter was hoping that his new interpretation of a centuries-old style of ceramics would be well received at the "Great Exhibition of the Industries of All Nations" set to open May 1 in London's Hyde Park.

Potter Herbert Minton had high hopes for his display. His father, Thomas Minton, founded a pottery works in the mid-1790s in Stoke-on-Trent, Staffordshire. Herbert Minton had designed a "new" line of pottery, and his chemist, Leon Arnoux, had developed a process that resulted in vibrant, colorful glazes that came to be called "majolica."

Trained as an engineer, Arnoux also studied the making of encaustic tiles, and had been appointed art director at Minton's works in 1848. His job was to introduce and promote new products. Victorian fascination with the natural world prompted Arnoux to reintroduce the work of Bernard Palissy, whose naturalistic, bright-colored "maiolica" wares had been created in the 16th century. But Arnoux used a thicker body to make pieces sturdier. This body was given a coating of opaque white glaze, which provided a surface for decoration.

Pieces were modeled in high relief, featuring butterflies and other insects, flowers and leaves, fruit, shells, animals and fish. Queen Victoria's endorsement of the new pottery prompted its acceptance by the general public.

When Minton introduced his wares at Philadelphia's 1876 Centennial Exhibition, American potters also began to produce majolica.

For more information on majolica, see *Warman's Majolica Identification and Price Guide* by Mark F. Moran.

English two-section "Pug" humidor, dog with yellow collar with pink bow, glossy brown glaze, unmarked, perfect condition, 8" h. **$375**

Mark Mussio, Humler & Nolan

English game dish, covered with quail on lid and sides, 19th century, 6" x 9-1/2" x 6-3/4". **$688**

Rago Arts and Auction Center

Wedgwood grape and vine punch set with large punch bowl, 10-1/2" dia., 6-1/2" h., and eight matching cups, strong color and detail to entire set, rare. **$1,500**

Delphin Massier grasshopper figural planter, early 20th century, signed, 6-1/2" x 12-3/4" x 3-1/2".. **$3,125**

Rago Arts and Auction Center

Two Continental centerpieces, 19th century, large oval bowl with bird decoration and bowl with satyr decoration, larger 6-1/2" x 20" x 11".......**$625**

Rago Arts and Auction Center

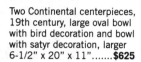

Delphin Massier vase, rooster alongside corn husk, early 20th century, signed, 13-1/2".. **$2,000**

Rago Arts and Auction Center

Hugo Lonitz compote, figural fish base, 19th century, impressed mark, 6-1/2" x 5-3/4" dia. .. **$313**

Rago Arts and Auction Center

Delphin Massier parrot perched on bamboo branch, early 20th century, signed, 14". **$1,750**

Rago Arts and Auction Center

Ceramic tobacco jar in form of bulldog in gentlemanly attire with pipe, German, late 19th century, impressed on bottom 6118 and 65, hairline along bottom, hairline from rim below arm with pipe, small chip on other arm's sleeve, 8" h. **$270**

Cowan's Auctions, Inc.

Turquoise strawberry server with flowers and leaves, twig handle and attached cream and sugar bowls, good color, 10" d.... **$225+**

Wedgwood ribbon and bow sauce dish, 7" w. .... **$150+**

CERAMICS

Three English Wedgwood fish plates with raised decoration, 19th century, stamped Wedgwood, 8-3/4" dia..**$250**

Rago Arts and Auction Center

Four English items, 19th century, footed oval tray with oval platter and two Wedgwood plates, largest 3" x 12-1/4" x 10-1/4".. **$313**

Rago Arts and Auction Center

Fielding fan and insect with scroll platter with turquoise pebble ground, good color, minor rim chip to back, 13" w. .... **$200+**

W. Schiller & Son jardiniere, circa 1900, 13" h. x 15" dia. **$175**

Kaminski Auctions

George Jones chestnut leaf tray with mottled center, hairline, 12" dia.. **$400+**

English sardine box, rectangular form, 19th century, stamped Jones, 3-3/4" x 5-3/4" x 4-3/4". **$375**

Rago Arts and Auction Center

MCCOY POTTERY

The first McCoy with clay under his fingernails was W. Nelson McCoy. With his uncle, W.F. McCoy, he founded a pottery works in Putnam, Ohio, in 1848, making stoneware crocks and jugs.

That same year, W. Nelson's son, James W., was born in Zanesville, Ohio. James established the J.W. McCoy Pottery Co. in Roseville, Ohio, in the fall of 1899. The J.W. McCoy plant was destroyed by fire in 1903 and was rebuilt two years later.

It was at this time that the first examples of Loy-Nel-Art wares were produced. The line's distinctive title came from the names of James McCoy's three sons, Lloyd, Nelson, and Arthur. Like other "standard" glazed pieces produced at this time by several Ohio potteries, Loy-Nel-Art has a glossy finish on a dark brown-

black body, but Loy-Nel-Art featured a splash of green color on the front and a burnt-orange splash on the back.

George Brush became general manager of J.W. McCoy Pottery Co. in 1909. The company became Brush-McCoy Pottery Co. in 1911, and in 1925 the name was shortened to Brush Pottery Co. This firm remained in business until 1982.

Separately, in 1910, Nelson McCoy, Sr. founded the Nelson McCoy Sanitary and Stoneware Co., also in Roseville. By the early 1930s, production had shifted from utilitarian wares to art pottery, and the company name was changed to Nelson McCoy Pottery.

Designer Sydney Cope was hired in 1934, and was joined by his son, Leslie, in 1936. The Copes' influence on McCoy wares continued until Sydney's death in 1966. That same year, Leslie opened a gallery devoted to his family's design heritage and featuring his own original art.

Nelson McCoy Sr. died in 1945, and was succeeded as company president by his nephew, Nelson McCoy Melick.

A fire destroyed the plant in 1950, but company officials—including Nelson McCoy, Jr., then 29—decided to rebuild, and the new Nelson McCoy Pottery Co. was up and running in just six months.

Nelson Melick died in 1954. Nelson, Jr. became company president, and oversaw the company's continued growth. In 1967, the operation was sold to entrepreneur David Chase. At this time, the words "Mt. Clemens Pottery" were added to the company marks. In 1974, Chase sold the company to Lancaster Colony Corp., and the company marks included a stylized "LCC" logo. Nelson Jr. and his wife, Billie, who had served as a products supervisor, left the company in 1981.

In 1985, the company was sold again, this time to Designer Accents. The McCoy pottery factory closed in 1990.

For more information on McCoy pottery, see *Warman's McCoy Pottery*, 2nd edition, by Mark F. Moran.

Green hanging planter basket, circa 1940s, 7" dia., 4-1/2" h. **$30**

J. Levine Auction & Appraisal LLC

 Visit www.AntiqueTrader.com

CERAMICS

Native American cookie jar, normal crazing, no chips or cracks, 11" h. **$210**

Showtime Auction Services

Arts & Crafts pottery umbrella stand, Brush McCoy, cylindrical form, decorated with repeating stylized lotus stems in ivory glaze on brown reserve, 16-3/4" h. **$270**

Leslie Hindman Auctioneers

Vintage unmarked art pottery dog dish, circa 1945, "MAN'S BEST FRIEND HIS DOG," green, unmarked, good condition, two darkened tight hairlines, 2-1/2" h. x 7-1/2" dia. **$45**

Pacific Galleries

Aqua and pink floral teapot, cream and sugar, circa 20th century, several fleabites and crack in sugar handle, 7" h. x 10" l. **$94**

Midwest Auction Galleries

Covered butter dish in glossy green, 1960s, McCoy USA mark ..**$30-$40**

Three vases in pink, no chips or damage, largest 9-1/4" h., 5-3/8" dia. **$30**

Mosby & Co. Auctions

Covered casserole, 1940s, McCoy USA, 6-1/2" d. ... **$55-$65**

Large Brush McCoy glazed stoneware jardinière, Amaryllis pattern, cream and green ivotint glaze, circa 1920s, glaze chip to rim, 9-1/2" h. x 11-1/2" dia. **$180**

Kaminski Auctions

Cherries and Leaves charger in glossy yellow, mid-1930s, unmarked, 11-1/4" d. .... **$550-$650**

Strap pitcher in glossy burgundy, late 1940s, McCoy mark ....**$75-$85**

Flowerpot in a skyscraper design, detached saucer, 1930s-1940s, found in other colors, unmarked, 9" h., 10-1/2" dia.. **$75+**

Two jardinières with applied leaves and berries, late 1940s, McCoy USA mark, 7-1/2" h.....**$200-$250 ea.**

McCoy flowerpot, ribbed with rose design, stoneware, 1920s, unmarked, 4" h., 5-1/2" dia. .... **$30+**

CERAMICS

Jardinière in a ring-ware design, stoneware, 1930s, unmarked, 9" h., 10" dia. opening .... **$100+**

Ivy jardinière in brown and green, early 1950s, unmarked, also found in a brighter glossy tan and green with matching pedestal, 8" h.............................**$350-$450**

Art pottery dog dish, blue mottled glaze, marked (incised) McCoy Made in USA, age appropriate wear, 3-1/4" h., 5" dia. top, 6-1/2" dia. base...................**$36**

Dargate Auction Galleries

Leaves and Berries jardinière and pedestal in matte brown and green; jardinière, 7-1/2" d.; pedestal, 6-3/4" h. ....**$225-$275/pair**

Pine Cone planter, mid-1940s, McCoy USA mark, 8" w., rare ....**$500-$600** (A slightly larger planter in rust glaze .... **$1,800-$2,000)**

Sand dollar vase in matte white, stoneware, 1940s, unmarked, also found in pastel colors, and brown and green........**$250-$300, depending on color**

Sunburst jardinière in a multicolored glaze, 1930s, unmarked, 6-3/4" h. ....**$50-$70**

Shrimp vase in traditional colors, 1950s, McCoy USA mark, 9" h. ......**$175+**

Large fish planter, found in other colors, 1950s, McCoy mark, 12" l. .... **$1,200-$1,400**

Basket-Weave jardinière and pedestal, peach glaze, late 1930s, NM USA mark, 13" and 7-1/2" h. .... **$250+ set**

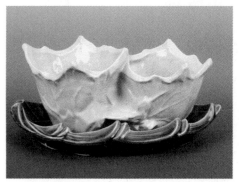

Hummingbird planter in green, late 1940s, McCoy USA mark, 10-1/2" w. ....**$125-$150**

Ring ware covered butter or cheese crock, 1920s, shield mark "M." ....**$90-$110**

Swan planting dish in rustic ivory and turquoise, 1950s, McCoy USA mark, 8-1/2" h..........**$700-$800**

Five sizes of Stone Craft mixing bowls (called pink and blue) ranging in diameter from 7" to 14" (also a 5" size), mid-1970s, McCoy LCC mark. ....**$225-$250 for complete set**

Apple wall pocket in gold trim, 1950s, unmarked, 7" l. ....**$200-$225**

Large centerpiece planter, 1950s, McCoy USA mark, found in other colors, 12" l ....**$90-$110**

Fancy Lily Bud wall pocket in matte aqua, 1940s, incised McCoy mark, 8" l......**$225-$250**

Blossomtime wall pocket in matte yellow, McCoy mark, 7-3/4" l. .... **$90-$110**

Bird on sunflower wall pocket, can also stand as planter, McCoy mark, came in a variety of glaze combinations, 6-1/2" h.............................. **$60-$75**

Floor vase in a blue onyx glaze, 24" h, unmarked ......**$700-$900**

Tall scroll vase in matte green (often found in glossy tan-brown), late 1940s, USA mark, 14" h. ....**$150-$200**

MEISSEN

Known for its finely detailed figurines and exceptional tableware, Meissen is recognized as the first European maker of fine porcelain.

The company owes its beginnings to Johann Friedrich Bottger's 1708 discovery of the process necessary for the manufacture of porcelain. "Rediscovery" might be a better term, since the secret of producing hard paste porcelain had been known to the Chinese for centuries. However, Bottger, a goldsmith and alchemist, was the first to successfully replicate the formula in Europe. Soon after, The Royal Saxon Porcelain Works set up shop in Dresden. Because Bottger's formula was highly sought after by would-be competitors, in 1710 the firm moved its base of operations to Albrechtburg Castle in Meissen, Saxony. There, in fortress-like surroundings, prying eyes could be successfully deflected. And, because of that move, the company name eventually became one with its locale: Meissen.

The earliest Meissen pieces were red stoneware, reminiscent of Chinese work, and incised with Chinese characters. Porcelain became the Meissen focus in 1713; early releases included figurines and teasets, the decorations reminiscent of baroque metal. In 1719, after Bottger's death, artist J.J. Horoldt took over the firm's direction. His Chinese-influenced designs, which employed a lavish use of color and decoration, are categorized as chinoiserie.

By the 1730s, Meissen employed nearly 100 workers, among them renowned modelers J.G. Kirchner and J.J. Kandler. The firm became known for its porcelain sculptures; subjects included birds, animals, and familiar figures from *commedia dell'arte*. Meissen dinnerware also won acclaim; in earlier attempts, the company's white porcelain had only managed to achieve off-white. Now, at last, there were dazzling white porcelain surfaces that proved ideal for the exquisite, richly colored decoration that became a Meissen trademark.

Following Horoldt's retirement in the mid-1700s, Victor Acier became Meissen's master modeler. Under Acier, the design focus relied heavily on mythological themes. By the early 1800s, however, Meissen's popularity began to wane. With production costs mounting and quality inconsistent, changes were instituted, especially technical improvements in production that allowed Meissen to operate more efficiently and profitably. More importantly, the Meissen designs, which had remained relatively stagnant for nearly a century, were refurbished. The goal: to connect with current popular culture. Meissen's artists (and its porcelain) proved perfectly capable of adapting to the prevailing tastes of the times. The range was wide: the ornate fussiness of the Rococo period; the more subdued Neoclassicism of the late 1700s; the nature-tinged voluptuousness of early 20th century Art Nouveau; and today's Meissen, which reinterprets, and builds on, all of these design eras. Despite diligent efforts, Meissen eventually found its work widely copied. A crossed-swords trademark, applied to Meissen pieces from

Porcelain figural footed compote with applied floral decoration, 19th/20th century, crossed swords mark, 19" x 14" x 11-1/2"................................... **$2,375**

Rago Arts and Auction Center

CERAMICS

1731 onward, is a good indicator of authenticity. However, even the markings had their imitators. Because Meissen originals, particularly those from the 18th and 19th centuries, are both rare and costly, the most reliable guarantee that a piece is authentic is to purchase from a reputable source.

Meissen porcelain is an acquired taste. Its gilded glory, lavish use of color, and almost overwhelmingly intricate detailing require just the right setting for effective display. Meissen is not background décor. These are three-dimensional artworks that demand full attention. Meissen pieces also often tell a story (although the plots may be long forgotten): a cherub and a woman in 18th century dress read a book, surrounded by a bevy of shepherdesses; the goddess Diana perches on a clock above a winged head of Father Time; the painted inset on a cobalt teacup depicts an ancient Dresden cathedral approached by devout churchgoers. Unforgettable images all, and all part of the miracle that is Meissen.

Hand-painted porcelain urn covered with applied putti and large floral finial, 19th century, crossed swords mark, 24" x 12" x 9-1/2".. **$4,063**

Rago Arts and Auction Center

Tureen and platter, German, in Blue Onion pattern, lidded tureen and shaped oval platter with handles, both with underglaze blue crossed swords mark, tureen missing ladle, small chip to handle of platter, platter 20" l....... **$510**

Cowan's Auctions, Inc.

Nine items with gilt and floral decoration, 19th/20th century: six round bowls, two-handled rectangular bowl and square serving tray, all marked, tray 16" sq. (four items shown)...... **$2,625**

Rago Arts and Auction Center

Gardener figure, German, 19th century, woman in 18th-century attire with basket of flowers, holding tool, standing beside rose-filled planter on circular base, marked with underglaze blue crossed swords, incised 122 on bottom, chip to rim of bonnet, minor losses to lace and flowers, missing blade of sickle, 8-1/2" h. **$900**

Cowan's Auctions, Inc.

Figural perforated vase with lid, 19th century, some damage, 12-1/2" h. **$950**

Kaminski Auctions

Figural grouping, German, late 18th/early 19th century, 15" h. x 8-1/2" w............................ **$500**

Kaminski Auctions

Leda and the Swan, German, late 19th century, marks: crossed swords, 433, some losses to top of toe on extended foot, floral garland, and tree leaves, 6-3/4" h. **$1,250**

Heritage Auctions

Hunter on horseback with dogs, German, late 19th century, marks: crossed swords, T 102, good condition with restoration to tail of one dog, 15-1/4" h. **$18,125**

Heritage Auctions

Two porcelain figures from "The Senses" series, German, late 19th century, representing taste and smell, both with woman in 18th-century attire, seated at a table, one smelling a rose and the other enjoying a pastry, each marked with underglaze blue crossed swords, "taste" incised 127 on bottom, "smell" incised 42 on bottom, both groups with minor losses, taller 5-1/2" h. **$1,920**

Cowan's Auctions, Inc.

Malabar Lady and Malabar Man, late 19th century, marks to female: crossed swords, 1519, 12-1/2" h. **$3,750**

Heritage Auctions

Cup and saucer, cup 2" h. x 3" dia., saucer 5" dia...**$50**

Kaminski Auctions

METTLACH

Ceramics with the name Mettlach were produced by Villeroy & Boch and other potteries in the Mettlach area of Germany. Villery & Boch's finest years of production are thought to be from about 1890-1910.

Pate sur pate charger of Three Graces, #7052, 21" dia. **$590**

Michaan's Auctions

Hofbrauhaus party stein, Mettlach #1909/1102 PUG, depicting people drinking at Hofbrauhaus, mint condition, half liter. **$207**

Fox Auctions

Etched stein #1916, cavaliers drinking, Harvey Murphy replaced lid, body mint condition, 2-1/2 liters. **$460**

Fox Auctions

Ornate punch bowl with colonial era scenes front and rear, two handles of fishlike creatures, basketweave designs and others in heavy white slip to body, impressed with Mettlach logo and notation "Gefnnachbildung, Seschutzi," 2088 and 98 with W in black slip and mark in green slip, one handle oversprayed, some staining to interior rim, 11-1/4" h. x 17" w. **$200**

Mark Mussio, Humler & Nolan

Etched plaque #2287, two cavalier knights shaking hands with verse, mint condition, 17". **$460**

Fox Auctions

NEWCOMB COLLEGE

This pottery was established in the art department of Newcomb College in New Orleans in 1897. Each piece was hand-thrown and bore the potter's mark and decorator's monogram on the base. It was always a studio business and never operated as a factory. Its pieces are, therefore, scarce, with the early wares eagerly sought. The pottery closed in 1940.

Anna Frances Simpson large scenic vase with Spanish moss, live oaks and full moon, 1922, marked NC/MO35/JM/AFS/211, 11-1/4" x 6-1/4"............$11,875

Rago Arts and Auction Center

Sadie Irvine vase with trumpet flowers, 1929, marked NC/236/RL24/SI, 7" x 3-3/4"....... **$2,750**

Rago Arts and Auction Center

Henrietta Bailey transitional chamberstick with paperwhites, 1911, marked NC/HB/JM/T/EN24, 6-1/4" x 4-1/4".............. **$1,625**

Rago Arts and Auction Center

Corinne M. Chalaron low bowl with stylized magnolia flowers, 1922, marked NC/JM55/CMC/MQ35, 2-1/4" x 7"..$1,063

Rago Arts and Auction Center

Mazie Teresa Ryan early two-handled vase with jasmine, 1905, marked NC/M.T. RYAN/AT94, 4-1/2" x 4-1/2". **$3,500**

Rago Arts and Auction Center

Henrietta Bailey vase with nicotina blossoms, 1917, marked NC/IY77/721A/HB, 4-1/4" x 4-3/4". **$1,625**

Rago Arts and Auction Center

Rare carved cabinet vase in oxblood glaze, 1932, marked NC/G1/TT38/JH/A, 2-3/4" x 3". **$1,625**

Rago Arts and Auction Center

Ada Wilt Lonnegan high glaze lidded creamer with incised and painted irises, lid incised with leaves, 1909, marked with Newcomb logo, date code for 1909 (DD 73), impressed initials of potter Joseph Meyer, and W for white clay body, excellent original condition, 4" h. **$3,200**

Mark Mussio, Humler & Nolan

Sadie Irvine cabinet vase with willow leaves, 1933, marked NC/UE8/KS/SI, 3-1/2" x 3-1/2". **$1,750**

Rago Arts and Auction Center

Sadie Irvine transitional vase with magnolia blossoms, 1907, marked NC/JM/SI/BX67, 5-1/2" x 3-1/4". **$1,375**

Rago Arts and Auction Center

Joseph Meyer vase with gloss black glaze, impressed on base with Newcomb insignia, excellent original condition, 3" h. **$225**

Mark Mussio, Humler & Nolan

Sadie Irvine vase with carved and painted decoration of flowering vines, marked with Newcomb logo, date code for 1929 (RS 93), monogram of potter Jonathan Hunt, and incised monogram of artist, excellent original condition, no apparent crazing, 6-1/2" h. **$1,400**

Mark Mussio, Humler & Nolan

Anna Frances Simpson small circular trivet with trumpet vine, 1924, marked NC/OC27/AFS, 4" dia. **$750**

Rago Arts and Auction Center

Henrietta Bailey rare seven-piece transitional tea set for two with pine trees, 1911, two teacups and saucers, teapot, sugar bowl, and creamer, all marked NC/HB/EI61, teapot 4" x 5-1/2". **$25,000**

Rago Arts and Auction Center

Sadie Irvine candleholder with pink lilies at top and bottom, 1918, impressed with Newcomb College logo, shape 232, and 1918 date code JM35, incised with artist's monogram, most of original Newcomb Pottery label present, bruise at rim and small firing separation to bottom, 7" h. .. **$850**

Mark Mussio, Humler & Nolan

Sadie Irvine rare transitional scenic vase with tall pines and full moon, 1915, marked NC/HO8/SI, 8" x 3-1/2".................... **$3,625**

Rago Arts and Auction Center

Sadie Irvine tall vase with pine trees and full moon, 1927, marked NC/SI/QP58/325/JM, 9-1/4" x 4".................... **$9,375**

Rago Arts and Auction Center

CERAMICS

NIPPON

"Nippon" is a term used to describe a wide range of porcelain wares produced in Japan from the late 19th century until about 1921. It was in 1891 that the United States implemented the McKinley Tariff Act, which required that all wares exported to the United States carry a marking indicating their country of origin. The Japanese chose to use "Nippon," their name for Japan. In 1921 the import laws were revised and the words "Made in" had to be added to the markings. Japan was also required to replace the "Nippon" with the English name "Japan" on all wares sent to the United States.

Many Japanese factories produced Nippon porcelain, much of it hand-painted with ornate floral or landscape decoration and heavy gold decoration, applied beading and slip-trailed designs referred to as "moriage." Be aware that a number of Nippon markings have been reproduced and used on new porcelain wares.

Painted urn decorated with Arabic scene, quarter-inch chip to one foot, wear to gold gilt, 17-3/4" h. **$830**

Pook & Pook, Inc.

Scenic vase, large two-handle tapering form hand painted with scenic reserve on both sides, extensive gilding, blue maple leaf mark, first quarter 20th century, 13" h. **$161**

Jeffrey S. Evans & Associates

Scenic cobalt vase, square baluster form with two open handles at shoulder and flared feet, hand-painted scenic reserves on all four sides, applied red beaded grapes, green M-in-wreath mark, first quarter 20th century, 9-1/2" h. **$288**

Jeffrey S. Evans & Associates

Floral vase, baluster form with two open handles at shoulder, hand painted with roses, blue maple leaf mark, first quarter 20th century, 13" h. **$431**

Jeffrey S. Evans & Associates

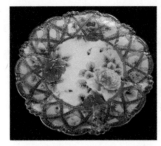

Plate with roses, 11" dia..... **$236**

Stevens Auction Co.

Two decorated vases, each of flattened pillow form with two handles, smaller vase painted with irises, larger vase painted with Art Nouveau poppies and water lilies surrounding a reserve featuring swans on a lake, M-in-wreath marks, one blue and one green, first quarter 20th century, 8" and 10" h. **$374**

Jeffrey S. Evans & Associates

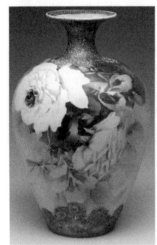

Floral vase, baluster form with everted lip, hand painted with roses, blue maple leaf mark, first quarter 20th century, 11" h. **$316**

Jeffrey S. Evans & Associates

Pair of floral vases, two-handle square baluster form with two open handles at shoulder and flared feet, raised moriage centering band of painted white dogwood flowers, green M-in-wreath marks, first quarter 20th century, 9-1/2" h. **$316**

Jeffrey S. Evans & Associates

Whiskey jug with hand-painted European cottage scene, stopper needs new cork, 6" h. **$100**

Kaminski Auctions

NORITAKE

Although Noritake is the long-recognized identifier for a particular brand of fine china, the firm began life in 1904 as Nippon Gomei Kaisha. The "Noritake" moniker came from the company's location in the village of Noritake, Japan. Because it was a geographic designation, the firm had to wait until the 1980s before receiving permission to officially register "Noritake" as a trade name.

Prior to the 1900s, Japan's "closed" society meant that relatively few domestically produced items found their way past the country's borders. Japanese artware was prized as much for its rarity as for its skillful execution. In the late 1800s, the easing of economic sanctions and growing interaction with the West meant that the rest of the world could appreciate the artistry of Japan.

Noritake was developed by Morimura Brothers, a distributorship founded in 1876. In its earliest years, Morimura operated as an exporter, bringing traditional Japanese giftware (paper lanterns, china, and a variety of decorative curio items) to buyers on American shores. The company eventually embraced the goal of producing a line of fine china dinnerware that, while Japanese-made, would prove irresistible in styling and execution to Western consumers.

Noritake dinnerware debuted in 1904. In 1914, when the product was deemed ready for a larger audience, exports began. The first Noritake pieces were hand-painted with extensive gold trim, which were both costly and time-consuming to produce. Additionally, much of the decorative work was farmed out to independent artisans throughout the region. Quality varied due to the differing skill levels of individual freelancers.

With the onset of mass production in the 1920s, Noritake was able to achieve consistency in its output, expand productivity, lower costs, and increase brand name recognition.

From the 1920s until World War II, Noritake achieved its greatest prominence. The inventory fell into two overall categories: dinnerware and fancy ware. Dinnerware, as the name implies, encompassed products made specifically for the table—plates, bowls, tea sets, condiment holders, and the like. Fancy ware covered everything else, from wall pockets and vases to elaborately decorated display platters.

Painted scenic bowl depicting landscape with cabin, trimmed in gilt with two handles, circa early 20th century, green leaf Noritake mark, 7" dia. x 2-1/4" h..**$48**

Midwest Auction Galleries

Hand-painted Art Deco porcelain covered dresser box depicting young woman with hand mirror, early 20th century, marked with green M-in-wreath backstamp, 3-3/4" dia..**$210**

Jackson's International

A major factor in Noritake's success was the Morimura brothers' early and aggressive use of advertising, cementing the brand in the minds of American buyers. Full-page Noritake ads graced major trade journals. Early on, the company also saw the value of such promotional efforts as premium tie-ins. During the 1920s, the Larkin Co., a New York mail-order distributor of various home and beauty products, offered buyers an assortment of Noritake china as a bonus when buying from the company's catalog. Among the most popular Larkin patterns was Azalea, still a favorite today.

The onset of World War II meant that, overnight, Noritake china was no longer available (or even welcome) in American homes. The company continued to produce china on a limited basis during the war, but only for domestic buyers.

During the American occupation of Japan (1945-1952), Noritake china became popular with servicemen stationed there; the company's increased production was one factor in assisting Japan along the road to economic recovery. The "Noritake China" name was, for a time, replaced with a more indeterminate "Rose China." The company indicated this was because the china was not yet at its pre-war level of quality; concerns about identifying the product too closely with a recent adversary may also have been a contributing factor.

In the years following the war, Noritake regained its previous worldwide reputation for quality. Whether lusterware of the 1920s, Art Deco stylings of the 1930s, or today's contemporary designs, Noritake porcelain reflects the artistic sensibilities of its creators, yet remains perfectly attuned to the specific cultural sensibilities of its intended audience.

Double-handled vase, parcel gilt, depicting group of maidens stringing flowers, 9" h................... **$213**

Leslie Hindman Auctioneers

Nippon hand-painted floral decorated vase, green maple leaf mark, 10-1/2" h. x 5-1/4" w. **$102**

Dirk Soulis Auctions

Three-piece hand-painted Art Deco porcelain group, handled perfume bottle with harlequin figure (stopper absent), blue luster wall pocket with blown out fruits, and two-sided figural peacock posy vase, early 20th century, first and third marked with red M-in-wreath backstamps, wall pocket with green Paulownia made in Japan flower mark, largest 8" l. **$150**

Jackson's International

Two hand-painted Art Deco porcelain cabinet plates, each depicting finely dressed young debutant with floral accents on turquoise luster ground, early 20th century, both marked with M-in-wreath backstamp, largest 8-3/4" dia. **$450**

Jackson's International

CERAMICS

GEORGE OHR

George Ohr, the eccentric potter of Biloxi, Mississippi, worked from about 1883 to 1906. Some think him to be one of the most expert throwers the craft will ever see. The majority of his works were hand-thrown, exceedingly thin-walled items, some of which have a crushed or folded appearance. He considered himself the foremost potter in the world and declined to sell much of his production, instead accumulating a great horde to leave as a legacy to his children. In 1972 this collection was purchased for resale by an antiques dealer.

Vase incised with Masonic temple and "E.E. Pattison, COAL, Chicago, S98," 1897-1900, stamped G.E. OHR, Biloxi, Miss., 4-1/4" x 3-1/4". **$7,500**

Rago Arts and Auction Center

Large bisque-fired vessel, in-body twist, folded rim, 1898-1910, script signature, 4-1/2" x 6-1/2". **$3,250**

Rago Arts and Auction Center

Cabinet vase with in-body twist, gunmetal glaze, circa 1897-1900, stamped G.E. OHR Biloxi Miss, 4-1/4" x 2-1/2". **$3,375**

Rago Arts and Auction Center

Curled bisque bank, 1897-1900, stamped G.E. OHR, Biloxi, Miss., 3-3/4" x 3-1/4"............. **$1,375**

Rago Arts and Auction Center

Barrel-shaped vase of scroddled clay with amber and cobalt glaze, 1880s-1900s, hand-incised OHR, Biloxi, 5-1/4" x 4"........... **$1,250**

Rago Arts and Auction Center

Large corseted bulbous vase, green, raspberry, cobalt, and yellow sponged-on glaze, 1897-1900, stamped G.E.OHR Biloxi, Miss., 7" x 4". **$3,250**

Rago Arts and Auction Center

Bottle-shaped vase with curled handles and incised with leafy sprig, brown and gunmetal glaze, 1897-1900, stamped G.E. OHR, Biloxi, Miss., 5" x 4". **$7,500**

Rago Arts and Auction Center

Vase, thin-walled construction, "tortured" form, pumpkin colored high glaze, impressed on base Geo. E. Ohr, Biloxi, Miss., excellent original condition, 3-1/8" h. **$1,600**

Mark Mussio, Humler & Nolan

Novelty spittoon inkwell, unusual green, oxblood, and amber glaze, 1892-1894, stamped GEO. E. OHR BILOXI, 1-1/2" x 3-1/2". **$813**

Rago Arts and Auction Center

Large unusual figural bisque bank, 1895-1896, stamped GEO. E. OHR BILOXI MISS., 5-1/2" x 3-1/2". **$2,000**

Rago Arts and Auction Center

CERAMICS

Bisque-fired vase, pinched and lobed, 1898-1910, script signature, 5" x 6".............................. **$3,750**

Rago Arts and Auction Center

TOP! LOT!

Spherical vase with folded rim, rare matte raspberry and emerald mottled glaze, 1897-1900, stamped G.E. OHR Biloxi, Miss., 6" x 6". **$13,750**

Rago Arts and Auction Center

"Burnt Baby" inkwell with snake, 1892-1894, unmarked, 3" x 2-3/4"....................... **$1,875**

Rago Arts and Auction Center

White bisque vessel, 1898-1910, script signature, 3-1/2"x 4-1/2".......... **$875**

Rago Arts and Auction Center

Bisque-fired vessel of scroddled clay, pinched, 1898-1910, script signature, 3-3/4" x 5-1/2"......... **$2,750**

Rago Arts and Auction Center

Large teapot with ear-shaped handle and snake spout, teal and brown sponged-on glaze, 1897-1900, stamped G.E. OHR, Biloxi, Miss., 6-1/2" x 9"..............**$10,000**

Rago Arts and Auction Center

OVERBECK

The Overbeck studio pottery was founded by four sisters, Hannah, Mary Francis, Elizabeth and Harriet, in the Overbeck family home in Cambridge City, Indiana, in 1911. A fifth sister, Margaret, who worked as a decorator at Zanesville Art Pottery in 1910, was the catalyst for establishing the pottery, but died the same year. Launching at the tail end of the Arts and Crafts movement, and believing "borrowed art is bad art," the sister potters dedicated themselves to producing unique, quality pieces with original design elements, which often were inspired by the natural world. Pieces can also be found worked in the Art Nouveau and Art Deco styles, as well as unique figurines and grotesques. The studio used several marks through the years, including an incised "O" and incised "OBK," often accompanied by the artist's initials. The pottery ceased production in 1955.

Barnyard goose with large pink feet, neck outstretched, "OBK" logo incised beneath, tip of beak has glaze chip and perimeter of feet has some glaze nicks. **$300**

Mark Mussio, Humler & Nolan

Grotesque figure of champion pacer Single G, so named for G on forehead, marked on bottom with Overbeck Pottery ink stamp, excellent original condition, 2-1/4" x 3". Single G, who was born in Cambridge City, Indiana in 1910, had a 16-year career as a successful harness racer. He died in 1940 and is buried in Cambridge City. **$700**

Mark Mussio, Humler & Nolan

Monochromatic vase with dozens of small clusters of flowers by sisters Elizabeth and Mary Frances Overbeck, incised marks include Overbeck logo and initials of two sisters, excellent original condition, 8-1/4" h. **$1,600**

Mark Mussio, Humler & Nolan

Pink and purple billy goat with black accents, incised "OBK" logo, both horns have been broken at crown and glued back, 3-5/8" h. **$200**

Mark Mussio, Humler & Nolan

CERAMICS

Skunk figure, impressed with Overbeck trademark, excellent original condition, 1-5/8" x 3-1/4"................................. **$350**

Mark Mussio, Humler & Nolan

Grotesque figure of gentleman outfitted in pink morning coat, blue pants, blue cravat, and blue top hat, impressed with Overbeck logo, excellent original condition, 4-1/2" h. **$140**

Mark Mussio, Humler & Nolan

Grotesque figure of Southern Belle in dress with hoop skirt and broad-brimmed hat, blue, pink and white, impressed with Overbeck logo, excellent original condition, 4-1/4" h. **$200**

Mark Mussio, Humler & Nolan

Grotesque figure of member of choir wearing hat with white feature, holding hymnal, impressed on sole of right foot with Overbeck emblem, excellent original condition, 5-1/4" h. **$250**

Mark Mussio, Humler & Nolan

Petite figure of Southern Belle with blond tresses, dressed in flowered dress and matching hat, impressed with Overbeck symbol, excellent original condition, 1-7/8" h. **$180**

Mark Mussio, Humler & Nolan

Grotesque figure of Dickensian lady colorfully dressed, impressed with Overbeck logo, excellent original condition, 3-1/2" h. . **$140**

Mark Mussio, Humler & Nolan

Cockatoo pin, white bird backlit by green disc, impressed with Overbeck logo, excellent original condition, 2-1/2" l............... **$190**

Mark Mussio, Humler & Nolan

Grotesque figure of wild dog in pink, green, blue, lavender and black, impressed with Overbeck symbol, small chips to front feet, 2" x 3-1/2"......................... **$180**

Mark Mussio, Humler & Nolan

Grotesque figure of wild dog in pink, brown, blue, green and black, impressed with Overbeck logo, excellent original condition, 2-1/4" x 3-1/2".................... **$325**

Mark Mussio, Humler & Nolan

OWENS

Owens pottery was the product of the J.B. Owens Pottery Co., which operated in Ohio from 1890 to 1929. In 1891 it was located in Zanesville and produced art pottery from 1896, introducing "Utopian" wares as its first art pottery. The company switched to tile after 1907. Efforts to rebuild after the factory burned in 1928 failed, and the company closed in 1929.

Feroza vase with molded jonquil design and brown metallic luster glaze, unmarked, excellent original condition, 8-1/4" h...**$275**

Mark Mussio, Humler & Nolan

Rare Utopian scenic vase showing heron standing on one leg in a marsh with lotus and cattail decoration by Mae Timberlake, impressed "J.B. Owens Utopian 798" on bottom and initialed by artist on side, 14-1/8"..**$1,300**

Mark Mussio, Humler & Nolan

Soudaneze mug decorated with grapes and leaves against mat black ground, impressed on base "Owens Soudaneze X 235," excellent original condition, 4-3/4" h. **$275**

Mark Mussio, Humler & Nolan

Miniature Utopian handled vase decorated with a pair of yellow clematis, impressed "JB Owens Utopian, 866" on bottom, 3-1/4" h. **$160**

Mark Mussio, Humler & Nolan

Three-piece tea set with metal mounts, 5-5/8" teapot, 4-1/4" sugar bowl and 4" cream pitcher, each impressed "J.B. Owens, Utopian, 1057," all with fine overall crazing, teapot with small chips at spout and tiny nicks below handles, sugar in excellent original condition, creamer with tiny nicks to two feet, each bears a sticker indicating it is "From the Collection of Frank L. Hahn," author of *Collector's Guide to Owens Pottery.* **$225**

Mark Mussio, Humler & Nolan

Wall pocket classified as "Green Ware," possibly part of Aqua Verde line, marked only with incised number 1017, chipping at hanger hole, minor nicks to back, 10-3/4" h. **$200**

Mark Mussio, Humler & Nolan

Utopian vase formed of North Dakota clay (a partnership between Owens Pottery and North Dakota School of Mines), decorated with wild roses, impressed with Owens Utopian logo, shape 108, 2 and 8 and marked "ND" in slip near base to identify the source of clay, 5-7/8" h. **$110**

Mark Mussio, Humler & Nolan

REDWARE

Red earthenware pottery was made in the American colonies from the late 1600s. Bowls, crocks, and all types of utilitarian wares were turned out in great abundance to supplement the pewter and hand-made treenware. The ready availability of the clay, the same used in making bricks and roof tiles, accounted for the vast production. The lead-glazed redware retained its reddish color, although a variety of colors could be obtained by adding various metals to the glaze. Interesting effects occurred accidentally through unsuspected impurities in the clay or uneven temperatures in the firing kiln, which sometimes resulted in streaks or mottled splotches.

Redware pottery was seldom marked by the maker.

Pennsylvania redware loaf dish with slip wavy line decoration, 19th century, 9-1/2" l. x 12-3/4" w.
.... **$1,304**

Pook & Pook, Inc.

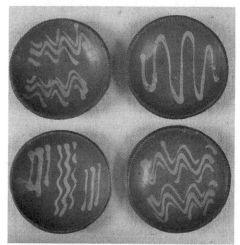

Four Pennsylvania slip decorated redware plates, mid-19th century, 7-1/4" dia............................ **$948**

Pook & Pook, Inc.

Pennsylvania redware bank, dated 1862, with dog finial and manganese splotching, inscribed on base AP 1862 PLM, 5-1/2" h. **$4,266**

Pook & Pook, Inc.

Pennsylvania redware colander with slip band and zigzag decoration, 19th century, 3-3/4" h. x 8-3/4" w.. **$2,607**

Pook & Pook, Inc.

CERAMICS

Pennsylvania redware pie plate with slip tulip decoration, 19th century, attributed to Dryville Pottery, 8-1/2" dia. **$1,896**

Pook & Pook, Inc.

York County, Pennsylvania redware figure of seated dog clutching basket of fruit, 19th century, attributed to Jesiah Shorb, West Manheim Township, York County, Pennsylvania, 4-1/4" h. ... **$4,029**

Pook & Pook, Inc.

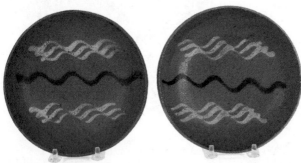

Pair of Pennsylvania redware pie plates with yellow and brown slip wavy line decoration, 19th century, 6-7/8" dia. **$1,541**

Pook & Pook, Inc.

Chester County, Pennsylvania redware crock, late 19th/early 20th century, inscribed Henry Schofield, 7-3/4" **$889**

Pook & Pook, Inc.

American redware pie plate with yellow slip ABC, 19th century, 10" dia. **$889**

Pook & Pook, Inc.

Pennsylvania redware charger with yellow slip wavy line decoration, 19th century, 10-3/4" dia. .. **$790**

Pook & Pook, Inc.

Pennsylvania redware wall pocket with manganese splash decoration, 19th century, 7-1/2" h. x 5-1/4" w.. **$267**

Pook & Pook, Inc.

Pennsylvania redware pie plate with green slip X decoration, 19th century, 8-1/4" dia. **$711**

Pook & Pook, Inc.

Pennsylvania redware spaniel bank, attributed to George Wagner, 6-3/4" h. **$1,541**

Pook & Pook, Inc.

Miniature Pennsylvania redware pie plate with yellow slip clef decoration, 19th century, 4-3/8" dia. **$1,007**

Pook & Pook, Inc.

Pennsylvania redware pie plate with slip tulip decoration, 19th century, 8" dia. **$2,370**

Pook & Pook, Inc.

Pennsylvania redware bird rattle, 19th century, attributed to William Maize, New Berlin, Union County, Pennsylvania, 3" h. **$1,778**

Pook & Pook, Inc.

TOP LOT!

Southeast Pennsylvania redware covered bowl with extensive slip star and tulip decoration, circa 1800, 5" h. x 8-1/2" dia. **$5,214**

Pook & Pook, Inc.

RED WING POTTERY

Various potteries operated in Red Wing, Minnesota, starting in 1868, the most successful being the Red Wing Stoneware Co., organized in 1877. Merged with other local potteries through the years, it became known as Red Wing Union Stoneware Co. in 1906 and was one of the largest producers of utilitarian stoneware items in the United States.

After a decline in the popularity of stoneware products, an art pottery line was introduced to compensate for the loss. This was reflected in a new name for the company, Red Wing Potteries, Inc., in 1936. Stoneware production ceased entirely in 1947, but vases, planters, cookie jars, and dinnerware of art pottery quality continued in production until 1967, when the pottery ceased operation altogether.

For more information on Red Wing pottery, see *Warman's Red Wing Pottery Identification and Price Guide* by Mark F. Moran.

White stoneware advertising crocks 5" and 3-3/4" h., unmarked. ....**$900-$1,200 ea.**

White stoneware advertising crocks 6-1/4" and 6" h., unmarked. ....**$900-$1,200 ea.**

Three brown-top mini jugs two with advertising and one a souvenir, each 4-1/4" h., found unmarked and with raised "R.W.S.W. Co." ...**$250+ ea., with a high range of $800 depending on markings**

Blue and white covered butter crock in a daisy pattern, left, 4-1/2" h. with lid, 5-1/2" dia. ..**$400+**
Blue and white bail-handle covered butter crock with advertising, 5-1/2" h. without handle. ....**$500+**

White stoneware bail-handle butter crock with advertising (cover missing), left, 7-1/4" h. without handle......................................**$400+**
Sponge-decorated butter crock with lid, 7" h., unmarked. ....**$300+**

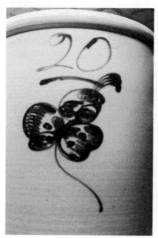

Close-up of the hand-decorated butterfly and flower on a 20-gallon salt-glaze crock. .. **$2,000-$2,500, signed**

Stoneware bread crock in glossy green glaze, also found with matte Brushed Ware surface, and in tan; lid missing, 11" h., 14" dia., rare. **$2,800+ (as is); with lid, $4,000+**

Ten-pound butter crock with Osage, Iowa, advertising, 6-3/4" h., otherwise unmarked. ... **$1,500**

Eight-gallon transitional zinc-glaze crock with stamped Minnesota oval and hand-decorated birch leaf. .... **$3,500+**
Twelve-gallon salt-glaze crock with large hand-decorated birch leaf pointing up. **$2,500**

Ten-gallon crock with Washington advertising that includes crockery, unusual. ....**$1,500+ if perfect**

Fifteen-gallon salt-glaze crock with cobalt decoration of "bowtie" and double leaves, circa 1890, 18-1/2" h., unmarked. (Collector Tip: The leaves seen here are precursors to the stenciled or stamped birch-leaf decoration used on white hand-thrown stoneware made just a few years later.) .... **$800-$1,000**

Eighth-pint fancy jug with rare blue sponge decoration, 2-3/4" h. .... **$1,800+**

CERAMICS

Three-gallon white stoneware crock with tilted birch leaves and original lid, and rarely seen "Minnesota Stoneware Company" oval mark, 10-3/4" h. without lid; lid, 11" dia. .... **$900+**

Transitional five-gallon crock with hand-decorated blue-black number and "bowtie," circa 1900, the glaze on this crock is between white and tan, 13-1/4" h., unmarked. .... **$300+**

Two-gallon crock with tilted birch leaves and oval stamp with "Minnesota Stoneware Company" (spelled out, commonly found as "Co."), 12" h. with lid, otherwise unmarked. .... **$1,500+**

Five-gallon white stoneware crock with oval and large wing, the most commonly found size for crocks and jugs. .... **$70+**

Four-gallon white stoneware crock with birch leaves called "elephant ears," and original lid, 11-1/2" h. without lid. .... **$150+**

Two-gallon crock with Washington advertising and original lid, 12" h. with lid. **$2,500**

Two-gallon white stoneware crock with tilted birch leaves, 10" h., impressed mark, "Minnesota Stoneware Co. Red Wing, Minn." .... **$70-$90**

White stoneware 20-pound butter crock with 4" wing, 7-1/2" h., 11-1/2" dia. .... **$1,000+**

White stoneware 20-pound butter crock with hand-decorated numbers, a transitional mark before stamping was regularly used, circa 1900, 8" h., 11-1/2" dia., raised mark on bottom, "Minnesota Stoneware Red Wing, Minn." .... **$800-$1,000**

White stoneware bail-handle jugs in three sizes with advertising; from left, 6", 10" and 7-1/2" h. ....**$300-$400 ea.**

Two brown-top stoneware jugs with small red wings; left, half gallon, 9" h.; right, one gallon, wide mouth, 10-1/2" h. ....**$150-$225 ea.**

Two white stoneware shoulder jugs with advertising; left, 10-1/2" h.; right, 8-1/2" h. .....**$275-$350 ea.**

Two white stoneware shoulder jugs one with elaborate advertising for a Chicago liquor store.
Left: 7-1/2" h., with rare mark, "Minn. S. Co. Red Wing, Minn." .... **$70+**
Right: 8-3/4" h., unmarked .... **$300-$500**

Wide-mouth, brown-top one-gallon jug left, with raised star on bottom, 10" h. ....**$75+**
Dome-top one-gallon jug with unglazed top, with raised letters, "Wm. R. Adams Microbe Killer," 10-1/2" h., unmarked. ....**$325+**

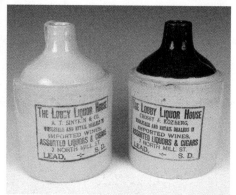

Two half-gallon shoulder jugs, one with a white top and one brown, late 19th and early 20th century, with advertising for the same liquor store in Lead, S.D., but identifying different owners, each 8-3/4" h.
.... **White, $500-$600; brown, $600-$800**

One-gallon brown-top stoneware jug with rare original paper label, 11" h. .... **$300+**

One-gallon 1915 Potters Excursion shoulder jug one gallon, 11" h. .... **$7,000+**

Half-gallon shoulder jug with Cannon Falls, Minn., advertising, 8-1/2" h., impressed bottom mark, "Minnesota Stoneware Co. Red Wing, Minn." .... **$500+**

Red (pink) and blue banded ribbed stoneware mixing bowls, complete set of eight, in sizes ranging from 4-1/4" to 12" dia., unmarked. .... **$90-$110 ea.**

Blue and white "Greek Key" stoneware mixing bowls, complete set of seven, in sizes ranging from 6" to 12" dia., unmarked. .... **6" to 10" size, $125+ ea.; 11" and 12", $250-$300 ea.**

Sponge-decorated paneled mixing bowls, complete set of seven, in diameters of 5", 6-1/4", 7-1/2", 8", 9", 10" and 11", unmarked except for impressed size number. ..... **5", $500+; other sizes, $125-$300 ea.**

White stoneware refrigerator jars, three sizes, with cobalt trim, each has a raised, footed base so that the same size jars could be stacked, seen here in diameters of 4-3/4", 5-3/4", and 6-3/4". ....**$250-$350 ea.**

Sponge-decorated umbrella stand, 17-3/4" h., unmarked. .... **$1,800-$2,200**

Floor vase No. 145, in a glaze called "Ripe Wheat," 15" h. .... **$550+**

Two one-gallon white stoneware shoulder jugs with cobalt trim, with narrow and wide mouths, 11" and 10-1/4" h., both marked on bottom, "Minnesota Stoneware Co. Red Wing, Minn.".....**$375-$450 ea.**

Sponge-decorated yellow ware bowls; left, two sizes, with advertising, 1930s, 7-1/2" and 5-1/2" dia.; right, Saffron Ware covered casserole with advertising, 7-1/2" dia. without handles, ink-stamped, "Red Wing Saffron Ware." ....**$300-$400 ea.**

Rooster vases in Fleck Zephyr Pink, two sizes, No. 1438 (Collector Tip: Also found marked No. M1438), designed by Charles Murphy, 9-3/4" and 14" h...**$200+ ea.**

Sponge-decorated pitchers, three sizes, two with advertising. Left, with cherry band, 8-1/2" h.**$1,800+**
Center, 9" tall ....**$400+**
Right, squat jug, with advertising inside, "Compliments of Farmers Co-op Creamery Association—Hull, Iowa," 6-1/2" h. ....**$1,500+**

Blue and white stoneware pitcher and basin with raised lily; pitcher, 10-1/2" h.; basin, 15-1/2" dia., unmarked. ....**$1,200+ set**

Sand jar with lily and cattail motif, made for both Red Wing and RumRill, No. 106, 15" h., unmarked. ....**$800+**

Belle Kogan planter called "The Nymphs," No. B2500, part of the "Deluxe Line," 16-1/2" w. x 6-3/4" h. ....**$180+**

CERAMICS

ROOKWOOD

Maria Longworth Nichols founded Rookwood Pottery in Cincinnati, Ohio in 1880. The name, she later reported, paid homage to the many crows (rooks) on her father's estate and was also designed to remind customers of Wedgwood. Production began on Thanksgiving Day 1880 when the first kiln was drawn.

Rookwood's earliest productions demonstrated a continued reliance on European precedents and the Japanese aesthetic. Although the firm offered a variety of wares (Dull Glaze, Cameo, and Limoges for example), it lacked a clearly defined artistic identity. With the introduction of what became known as its "standard glaze" in 1884, Rookwood inaugurated a period in which the company won consistent recognition for its artistic merit and technical innovation.

Rookwood's first decade ended on a high note when the company was awarded two gold medals: one at the Exhibition of American Art Industry in Philadelphia and another later in the year at the Exposition Universelle in Paris. Significant, too, was Maria Longworth Nichols' decision to transfer her interest in the company to William W. Taylor, who had been the firm's manager since 1883. In May 1890, the board of a newly reorganized Rookwood Pottery Co. purchased "the real estate, personal property, goodwill, patents, trade-marks... now the sole property of William W. Taylor" for $40,000.

Under Taylor's leadership, Rookwood was transformed from a fledgling startup to successful business that expanded throughout the following decades to meet rising demand.

Throughout the 1890s, Rookwood continued to attract critical notice as it kept the tradition of innovation alive. Taylor rolled out three new glaze lines—Iris, Sea Green and Aerial Blue—from late 1894 into early 1895.

At the Paris Exposition in 1900, Rookwood cemented its reputation by winning the Grand Prix, a feat largely due to the favorable reception of the new Iris glaze and its variants.

Over the next several years, Rookwood's record of achievement at domestic and international exhibitions remained unmatched.

Throughout the 1910s, Rookwood continued in a similar vein and began to more thoroughly embrace the simplified aesthetic promoted by many Arts and Crafts figures. Production of the Iris line, which had been instrumental in the firm's success at the Paris Exposition in 1900, ceased around 1912. Not only did the company abandon its older, fussier underglaze wares, but the newer lines the pottery introduced also trended toward simplicity.

Unfortunately, the collapse of the stock market in October 1929 and ensuing economic depression dealt Rookwood a blow from which it did not recover. The Great Depression took a toll on the company and eventually led to bankruptcy in April 1941.

Rookwood's history might have ended there were it not for the purchase of the firm by a group of investors led by automobile dealer Walter E. Schott and his wife, Margaret. Production started once again. In the years that followed, Rookwood changed hands a number of times before being moved to Starkville, Mississippi, in 1960. It finally closed its doors there in 1967.

Standard Glaze ewer decorated by William McDonald in 1891 with hawthorn blossoms, impressed with Rookwood symbol, which provides date, shape 527 D, and a "W" for white clay, incised with an "L" for Light Standard Glaze and artist's monogram, fine overall crazing, 10" h. **$400**

Mark Mussio, Humler & Nolan

ROOKWOOD MARKS

Rookwood employed a number of marks on the bottom of its vessels that denoted everything from the shape number, to the size, date, and color of the body, to the type of glaze to be used.

Company Marks

1880-1882

In this early period, a number of marks were used to identify the wares.

1. "ROOKWOOD" followed by the initials of the decorator, painted in gold. This is likely the earliest mark, and though the wares are not dated, it seems to have been discontinued by 1881-1882.
2. "ROOKWOOD / POTTERY. / [DATE] CIN. O." In Marks of American Potters (1904), Edwin AtLee Barber states, "The most common marks prior to 1882 were the name of the pottery and the date of manufacture, which were painted or incised on the base of each piece by the decorator."
3. "R. P. C. O. M. L. N." These initials stand for "Rookwood Pottery, Cincinnati, Ohio, Maria Longworth Nichols," and were either painted or incised on the base.
4. Kiln and crows stamp. Barber notes that in 1881 and 1882, the trademark designed by the artist Henry Farny was printed beneath the glaze.
5. Anchor stamp: Barber notes that this mark is "one of the rarest."
6. Oval stamp.
7. Ribbon or banner stamp: According to Barber, "In 1882 a special mark was used on a trade piece... the letters were impressed in a raised ribbon."
8. Ribbon or banner stamp II: A simpler variation of the above stamp, recorded by Herbert Peck.

1883-1886

1. Stamped name and date.
2. Impressed kiln: Appears only in 1883.

1886-1960

Virtually all of the pieces feature the conjoined RP monogram. Pieces fired in the anniversary kilns carry a special kiln-shaped mark with the number of the anniversary inside of it.

1955

A diamond-shaped mark that reads: "ROOKWOOD / 75th / ANNIVERSARY / POTTERY" was printed on wares.

1960-1967

Occasionally pieces are marked "ROOKWOOD POTTERY / STARKVILLE MISS"; from 1962 to 1967 a small "®" occasionally follows the monogram.

Date Marks

Unlike many of their contemporaries, Rookwood seems very early on to have adopted a method of marking its pottery that was accurate and easy to understand.

From 1882-1885, the company impressed the date, often with the company name, in block letters (see 1883-86, No. 1).

Although the date traditionally given for the conjoined RP mark is June 23, 1886, this marks the official introduction of the monogram rather than the first use.

Stanley Burt, in his record of the Rookwood at the Cincinnati Museum, noted two pieces from 1883 (Nos. 2 and 3) that used the monogram. The monogram was likely designed by Alfred Brennan, since it first appears on his work.

From 1886 on, the date of the object was coded in the conjoined "RP" monogram.

1886: conjoined "RP" no additional flame marks.

1887-1900: conjoined "RP" with a flame added for each subsequent year. Thus, a monogram with seven flames would represent 1893.

1900-1967: conjoined "RP" with 14 flames and a Roman numeral below the mark to indicate the year after 1900. Thus, a monogram with 14 flames and the letters "XXXVI" below it signifies 1936.

Clay-Type Marks

From 1880 until around 1895, Rookwood used a number of different colored bodies for production and marked each color with a letter code. These letters were impressed and usually found grouped together with the shape number, sometimes following it, but more often below it.

The letter "S" is a particularly vexing designation since the same initial was used for two other unrelated designations. As a result, it is particularly important to take into account the relative position of the impressed letter.

R = Red
Y = Yellow
S = Sage
G = Ginger
W = White
O = Olive
P = From 1915 on Rookwood used an impressed "P" (often found perpendicular to the orientation of the other marks) to denote the soft porcelain body.

Size and Shape Marks

Almost all Rookwood pieces have a shape code consisting of three or four numbers, followed by a size letter. "A" denotes the largest available size, "F" is the smallest. According to Herbert Peck, initial designs were given a "C" or "D" designation so that variations could be made. Not every shape model, however, features a variation in every size.

Glaze Marks

In addition to marking the size, shape and year of the piece, Rookwood's decorators also used a number of letters to designate the type of glaze to be used upon a piece. Generally speaking, these marks are either incised or impressed.

"S" = Standard Glaze to be used. (Incised.)
"L" = Decorators would often incise an "L" near their monogram to indicate that the light variation of the Standard Glaze was to be used. (Incised.)
"SG" = Sea Green Glaze to be used.
"Z" = from 1900-1904 designated any piece with a Mat Glaze. (Impressed.)
"W" = Iris Glaze to be used.
"V" = Vellum Glaze to be used; variations include "GV" for Green Vellum and "YV" for Yellow Vellum.

Other Marks

"S" = If found away from the shape number, this generally indicates a piece that was specially thrown at the pottery in the presence of visitors. (Impressed.)
"S" = If this precedes the shape number than it denotes a piece that was specifically thrown and decorated from a sketch with a corresponding number. Because of the size and quality of pieces this letter has been found on, this probably signifies a piece made specifically for an important exhibition.
"X" = Rookwood used a wheel ground "x" to indicate items that were not of first quality. There

has been some suggestion that decorators and salespersons might have conspired to "x" certain pieces that they liked, since this designation would reduce the price. Since there are a number of items that appear to have been marked for no apparent reason, there may be some truth to this idea. Unfortunately, as this idea has gained credence, many pieces with obvious flaws have been listed as "marked x for no apparent reason," and collectors should be cautious.

Generally, the mark reduces the value and appeal of the piece. Peck describes a variation of the "x" that resembles an asterisk as indicating a piece that could be given away to employees.

> "T" = An impressed T that precedes a shape number indicates a trial piece.
>
> ◗ ◆ ▲ = These shapes (crescents, diamonds, and triangles) are used to indicate a glaze trial.
>
> "K1" and "K3" = c. 1922, used for matching teacups and saucers
>
> "SC" = Cream and Sugar sets, c. 1946-50
>
> "2800" = Impressed on ship pattern tableware

Some Lines of Note

AERIAL BLUE: Commercially, this line was among the least successful. As a result, there are a limited number of pieces, and this scarcity has increased their values relative to other wares.

BLACK IRIS: This line is among the most sought after by collectors, commanding significantly more than examples of similar size and design in virtually any other glaze. In fact, the current auction record for Rookwood—over $350,000—was set in 2004 for a Black Iris vase decorated by Kitaro Shirayamadani in 1900.

IRIS: Uncrazed examples are exceptionally rare, with large pieces featuring conventional designs commanding the highest prices. Smaller, naturalistically painted examples, though still desirable, are gradually becoming more affordable for the less advanced collector.

PRODUCTION WARE: This commercial and mass-produced artware is significantly less expensive than pieces in most other lines.

STANDARD GLAZE: These wares peaked in the 1970s-1980s, and the market has remained thin in recent years, but regardless of the state of the market, examples of superlative quality, including those with silver overlay, have found their places in the finest of collections.

WAX MAT: This is among the most affordable of the hand-decorated lines.

Standard Glaze cache pot, decorated by Ed Abel in 1893 with wildflowers front and rear, impressed with Rookwood symbol, which indicates date, shape 519 and a "W" for white clay body, incised with artist's monogram, fine light crazing, excellent original condition, 5-1/2" h. **$300**

Mark Mussio, Humler & Nolan

Limoges style pitcher decorated in 1885 by Albert R. Valentien, trio of birds flying beneath clouds and above Oriental grasses, impressed Rookwood in block letters with date, shape number 56, small kiln mark, a "G" for ginger clay, incised with decorator's monogram, fine light crazing, restoration to chip at rim, 9-1/2" h. **$400**

Mark Mussio, Humler & Nolan

Dull Finish vase dated 1882, incised with vines, leaves and berries by a decorator with initials M.E.B., impressed Rookwood in block letters, date, number 68 3 and a "C" and incised with artist's initials, excellent original condition, 7-3/4" h. **$275**

Mark Mussio, Humler & Nolan

Dull Finish vase decorated in 1886 by Albert Valentien, two small birds flying around branch of tree, band of gold encircling vessel at shoulder, impressed Rookwood in block letters, with date, shape 117 C and a "Y" to indicate yellow clay body, excellent original condition, 8-1/4" h. **$500**

Mark Mussio, Humler & Nolan

Wax Mat vase with Greek key pattern, designed by Wilhelmina Rhem, 1945, flame mark XLV/ 6696/WR, 11-1/2" x 9"... **$1,000**

Rago Arts and Auction Center

Dull Finish (Smear Glaze) pitcher decorated by Albert Valentien in 1884 in Chaplet style, incised clouds and flowers, clouds outlined in gold and colored brown, impressed Rookwood in block letters, date, a "G" for ginger clay and a kiln mark, Cincinnati Art Museum numbers in red, artist monogram in black slip, excellent original condition, 8-1/8" h. This item sold as Lot 281 in the historic Glover Collection Auction in 1991.. **$700**

Mark Mussio, Humler & Nolan

Dull Finish ewer decorated by Martin Rettig in 1884, bird flying above trees, impressed Rookwood in block letters with date, shape 101 A and a "G" for ginger clay, incised with artist's monogram, excellent original condition, 11-3/8" h. **$500**

Mark Mussio, Humler & Nolan

Standard Glaze teapot decorated by Lisbeth Lincoln in 1902 with yellow daffodils, base impressed with Rookwood symbol, date and shape 771 B, incised with Lincoln's monogram, fine overall crazing, chip to inner portion of lid from which cracks emanate, none visible with lid in place, 9-3/4" h. **$275**

Mark Mussio, Humler & Nolan

Dull Finish vase with incised leaves by Nettie Wenderoth, circa 1881, incised with artist's monogram and notation Rookwood Pottery in script, decoration outlined in gold, the name Collins and a monogram, both in gold slip, are also on base, excellent original condition, 7" h. **$300**

Mark Mussio, Humler & Nolan

Early Standard Glaze cruet, circa 1886-1888, decorated with flowering branch of rose bush, white clay body, bottom has been ground so no marks remain, light crazing and some small grinding chips at base, 5-3/4" h. **$180**

Mark Mussio, Humler & Nolan

Coromandel Glaze vase made in 1932, glossy red tinted aventurine glaze with metallic gray dripped from rim, impressed with Rookwood logo, date and shape 6315, excellent original condition, 6-1/4" h. **$550**

Mark Mussio, Humler & Nolan

Cat paperweight designed by Louise Abel, cast in 1946, chartreuse high glaze, impressed with Rookwood logo, date, shape 6182, and designer's mold monogram, overall crazing, excellent original condition, 6-3/4". **$200**

Mark Mussio, Humler & Nolan

Perfume jug decorated by Harriet Wenderoth in 1882 with carved flowers and leaves, green high glaze, impressed Rookwood in block letters, with date, shape 61 and a kiln mark, incised with artist's mark, light crazing, excellent original condition, 4-3/4" h. **$250**

Mark Mussio, Humler & Nolan

◄ Early Standard Glaze cream pitcher decorated by Martin Rettig in 1885 with a butterfly on one side and Oriental grasses on the other, impressed Rookwood in block letters, with date, shape 79 and an "S" for sage clay body, incised with Rettig's cipher, fine overall crazing, excellent original condition, 3" h. **$250**

Mark Mussio, Humler & Nolan

Standard Glaze tyg decorated by Matt Daly in 1894 with portrait of a laughing man on front and woven basket on rear, impressed with Rookwood symbol, date, shape 659 and a "W" for white clay, incised with artist's monogram, fine, light crazing, overspray indicative of restoration, 8" h. **$300**

Mark Mussio, Humler & Nolan

Squat jewel porcelain vase with horses, designed by Jens Jensen, 1933, flame mark XXXIII/S/artist's cipher, 4-1/4" x 5-1/2". **$875**

Rago Arts and Auction Center

Dull Finish lidded box decorated by Albert Valentien in 1882 with beetles flying around Oriental style branches with gold accents, impressed Rookwood in block letters, with 1882 date, shape 21 and a "Y" for yellow clay body, artist's monogram in black slip, label identifying this as lot 0976 from historic Glover Collection Auction in June, 1991, line to lid and crazing confined to interior, 3" x 5". **$500**

Mark Mussio, Humler & Nolan

Calendar holder made during the 1920s, Mat blue glaze, impressed only with Rookwood symbol, excellent original condition, accompanied by original perpetual calendar insert, 6-3/4" h. **$425**

Mark Mussio, Humler & Nolan

Rookwood architectural faience tile depicting a sailing ship, impressed Rookwood Faience 1177 Y, fine original condition with light crazing and a couple of pinpoint burst glaze bubbles, 6" x 6", oak frame. **$400**

Mark Mussio, Humler & Nolan

Seated elephant paperweight, designed by Shirayamadani, cast in 1945, Wine Madder glaze, impressed with Rookwood logo, date, and shape 6490, tiny glaze bubbles at base, 3-3/4". **$200**

Mark Mussio, Humler & Nolan

Glaze effect vase made in 1939, crystalline green over brown high glaze, impressed with Rookwood logo, date and an "s" to indicate special shape, fine original condition, 5" h. **$650**

Mark Mussio, Humler & Nolan

Designed Crystal vase decorated by Flora King in 1946 with horse standing in field, impressed with Rookwood symbol, date and shape 6292 C, incised with number 252 and King's initials, overall crazing, excellent original condition, 7-1/2" h. **$475**

Mark Mussio, Humler & Nolan

Standard Glaze vase decorated by Sallie Coyne in 1900 with buckeyes, impressed with Rookwood symbol, which indicates date shape 762 C, incised with artist's monogram, fine overall crazing, excellent original condition, 5-1/2" h. **$500**

Mark Mussio, Humler & Nolan

Kitten paperweight designed by David Seyler, cast in 1943, crystalline blue Mat Glaze that permits portions of white body to show through, impressed with Rookwood logo, date and shape 6661, excellent original condition, 1-1/4" x 3-3/4"..............**$400**

Mark Mussio, Humler & Nolan

Five-piece desk set consisting of 4" x 5" letter holder, 3-1/8" inkwell with liner, 1" x 2-3/4" lidded box, 2-1/4" x 5" blotter roller, and 1-7/8" unknown item, each impressed with Rookwood logo and shape 2747, each dated 1924 except for last piece dated 1925, all in excellent original condition, each covered with speckled brown glaze. **$375**

Mark Mussio, Humler & Nolan

Mat Glaze lamp deeply incised with designs by Rose Fechheimer in 1906, lamp with olive green glaze with brown highlights, some panels colored in darker green by artist, impressed with Rookwood symbol, date and shape 822 A, signed on side with an "F" in a box, an alternative cipher for Fechheimer, lamp base in excellent original condition, contemporary mica shade, ceramic portion 11-3/8" h. **$750**

Mark Mussio, Humler & Nolan

Porcelain vase decorated by Lorinda Epply in 1931 with stylized flowers and glaze dripping over rim and covering interior, impressed with Rookwood logo, date and shape 2254 E, with Epply's monogram in black slip, excellent original condition, 4-1/2" h. x 5-1/4" dia. **$700**

Mark Mussio, Humler & Nolan

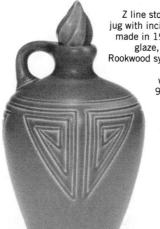

Z line stoppered whiskey jug with incised decoration, made in 1904, Mat Green glaze, impressed with Rookwood symbol, date and shape 765 BZ, wheel ground X, 9-1/4" h....**$450**

*Mark Mussio,
Humler & Nolan*

Mat green bowl with lizard crawling up side, Shirayamadani design, cast in 1904, impressed with Rookwood symbol, date and shape 630 Z, excellent original condition, 1" x 3"...........................**$325**

Mark Mussio, Humler & Nolan

Dull Finish vase decorated in 1887 by A.R. Valentien, bird seated on tree branch looking upward, impressed with Rookwood monogram, which indicates date, shape 30 B and an "S" for sage clay, incised with artist's symbol, excellent original condition, 12" h.....**$750**

Mark Mussio, Humler & Nolan

Butterfat Glaze vase decorated by Wilhelmine Rehm in 1945 with flowers, Butterfat Glaze in white over brown, lined in mottled brown, impressed with Rookwood logo, date and shape 6868, incised with number 7085 and Rehm's monogram, excellent original condition, 9" h. **$375**

Mark Mussio, Humler & Nolan

Decorated Mat Glaze vase with vine with blueberries and green leaves, the work of Sallie Coyne in 1925, impressed with Rookwood logo, date and shape 907 F, Coyne's monogram in black slip, excellent original condition with some tiny color misses at base, stray color spot, 7-3/4" h. **$350**

Mark Mussio, Humler & Nolan

Early vase decorated by Alfred Laurens Brennan in 1885, bird in flight above Oriental grasses, Limoges style, impressed Rookwood in block letters with date, shape 126 C and an "R" for red clay, incised with Brennan's monogram, fine light crazing, excellent original condition, 9-1/2" h. **$300**

Mark Mussio, Humler & Nolan

Standard Glaze vase decorated by Harriet Wilcox in 1898 with dandelions against shaded gold to brown ground, impressed with Rookwood monogram, which indicates date, shape 583 D and an esoteric mark, incised with Wilcox's initials, fine light crazing, excellent original condition, 8-1/2" h. **$650**

Mark Mussio, Humler & Nolan

Dull Finish vase decorated in 1885 by Matthew Daly, trio of turtles at shoreline, impressed Rookwood in block letters and with date and shape 241, incised with Daly's mark, 1-1/2" x 3/8" chip at rim, which has been glued into place, 13-1/4" h. **$650**

Mark Mussio, Humler & Nolan

Iris Glaze vase decorated with yellow tulips, the work of Sara Sax in 1893, impressed with Rookwood symbol, which indicates date, partial shape number and Sax's monogram, incised with a "W" to indicate white (Iris) glaze, crazing, drill hole to bottom, which removed part of shape number and has been plugged, 8-1/8" h...**$550**

Mark Mussio, Humler & Nolan

Production candlestick encircled with tulips, cast in 1910, brown over green Mat Glaze, impressed with Rookwood symbol, date, a "V" for Vellum body, and shape number 1830, small chip at base, 10" h........**$150**

Mark Mussio, Humler & Nolan

Rare Deco style ashtray featuring a fish lying across bowl resting its snout on a wall, a Shirayamadani design, cast in 1936, ivory Mat Glaze, impressed with Rookwood logo, date and shape 6554, single burst glaze bubble at top of wall, 2-1/4" x 5-3/4"..................**$170**

Mark Mussio, Humler & Nolan

Panther figure designed by William McDonald, Mat black glaze, no marks visible, excellent original condition, 2-3/8" x 6-1/4".............................**$400**

Mark Mussio, Humler & Nolan

Mat Glaze card tray lightly modeled with flower and swirls, flower in pink against green ground, the work of Anna Valentien in 1904, impressed with Rookwood symbol, date, shape 689 Z and experimental designation X 1206 X, with artist's monogram in black slip, excellent original condition with mild peppering, 1/2" x 5-5/8".....**$200**

Mark Mussio, Humler & Nolan

Petite dragon bowl designed by Shirayamadani, cast in 1905, yellow Mat Glaze with some red hazing, impressed with Rookwood logo, date and shape 1080, excellent original condition with small, stray glaze spot, 1" x 3".............**$425**

Mark Mussio, Humler & Nolan

Ballerina flower holder designed by Louise Abel, cast in 1923, Mat gray green glaze with some crystals, impressed with Rookwood logo, date and shape 2538, wheel ground X, two tiny glaze nicks at base, 6-7/8" h....................**$180**

Mark Mussio, Humler & Nolan

Rookwood Vellum vase with carved and stylized peacock feathers done in 1905 by Sara Sax, marks include company logo, date, shape number 942 E, impressed "V," incised "V" for Vellum glaze, impressed monogram of artist, faint crazing and tight half-inch line at rim, 4-3/4" h. **$375**

Mark Mussio, Humler & Nolan

Pelican ash receiver cast in 1930, blue and tan Mat Glaze, impressed with Rookwood symbol, date, shape 6149 and fan-shaped esoteric mark, excellent original condition, 4-1/8" x 6-1/8". . **$350**

Mark Mussio, Humler & Nolan

Pair of Rookwood lamps cast in 1937, Coromandel Glaze, impressed with Rookwood logo, date and shape 6311, excellent original condition, original fittings present but lamps need to be rewired, ceramic portion 7-3/8" h. **$800**

Mark Mussio, Humler & Nolan

Pair of Dolphin candlesticks, cast in 1919, Mat green glaze, each impressed with Rookwood symbol, date and shape 2464, excellent original condition, 11-1/4" h. . **$475**

Mark Mussio, Humler & Nolan

Modeled Mat vase featuring lotus flowers, carved by Rose Fechheimer in 1906, green Mat Glaze, impressed with Rookwood logo, date and shape 942 D, incised with artist's monogram, excellent original condition, 6-3/8" h. **$900**

Mark Mussio, Humler & Nolan

CERAMICS

Standard Glaze mug decorated by Matt Daly in 1889 with a pair of frogs in tutus, impressed with Rookwood logo, which indicates date, shape 422 and an "S" for sage green clay, incised with Daly's monogram, restoration to line at rim, 5-7/8" h......**$850**

Mark Mussio, Humler & Nolan

Five-sided pencil holder, each side panel showing a rook seated beneath a branch, cast in 1912, green Mat Glaze with red highlights, impressed with Rookwood symbol, date and shape 1795, excellent original condition, 4-5/8" h. **$350**

Mark Mussio, Humler & Nolan

Early Rookwood production piece described as "Persian Pitcher," made in 1882, cobalt blue high glaze with two angular handles, marks include Rookwood in block letters, date, shape number 26 and "W" for white clay, excellent original condition, 11-3/4" h........**$500**

Mark Mussio, Humler & Nolan

Jens Jensen Wax Mat vase with yucca plants in heavy glazes on opposing sides, painted at Rookwood in 1943, squeeze bag wavy lines run vertically up each side, marks include company logo, date, shape number 2194 and incised monogram of artist, 9-3/8" h.......**$450**

Mark Mussio, Humler & Nolan

Figure of a colonial woman, cast in 1946, uncrazed green high glaze, impressed with Rookwood symbol, date and shape 6907, wheel ground X to base, excellent original condition, 7-1/2" h..**$110**

Mark Mussio, Humler & Nolan

Mahogany Glaze vase decorated by Kataro Shirayamadani in 1889 with trumpet vines, impressed with Rookwood insignia, which discloses date, shape number 488 D and an "R" for red clay, incised with Shirayamadani's Japanese script signature, fine overall crazing, restoration at rim, 14-1/2" h. (Mahogany Glaze is formed by the application of Standard Glaze onto red clay body.) **$950**

Mark Mussio, Humler & Nolan

Dull Finish ewer decorated by M.A. Daly in 1887 with bough of flowering magnolias, impressed with Rookwood logo, which indicates date, shape 806 A, and 7 A, designating a type of white clay, with an "S" to indicate Daly's preference for Smear Glaze (dull finish) and his monogram, both in slip, some crazing, restoration at rim and where the handle attaches to neck, 23-1/4" h. **$800**

Mark Mussio, Humler & Nolan

Dull Finish ewer decorated by Martin Rettig during first half of 1880s with chrysanthemums, incised with Rettig's monogram and an "S" to indicate Smear Glaze (Dull Finish), impressed with shape number 101 A and 7 W for a type of white clay, fine original condition with a small color miss on handle, 10-1/2" h. **$400**

Mark Mussio, Humler & Nolan

ROSEVILLE POTTERY

Roseville is one of the most widely recognizable potteries across the United States. Having been sold in flower shops and drug stores around the country, its art and production wares became a staple in American homes through the time Roseville closed in the 1950s.

The Roseville Pottery Co., located in Roseville, Ohio, was incorporated on Jan. 4, 1892, with George F. Young as general manager. The company had been producing stoneware since 1890, when it purchased the J. B. Owens Pottery, also of Roseville.

The popularity of Roseville Pottery's original lines of stoneware continued to grow. The company acquired new plants in 1892 and 1898, and production started to shift to Zanesville, just a few miles away. By about 1910, all of the work was centered in Zanesville, but the company name was unchanged.

Young hired Ross C. Purdy as artistic designer in 1900, and Purdy created Rozane—a contraction of the words "Roseville" and "Zanesville." The first Roseville artwork pieces were marked either Rozane or RPCO, both impressed or ink-stamped on the bottom.

In 1902, a line was developed called Azurean. Some pieces were marked Azurean, but often RPCO. In 1904 at the St. Louis Exposition, Roseville's Rozane Mongol, a high-gloss oxblood red line, captured first prize, gaining recognition for the firm and its creator, John Herold.

Many Roseville lines were a response to the innovations of Weller Pottery, and in 1904 Frederick Rhead was hired away from Weller as artistic director. He created the Olympic and Della Robbia lines for Roseville. His brother Harry took over as artistic director in 1908, and in 1915 he introduced the popular Donatello line.

By 1908, all handcrafting ended except for Rozane Royal. Roseville was the first pottery in Ohio to install a tunnel kiln, which increased its production capacity.

Frank Ferrell, who was a top decorator at the Weller Pottery by 1904, was Roseville's artistic director from 1917 until 1954. This Zanesville native created many of the most popular lines, including Pine Cone, which had scores of individual pieces.

Many collectors believe Roseville's circa 1925 glazes were the best of any Zanesville pottery. George Krause, who had become Roseville's technical supervisor, responsible for glaze, in 1915, remained with Roseville until the 1950s.

Company sales declined after World War II, especially in the early 1950s when cheap Japanese imports began to replace American wares, and a simpler, more modern style made many of Roseville's elaborate floral designs seem old-fashioned.

In the late 1940s, Roseville began to issue lines with glossy glazes. Roseville tried to offset its flagging artware sales by launching a dinnerware line—Raymor—in 1953. The line was a commercial failure.

Roseville issued its last new designs in 1953. On Nov. 29, 1954, the facilities of Roseville were sold to the Mosaic Tile Co. For more information on Roseville, see *Warman's Roseville Pottery*, 2nd edition, by Denise Rago.

▶ Azurean vase, shape 892-8-1/2", decorated with pansies, impressed Azurean in block letters, shape 892 and RP Co., light crazing and some glaze inclusions on neck, 8-3/8" h. **$375**

Mark Mussio, Humler & Nolan

Impressed mark on Azurean vase, 8" h.

Raised mark on a Bushberry vase.

Bottom Marks

There is no consistency to Roseville bottom marks. Even within a single popular pattern like Pine Cone, the marks vary.

Several shape numbering systems were implemented during the company's almost 70-year history, with some denoting a vessel style and some applied to separate lines. Though many pieces are unmarked, from 1900 until the late teens or early 1920s, Roseville used a variety of marks including "RPCo," "Roseville Pottery Company," and the word "Rozane," the last often with a line name, i.e., "Egypto."

The underglaze ink script "Rv" mark was used on lines introduced from the mid-to-late teens through the mid-1920s. Around 1926 or 1927, Roseville began to use a small, triangular black paper label on lines such as Futura and Imperial II. Silver or gold foil labels began to appear around 1930, continuing for several years on lines such as Blackberry and Tourmaline, and on some early Pine Cone.

From 1932 to 1937, an impressed script mark was added to the molds used on new lines, and around 1937 the raised script mark was added to the molds of new lines. The relief mark includes "U.S.A."

All of the following bottom mark images appear courtesy of Adamstown Antique Gallery, Adamstown, Pennsylvania.

Ink stamp on a Cherry Blossom pink vase, 10" h.

Gold foil label and grease pencil marks on an Imperial II vase, 10" h.

Impressed mark on an Iris vase.

Wafer mark on a Della Robbia vase, 10-1/2" h.

Ink stamps on a Wisteria bowl, 5" h.

Impressed marks on a Rozane portrait vase, 13" h.

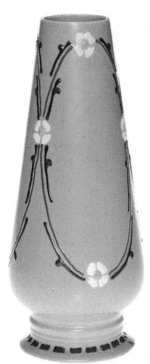

Handled Baneda vase, shape 596 in green overlaid in blue with panel displaying orange pumpkins and yellow flowers on green vines, beneath is gold foil Roseville sticker, shape number in red crayon, perfect condition, 9-1/4" h.. **$600**

Mark Mussio, Humler & Nolan

Aztec vase with small white flowers and decorative piping applied with pastry bag, gray-blue ground, marked with R on foot, two small chips at base, one glazed over, 10-3/4" h. **$200**

Mark Mussio, Humler & Nolan

Wisteria vase, shape 637-6-1/2", Roseville silver foil sticker, sticker from retailer Fowler, Dick and Walker, Inc., number 637 in orange crayon, excellent original condition, 6-1/2" x 8-1/2". . **$600**

Mark Mussio, Humler & Nolan

Azurean vase, shape 955-17, peonies, impressed with shape number, RPCo 1, some restoration at rim, oversprayed, tight spider to base, crazing, 17-1/4" h. **$350**

Mark Mussio, Humler & Nolan

Carnelian II scroll-handled vase in pink with variations of green, excellent condition, 10-1/4" h. **$225**

Mark Mussio, Humler & Nolan

Rozane Royal Dark letter holder decorated by Tot Steele, raised Rozane Ware Royal wafer and signed Steele on side, crazing and two small base chips, 3-5/8" x 4-3/4". **$80**

Mark Mussio, Humler & Nolan

Large Crystalis vase with two handles and orange crystalline glaze, marked with Rozane Ware wafer seal, restoration to rim chips, 11-1/8" h. **$400**

Mark Mussio, Humler & Nolan

Creamware smoking set consisting of lid crested by match holder and base with jar for tobacco fused to ashtray base, tobacco jar encircled by decal that shows an Indian smoking a pipe, unmarked, overall crazing, tight line at rim of jar, tight firing line to interior side, bruise at rim of lid, 7" h. **$300**

Mark Mussio, Humler & Nolan

Azurean pitcher decorated with flower and berry design, perhaps by Claude Leffler, impressed on bottom RPCo 937 F 1 and bearing artist monogram to right of handle, fine crazing, 3-1/2" h. **$300**

Mark Mussio, Humler & Nolan

Azurean humidor decorated with pipe and matches, impressed RPCo, F, 897 and 2, lid and base over-sprayed, tight line at rim, crazing, 5-1/4" h....... **$150**

Mark Mussio, Humler & Nolan

Egypto inkwell with lid, encircled with classical molded design and covered with fine mat green glaze, marked with raised Rozane Egypto wafer, excellent original condition, 3-3/4" h. **$500**

Mark Mussio, Humler & Nolan

Dealer advertising sign, 1930s Art Deco style, mat pink glaze, marked Roseville on front, excellent original condition, 2" x 6-1/4".......................**$700**

Mark Mussio, Humler & Nolan

Dealer sign bearing the name Roseville Pottery, gray green mat glaze with brown showing through in places, marked only on front of sign, chips to two corners, 4-1/4" x 9-1/4". **$800**

Mark Mussio, Humler & Nolan

Earlam sand jar, 1930s, foil label, 14-1/2" x 11-1/2". **$2,125**

Rago Arts and Auction Center

Imperial II vase in blues and yellows, shape 484-11, black paper label, excellent original condition, crystals in glaze, 11-1/4" h. **$650**

Mark Mussio, Humler & Nolan

Fudji vase, circa 1906, garnished with enameled yellow flowers front and rear on bisque ground, marked with green Fujiyama ink stamp, minor staining, 6" h. **$300**

Mark Mussio, Humler & Nolan

Fuchsia vase in green, shape 904-15", impressed Roseville 904-15, some restoration at the rim, 15-1/2" h. **$140**

Mark Mussio, Humler & Nolan

Futura "Sand Toy" bowl, shape 189-4-6", unmarked, tiny nick at base, 4-1/8" x 5". **$300**

Mark Mussio, Humler & Nolan

Early pitcher, each side decorated with two tulips, one pink and white, the other pink and yellow, attributed to L. Metzberger, a decorator and molder at Roseville, marked "LM" on bottom in slip, 7-3/8" h. **$325**

Mark Mussio, Humler & Nolan

Iris vase in blue, impressed Roseville 929-15", excellent original condition, 15-1/4" h. **$350**

Mark Mussio, Humler & Nolan

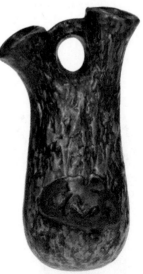

Imperial I wall pocket, shape 1222-9", unmarked, excellent original condition, 10-1/8" h. **$200**

Mark Mussio, Humler & Nolan

Matt Green covered bowl, cover acting as flower holder and covered with matt green glaze, unmarked, small chip to rim of bowl, which is covered when the top is in place, 3-5/8" x 7-1/4" w. **$110**

Mark Mussio, Humler & Nolan

Laurel vase, shape 674, mustard brown glaze, black highlights, marked with number 5 in black slip below base, excellent original condition, 9" h. **$400**

Mark Mussio, Humler & Nolan

Pine Cone bowl in blue, shape 632-3", lightly impressed with Roseville logo and shape number and marked D 8 in blue slip, fine original condition, 3". **$110**

Mark Mussio, Humler & Nolan

Rosecraft Panel Nude vase in brown, four panels each depicting a female nude in Art Nouveau style, unmarked, small chip to underside of rim, 10-1/2" h. **$500**

Mark Mussio, Humler & Nolan

Pauleo vase in red metallic luster glaze, marked with number 130 in black slip, excellent original condition, 14" h. **$500**

Mark Mussio, Humler & Nolan

Quaker humidor encircled by 2" wide red band with repeating pattern of two Quaker men in tricornered hats and white wigs, trimmed with black piping, unmarked, base has crazing, lid does not, 5-1/2" h. **$200**

Mark Mussio, Humler & Nolan

Mara vase in colorful iridescent glaze, marked with impressed number 13, excellent original condition with two minor scratches, 5-3/8" h. **$950**

Mark Mussio, Humler & Nolan

Poppy ewer, shape 880-18", mat pink, impressed with Roseville logo and shape number and marked with a B in blue slip, fine original condition, 18-1/4" h. **$325**

Mark Mussio, Humler & Nolan

Rozane Dark tyg decorated with leaves and berries, marked with Rozane raised wafer, overall crazing, fine original condition, 5-7/8" h. **$225**

Mark Mussio, Humler & Nolan

Royal Capri vase with gold finish, shape 578-7", marked with stylized R, U.S.A. and the shape number, excellent original condition, little or no wear, 7-3/8" h. Original advertising piece shows the vase is covered with "22 carat stippled gold." **$190**

Mark Mussio, Humler & Nolan

Rosecraft Panel Nude fan vase in green, each side depicting a different female nude posing with scarves in Art Nouveau tradition, marked with blue Rv inkstamp, excellent original condition, 8" h. **$500**

Mark Mussio, Humler & Nolan

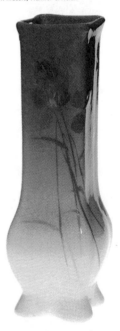

Rozane Woodland vase decorated with flowers in autumnal colors on bisque-like ground, unmarked, some staining, 13" h. **$750**

Mark Mussio, Humler & Nolan

Rozane Dark ewer covered with silver overlay, impressed on base Rozane 930 RPCo. 4 and marked JW in black slip, fine crazing, 4-5/8" h. **$200**

Mark Mussio, Humler & Nolan

Rozane Royal Light vase decorated with red clover, Rozane Royal wafer seal and impressed with numbers 36 and 4, heavy dark crazing to lower portion of base, 11" h. **$200**

Mark Mussio, Humler & Nolan

Two Woodland vases with tulips, circa 1905, both with Rozane Ware medallion, 9-1/4" h. and 13-1/4" h.**$1,250**

Rago Arts and Auction Center

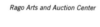

Rozane Royal Light vase with orchid, 1900s, Mae Timberlake, raised Rozane Ware, royal seal, artist's signature to body, 10-1/2" x 3".........**$625**

Rago Arts and Auction Center

Rozane Royal Light vase decorated by Lillie Mitchell, blackberry vines, marked with raised Rozane Ware wafer seal partially effaced, indicating a "second," impressed 7 L and signed by artist in slip on side, fine, light crazing and some minor roughness at base, 12-1/4" h. **$325**

Mark Mussio, Humler & Nolan

Blackberry vase, shape 576-8", unmarked, fine original condition, mold and color appear average, 8" h. **$325**

Mark Mussio, Humler & Nolan

Pillow vase with fluted rim and two handles, decorated by Fred Steele with a vignette depicting two English spaniels, impressed on base Rozane 88 RPCo 4 and signed "F Steele" by artist to lower left of picture, fine crazing, some restoration at rim evidenced by overspray, chip to foot ring not visible from side, 9" x 11-1/4". **$400**

Mark Mussio, Humler & Nolan

Rozane vase with portrait of goat, impressed Rozane RPCo on base, no artist mark visible, oversprayed and deteriorating, few glaze bubbles, crazing, 8-1/4" h... **$150**

Mark Mussio, Humler & Nolan

Rozane vase decorated by Arthur Williams with portrait of a man done in Old Masters style, impressed on base Rozane, 212 RPCo X, signed on side near base by artist, fine crazing, burst glaze bubble toward rear of vase, 13" h. **$650**

Mark Mussio, Humler & Nolan

Rozane Woodland vase with two enameled flowers on bisque-like ground, raised Rozane Woodland disc, excellent original condition, 8-7/8" h. **$400**

Mark Mussio, Humler & Nolan

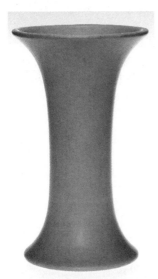

Rozane Dark vase decorated by Arthur Williams, portrait of Native American male in profile, unmarked, bearing a sticker from White Pillars Museum, overall crazing, restoration from middle of vase to base, 13-3/4" h....... **$800**

Mark Mussio, Humler & Nolan

Vase covered with organic mat green glaze, impressed with a "C" on bottom, 12" h............... **$170**

Mark Mussio, Humler & Nolan

Rare vase with iris design covered with black luster glaze, unmarked, oversprayed, pinhead-size glaze bubbles, light crazing, possibly part of Rozane line dating from first decade of 20th century, 14" h.. **$350**

Mark Mussio, Humler & Nolan

R.S. PRUSSIA

Ornately decorated china marked "R.S. Prussia" and "R.S. Germany" continues to grow in popularity. According to the Third Series of Mary Frank Gaston's *Encyclopedia of R.S. Prussia* (Collector Books, Paducah, Kentucky), these marks were used by the Reinhold Schlegelmilch porcelain factories located in Suhl in the Germanic regions known as "Prussia" prior to World War I, and in Tillowitz, Silesia, which became part of Poland after World War II. Other marks sought by collectors include "R.S. Suhl," "R.S." steeple or church marks, and "R.S. Poland."

The Suhl factory was founded by Reinhold Schlegelmilch in 1869 and closed in 1917. The Tillowitz factory was established in 1895 by Erhard Schlegelmilch, Reinhold's son. This china customarily bears the phrase "R.S. Germany" and "R.S. Tillowitz." The Tillowitz factory closed in 1945, but it was reopened for a few years under Polish administration.

Prices are high and collectors should beware of the forgeries that sometimes find their way onto the market. Mold names and numbers are taken from Mary Frank Gaston's books on R.S. Prussia.

The "Prussia" and "R.S. Suhl" marks have been reproduced, so buy with care. Later copies of these marks are well done, but quality of porcelain is inferior to the production in the 1890-1920 era.

Collectors are also interested in the porcelain products made by the Erdmann Schlegelmilch factory. This factory was founded by three brothers in Suhl in 1861. They named the factory in honor of their father, Erdmann Schlegelmilch. A variety of marks incorporating the "E.S." initials were used. The factory closed circa 1935. The Erdmann Schlegelmilch factory was an earlier and entirely separate business from the Reinhold Schlegelmilch factory. The two were not related to each other.

Floral-decorated tankard pitcher, mold 82 transfer-printed with poppies on both sides, red and green wreath-and-star mark, professional restoration to one foot, late 19th/early 20th century, 14" h. overall...........................**$288**

Jeffrey S. Evans & Associates

Floral-decorated tankard pitcher, "Carnation" mold 526 transfer-printed with roses on both sides, red and green wreath-and-star mark, late 19th/early 20th century, undamaged except for light chip under base, 11" h. overall. **$345**

Jeffrey S. Evans & Associates

Floral-decorated tankard pitcher, "Iris Variation" mold 514 transfer-printed with floral bouquet, late 19th/early 20th century, unmarked, undamaged, 10" h. overall. **$184**

Jeffrey S. Evans & Associates

"Ostriches" serving bowl, scalloped-rim mold 182, transfer-printed with two ostriches in a landscape, red and green wreath-and-star mark, late 19th/early 20th century, 9-3/8" dia. **$920**

Jeffrey S. Evans & Associates

Winter season serving bowl, eight-lobe form with scalloped and molded rim, center transfer-printed with woman in snowy landscape, pearlized finish with shadow star transfers, unmarked, late 19th/early 20th century, 10-1/2" dia. **$575**

Jeffrey S. Evans & Associates

Scenic cake plate, "Icicle" mold 7 transfer-printed with Man in Mountain, sailboat and castle on cliff, red and green wreath-and-star mark, late 19th/early 20th century, 10-1/4" dia. **$375**

Jeffrey S. Evans & Associates

Floral-decorated chocolate set, nine pieces, pot with four cups and saucers, mold 82 transfer-printed with roses, red and green wreath-and-star marks, late 19th/early 20th century, pot 8-1/2" h. overall.........**$374**

Jeffrey S. Evans & Associates

Nine-piece demitasse set, floral decoration, pot 9-1/2" h., cups 2" h.....................................**$295**

Turkey Creek Auctions, Inc.

"Melon Boys" plate with decorative gold trim, 8-3/4", and ball-footed urn with Grecian women in a garden setting, closed ring handles, 4-3/8"; red back stamp logo on bottom of both pieces, wear to areas on each. **$80**

Mark Mussio, Humler & Nolan

Floral-decorated beverage items, 14, chocolate pot with five cups and saucers, three-piece tea set, pot lacking cover, all mold 501 with matching transfer-printed roses and bronze/gilt shoulder band, satin finish, unmarked, late 19th/early 20th century, pot 9-1/2" h. overall...**$518**

Jeffrey S. Evans & Associates

SATURDAY EVENING GIRLS

Saturday Evening Girls (Paul Revere) pottery was established in Boston, Massachusetts, in 1906, by a group of philanthropists seeking to establish better conditions for underprivileged young girls of the area. Edith Brown served as supervisor of the small "Saturday Evening Girls Club" pottery operation, which was moved in 1912 to a house close to the Old North Church where Paul Revere's signal lanterns had been placed. The wares were mostly hand decorated in mineral colors, and both sgraffito and molded decorations were employed. Although it became popular, it was never a profitable operation and always depended on financial contributions to operate. After the death of Edith Brown in 1932, the pottery foundered and finally closed in 1942.

S.E.G.

Fannie Levine, Sara Galner, 1914, chamberstick with Greek key pattern and faceted paperweight with swan, both signed and dated, 2" x 6", 2-1/2" sq..**$1,188**

Rago Arts and Auction Center

Flaring bowl painted with tulips in cuerda seca, circa 1925, Paul Revere Pottery medallion/ PRP/?MD/11-2-?, 3" x 7-1/2". **$1,000**

Rago Arts and Auction Center

Albina Mangini plate and pitcher with running rabbits, "Caroline"s Plate," 1913, signed AM/ SEG/10/13/December 25, 1913, 4-1/4" x 4-1/2", plate 7-3/4" dia. **$2,125**

Rago Arts and Auction Center

Vase painted with lotus in cuerda seca, circa 1925, Paul Revere Pottery medallion, 6-1/2" x 3-1/2"...........................**$2,125**

Rago Arts and Auction Center

Cream pitcher depicting white rabbit on either side and the name Joan Audrey Carlson in a band beneath, marked with Paul Revere Pottery circular paper label, excellent original condition, 4-1/4" h. **$375**

Mark Mussio, Humler & Nolan

SPATTERWARE

Spatterware takes its name from the "spattered" decoration, in various colors, used to trim pieces hand painted with rustic center designs of flowers, birds, houses, etc. Popular in the early 19th century, most was imported from England.

Related wares, called "stick spatter," had freehand designs applied with pieces of cut sponge attached to sticks, hence the name. Examples date from the 19th and early 20th century and were produced in England, Europe, and America.

Some early spatter-decorated wares were marked by the manufacturers, but not many. Twentieth century reproductions are also sometimes marked, including those produced by Boleslaw Cybis.

Rainbow spatterware coffeepot in blue and red, repairs to lid and tip of spout, 9" h. **$300**

Dan Morphy Auctions

Bowl, 19th century, original blue and yellow tulip decoration, extremely rare, no imperfections or paint loss, 13-1/2" dia. **$330**

Dan Morphy Auctions

Rare cup and saucer, 19th century, double brown acorn decoration, original red spatterware decoration, both pieces with no loss or repairs, largest 6" dia......... **$960**

Dan Morphy Auctions

Pair of red spatterware peafowl plates with large peafowls surrounded by strong red spatter decoration, larger plate 9-1/2" dia. **$360**

Dan Morphy Auctions

Plate, 19th century, Thistle pattern, strong yellow border, numerous repairs to rim, 8-1/4" dia. **$420**

Dan Morphy Auctions

Red spatterware with peafowl decoration, two small cups and saucer, American, 19th century, saucer 4-1/2" dia., larger cup 3-3/4" h... **$180**

Cowan's Auctions, Inc.

Large milk pitcher, 19th century, fort or castle pattern, strong blue decoration, 8-1/2" h. **$270**

Dan Morphy Auctions

Group of spatterware: yellow spatterware sugar bowl with thistle pattern (missing cover), rainbow milk pitcher, blue and purple glazed octagonal plate, American, 19th century, plate 10" x 7-1/4", sugar bowl 5-1/2" h. **$480**

Cowan's Auctions, Inc.

Large water pitcher, 19th century, strong blue spatter, original red, orange, and green peafowl decoration, colors on peafowl are unusual, pitcher has no imperfections, 10" h.......... **$570**

Dan Morphy Auctions

Rainbow spatterware octagon platter, 19th century, green and red, no imperfections or loss, 14" x 17-3/4". **$900**

Dan Morphy Auctions

SPONGEWARE

Spongeware: The name says it all. A sponge dipped in colored pigment is daubed onto a piece of earthenware pottery of a contrasting color, creating an overall mottled, "sponged" pattern. A clear glaze is applied, and the piece fired. The final product, with its seemingly random, somewhat smudged coloration, conveys an overall impression of handmade folk art.

Most spongeware, however, was factory-made from the mid-1800s well into the 1930s. Any folk art appeal was secondary, the result of design simplicity intended to facilitate maximum production at minimum cost. Although mass-manufacturing produced most spongeware, it did in fact originate in the work of independent potters. Glasgow, Scotland, circa 1835, is recognized as the birthplace of spongeware. The goal: the production of utilitarian everyday pottery with appeal to the budget-conscious. Sponged surface decorations were a means of adding visual interest both easily and inexpensively.

Since early spongeware was quickly made, usually by amateur artisans, the base pottery was often insubstantial and the sponging perfunctory. However, due to its general usefulness, and especially because of its low cost, spongeware quickly found an audience. Production spread across Great Britain and Europe, finally reaching the United States. Eventually, quality improved, as even frugal buyers demanded more for their money.

The terms "spongeware" and "spatterware" are often used interchangeably. Spatterware took its name from the initial means of application: A pipe was used to blow colored pigment onto a piece of pottery, creating a spattered coloration. Since the process was tedious, sponging soon became the preferred means of color application, although the "spatterware" designation remained in use. Specific patterns were achieved by means of sponge printing (aka "stick spatter"): A small piece of sponge was cut in the pattern shape desired, attached to a stick, then dipped in color. The stick served as a more precise means of application, giving the decorator more control, creating designs with greater border definition. Applied colors varied, with blue (on white) proving most popular. Other colors included red, black, green, pink, yellow, brown, tan, and purple.

Because of the overlap in style, there really is no "right or wrong" in classifying a particular object as "spongeware" or "spatterware"; often the manufacturer's advertising designation is the one used. Spatterware, however, has become more closely identified with pottery in which

Butter crock, covered, dark blue sponging around oval reserved printed "BUTTER," 6" dia., 5" h. .... $80-$150

Butter crock, no cover, blue sponging, printed on front in black, "Butter," 6" dia., 5" h. $115

the mottled color pattern (whether spattered or sponged) surrounds a central image, either stamped or painted free-hand. Spongeware usually has no central image; the entire visual consists of the applied "splotching." Any break in that pattern comes in the form of contrasting bands, either in a solid color matching the mottling, or in a portion of the base earthenware kept free of applied color. Some spongeware pieces also carry stampings indicating the name of an advertiser, or the use intent of a specific object ("Butter," "Coffee," "1 Qt.").

Vegetable dish, shallow rectangular shape with rounded corners, overall dark blue sponging, wear, minor clay separation at rim, 9-3/4" l...........**$120**

Much of what is classified as spatterware has a certain delicacy of purpose: tea sets, cups and saucers, sugar bowls, and the like. Spongeware is more down-to-earth, both in intended usage and sturdiness. Among the many examples of no-nonsense spongeware: crocks, washbowl and pitcher sets, jugs, jars, canisters, soap dishes, shaving mugs, spittoons, umbrella stands, washboards, and even chamber pots. These are pottery pieces that mean business; their shapes, stylings, and simple decoration are devoid of fussiness.

Spongeware was usually a secondary operation for the many companies that produced it, and was marketed as bargain-priced service ware; it's seldom marked. Today, spongeware is an ideal collectible for those whose taste in 19th century pottery veers away from the overly detailed and ornate. Spongeware's major appeal is due in large part to the minimalism it represents.

Pitcher, embossed Pine Cone pattern, cylindrical with D-form handle, heavy overall dark blue sponging, Burley-Winter Pottery Co., 9-1/2" h...............**$800**

Pitcher, slightly tapering cylindrical body with rim spout and C-form applied handle, overall dark blue sponging, a few tight hairlines, 8-3/4" h.......**$175**

Canister, covered, footed cylindrical shape with domed cover with knob finial, dark blue large sponging around zigzag oval reserved printed in fancy script, "Coffee," 6" h................. **$1,000**

Canister, open, advertising-type, heavy dark blue sponging around reserve printed in dark blue fancy lettering, "Old Honesty Coffee," 6" h............................. **$1,000**

Umbrella stand, cylindrical, decorated with narrow blue sponged bands around rim and base, each flanked by two wide blue bands, two wide blue sponged bands around middle flanked by two dark blue bands, 21" h............................. **$2,000**

Pitcher, slender ovoid body with pinched rim spout and pointed arched handle, overall dark blue patterned sponging, 8-1/4" h.
.... **$250**

Pitcher, Hallboy-type, blue sponged bands around rim and base, wide dark blue body band flanked by pinstripe bands, angular handle, 6" h........... **$250**

Water filter, wide cylindrical body with stepped domed cover, heavy dark blue sponging with two thin bands near top, rectangular white panel printed "No. 7," large shield-form mark on lower front reading "Improved Natural Stone Germ Proof Filter – Fulper Pottery Co., Flemington, N.J. Est. 1895," crack at rim and chip on cover, 12-1/2" h. **$230**

Batter pitcher, no cover, dark blue sponging, printed on front "1 Qt." **$625**

Batter pitcher, no cover, dark blue sponging, printed on front "1 1/2 Qt." **$625**

CERAMICS

SUMIDA GAWA POTTERY

Sumida Gawa wares were made in Japan for Western export from the late 19th century through 1941. The pottery pieces, the popular forms of which include teapots, bowls, vases, jugs and tankards, are often heavy, brightly glazed and covered with figures in relief. Inscribed in kanji, more than 70 different marks are known, but not all pieces are marked. Pieces marked "Nippon" date to 1890-1921; pieces marked "Foreign" were made for export to England.

Elephant-form candleholder with child reading book, early 20th century, illegible mark, 7-1/8" x 7-1/4" x 4-1/2"................. **$875**

Rago Arts and Auction Center

Bulbous vase with bird on flowering vine in relief on deep red glossy ground, early 20th century, unidentified mark, 11-1/4".. **$250**

Rago Arts and Auction Center

Covered house-shaped tea box with female figure at top on black ground, early 20th century, unidentified, mark 6".......... **$250**

Rago Arts and Auction Center

Pitcher with two figures on rock formations in mountain landscape, circa 1900, mark of Ryosai, 12-3/8".............................. **$250**

Rago Arts and Auction Center

Urn-shaped vase with applied decorations of Japanese ceramics on black ground, circa 1900, Ryosai mark, 18-1/4". **$3,000**

Rago Arts and Auction Center

Figure of Girogin, god of longevity, with scroll in hand, circa 1900, unmarked, 9"....................**$313**

Rago Arts and Auction Center

Jardiniere with figures pulling cart along path on orange ground, circa 1900, mark of Ryosai, 9" x 12".....**$375**

Rago Arts and Auction Center

Vase with bamboo stem and crane, early 20th century, Hara mark, 7-1/2"...............................**$375**

Rago Arts and Auction Center

Pair of vases with woman and child in relief on brown and red ground, early 20th century, illegibly marked, 8-1/4"...**$438**

Rago Arts and Auction Center

Diorama bowl with seven figures on ledge in relief on brown ground, early 20th century, unsigned, 5-1/4"..**$600-$800**

Rago Arts and Auction Center

CERAMICS

Urn-form vase with pot of flowers with mother-of-pearl petals surrounded by porcelain vases on black ground, early 20th century, mark of Ryosai, 12"............ **$406**

Rago Arts and Auction Center

Cylindrical form vase with figures and vines in relief on orange ground, circa 1900-1910, mark of Ryosai, 13-7/8".................. **$313**

Rago Arts and Auction Center

Lidded vessel with handles and pouring spout with figures and thatched hut in relief on red ground, circa 1900, Ryosai mark, 18"................................... **$750**

Rago Arts and Auction Center

Three pots with figures in relief on red ground, early 20th century, chocolate pot with figural head, teapot with figures in relief and covered pot with pouring spout, all marked, tallest 9". **$1,125**

Rago Arts and Auction Center

Gourd vase with figures and creatures in celebratory poses on matte dark red ground, circa 1900, unidentified mark, 9" x 12"........................... **$1,625**

Rago Arts and Auction Center

VAN BRIGGLE POTTERY

The Van Briggle Pottery was established by Artus Van Briggle, who formerly worked for Rookwood Pottery, in Colorado Springs, Colorado at the turn of the 20th century. He died in 1904, but the pottery was carried on by his widow and others. From 1900 until 1920, the pieces were dated. It remains in production today, specializing in art pottery.

Rare copper-clad vessel with chameleon handles, 1907, signed AA/11/15/Van Briggle/Colo. Springs/702.S.W., 5" x 8"... **$2,250**

Rago Arts and Auction Center

Humidor encircled by red tulips against green ground with red accents at top and lined in red, 1902, marked with Van Briggle logo, name, 1902 date, Roman numeral III for clay type and number 90, probably a process number; small glaze nick to tip of one leaf, open glaze bubble, 6-1/4" h. **$3,700**

Mark Mussio, Humler & Nolan

Early vase with tulips, chartreuse and indigo glaze, 1903, signed AA/VAN BRIGGLE/1903/141/III, 8" x 3" **$5,625**

Rago Arts and Auction Center

Vase with dark mat black-green glaze, 1916, marked in blue slip with Van Briggle logo and 1916 date, glaze skip at rim and base, 6-3/4" h. **$150**

Mark Mussio, Humler & Nolan

Early bulbous vase with poppy pods, mauve glaze, 1905, incised AA/VAN BRIGGLE/1905/V/21, 3-3/4" x 4" **$625**

Rago Arts and Auction Center

Vase with trefoil, green glaze, 1907, marked AA VAN BRIGGLE COLO. SPGS. 1907, 60?, 8-3/4" x 7-1/2". **$1,750**

Rago Arts and Auction Center

Butterfly vase with two embossed swallowtails in rose over green mat glaze, AA and Van Briggle name visible, restoration to small rim chip, 3-3/4" h. **$200**

Mark Mussio, Humler & Nolan

Early vessel with flowers and buds, lilac and green glaze, 1905, incised AA VAN BRIGGLE/354/ VY/1905, 4-1/2" x 7". **$625**

Rago Arts and Auction Center

Large squat vessel with arrowroot leaves, matte green glaze, 1906, signed AA/VAN BRIGGLE/3/1906/439, 5-1/2" x 11-1/2". **$3,125**

Rago Arts and Auction Center

Early vase with daffodils, matte green glaze, 1903, signed AA/VAN BRIGGLE/1903, 8-1/4" x 3". **$1,875**

Rago Arts and Auction Center

Vase with poppy pods, thick matte green glaze, 1906, marked AA VAN BRIGGLE/illegible numbers/1906/X, 3-1/2" x 5-1/2". **$813**

Rago Arts and Auction Center

Mug with embossed image of attacking eagle in light green mat glaze, 1905, incised marks include AA, company name, number 3 in circle, and date, impressed is shape number 355 B, excellent original condition, 4-3/4" h. **$325**

Mark Mussio, Humler & Nolan

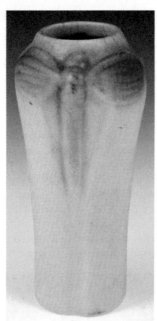

Art Nouveau pottery vase, dragonfly, Kathryn Hall, circa 1910, 7-1/4" h. x 3-1/4" dia..........**$275**

Kaminski Auctions

Early vase with stylized flowers, matte purple and green glazes, 1903, signed AA/1903/III/219, 6-1/2" x 4"......................**$2,125**

Rago Arts and Auction Center

Small vessel with anemone, light green and blue glaze, 1906, incised AA VAN BRIGGLE/323/1906/4, 3-1/2" x 4-3/4".................................**$500**

Rago Arts and Auction Center

Bowl with arrowroot design, mulberry mat glaze, 1920, marked on bottom with Van Briggle logo, name "Van Briggle" and "20" for date, excellent original condition, 4-7/8" x 9-1/2".....................**$275**

Mark Mussio, Humler & Nolan

Two-handled vase with peacock feathers, sheer mottled indigo glaze on brown ground, 1906, signed AA/VAN BRIGGLE/COLO SPRINGS/1906, 6-1/2" x 3-1/4"..............................**$1,500**

Rago Arts and Auction Center

Lorelei vase, Art Nouveau woman grasping top of vase, her hair flowing forward and long gown flowing around side of vase, green shading to blue glaze, signed on underside with Van Briggle logo, "Van Briggle Colo Spgs" and artist initials "HVM," very good to excellent condition, 11" h.....**$403**

James D. Julia, Inc.

CERAMICS

WEDGWOOD

The name "Wedgwood" has, over the years, become nearly synonymous with "Jasperware," a specific pottery line produced by this British firm. But **WEDGWOOD**

while Jasperware may be Wedgwood's most enduring contribution to the world of pottery, it is by no means the only one.

Wedgwood was founded in 1759 by Josiah Wedgwood in Burslem, England. The earliest Wedgwood efforts were focused on utilitarian earthenware. Ornamental pottery made its debut in 1770, with the opening of new production facilities in Etruria. Jasperware became the company's first artware success.

Wedgwood's Jasperware has been so often imitated that a brief description immediately conjures up its basics: solid-color, unglazed stoneware, the decoration consisting of white, bas-relief "classic" figures encircling the object. The most common Jasperware color is blue, although other shades have included black, white, yellow, green, and even lilac. Most pieces are single-color, but some of the most striking examples of Jasperware use three or more alternating colors.

Once established, the Jasperware format remained quite consistent. The reason was simple: It filled a niche for the sort of elegant yet relatively inexpensive décor pieces that buyers craved. The Jasperware

Fairyland lustre geisha bowl, octagonal, decorated on exterior with Geisha or Angels pattern, interior decorated with running figures, signed with Portland vase mark "MADE IN ENGLAND Z-4968," very good to excellent condition. .... **$5,000-$7,000**

James D. Julia, Inc.

Fairyland lustre plate with center decoration of Thumbelina floating on a leaf, holding a stick with an insect on top, finished with Twyford border, signed on underside with Portland vase mark "WEDGWOOD MADE IN ENGLAND," no "Z" number, very good to excellent condition, 10-1/2" dia..................... **$7,188**

James D. Julia, Inc.

Chase dish in lilac jasperware, 10-1/2" h. x 10"dia............ **$175**

Kaminski Auctions

Fairyland lustre Nizami plate decorated with center medallion depicting Persian gentleman cutting down a tree, center medallion and gilded trim set against a moonlight blue background with mother of pearl lustre, signed on underside with Portland vase mark "WEDGWOOD MADE IN ENGLAND Z-5494," very good to excellent condition, 3-3/4" dia........ **$1,553**

James D. Julia, Inc.

Three Jasperware pieces including two pitchers with England only markings, 20th century, undamaged, large pitcher with firing separation at base of tree below spout, 3" to 8-3/4" h.......... **$184**

Jeffrey S. Evans & Associates

Fairyland lustre plate decorated with Roc Centre variation of Imps on a Bridge, scene depicts maroon imps walking across arched bridge with Roc bird flying above and other imps looking on, finished with blue and white floral rim, signed on underside with Portland vase mark "WEDGWOOD MADE IN ENGLAND," very good to excellent condition, 10-1/2" dia. **$5,750**

James D. Julia, Inc.

Fairyland lustre plaque decorated with Picnic By a River design showing orange and green elves against lavender background with green river, green Roc bird and flame lustre sky, signed on reverse with gold Portland vase mark, "Wedgwood Made in England," black lacquered frame, very good to excellent condition, plaque 4-1/2" x 10", 7" x 12-3/4" overall. .... **$5,000-$7,000**

James D. Julia, Inc.

Fairyland lustre chalice bowl decorated on exterior with Twyford Garlands pattern against flame background, interior decorated with variation of Fairy Gondola against flame background, signed on underside with Portland vase mark "WEDGWOOD MADE IN ENGLAND Z-5360," very good to excellent condition with minor scratches to interior bottom of bowl, 10-3/4" dia. **$10,350**

James D. Julia, Inc.

Fairyland lustre melba center bowl decorated on exterior with Garden of Paradise pattern against pink sky, interior decorated with Jumping Fawn pattern, signed on underside with Portland vase mark "MADE IN ENGLAND Z-4968," very good to excellent condition, 8" dia. .... **$5,000-$8,000**

James D. Julia, Inc.

Fairyland lustre vase decorated with Pillar pattern against creamy background, signed on underside with Portland vase mark "WEDGWOOD MADE IN ENGLAND Z-4968," very good to excellent condition, 14" h.......................**$10,925**

James D. Julia, Inc.

Fairyland lustre vase decorated with panels of Pillar design on shape 3451, finished with floral decoration around inside lip, signed on underside with Portland vase mark "MADE IN ENGLAND Z-4968," very good to excellent condition, 11-3/4" h. **$12,650**

James D. Julia, Inc.

Pitcher with image of Thomas Carlyle, 19th century, 8" x 7-1/2". **$150**

Kaminski Auctions

Bowl, Dragon Lustre, low flaring round foot below deep flaring bell-form bowl, exterior in mottled blue and green with enameled gold dragons and red highlights, interior bottom with Oriental medallion in blue, green, red, and gold, Portland vase mark on bottom, 9" dia., 5-1/2" h. **$210**

Teapot, covered, footed squatty bulbous body in creamy white with short angled spout, upright squared handle and tapering domed cover with knob finial, applied light blue grapevine band around shoulder and cover, marked "Wedgwood Embossed Queens Ware of Etruria & Barlaston," Josiah Wedgwood & Sons, England, circa 1940, 8-3/4" l., 5" h..........**$70**

CERAMICS

appeal is particularly understandable during the Victorian era, as adventurers unearthed the wonders of ancient Greece and Rome. Jasperware's images of toga-clad warriors and water-bearing maidens effectively romanticized a theme occupying the public interest, presenting civilizations of the past at their most civilized.

Bowl, Butterfly Lustre, footed octagonal form, exterior in pale blue lustre with large blue and gold butterflies, interior in deep gold lustre, 6-1/2" w. **$463**

As noted, Jasperware was just one of the Wedgwood successes. Among the others:

• **Creamware.** Of a lighter weight than traditional china, this Wedgwood line proved less expensive both to produce and transport. Creamware was so acclaimed that Queen Charlotte of England eventually permitted it to be marketed as "Queen's Ware."

• **Moonlight Lustre.** Produced from 1805-1815, the "moonlight" decorative effect was achieved by varied colors, (pink, gray, brown, and sometimes yellow), intermingled and "splashed" across the ware.

• **Varied lustrewares.** In the early 20th century, Wedgwood produced an in-demand line of pottery in assorted lustre finishes, their names and multicolored hues once again stressing the romantic: Butterfly, Dragon, and Fairyland. Within each series, designs held true to the theme: Fairyland, for example, featured such pattern images as Woodland Elves, Fairy in a Cage, and Toad and Dwarf. The overall, dreamlike effect was often enhanced by the use of mottled colors and hypnotically repeating borders. Decades later, similarities to the Fairyland decorative technique could be found in the psychedelic stylings of the 1960s.

During its long history, Wedgwood also experimented, to alternating effect, with other processes and treatments. These included fine porcelain, bone china, stone china, majolica, and Pearlware.

Fortunately for collectors, most Wedgwood pieces carry the marking "Wedgwood." In 1891, the additional identifier "England" was added (later pieces are marked "Made In England"). A limited line of artware, produced from 1769 to 1780, carries the marking "Wedgwood & Bentley"; during that time Josiah Wedgwood was in partnership with Thomas Bentley.

Pottery marked "Wedgwood & Co." and "Wedgewood" (note the additional "e") was the work of competitors, hoping to capitalize on Josiah Wedgwood's fame. They have no relation to the Wedgwood firm; the only advantage of owning one of these pieces would be for its curiosity value.

Wedgwood has certainly set the record for endurance: Jasperware has remained in continuous production since first being introduced in the 1700s. Collectors remain drawn to this line, thanks to its eye-catching juxtaposition of vivid base colors with the stark-white relief images. And, while many are first exposed to the Wedgwood legacy through Jasperware, a significant number delight in exploring the many other directions in pottery the company has taken during its 250-year history.

Fairyland lustre bowl decorated on exterior with Fairy with Large Hat pattern with dark blue water and flame sky, interior decorated with Woodland Bridge pattern in a variation with no elves present, signed on underside with Portland vase mark "WEDGWOOD MADE IN ENGLAND Z-5360," very good to excellent condition, 6-1/2" dia. **$5,750**

Fairyland lustre octagonal bowl decorated on exterior with gold castles against light blue sky, interior decorated with gnomes, toadstools and fairies, signed on underside with Portland vase mark "WEDGWOOD ENGLAND Z-5125," very good to excellent condition with minor wear to gilding in bottom of bowl, 4-3/4" dia. **$2,875**

James D. Julia, Inc.

Fairyland lustre plate decorated with Firbolgs IV pattern showing purple Firbolgs in various stages of falling out of a tree, finished with border rim of blue and white flowers and gilded leaves against black border, signed on underside with Portland vase mark "WEDGWOOD MADE IN ENGLAND W-557," very good to excellent condition, 10-1/2" dia. **$5,750**

James D. Julia, Inc.

CERAMICS

WELLER

Weller Pottery was made from 1872-1945 at a pottery established originally by Samuel A. Weller at Fultonham, Ohio and moved in 1882 to Zanesville, Ohio.

Mr. Weller's famous pottery slugged it out with several other important Zanesville potteries for decades. Cross-town rivals such as Roseville, Owens, La Moro, and McCoy were all serious fish in a fairly small and well-stocked lake. While Mr. Weller occasionally landed some solid body punches with many of his better art lines, the prevailing thought was that his later production ware just wasn't up to snuff.

Samuel Weller was a notorious copier and, it is said, a bit of a scallywag. He paid designers such as William Long to bring their famous discoveries to Zanesville. He then attempted to steal their secrets, and, when successful, renamed them and made them his own.

After World War I, when the cost of materials became less expensive than the cost of labor, many companies, including the famous Rookwood Pottery, increased their output of less expensive production ware. Weller Pottery followed along in the trend of production ware by introducing scores of interesting and unique lines, the likes of which have never been created anywhere else, before or since.

In addition to a number of noteworthy production lines, Weller continued in the creation of hand-painted ware long after Roseville abandoned them. Some of the more interesting Hudson pieces, for example, are post-World War I pieces. Even later lines, such as Bonito, were hand painted and often signed by important artists such as Hester Pillsbury. The closer you look at Weller's output after 1920, the more obvious the fact that it was the only Zanesville company still producing both quality art ware and quality production ware.

For more information on Weller pottery, see *Warman's Weller Pottery Identification and Price Guide* by Denise Rago and David Rago.

Eocean tankard displaying trio of red peonies in full bloom on long arched stems, impressed 580 below base, 12" h. **$200**

Mark Mussio, Humler & Nolan

Chase vase depicting white horse, rider and three hounds with a tree to side, in thickly applied white slip on dark blue ground, Weller Pottery incised mark and a W, excellent original condition, 11-3/4" h.......**$150**

Mark Mussio, Humler & Nolan

First Line Dickensware oil lamp decorated by Laura Cline with leaves and berries, impressed 385 on bottom and initialed by artist on side amid leaves, excellent original condition, original Bradley and Hubbard copper oil font, 5-1/4" x 8-1/2". A letter, dated 1975, from early dealers Gladys and Foster Hall, authors of *Halls' Pricing Formulas*, identifies this as a rare piece of Roseville Blue Ware......................**$425**

Mark Mussio, Humler & Nolan

Tall Aurelian vase decorated by Frank Ferrell, grape decor, incised Aurelian Weller K and impressed 518 10 on base and signed "Ferrell" in slip on side near base, exterior oversprayed, which indicates restoration of some sort, 20" h. ...**$325**

Mark Mussio, Humler & Nolan

Flemish vase with magnolia decoration encircling vase, unmarked, excellent original condition, 14" h.............**$275**

Mark Mussio, Humler & Nolan

Eocean iris vase of cylindrical form with flaring neck, marked Weller / Eocean / 305 on bottom, 12-3/4" h. .**$330**

Cowan's Auctions, Inc.

Dickensware "Chinaman" humidor, underside of lid incised "Dickens Weller," bottom bears a sticker identifying piece as being from White Pillars Museum, deteriorating restoration to top, small chip to inner rim of base, 6-1/4" h. **$120**

Mark Mussio, Humler & Nolan

Dickensware "The Irishman" humidor, incised "Dickens Weller," several chips to edge of top, label affixed to bottom and certificate within that indicates this came from White Pillars Museum, 6-1/2" h..................**$150**

Mark Mussio, Humler & Nolan

Glendale vase with small bird seated in tree looking over nest containing four eggs, bears name McLaughlin in raised letters on back near base, restoration at rim, 10-1/8" h. **$275**

Mark Mussio, Humler & Nolan

Dedonatis vase encircled with Italianesque freehand floral design by Frank Dedonatis, impressed with "Weller Script" mark and marked "255 BPU," artist's monogram in blue slip, very fine crazing, excellent original condition, 8-3/4" h. **$375**

Mark Mussio, Humler & Nolan

Three art pottery vases, including two pieces of Baldin, one signed, first half 20th century, undamaged except for minute flake to one leaf of largest example, 6" to 7-1/4" h. **$287**

Jeffrey S. Evans & Associates

Second line Dickensware jug, front with vignette of Dombey and son seated at a table with crystal flacon and glass on top, on rear of flat vessel is name "Dombey and Son" in white slip, base incised 504 Dickens Weller, excellent original condition, 7-1/4" h. **$300**

Mark Mussio, Humler & Nolan

Dickensware "The Turk" humidor, incised "Dickens Weller," a few minor nicks to top and base, 7-1/2" h. **$200**

Mark Mussio, Humler & Nolan

Hudson white and decorated vase with flower and berry decoration, impressed Weller in block letters with label from White Pillars Museum, overall fine crazing, 10-5/8" h. Warranty card from White Pillars Museum accompanies vase................ **$190**

Mark Mussio, Humler & Nolan

Aurelian jug decorated with cherries, incised Aurelian Weller on base, roughness at spout, broad crazing, 6" h. **$80**

Mark Mussio, Humler & Nolan

Tutone vase with four loop handles in signature maroon mat with green accents color scheme, unmarked, excellent original condition, 12-7/8" h. **$190**

Mark Mussio, Humler & Nolan

Three Hobart art pottery pieces, turquoise glaze, putti with grapes flower frog, girl with duck flower frog, and kneeling nude female two-part flower frog/bowl, first two marked, circa 1925, boy undamaged, girl marked second with glaze pops to head, nude with restoration to nose, each with some normal crazing, 4-1/4" to 7" h...**$126**

Jeffrey S. Evans & Associates

Two art pottery articles, comprising Knifewood vase with canaries and small Woodrose jardinière, each marked under base, first half 20th century, undamaged, 5" h. **$230**

Jeffrey S. Evans & Associates

Two Hobart/Lavonia art pottery pieces, lilac to turquoise glaze, semi-nude female two-compartment vase and wall pocket, latter with ink-stamp mark, circa 1925, vase undamaged with light crazing around base, pocket with minor flake to side rim and moderate crazing, 10-1/2" and 8-1/2" h...........**$184**

Jeffrey S. Evans & Associates

Tall LaSa vase with pine tree decoration, some painted, some incised, allowing white clay body to show through, incised Weller LaSa near base, some wear, mostly at base, 13-3/8" h......**$200**

Mark Mussio, Humler & Nolan

Louwelsa vase with long stem flowers in green glaze, shape number 555, marked Louwelsa/ Weller/555 on underside, 8-1/2" h. **$360**

Cowan's Auctions, Inc.

LaSa vase showing trees by side of river, signed Weller LaSa near base, wear at rim and near base, several small scratches, 11-1/4" h................**$325**

Mark Mussio, Humler & Nolan

Ragenda vase, suggestive of draped fabric, early 1930s, dark maroon mat glaze, unmarked, in excellent original condition, 9-3/4" h. **$200**

Mark Mussio, Humler & Nolan

Lorbeek flower frog in lavender glaze, marked with Weller Ware full kiln ink stamp, excellent original condition, 5-1/4" h. **$140**

Mark Mussio, Humler & Nolan

Rhead Faience vase of Geisha wearing formal garment kneeling beneath a canopy of trees, squeeze bag and hand painting techniques, monogram "VMH," unidentified artist appears on side, hand incised "Rhead, X, 504" beneath, crazed, a few surface scratches, otherwise excellent condition, 6-7/8" h. **$400**

Mark Mussio, Humler & Nolan

Kenova vase with relief decoration of flowering branch, flowers hand colored, impressed with 8 on bottom, excellent original condition, 8-3/4" h. **$350**

Mark Mussio, Humler & Nolan

Small pop-eyed dog figure, impressed with Weller script mark, fine crazing, excellent original condition, 4-1/8" h. **$250**

Mark Mussio, Humler & Nolan

Rosemont vase with lilac tinted cockatoo swinging on hoop front and back, connected by bows and rose bouquets set against ebony backdrop, Weller in block letters is impressed beneath, 8-1/2" h. **$300**

Mark Mussio, Humler & Nolan

Matt glaze 6-1/4 inch humidor encircled with molded band of animals, unmarked, some chips to lid. **$80**

Mark Mussio, Humler & Nolan

Unusual Hunter whiskey jug with two fish and lots of hand incising in design, incised "Hunter" on bottom along with paper label that reads "From White Pillars Museum," professional restoration to handle and spout, 5-5/8" h. **$180**

Mark Mussio, Humler & Nolan

Matt ware squat vase decorated with white daisies against mat green ground, unmarked, crazing, excellent overall condition, 3-1/4" x 5-3/8." **$130**

Mark Mussio, Humler & Nolan

Muskota bowl with trio of white geese clustered at one end, marked with Weller Pottery ink stamp, crazing and chip to end of one reed, 6-5/8" x 10" h..... **$250**

Mark Mussio, Humler & Nolan

Rosemont planter, each side picturing a bluebird and branches with pink flowers, impressed Weller in block letters, excellent original condition, 6-5/8" h. **$200**

Mark Mussio, Humler & Nolan

Pottery vase made for 1904 World's Fair in St. Louis, two slip decorated Jerusalem flowers and word Jerusalem, also in slip, no other markings , 2-1/2" h.... **$225**

Mark Mussio, Humler & Nolan

Sicard vase covered with flower and leaf design, signed Sicard Weller on side and incised 94 on base, tight line on side, 8-7/8" h. **$350**

Mark Mussio, Humler & Nolan

Miniature Sicard pear-shape vase encompassed with leaves of dandelion, signed "Weller Sicard" on side, glaze nick at rim, minor surface scratches, 3-1/8" h. **$325**

Mark Mussio, Humler & Nolan

Brighton kingfisher flower frog, bright colors, impressed Weller in block letters, excellent original condition, 9" h......**$300**

Mark Mussio, Humler & Nolan

Brighton butterfly, blue and white with accents in pink, green and black, unmarked, fine overall crazing, 2-1/4" x 3" h.........**$140**

Mark Mussio, Humler & Nolan

Chalkware

Chalkware figures are made of sculpted gypsum or cast from plaster molds and painted with watercolors. Portraying everything from whimsical animals to historical characters, chalkware was made from the late 18th century through the beginning of the 20th century, and again during the Great Depression. Early chalkware was often hollow and can be difficult to find unblemished.

Pair of comic figures, Happy Hooligan and Gloomy Gus, early 20th century, created by celebrated cartoonist Frederick Burr Opper in 1900, detailed and painted with lifelike appearance, overall very good plus condition, both have repairs to neck, approximately 10-1/2" h. each. Happy Hooligan and Gloomy Gus were popular in newspapers and portrayed in toys. Happy Hooligan was a street person or hobo. His brother, Gloomy Gus, traveled with his brother and never wore a happy expression. **$177**

James D. Julia, Inc.

Victorian bust of Eastern woman with intaglio cut eyes and elaborate headpiece with coin necklaces and draping garment, all on a round plinth, overall very good condition with scattered paint chips and some touch-up, 26-1/2" h. x 17" w. **$575**

James D. Julia, Inc.

1940s Mazzolini Cleveland Indians Chief Wahoo statue made by Mazzolini Artcraft Co. for Cleveland Indians, great coloring, few paint chips on back of base, marked on back, copyright C.B.C. on front of base, 8-1/4" h. x 6" w. at base. **$425**

Fusco Auctions

Hiawatha Indian bust, 20" h...**$150**

Blanchards Auction Service

Cat head toothpick holder, late 19th century, minor roughness to ears, minor surface dirt, 1" scratch to back side, 3" h **$125**

Pook & Pook, Inc.

Marwal by Brower, 1965 Oriental bust, small chip to back of head, 11-1/2" h. x 7-1/2" w............**$30**

Fusco Auctions

Painted squirrel mantel figure and small bandbox, American, 19th century, molded squirrel figure highlighted with red, brown and yellow paint, small round bandbox with green, pink, and black varnished foliate designs on white ground, squirrel 6-1/2" h., box 3-1/4" h., 4-1/2" dia. **$246**

Skinner, Inc., www.skinnerinc.com

Pair of Pennsylvania stags, 19th century, 10-1/4" h. x 9-3/4" w. **$356**

Pook & Pook, Inc.

St. Roche statue, paint chips through-out, 17-1/2" h. x 5-1/2" dia.......**$100**

Great Expectations Auction Co., LLC

American balloon bank, circa 1876, rare survivor of Centennial era with vivid coloration, minor surface cracking, 7" h. **$500**

Heritage Auctions

Early reindeer, 11" h. x 9" w...**$110**

Hartzell's Auction Gallery, Inc.

Early pug, 6" h. x 7" w........ **$120**

Hartzell's Auction Gallery, Inc.

Popeye carnival figure with tattoo on right forearm, hole for pipe, appears to have restoration around neck, and 1926 "Genuine Pop Eye Bif Bat" with red and blue paint, 16" h................................ **$80**

Saco River Auction

Art Deco bust of young woman, 1920s, chip at base, 20-1/4" h. x 7-1/2" w. x 8-1/2" d. **$225**

Austin Auction Gallery

Circus Collectibles

The 200th anniversary of Phineas Taylor Barnum's birth in 2010 triggered a renewed interest in collecting circus memorabilia. Collectibles range from broadsides announcing the circus is coming to town, to banners with brightly embellished visages of freakish sideshow acts, to windup tin toys depicting the lions, tigers, elephants and clowns that no circus or sideshow would be complete without.

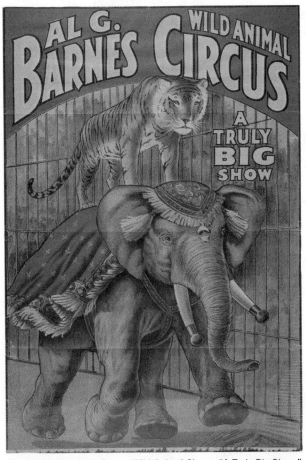

Circus poster for Al G. Barnes Wild Animal Circus, "A Truly Big Show," tiger atop elephant, some horizontal creases, small 2" separation at top and bottom, originally had a paper attached that probably gave address of circus, approximately 38-3/4" h. x 26" w.............. **$460**

James D. Julia, Inc.

Ringling Brothers "The Field of the Cloth of Gold" litho, colorful four-paneled elongated poster dated 1905, printed by Strombridge Litho Co., each panel depicting scenes with hundreds of participants, some horizontal creases, edges reinforced with tape, 1906 written on front of poster, 33-1/3" h. x 11-3/4" w.............**$350-$650**

James D. Julia, Inc.

Clockwork George Brown circus cage wagon, American, tin, latter part of 19th century, recently discovered in Rhode Island. When clockwork mechanism is activated, the toy will roll while lion enclosed within cage appears to pace to and fro. One of the finest known original examples to exist today. Painted in red, blue, black, apricot and white with japanned highlights, overall excellent condition, minimal inpainting to white crossbar on hitch and small areas where crossbar is attached/soldered to horses, minimal repair to a couple of solder joints, two vertical bars on rear of cage door replaced, cage wagon appears to be completely original other than two replaced slats, 13-1/2" l. overall. ... **$76,700**

James D. Julia, Inc.

Pair of German clowns, papier maché socket heads with molded and painted features on papier maché bodies, jointed at wrists, shoulders and hips, both wearing original factory costumes depicting clowns and faces painted on sun, etc., one has blue felt slippers and the other wears oilcloth shoes, both very good condition, slight surface dust, one doll needs hand restrung and is probably missing red yarn pompom on top of head, 15" each...**$862**

James D. Julia, Inc.

Carved wood carnival or carousel plaque depicting stylized face of mustachioed man in gold with intaglio cut eyes and mouth agape, edges of his face sweep into fleur de lis, surrounded by demilune framework border of same, overall very good condition, likely with at least one layer of overpaint or touch-up due to its exposure to elements, some splits to seam, missing a few slivers of wood, 35" w. x 25-1/2" h. **$977**

James D. Julia, Inc.

Early carved wooden head, appears to be a carnival element with grotesque face wrought with emotion, fitted with display stand of more recent vintage, fair to good condition with several layers of paint traces, a few wood chips, 9-1/2" h. **$575**

James D. Julia, Inc.

"Spidora" original, weathered canvas circus sideshow banner, circa 1940s-1950s, captioned "Spidora – Alive," spider with woman's face, heavy leather reinforced corners with steel rings for tie-downs, stenciled "Snap Wyatt, Tampa, Fla.," two canvas tears that appear to be intentional to allow for wind to go through, overall 9' 8" x 7' 8" h. Born David C. Wyatt in Asheville, North Carolina, Snap Wyatt began painting canvas backdrops after studying at Cooper Union in New York City from 1930-1934. His body of work is regarded today to be among the most collectible and sought-after circus art. **$633**

James D. Julia, Inc.

Large grouping of Schoenhut circus animals, people and accessories, eight clowns (two reduced), bisque-headed female acrobat, four clowns (early mask-faced versions), seven animals consisting of glass-eyed white horse and painted-eye brown horse, donkey, elephant, three reduced pieces, five chairs, two barrels, large pedestal, and pair of ladders, poor to very good condition, acrobat has small flake to bisque at stringing hole on top of head, sizes vary..**$805**

James D. Julia, Inc.

Civil War Collectibles

The Civil War began on April 12, 1861, at Fort Sumter, the Confederates surrendered at Appomattox Courthouse on April 9, 1865, and all official fighting ceased on May 26, 1865.

Between the beginning and end of the Civil War, the way wars were fought and the tools soldiers used changed irrevocably. When troops first formed battle lines to face each other near Bull Run Creek in Virginia on June 21, 1861, they were dressed in a widely disparate assemblage of uniforms. They carried state-issued, federally supplied, or brought-from-home weapons, some of which dated back to the Revolutionary War, and marched to the orders and rhythms of tactics that had served land forces for at least the previous 100 years. Four short years later, the generals and soldiers had made major leaps in the art of warfare on the North American continent, having developed the repeating rifle, the movement of siege artillery by rail, the extensive employment of trenches and field fortifications, the use of ironclad ships for naval combat, the widespread use of portable telegraph units on the battlefield, the draft, the organized use of African-American troops in combat, and even the levying of an income tax to finance the war.

For some Civil War enthusiasts, collecting war relics is the best way to understand the heritage and role of thousands who served. Collecting mementos and artifacts from the Civil War is not a new hobby. Even before the war ended, people were gathering remembrances. As with any period of warfare, the first collectors were the participants themselves. Soldiers sent home scraps of flags, collected minie-ball shattered logs, purchased privately marketed unit insignias, or obtained a musket or carbine for their own use after the war. Civilians wrote to prominent officers asking for autographs, exchanged photographs ("carte de visites") with soldiers, or kept scrapbooks of items that represented the progress of the conflict.

Post-Civil War carbon print of Gen. Robert E. Lee atop his war horse, Traveller, circa 1880s, marked with Miley & Son, Lexington, VA, includes penciled inscription with, among other information: "This picture of Gen. Robt. E. Lee was given to Miss Mattie P. Harris by Robt. E. Lee, grandson of Gen. Robert E. Lee," 16-1/4" x 19" photo and 25" x 30" with mount...............**$3,500**

Cowan's Auctions

After the war, the passion for owning a piece of it did not subside. Early collectors gathered representative weapons, collected battlefield-found relics, and created personal or public memorials to the veterans. Simultaneously, surplus sales emerged on a grand scale. This was the heyday of Civil War collecting. Dealers such as Francis Bannerman made hundreds of Civil War relics available to the general public.

Following World War II, a new wave of collecting emerged. Reveling in the victories in Japan and in Europe, Americans were charged with a renewed sense of patriotism and heritage. At the same time, newspapers started to track the passing of the last few veterans of the Civil War. As the nation paid tribute to the few survivors of the Rebellion, it also acknowledged that the 100-year anniversary of the war was fast upon them. In an effort to capture a sense of the heritage, Civil War buffs began collecting in earnest.

During the Civil War Centennial in the 1960s, thousands of outstanding relics emerged from closets, attics, and long-forgotten chests, while collectors eagerly bought and sold firearms, swords, and uniforms. It was during this time that metal detectors first played a large role in Civil War collecting, as hundreds donned headphones and swept battlefields and campsites, uncovering thousands of spent bullets, buttons, belt plates, and artillery projectiles.

By the 1970s, as this first wave of prominent and easily recognized collectibles disappeared into collections, Civil War buffs discovered carte-de-visites, tintypes, and ambrotypes. Accoutrements reached prices that far outstretched what surplus dealers could have only hoped for just a few years prior. The demand for soldiers' letters and diaries prompted people to open boxes and drawers to rediscover long-forgotten manuscript records of battles and campaigns.

By the end of the 20th century, collectors who had once provided good homes for the objects began to disperse their collections, and Civil War relics reemerged on the market. It is this era of Civil War relic reemergence in which we currently live. The fabulous collections assembled in the late 1940s and early 1950s are reappearing.

It has become commonplace to have major sales of Civil War artifacts by a few major auction houses, in addition to the private trading, local auctions and Internet sales of these items. These auction houses handle the majority of significant Civil War items coming to the marketplace.

The majority of these valuable items are in repositories of museums,

Political presidential campaign chart, circa 1860, hand-colored illustrated broadside with map of United States surrounded by portraits and platforms of Republican and Democratic candidates and vignettes of 15 previous presidents, framed, 39" x 30-1/2"..**$600-$800**

Leslie Hindman Auctioneers

universities, and colleges, but many items were also traded between private citizens. Items that are being released by museums and from private collections make up the base of items currently being traded and sold to collectors of Civil War material culture. In addition, many family collections that were compiled over the years have been recently coming to the marketplace as new generations have decided to liquidate some of them.

Civil War items are now acquired by collectors in the same fashion as any material cultural item. Individuals interested in antiques and collectibles find items at farm auction sales, yard sales, estate sales, specialized auctions, private collectors trading or selling items, and the Internet and online auction sales.

Provenance is important in Civil War collectibles – maybe even more important than with most other collectibles. Also, many Civil War items have well-documented provenance as they come from family collections or their authenticity has been previously documented by auction houses, museums or other experts in the field.

For more information on Civil War memorabilia, see *Warman's Civil War Collectibles Identification and Price Guide*, 3rd edition, by Russell L. Lewis.

Civil War soldier inscribed Colt model 1851 Navy percussion-operated single action with 6-shot cylinder, blued steel, brass on upper and lower tangs, smooth wood grip panels, brass tang at back of grip inscribed "T.H. BISCOE 5th LA. VOL." and "FOREVER ASHLEY" inscribed on brass butt of grip, Texas battle scene etched onto cylinder..........**$3,250**

Cordier Auctions

◄ Smith & Wesson No. 2 Army Revolver, circa 1865, features nearly 98% strong original blue and caseharded finish, barrel and cylinder markings are crisp; popular personal hand-gun during Civil War and among famous military and western figures of the day including James Butler "Wild Bill" Hickok, who was said to be carrying one when he was killed in Dead-wood, Dakota Territory in 1874.
....................**$5,500-$8,500**

Rock Island Auctions

Group of U.S. Civil War Union artifacts, including Union army bayonet with scabbard, U.S. belt buckle, leather belt and pouch; bayonet in good shape, overall 19", scabbard 18", belt buckle complete with all three tabs on back, 2-1/4" x 3", leather pouch well worn, 1-1/2" x 3" x 3-1/2". ....**$300-$600**

Nest Egg Auctions

Civil War soldier's footlocker identified on front as Lieutenant R.W. Hinman Company A 23rd Artillery division, 27" x 14" x 14"......................**$200-$300**

Saco River Auction

John Quincy Adams autographed letter, circa 1837, on congressional stationery, to Elijah Hayward thanking him for his support and explaining his objection to slavery, letter has old folds and a round spot impression, likely from the original sealing wax, 7-3/4" w. x 10" h. folded. **$70,000**

Skinner, Inc., www.skinnerinc.com

U.S. Civil War 35-star flag, white stars machine sewn in configuration of irregularly shaped five-pointed star, faded blue field, red and white panels separately sewn, some wear and mothing, white border has rope and loop ends, lower right corner is tattered and shows some tar stains, 82" w. x 138" l............**$675**

Mohawk Arms

Colt 3rd Model Dragoon percussion revolver, all metal generally smooth and gray, grass straps excellent with soft light patina, grip excellent condition, with notarized affidavit from a direct descendent that pistol was once owned by Lt. Col. Thomas J. Jackson of 42nd Indiana and 11th U.S. Colored Infantry, with period inked inscription on reverse listing the battles he participated in...$13,145

Heritage Auctions

Spencer Army Model repeating rifle, circa 1864, original Civil War configuration, does not have Stabler magazine cut-off retrofitted to many Spencer rifles and carbines after the Civil War. This model of firearm was first issued to Federal cavalry and mounted infantry units in 1863; it was an immediate success and paved the way for the subsequent adoption of the Spencer Model 1860 carbine as the standard weapon for the Federal cavalry regiments by the end of the Civil War..............$20,000-$30,000

Rock Island Auctions

Carved staghorn cane of Civil War soldier wearing a kepi hat sitting on a stone and rubbing his feet, circa 1860, thin horn separator on coconut wood shaft, carved staghorn is 3" x 3/4" at its widest, overall length 36-1/4"............**$600-$800**

Tradewinds Antiques

Artillery priming or gunner's powder horn, 19th century, brass and hardwood threaded stopper, leather carry strap attached to horn with swivel at base and eyelet at tip, 16" l., with stopper 18-1/2" l. **$375**

Cordier Antiques & Fine Art

Civil War era fighting knife, Bowie-style blade with wood handle held in place with two rivet-style nails, significant wear on blade and crack on grip, blade 11-3/4" l., knife 18-3/8" l. overall.............................. **$300**

Cordier Auctions

Civil War mortar and pestle, iron, used to mix and grind medications into powder while on the battlefield, 12-1/4" h. **$125**

Kaminski Auctions

Ulysses S. Grant liberty cap ferrotype badge (Grant ferrotypes are plentiful, but examples from 1872 are scarce), gilt brass shell badge with ferrotype portrait of Grant, includes inscription 1776 with laurel wreath and fasces, border surrounding ferrotype reads "1861 1872 Liberty Loyalty" meant to appeal to the loyalty of men who fought for the North in the Civil War. **$896**

Heritage Auctions

Harper's Pictorial History of the Civil War, two volumes, McDonnell Bros., Chicago, circa 1866, stamped brown cloth covers with gilt text, extensive illustrations in both volumes, 16-1/4" x 11-1/2". **$250**

Corider Auctions

Civil War trunk marked Lieut. Coln over 10th Regt. W.V., volunteer regiment was organized in 1862 and mustered out 1865, metal clasp and brackets on trunk are solid, 36" w. x 22-3/8" x 19-3/4". **$800**

Cordier Auctions

U.S. 4-1/2" 12-pounder canister, standard canister used extensively during Civil War by Federal batteries, fired from 12-pounder smoothbore 4.62" caliber gun, minor chip on wood sabot, minor dent on tin cylinder, rare projectile.... **$4,481**

Heritage Auctions

Regulation Civil War Navy Officer's jacket and belt with a rollover collar, lined with black silk serge, sleeves feature typical Civil War era flared elbows and narrow cuffs and are lined in white cotton with thin red striping, includes two rows of nine Navy officer buttons on each side, accompanied by naval officer's sword belt, circa 1864................................. **$4,500-$7,500**

Universal Live

Collection of Confederate materials, including two veteran's tunic buttons and similar cuff button; modern Texas state tunic button; reproduction Confederate Navy tunic button; dug waist belt buckle with a note identifying it as having come from Fredericksburg, Virginia; and a Southern Cross of Honor. . **$203**

Heritage Auctions

Civil War oak water barrel used in conjunction with medical transports/treatment, brass on spiget, connects wooden handle to barrel, 14" x 21" x 10" dia. **$350**

Great Gatsby's Antiques and Auctions

U.S. Model 1841 "Mississippi" percussion rifle with buff sling, unfired and in excellent condition, original .54 caliber round ball configuration when issued, brass buttplate, patch box, trigger guard, side plate and barrel bands, lock plate roll stamped "N.Haven/1850." The Model 1841, considered to be the best designed and most handsome of all U.S. percussion longarms, gained fame during the Mexican War and went on to be a critical firearm used by the Union and Confederate armies during the Civil War. **$22,500**

Rock Island Auctions

Two Warren & Steele Albany saw handle percussion guns, both with fixed sights with empty dovetail slot behind front sight, fish hammer with floral engraving, stock with pewter forend cap, German silver band at butt, one owned by Union Army surgeon and the other by famed New York gunmaker Nelson Lewis. .... **$2,500-$4,500**

Rock Island Auctions

12mm single-action pinfire revolver, circa 1854, very rare, bore in excellent condition with strong and shiny rifling, chambers in excellent condition, strong action, silver engraving on barrel believed to be the name of the man who manufactured the gun, Manuel Ma Sanchez Oviedo. **$300**

Cuevas Auctions LLC

Civil War era traveling utensils, rosewood handled knife and fork sets, one set stamped "W.H. Wrags Patentee," one unmarked, and one "Emigrant Knife W.H. Wrags Patentee," set includes knife, spoon and two-tine fork combination, partially legible maker's stamp "xxx Knife Union," plus three ivory-handled folding forks, unmarked, ivory shows cracks. **$418**

Heritage Auctions

TOP LOT!

Carte-de-visite of a federal soldier with a young servant boy, likely Western theater with knee high boots, black slouch hat on his lap, smoking a clap pipe, wearing a nine-button frock coat; seated at his side, with his head leaning against soldier's shoulder, is a black youth with forage cap with rain cover, visor turned up, four-button blouse with sleeves rolled up, light-colored trousers, one foot visible wearing what appears to be standard Jefferson bootee; no backmark, pristine condition. **$3,346**

Heritage Auctions

Bible found in pocket of Pvt. Edwin C. Hall of 10th Vermont Volunteer Infantry, where it was struck by a Confederate minie ball at the battle of Sailor's Creek on April 6, 1865; 3" x 4" bible stopped the bullet, which remains imbedded in it, preventing the soldier's death. Bible is accompanied by Aug. 13, 1897 edition of the *Boston Weekly* newspaper in which it was wrapped, along with a letter from Hall to a gentleman, written April 1, 1898, explaining the story of the bible saving his life, and his request that it be placed in a museum. **$15,535**

Heritage Auctions

Brady Album gallery portrait of officers of U.S.S. Monitor, casual pose in front of turret of Monitor, including Commodore Worden seated at center, rare, image 3" x 4-1/2", mount 3-11/16 x 5-7/8". **$2,031**

Heritage Auctions

Regulation-style company grade drum, maple body, red painted hoops and brass tack decoration with incised five-pointed star surrounding air hole, rope heads and tighteners all appear to be original and in near perfect condition, 15" h. x 16" dia., owned by Klineyoung, a musician in Company D of the 30th Infantry Regiment (1st Regiment Reserves), serving from June 8, 1861 until June 13, 1864, having seen action at Mechanicsville, Antietam, Fredericksburg and Gettysburg. **$5,676**

Heritage Auctions

Civil War wooden Army canteen with leather patch of period used to cover plug hole, obverse includes museum paper tag that reads, "Cedar Canteen/Confederate/Found on Chickamauga/Battlefield," wood is dry from age and staves are loosening, 7-1/2" x 2-1/2". **$2,629**

Heritage Auctions

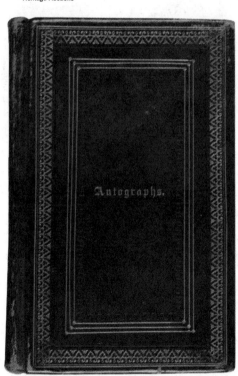

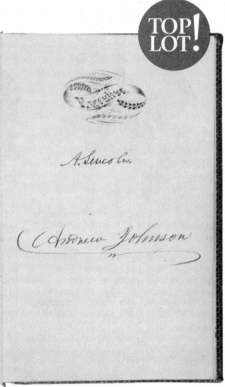

TOP LOT!

Civil War leather-bound autograph album with collection of signatures collected by Charles A. Munger, enlisted soldier with 117th Regiment N.Y. Volunteers; approximately 185 names in all, including President Abraham Lincoln, signed "A. Lincoln," and Vice President Andrew Johnson; other signatures include Ulysses S. Grant, William T. Sherman, Henry W. Halleck, among many other military figures, members of Lincoln's cabinet, Supreme Court justices, U.S. senators and representatives, ambassadors, plus abolitionists and social reformers, as well as George Armstrong Custer, which represents one of few examples where Lincoln and Custer signed the same album. **$17,925**

Heritage Auctions

Officer's cartridge box, sling and baldric, used primarily by elite militia units prior to and during Civil War, alternating bands of red and gold bullion mark 2-1/8" w. baldric/sling with large gilt brass buckle, loop and sling tip, baldric includes die-struck lion's head with three brass chains suspended at month, attached to brass shield featuring spread-wing eagle with clouds and sun rays, box bound with gilded brass with 3-1/8" spread-wing eagle affixed to front flap. **$2,868**

Heritage Auctions

New York Zouave officer's kepi; one of the Civil War's most colorful items of headgear were the caps worn by various zouave units; scarlet body sewn to tall blue band with three wide strips of gold lace on front, back and sides, front rises 4" from visor, two State of N.Y. "Excelsior" buttons affixed to blue band, infantry bugle sewn to front with metallic numeral 5 in bend. **$6,572**

Heritage Auctions

U.S. Model 1859 McClellan Civil War saddle and bridle ensemble with rawhide-covered tree, ornate original hooded stirrups, carbine boot, saddlebags and U.S. Model 1859 cavalry bit with re-leathered headstall, saddle bears its original die-struck brass oval maker's label reading: P. Ambler & S./3/ Bridgeport, Conn., located on left pommel, grass shield-shaped escutcheon on pommel marked 11 1/2" / Seat. **$3,107**

Heritage Auctions

Confederate militia uniform worn by Capt. Peyton N. Hale F "Grayson Dare Devils" 4th Virginia Inf., heavy double-breasted butternut wool tailcoat with extra gray wool liner inside, trousers with brass rivet-type buttons used for suspenders and fly and painted composition buttons to close the pockets, butternut gray wool kepi stands just over 4-1/2" tall at front, thick and rather large with elaborate stamped brass adjusting buckle, all in very good to excellent condition, with some worn areas. **$23,900**

Heritage Auctions

U.S. medical staff officer's sword, circa 1840, regulation form, etched for three-fourths of its length with acorns and oak leaves with "United States Medical Staff" central panel on obverse with maker name "Horstman & Son Philadelphia" and American eagle on reverse, brass on grip, oak leaf and eagle, sword carried by all medical officers during the Civil War, 27-3/4" double edge blade, elliptical in cross section, 5/8" wide at ricasso. **$2,629**

Heritage Auctions

Civil War veteran reserve corps jacket, "of sky-blue kersey, with dark-blue trimmings, cut like the jacket of the U.S. Cavalry," mint condition, retaining all 12 original small general service buttons down the front, two at collar and one at each shoulder strap, each sleeve marked with two "size dots," one bears the inspector's stamp "J2" and the other "2/SA" indicating it was contracted for the Schuylkill Arsenal in Philadelphia.......**$5,377**

Heritage Auctions

Set of material belonging to Lt. John Edward Rastall, Wisconsin abolitionist and military figure who became a 1st Lt. and Adjutant of the 1st Maryland Eastern Shore Infantry. Group includes Rastall's regulation single-breasted wool frock coat with embroidered label "Rockhill & Wilson/Army & Navy Clothing/603 & 605 Chestnut St./Philadelphia"; beaver hat with 3" wide brim and crown that rises 5-1/2" with 3" sweatband; doeskin leather gauntlets with flared cuffs and red morocco leather lining; high boots on which are still affixed a pair of regulation and complete brass cavalry spurs; regulation sword belt with high-relief M. 1851 officers' sword belt plate; with the set is a recently framed, 19th century copy of a photo of a group of 14 Union officers; a letter of provenance from the consignor accompanies the set. **$16,730**

Heritage Auctions

Civil War leather artillery gunner's pouch, marked Watertown Arsenal 1865 on the inner flap covering main compartment, leather strap closure and brass finial, 6" x 8"......**$300**

Cordier Auctions

Civil War naval officer's service dress frock coat, circa 1864, deep blue/black wool body, rolling collar, black silk serge lining, two rows of nine original naval buttons on front, two strips of Navy gold lace at each cuff, original shoulder straps for assistant paymaster affixed to coat, oak spring embroidered on black background. **$4,481**

Heritage Auctions

Clocks

The measurement and recording of time has been a vital part of human civilization for thousands of years, and the clock, an instrument that measures and shows time, is one of the oldest human inventions.

Mechanical, weight-driven clocks were first developed and came into use in the Middle Ages. Since the 16th century, Western societies have become more concerned with keeping accurate time and developing timekeeping devices that were available to a wider public. By the mid-1600s, spring-driven clocks were keeping much more accurate time using minute and seconds hands. The clock became a common object in most households in the early 19th century.

Clocks are a prime example of form following function. In its earliest incarnations, the functionality of a timepiece was of paramount importance. Was it telling the time? More importantly, was it telling the correct time? Once those basic questions had been answered, designers could experiment with form. With the introduction of electronics in the 20th century, almost all traditional clockwork parts were eliminated, allowing clocks to become much more compact and stylistically adaptable.

In lavish Art Deco styles of the 1920s and '30s, clocks featured the same attention to exterior detail as a painting or sculpture. Fashioned of materials ranging from exotic woods to marble, bronze, and even wedges of Bakelite, Art Deco clocks were so lovely that it was actually an unexpected bonus if they kept perfect time. The Parisian firm, Leon Hatot, for instance, offered a clear glass stunner with hands and numerals of silver.

For the budget-conscious, particularly during the 1930s Depression years, inexpensive novelty clocks found favor. Prominent among these were molded-wood clocks by Syroco (Syracuse Ornamental Co.). Offering the look of hand-carving at a fraction of the cost, Syroco clocks featured an interior mechanism by Lux.

Also popular: affordable clocks ideally suited for a specific room in the home, such as the Seth Thomas line of kitchen-ready "Red Apple" clocks. Other companies specialized in attractively priced clocks with added whimsy. Haddon's "Ship Ahoy" clock lamp had a sailboat rocking on its painted waves, while MasterCrafters ceramic clocks replicated a pendulum effect with moving figures, such as children on swings or old folks in rocking chairs.

English triple fusee eight-bell bracket clock, pierced painted black hands, silvered 7" chapter ring with black Roman hour numerals and Arabic five-minute markers, pierced gilt brass floral spandrel, eight silvered bells, chains, brass pendulum and rod, coiled quarter hour cathedral gong, ebonized frame, 29" x 16" x 10-1/2"..............................**$5,310**

Fontaine's Auction Gallery

Another best-seller, still in production today, is the "Kit-Cat Clock" with pendulum tail and hypnotic moving eyes.

And possessing an irresistible kitschy charm: "souvenir" clocks from locales as diverse as New York and Las Vegas. What better way to travel back in time than with a "Statue of Liberty Clock" (complete with glowing torch) or a sparkly Vegas version with casino dice marking the hours?

After the production restraints of World War II, postwar clock designers found inspiration in fresh shapes and materials. Among the most unusual: "clock lamps" by San Francisco's Moss Manufacturing. These Plexiglas eye-poppers exhibit a mastery of multi-purposing. They tell time. They light up. They hold flowers. Many even include a rotating platform: Flick the switch, and a ceramic figurine (often by a prominent design name, such as deLee, Hedi Schoop, or Lefton) begins to twirl.

Equally modern yet less over-the-top were fused glass clocks by Higgins Glass Studio of Chicago. Although artisans such as Georges Briard also designed glass clocks, those by Michael and Frances Higgins are among the mid-century's most innovative. Clocks were a natural outgrowth for these pioneers of practical design, whose decorative housewares ran the gamut from cigarette boxes to candleholders.

According to Michael Higgins, "We try to make things which may be thought beautiful. But we are not ashamed if our pieces are useful. It makes them easier to sell."

A 1954 Higgins clock for GE, featuring ball-tipped rays radiating outward on the glass face, is as unexpectedly glorious as an alien sun. A later line of glass-on-glass clocks was created for Haddon during the Higgins' stay at Dearborn Glass Co. The hours are indicated by colorful glass chunks fused to a vibrantly patterned glass slab. While from the mid-century, a Higgins clock is not of the mid-century. Simplicity and clarity of line, coupled with a bold use of color, make Higgins clocks right at home in any age.

There's no time like the present to explore the limitless treasure trove of mid-20th century clocks. Which will be your favorite? Only time will tell.

Chelsea tambour clock, 5-1/2" silvered dial with original blued hands, signed Tiffany & Co. New York, brass spring-driven ship's bell movement strikes hour on coiled gong and once on half hour, bronze tambour style case with deep green-brown patina, 12" h. x 23" w. x 7" d. **$767**

Fontaine's Auction Gallery

French walnut grandfather clock, Herter Bros. and Tiffany & Co. Makers, circa 1869, 12" bronze dial, swirling brass hands, brass weight-driven movement, rack and snail strike mechanism on five coiled gongs, progressive Westminster chime, French walnut case with scrolling broken arch crest with larger sphere and flame-turned finial at top of reeded pilaster with hanging garland and drapery, four turned finials at corners, shell carved spandrels with ribbons around beveled dial, original finish, 98" h. x 24-1/2" w. x 12-1/2" d. **$38,350**

German table model cuckoo clock, fancy pierced carved hands, triple spring-driven movement, count wheel strike mechanisms, double cuckoo mechanism with three whistles and bellows in good working condition, petite sonnerie strike with two coiled gongs, strikes quarter hour and hour, birds chirp simultaneously with each gong strike, carved walnut case with architectural roof, carved corbels, turned half columns and applied rosettes, 21-1/2" h. x 16" w. x 8-1/2" d. **$1,534**

Fontaine's Auction Gallery

TOP! LOT!

French industrial steam engine clock, large central cylinder and piston with vertical connecting rod that powers flywheel, cylinder with two large fireboxes on either side mounted with boilers, barometer over right firebox and thermometer behind cylinder, gilt, silvered, and patinated three-tone bronze finish on rouge marble base, 18" x 14-1/2" x 7-1/2"............**$30,680**

Fontaine's Auction Gallery

E. Howard & Co. No. 60 wall regulator clock, silvered dial with black incised Roman hour numerals, Arabic five-minute markers outside, original pierced diamond hands, walnut bezel, signed E. Howard & Co., Boston, Mass., four steel jar mercurial pendulum with long steel rod, carved walnut case, no breaks or repairs, 80" h. x 27" w. x 13" d. **$59,000**

Fontaine's Auction Gallery

Birge & Fuller mahogany double steeple shelf clock, circa 1850, spring-driven movement, painted metal dial and tablets, 26" h. **$1,126**

Pook and Pook, Inc.

Tiffany Studios Spanish bronze desk clock, circa 1910, gold tone face and black enamel numbers and notches, 2-3/4" h., 1,273 g. **$1,500**

Elite Decorative Arts

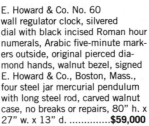

Chelsea No. 1 pendulum clock, 12" dial, eight-day time-only brass movement, wood pendulum stick, brass bob, lead weight and lock down hardware, cherry case with original finish, 34" h.......... **$826**

Fontaine's Auction Gallery

Bradley & Hubbard blinking eye clock, figural painted cast iron case with paper dial with black Roman hour numerals and fancy black hands, 30-hour brass, spring-driven, lever attached to escapement rocks eyes open and closed, 16" h. **$1,180**

Fontaine's Auction Gallery

English gothic carved fusee tavern wall clock, 12" painted metal dial, spade hour hand and pointer minute hand, brass pendulum bob and stick, exterior of gothic carved oak wallhanging case in dark finish with gold undertones, spire-shaped crest and base with filigree carvings, heavy beveled door glass, 38" h. x 21" w. x 6-1/2" d. . **$560**

Fontaine Auction Gallery

Black Forest cuckoo clock, heavily carved case with figural bird on crest, large oak leaves and branches on front with carved birds on side, bird's nest below 6" dial with applied Roman numerals and fancy hands, pierced brass movement with lyre-shaped cutout, 30" h. x 22" w. x 9" d. **$649**

Fontaine's Auction Gallery

Elmer Stennes pillar and scroll clock, circa 1814, painted metal dial with 10" chapter ring with black Arabic hour numbers, gilt beaded minute markers, floral spandrels and pierced black hands, brass spring-driven movement with rack and snail strike mechanism, strikes on single strait chime, brass pendulum, mahogany pillar and scroll case with maple inlay in crest, 30" h. x 17-1/4" w. x 4" d. **$472**

Fontaine's Auction Gallery

Alpha Hart Splat & Column mantle clock, floral painted spandrels, gilt wreath center and open hands, wooden works movement with count wheel strike mechanism, iron bell, brass-covered pendulum bob and conical iron weights, mahogany case with ebony crest with gilt stenciled fruit basket and original reverse-painted scenic tablet with building, 27" h. x 15-1/2" w. x 6" w. **$708**

Fontaine's Auction Gallery

Lucius B. Bradley mantle clock in carved mahogany case, label of Charles Platt (clock case maker) No. 66 Beekman St. New York, 1810 date in pencil, brass works, dial with raised gilt bead spandrels, paint loss on VIII, tabernacle glass cracked, clock key and case key present, 28-3/4" h. x 18" w. x 6-1/4" d...... **$5,000**

Kaminski Auctions

CLOCKS

Early 19th century Kentucky grandfather clock, inlays with moon face dial. **$11,115**

Kaminski Auctions

Three-piece musical gothic gargoyle figural clock, large winged demonic figure seated on top of base drum on stand holding mallet in one hand raised overhead and cymbal strapped to other, drum mounted on stand formed from branches tied together, and winged griffin side mounts; candlestick side pieces have matching figures leaning on lampposts with candleholder top; timepiece contained within base drum, half-hour strike on steel bell, primary piece 19" x 15" x 8". **$4,130**

Fontaine's Auction Gallery

Walter Durfee nine-tube mahogany grandfather clock, large brass dial with silvered 12" chapter ring with applied gilt brass Arabic hour numbers, scrolling gilt engraved center and spandrels, silvered sub seconds dial, sub dials for Chime-Silent & Westminster-Whitington, nautical moon phase dial, quarter-hour strike, signed Walter H. Durfee, Providence, RI on top of back plate, mahogany case with broken arched crest with applied brass rosettes and spun brass finials, spiral-turned columns, beveled glass door glass, claw feet, 103" x 23" x 15".......... **$23,600**

Fontaine's Auction Gallery

Pennsylvania walnut miniature tall case clock, early 19th century, made by Hy (Henry) Bower, F. (Feste) Swome... **$31,625**

Stephenson's Auctioneers

E. Howard & Co. Astronomical Regulator No. 46, 16" reverse-painted glass astronomical dial with Arabic five-minute numbers on chapter ring, sub hour dial with Roman numerals and sub seconds dial with walnut bezel, circa 1888, eight-day brass pulleys, brass weight and four jar mercurial pendulum, walnut case with carved crest, arched center with figural pediment bust of woman, pierced carved side pieces and carved finials, pierced carved corbel supports under cornice top, walnut burl and rosettes throughout body, base with burled panels with bordering trim and central carved fox head, 126" h. x 41" w. x 16" d.. **$230,100**

Fontaine's Auction Gallery

American presentation banjo clock, brass, eight-day time-only movement, brass pulley and covered pendulum bob, mahogany presentation banjo case with gilt brass eagle finial and pierced side arms, 37" h. ...**$708**

Fontaine's Auction Gallery

French marble and bronze lyre swing clock, two-tone gilt and dore bronze on lyre-shaped case with pierced leaf and berry decoration within frame, maiden's head at crest, hanging garland on oval white marble base with beaded and filigree decoration and feet, brass spring-driven movement has hour and half-hour strike mechanism with bell, 23" x 8" x 4".... **$16,520**

Fontaine's Auction Gallery

Tiffany & Co. weight-driven grandfather clock, 10" silvered metal dial with incised black Arabic hour numbers and five-minute markers outside, fancy pierced black hands and dial signed Tiffany & Co., brass weight-driven movement, hour strike mechanism with coiled gong, tall oak case with overhanging top, tapered below bonnet with silver-plated Art Nouveau leaf overlays on glass, 83" x 23" x 12". **$1,475**

Fontaine's Auction Gallery

Killam & Co. mahogany and giltwood banjo clock, circa 1860, 42-1/2" h. **$2,844**

Pook and Pook, Inc.

Wheel skeleton clock, brass with pierced diamond shape at top, Roman hour numerals and black open moon hands, spring-driven movement, silk thread suspension and brass pendulum bob, oval mahogany base with glass dome, 20" h. x 14" w. x 8" d. **$885**

Fontaine's Auction Gallery

Ansonia La Vendee china mantle clock, Royal Bonn case with three pansies with leaves and gilt decoration on pink background, beveled glass on door, half-hour gong strike, 15" h. x 13" w. x 5" d..............**$1,003**

Fontaine's Auction Gallery

Somers Coca-Cola advertising wall clock, paper dial, black Roman hour numerals on face, pierced hands and brass bezel, time movement with pendulum rod and brass-covered bob, painted wood figure-eight style case with raised lettering of Coca-Cola, The Ideal Brain Tonic around dial, lower door of clock has words Delightful Beverage Relieves Exhaustion, 30-1/2" h. x 18-1/4" w. x 4-3/4" d. .... **$4,500-$6,000**

Fontaine's Auction Gallery

Marble dial wall clock, circa 1858-1875, Howard & Davis (E. Howard & Co.), white marble front with gray striations, 20" dial with Roman hour numerals, eight-day weight-driven movement, wood pendulum with brass covered ball, 34" x 20"....................**$2,065**

Fontaine's Auction Gallery

Tall case clock, late 19th century, bronze mythological ram's heads and other embellishments including ornate bronze urn finial, maker's mark "LSF," produced by Lenzkirch, 94" h. **$10,350**

Don Presley Auction

James Doutt grandfather clock, circa 1890, figured mahogany case with bird's-eye maple panels, silver appointments, trimmings, and hinges, compensated pendulum, unusual seat board and eight-day time and strike, 97" x 20" x 10-1/2". **$4,720**

Fontaine's Auction Gallery

J.J. Beals Boston banjo clock, circa 1838-1874, period open moon hands, brass banjo clock movement, recoil escapement, steel pendulum rod with brass bob, weight baffle and iron weight, mahogany banjo-style case with carved and scrolling sidearms and original reverse-painted black and gilt glasses with banded inlaid boarders and brass eagle and ball finial, 35" h. x 10" w. x 4-1/2" d. **$590**

Fontaine's Auction Gallery

Rare Diana conical pendulum mystery clock, standing bronze figure of Diana the Huntress holding bow with quiver of arrows and pendulum, hanging from three chains, under a large four-spring suspension cluster, is a cobalt sphere containing spring-driven movement with conical platform at top, hour and half-hour bell strike, 27-1/2" h. **$8,850**

Fontaine's Auction Gallery

Black marble triple-dial mantle clock, large inset dial on center clock, blue open moon hands and exposed Brocot with jeweled pallet, half-hour strike, calendar mechanism on left, aneroid barometer on right, 19" h. x 27-1/2" w. x 6" d. overall. **$1,298**

Fontaine's Auction Gallery

Georgian fruitwood shelf clock, 18th century, brass face, inscribed Edwd Barlon Oldham, 13-1/2" h. **$385**

Pook and Pook, Inc.

Rare 19th century Sevres clock in urn form, hand-painted and artist-signed, 26" x 15". **$7,250**

Stevens Auctions

MODERN CLOCKS

Wall clock, Zeeland, Michigan, 1950s, screen-printed plate glass, brass, enameled aluminum, manufacturer's paper label to back, designed by George Nelson & Associates, manufactured by Howard Miller Clock Co., 18" dia. **$1,125**

Rago Arts and Auction Center

Flock of Butterflies clock (no. 2226), United States, 1950s, brushed and enameled metal, painted wood, manufacturer's label and stamp, designed by George Nelson & Associates, manufactured by Howard Miller Clock Co., 24" dia. x 2-1/2" **$3,125**

Rago Arts and Auction Center

Sunflower wall clock (no. 2261), United States, 1950s, laminated walnut, birch, brass, enameled aluminum, manufacturer's decal, designed by George Nelson & Associates, manufactured by Howard Miller Clock Co., 29-1/2" dia. **$2,375**

Rago Arts and Auction Center

Clock used to advertise Write Co. coffee, slogan on face "Wright Co. Celebrated Boston Roasted Coffee Ja-Vo Blend," wood case with glass face, some warping, 16" dia. **$325**

Rich Penn Auctions

Two microcar clocks, plastic frames, made in England, approximately 8" l. **$518**

RM Auctions

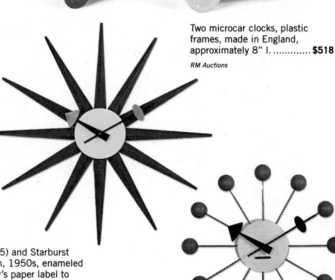

Two wall clocks, Ball (no. 4755) and Starburst (no. 2202), Zeeland, Michigan, 1950s, enameled wood and metal, manufacturer's paper label to both, designed by George Nelson & Associates, manufactured by Howard Miller Clock Co., Starburst 19" dia. **$1,625**

Rago Arts and Auction Center

Coca-Cola & Other Soda Pop Collectibles

Collectibles provide a nostalgic look at our youth and a time when things were simpler and easier to understand. Through collecting, many adults try to recapture this time loaded with fond memories.

The American soft drink industry has always been part of this collectible nostalgia phenomenon. It fits all the criteria associated with the good times, fond memories, and fun. The world of soda pop collecting has been one of the mainstays of modern collectibles since the start of the genre.

Can soda pop advertising be considered true art? Without a doubt! The very best artists in America were an integral part of that honorary place in art history. Renowned artists like Rockwell, Sundbloom, Elvgren, and Wyeth helped take a quality product and advance it to the status of an American icon and all that exemplifies the very best about America.

This beautiful advertising directly reflects the history of our country: its styles and fashion, patriotism, family life, the best of times, and the worst of times. Nearly everything this country has gone through can be seen in these wonderful images.

Organized Coca-Cola collecting began in the early 1970s. The Coca-Cola Co., since its conception in 1886, has taken advertising to a whole new level. This advertising art, which used to be thought of as a simple area of collecting, has reached a whole new level of appreciation. So much so, that it has been studied and dissected by scholars as to why it has proved to be so successful for more than 120 years.

For more information on Coca-Cola collectibles, see *Petretti's Coca-Cola Collectibles Price Guide*, 12th edition, by Allan Petretti.

Coca-Cola "Yes!" cardboard sign, circa 1944, large version sign in original frame, wartime theme of woman being handed a cold bottle of Coke by her military officer beau, remarkable condition, some light scattered scuffs, 62-1/2" w. x 34" h. **$460**

James D. Julia, Inc.

Red leather Coca-Cola change purse with gilt stamping, double-snap closure, some wear to leather and gilt, circa 1907, 2-3/8" x 2-7/8". .....**$150-$250**

Ivy Auctions

Coca Cola cast pencil sharpener, hard to find in any condition, 1-1/2". **$100**

Sullivan & Son Auctions

Coca-Cola offset print by Andy Warhol, circa 1965, hand-signed by Warhol in black pen, 10-3/4" x 8". ....**$900-$1,800**

Frey's Assets

7Up light-up motion sign, metal and plastic, by Everbrite Electric Signs Inc., circa 1960s, excellent condition, 22-1/4". **$300**

Rich Penn Auctions

B-1 Lemon-Lime Soda sign, promoting the slogan of B-1, to be mounted on a bus or as a free-standing display, a few spots and scrapes, 28" x 11". **$60**

Paige Auctions

Coca-Cola syrup urn, circa 1896, normal crazing, spotting and mild to medium wear, small nick on one ear of bowl, long running hidden crack on base of bowl that appears to have been created that way, spigot is not original, 22". **$7,000**

Richard Opfer Auctioneering, Inc.

Red lacquer and abalone inlaid Coca-Cola advertising tray from estate of John Talley, past president and CEO of Coca-Cola European and Asian operations, presentation inscription on reverse, 13-1/2". ....**$300-$600**

A-1 Auction

Original Coca-Cola pencil sketch by Andy Warhol, signed lower left and dated '75, very good condition with framing hinge remnants on reverse, 30" x 22-1/8". .... **$2,000-$4,000**

Preston Hall Gallery

Coca-Cola trolley sign, circa 1905, cardboard sign is earliest known in series of trolley cards used for advertising Coca-Cola, condition is good to very good, some cardboard loss at upper corners, 21" x 11". **$2,127**

James D. Julia, Inc.

Fowler's Cherry Smash ceramic syrup dispenser with original pump top and slogan "Our Nation's Beverage," paint in excellent condition, dispenser has one small chip at mouth, 15". **$2,100**

Matthews Auctions

Ward's Lemon Crush ceramic syrup dispenser, no chips cracks or repairs, front in good shape with good color, reverse has some wear to paint, 13". **$1,400**

Matthews Auctions

Pepsi-Cola sign, circa 1930s, early celluloid over cardboard sign with double dot Pepsi bottle with "Pepsi-Cola" across top, "5¢, 12-ounces" with "A Nickel Drink - Worth A Dime" across bottom of sign, 5-1/4" x 12-1/4". **$525**

Sullivan Auctioneers, LLC

Dad's Root Beer bottle cap-shaped celluloid sign with slogan "you'll love Dad's...tastes like ROOT BEER should!", minor scratches, 30". **$275**

Matthews Auctions

Pepsi-Cola logo on bottle cap-shaped celluloid button, good condition with some minor scuffing, 9" dia. **$100**

Matthews Auctions

Rochester Root Beer Soda Selmix fountain dispenser, circa 1940s, metal badge-type emblems on three sides, nice condition, 17" x 22" x 12". **$250**

Sullivan & Son Auction

Coca-Cola metal toy truck, circa 1950s, battery operated, original box, moderate overall wear and soiling to box, minor chips, nicks and scratches to truck, 12". **$475**

Richard Opfer Auctioneering, Inc.

Antique Apparatus Model CCD4 Coca-Cola jukebox, plays CDs with key. **$3,750**

Victorian Casino Antiques

Animated Mountain Dew "Willy the Hillbilly" store display with jug of "Dew," made of papier mache, circa 1950s, 40" x 17". **$1,300**

Matthews Auctions

Coca-Cola in Bottles Ingraham clock, wood case, working condition, 35" x 18" x 4". **$375**

Matthews Auctions

COCA-COLA & OTHER SODA POP

Coca-Cola milestone cardboard sign, hand-lettered in 1944 to commemorate one-billionth gallon of Coca-Cola syrup, bottom of sign says "Presented to Mr. Chas Howard Candler, son of the founder of Coca-Cola and former president of the Coca-Cola Company," in good condition with flattened crease at bottom, 10-3/4" x 10-3/4"............................$230

James D. Julia, Inc.

Drink Coca-Cola neon clock with lighted marquee with "Sign of Good Taste" slogan, marked with Electric Neon Clock Co., Cleveland Ohio, clock operational and lights up, good color, no cracks or breaks, some wear and light scratches to dial and rust on case, 31" x 36" x 7"................ **$1,300**

Matthews Auctions

Coca-Cola tin "turtle" die-cut sign, circa 1920s, embossed sign with chain hanger with caption "DRINK Coca-Cola THE DELICIOUS BEVERAGE," good to very good condition with some bubbling to surface paint, a few soft bends. ... **$1,150**

James D. Julia, Inc.

Seven-Up with Gin light motion sign with pouring bottle action, plastic sign, good condition with minor wear, 9" x 12" x 3-1/2". **$375**

Matthews Auctions

Original artwork for Pepsi-Cola with marketing slogan "The Light Refreshment-Refreshes Without Filling," mixed media on artist board, good condition, minor water stains in lower field, bottle cap is applied over painting, 21" x 40". $2,300

Matthews Auctions

Pepsi-Cola marquee bubble face neon clock, operates and lights up properly, 36" x 31" x 8". **$2,300**

Matthews Auctions

Coca-Cola light-up clock, some wear to frame, good working condition, 11" x 12" x 3". ..**$350-$750**

Showtime Auctions

Cast bronze Coca-Cola bookends, circa 1963, gold wash finish, 5-1/4" x 8-1/4".................... **$57**

James D. Julia, Inc.

Rare Coca-Cola button flange drugstore sign, excellent condition, minor edge wear, 18" x 22-1/2".
.... **$1,500-$2,500**

Showtime Auctions

Early Coca-Cola tin sign, circa 1899, embossed tin advertisement manufactured by Standard Adv. Co., Coshocton, Ohio, with slogan "Delicious Refreshing DRINK Coca-Cola AT ALL SODA FOUNTAINS," piece vertically cut in half at one point, 17-1/4" x 25-3/4". **$1,265**

James D. Julia, Inc.

Scarce Coca-Cola bottle-shaped lamp, circa 1920s, line-for-line scale model of official Coke bottle, complete with metal cap, trademark and registration notice below official logo, 20-1/4". **$12,000**

Morphy Auctions

Coca-Cola display octagon sign, near mint condition, 10" x 10". .... **$500-$1,000**

Showtime Auctions

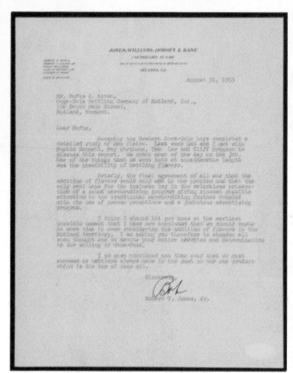

Letter from Golden Age golf legend Bobby "Bob" Jones to Coca-Cola's Mr. Rufus E. Brown, offering his opinion about the soft drink and the direction in which the company should progress in regards to expanding the line to include other bottling flavor, with his recommendation to step up the marketing plan for the original soda instead of expanding the line; 8-1/2" x 11" paper, featuring the signature "Bob" in black ink, signed on Jones, Williams, Dorsey & Kane letterhead. **$1,195**

Heritage Auctions

Coca-Cola embossed tin sign, circa 1902, scarce version of sign says "5¢ IN BOTTLES 5¢," manufactured by N.Y. Metal Ceiling Co., N.Y., very good condition with some paint loss to relief lettering, 13-1/2" x 9-1/2". **$575**

James D. Julia, Inc.

Coca-Cola leaded glass shade, authentic circa 1920s, Tiffany-style, one of the most sought after Coca-Cola collectibles, with words "Property of Coca-Cola Co. to be returned on demand" stamped in two locations, very good to near excellent condition with a few small pieces in lower section with cracks, 16"..............**$3,220**

James D. Julia, Inc.

◄ Rare Coca-Cola tray from 1908 depicting partially clad young woman. .. **$5,000-$10,000**

Showtime Auctions

Coin Ops & Trade Stimulators

Coin-operated devices fall into three main categories: amusement or arcade games, trade stimulators, and vending machines.

O.D. Jennings coin drop trade stimulator, horse race theme depicted on aluminum castings; depending upon where penny landed, player received anywhere from 0 to 25 points and a gumball. Original finish to wood and aluminum castings with some minor paint enhancement to lower front panel, overall very fine plus condition, replacement aluminum cap at gum fill opening, original tin coin box no longer present, 12-1/2" d. x 14" w. x 20" h. **$2,300**

James D. Julia, Inc.

The Official Sweepstakes horse race machine, front casting is elaborate cast aluminum; sides, base, and top appear to be maple and finished naturally, interior depicts three-sided horse racing scene with track and bleachers. All original, lacking lock to rear door, overall very fine plus condition, top wooden board reversed, top of rear door trimmed to fit and close, 15" w. x 13" d. x 12" h. **$4,600**

James D. Julia, Inc.

Sun Manufacturing Co. two-wheel bicycle trade stimulator, circa 1900, overall original with paint restoration to bicycle and new papers (award card, instructions, etc.), overall very good plus condition, lacking some rope twist columns on rear corners of machine, 20-1/2" w. x 13" h. x 5-1/2" d. **$9,200**

James D. Julia, Inc.

5¢ Buckley Bones dice cash payout machine (craps simulator), restored, overall very fine appearance/ restoration, appears to be in full functional operating condition, replacement sheet metal backdoor and cash box, done to factory specs, approximately 15-1/2" w. x 11-1/2" d. x 13" h. **$2,300**

James D. Julia, Inc.

Sun Manufacturing Co. bicycle trade stimulator, circa 1890s; dropped coin would free lever to set bicycle wheels spinning, which would then stop adjacent to a number on paper-sided wheels; sum of the two numbers would determine the value of store credit award. Very good to excellent condition, locking coin box and slide missing, mechanism needs adjustment, 17-1/2" w. x 13" h................................. **$5,500**

Noel Barrett Auctions

Gottlieb Frontiersman pinball machine, vintage wood case, one leg with vertical stress split, original 5¢ coin mechanism present but set for free play, lacking key, presently unlocked, a few replaced bumpers with some celluloid bumper tops showing much distress, 54" l. x 66" h. x 25" w. **$374**

James D. Julia, Inc.

O.D. Jennings Rockaway "Jacks" trade stimulator. When a coin is deposited and plunger pushed, coin drops into pinned spinning see-saw dial, then cascades down through a series of pins, possibly landing in a payout pocket. If coin lands in payout pocket, player is entitled to all the coins in corresponding window below pocket. This particular machine also would have vended gumballs with each play. Overall very good plus restored condition, back door is quality wood replacement with replica instruction sheet on interior panel, lacking gum mechanism, 15" w. x 12" d. x 22" h.**$1,553**

James D. Julia, Inc.

Mutoscope Skyscraper traveling crane digger machine, 1920s, large front aluminum plaque with manufacturer's name and indicating machine was sold by Mills Sales Co. of Oakland, California, front compartment facades picture Empire State Building, possibly repainted more than 50 years ago, mechanics untested, appear complete, original coin entry likely functional on 1¢ and updated with 5¢ coin entry, replacement coin entry does not fit perfectly over original void, 42" h. x 23" w. x 20" d. **$1,093**

James D. Julia, Inc.

5¢ Pace "Fancy Front" Comet slot machine, 1930s, elaborate aluminum front castings, older restoration with what appear to be all original parts including slide behind goose neck, reel strips, back door, etc., overall very good functional working order in need of minor lubrication and fine tuning, original Pace lock with keys included, in cash box needs to be reattached to back door with two carriage bolts, small chips to jackpot center post, 16" w. x 15" d. x 24" h. **$575**

James D. Julia, Inc.

► Cast iron Mutoscope clam shell viewer with many layers of paint, top layer gold, cast iron marquee broken and in need of professional repair, small breaks and missing pieces to iron castings, overall machine intact and in very good condition, reel bundle and marquee card feature Felix the Cat, operational condition, glass over viewing cards damaged, reel bundle in good to very good condition, lacking key for side door, overall 76" h. x 20" d. x 15" w. **$5,310**

James D. Julia, Inc.

Countertop Five Star Final pinball machine, circa 1930s, precursor to modern day pinball machines; player deposits nickel in coin slot, pushes plunger, and receives five balls; depending on tension of plunger, player would launch each ball through a series of pins into scoring holes. Overall very fine plus condition, 17" w. x 31" l. **$460**

James D. Julia, Inc.

Mills 5¢ Futurity, 1930s, restored, reproduction wooden base, reproduction cash box, overall 61" h., machine is approximately 16" w. x 15" d. x 27" h... **$13,800**

James D. Julia, Inc.

◄ 5¢ International Mutoscope featuring Hoot Gibson movie cowboy. For a nickel player would crank handle, light would come on, and cowboy scene viewed. Stamped steel and iron machine with cast iron marquee, machine restored, in operating condition, overall very fine restored condition, reel bundle appears to be excellent, overall 52" h., approximately 13" d. x 8" w. **$1,298**

James D. Julia, Inc.

Mills 5¢ Black Cherry slot machine produced originally in late 1930s, mechanically sound, overall very good working order, jackpot intact but needs lubrication, original finish to aluminum castings, wooden cabinet appears to have second coat of black paint applied, overall very sound, lacking original metal back door, now with wooden hinged door, 16" l. x 16" d. x 23" h. **$920**

James D. Julia, Inc.

1¢ O.D. Jennings "Little Duke" slot machine with side vendor, unusual three-reel slot machine: three reels are concentric discs with first reel being the middle disc; functional working condition, retains original trapezoidal cash box, overall very fine restored condition, 22" h. x 11" d. x 17" w. **$2,013**

James D. Julia, Inc.

Wooden 1¢ penny drop, oak wood cabinet and front door containing cash box with separate columns indicating various winning positions, overall very good condition, replacement lock to front door, 13-1/2" w. x 8" d. x 20" h. **$1,265**

James D. Julia, Inc.

Mills 5¢ Brownie slot machine, largest of countertop color wheels produced by Mills from the early 20th century; wheel altered, machine is a token payout and not a cash payout machine, original finish to both wood and castings, including original wood backdoor and cloth money bag. Very fine plus condition, coin head currently jammed, lacking key for coin head lock but machine in functional working order, iron payout cup has some deterioration to front lip due to oxidation, 21" w. x 29" h. x 11" d..**$9,775**

James D. Julia, Inc.

25¢ Mills Poinsettia slot machine, 1920s, original finish except back door, coin box, and metal slide behind goose neck, which are replacements, includes nickel-plated fanciful of more recent vintage (approximately 30" h.), overall clean original condition, tin reel strips somewhat darkened, aged black paint to wooden base, 24" h. **$863**

James D. Julia, Inc.

5¢ Mills floor model slot machine, 1930s, restored, mechanics in functional working order, full working jackpot, original back door and coin box, reel strips are appropriate replacements, overall very fine restored condition, missing lower back wood panel on cabinet, 60" h. **$1,150**

James D. Julia, Inc.

25¢ Bally Reliance payout dice machine (craps simulator), very good, all-original, untouched condition, in need of some light lubrication, retains original back door with instruction sheet and cash box, 15-1/2" w. x 11-1/2" d. x 17" h. **$6,900**

James D. Julia, Inc.

Chocolat Menier tin lithographed bank, six-sided dome-top bank with pointed top and filigree crest, panels depict various advertisements in French and a girl writing "Chocolat Menier." Slot in top of bank accepts coin, and when lever is pulled, a small piece of chocolate is dispensed. Overall discoloration and minor chipping, but otherwise generally good to very good condition, 10-1/2" h. **$518**

James D. Julia, Inc.

10 Things You Didn't Know About Coin-Op Antiques

1 Artifacts reveal the presence of coin-operated machines as far back as the 1st century A.D.; and the very thing they dispensed might surprise you: They were used to control the amount of holy water distributed at temples.

2 Coin-operated machines continue to draw much attention and interest at auctions. In 2012, the following made headlines: A working, dual vend Chiclets Stollwerck chocolate vending machine (estimated at $10,000-$15,000) sold for $28,200, and a Rol-A-Top cherry front 10-cent coin-op machine brought $6,000 at Morphy's Auctions in August; plus, a Buckley Bones dice cash payout went for $13,800 and a Sun Manufacturing Co. Two-Wheel Bicycle Trade Simulator for $9,200 in June at James D. Julia's toy, doll and advertising auction.

3 Coin-operated machines dispense many things, but the most unusual items have included gold bars at airports, live lobster catching games, live bait (for the next fishing excursion), and fresh eggs.

A working, dual vend Chiclets Stollwerck chocolate vending machine (estimated at $10,000-$15,000) sold for $28,200 at Morphy's Auctions in August 2012.

4 The Penny Arcadia, associated with the International Arcade Museum, is a living showcase of several hundred coin-op machines and video games, including an early 1800s coin-operated tobacco honor box and the first coin-operated kiddie ride of the 1920s. Also featured are the popular pinball machines of the 1960s and the game-changing arcade video games like Asteroids. The Arcadia's owners are looking for a permanent facility for the massive collection, but for now it is displayed at various public exhibitions. To learn more, visit www.arcade-museum.com/penny-arcadia.

5 Coin-operated arcade games have long been popular collectibles and they got their start in 1971 when The Galaxy Game made its debut on the campus of Stanford University.

6 The largest club for people who enjoy coin-op machines is the Coin Operated Collector's Association (C.O.C.A.), a non-profit organization with a membership of more than 700. For more information or to join, visit www.coinopclub.org.

7 Various types of coin-operated machines exist, but among the most popular are gambling devices and vending machines, according to Doug Cain, president of C.O.C.A. Slot machines are popular gambling units, while the most collectible vending machines distribute gum or peanuts.

8 Among the most sought after coin-op machines are those manufactured in the late 1800s through the early 1900s.

9 Like most collectibles, age, rarity and originality are key features collectors look for in coin-op machines. And the most preferred among serious coin-op collectors are those that have not been restored and are 100 percent original.

10 There are no less than seven different books about collecting coin-operated machines still in print today. One of the most popular, and a pioneer of these guides is the book *Drop Coin Here*, which was first published in 1979.

10 THINGS

Compiled by Antoinette Rahn. Sources: Kovels, Smithsonian.com – *Smithsonian Magazine*, coinopclub.org, Doug Cain of C.O.C.A, International Arcade Museum, Morphy's Auctions, James D. Julia Auctions.

Coins & Currency

Coin collecting and the study of numismatics has long been one of the most respected and honored aspects of the collecting world. Today it still holds fascination as new collectors come onto the scene every day. The 50 State Quarters series, issued from 1999 to 2008, spurred many to save quarters again and encouraged all types of coin collecting.

The United States has a rich history of coinage. Many of the early states created their own coins until April 1792, when Congress passed an act establishing the U.S. Mint. By 1796, in addition to half cents and cents, the Mint was producing silver half dimes, dimes, quarters, half dollars, and dollars, and gold $2.50, $5, and $10 coins. By the mid-1800s, the Mint was producing about 17 million coins annually in 12 denominations.

The Coinage Act of 1873 brought sweeping changes to the U.S. monetary and coinage systems, and to the Mint's governing structure. The act established the main mint at Philadelphia. President Theodore Roosevelt is credited with encouraging Congress to pass legislation for providing new coin designs. Designs on coins continue to change to reflect events.

Over the years, the Mint has made various adjustments and revisions to U.S. coinage in response to economic conditions prevailing at the time and the cost and supply of the metals from which the coins are produced.

A coin collection can be whatever an individual wants it to be. Collect the kind of coins and paper money you like and what brings you pleasure as a leisure-time hobby. It's also good to have a strategy and a road map to your collecting pursuits. Here are some tips and comments on traditional collecting strategies.

BY SERIES. The traditional coin-collecting pursuit of acquiring one example of each date and mint mark within a particular series may seem daunting at first considering the long runs of some U.S. coin series. To get started, a collector can break down a series into smaller parts. For example, a collector interested in Lincoln cents can start with those depicting the Lincoln Memorial on the reverse, which began in 1959. A collector can also get started by collecting simply one date of each Lincoln Memorial cent rather than seeking an example of every mint mark of a particular date.

1882 bronze Indian head cent .... **$5-$20**

BY TYPE. Rather than seeking an example of every date and mint mark within a series, many collectors seek just one example of each type of coin within a particular focus. For example, a collector assembling a 20th century type set of U.S. 5-cent coins would seek one Liberty nickel, one Buffalo nickel, and one Jefferson nickel. The representative coins could be of any date and mint mark within each series, thus accommodating any collecting budget.

BY THEME. The proliferation of modern commemorative and circulating commemorative coins gave rise to collecting coins with a common theme. Examples include coins that depict animals or ships, coins that commemorate a certain event, or coins of a certain date, such as 2000.

BY COLLECTOR'S CHOICE. Various aspects of the listed strategies overlap and can be combined and mixed to form a goal that interests an individual collector. The result should be a coin collection that is affordable and attainable for the collector, and a collection that brings enjoyment and satisfaction.

The first paper money to circulate in the United States was issued during the Colonial era. During the Revolutionary War, the states and Continental Congress continued to issue paper money, but its backing in hard currency was spotty at best.

Demand notes of 1861 were the first paper money issued by the U.S. government, as an emergency measure during the Civil War. The nickname "greenback" for paper money began with these notes, which have a distinctive green back.

The Federal Reserve System was created in 1913. It consists of 12 Federal Reserve banks governed in part by the U.S. government through the Federal Reserve Board. The paper money used today in the United States is issued by the Federal Reserve banks. Federal Reserve notes are produced at the Bureau of Engraving and Printing's main facility in Washington, D.C., and at its Western Currency Facility in Fort Worth, Texas.

For more information on U.S. coins and currency, see *Warman's U.S. Coins & Currency Field Guide*, 5th edition, by Arlyn G. Sieber.

1825 half cent with classic head...**$75-$110**

1828 large cent with coronet **$35-$80**

1840 large cent with braided hair .... **$30-$35**

1902 bronze Indian head cent ..**$2.50-$10**

1943-S Lincoln cents were produced in zinc-coated steel during World War II. ....65¢-$4

1964-D Lincoln cent with Lincoln Memorial reverse..........$7

1863 silver three-cent piece with double border around star ..$450-$520

1865 nickel three-cent piece... $17.50-$35

1896 Liberty nickel. $40-$100

1913-D buffalo nickel. .... $180-$285

1939 Jefferson
nickel 20¢.**$1.75**

2005-D Jefferson
nickel with bison
reverse..... **$1.50**

1863 Seated
Liberty half dime
with legend on
obverse.
........**$300-$485**

1877 Seated
Liberty dime
with legend on
obverse.
.... **$20-$25**

1898-S Barber
dime. ..**$35-$80**

1916-D
Mercury dime...
$3,950-$13,200

1964 Roosevelt dime. .. **$4-$7.50**

1873 Seated Liberty quarter, open 3, with motto above eagle. ..**$45-$130**

1903 Barber quarter...**$20-$60**

1916 Standing Liberty quarter..... **$6,900-$10,000**

1945 Washington quarter..**$6-$7.50**

1966 Washington quarter. ... **$7.50**

Delaware State Quarter
(1999) .... **$2-$8**

1976-D Kennedy
half dollar with
Bicentennial
reverse........ **$14**

1921-D Walking Liberty half
dollar...................... **$550-$2,200**

1858-S Seated Liberty half dollar
with arrows removed from date
...................................**$65-$140**

1871 Seated Liberty dollar with motto above eagle .... **$330-$545**

1974-D Eisenhower dollar....... **$7.50**

George Washington Presidential dollar. **$2**

1911-D gold $2.50 with Indian head. ......**$1,100-$2,850**

1850 gold $20 with Liberty head. ...**$1,945-$2,025**

1892-S Morgan dollar............... **$135-$44,500**

1903 gold $20 with Liberty head. ...**$1,780-$1,800**

1992-S half-dollar Commemorative Olympics...**$8.50**

Philadelphia $5 demand note, Series 1861... **$3,300-$4,500**

$50 national bank note, Third Charter.....................**$700-$825**

$10 large-size United States note, Series 1901...............**$600-$2,000**

$10 small-size gold certificate, Series 1928.............. **$145-$200**

$2 large-size silver certificate, Series 1896.............................. **$625-$2,550**

$10 small-size silver certificate, special yellow seal, Series 1934A .... **$320-$400**

$10 large-size Federal Reserve Note, red seal, Series 1914 .... **$400-$1,250**

$10 large-size Federal Reserve Note, blue seal, Series 1914 .... **$85-$250**

$5 small-size Federal Reserve Note, green seal, Series 1928A .... **$15-$75**

$10 small-size Federal Reserve Note, green seal, Series 2003 .... **$15**

$50 small-size Federal Reserve Note, green seal, Series 1969A .... **$75-$100**

$1 large-size Federal Reserve Bank Note, blue seal, Series 1918 .... **$125-$250**

Comics

Values for scarce, high-condition comic books saw an exponential increase in auction values in 2012 and 2013. Surprisingly, it's not always collectors who are driving this growth as more investors are turning to comic books as a store of wealth. In February 2012, a 6.5-graded copy of Detective Comics #27, the first appearance of Batman, sold for $522,813. The same book in the same condition sold in February 2013 for an additional $44,812 to realize $567,625.

Presented here are mostly slabbed versions of scarce or rare comic books. This is a departure from previous editions, but for a very good reason. Just as we present the finest of condition across every other category in the *Antique Trader Antiques & Collectibles Price Guide*, we are presenting the best examples of these comic books that have sold in the last year. These copies are the best examples to objectively evaluate your copy using the grading scale in this section to check off as many defects as possible. To effectively grade comic books, you must be honest – nay, downright persnickety – in pointing out unique characteristics about each copy. With so many millions of comic books printed, slabbed books are the most likely to hold their value over the long term. If you are a new collector or otherwise not yet familiar with slabbed books, now's the time to learn more about this service and how it can exponentially improve the value of your collection.

As the comic book collecting hobby matures, collectors are finding new interest in collecting the original works of specific writers and artists. As more and more collectors complete runs of their favorite titles, many are expanding into rare and original, hand-drawn art. These prices catch the eye of investors and enthusiasts and the cycle repeats itself.

Original comic art can be found the world over. The original artwork for *Tintin in America*, featuring the French comic strip character Tintin by Hergé, sold at a Paris auction for more than $1.6 million in 2008. In early 2013, a collector paid just $1 at a California garage sale for a piece of original art from a Flash Gordon newspaper strip estimated to be worth $1,500 to $2,000. Like any original art, the works of well-known and popular artists command the most dollars at auction. The works do not have to be vintage art to garner six-figure sale prices. Works produced in the 1990s, at the height of the "collector's edition craze," by Todd McFarlane or John Romita, Sr.'s work from the 1970s or Jerry Robinson's Batman covers from the 1940s command prices in excess of $200,000.

CONDITION MATTERS

Consider the difference between these two copies of *The Amazing Spider-Man* #21. The comic book is significant to Spider-Man collectors because of its dynamic cover art and because the Human Torch makes a crossover appearance when the Beetle (in his second appearance) kidnaps his girlfriend. The issue also features a Spider-Man pin-up. Perhaps more importantly, it features one of the most popular Spider-Man artists of all time, Steve Ditko, whose art appears on both the cover and on the inside stories.

In this example, the auction value of a copy of *The Amazing Spider-Man* #21 graded as a 9.6 resulted in a 45 percent increase in the auction value compared to a copy graded as a 9.4. The leading third-party comic book grader, Certified Guaranty Company, LLC, (CGC) not only grades books but also maintains a census of each copy it sees. CGC data shows that 11 copies

COMICS

of this issue are known to exist with a grade of 9.6, and just three copies are graded higher. Collectors factor this information when deciding how much to spend on a slabbed comic book.

The Amazing Spider-Man #21 (Marvel, 1965), CGC NM+ 9.6, white pages, Steve Ditko cover and art..........................**$2,629**

The Amazing Spider-Man #21 (Marvel, 1965), CGC NM 9.4, off-white to white pages, Steve Ditko cover and art. **$1,434**

Here's another example of how condition drastically affects values for scarce comic books.

Teenage Mutant Ninja Turtles #1 first printing (Mirage Studios, 1984), CGC NM/ MT 9.8, white pages, origins and first appearances of the Teenage Mutant Ninja Turtles, Splinter, and Shredder, initial print run of 3,000 copies, wraparound cover is by Kevin Eastman, story and interior art by Eastman and Peter Laird. **$17,929**

The condition of this copy, even by a relatively small margin, resulted in a significant decrease in value as the same issue graded a 9.2 and offered in the same auction sold for just **$2,868.**

Comic Book Grading Guide

Coming to a consensus on what grade a given comic book is in has been a topic of heated discussion among collectors for many years. When you compare your comics with the images provided here, it's easy to see there are many comics that fall between categories in something of an infinite gradation.

For example, a "Fair" condition comic book (which falls between "Good" and "Poor") may have a soiled, slightly damaged cover, a badly rolled spine, cover flaking, corners gone, tears, etc. It is an issue with multiple problems but it is intact — and some collectors enjoy collecting in this grade for the fun of it. Tape may be present and is always considered a defect. In addition to the grades shown, any defects must be taken into account.

The condition of a comic book is a vital factor in determining its price.

MINT *(Abbreviated M, Mt)*

This is a perfect comic book. Its cover has full luster with edges sharp and pages like new. There are no signs of wear or aging. It is not imperfectly printed or off-center. "Mint" means just what it says. [The term for this grade is the same one used for CGC's 10.0 grade.]

NEAR MINT *(NM)*

This is a nearly perfect comic book. Its cover shows barely perceptible signs of wear. Its spine is tight, and its cover has only minor loss of luster and only minor printing defects. Some discoloration is acceptable in older comics — as are signs of aging. [The term for this grade is the same one used for CGC's 9.4 grade.]

VERY FINE *(VF)*

This is a nice comic book with beginning signs of wear. There can be slight creases and wrinkles at the staples, but it is a flat, clean issue with definite signs of being read a few times. There is some loss of the original gloss, but it is in general an attractive comic book. [The term for this grade is the same one used for CGC's 8.0 grade.]

FINE *(F, Fn)*

This comic book's cover is worn but flat and clean with no deface-ment. There is usually no cover writing or tape repair. Stress lines around the staples and more rounded corners are permit-ted. It is a good-looking issue at first glance. [The term for this grade is the same one used for CGC's 6.0 grade.]

VERY GOOD *(VG, VGD)*

Most of the original gloss is gone from this well-read issue. There are minor markings, discoloration, and/or heavier stress lines around the staples and spine. The cover may have minor tears and/or corner creases, and spine-rolling is permissible. [The term for this grade is the same one used for CGC's 4.0 grade.]

GOOD *(G, Gd)*

This is a very worn comic book with nothing missing. Creases, minor tears, rolled spine, and cover flaking are permissible. Older Golden Age comic books often come in this grade. [The term for this grade is the same one used for CGC's 2.0 grade.]

FAIR *(FA, Fr)*

This comic book has multiple problems but is structurally intact. Copies may have a soiled, slightly damaged cover, a badly rolled spine, cover flaking, corners gone, and tears. Tape may be present and is always considered a defect. [The term for this grade is the same one used for CGC's 1.0 grade.]

POOR *(P, Pr)*

This issue is damaged and generally considered unsuitable for collecting. While the copy may still contain some readable stories, major defects get in the way. Copies may be in the process of disintegrating and may do so with even light handling. [The term for this grade is the same one used for CGC's 0.5 grade.]

COMICS

Detective Comics #27 (DC, 1939), CGC FN+ 6.5, off-white to white pages, first appearance of Batman. **$567,625**

Batman #1 (DC, 1940), CGC FN/VF 7.0, off-white to white pages, origin of the Joker and Catwoman, Batman's origin story......**$107,550**

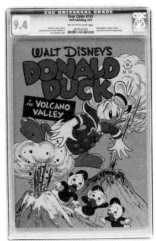

Four Color #147 Donald Duck (Dell, 1947), CGC NM 9.4, off-white to white pages, Carl Buettner cover, Carl Barks story and art, Jack Hannah art... **$2,629**

Dagar, Desert Hawk #14 (Fox Features Syndicate, 1948), CGC NM 9.4, off-white pages, Tangi and Safari Cary stories begin, Ed Good and Jack Kamen interior art......................... **$1,314**

Daredevil Comics #37 Mile High pedigree (Lev Gleason, 1946), CGC NM+ 9.6, off-white to white pages, Charles Biro story and cover, Norman Maurer and Carl Hubbell art. **$1,314**

Action Comics #114 (DC, 1947), CGC NM 9.4, off-white to white pages, Superman cover by Wayne Boring, Ed Smalle and George Papp art. **$1,374**

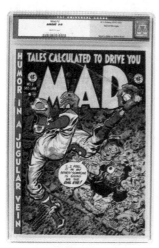

Mad #2 Gaines File pedigree (EC, 1952), CGC NM/MT 9.8, off-white pages, John Severin, Bill Elder, Harvey Kurtzman, and Wally Wood art.................................. **$2,629**

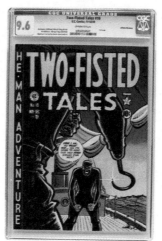

Two-Fisted Tales #18 Gaines File pedigree 2/7 Plus Bonus EC Slipcases (EC, 1950), CGC NM+ 9.6, off-white pages, first issue of title (which had numbering continued from Haunt of Fear), Harvey Kurtzman cover....... **$3,107**

The Amazing Spider-Man #19 (Marvel, 1964), CGC NM+ 9.6, cream to off-white pages, Steve Ditko cover and art............ **$1,673**

The Green Hornet #3 Boston pedigree (Gold Key, 1967), CGC NM/MT 9.8, white pages, Van Williams and Bruce Lee photo cover, Green Hornet and Kato back cover pin-up, Dan Spiegle art....................................... **$657**

The Amazing Spider-Man #300 Signature Series (Marvel, 1988), CGC NM/MT 9.8, white pages, origin and first full appearance of Venom, last time Spider-Man wears the black "alien" costume, and The Thing appears; Todd McFarlane cover and art, signed by Todd McFarlane on 10/5/12 and Stan Lee on 10/20/12....... **$1,434**

The Incredible Hulk #181 (Marvel, 1974), CGC NM+ 9.6, off-white to white pages, first full appearance of future X-Men star Wolverine, Wendigo appearance, Herb Trimpe cover and art.................... **$4,182**

Dell Giants #48 The Flintstones (Dell, 1961), CGC NM/MT 9.8, off-white to white pages, considered The Flintstones #1, first appearance of the Flintstones in comic book form, contains photos of Bill Hanna and Joe Barbera. **$2,629**

Superman's Girlfriend Lois Lane #29 (DC, 1961), CGC NM+ 9.6, off-white to white pages, Aquaman, Batman, and Green Arrow appearances, last 10¢ issue, Curt Swan cover and art. **$1,195**

Thor #168 (Marvel, 1969), CGC NM/MT 9.8, white pages, origin of Galactus, Jack Kirby cover and art. **$2,629**

Action Comics #317 Twin Cities pedigree (DC, 1964), CGC NM+ 9.6, white pages, text story on Lena Thorul (Lex Luthor's sister), Lena Thorul's marriage, Curt Swan cover, Al Plastino and Jim Mooney art....................................... **$433**

Little Lulu #260 (Whitman, 1980), CGC NM/MT 9.8, off-white to white pages, one of the rarest Whitman comics, distributed in multi-packs only, low distribution. **$388**

Action Comics #23 (DC, 1940), CGC FN+ 6.5, off-white pages, first appearance of Lex Luthor (who appears with red hair), first mention of the Daily Planet, Joe Shuster cover and interior art and Sheldon Moldoff, Bernard Baily, and Fred Guardineer added interior art........................ **$8,365**

Amazing Mystery Funnies V1#1 Billy Wright pedigree (Centaur, 1938), CGC VG+ 4.5, off-white pages, first published comic book work of Bill Everett, cover art by Everett.................................. **$836**

Batman #14 (DC, 1943), CGC VF- 7.5 Off-white to white pages, second appearance of The Penguin, Jerry Robinson cover and art, Bob Kane and Jack Burnley art.................................... **$3,883**

Batman #20 (DC, 1943), CGC VF- 7.5, cream to off-white pages, first time the Batmobile appeared on a comic book cover, cover by Dick Sprang, interior art by Bob Kane and Jack Burnley. **$1,314**

Barbie and Ken #1 File Copy (Dell, 1962), CGC NM+ 9.6, cream to off-white pages, photo cover. **$1,195**

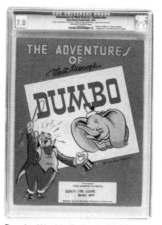

Dumbo Weekly Collector Folder (Walt Disney Productions, 1942), CGC FN/VF 7.0, off-white to white pages, collector folder for Dumbo Weekly, a promotional magazine supplied by Diamond D-X Gas Stations, includes Dumbo Weekly issues #1-8 ("County Line Garage, Covert, Mich." stamp on cover and issue #1). **$262**

Hansi, The Girl Who Loved the Swastika #nn (Spire Christian Comics, 1976), CGC NM/MT 9.8, white pages, this is the 39¢ 1976 reprint issue (a 49¢ version also exists), Al Hartley cover. **$250**

COMICS

Startling Comics #49 (Better Publications, 1948), CGC VG+ 4.5, off-white pages, Alex Schomburg robot cover, Hal Sherman art. **$1,912**

Popeye Plays Nursemaid to Sweet Pea #nn File Copy (Whitman, 1937), CGC VF 8.0, cream to off-white pages, picture book. **$131**

Batman #10 (DC, 1942), condition GD+, Catwoman appearance in a new costume, Jerry Robinson cover, Robinson and Bob Kane interior art. **$310**

X-Men #138 (Marvel, 1980), CGC NM/MT 9.8, white pages, Cyclops leaves the X-Men, funeral of Jean Grey, Dazzler appearance, John Byrne and Terry Austin cover and art....................................... **$179**

The Amazing Spider-Man #365 (Marvel, 1992), CGC NM/MT 9.8, white pages, first appearance of Spider-Man 2099, gatefold Venom/Carnage poster by Mark Bagley, hologram cover, Bagley, John Romita Jr., and Rick Leonardi art. **$102**

Batman: The Killing Joke #nn (DC, 1988), CGC NM/MT 9.8, white pages, Joker cripples Barbara Gordon (Batgirl), story by Alan Moore, embossed cover and art by Brian Bolland, green logo. From the Empire Comics Collection. **$102**

COMICS

Walking Dead #1 (Image, 2003), CGC NM/MT 9.8, white pages, inspired the AMC TV series but predates it by seven years... **$1,434**

Walking Dead #19 (Image, 2005), CGC NM/MT 9.8, white pages, first appearance of Michonne, "Death" of Dexter. **$657**

Batman: Gotham by Gaslight #nn (DC, 1989), CGC NM 9.4, white pages, Mike Mignola art, introduction by Robert Bloch. .**$20**

The Amazing Spider-Man #325 (Marvel, 1989), CGC NM/MT 9.8, white pages, Captain America, Silver Sable, and Red Skull appearances, Todd McFarlane cover and art. **$86**

Justice League #1 (DC, 1987), CGC NM/MT 9.8, white pages, first appearance of Maxwell Lord (the Black King), Kevin Maguire and Terry Austin cover and art. **$60**

Sheena, Queen of the Jungle #16 (Fiction House, 1952), CGC VF 8.0, off-white to white pages, Maurice Whitman cover, Robert Webb and Charles Sultan art. **$179**

Brown's Blue Ribbon Book of Jokes and Jingles (Brown's Shoe Co., 1904), CGC FN- 5.5, white pages. This is the very first Buster Brown comic book premium with a Yellow Kid cameo on the back cover. R. F. Outcault art............**$597**

Iron Man #170 (Marvel, 1983), CGC NM+ 9.6, off-white to white pages, first full appearance of James Rhodes as Iron Man. **$51**

X-Men #244 (Marvel, 1989), CGC NM/MT 9.8, white pages, first appearance of Jubilee, Marc Silvestri cover and art. **$76**

Batman: Vengeance of Bane Special #1 (DC, 1993), CGC NM/MT 9.8, white pages, origin and first appearance of Bane.......**$173**

X-Men #141 (Marvel, 1981), CGC NM+ 9.6, white pages, features "Days of Future Past" story, first appearances of Rachel (Phoenix II), Pyro, Destiny, and Avalanche; Mystique, Blob, and Robert Kelly appearances, John Byrne cover and art. **$197**

The Amazing Spider-Man #274 (Marvel, 1986), CGC NM/MT 9.8, white pages, Zarathos, Beyonder, Mephisto, and Kingpin appearances, John Romita Sr. cover and art. **$47**

Spider-Man #1 Platinum Edition (Marvel, 1990), CGC NM+ 9.6, white pages, Lizard appearance, Todd McFarlane story, cover, and art. This edition was mailed to retailers only (print run of 10,000 copies). New McFarlane art and editorial material in place of the ads found in all other editions of the issue. Stiff cover with no price. **$250**

ORIGINAL COMIC BOOK & COMIC STRIP ART

Al Feldstein, Weird Science-Fantasy Annual #1 cover original art (EC, 1952), 13-1/2" x 19-1/2". From the Jerry Weist Collection. **$77,675**

"HOW DO YOU OPEN THIS THING? YOU JUST SUCKED UP SIX VALUABLE COMIC STAMPS AND MY COLLECTION OF DEAD SPIDERS!"

Hank Ketcham, Dennis the Menace daily comic strip original art dated 1-15-52 (Post-Hall Syndicate, 1952), 6-1/2" x 8"........... **$1,105**

Brian Bolland, Batman: The Killing Joke page 38 original art (DC, 1988), 10" x 15-3/4". **$47,800**

Jack Davis, Tales from the Crypt #26 complete eight-page story, "Drawn and Quartered" Original Art (EC, 1951), 13" x 18".... **$19,120**

Dave Gibbons, Watchmen #1 "Bloody Smiley Face/Doomsday Clock" cover original art (DC, 1986). Widely considered to be one of the greatest stories in modern comics history, 10" x 15". From the Shamus Modern Masterworks Collection...**$155,350**

TOP LOT!

Todd McFarlane, The Amazing Spider-Man #328 cover original art (Marvel, 1990), 10" x 15". From the Shamus Modern Masterworks Collection...**$657,250**

Wayne Boring, Superman daily comic strip #8153 original art dated 2-3-65 (Bell-McClure Syndicate, 1965), 16-3/4" x 4-3/4"..**$418**

COMICS

Alex Ross, Wizard the Comics Magazine #42 Marvel Heroes triple-panel cover original art (Wizard, 1995), 33" x 16". From the Shamus Modern Masterworks Collection...**$68,712**

Mike Deodato, Jr., Incredible Hulk #65 cover original art (Marvel, 2003), 10" x 15".............. **$1,314**

John Romita, Sr., Amazing Spider-Man #121 "The Night Gwen Stacy Died" cover original art (Marvel, 1973). Some say the death of Gwen Stacy marked the end of the Silver Age of comics (1956 to circa 1972), 10" x 15".........**$286,800**

Mike Zeck, Robin III, Cry of the Huntress #6 cover original art (DC, 1993), 10" x 15". From the Shamus Modern Masterworks Collection. **$1,314**

Curt Swan and Bob Oksner, Action Comics #459 Splash page 1 original art (DC, 1976), 10" x 15"................................. **$1,434**

Woody Kimbrell, Little Lulu daily comic strip original art dated 8-25-58 (Chicago Tribune-N.Y. News Syndicate, 1958), 19-3/4" x 6"........ **$262**

Eldon Dedini, cartoon original art (undated), Caption: "The pecan pie with ice cream looks delicious." Ink and wash cartoon illustration by Playboy/New Yorker cartoonist Eldon Dedini, 10-1/2" x 13-1/2"............................. **$358**

Bill Watterson, Calvin and Hobbes daily comic strip original art dated 11-3-86 (Universal Press Syndicate, 1986), ink and graphite on bristol, 12" x 3-3/4", 16-1/2" x 8-3/4". **$65,725**

Bob Montana, Archie daily comic strip original art, dated 6-26-65 (King Features Syndicate, 1965), 18" x 5". From the Jerry Weist Collection. **$203**

Bud Sagendorf, Popeye Sunday comic strip original art dated 9-16-73 (King Features Syndicate, 1973), 21" x 14". **$358**

Cookie Jars

Cookie jars evolved from the elegant British biscuit jars found on Victorian-era tables. These containers featured bail handles, and were often made of sterling silver and cut crystal.

As the biscuit jar was adapted for use in America, it migrated from the dining table to the kitchen and, by the late 1920s, it was common to find a green-glass jar (or pink or clear), often with an applied label and a screw-top lid, on kitchen counters in the typical American home.

During the Great Depression—when stoneware was still popular, but before the arrival of widespread electric refrigeration—cookie jars in round and barrel shapes arrived. These heavy-bodied jars could be hand-painted after firing. This decoration was easily worn away by eager hands reaching for Mom's bakery. The lids of many stoneware jars typically had small tapering finials or knobs that also contributed to cracks and chips.

The golden age of cookie jars began in the 1940s and lasted for less than three decades, but the examples that survive represent an exuberance and style that have captivated collectors.

It wasn't until the 1970s that many collectors decided—instead of hiding their money in cookie jars—to invest their money in cookie jars. It was also at this time that cookie jars ceased to be simply storage vessels for bakery and evolved into a contemporary art form. And it's because of this evolution from utility to art that—with some exceptions—we have limited the scope of this section to jars made from the 1930s to the early 1970s.

The Brush Pottery Co. of Zanesville, Ohio, produced one of the first ceramic cookie jars in about 1929, and Red Wing's spongeware line from the late 1920s also included a ridged, barrel-shaped jar. Many established potteries began adding a selection of cookie jars in the 1930s.

Debutante by Metlox, 12-3/4" h., late 1950s, unmarked, also found with foil label, and in other colors. ....**$275-$450**

The 1940s saw the arrival of two of the most famous cookie jars: Shawnee's Smiley and Winnie, two portly, bashful little pigs who stand with eyes closed and heads cocked, he in overalls and bandana, she in flowered hat and long coat. And a host of Disney characters also made their way into American kitchens.

In the 1950s, the first television-influenced jars appeared, including images of Davy Crockett and Popeye. This decade also saw the end of several prominent American potteries (including Roseville) and the continued rise of imported ceramics.

A new collection of cartoon-inspired jars was popular in the 1960s, featuring characters drawn from the Flintstones, Yogi Bear, Woody Woodpecker, and Casper the Friendly Ghost. Jars reflecting the race for space included examples from McCoy and American Bisque. This decade also marked the peak production era for a host of West Coast manufacturers, led by the twin brothers Don and Ross Winton.

For more information on cookie jars, see *Warman's Cookie Jars Identification and Price Guide* by Mark F. Moran.

Mother Goose by Abingdon, 12-1/4" h., 1950s, ink-stamped, "Abingdon USA," and impressed, "695." .... **$325+**

Wigwam by Abingdon, 11-3/8" h., 1949, ink-stamped "Abingdon U.S.A." and impressed "665." .... **$395-$650**

Witch by Abingdon, 11-1/4" h., 1950s, with original foil label, "Abingdon Made in USA," ink-stamped "Abingdon U.S.A." and impressed "692." **$715**

Cookie Truck by American Bisque, 11-3/4" h., 1960s, marked on side, "U.S.A. 744," also found in larger size close to 13" h. This example................................. **$85**

Cowboy Boots by American Bisque, 12" h., 1950s, marked on back, "U.S.A. 742." .... **$50-$180**

Daisy by American Bisque, 12" h., 1950s, impressed on reverse, "U.S.A." .... **$60-$70**

Circus Horse by Brush, 11-1/2" long, early 1950s, unmarked. (Found in other color combinations.) **$600**

Rubble House by American Bisque, 9-1/2" h., 1960s, impressed mark on back, "U.S.A." (Ranging in size up to about 10" h., beware of smaller reproductions.) .... **$150-$200**

Fruit with Cookie Tray Lid by American Bisque, 6-3/4" h., lid 9-1/4" wide, 1950s, marked on bottom, "U.S.A.-602." ...... **$200+**

Squirrel with Top Hat by Brush, 11-1/4" h., 1950s, marked, "W15 USA."................................ **$300+**

Cookie Clock by Brush, impressed on side, "Tick Tock the Cookie Clock, to help yourself just lift the top!", 10" h., early 1950s, impressed mark on bottom, "W20 Brush USA." .... **$40-$75**

Potbellied Stove by California Cleminsons, 8-3/4" h., 1950s, unmarked. Found in other color combinations. ....**$100-$175**

Little Audrey by American Bisque, 13-1/2" h., early 1960s, unmarked, also found with "USA" mark. Beware of reproductions. **$2,500**

Elephant with Monkey (lid missing) by Brush, cold-paint decoration, 8-3/8" h. as is, late 1930s (?), unmarked. If complete .... **$2,000+**

Dice by Doranne of California, 8-1/2" h., 1960s, impressed mark, "J-70 Copyright (symbol) USA."................................. **$75+**

Pigeon by Fredericksburg Art Pottery, 7-1/4" h., 1940s, marked, "U.S.A. F.A.P. Co."............... **$80+**

Telephone distributed by Cardinal, 11-1/2" h., 1950s, marked on reverse, "Cardinal © 311 USA." .... **$100+**

Davy Crockett by American Bisque, 12" h., 1950s, unmarked. ....**$180-$250**

COOKIE JARS

Cookie Bear by Ludowici Celadon (?), with worn cold paint, 11-3/4" h., 1950s, marked, "Royal Ware." **$80**

Bundle of Corn by Metlox, 10-3/4" h., late 1960s, impressed mark on bottom, "Made in Poppytrail Calif." (Also found with a golden-brown glaze on cobs as though they had been grilled. In either glaze combination, it is common for the lid and base to appear slightly mismatched because they were produced separately.).........**$300+**

Little Red Riding Hood by Pottery Guild of America, 12-1/2" h., 1940s, unmarked.........**$60-$125**

Pear by McCoy, a lunch-hour piece with a cat finial that was intended for use on a planter called "Pussy at the Well," 1950s. .....**$70-$120**

King by Hedi Schoop, 12" h., 1950s, marked inside lid, "Hedi Schoop 15," with original label, "Hedi Schoop Hand Made in California." ....**$700-$800**

Tommy Turtle by Twin Winton, 13-1/8" h., late 1950s (?), unmarked, in glossy glaze; also found in wood tone. ....**$75-$110**

Basket with Flowers by Metlox, 10-3/4" h., 1960s, remnant of foil label................................**$100+**

Cookie House by McCoy, late 1950s, McCoy USA mark, with split roof lid, easily damaged, with glaze and cold paint. ....**$100-$140**

Mr. and Mrs. Owl 1950s, McCoy USA mark, cold-painted details. ....**$20-$135**

Barrel jars with stepped profiles by Red Wing. Left, with three blue lines, 7-3/8" h., late 1930s, unmarked. ....**$200+**
Right, with hand-painted flowers, 9" h., late 1930s, ink-stamped, "Red Wing Saffron Ware" in a circle...**$150+**

Banana by McCoy, 1948, McCoy mark. Left is the more typical glaze. Often found with damage to lid points............................**$40-$75, depending on color**

Flat-leaf Apple in glossy maroon, 1930s, McCoy..**$150-$200**

Elephant with Straw Hat by Metlox, 11-7/8" h., late 1950s, unmarked...**$750**

Turkey with Chick attributed to Morton Pottery, 9" h., 1960s, unmarked. .... **$50-$75**

Baking Angel, unmarked, probably by Pearl China (identified in a Pearl China catalog). **$300**

Bear with Cookie in Vest by McCoy, in atypical yellow and brown, 10-3/4" h., 1950s, impressed mark on bottom, "McCoy." **$300+**

Cookie Cop by Pfaltzgraff, 10-3/4" h., 1950s, unmarked; shown with chipping. If perfect........... **$500+**

Spaceship by Metlox, 13" h., late 1950s, impressed mark, "Made in USA." .... **$400-$600**

Old King Cole by Robinson Ransbottom, 10-1/2" h., 1950s, impressed mark, "RRPCo. USA Roseville O." .... **$70-$120**

Little Red Riding Hood by Regal China with closed basket, large transfer-decorated flowers, and gold trim, brown shoes, 13" h., 1940s, marked on bottom, "Little Red Riding Hood Patent Design No. 135889 USA." .... **$200+**

Barn by Regal China, 9" l., 1960s (?), impressed mark, "Pat. Pending." .... **$75+**

Clematis brown (3-8") by Roseville, bruise and small nicks to lid, and bruises and nicks to jar, marked. .... **$140-$300**

COOKIE JARS

Mother Goose by Metlox, 13" h., late 1960s, marked on bottom, "Made in Poppytrail California" over an outline of the state...................................**$235-$300**

Cattails in glossy green and aqua by Red Wing, both 9" h., with "Cookies" in raised lettering, showing two different knob configurations, 1940s, both ink-stamped, "Red Wing Art Pottery," also found unmarked. .... **$150-$250 each**

Dancing Peasants by Red Wing, in glossy sage green and white, with cold-paint decoration, showing variations in mold crispness, left 10" h., right 9-3/4" h., early 1940s, unmarked (also found with impressed "Red Wing USA"). ....**$40-$80 each**

Stoneware "spool" form by Red Wing with hand-painted flowers and "Cookies" in raised lettering, 1930s. Left, 8-5/8" h., unmarked. ....**$150+** Right, 9-1/4" h., ink-stamped, "Red Wing Saffron Ware." ....**$200+**

Magnolia blue (2-8") by Roseville, a couple of small chips, bruises, and burst bubbles, raised mark. ....**$110-$240**

Streetcar by Sierra-Vista, 11" l., 1950s, impressed mark, "Sierra-Vista © 54 California," and written in grease pencil, "Macy's exclusive."................**$250+**

Great Northern Dutch Girl by Shawnee, 10-1/2" h., 1950s, raised mark on bottom, "Great Northern U.S.A." and impressed "1026." ....**$125-$300**

Puss-n-Boots by Shawnee with gold trim, transfer-decorated flowers, detailed under-glaze decoration, tail behind foot, 10-1/2" h., 1940s, marked, "Patented Puss-n-Boots U.S.A." ....**$125-$400**

Goldilocks with Baby Bear by Regal China, 12-1/4" h., 1950s, cold paint and under-glaze colors, impressed mark on bottom, "Goldilocks Pat. Pending #405."...........**$150-$300**

Corn King by Shawnee, 10-1/4" h., 1940s, with original foil label, "Corn King Oven Proof Shawnee," raised mark on bottom, "Shawnee U.S.A.," and impressed "66." ....**$200-$400**

Poodle by Sierra-Vista, 13" h., introduced in 1956, impressed mark on bottom, "Sierra-Vista Ceramics Calif. © 56."... **$70-$90**

Darner Doll, 12" h., late 1960s, impressed mark, "Los Angeles Potteries © 62 #54 Hand Crafted Calif. USA." ....**$75-$100**

COOKIE JARS

10
THINGS

10 Things You Didn't Know About Advertising Cookie Jars

1 Cookie jars have been used to peddle everything from pancakes and green beans to soft drinks, cars, and dog treats, among other things.

2 It's said cookie jars (called biscuit barrels or jars) first came on the scene in England in the late 18th century. They became popular in the United States during the Great Depression, and the 1930s saw the Brush Pottery Co. create the first ceramic cookie jar (prior to that they were mostly glass or tin). As early as the 1940s, companies started using cookie jars to bring their brands into the homes and minds of Americans.

The Hamm's Beer company made a smart call when it added its "Beer Bear" to its advertising campaign. This 1970s cookie jar, in the shape of the Hamm's Bear "Sascha," carries a value of $225-$250.

3 Early on, American companies would fill cookie jars with their product and sell the entire container. It was an easy and popular way to promote their brands and products.

4 Disney celebrated its family of characters and advertised its movies with cookie jars featuring Dumbo, Beauty and the Beast, and Mickey Mouse, among others.

5 To avoid the multitude of reproduction cookie jars out there, measure the size of the jar and turn to a reputable cookie jar guide to check the dimensions listed for original jars – fakes are often smaller than originals. Also, check the bottom and the lip of antique cookie jars for scratches – over the years a truly vintage jar rarely remains free from even small scratches.

6 One of the earliest companies to use cookie jars in advertising was Aunt Jemima Pancake Flour. The jars were offered as a premium in the 1920s and 1930s (a popular practice during this era).

7 A popular site for cookie jar collectors to talk jars and learn more is http://thecookiejar.net.

8 Various outlets sell cookie jars, but Remember When Relics in Delavan, Wisconsin not only sells cookie jars, but is also home to an extensive cookie jar museum.

9 The late Andy Warhol was a fan of cookie jars, amassing a collection of several hundred jars. The collection sold for nearly $250,000 in 1988.

10 Hollywood has turned to these timeless treat containers to help promote movies and starlets.

Often believed to be McCoy-made, this popular Quaker Oats cookie jar, circa 1970, was actually made by Regal China. It's valued at $500-$600 in near mint condition.

Compiled by Antoinette Rahn. Sources: About.com Collectibles (Barbara Crews); The Old Cookie Jar Shop http://www.the-old-cookie-jar-shop.com; Collector Cookie Jars (collectorcookiejars.com); *The New York Times*, "Warhol Cookie Jars Sell for $247,830" by Rita Reif; www.MountainStatesCollector.com, "Cookie Jars That Advertised" by Robert Reed; Remember When Relics: www.rememberwhenllc.com; *Warman's Cookie Jars Identification and Price Guide*.

Country Store

Few categories of fine collectibles are as fun and colorful as country store memorabilia. The staple of quality antiques shows and shops nationwide, the phrase often refers to such an expansive field of items that it's often difficult to decide where "country store collectibles" begin and "advertising collectibles" end. That's one of the very reasons why the category remains so popular and one of the two reasons why this market is growing in value and appeal.

Country store collectibles are associated with items in use in general or frontier retail establishments dating from the mid-1800s to well into the 1940s. The country store was a natural evolution of the pioneer trading post as the more affordable source of day-to-day living items, baking and cooking supplies, or goods for general household and home garden use. Country store furniture is rare, but larger pieces usually include retail countertops and dry goods bins.

The appeal of country store memorabilia has never really waned during the last 40 years, and the emergence of online trading in the late 1990s redefined items dealers once described as rare. Much like how mid-20th century rock and roll and entertainment memorabilia is used to decorate Applebee's Bar and Grill restaurants, so have

Bill and Kathie Gasperino displayed their 35-year collection of country store collectibles in a building next to their home in Washington State. The two worked as a team, traveling across Idaho, Montana and Oregon, inspecting attics and basements of shuttered stores to amass the collection.

country store collectibles been used to line the walls of Cracker Barrel Restaurant and Old Country Store establishments to stoke big appetites for comfort food.

Among items in high demand are original and complete store displays in top condition. These displays were originally intended to hold the product sold to customers and were not generally available for private ownership. Those that survive are highly sought after by collectors for their graphic appeal and their rarity. Until recently, restoration of these items would negatively impact auction prices. However, recent auction results show strong prices for these items if they are rare and retain at least most of the original graphics.

A great deal of time, talent and production value was invested in these store displays. Think of them as the Super Bowl commercials of their day. With limited counter space and a captive audience, marketers used every technique and theme available to catch customers' eyes. And here is where the appeal of country store collectibles crosses over so many different categories of collectibles. A store display of a fine paper poster advertising DeLaval Cream Separators may appeal to those who collect farming items, cows, and country maidens in addition to country store items. The same principle applies to store displays. Are they collected as country store items or as well-preserved examples of vintage advertising, or both? The definition takes shape

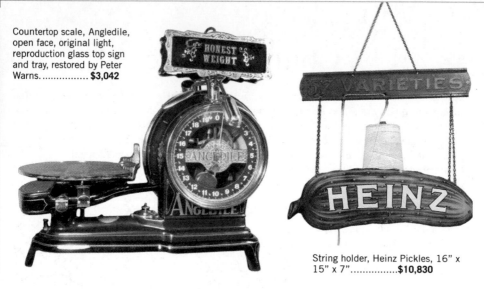

Countertop scale, Angledile, open face, original light, reproduction glass top sign and tray, restored by Peter Warns. **$3,042**

String holder, Heinz Pickles, 16" x 15" x 7". **$10,830**

when the items are added to a well-curated collection, like the one Bill and Kathie Gasperino amassed over the last 35 years.

The couple sold off the collection in April 2013 with Showtime Auction Services, as part of a massive collectibles event that realized more than $2.2 million. Together the couple happily traveled across the Pacific Northwest and beyond cultivating a collection of obscure and unusual items. It was a true team effort. "Kathie and I drove all over – Montana, Idaho and Oregon," Bill said. "Half the fun was finding the stuff. We loved crawling around attics and basements of old stores finding things."

The Gasperino collection was displayed next to the couple's Washington state home in a large building designed to look like a circa 1880s country store. "We had dry goods on one side, and on the other was a combination of things you'd find in a store of that period," Bill said. The two began branching out to larger and larger items, such as country spool cabinets and eventually back bars, a bank teller booth, and even a 19th century soda fountain.

When it came time to downsize, the Gasperino collection hit the hobby like a comet. It remains one of the most important collections offered in recent years. Even the Gasperinos were surprised at the prices collectors were willing to pay for especially rare items in top condition.

"People called us and let us know how much they appreciated the collection and the quality," said Bill, a retired police officer. "We knew it was special to us, but it was interesting to hear from collectors who said they hadn't seen some of these items."

The Gasperino Collection is a good example of why the country store collectibles category continues to hold its own. The category was extremely popular between the late 1970s and the mid-1990s. It appears the hobby is reaching a point at which longtime collectors are ready to begin a new phase of their lives – one that requires fewer items and less space – and are offering these collections for the first time in decades.

So if the old adage, "The best time to buy an antique is when you see it" is true, the country store collectibles category stands to grow as these large collections come to market, and the crossover appeal catches the attention of a wide variety of collectors.

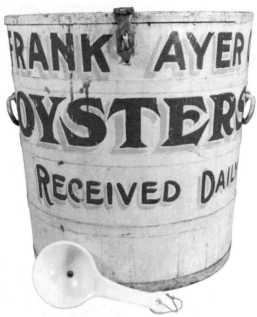

String holder, Lipton Tea, tin, 13-3/4" x 20"................. **$2,565**

Store display, Frank Ayer oyster barrel, original milk glass draining scoop, 19-1/2" h. x 19" dia. **$2,850**

Sign, Snider's Pork and Beans, linen, framed under glass, 38" x 12"... **$371**

Cheese safe, cast iron with glass dome and counter balance lift, Edward R. Smith, Oshkosh, Wisconsin, rare, 19" x 41-1/2" x 23"................................ **$4,500**

Spice cabinet, country store floor model, 16 drawers with beveled mirror fronts and four pull-out bins with glass fronts, original decals, 77" x 48" x 21-1/2". **$1,565**

Bag holder, Swifts Arrow Borax Soap and Wool Soap Chips, dated 1900, two sided, 39-1/2" x 13-1/2". **$969**

Store display, Old Quaker Oats, tin, die-cut light-up, with three boxes of Quaker Quick Oats as props, 19-1/2" x 24-1/2" x 7". **$1,368**

Banner, Gold Dust Washing Powder, cardboard, rare, 11' fully extended, letters: 8" w. x 16" l. **$2,265**

Bag holder, KC Baking Powder, rare, 28" x 42". **$684**

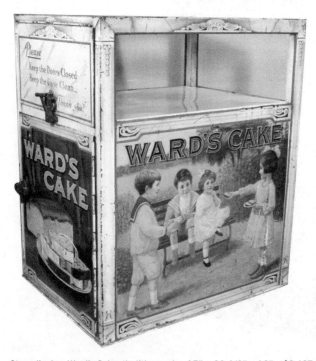

Store display, Ward's Cake, tin lithography, 17" x 20-1/2" x 13"...**$3,135**

Cheese safe, wood and wire, 14" h. x 24" dia. **$171**

Sign, Kellogg's Toasted Corn Flakes, die-cut cardboard, 14-1/2" x 24-1/2". **$456**

Barrel label, Heinz 57, 11" dia. **$29**

Sign, Snider's Catsup, tin, embossed, 19-1/2" x 3-3/4". **$257**

Trade sign bracket, butcher, cast iron, painted, 24" x 28". **$2,964**

Sign, Campbell's Soup, tin, embossed, well-known and highly sought after by collectors of both advertising signs and folk art items, rare, 40" x 27-1/2". **$54,000**

TOP LOT!

Store bin, Japan Tea, tin, 15-1/2" w. x 16" l. x 15" d............. **$570**

Banner, Howdy Orange Soda, paper, no dimensions available. **$150**

Cabinet, Peerless Dyes, tombstone top, tin front, tambour door, also found made of composite material, rare, 19" x 32" x 11". **$285**

Store display, C / B A'La Spirite Corsets, original etched and gold leaf on front of case, mannequin original, 23-1/2" x 42" x 20"................................**$17,100**

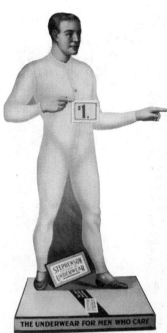

Store display, Stephenson Underwear, tin, die-cut, rare, 16-1/2" x 38" x 10". **$3,705**

Clock, Walkden's Inks, manufactured by Baird Clock, pendulum, no key, 18" w. x 30" l. x 4-1/2" d.......................... **$1,800**

Sign, Hy-Quality Coffee, die-cut cardboard string hanging sign, 16" w. x 38-1/2" l..................... **$684**

Syrup dispenser, Mission Fruit Orange/Grapefruit, porcelain with light-up center, indentation in lid top likely to display fresh fruit, rare...................... **$3,420**

Store display, Bow-Legs White Metal Clothes Pins, with 14 boxes of product and brochures, 9-3/4" w. x 3-1/2" l. x 8-1/4" d............ **$399**

Sign, Allens Red Tame Cherry Co., tin, circa 1910, die cut embossed, metal easel back, American Art Works, Coshocton, Ohio, accompanied by history of artist and subjects, 23-1/2" w. x 35-1/4" l. ..**$11,400**

Store display, roll of cigars and chewing tobacco, rare. **$285**

Store display, Moth-Ene, cardboard with easel back, six tins, 12-1/2" w. x 7-1/2" h. **$285**

Sign, Whistle soda, die-cut cardboard depicting boy on bicycle, 20-1/2" w. x 21-1/2" l. **$450**

Popcorn wagon/peanut roaster, circa 1907, made by The R.O. Stutsman Co., "The Ideal" model, discovered in Lewistown, Montana, original working condition, fueled with white gas, 51" w. x 30" d. x 80" h. **$8,550**

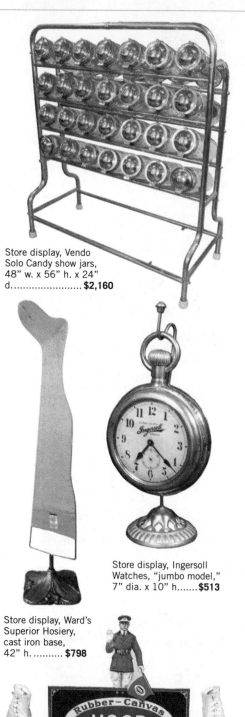

Store display, Vendo Solo Candy show jars, 48" w. x 56" h. x 24" d. **$2,160**

Store display, Ingersoll Watches, "jumbo model," 7" dia. x 10" h. **$513**

Store display, Ward's Superior Hosiery, cast iron base, 42" h. **$798**

Sign, Coca-Cola button flange, drugstore, rare, 18" x 22-1/2". **$2,160**

Store display, Hood Footwear, tin, die-cut, counter top display, with pair of shoes, 14" x 13-1/2" x 5". **$5,130**

Meat rack, Gus. V. Brecht, B.S. Co. Mfg., St. Louis, patent 1892, nickel-plated cast iron and steel, three-tier, decorated with steer horns and Buffalo Bill roping a steer, original wall hanging brackets, 9' w. with adjustable height............................. **$6,840**

Mannequin, male youth, German, dressed in wool suit, wax head, porcelain teeth, human hair and eye lashes, composite body, rare, 52" h. **$7,200**

Soda fountain, quarter-sawn oak, circa late 1800s, marble top, icebox compartments, six stools, original slag glass lamps and 5 Cent Brazilla lamp globe, original fountain on front bar with onyx dispenser handles, 8'-1" x 101" x 20", front bar 80-1/2" x 41" x 24"....................**$6,600**

Store display, Munsingwear, tin, die-cut, with three boxes of product, 9-1/2" square base x 45" h. **$9,120**

Store showcase, general store ribbon cabinet manufactured by Exhibition Showcase Co., Erie, Pennsylvania, circa 1882, discovered in Judith Gap, Montana, eight tiers, one of the largest spool cabinets ever made, 32" w. x 47-1/2" l. x 27-1/2" d......... **$969**

Corner sign, Buffalo Lager, reverse painted glass, original metal frame painted gold, rare, 16" w. x 26" h. x 8" d............................**$12,540**

Sign, Walden Eddy Plows, outdoor stand-style sign, Greenwich, New York, rare, 59" w. x 24" h. ..**$18,000**

Sign, Mitchell, Lewis & Co. Wagon Manufacturing, Racine, Wisconsin, paper lithography, depicting circling of wagons and American Indian attack, cameos depict 1834 Chicago factory and 1883 Racine factory, dime-size restoration in far right wagon canopy, only known example, framed under glass in walnut recessed frame, 32" w. x 26" h. **$25,650**

Window display, Wrigley's Gum, die cut cardboard, dimensional in two pieces, 37" w. x 29" h. **$1,920**

Sign, Castle Hall, die cut tin string hanging sign, rare, 27-1/2" w. x 9-1/2" h. **$1,140**

Store showcase, double tower, cathedral-style, curved glass, oak with nickel corners and glass top, rare at this width, 72" w. x 42" l. x 26" d. **$10,260**

Poster, Deering All-Steel Binder, paper, titled "Harvest isn't what it used to be," Wm Deering & Co., Chicago, dealer James Rork & Bro., North Lansing, Mich., repaired tear, 27-3/4" w. x 21-3/4" h. **$2,280**

Store display, Albright Rubberset, tin, with seven brushes not original to display, 15-1/2" w. x 12-1/2" l. x 6" d. **$2,280**

Store bin, Wilbur's Food wood store bin, original stenciling, 17-1/2" w. x 36-1/2" l. x 20" h. **$5,700**

Sign, DeLaval Cream Separators, red version, original gesso frame, 29-3/4" w. x 40-3/4" h. **$3,900**

Store display, Rat Bis-Kit, papier maché, discovered in Virginia City, Montana, rare, 12-3/4" w. x 20" l. x 13" d.......................... **$5,700**

Counter display, mechanical dairy cow, electrical, covered papier maché, head and mouth move, which rings bell around neck, missing one teat, 30" w. x 17" l. x 8" h.............. **$2,565**

Store bin, Choice Imperial Coffee, original stenciling, 15" w. x 41" l. x 13" d.......................... **$8,550**

Window display, Hills Bros. Coffee, die-cut cardboard, easel back, 24" w. x 60-1/2" l. **$1,254**

Store display, Auto-Strop Safety Razor, battery operated, rare, 17-1/2" w. x 31" l. x 7" d. **$3,500**

Decoys

The origin of the decoy in America lies in early American history, pre-dating the American pioneer by at least 1,000, perhaps 2,000 years. In 1924, at an archeological site in Nevada, the Lovelock Cave excavations yielded a group of 11 decoys preserved in protective containers. The careful manner of their storage preserved them for us to enjoy an estimated 1,000 to 2,000 years later.

When the first settlers came to North America, their survival was just as dependent upon hunting wild game for food as it was for the Indians. They began to fashion likenesses of their prey out of different materials, ultimately finding that wood was an ideal raw material. Thus the carving of wildfowl decoys was born out of necessity for food.

Historical records indicate wooden decoys were in general use as early as the 1770s, but it seems likely that they would have been widely used before then.

Until the middle of the 1800s, there was not sufficient commercial demand for decoys to enable carvers to make a living selling them, so most decoys were made for themselves and friends. Then the middle of the 19th century saw the birth of the market gunners. During the market-gunning period, many carvers began making a living with their decoys, and the first factory-made decoys came into existence. The huge numbers of decoys needed to supply the market hunters and the rising numbers of hunters for sport or sustenance made commercial decoy carving possible.

The market hunters and other hunters killed anything that flew. This indiscriminate destruction of wildfowl was the coup de grace for many bird species, rendering them extinct.

The United States Congress, with the passage of the Migratory Bird Treaty Act in 1918, outlawed the killing of waterfowl for sale. Following the passage of the 1918 act came the demise of the factory decoys of the day.

Today a few contemporary carvers carry on their tradition. They produce incredibly intricate, lifelike birds. What these contemporary carvings represent is that decoy carving is one of the few early American folk arts that has survived into our modern times and is still being pursued.

For more information on decoys, see *Warman's Duck Decoys* by Russell E. Lewis.

Rare hollow carved gadwall hen, Cigar Daisy, Chincoteague, Virginia, branded and signed, relief wing tip carving, very good and original condition......**$4,000**

Guyette, Schmidt & Deeter

Large plover carved in the Virginia style,
Mark McNair, Craddockville, Virginia,
relief wing carving and slightly turned
head, original paint that has been aged,
small "in the making" crack in back and
underside....................................**$800**

Guyette, Schmidt & Deeter

Two whimbrels with turned heads, Cigar Daisey, Chincoteague,
Virginia, both have carved crossed wing tips and carved
secondaries, unsigned, very good and original condition. **$750**

Guyette, Schmidt & Deeter

Oversize hollow merganser carved in
the Maine tradition, Mark McNair,
Craddockville, Virginia, inlet head,
signed and dated 1996, original and
good condition...........................**$2,500**

Guyette, Schmidt & Deeter

Coot, Cigar Daisey, Chincoteague, Virginia, branded and signed,
very good and original condition. **$550**

Guyette, Schmidt & Deeter

Classic 1936 model canvasback drake,
Ward Brothers, Crisfield, Maryland,
signed at a later date, original paint with
minor wear on much of the decoy, crack
partway through neck, small rough area
on one edge of bill, chip missing from
one edge of tail, old repair to several
chips at neck base...................**$30,000**

Guyette, Schmidt & Deeter

Rare magnum mallard drake, Cigar Daisey, Chincoteague, Virginia,
branded "Cigar," hollow carved with relief wing tip carving, small
cracks in tail, otherwise very good and original condition. .. **$1,000**

Guyette, Schmidt & Deeter

Rigmate pair of canvasbacks, Ward Brothers, Crisfield, Maryland, circa 1940, both have slightly turned heads and are signed, paint restored by Ward Brothers at a later date, few small dents, small chip missing from one side of drake's bill. **$5,500**

Guyette, Schmidt & Deeter

Canvasback drake, John Daddy Holly, Havre de Grace, Maryland, third quarter 19th century, from Carroll's Island Club, club brand in underside, old in use repaint, neck crack repair, small cracks and dents. **$2,500**

Guyette, Schmidt & Deeter

Widgeon hen, Lee Dudley, Knott's Island, North Carolina, last quarter 19th century, branded "L.D." on underside, old in use repaint, cracks in neck and body, old bill repair. **$8,500**

Guyette, Schmidt & Deeter

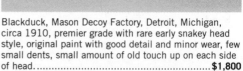

Rare mallard drake, Ned Burgess, Churches Island, North Carolina, first quarter 20th century, original paint with minor wear, filler and two finish nails added to crack in neck, cracks in underside............................**$3,000**

Guyette, Schmidt & Deeter

Blackduck, Mason Decoy Factory, Detroit, Michigan, circa 1910, premier grade with rare early snakey head style, original paint with good detail and minor wear, few small dents, small amount of old touch up on each side of head. **$1,800**

Guyette, Schmidt & Deeter

Preening whimbrel, Elmer Crowell, East Harwich, Massachusetts, Crowell's rectangular stamp is in underside, fine feather paint detail and excellent patina, original paint with minor shrinkage, small crack through one jesso thigh. **$30,000**

Guyette, Schmidt & Deeter

Full size decorative sandpiper, Elmer Crowell, East Harwich, Massachusetts, signed and dated 1940, fine feather paint detail, very good and original. **$3,500**

Guyette, Schmidt & Deeter

Full-size standing widgeon drake, Oliver Lawson Crisfield, Maryland, signed and dated 1965, fine carving detail with raised wings and fluted tail, few tiny rubs, otherwise very good and original..**$7,000**

Guyette, Schmidt & Deeter

Rare early "drop wing" style greater yellowlegs, Elmer Crowell, East Harwich, Massachusetts, circa 1910, Crowell's oval brand is in underside, one of Crowell's earlier decoratives with paint pattern reminiscent of decoys from the Parker Whittamore hunting rig, Essex, Massachusetts, carved clam shell base, near mint original paint with good patina, several tiny cracks in jesso. **$16,000**

Guyette, Schmidt & Deeter

Full size killdeer plover, Elmer Crowell, East Harwich, Massachusetts, Crowell's rectangular stamp is in the base, signed "Killdeer Plover," slightly turned head, fine and precise feather paint detail with incredible color, tiny dent in one side of tail. **$10,000**

Guyette, Schmidt & Deeter

Classic mallard hen, Robert Elliston, Bureau, Illinois, circa 1880s, retains Elliston weight, fine paint detail, original paint with minor wear, few small dents..**$3,750**

Guyette, Schmidt & Deeter

Hollow carved redhead drake, Tom Chambers, Toronto, Ontario, first quarter 20th century, branded "J.T. McMillan" in underside for James T. McMillan, St. Clair Flats shooting company member, 1913-1946; original paint with good patina and minor wear, few small dents.**$1,700**

Guyette, Schmidt & Deeter

Pair of hollow carved mallards, William Gibian, Onancock, Virginia, both signed, both have slightly turned heads, raised wing tip carving and fluted tails, very good and original..................................... **$1,500**

Guyette, Schmidt & Deeter

Hollow carved redhead hen, Davison Hawthorne, Greenville, Delaware, signed and dated 2009, fine wing tip carving detail and fluted tail, very good and original. **$300**

Guyette, Schmidt & Deeter

Sleeping Bluebill hen, Keith Mueller, Killingsworth, Connecticut, bill is buried in feathers, original paint with minor wear, few tiny dents.......**$425**

Guyette, Schmidt & Deeter

Rare solid body scoter, Joseph Lincoln, Accord, Massachusetts, circa 1900, original paint with moderate wear, several cracks and shot marks. **$1,700**

Guyette, Schmidt & Deeter

Rare bluebill drake, Levi Rhodes Truex, Absecon, New Jersey, first quarter 20th century, good feather paint detail on back, original paint with good patina and minor wear, slight separation at body seam. **$1,200**

Guyette, Schmidt & Deeter

Rare hollow brant, Mark Kears, Linwood, New Jersey, first to second quarters 20th century, outstanding dry original scratch paint shows minor wear, wonderful patina, excellent structural condition..............**$2,600**

Guyette, Schmidt & Deeter

Hollow carved oversize Canada goose, circa 1900, found in Eastville, Virginia, raised neck seat and ice dip behind head, weathered and worn, crack through neck, small cracks in body, minor roughness to end of bill.........................**$1,100**

Guyette, Schmidt & Deeter

Hollow bluebill hen, H.V. Shourds, Tuckerton, New Jersey, last quarter 19th century, branded "H.W. GODFREY" twice on bottom, original paint shows moderate wear and some flaking to bare wood, some filler has popped out of body seam, overall sound structurally...**$2,000**

Guyette, Schmidt & Deeter

Rare pintail drake, Ira Hudson, Chincoteague, Virginia, first quarter 20th century, round body style with banjo tail, slightly turned head and good scratch paint detail, original paint with minor wear, cracks in underside, chip missing from end of tail, small dents, most of bill is a professional replacement...**$4,000**

Guyette, Schmidt & Deeter

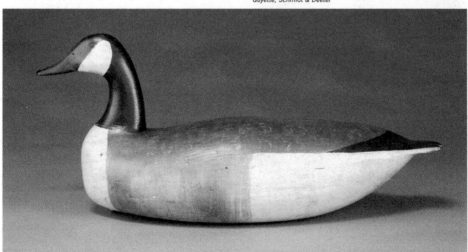

Hollow Canada goose, Levi Rhodes Truex, Atlantic City, New Jersey, first quarter 20th century, from gunning rig of Earl Leeds, Pleasantville, New Jersey, stamped with his name and address, outstanding dry original condition. **$5,750**

Guyette, Schmidt & Deeter

Black bellied plover by a member of Verity family, Seaford, Long Island, New York, last quarter 19th century, relief wing carving with extended wing tips, original paint with good detail and minor wear on most of the decoy, old repaint on black areas and white on underside, lightly hit by shot. **$1,400**

Guyette, Schmidt & Deeter

Two decoys, Doug Jester, Chincoteague, Virginia, 1st quarter 20th century, old in use repaint, cracks and filled rough areas in bodies.............................**$300**

Guyette, Schmidt & Deeter

Flat sided yellowlegs from Hatteras, North Carolina, circa 1920, original paint with minor wear, structurally good..**$900**

Guyette, Schmidt & Deeter

Yellowlegs, John Fosdick, Massapequa, Long Island, New York, circa 1910, in feeding pose, branded "J.S. Fosdick," original paint with minor discoloration and wear, bill is an old replacement.......................**$475**

Guyette, Schmidt & Deeter

Robin snipe in spring plumage, Harry V. Shourds, Tuckerton, New Jersey, first quarter 20th century, worn original paint, lightly hit by shot, bill is an old replacement...**$650**

Guyette, Schmidt & Deeter

Hollow carved brant, Charles Birch, Willis Wharf, Virginia, second quarter 20th century, worn old paint, crack through neck and in underside, small dents. **$1,000**

Guyette, Schmidt & Deeter

Blackduck from Cobb Island, Virginia, last quarter 19th century, hollow carved with raised "V" wing carving, raised neck seat and tack eyes, old in use repaint, reglued cracks in neck, lightly hit by shot, crack in underside. **$400**

Guyette, Schmidt & Deeter

Two blackducks found in Eastville, Virginia, both have raised neck seats and slightly turned heads, old in use repaint, small cracks. **$300**

Guyette, Schmidt & Deeter

Rare widgeon drake, Miles Hancock, Chincoteague, Virginia, original paint with minor wear, mostly on breast, few small dents. **$550**

Guyette, Schmidt & Deeter

Dowitcher in fall plumage, John Dilley, Quogue, Long Island, New York, "Dilley" and "Dowitcher" written in pencil on underside below stick hole, believed to have been done by the maker, intricate feather paint detail, original paint showing some wear and flaking with some light inpainting to one side of stick hole running part way up breast, original bill has second coat of paint, one or two small chips in bill. ..**$2,750**

Guyette, Schmidt & Deeter

Robin snipe from Kitty Hawk, North Carolina, circa 1900, flat sided, branded "J.H.D." for John Dunham, Boulder, Colorado, excellent original paint, lightly hit by shot, chip missing from end of bill, crack in underside...**$650**

Guyette, Schmidt & Deeter

Two blackducks, Doug Jester, Chincoteague, Virginia, first quarter 20th century, old in use repaint by Jester, minor wear, minor roughness to edges of tails. ...**$325**

Guyette, Schmidt & Deeter

Pintail drake working duck decoy, A. Elmer Crowell (1862-1952), East Harwich, Massachusetts, slightly turned head, impressed owner's name on base "E.FLAGG," (imperfections), 7" h. x 6-1/2" w. x 16" l. **$840**

Skinner, Inc., www.skinnerinc.com

Pair of hollow mallard decoys, Charles Perdew (1874-1963), Henry, Illinois, early 20th century, hen with turned head, both with inset glass eyes, delineated bills, distinctive shaped tail, drake with applied weight, varnished, 6-3/4", 7-1/2" h., 14", 17" l., respectively. **$8,400**

Skinner, Inc., www.skinnerinc.com

TOP LOT!

Pair of rare Ward Brothers widgeon decoys, Lemuel T. Ward (1896-1983) and Stephen Ward (1895-1976), Crisfield, Maryland, early 20th century, turned-head figures with original paint, minor losses, repairs, both inscribed on bottom with black marker "WARD BROS. CRISFIELD MD.," wood used is possibly balsam fir, 15-1/2" l...**$132,000**

Skinner, Inc., www.skinnerinc.com

Black bellied plover, George Boyd, Seabrook, New Hampshire, first quarter 20th century, exceptional paint detail, dry original paint, excellent structural condition. **$5,250**

Guyette, Schmidt & Deeter

Two canvas over wooden framed coots from North Carolina, first quarter 20th century, old in use repaint, small amount of roughness on one head... **$175**

Guyette, Schmidt & Deeter

Illinois River mallard drake decoy, reportedly by Edward Shirtz, Henry, Illinois, circa 1936, hollow decoy with painted relief-carved eyes, base inscribed "ES" with applied weight with raised manufacturer inscription "Raymond Lead Co. Chicago, ILL.," paint appears original, paint loss, 7" h., 16-3/4" l. ...**$738**

Skinner, Inc., www.skinnerinc.com

Canvasback drake from Susquehanna River, first quarter 20th century, old in use repaint, crack through neck.. **$275**

Guyette, Schmidt & Deeter

Folk carved and painted hooded merganser decoy, possibly Virginia, early to mid-20th century, applied glass eyes, imperfections, 5-7/8" h., 12-1/2" l.... **$840**

Skinner, Inc., www.skinnerinc.com

Three small carved and painted duck decoys, America, early 20th century, hollow blue wing teal hen, possibly by Charles Perdew (1874-1963), Henry, Illinois, the name "S. WILCOX" impressed on bottom; bluebill hen reportedly by "Clarence Krieser, Manitowac [sic], Wisconsin, c. 1936," according to label on bottom; possible Oldsquaw with "JS" and indistinct inscription on base, imperfections, 4" to 5" h., 11" to 13" l......... **$2,280**

Skinner, Inc., www.skinnerinc.com

Pair of miniature mallard duck decoys, reportedly made by Charles Perdew (1874-1963), Henry, Illinois, early 20th century, turned-head drake and hen with painted eyes and delineated bills, 3-1/2" h., 3-5/8" h., 7" l., 7-1/2" l., respectively. **$5,700**

Skinner, Inc., www.skinnerinc.com

Six carved and painted fish decoys, America, early to mid-20th century, five with applied sheet metal fins, painted or tack eyes, one painted red, yellow, and white attributed to John Tax, Osakis, Minnesota, one painted red and white with applied gold glitter attributed to Henry Max (1903-1978), Fergus Falls, Minnesota, wear, 4-1/2" to 6-1/4" l......................**$420**

Skinner, Inc., www.skinnerinc.com

Disney

Collectibles that feature Mickey Mouse, Donald Duck, and other famous characters of cartoon icon Walt Disney are everywhere. They can be found with little effort at flea markets, garage sales, local antiques and toys shows, and online as well as through auction houses and specialty catalogs.

Of the Disney toys, comic books, posters, and other items produced from the 1930s through the 1960s, prewar Disney material is by far the most desirable.

The Art of Animation by Bob Thomas, 1958, autographed by Walt Disney, signature located on page facing title page...............**$4,800**

Swann Galleries

Walt Disney Mickey and Minnie Mouse teaset with images of Mickey stirring tea and/or Minnie enjoying a piece of cake on surface of items made of French ceramic with silver highlights, large teapot, lidded sugar, creamer, six plates and six cups, in very good condition with some minor rubs to finish, largest item 8" h. **$115**

James D. Julia, Inc.

Artist's proof large-scale Mickey Mouse figure, hollow, wooden, carved, vibrantly painted parts, body, nose, eyes, ears and mouth, and unpainted varnished spots, marked "04/10" and "A/P" on heel of left foot, 59" h. on 32-1/2" base **$3,000**

Profiles in History

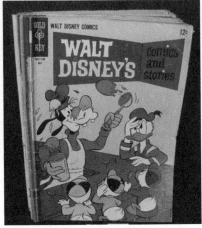

Walt Disney Xylophone with original box, circa 1960s, manufactured by Tudor Metal Products, very little wear, dents or nicks, vibrant colors, 12-1/4" x 4-1/4"............**$35**

Matthews Auctions

Disney comic books, 12, circa late 1960s, published by Dell and Gold Key, both of which came into their own and thrived in the 1960s by teaming up with popular television and film studios to features stories in comic books. **$150**

Toronto Toy Auction

Assorted Disney tin items, red-striped garbage pail, Walt Disney World lunch box, Disney school bus lunch pail, Pinocchio red cylinder tin, and independent spinning globe. **$45**

Toronto Toy Auction

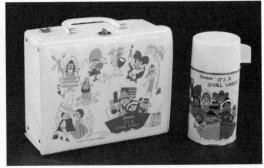

Hamilton Enterprises Mickey Mouse gumball machine, coin-operated, circa 1938, considered a "3-way vendor" to dispense gumballs, candy or nuts, decal depicts Disney graphics of Mickey Mouse, Goofy, Donald, Pluto on green porcelain/enamel body with silver metal chute lid, rubber feet on metal base are intact, excellent condition......**$1,800**

Profiles in History

Disney "It's a Small World" vinyl lunch box and bottle, never used, mint condition, 1968, manufactured by Aladdin, artwork on box and bottle with caricatures featured on multi-cultural Disneyland and Disneyworld ride. **$250**

Profiles in History

Mickey Mouse silver-plated children's cereal spoons on display card, circa 1930s, with Mickey Mouse's image cast on handle, awarded as premiums for buying packages of Post's Bran Flakes and Grape Nuts Flakes, entire package in excellent condition..**$600**

Profiles in History

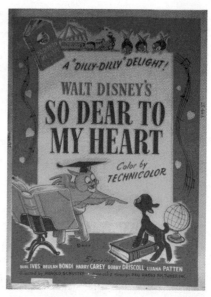

Walt Disney's So Dear to My Heart movie poster, circa 1949, heavy cardstock, unmounted, some edge wear and pinholes to border and 2" tear to top center, 30" x 40". **$225**

Mosby & Co. Auctions

Pen and ink illustration of Donald Duck and one of his nephews, original piece by Jack Hannah, a U.S. First Day Cover for Joel Chandler Harris, commemorative piece dated 12-9-1948. ....**$250**

Philip Weiss Auctions

Limited edition Who Framed Roger Rabbit? celluloid, framed and signed by artist with inscription "Happy 10th Anniversary 'Roger Rabbit,'" edition No. 62 of 250, 21" x 22" with mat. **$290**

Philip Weiss Auctions

Trio of Disney collectibles including bookends featuring the Seven Dwarfs, goose egg featuring Dumbo, and Donald Duck Diner toy. **$240**

Philip Weiss Auctions

Silver-plated Mickey Mouse radio, circa 1930s, tube radio with Art Deco silver styling and embossed image of Mickey marching and playing big bass drum, back of piece reveals a partially visible maker's name, "Ramsco Corp., New York, USA," very good condition, some tarnish, 9" x 6-1/2" x 4". **$2,300**

James D. Julia, Inc.

Celluloid of Disney's "Little Toot," circa 1950s, on a specially prepared background, probably courvoisier, presented to Hardie Gramatky by Walt Disney, inscribed "To Hardie from Walt" by hand on mat, 8" x 14-1/2"..**$7,500**

Philip Weiss Auctions

Lionel Mickey Mouse steel clockwork handcar with Mickey and Minnie pumping around accompanying tin track, good condition, 8" l............**$402**

James D. Julia, Inc.

Dolls

Dolls have been children's playthings for centuries. Dolls also have served other functions. From the 14th through 18th centuries, doll making was centered in Europe, mainly in Germany and France. The French dolls produced in this era were representations of adults and dressed in the latest styles. They were not children's toys.

During the mid-19th century, child and baby dolls made of wax, cloth, bisque and porcelain were introduced. Facial features were hand painted, wigs were made of mohair and human hair, and the dolls were dressed in the current fashions for babies or children.

Doll making in the United States began to flourish in the 1900s with companies such as Effanbee, Madame Alexander, and Ideal.

Recognizing the Beauty of a Good Name

During the years of World War II, the development of new manmade products in the scientific community was centered on items allocated for military use. After the war, the emphasis changed.

Manmade products that had been put on hold because of the war or that had been used by the military were now made available for general use. Petroleum-based fibers such as nylon and later Dacron and Orlon were introduced to the clothing industry, and their ease of care and cleaning made life much easier for women who had worked so hard and sacrificed so much during the war years. Other petroleum-based products such as hard plastic were now more available, and vinyl was soon to follow.

These new manmade products did not go unnoticed by doll manufacturers. The development of new and innovative dolls had not been a priority for several years, but things were about to change. The new manmade products were exactly what the doll world had been waiting for. During the 1940s, hard plastic was being used in limited supply. Shortly after the war, a variation of plastic – called vinyl – was developed. Hard plastic, vinyl, or a combination of the two became the material of choice for doll manufacturers in the late 1940s and 1950s.

The major American doll companies now had what they needed to manufacturer a quality product, but how could they sell this product to a generation that had learned to do without?

The manufacturers looked at their major consumers: the women of America. These women were no longer restrained from buying as they had been. Many now had families with young children, nice homes, husbands

Ideal, hard plastic Toni doll, fully marked "P-90 Ideal Doll Made in USA" with matte unplayed-with finish, lashed blue sleeping eyes, original platinum blonde nylon wig in original set, factory original tagged dress with attached slip, panties and shoes with wrist tag; original box with Toni Play Wave set including curlers, lotion, shampoo, comb and directions; excellent condition, original box has some wear and breaking; 14" h. **$650**

Dan Morphy Auctions

Ideal, Harriet Hubbard Ayer doll in box, 1953, marks: Ideal Doll//P-90 on body, five-piece hard plastic body, soft vinyl head, sleep eyes, blonde wig, red tulle over taffeta gown, matching headpiece; in box with some original makeup; 14". $125

McMasters Harris Auction Co.

with good jobs and good salaries, cars and, for the first time in many years, they were being exposed to glamour and fashion. Magazines and newspapers were filled with advertisements for beauty products and stylish couture. No more painting seams on legs to represent stockings. No more coats and jackets made from blankets. No more dresses made and remade from old fabric. No more fingernails worn down because of work on military machinery, and no more hair hidden under bandanas. After five years of drabness, it was now time to shine – not only for ladies but also for dolls.

The doll manufacturers observed the popularity of the beauty products and the fashions flooding the pages of magazines and newspapers. The marketing people also realized that associating their dolls with a popular product would certainly increase sales. A popular product name would mean a popular product – at least that was the plan.

One of the earliest doll manufacturers to take advantage of this sales idea was the Ideal Toy Co. Ideal was known for its fine dolls and had been in business since the early 1900s, but the postwar period was a new market and the company was eager to compete.

Toni Home Permanents had become an overnight sensation for ladies and children. Now, home permanents could be done in the comfort of your home, and if the mother could give a permanent, why not the child? The Toni Co. allowed the Ideal Toy Co. to produce a doll that had hair that could be combed, washed and curled with a perm-type solution (not harmful). The perm rods and perm box looked just like the adult version. It even came with perm papers. While the perms were not always satisfactory, the sales proved very successful for Ideal and the idea spread.

A variation of the Toni doll was the Harriet Hubbard Ayer doll. This doll by Ideal used the Toni body but had a vinyl head and vinyl arms. The Harriet Hubbard Ayer Cosmetic Co. provided a cosmetic kit with each doll. "Child safe" makeup including eyebrow pencil, eyeliner, rouge, lipstick and fingernail polish came with the doll and could be applied to the vinyl face and to the very unusual long fingernails. The popularity of these dolls was more limited than the Toni doll because the makeup was difficult to remove completely, and often the results were not pretty.

Revlon Cosmetics lent its name to another Ideal doll, the Revlon doll. Unlike the Toni doll,

Ideal, Harriet Hubbard Ayers make-up doll, vinyl socket head doll with five-piece jointed body, rooted blonde hair, sleep eyes, gray cotton pique dress, red/white striped pinafore, black vinyl shoes; original illustrated box with hair curlers, booklet and make-up kit; mint-in-box condition with complete accessories; 14".............**$400-$500**

Frasher's Doll Auctions

which represented a child, the Revlon doll had a lady's figure with a small waist and a bust, and she wore high heels. She could wear the high fashions seen in magazines, plus she could wear high heels and hose. Her fashions were influenced by designers such as Dior, but the names for the fashions were influenced by the names from the Revlon Cosmetic line. Names such as "Cherries a la Mode" given to one of the most popular Revlon doll outfits came directly for the introduction of the Revlon lipstick and nail polish color.

Like Ideal, the Arranbee Doll Co. needed a glamorous name association and formed an alliance with Coty Cosmetics. While Coty did not influence the doll directly, the name association paid off, and the little fashion ladies were quite popular in the late 1950s.

One of the largest doll manufacturers, Madame Alexander Doll Co., also saw the advantages of name recognition. Madame Alexander was a masterful businesswoman and drew up an agreement with the Yardley Cosmetic Co. A selection of the popular Cissy lady dolls were to be used in the Yardley advertisements, which were seen in many popular ladies magazines. This proved to be a great sales boost to both Yardley Cosmetics and the Madame Alexander Cissy doll.

A child doll by Alexander was not to be left out. A "Little Lady" 8" Wendy Kin was produced that came with "Little Lady" cosmetics, including toilet water, bubble bath and perfume.

Partnering the name of a doll firm with a name associated with beauty was a brilliant move. This, plus the utilization of manmade advances in manufacturing technology, established the U.S. doll industry as the best in the world.

— *Sherry Minton*

For information on the Barbie doll, please see the separate section titled "Barbie."

DOLLS

Early E.J. Jumeau Bebe, incised "E.J." over "6," large brown paperweight eyes, closed mouth with white molded space between highlighted lips, pierced ears on early French wood and composition body with eight separate ball joints; costume in pink silk with burgundy velvet trim and ecru lace, antique undergarments, antique brown leather French shoes (worn); replacement hair wig; very good condition, 16"....................**$6325**

James D. Julia, Inc.

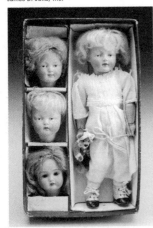

Kestner character doll with interchangeable heads, 1910 era ensemble with one complete doll and three additional heads; head on complete doll incised "178"; other painted eye heads are unmarked, smiling face is "185" mold and somber face boy is "184" mold; open mouth head has brown glass sleep eyes, incised "Made in Germany 174"; all four heads have their original mohair wigs; complete doll has original body with original finish; chemise is factory issued, two-tone leather shoes; original red box with paper label bearing Kestner crown mark and "Charakterpuppe No. 3439"; very good to excellent condition; 11"...........................**$4,025**

James D. Julia, Inc.

Cabinet-size Bru Bebe bisque socket head with blue paperweight eyes, open/closed mouth with molded tongue tip, incised on head and shoulder "Bru Jne 2," white leather "Chevrot"-style body with hinged joints at elbows and knees, wooden lower legs and bisque forearms; cranberry silk dress, burgundy straw hat, black cotton stockings and original Bru black leather shoes impressed on soles "2" and "Bru Jne Paris"; original blond mohair wig over cork pate; overall excellent condition; 12-1/2".........**$25,300**

James D. Julia, Inc.

Unmarked French bisque boy doll resembling Toto with inset blue glass eyes, open/closed mouth with two rows of molded and painted teeth, protruding ears with dimples in cheeks on a five-piece composition straight leg body; appropriately redressed in black velvet with large white collar; newer blond human hair wig; very good condition; 22"......................**$173**

James D. Julia, Inc.

Hertel Schwab googly eyes baby, bisque head incised "173-4" with closed smiling mouth, blue glass eyes that move from side to side and are attached to wire lever; five-piece bent limb composition body; red and white crocheted costume with matching nightcap, pair of leather boxing gloves; mohair wig sparse and ragged, head is very good condition, partial repaint to the hands; 13". **$3,220**

James D. Julia, Inc.

Kammer & Reinhardt character baby, head incised "K*R Simon & Halbig 122 32" with brown glass sleeping eyes, wide open mouth with two upper teeth and separately molded tongue, dimples in both cheeks and chin, on original five-piece bent limb composition body; auburn curly lamb's wool wig (not removed); white linen shirt and brown velvet pants; very good condition; 12-1/2"...............................**$345**

James D. Julia, Inc.

Carved English wooden doll, Queen Anne, mid-18th century, gesso covered and painted head, lower arms and legs with one-piece head and torso, black glass eyes, long neck, finely carved nose, chin and ears, jointed at shoulders, elbows, hips and knees; two-piece gold silk costume with train, quilted linen undergarments, green and gold antique brocade slippers; brown human hair wig with mop cap; some paint wear on forehead, nose tip and upper lip; 24" to top of wig. **$34,500**

James D. Julia, Inc.

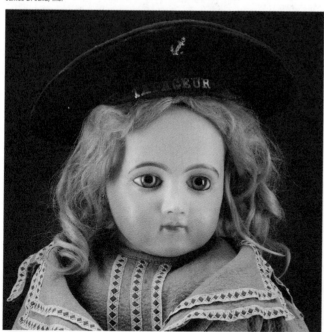

Unusual portrait-type Jumeau, incised "12" with large blue paperweight eyes, pierced applied ears, double chin with deep modeling around mouth and lower chin area; fully jointed wood and composition French body, unmarked; two-piece lavender felt wool costume with ribbon trim, authentic Jumeau shoes impressed on sole "12 Paris Depose," original white leather French gloves, navy blue wool sailor's cap with gold lettering "Tapageur," 25"; antique blond mohair wig and cork pate; very good condition, minor surface scratch on right side of forehead, stringing is loose **$16,100**

James D. Julia, Inc.

Presentation box with all-bisque doll and wardrobe from "Galeries LaFayette," closed mouth, swivel neck, glass eyes, molded and painted shoes and socks; three additional dresses with hats, toiletries in four compartments in box; excellent condition; 7-1/2", box 14-1/2" w. x 11-1/2" h. **$1,955**

James D. Julia, Inc.

All-original Bruno Schmidt Wendy, larger than average, head incised "2033," "BSW" in a heart, "537," brown glass sleep eyes, closed mouth with full pouty upper lip, painted eyelashes and brows, dimple in chin; fully jointed wood and composition body with fine original finish; blue gauze pleated factory dress, antique undergarments, socks and black oilcloth shoes; dark human hair wig with blue silk bow; remnants of cardboard store box, lacking lid; excellent condition; 17"... **$17,250**

James D. Julia, Inc.

Diminutive French fashion doll (possibly Jumeau), unmarked bisque socket head on separate bisque shoulder plate with large blue glass eyes, closed mouth with hint of a smile and pierced ears with possibly original earrings; striped silk antique dress with original Jumeau chemise underneath, antique black leather shoes, gold bead necklace; auburn mohair wig appears to be original; very good with slight discoloration to body; 12". **$1,610**

James D. Julia, Inc.

Gaultier fashion doll in trunk with wardrobe and accessories, doll incised "7" with separate bisque shoulder head, blue threaded eyes, highlighted lips, even coloring; original honey-colored human wig on cloth body with white kid forearms and individually stitched fingers; bridal costume of ivory silk with veil and newer white leather shoes; large wooden trunk with leather handles with separate compartment at top, pullout drawer with glove box to one side; five additional costumes, bonnets, various accessories; very good condition; doll 23-1/2", trunk 26" l. x 14" w. x 12" h... **$3,163**

James D. Julia, Inc.

German child doll, head incised "Simon & Halbig 1079 Dep" with brown glass sleep eyes, open mouth with four upper teeth (possibly replaced) on fully jointed wood and composition body; white organdy and lace dress, child's black patent leather shoes, parasol; antique honey human hair wig; 33".......... **$345**

James D. Julia, Inc.

Gebruder Heubach character doll, head incised "5" and "Heubach" within square with brown glass sleep eyes, open smiling mouth with two upper teeth, flat cut neck socket over ball swivel joint attached to five-piece German composition toddler body with diagonal hip joints; very good condition; 14". **$345**

James D. Julia, Inc.

Kestner twins, both heads incised "L Made in Germany 15 1/2 171," both with brown glass sleep eyes, one set in stationary position; both with fully jointed wood and composition bodies; dressed as identical twins in pink gingham costumes with matching hats and homemade purses containing panda bears; head on sleep-eyed doll restored; 29". **$230**

James D. Julia, Inc.

1890s-era Jumeau Bebe, incised "11" at base of neck and a few red artist marks, large blue paperweight eyes, thick multi-stroked eyebrows and tiny painted eyelashes, well painted closed mouth with dimple in center of chin, original fully jointed wood and composition body bearing oval-shaped paper label on torso reading "Bebe Jumeau Diplomme d'Honneur"; slightly worn magenta pleated silk dress with gold braid trim, antique undergarments and socks, no shoes; blond human hair replacement wig over replaced cardboard pate; overall very good condition; 23"... **$2,990**

James D. Julia, Inc.

◄ Munich Art girl character doll, early 20th century, by Marion Kaulitz, fully jointed marked Kestner body, dark hair, facial coloring and high-waisted dress; overall very fine condition, original condition facial painting and clothing; 18". **$3,738**

James D. Julia, Inc.

Pair of black cloth dolls pictured in Collecting Black Americana by Dawn E. Reno. Larger girl doll is 21" with black sateen face and covered body with embroidered features, individually stitched ears and black caracal hair; 1910 period cotton gauze two-piece undergarment with two-piece dress with white cotton blouse and blue and white striped linen skirt and printed cotton pleated dress of same era, blue and white striped ribbed cotton stockings. Smaller boy doll is 19-1/2" with hand-stitched facial features; wig and eyebrows of black wool yarn; checkered hat, paisley jacket, red and white striped pants and paisley shoes. Both in very good condition. **$460**

James D. Julia, Inc.

Bru Bebe, bisque socket head with blue paperweight eyes, closed mouth with slight molded space between lips, pierced ears, multi-stroked eyelashes, head incised "Bru-Jne 7" on bisque shoulder plate, incised "Bru-Jne" on left side of shoulder and "5" on right side of shoulder, gusseted body with original paper label on torso, kid over metal upper arms, lower legs and lower arms of wood; antique French blond mohair wig over cork pate; possibly original undergarments, original cordovan leather shoes incised on soles "Bru-Jne Paris 7," two dresses, one antique cotton and lace, the other a party dress, antique black wool hat, gloves; excellent condition; 17" **$11,500**

James D. Julia, Inc.

Lenci female equestrian doll, molded and pressed felt, green eyes glancing to the side, yellow mohair bobbed wig; white felt shirt with black felt tie, black and white diamond checkered jodhpurs, high leather boot, riding crop on right wrist, leather jockey hat matches boots, green riding coat (possible replacement); fair to good condition; 27-1/2". **$5,750**

James D. Julia, Inc.

TOP LOT!

Carved English wooden doll from William & Mary period, late 17th century, one-piece head, torso and hips with articulation at hips and knees, upper arms of cloth and lower arms of carved wood with individually carved fingers, head has painted long arched eyebrows with tiny dots above, eyelashes are painted in similar manner, mouth is three-dimensional with individually painted lips, black painted beauty spot on forehead, lower legs painted black; rose-colored brocade skirt with cloth flowers and silver braid trim, pieces of lace cover joint at elbow; very good condition, upper body repainted; 19".. **$13,750**

James D. Julia, Inc.

Open-mouth Jumeau, head stamped in red "Tete Jumeau" with blue glass sleep eyes, open mouth with six upper teeth on original fully jointed French wood and composition body with original finish, re-costumed in maroon taffeta knee-length dress trimmed in lamb's wool faux fur with antique fur muff, antique dark leather shoes; antique brown human hair wig over cork pate; very good condition; 26"... **$575**

James D. Julia, Inc.

Mattel Chatty Cathy dolls, plastic and vinyl, pull-string talkers (all mute), circa-1963; one brown-eyed brunette, three blondes, two redheads, and one light brunette; one pair of shoes is original; three dolls have no teeth; very good condition; 20" h. each. **$180**

Morphy Auctions

Large size Hertel Schwab googly eyes doll, head incised "163-6" with blue glass side-glancing stationary eyes, closed smiling "watermelon slice" mouth, reddish molded and painted hair on fully jointed wood and composition toddler body with diagonal hip joints; period pale green organdy and print dress, antique undergarments, socks and black oil cloth shoes; excellent condition; 16"................... **$7,080**

James D. Julia, Inc.

Assorted advertising dolls, one Elsie the Cow of pink plush and vinyl; one Campbell kid, jointed composition, redressed; one Campbell kid premium doll, all original with tag, circa-1955; very good-excellent condition; largest 13". **$48**

Morphy Auctions

Unusual Lanternier bisque socket head lady doll, early 20th century, inset blue glass eyes, open/closed mouth with four molded and painted teeth, incised in back of head "Lorraine N20 AL & Co," a line, "Limoges" below; composition body with narrow waist and joints at shoulders and elbows, hips with a diagonal slanted joint, also at knees, painted brown gloves, beaded bracelet on right wrist, matching necklace; brown human hair wig with cloth flowers; two-piece gold silk party dress with puffed sleeves and ecru lace, antique brown leather fashion boots; very good condition; 17". $575

James D. Julia, Inc.

Large Hertel & Schwab googly eye, head incised "173-9," brown glass side-glancing sleep eyes, wide narrow smiling mouth, protruding ears, multi-stroke eyebrows, tiny eyelashes surrounding eye sockets, pale bisque, fully jointed German toddler body with diagonal hip joints; green organdy dress with matching pantaloons, silk and suede cape with rabbit fur trim, antique blond mohair wig, leather shoes; overall very good condition, body finish is original; 18". $5,175

James D. Julia, Inc.

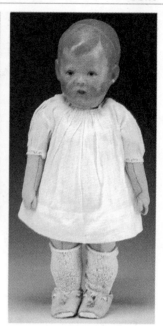

Kathe Kruse Doll I, molded and painted facial features, muslin body with separate fingers and separately molded thumb, diagonal disc hip joints; white cotton dress, white cotton stockings, felt replacement shoes; some paint loss on right back of head; 17".........................$4,600

James D. Julia, Inc.

Black gutta percha peddler doll in glass dome, circa 1870s, head is mask type with inset glass eyes on black kid body; vintage cotton print clothing, molded hair with braided buns, open/closed mouth; overall very fine condition; 14". $575

James D. Julia, Inc.

Door of Hope kindergarten child, all original; cotton and silk outfit with animal-faced slippers; near mint condition; 5-1/4". $4,600

James D. Julia, Inc.

Armand Marseille googly eye, pale bisque head incised "Germany 323 A.O.M." with blue side-glancing sleep eyes, closed smiling mouth, one stroke eyebrows with painted lashes surrounding eye sockets mounted to antique German wood and composition body with diagonal hip joints; antique white cotton and lace dress with newer oil cloth shoes; antique blond mohair bobbed wig; very good condition; 13-1/2".............................$1,150

James D. Julia, Inc.

DOLLS

Jumeau walking doll stamped in red "De-pose Tete Jumeau 7" on body with key-wind mechanism, metal feet with leather shoe tops covering top of feet, blue paperweight eyes, closed mouth; quality replacement costume; light human hair replacement wig; very good condition; 16"..................... **$2,875**

James D. Julia, Inc.

Size 1 Tete Jumeau Bebe, bisque head stamped in red "DE-POSE TETE JUMEAU Bte S.G.D.G. 1," large blue paperweight eyes, closed mouth, pierced ears, evenly arched multi-stroked eyebrows, original fully jointed wood and composition body stamped in blue "JUMEAU MEDAILLE D'OR PARIS"; re-cos-tumed in cream cotton and lace overlay dress with newer brown human hair wig (lacking cork pate), original Jumeau shoes of pink silk, fully marked on soles with gold lettering, markings cor-respond with markings on back of head; 9-1/2". **$3,335**

James D. Julia, Inc.

SFBJ child, first quarter 20th century, by Fran-cisque Poulbot, with three additional outfits and book about the artist and the work he did for dis-advantaged youth; bisque head on original five-piece composition body, original amber glass eyes with original plaster setting; blond mohair wig appears to be original, as do shoes and socks; overall very fine original condition; 14". **$6,325**

James D. Julia, Inc.

Brown bisque Jumeau child doll, unmarked, open mouth, brown paperweight eyes, painted lashes and brows, pierced ears, fully jointed wood and composition body; ethnic costume with gold coin necklace, brass hoop earrings; original black mohair wig over cork pate; very good condition; 10"..... **$1,725**

James D. Julia, Inc.

Door of Hope policeman, carved and painted head, wooden forearms; heavy black cotton costume with belt, brass buttons and white embroidered designs on sleeves and high collar, hat is missing; very good condition; 11-1/2". **$1,380**

James D. Julia, Inc.

Mollye Raggedy Ann doll, painted facial features and red yarn hair, original clothes; good condition; 18". **$460**

James D. Julia, Inc.

Door of Hope priest, carved and painted head with wooden spoon arms; traditional pale lime green costume that comes to ankle to right side with boots made of same material; 11-1/2". ... **$805**

James D. Julia, Inc.

Schoenhut boy with carved hair, spring jointed all-wooden doll, carved and painted features; replacement World War I-era style clothing and reproduction Schoenhut boots; significant loss of paint, some probable repaint; 15". **$230**

James D. Julia, Inc.

Wide-Eyed Jumeau Bebe, head stamped in red "Depose Tete Jumeau Bte S.G.D.G. 10" with incised "10" marking at base of neck socket, blue paperweight eyes, closed mouth with slight molded space between the lips, on original fully jointed wood and composition body stamped on torso in blue "Bebe Jumeau Diplomme d'Honneur"; antique blue plaid silk costume with dropped sash waist, dark blue velvet panels on jacket, replaced antique brown leather shoes; replacement dark human hair wig over cork pate; overall very good condition; 22".................**$2,875**

James D. Julia, Inc.

French fashion doll, fully jointed wooden body, head and shoulder incised "2" with pale bisque head, blue glass eyes, closed mouth and pierced ears on original fully articulated French fashion body with joints at shoulders, elbows, wrist, waist, hips and knees; antique two-piece white cotton gauze walking dress with blue silk ribbon bows, antique brown leather boots with brass buttons; antique blond human hair wig with black snood and antique straw bonnet; very good condition; 15-1/2"...........................**$4,600**

James D. Julia, Inc.

German glass-eyed china shoulder head doll, 1850s-era, glazed porcelain head with inset brown glass eyes, painted upper and lower lashes, rosy cheeks, closed mouth with slight smile, molded and painted black hair with center part with short curls, body stuffed muslin with brown leather forearms; off-the-shoulder printed wool dress of the period; head is very good condition with a few minor kiln dust specks and pitting, arms have deteriorated, left arm missing and body is broken at both ankles, dress has considerable moth damage; 19"............**$1,610**

James D. Julia, Inc.

French glass-eyed papier maché doll, possibly 1830s, shoulder head with inset glass eyes without pupils, wide nose, tiny closed mouth with pursed smile wearing original human hair wig with side curls and braids on top; narrow-waisted firm leather body with wooden forearms and wooden legs with painted orange shoes; period off-the-shoulder dress with puff sleeves, linen undergarments; very good condition; 17".........**$2,588**

James D. Julia, Inc.

Large Kammer & Reinhardt character doll, head incised "K*R Simon & Halbig 117n 80" with blue glass eyes that both sleep and flirt from side to side with open mouth and four upper teeth on fully jointed wood and composition body, diagonal hip joints and high knee joints; navy blue dress with white cotton pinafore and white leather children's shoes; human hair replacement wig; very good condition; 32"..................**$1,150**

James D. Julia, Inc.

Carl Bergner three-face Little Red Riding Hood and cloth wolf, socket head doll with three faces: glass-eyed smiling girl, painted-eye sleeping girl, and glass-eyed crying girl, carton torso with composition arms and lower legs, head contained within a papier maché cap with handle on top, red cape; felt wolf doll by artist Patricia Cain Blair, mohair head with glass eyes, felt body jointed at shoulders and hips; both in very good condition; 12-1/2" and 16-1/2", respectively. **$863**

James D. Julia, Inc.

Simon & Halbig Asian child doll, olive tinted bisque head incised "Simon & Halbig Germany 1329 6" with brown glass sleep eyes, open mouth with four upper teeth, protruding ears, original light brown painted wood and composition fully jointed body; dressed in two-piece orange brocade costume with high collar and braid trim buttons; small black mohair queue glued to inside of boy's blue hat; overall good condition; 15"............**$633**

James D. Julia, Inc.

Early Georgene Beloved Belindy with Volland book, stamped on back of head, printed/painted face on brown cloth body, button eyes, tin buttons on dress, 1926, 18"..**$375**

McMasters Harris Apple Tree Auctions

Early Jumeau Bebe, head incised "Depose E11J," straight wrist wood and composition body with eight separate ball joints, stamped on torso in blue "Jumeau Medaille d'or Paris"; blue paperweight eyes, pierced applied ears, closed mouth; off white silk costume with pleated maroon silk sash ribbon bow with antique buttons and original shoes stamped "11 Paris Bebe"; replacement blond mohair wig over original cork pate; overall very good condition; 24".................**$3,335**

James D. Julia, Inc.

Brown bisque child doll, fired-in color, incised "2 Walkure Germany" from Kley & Hahn with brown glass sleep eyes, enameled eyebrows, open mouth with upper teeth, fully jointed wood and composition body; purple cotton print dress, antique magenta velvet purse; newer black mohair wig; very good condition; 13".......**$230**

James D. Julia, Inc.

Simon & Halbig brown bisque doll, head incised "S13H 739 DEP" with originally set fixed brown eyes, open mouth with four upper teeth, pierced ears on fully jointed wood and composition body with straight wrists; tight black curly mohair wig is original; white cotton dress with printed flowers (faded); very good condition; 22"..................**$1,265**

James D. Julia, Inc.

Moritz doll, head incised "32.11/0," attributed to Recknagel, molded and painted features, reddish bobbed hair with curl on top, side-glancing intaglio eyes, grin, five-piece composition with joints at shoulders and hips with molded and painted shoes and stockings; cotton dress with blue ribbon inserts, antique undergarments; very good condition with possible repair and repaint to left ankle and stocking; 9"....................................**$1,035**

James D. Julia, Inc.

Ideal Shirley Temple composition doll; sailor outfit marked on rear of head and shoulder; original clothing, shoes and socks, newer button and ribbon; overall light crazing, eyes intact; 15".....**$460**

James D. Julia, Inc.

Armand Marseille googly eye, head incised "Germany 323 A.11/0.M.," blue glass eyes fixed in stationary position facing right, body is original composition jointed at shoulders and hips with molded and painted shoes and stockings; red mohair replacement wig with braid in back, 1st Place blue ribbon from a UFDC show; 7"..........**$345**

James D. Julia, Inc.

DOLL HOUSES

Christian Hacker mansard roof doll house, circa 1880, cream with salmon accents, roof is lithographed paper simulating blue shingles, two brick chimneys with three dormer windows, center doorway leads to balcony flanked by two double windows, painted center door with ormolu door knocker and metal handle, simulated coining, opens to reveal two lower rooms and hallway; kitchen has original shelving and stove; upper level is one large room. Top of mansard roof reveals two additional rooms with dividing wall. All rooms appear to have original wallpaper; overall very good plus condition; 30" h. x 25-3/4" w. x 12-3/4" d...................... **$4,600**

James D. Julia, Inc.

Lines doll house, circa 1908, English cottage with papered roof simulating shingles, two chimneys, sides and back papered with simulated brick, front painted off-white with dark brown trim, two upper windows and one lower, door to left. House opens from front to reveal two rooms covered in original papers. Papered areas in good condition; 25" l. x 15-1/2" w. x 13-1/2" d....................**$230**

James D. Julia, Inc.

Heston Higgenbothom doll house, circa 1890, replica of a South New Jersey home, mansard shingled roof, exposed faux brick front porch and chimneys, metal railing at top, clapboard sides with both front and back door entry, wood decoration at top of roof. Mansard portion of roof is removable for access to second floor with four rooms and central staircase, second floor walls are hinged to create four smaller rooms or two larger rooms, raised panel doors, double sash windows, electrified for lighting. Very good condition with minor wear; 31" h. x 25" w. x 26" d...............**$2,419**

James D. Julia, Inc.

Schoenhut doll house, circa 1931, gray base with tan exterior with two upper dormers, three upper windows with window boxes, cardboard shutters, half roof above first floor, center wooden door, lower level has two windows with window boxes. Front opens to reveal four rooms with staircase, doors between rooms, interior rooms with original wallpaper, roof flips up to reveal attic. Overall very good condition; 20" h. x 18-1/2" w. x 9-3/4" d......................**$345**

James D. Julia, Inc.

Scarce Tynietoy two-room South County cottage, circa 1920, faux painted with three windows and door and natural wood-finished sloped roof hinged at center. When roof is lifted, bottom half opens to reveal walkway, garden, two interior rooms, one with wooden fireplace, each room with upper and lower window on exterior walls. Generally good condition; 25-1/2" w. x 14" h. x 12" d. **$920**

James D. Julia, Inc.

Bliss seaside doll house, circa 1900, marked "Bliss" above center doorway, three different levels of roofing, upper balconies, three dormer windows, front porch, two front doors, turned posts, set of wooden detachable steps, entire house lithographed in a variety of colors. House opens from front and from left side. Overall good condition; 24" h. x 19" w. x 10-1/4" d. **$747**

James D. Julia, Inc.

Early Silber & Fleming doll house with contents, faux stone block first story and simulated brick second story with yellow coining, opens to reveal two rooms with original wallpaper, both rooms with center fireplaces made by Evans & Cartwright, house has been electrified. Accompanied by an assortment of Biedermeier furniture including sideboard, stepback hutch, chest of drawers, marble top sideboard, as well as soft metal pieces, two small early dolls, birdcage, and other miscellaneous items. House in overall good condition, furniture in good to very good condition; first floor room 8" h. x 13" w. x 7-3/4" d., upper floor room 8-1/4" h. x 13" w. x 7-3/4" d. **$4,140**

James D. Julia, Inc.

Regency English yellow stone doll house, circa 1840, side bale handles for carrying, yellow faux brick with dark green roof with four large windows with demilune windows above and two smaller attic windows, lower story entry with second floor balcony; yellow exterior not original, original brick pattern remains underneath and exposed in one section. Split front opens in center to reveal four large rooms and center hallway with staircase, rooms all have opening wood doors, privy beneath stairs on front level; roof has pointed finial; many rooms covered with early papers, two rooms repapered. Overall very good condition; 42" h. x 43" w. x 19" d., upper rooms 12" h. x 12" w. x 15-1/2" d., lower rooms 14" h. x 15" w. x 15-1/2" d. **$690**

James D. Julia, Inc.

Farm Collectibles

American farming is steeped in family and the tradition of hard work. Many current farming collectibles were invented prior to 1900, and examples are still readily found for sale, with some of the items still in use on farms.

Farm collectibles – items related to farming and farming households in America – covers items related to farming in North America from the period beginning shortly after the Civil War until approximately 1965. These dates correspond to the beginning impact of the industrial revolution on farming in America and the manufacture of many items that have now today become collectibles and antiques of interest to many, not just to farmers and those individuals who were raised on a farm.

The time period selected represents the evolution from a truly agrarian society to an urban society in America. Many people now find farm collectibles of interest partly due to the romantic ideal of an agrarian society.

Many farm items did not change greatly once invented in the late 1800s or early 1900s, such as fence stretching tools, feeding equipment, and implements, until the advent of the tractor in the 1920s. A review of the Montgomery Ward Farm Catalog of 1964 demonstrates that many of the early 1900s items are still in use and in demand.

The information presented here should help assist in dating items to prevent collectors from buying so-called "antique" items that are really only a few years old. Some of the more recent items are still highly collectible, but the buyer should be aware of how long many of the farm items of a collectible nature were actually manufactured.

For more information on farm collectibles, see *American Farm Collectibles Identification and Price Guide* by Russell E. Lewis.

Colored crate end labels for fruits and vegetables are becoming highly collectible. Values generally begin at $4 each and can go as high as $200 if the label is rare and/or has exceptionally interesting graphics. Vandalia Brand label........................**$5-$15**

Egg crate made of aluminum, holds three dozen eggs. ....**$35-$50**

VanAlstine Collection

Early grading scoop for use with horses............. **$100**

John Deere sulky plow. **$425**

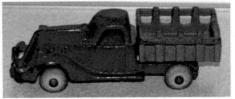

Small Hubley farm truck, mint condition............. **$80**

Art Smith Collection

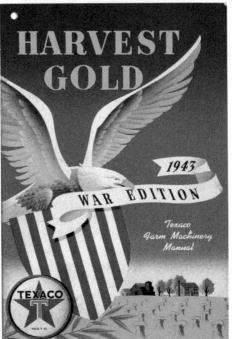

Harvest Gold booklet from 1943 shows the patriotism of the farm community during the war era. The contents include a complete listing of all farm tractors and machinery companies in business in 1943 and all major equipment made, as it was needed for the lubrication guide furnished by Texaco. Also, the booklet has many fine line drawings of equipment and photos of the types of oil containers from the era. **$8**

Cast iron implement seat marked #147 with no other marks. ....**$100+**

Art Smith Collection

Lunch box is a fine example of tin lithography and shows the romantic ideals of farm life around a barn...............................**$50+**

Die-cast John Deere Model A and driver from about 1952 in pristine condition. ....**$300-$500**

Art Smith Collection

Old cast well water pulley with ornate design. ....**$20+**

Art Smith Collection

Hat rack produced by MoorMan's in the image of its trademarked cow. **$25**

Lewis Collection

Large pair of ice tongs made of wrought iron.........................**$35**

Art Smith Collection

Feedbag cart. **$12**

Primitive barn scraper. ... **$15-$20**

Nerbonne Collection

Conneaut #3 shovel. ....**$25+**

Lewis Collection

FARM COLLECTIBLES

Cow number tag, Hasco brand, brass. The number would hang from a chain around a cow's neck for identification. Value depends on materials used to make the tag. .... **$5-$15**

Small cowbell........................**$25**

Lewis Collection

Calf trainer used to wean a calf from nursing; the little points went into the calf's nose and hurt when it tried to suckle its mother.......................... **$10-$25**

VanAlstine Collection

Hay spear made by Myers of Ashland, Wisconsin........ **$25-$50**

Lewis Collection

Egg scale, Jiffy-Way, sold by Sears and Wards..........................**$25+**

Lewis Collection

1940 Farmall H tractor. ... **$2,400**

1964 John Deere Model 1010 tractor. **$3,050**

Antique bread box from England. .... **$100+**

VanAlstine Collection

Primitive milk stool with four legs, nice condition. .... **$25-$50**

Nerbonne Collection

Copper barn light from a dairy barn near Coopersville, Michigan...**$300**

Lewis Collection

Figurines

HOLT-HOWARD

The 1950s was a time of expansion. New homes were cropping up everywhere, affording people the luxury of space, both indoors and out. As a result, many families now had full-size kitchens, dining rooms, and dens to display their cherished belongings and collectibles.

The Holt-Howard Co., started in 1949 by brothers John and Robert Howard and Grant Holt, concentrated on producing Christmas items in the early years. Then the company branched out into kitchen-related items. Christmas and kitchen items were the company's most popular commodities in the 1950s. The firm's confidence in the success of kitchen-related items was the catalyst that led to the creation of the famous Pixieware line in the late 1950s, a new concept in deep-glazed ceramics. These products featured whimsical pixie heads.

Due to the huge success of Pixiewares, other novelty companies such as Davar, Lefton, Lipper & Mann, and Napco all began to copy Holt-Howard's style. While each company made creative items, the Davar Co. practically copied the Pixieware copyrighted design. They were all competing for sales around the same time — the 1950s and early 1960s. Today, many of these items have also become highly collectible and some are commanding top dollar at antiques and collectibles shows.

About the Prices

The prices in this section were formulated as guidelines and should not be used to establish a fixed price. The prices are a compilation of averages from different parts of the country. Prices vary from region to region. In certain areas of the country, Holt-Howard and other collectibles are more plentiful than in others, so supply-and-demand can affect prices. Scarcity of a highly desirable collectible influences the price that a collector is willing to pay. Rare pieces will always command more money than common ones. Rare pieces are generally the result of a limited production of an item, or the piece's fragility (causing it to break easily and almost become extinct over the years).

Another factor governing the value of a piece is its condition. Any collectible that is chipped, cracked, or faded should not be bought or sold at top dollar, as if it were in perfect condition.

Signatures and Stickers

Holt-Howard marked and copyright dated most of its collectibles with an ink stamp. However, certain tiny pieces were not marked because of a lack of space, so a foil sticker was sometimes applied instead. These items may have just read "HH" or nothing at all.

On Holt-Howard collectibles made abroad, the word "Japan" was included as part of the ink backstamp or printed on the foil label. Occasionally, Holt-Howard used numeric identification codes such as 6128L or 6457 to identify its merchandise.

Foil labels were used on many Holt-Howard items, especially on collectibles from the late 1950s and early 1960s. The label color schemes included black and gold, silver and gold, and red and gold. Most Pixieware pieces had the black and gold label. The Christmas collectibles usually had the red and gold version of this label, but during the early 1960s, the rectangular silver and gold foil label was also used.

For more information on Holt-Howard, see *Price Guide to Holt-Howard Collectibles*, second edition, by Walter Dworkin.

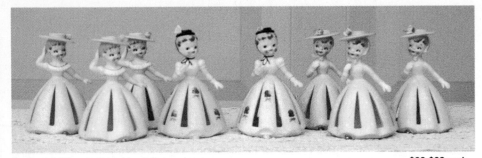

Sunbonnet Miss napkin holder dolls ....**$80-$90 each**

Bobbie Bryson, from *Collectibles for the Kitchen, Bath, & Beyond, A Pictorial Guide,* Krause Publications

Santa locomotive candleholder.................... **$30-$40**

Collection of and photo by Jason Wormington and John Frownfelter

Snow Babies candy holders ....**$15-$20**
Snow Babies planters......................**$23-$28 each**

Dworkin collection, photo by Brenner Lennon Photo Productions

Winking Santa punch bowl set ....**$140-$150 for set**

Dworkin collection, photo by Van Blerck Photography

Minnie and Moby sea horse wall planters
.... **$90-$105 each**

Collection of and photo by Evan Pazol

Totem Pole Rabbits candleholders............... **$45-$55**
Matching shakers.................................. **$25-$35 pair**

Dworkin collection, photo by Brenner Lennon Photo Productions

Minnie cotton ball dispenser
.... **$80-$90**

Collection of and photo by Hall/Glascock

Winking Wabbits shakers
............................**$58-$68 for set**

Collection of and photo by Darline Comisky

"Chris Moose" candleholder
.... **$30-$35**

*Dworkin collection, photo by Brenner
Lennon Photo Productions*

Tiger cookie jar .... **$38-$48**

*Dworkin collection, photo by Brenner
Lennon Photo Productions*

Honey Bunny candle climbers
............................**$35-$45 for set**

*Dworkin collection, photo by Brenner
Lennon Photo Productions*

Carolers Trio candleholder
.... **$23-$33**

*Dworkin collection, photo by
Van Blerck Photography*

Humpty Dumpty puppet
planter.......................... **$35-$45**

*Dworkin collection, photo by Brenner
Lennon Photo Productions*

Girl Christmas Tree wick air
freshener ....
$35-$45

*Dworkin collection, photo by Brenner
Lennon Photo Productions*

Snowie Clips, set of four with original Box.... **$38-$43**

Collection of and photo by Jason Wormington and John Frownfelter

Ermine Angels salt and peppers ....**$25-$30 for set**

Dworkin collection, photo by Van Blerck Photography

Wee Three Kings candleholders
.....................................**$50-$60 for three-piece set**

Dworkin collection, photo by Van Blerck Photography

Elf Girl NOEL candleholders .... **$33-$38 for set**

Dworkin collection, photo by Van Blerck Photography

Huge Santa planter..............................**$245-$250**

Dworkin collection, photo by Brenner Lennon Photo Productions

Santa on Candy Canes candleholders........**$40-$50**

Dworkin collection, photo by Brenner Lennon Photo Productions

Santa Boys ornaments
.... **$12-$15 each; $50 for complete set**

Collection of and photo by Jason Wormington and John Frownfelter

Holly Elf Climbing Boot planter .... **$28-$32**
Holly Elf pitcher .... **$38-$48**

Dworkin collection, photo by Brenner Lennon Photo Productions

Trio of Chicks nesting trays .... **$38-$48 for set of three**

Dworkin collection, photo by Brenner Lennon Photo Productions

Christmas Choirboys .... **$10-$12 each**

Dworkin collection, photo by Brenner Lennon Photo Productions

Snow Babies ashtray .... **$25-$30**
Snow Babies figurines .... **$4-$8 each**

Dworkin collection, photo by Brenner Lennon Photo Productions

Santa King decanter and glasses .. **$95-$100 for set**

Dworkin collection, photo by Brenner Lennon Photo Productions

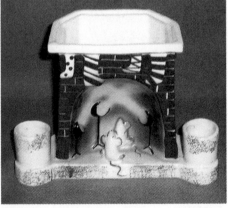

Mice-in-Fireplace planter.......................... **$15-$20**

Collection of and photo by Jason Wormington and John Frownfelter

HUMMEL FIGURINES & COLLECTIBLES

The Goebel Co. of Oeslau, Germany, first produced M.I. Hummel porcelain figurines in 1934, having obtained the rights to adapt the beautiful pastel sketches of children by Sister Maria Innocentia (Berta) Hummel. Every design by the Goebel artisans was approved by the nun until her death in 1946. Goebel produced these charming collectibles until Sept. 30, 2008. Manufaktur Rödental GmbH resumed production in 2009.

For more information on M.I. Hummel collectibles, see *The Official M.I. Hummel Price Guide* by Heidi Ann von Recklinghausen.

Hummel Trademarks

Since 1935, there have been several changes in the trademarks on M.I. Hummel items. In later years of production, each new trademark design merely replaced the old one, but in the earlier years, frequently the new design trademark would be placed on a figurine that already bore the older style trademark.

• The Crown Mark (TMK-1): 1934-1950

The Crown Mark (TMK-1 or CM), sometimes referred to as the "Crown-WG," was used by Goebel on all of its products in 1935, when M.I. Hummel figurines were first made commercially available. The letters WG below the crown in the mark are the initials of William Goebel, one of the founders of the company. The crown signifies his loyalty to the imperial family of Germany at the time of the mark's design, around 1900. The mark is sometimes found in an incised circle.

Another Crown-type mark is sometimes confusing to collectors; some refer to it as the "Narrow Crown" and others the "Wide Ducal Crown." This mark was introduced by Goebel in 1937 and used on many of its products.

Often, the Crown Mark will appear twice on the same piece, more often one mark incised and the other stamped. This is, as we know, the "Double Crown."

When World War II ended and the United States Occupation Forces allowed Goebel to begin exporting, the pieces were marked as having been made in the occupied zone.

These marks were applied to the bases of the figurines, along with the other markings, from 1946 through 1948. They were sometimes applied under the glaze and often over the glaze. Between 1948 and 1949, the U.S. Zone mark requirement was dropped, and the word "Germany" took its place. With the partitioning of Germany into East and West, "W. Germany," "West Germany," or "Western Germany" began to appear most of the time instead.

Incised
Crown Mark

Stamped
Crown Mark

Wide Ducal
Crown Mark

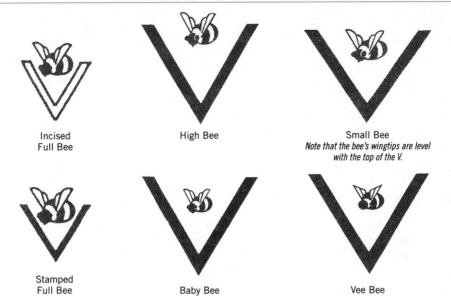

Incised Full Bee	High Bee	Small Bee *Note that the bee's wingtips are level with the top of the V.*
Stamped Full Bee	Baby Bee	Vee Bee

• The Full Bee Mark (TMK-2): 1940-1959

In 1950, Goebel made a major change in its trademark. The company incorporated a bee in a V. It is thought that the bumblebee part of the mark was derived from a childhood nickname of Sister Maria Innocentia Hummel, meaning bumblebee. The bee flies within a V, which is the first letter of the German word for distributing company, Verkaufsgesellschaft.

There are actually 12 variations of the Bee marks to be found on Goebel-produced M.I. Hummel items.

The Full Bee mark, also referred to as TMK-2 or abbreviated FB, is the first of the Bee marks to appear. The mark evolved over nearly 20 years until the company began to modernize it. It is sometimes found in an incised circle.

The very large bee flying in the V remained until around 1956, when the bee was reduced in size and lowered into the V. It can be found incised, stamped in black, or stamped in blue, in that order, through its evolution.

• The Stylized Bee (TMK-3): 1958-1972

A major change in the way the bee is rendered in the trademark made its appearance in 1960. The Stylized Bee (TMK-3), sometimes abbreviated as Sty-Bee, as the major component of the trademark appeared in three basic forms through 1972. The first two are both classified as the Stylized Bee (TMK-3), but the third is considered a fourth step in the evolution, the Three Line Mark (TMK-4).

W. Germany

Large Stylized Bee

The Large Stylized Bee: This trademark was used primarily from 1960 through 1963. The color of the mark will be black or blue. It is sometimes found inside an incised circle. When you find the Large Stylized Bee mark, you will normally find a stamped "West" or "Western Germany" in black elsewhere on the base, but not always.

W. Germany

Small Stylized Bee

The Small Stylized Bee: This mark is also considered to be TMK-3. It was used concurrently with the Large Stylized Bee from about 1960 and continued in this use until about 1972. The mark is usually rendered in blue, and it too is often accompanied by a stamped black "West" or "Western Germany." Collectors and dealers sometimes refer to the mark as the One Line Mark.

• The Three Line Mark (TMK-4): 1964-1972

This trademark is sometimes abbreviated 3-line or 3LM in print. The trademark used the same stylized V and bee as the others, but also included three lines of wording beside it. This major change appeared in blue.

Three Line Mark

• The Last Bee Mark (TMK-5): 1972-1979

Developed and occasionally used as early as 1970, this major change was known by some collectors as the Last Bee Mark because the next change in the trademark no longer incorporated any form of the V and the bee. However, with the reinstatement of a bee in TMK-8 with the turn of the century, TMK-5 is not technically the "Last Bee" any longer. The mark was used until about mid-1979. There are three minor variations in the mark shown in the illustration. Generally, the mark was placed under the glaze from 1972 through 1976 and is found placed over the glaze from 1976 through 1979.

Last Bee Mark

• The Missing Bee Mark (TMK 6): 1979-1991

The transition to this trademark began in 1979 and was complete by mid-1980. Goebel removed the V and bee from the mark altogether, calling it the Missing Bee. In conjunction with this change, the company instituted the practice of adding to the traditional artist's mark the date the artist finished painting the piece.

Missing Bee Mark

• The Hummel Mark (TMK-7): 1991-1999

In 1991, Goebel changed the trademark once again. This time, the change was not only symbolic of the reunification of the two Germanys by removal of the "West" from the mark, but very significant in another way. Until then, Goebel used the same trademark on virtually all of its products. The mark illustrated here was for exclusive use on Goebel products made from the paintings and drawings of M.I. Hummel.

Hummel Mark

• The Millennium Bee (TMK-8): 2000-2008

Goebel decided to celebrate the beginning of a new century with a revival in a bee-adorned trademark. Seeking once again to honor the memory of Sister Maria Innocentia Hummel, a bumblebee, this time flying solo without the V, was reinstated into the mark in 2000 and ended in 2008. Goebel stopped production of the M.I. Hummel figurines on Sept. 30, 2008.

Millennium Bee Mark

• The Manufaktur Rödental Mark (TKM-9): 2009-Present

Manufaktur Rödental purchased the rights to produce M.I. Hummel figurines from Goebel in 2009. This trademark signifies a new era for Hummel figurines while maintaining the same quality and workmanship from the master sculptors and master painters at the Rödental factory. This trademark has a full bee using yellow and black for the bumblebee, which circles around the words "Original M.I. Hummel Germany" with the copyright sign next to M.I. Hummel. Manufaktur Rödental is underneath the circle with a copyright sign.

Manufaktur Rödental Mark

For purposes of simplification, the various trademarks have been abbreviated in the list below. Generally speaking, earlier trademarks are worth more than later trademarks.

TRADEMARK	ABBREVIATIONS	DATES
Crown	TMK-1	1934-1950
Full Bee	TMK-2	1940-1959
Stylized Bee	TMK-3	1958-1972
Three Line Mark	TMK-4	1964-1972
Last Bee	TMK-5	1972-1979
Missing Bee	TMK-6	1979-1991
Hummel Mark	TMK-7	1991-1999
Millennium Bee/Goebel Bee	TMK-8	2000-2008
Manufaktur Rödental Mark	TMK-9	2009-present

Hum 1: Puppy Love, trademarks 1-6 .... **$200-$2,900**

Hum 2: Little Fiddler, trademarks 1-8 .... **$175-$2,000**

Hum 3: Book Worm, trademarks 1-8................................ **$200-$2,500**

Hum 5: Strolling Along,
trademarks 1-6...........**$150-$425**

Hum 7: Merry Wanderer, trademarks 1-8 ....**$200-$25,000**

Hum 6: Sensitive Hunter,
trademarks 1-8........**$125-$1,500**

Hum 9: Begging His Share,
trademarks 1-7...........**$150-$550**

Hum 12: Chimney Sweep,
trademarks 1-8.............**$99-$550**

Hum 13: Meditation, trademarks
1-8 ....**$99-$2,500**

Hum 15: Hear Ye, Hear Ye,
trademarks 1-8...........**$125-$650**

Hum 20: Prayer Before Battle,
trademarks 1-8...........**$200-$450**

Hum 16: Little Hiker, trademarks
1-8 ....**$140-$500**

Hum 17: Congratulations,
trademarks 1-7........**$225-$2,000**

Hum 21: Heavenly Angel,
trademarks 1-8...........**$100-$800**

Hum 32: Little Gabriel,
trademarks 1-7........**$150-$1,300**

Hum 27: Joyous News, trademarks
1-7 ....**$225-$750**

Hum 23: Adoration, trademarks 1-8 ....**$250-$900**

Hum 28: Wayside Devotion, trademarks 1-8 ....**$275-$1,100**

Hum 42: Good Shepherd, trademarks 1-7 ....**$195-$5,500**

Hum 43: March Winds, trademarks 1-8 ......**$55-$400**

Hum 57: Chick Girl, trademarks
1-8 ....**$110-$630**

Hum 47: Goose Girl, trademarks
1-8 ....**$120-$780**

Hum 49: To Market, trademarks
1-8 ....**$110-$1,020**

Hum 52: Going to Grandma's,
trademarks 1-8..........**$150-$960**

Hum 53: Joyful, trademarks 1-4,
6-7 ....**$85-$270**

Hum 51: Village Boy, trademarks
1-8 ....**$55-$690**

Hum 72: Spring Cheer, trademarks
1-6 ....**$120-$390**

Hum 50: Volunteers, trademarks
1-8 ....**$140-$900**

Hum 58: Playmates, trademarks
1-8 ....**$115-$600**

Hum 59: Skier, trademarks
1-8 ....$119-$515

Hum 67: Doll Mother, trademarks
1-8 ....$150-510

Hum 65: Farewell, trademarks
1-7 ....$170-$4,800

Hum 63: Singing Lesson,
trademarks 1-8.............$90-$300

Hum 68: Lost Sheep, trademarks
1-7 ....$99-$460

Hum 66: Farm Boy, trademarks
1-8 ....$170-$540

Hum 64: Shepherd's Boy,
trademarks 1-8........$170-$1,200

Hum 69: Happy Pastime,
trademarks 1-7...........$115-$390

Hum 74: Little Gardener,
trademarks 1-8.............$90-$450

Hum 79: Globe Trotter, trademarks
1-7 ....**$120-$499**

Hum 71: Stormy Weather,
trademarks 1-8...........**$210-$785**

Hum 73: Little Helper, trademarks
1-8 ....**$85-$300**

Hum 80: Little Scholar,
trademarks 1-8...........**$135-$480**

Hum 86: Happiness, trademarks
1-8 ....**$95-$300**

Hum 84: Worship, trademarks
1-8 ....**$115-$1,800**

Hum 81: School Girl, trademarks
1-8 ....**$105-$420**

Hum 82: School Boy, trademarks
1-8 ....**$105-$960**

Hum 85: Serenade, trademarks
1-8 ....**$70-$1,550**

Hum 87: For Father, trademarks
1-8 ....**$165-$480**

Hum 88: Heavenly Protection,
trademarks 1-8........**$315-$1,440**

Hum 89: Little Cellist, trademarks
1-8 ....**$155-$1,025**

Hum 94: Surprise, trademarks
1-8 ....**$105-$600**

Hum 96: Little Shopper,
trademarks 1-8...........**$105-$330**

Hum 95: Brother, trademarks
1-8 ....**$145-$480**

Hum 97: Trumpet Boy, trademarks
1-7 ....**$90-$315**

Hum 98: Sister, trademarks
1-8 ....**$55-$420**

Hum 99: Eventide, trademarks
1-7 ....**$220-$2,100**

LADY HEAD VASES

"Lady head vases," also known as "lady head planters" or simply "head vases," reached their zenith of popularity in the 1950s and 1960s, when florist shops found them a novel and inexpensive means of boosting sales. Flower overstock (which would normally be discarded) was gathered in small bouquets and used to adorn the hats of these ceramic figural novelties. Although initially a floral industry sideline, head vases quickly became collectible in their own right as consumers became attracted to their imaginative styling and seemingly infinite variations.

The term "lady head vase" was a natural identifier, since many of the most popular early vases depict beauties of the Gay Nineties era decked out in large picture hats with openings in the crown (the better to display their floral bounty). Thanks to public demand, however, head vases soon celebrated every theme and nationality: clowns, children, Disney and nursery rhyme characters, holiday figures, Asians, Africans, and favorites from television and the movies. With the introduction of male figures, the "lady head" label became somewhat inaccurate. Although often just a companion piece, the gentlemen sometimes branched out on their own in depictions ranging from cowboys to Howdy Doody.

Four ceramic figural lady head vases, two with earrings and necklaces, two marked for Napco and two for Relpo, Japan, 20th century, large example with hairline crack, otherwise undamaged, 5-1/2" to 7" h...............................**$126**

Jeffrey S. Evans & Associates

Six ceramic figural lady head vases, including Marilyn Monroe reissue and dog marked for Napco, Japan, 20th century, green example with chip, dog with light hairline, remainder undamaged, 3" to 6" h. **$126**

Jeffrey S. Evans & Associates

The function of a head vase also expanded. Variations included "umbrella girls," each holding an umbrella in an upraised hand; head vase lamps; and figures with jewelry and other accent pieces added after firing.

Due to import restrictions during World War II, the United States initially led the parade of head vase production. Domestic firms such as Ceramic Arts Studio, Betty Lou Nichols, Dorothy Kindell, Royal Copley, Florence, and many more all turned their talents, at one time or another, to head vase design. Head vases can even be found bearing the marks of such unlikely producers as Van Briggle and Roseville.

The opening of overseas markets in the early 1950s eventually reduced U.S. head vase manufacture to a trickle, as imports, many from Japan, cornered the market. Unhampered by copyrights, these mass-produced vases often directly imitated their United States counterparts, but at a lower cost (and quality).

Originality resurfaced, however, with the ongoing consumer appetite for variety. The 1960s fad for bouffant hairdos, for instance, resulted in a seemingly endless series of head vases that abandoned hats entirely; the floral opening was placed directly in the hair or as part of a bow or headband.

As new celebrities took center stage, they also found themselves achieving head vase immortality. A weeping Jacqueline Kennedy (complete with miniature figures of her children) remains one of the most in-demand head vases, as are those celebrating such timeless personalities as Marilyn Monroe and Lucille Ball.

By the early 1970s, head vases, along with many other mid-century figural ceramics,

Two vintage lady head vases, 7" h. Relpo K1633 lady with white glove, pearl necklace and earrings, gold foil Relpo label; 5-1/2" h. Napcoware C3307 lady with hand, pearl necklace, missing earrings, red hat brim with gold flecked top..**$47**

Phoebus Auction Gallery

began to fade from the popular consciousness. If thought of at all, they were regarded as dime-store relics of an earlier time.

In recent years there's been a head vase renaissance, due largely to the efforts of such authors as Maddy Gordon, Kathleen Cole, David Barron, and, most notably, the Head Hunters Collectors Association.

Each year, the Head Hunters sponsor a convention with thousands of head vases available for purchase; avid collectors are kept happy year-round with a quarterly newsletter. The Head Hunters have also championed the cause of new head vase production, with the annual release of a limited edition convention commemorative.

Today, collectors worldwide are once again appreciating the artistry and whimsical imagination that went into head vase creation. Whether put to their original use, stuffed with netting, used as pencil or eyeglass holders, or simply left unadorned, ceramic head vases retain the same appeal they held in the 1950s.

Porcelain lady head vase,
6" h. **$19**

Pioneer Auction Gallery

Lady head vase, NAPCO 1958, C3343 marking, heavy eyelashes, green drape of dress at shoulder, large hat with opening for flowers, hand with red nails in front, 4-1/4" h. x 3-3/4" w. **$35**

John Coker, LTD

Lady head vase with green hat, tied red scarf, and eyelashes...**$12**

Premier Auction Galleries

LLADRÓ

Lladró figurines—distinctive, elegant creations often glazed in the trademark colors of blue and white—hail from a Spanish company founded by three brothers nearly 60 years ago.

Juan, José, and Vicente Lladró began producing ceramic sculptures in their parents' home near Valencia, Spain in the mid-1950s. By 1955 they had established their own retail shop where they sold some of their earliest wares. In 1958 they moved to a factory in the town of Tavernes Blanques.

The 1960s were a decade of such strong growth and development, the Lladró company enlarged its facilities seven times before finally breaking ground for a new factory in 1967. This factory/office building complex, known as the City of Porcelain, was inaugurated in October 1969.

The 1970s were marked by Lladró's consolidation in the American market. In 1974, the first blue emblem—a bellflower and an ancient chemical symbol—appeared on the sculptures.

Lladró's success continued into the 1980s, and in 1985, the Lladró Collectors Society was launched. It lasted for more than 15 years. During the 1990s the Lladró brothers received several awards for their creations, which were exhibited in several cities throughout the world, and the company continued expanding. In 2001, the Lladró Collectors Society gave way to Lladró Privilege, a customer loyalty program.

Today Lladró—still headquartered at the City of Porcelain—employs 2,000 people and markets its creations in more than 100 countries across the globe.

A "G" after the identification number refers to a glazed finish; "M" refers to a matte finish. "G/M" means both glazed and matte finishes.

Flowers of the Season (#1454G) is one of Lladró's most famous creations, first issued in 1983 at a retail price of $1,460. The sculptor for this model was J. Puche, but creation of the parasol and flowerwork would have been largely the responsibility of Lladró's decoration and design staff. .... **$2,475-$3,500**

Sculptor Salvador Furió's Little Flower Seller (#5082G) was available from 1980 through 1985. .... **$2,000-$3,000**

All photos courtesy Lladró USA, Inc.

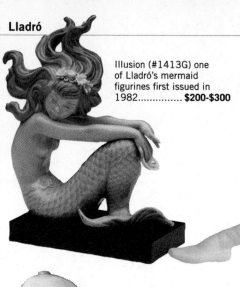

Illusion (#1413G) one of Lladró's mermaid figurines first issued in 1982............... **$200-$300**

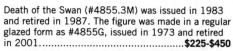

Death of the Swan (#4855.3M) was issued in 1983 and retired in 1987. The figure was made in a regular glazed form as #4855G, issued in 1973 and retired in 2001..**$225-$450**

"All Aboard" (#7619G) was the Lladró Society figurine for 1992........**$175-$300**

Eighteenth Century Coach (#1485) had an edition size of only 500, first issued in 1985....... **$14,000-18,000**

► "'A' is for Amy" (#5145G), part of a five "Vowel" figurine series available from 1982-1985, is the most difficult to find. ....**$375-$500**

"Woman Painting Vase" (#5079G) was issued in 1980 and retired in 1985. ....**$600-$700**

FIGURINES

Dutch Couple with Tulips (#5124G/M) was available from 1982 through 1985....**$450-$500**

Cathy and her Doll (#1380G) was issued in 1978 and retired in 1985..........................**$250-$400**

Wrath of Don Quixote (#1343G) was issued in 1977 in both glazed and matte finishes and was retired in 1989...................**$385-$1,300**

Sculptor Salvador Furió's Sharpening Cutlery (#5204G) was available from 1984 through 1988..........................**$300-$400**

Sheriff Puppet (#4969G) was issued in 1977 and retired in 1985..........................**$300-$500**

The Gossips (#4984G), sculpted by J. Roig, was available from 1978 through 1985....**$280-$600**

Valencian Boy (#1400G) was issued in 1982 and retired in 1988..........................**$250-$385**

Sculptor Francisco Catalá's Watching the Pigs (#4892G) was available from 1974 to 1978 and was retired in 1981..... **$1,200-$1,300**

Herons (also known as Ibis, #1319G) was first issued in 1976, 23" h. .... **$1,500-$2,500**

FIGURINES

Woman with Mandolin (#2107) is a Gres half-figure issued in 1978 and retired in 1981. The English title is inaccurate. The original Spanish title of the piece translates to maiden with musical wind instrument. .. **$1,700-$1,800**

Racing Motorcyclist (#5270G) was issued in 1985 and retired in 1988...................... **$800-$1,200**

Cow and Pig (#4640G/M) was sculpted by Vicente Martinez. Issued in the late 1960s, it was retired in 1981............**$400-$500**

Mirage (#1415G), last in a popular series of three Lladró mermaids issued in 1982............**$150-$300**

"Can I Help?" (#5689G) was issued in 1990 and retired in 1997. It was sculpted by Francisco Catalá. ....**$200-$350**

Woman with Cow and Calf (#4953G) was available from 1977 to 1979....... **$1,500-$4,000**

Fantasy (#1414G), second in a series of three popular mermaid models first issued in 1982.
................................**$300-$350**

Act II (#5035G/M) was issued in 1979. The glazed version was retired in 2004; the matte version in 1991............... **$1,000-$1,500**

Dutch Mother (#5083G), also known as Lullaby and Goodnight, was available from 1980 to 1983.........................**$200-$400**

"Puppet Show" (#5736G) was issued in 1991 and retired in 1996.........................**$200-$400**

Fishing with Gramps (#5215G/M) was issued in 1984. The matte version was retired in 1991. The piece was also produced in Gres (#2351) and was retired in 2001..........................**$300-$500**

Playful Horses (#4597G/M), whose original model was sculpted by Fulgencio Garcia, was issued in the late 1960s and retired in 1990......................**$800-$1,200**

Afghan (#1069G/M) was issued in the mid-to-late 1960s and retired in 1985......................**$200-$300** A glazed standing version of the dog, #1282G, was issued in 1974 and retired in 1985. ...**$250-$300**

Romeo and Juliet (#4750G/M) was issued in 1971 in both glazed and matte finishes. The matte version was retired in 1989, the glazed in 2005........**$800-$1,200**

Giraffe Group (#1005G) is small, given its subject, reaching a little over 6" h. It was available from 1969 to 1970......**$1,700-$1,775**

Snow White With Apple (#5067G) was issued in 1980 and retired in 1983......................**$450-$1,200**

Botanic (#1351G), sculpted by Salvador Furió, was available from 1979-1980. ....**$800-$1,720**

Lamplighter (#5205G), a tall figurine at 18-1/2", was first issued in 1984. The sculptor was Salvador Furió. ....**$200-$400**

ROYAL DOULTON

Doulton & Co., Ltd., was founded in Lambeth, London, in about 1858. It operated there until 1956 and often incorporated the words "Doulton" and "Lambeth" in its marks. Pinder, Bourne & Co., Burslem, was purchased by the Doultons in 1878 and in 1882 became Doulton & Co., Ltd. It added porcelain to its earthenware production in 1884. The "Royal Doulton" mark has been used since 1902 by this factory, which is still in operation. Character jugs and figurines are commanding great attention from collectors at the present time.

John Doulton, the founder, was born in 1793. He became an apprentice at the age of 12 to a potter in south London. Five years later he was employed in another small pottery near Lambeth. His two sons, John and Henry, subsequently joined their father in 1830 in a partnership he had formed with the name of Doulton & Watts. Watts retired in 1864 and the partnership was dissolved. Henry formed a new company that traded as Doulton and Co.

In the early 1870s the proprietor of the Pinder Bourne & Co., located in Burslem, Staffordshire, offered Henry a partnership. The Pinder Bourne & Co. was purchased by Henry in 1878 and became part of Doulton & Co. in 1882.

Five young women figurines, Nicola, HN 2839; Dawn, HN 3258, Alexandra, HN 3286; Elyse, HN 2474; and Sarah, HN 3380, underside signed in gold "Michael Doulton/11 Mar 1993"; 1971 to 1992, undamaged, 6-3/8" to 9" h. overall... **$207**

Jeffrey S. Evans & Associates

With the passage of time, the demand for the Lambeth industrial and decorative stoneware declined whereas demand for the Burslem manufactured and decorated bone china wares increased.

Doulton & Co. was incorporated as a limited liability company in 1899. In 1901 the company was allowed to use the word "Royal" on its trademarks by Royal Charter. The well known "lion on crown" logo came into use in 1902. In 2000 the logo was changed on the company's advertising literature to one showing a more stylized lion's head in profile.

Today Royal Doulton is one of the world's leading manufacturers and distributors of premium grade ceramic tabletop wares and collectibles. The Doulton Group comprises Minton, Royal Albert, Caithness Glass, Holland Studio Craft and Royal Doulton. Royal Crown Derby was part of the group from 1971 until 2000 when it became an independent company. These companies market collectibles using their own brand names.

Figurines

Four O'Clock, HN 1760, modeled by Leslie Harradine, 1936-1949, rare. **$2,000**

Auctioneer (The), HN 2988, black, grey and brown, 1986, R.D.I.C.C. Series. **$325**

Bedtime, HN 1978, white with black base, 1945-1997. .... **$80**

Autumn Breezes, HN 2131, orange, yellow and black, 1990-1994 .... **$150**

Fortune Teller, HN 2159, multicolor, 1955-1967. ...... **$400**

Sleeping Beauty, HN 3079, green, 1987-1989. .... **$225**

Huntsman (The), HN 2492, grey coat, cream pants, black hat and boots, 1974-1979. .... **$350**

Lambing Time, HN 1890, light brown, 1938-1980. .... **$115**

FIGURINES

Christmas Parcels, HN 2851, black, 1978-1982.............. **$225**

Three figurines, Balloon Man, HN 1954; The Old Balloon Seller, HN 1315; and Biddy Penny Farthin, HN 1843; 1937 to 1954, undamaged, 7-1/2" to 9" h. overall. **$149**

Jeffrey S. Evans & Associates

Shepherd (The), HN 1975, light brown, 1945-1975............. **$145**

Three figurines, Flora, HN 2349; A Stitch in Time, HN 2352; and Teatime, HN 2255; 1965 to 1966, two examples undamaged, Flora professionally repaired, 7-1/2" to 8" h. overall. **$149**

Jeffrey S. Evans & Associates

Two figurines, Rest Awhile, HN 2728 and Embroidering, HN 2855; 1979 and 1980, undamaged, 8" to 9" h. overall........................... **$92**

Jeffrey S. Evans & Associates

Pride & Joy, HN 2945, brown, gold and green, RDICC, 1984. .... **$275**

Top 'O The Hill, HN 2126, mauve and green, 1988, miniature.... **$125**

Wintertime, HN 3060, 1985, RDICC. **$325**

Harmony, HN 2824, grey dress, 1978-1984. **$275**

Cissie, HN 1809, pink dress, 1937-1993. **$100**

Thanks Doc, HN 2731, white and brown, 1975-1990..................... **$375**

Two figurines, The Orange Lady, HN 1953 and Silks and Ribbons, HN 2017; 1948 to 1978, minor glaze crazing to underside of dress on The Orange Lady, 6-1/2" to 9" h. overall. **$92**

Jeffrey S. Evans & Associates

Two figurines, Nanny, HN 2221 and Twilight, HN 2256, 1975, Nanny has loss of three spots of enamel to rocker, 4-1/2" to 5-12" h. overall........**$92**

Beatrix Potter

Hunca Munca Sweeping, P2584, brown dustpan, crown backstamp, 1977-2002. ....$70

Appley Dappley, P2333, bottle in, brown line backstamp, 1975-2002.....................................$60

Cecily Parsley, P1941, gold circle/oval backstamp, 1965-1993...................................$200

Mr. Benjamin Bunny & Peter Rabbit, P2509, brown line backstamp, 1975-1995.........$90

Christmas Stocking, P3257, crown backstamp, 1991-1994.......$250

Mr. Alderman Ptolemy, P2424, crown backstamp, 1973-1997..................................$135

Jemima Puddle-Duck Made a Feather Nest, P2823, brown line backstamp, 1983-1997........$50

Anna Maria, P1851, gold circle/oval backstamp, 1963-1983. ......$175

Hunca Munca, P1198, crown backstamp, 1951-2000........$60

Flopsy, Mopsy & Cottontail, P1274, John Beswick script backstamp, 1954-1997........$80

Old Mr. Brown, P1796, brown owl, gold circle/oval backstamp, 1963-1999....................................$60

FIGURINES

Mrs. Rabbit & Bunnies, P2543, brown line backstamp, 1976-1997....................................**$70**

Aunt Pettitoes, P2276, gold circle/oval backstamp, 1970-1993.................................. **$450**

And This Pig Had None, P3319, crown backstamp, 1992-1998.....................................**$60**

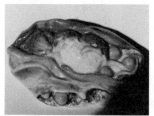

Timmy Willie Sleeping, P2996, brown line backstamp, 1986-1996................................. **$150**

Cousin Ribby, P2284, gold circle/oval backstamp, 1970-1993.................................. **$430**

Jemima Puddle-Duck, P1092, yellow scarf clip, Beswick Made in England backstamp, 1948-2002....................................**$50**

Mrs. Tiggy-Winkle, P1107, plaid dress, crown backstamp, 1972-2000.................................. **$180**

Squirrel Nutkin, P1102, red-brown squirrel, brown line backstamp, 1983-1989. ....**$40**

Timmy Tiptoes, P1101, gold circle/oval backstamp, 1948-1980................................. **$115**

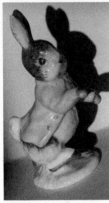

Peter Rabbit, P1098, gold circle/oval backstamp, 1948-1980. .... **$200**

Poorly Peter Rabbit, P2560, brown line backstamp, 1976-1997 .... **$50**

Pigling Bland, P1365, lilac jacket, brown line backstamp, 1975-1998 .... **$50**

Susan, P2716, brown line backstamp, 1983-1989 .... **$200**

Mr. Jeremy Fisher, P1157, large spots on head, striped legs, crown backstamp, 1950-2002 .... **$45**

Goody Tiptoes, P1675, gold circle/oval backstamp, 1961-1967 .. **$50**

Mrs. Rabbit, P1200, umbrella in, crown backstamp, 1975-2002 .. **$50**

Tabitha Twitchit & Miss Moppet, P2544, crown backstamp, 1976-1993. .... **$120**

Peter Rabbit, P1098, light blue jacket, brown line backstamp, 1980-2002 .... **$70**

Tom Kitten, P1100, light blue suit, crown backstamp, 1980-1999 .... **$60**

Tommy Brock, P1348, large eye patch, spade handle in, Beswick Made in England backstamp, 1975-2002. .... **$50**

Old Woman Who Lived in a Shoe Knitting (The), P2804, Beswick Made in England backstamp, 1983-2002. .... **$130**

Pig-Wig, P2381, black pig, brown line backstamp, 1972-1998. .... **$400**

Fierce Bad Rabbit, P2586, feet in, light brown rabbit, crown backstamp, 1980-1997.................... **$110**

Mr. Benjamin Bunny, P1940, pipe in, lilac jacket, brown line backstamp, 1975-2000.. **$50**

Pickles, P2324, gold circle/oval backstamp, 1971-1982. .... **$300**

Benjamin Bunny, P1105, ears in, shoes in, gold circle/oval backstamp, 1980-2000. .... **$60**

Amiable Guinea Pig, P2061, tan jacket, gold circle or oval backstamp, 1967-1983. .... **$230**

Lady Mouse, P1183, crown backstamp, 1950-2000...................... **$45**

Tailor of Gloucester, P1108, John Beswick script backstamp, 1949-2002...................... **$45**

Simpkin, P2508, brown line backstamp, 1975-1983.................... **$550**

Sir Isaac Newton, P2425, brown line backstamp, 1973-1984........... **$360**

Benjamin Bunny Sat on a Bank, P2803, head down, brown jacket, brown line backstamp, 1983-1985. .... **$70**

Foxy Whiskered Gentleman, P1277, crown backstamp, 1954-2002.................... **$140**

Fine Art

As the global economy continues to fluctuate, the art market continues to see expansion of its buyer pool and growth of some genres – with modern art commanding attention in the leader spot in terms of popularity and prices paid, especially among the world's wealthiest buyers.

In May 2013, Christie's, the global leader of fine art sales, saw its post war and contemporary fine art auction finish at $640 million in one week, a new auction record for value sold at auction, in any collecting category. In this one auction, 37 new fine art auction records were set. Claiming the spot as top lot of this record-setting auction was Jackson Pollock's "Number 19," which sold for $58.3 million, followed by "Woman with Flowered Hat" by Roy Lichtenstein, which fetched $56.1 million.

Bronze and silver sculptures are also garnering increased attention and appreciation, with Sotheby's reporting the sale of Auguste Rodin's "The Thinker" sculpture selling for $15.3 million – a new record for sale of this bronze figure.

Fine art continues to offer some ground for diversifying investments, however, as with any collectible item, the purpose should be steeped more in enjoyment and appreciation than profit.

Limited edition woodcut print, Ronnie Wood, portrait of Keith Richards, signed, titled and numbered "PP III/VI" in pencil in margin, 44" x 36" framed.................. **$4,375**

Julien's Auctions

Oil on canvas, Georges Washington (French), "Orientalist Battle Scene," 19th century. **$21,420**

Clars Auction Gallery

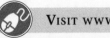

Hanging scroll, ink and color on paper, two tigers, 19th century, signed Zaobin with two seals of artist that state Hushi zhizhang and Zaobin xiehu, 57-3/4" x 26-1/4". **$3,750**

Bonhams

Oil on canvas of Aurora, after Guido Reni, deaccessioned from Reading Public Museum, 26-1/2" x 62-1/4"... **$1,304**

Pook and Pook, Inc.

Set of 18 offset lithographs, Andy Warhol in collaboration with interior designer Suzie Frankfurt, "Wild Raspberries," circa 1959, comprising 17 pieces with hand-coloring, some with applied gold leaf, fuchsia tissue interleafing, on laid paper, and fuchsia buckram boards; inscribed "To Gerald Kornblau/Andy Warhol," accompanied by two letters to Mr. Kornblau from Jane Opper, Executive Editor of Panache Press at Random House, detailing permission rights of material to be exhibited in book Pre-Pop Warhol..........................**$20,000-$30,000**

Woodbury Auctions

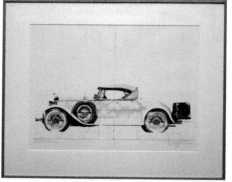

Graphite pre-study, 1930 Packard Elegant, presented for 1989 Meadow Brook Concours d'Elegance by Peter F. Maier, 41" x 51". **$1,725**

RM Auctions

Continental School oil, tag on painting reads "Portrait of a Lady at a Spinet, painted by D. Hams, England 1780," 37-3/4" x 32-1/2". **$2,655**

Michaan's Auctions

Lithograph, Aristide Bruant, "Ambassadeurs," circa 1892, colors on two sheets of wove paper backed with wove support, printed by Edward Ancourt, Paris, framed, sheet 53-3/8" x 35-7/8". ....**$20,000-$30,000**

Bonhams

Oil on canvas of harbor scene, Bernard Buffet, circa 1959, signed and dated "Bernard Buffet 59," upper left, 37-1/2" x 21-1/2". **$4,100**

Kaminski Auctions

Chinese reverse painting of woman, mid-19th century, 15-3/4" x 11-3/4". **$2,607**

Pook and Pook, Inc.

Watercolor illustration of two children and a dog, Tasha Tudor, 6-1/2" x 8". **$2,607**

Pook and Pook, Inc.

Oil on canvas landscape painting, Mary B. Leisz (American), signed lower right, 14" x 18"......**$356**

Pook and Pook, Inc.

Oil on canvas, Antoine Blanchard, street scene of people, carriages, trolleys, buildings and trees, signed lower right, mounted in gilded wood frame, 20" x 24"........**$3,000**

Elite Decorative Arts

Color lithograph on German etching paper under glass, "Dog Barking at Moon (Perro ladrando a la luna)," signed in pencil lower right R. Tamayo (Rufino Tamayo) and numbered in pencil lower left iii/xxv, with printer's intaglio "EP" with star, 22-1/2" h. x 30" w. **$5,197**

John Moran Auctioneers

FINE ART

Oil on canvas, Sir John Lavery, "Mrs. Rosen's Bedroom," early 20th century, signed. **$115,000**

Thomaston Place Auction Galleries

Signed oil on canvas, Fern Isable Coppedge, "Autumn From Music Circus Hill, Lambertville," circa 20th century, 25" x 30-1/2". **$65,175**

Pook and Pook, Inc.

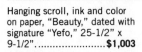

Hanging scroll, ink and color on paper, "Beauty," dated with signature "Yefo," 25-1/2" x 9-1/2". **$1,003**

Michaan's Auctions

Woodcut in colors on Tosa Koza paper, Wayne Thiebaud, "Candy Apples," 1987, signed, dated and numbered 80/200, signed in Japanese by printer, Tadashi Toda at Shi-un-do Print Shop, Kyoto, print 15-1/4" x 16-1/2". **$40,000**

Bonhams

Color lithograph on beige wove paper, "La passagère du 54 - Promenade en yacht," circa 1896, commissioned as a poster by La Plume for exhibition at Salon des Cent, 3-5/8" x 15-3/4". **$22,500**

Bonhams

Three woodblock prints on handmade paper, Wharton Esherick (American, 1887-1970), "Solomon Had a Vineyard," 1927 (framed), "Upon the Hills," and "Sky," 1928, all signed and titled, "Upon the Hills" numbered 8/20, image 4-1/2" sq., 2-1/2" x 2", 5-1/2" x 2"..**$2,125**

Rago Arts and Auction Center

Oil on canvas of abstract tree, David Alfaro Siquerios, 20th century, 32-1/2" h. x 26-1/4" w.. **$7,000**

Kaminski Auctions

Lithograph in colors, Henri de Toulouse-Lautrec, "Toulouse Le Jockey," circa 1899, 20-3/8" x 14-1/4"......................................**$50,000-$70,000**

Bonhams

Oil on canvas, Alexander Charles Stuart, seascape of American frigate off Delaware coast, signed lower left, 30" x 50"...**$7,703**

Pook and Pook, Inc.

Watercolor view of bridge on River Goblins, Lewis Miller (American), 19th century, 3" x 6"...........**$304**

Pook and Pook, Inc.

Oil on canvas, Charles Watson, "Highland Sheep," dated and signed, 15-1/2" x 23-1/2". **$4,500**

Kaminski Auctions

Unframed oil on cigar box lid, foothill mountain landscape, signed lower right H. Puthuff, dated verso: 5-10-15, 5-1/2" h. x 8" w.........................**$3,000**

John Moran Auctioneers

Oil on canvas coastal scene, William Stone, signed on lower left corner and dated 1889, 20" x 30"...**$593**

Pook and Pook, Inc.

SCULPTURES

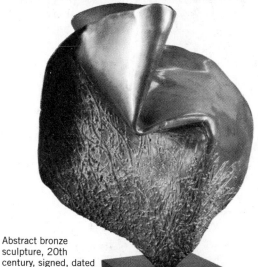

Abstract bronze sculpture, 20th century, signed, dated on reverse Rubino '82, positioned on revolving base, 19-3/4" h. x 17" w. x 8-1/2" d. **$700**

Woodbury Auctions

Bronze sculpture, Albert Ernest Belleuse (French), "Melodie," mid-19th century, female sculpture holds lyre, title plaque inscribed "Melodie Par Carrier Belleuse (Sculp)," signed "A. Carrier Belleuse/Hors Concours," 31" h.....**$8,000-$12,000**

Don Presley Auctions

Art Deco gilt bronze figure, Paul Manship, "Nude Study," circa 1927, set on brown banded onyx base, signed, 19" h. x 6-1/2" w. **$8,500**

Schwenke Auction Gallery

Automotive bronze, Stanley Wanlass, 1907 Thomas Flyer, 1982, mounted on walnut base, number 17 of 30, 34" l. **$13,800**

RM Auctions

Bronze, Earl E. Heikka, "Changing Riders on the Pony Express," inscribed "E. E. Heikka -3," marked "© H. METTLER CONS, J. G. STEVENS CONS 28/35 1976," 15-1/2" x 23" x 8-1/2," Powell Bronze (Kalispell, Montana) medallion. .... **$8,000-$12,000**

Manitou Galleries and The Coeur d'Alene Art Auction

Rare cast bronze, unawarded production model of Heisman Memorial Trophy, 20th century, Roman Bronze Works, unsigned, trophy is among the most iconic American sports awards, 13-3/4" h. x 12-1/2" w. x 6" d. ....**$75,000-$95,000**

Woodbury Auction

Patinated bronze portrait bust of Czar Nicholas II, based on model by Leopold Bernhard Bernstamm, 20th century, depicted half length wearing military regalia and cape, 18-1/2". **$6,875**

Bonhams

WESTERN ART

For the last five years, the market's interest in Western art was a lot like striking a match. From 2009 through 2010 the market moved slowly, giving off a few sparks for well-known artists. But in 2012 and 2013, auction houses nationwide marked the return of white-hot prices for the best works.

Western art is generally defined as paintings and sculpture that celebrate the history, lifestyles, cultures, and artists living in the American West. Popular subjects include cowboys, American Indians, women, floral still lifes, settlers, and landscapes. Famous artists include Frederic Remington, Albert Bierstadt and Charles M. Russell. A notable subset of Western art is Southwest art, made famous by E. Irving Couse and his contemporaries from northern New Mexico's Taos Founders or the Taos School.

Western art remains a bright spot in a global market. The Mei Moses World All Art Index showed the global art market actually shrunk by 3.28% in 2012. Yet a steady stream of records were set at annual Western and wildlife art auctions, such as Scottsdale Art Auction, Jackson Hole Art Auction, Santa Fe Art Auction, and Coeur d'Alene Art Auction.

Oil on canvas, Albert Bierstadt (American, 1830-1902), "Mount Brewer from King's River Canyon, California," 1872, signed lower left: A Bierstadt, 36" x 47". **$602,500**
Heritage Auctions

Bronze with patina, Grant Speed (American, 1930-2011), "Over the Cutback," 1972, signed and dated on base: "UG Speed / CA 1972," ed. 3/20, 22" h. **$9,375**
Heritage Auctions

Who's the hottest Western artist alive today? Howard Terpning.

"Terpning is celebrated because of his realism, accuracy and attention to detail," said Kirsty Buchanan, Associate Director of Western Art at Heritage Auctions. "He captures an authentic visual narrative in his paintings. In their hearts, Western collectors are history buffs, so the more accurate and realistic a work is in depicting those life and times, then the more it's going to be highly collectible."

Buchanan oversaw the late 2012 sale of Terpning's "Plunder from Sonora" for $962,500. The sale realized $8.78 million and set a number of artist records, including one for the late Grant Speed. His bronze, "Half Breed," is considered the Texas artist's signature work when it sold for $50,000. Earlier in 2012, Heritage set a record for H.H. Cross' "Sitting Bull," a portrait painted from life in 1882, which sold for $83,650.

FINE ART

Oil on canvas, Howard A. Terpning (American, b. 1927), "Plunder From Sonora," 1982, signed lower right: Terpning, 30" x 48"...**$962,500**

Heritage Auctions

Oil on board, Albert Bierstadt (American, 1830-1902), "Sundown on the Lake" (thought to be Lake Tahoe), initialed lower right: AB, 7-1/4" x 10-3/4"... **$8,750**

Heritage Auctions

Oil on canvas, Frank Earle Schoonover (American, 1877-1972), "Two Sweat Lodges," 1927, initialed and dated lower right: F.E.S. '27, 26" x 38"..........**$10,000**

Heritage Auctions

Oil on canvas, Thomas Hill (British/American, 1829-1908), "Gates of Yosemite," signed lower left: T. Hill, 16" x 24".. **$6,875**

Heritage Auctions

Oil on board, Tom Lovell (American, 1909-1997), "The Thaw," 1975, signed lower left: Tom Lovell, 27" x 40"...**$230,500**

Heritage Auctions

Oil on canvas, Howard A. Terpning (American, b. 1927), "Crow Country," 1978, signed and dated lower left: Terpning/1978, 30" x 46"..**$662,500**

Heritage Auctions

Watercolor on paper, David Allen Halbach (American, b. 1931), "Earth is Sky," signed lower right: DAVID HALBACH, titled and signed verso: "EARTH IS SKY"/ DAVID HALBACH, 27-1/2" x 33-1/2"............ **$8,750**

Heritage Auctions

Oil on canvas, William Robinson Leigh (American, 1866-1955), "One Good Turn Deserves Another," 1944, signed and dated lower left: W.R. Leigh, 1944, 28" x 22".......................................**$290,500**

Heritage Auctions

Firearms

Gun collecting has been going on since the first chunks of lead were fired out of old muskets, but it wasn't until the Industrial Revolution that things got interesting. Early manufacturers and inventors changed the way firearms were produced and conceived and, as a result, hundreds of makes and models of handguns, shotguns, and rifles have been produced. Some of these guns have changed the world through their use in wars, exploration, and hunting.

Collectible guns receiving the most attention are ones used by both famous and infamous people alike. In the last decade, the guns of Theodore Roosevelt, Ernest Hemingway, and baseball great Ted Williams have sold for staggering amounts of money. For example, Roosevelt's specially made double-barreled shotgun set a world record when it sold for $862,500 at a James D. Julia auction in 2010, while a Hemingway-owned Westley Richards side-by-side safari rifle sold for $340,000 at auction in 2011. Two pistols found on the bodies of famed Depression-era outlaws Bonnie Parker and Clyde Barrow, after they were killed in 1934, sold for $504,000 at an RR Auction sale in 2012.

In these rare cases provenance is everything, according to Wes Dillon, head of James D. Julia Rare Firearm & Military Division. "The results (from the Roosevelt sale) were a direct reflection of the significance and importance of the man and his gun," Dillon said.

Keep in mind, however, that these are exceptional, historical finds in the gun-collecting world and command extraordinary prices befitting the historical figure associated with the weapon. Some of these high prices are certainly driven by vanity – the desire to own a one-of-a-kind gun – while others are seen as investments. Either way, the right gun with the right history can realize staggering results at auction.

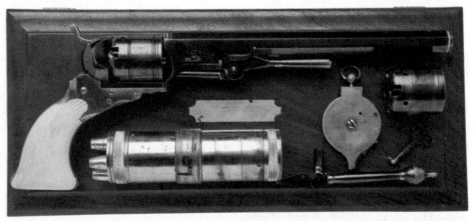

Colt Holster Model Paterson Revolver No. 5 SN 515, .36-caliber, 5-shot cylinder with stagecoach holdup roll scene and shell-carved ivory grips. About 1,000 of these revolvers were manufactured from 1838-1940. Also known as the Texas Paterson, this revolver has great appeal to collectors because of its size (9-inch barrel), relatively heavy caliber and the association of the type with the Texas Ranger Jack Hays and verified use by military and civilians on the frontier...**$977,500**

Heritage Auctions

Understanding Value

Like any collectible item, it is important to understand that the value of a used firearm greatly depends on its condition. There are six grades of gun conditions, and how a gun is graded is key to its value:

New in Box: The gun is in its original box with the papers that came with it. But this grade also means that the gun has never been fired, and there is no sign whatsoever that the gun has been handled or used. This is the highest grade for a used gun.

Excellent: The gun may have been used but so gently and lightly that 98 percent of its finish remains as if it were brand new. All of its parts are still original and have not been swapped out with foreign ones. That includes no repairs or alternations.

Very Good: The gun is in good working order and 100 percent original but may have had some minor repair work or alterations. Finish should be around 92 percent.

Good: The gun must have 80 percent of its original finish remaining. Alterations, repairs, or additions are acceptable as long as they are not major ones. Must be safe to fire and in decent working condition.

Fair: The gun is safe and in working order but only about 30 percent of its original finish remains. May have had a major overhaul in a refinishing process or some other kind of alteration.

Poor: Gun is piece of junk and unsafe to fire – rusty, cracked wood. Unless the gun has some incredible historical significance, it is not worth your time or money to mess around with other than hanging it above a fireplace as a conversation piece.

It is important not to deceive yourself about a gun's value. Professional gun appraisers will notice small details that were missed in your amateur inspection. If you think you have an old gun of value, or you are contemplating buying one, please do your homework. The landscape is pockmarked with unscrupulous people more than happy to separate you from your hard-earned money for something of dubious value. As always, knowledge is power. An excellent reference for antique American arms is *Flayderman's Guide to Antique American Firearms... and Their Values*. Norm Flayderman is arguably the world's best-known antique arms dealer and authority. Gun collectors and historians have long considered his book an indispensable tool. Other excellent resources are the *Standard Catalog of Firearms* and *The Blue Book of Gun Values*. Both offer an impressive depth and breadth of knowledge to the gun-collecting hobby.

Even with the help of a dependable reference such as *Flayderman's*, you may be well served getting the advice of a professional gun appraiser, especially if you think there is something unique or special about the gun you have or are considering buying. Armed with that knowledge, you can make an intelligent buying or selling decision.

Collectible Guns as an Investment

On Internet message boards, there is considerable debate about collectible guns as an investment. There are arguments for and against the idea that acquiring guns could enhance your financial portfolio. It's true that certain collectible firearms have realized substantial return on investment. As with any investment, however, there is risk.

Here are some points to consider before you decide to include collectible firearms in your investment portfolio:

• Don't venture into gun collecting as an investment unless you know what you're doing. To get to the point of knowing could take years of study of both guns and the marketplace.

• If you decide to invest in firearms, it's often wise to choose a specialty, preferably with a type of gun that you are personally interested in. There are numerous manufacturer-specific gun collector associations and they are a great place to start your research.

• Investing in anything entails risk.

— James Card, Editor, Gun Digest the Magazine

FIREARMS

!

TOP
LOT!

BONNIE PARKER-ALIAS-MRS. CLYDE BARROW.

Death Car

Notorious Depression-era criminal Bonnie Parker, who along with boyfriend Clyde Barrow gained fame as outlaws Bonnie and Clyde, carried this Colt Detective .38 revolver at the time of her death in 1934. Parker had the gun taped to the inside of her thigh when she and Parker were ambushed and killed by law officers on a rural road in Bienville Parish, Louisiana. Many of the guns carried by Bonnie and Clyde ended up in the estate of Texas Ranger Captain Frank Hamer, who led the six-man posse that performed the ambush on May 23, 1934. As an unexpected bonus for his service, Hamer was promised that he could take anything the outlaws had in their possession at the time of their capture. This .38 Special, concealed beneath Bonnie's red dress that morning – the same way she concealed the gun that enabled Clyde to bust out of prison in 1930 – was one that he kept. **$264,000**

RR Auction

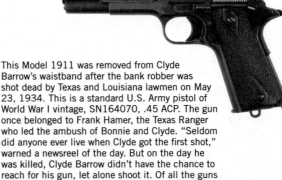

Clyde Barrow

This Model 1911 was removed from Clyde Barrow's waistband after the bank robber was shot dead by Texas and Louisiana lawmen on May 23, 1934. This is a standard U.S. Army pistol of World War I vintage, SN164070, .45 ACP. The gun once belonged to Frank Hamer, the Texas Ranger who led the ambush of Bonnie and Clyde. "Seldom did anyone ever live when Clyde got the first shot," warned a newsreel of the day. But on the day he was killed, Clyde Barrow didn't have the chance to reach for his gun, let alone shoot it. Of all the guns found in their death car, this is the most closely related to Clyde Barrow and accordingly, the most fascinating and valuable........................**$240,000**

HANDGUNS

Deluxe engraved presentation Colt Model 1849 Pocket Revolver, SN 33598, presented to gunsmith Anson Chase from inventor Col. Samuel Colt. Chase made prototype guns for Samuel Colt in the early 1930s. This presentation set honors the principal gun maker who built the first of the Colt revolvers. **$195,000**

Heritage Auctions

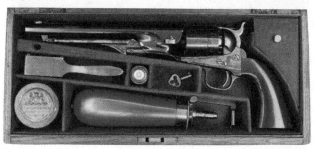

Colt Model 1860 Army Revolver, SN 154572, .44 caliber with 8" round barrel. About 200,500 revolvers were produced from 1860-1873. It was the major revolver in use by U.S. troops during the Civil War, with 127,156 of the Model 1860 Army acquired by the Union government for the war. Accompanied by an original English oak case. This revolver was manufactured and shipped to England at the height of Great Britain's Asian and African wars. **$57,500**

James D. Julia, Inc.

▲ Colt Walker Revolver, SN D COMPANY NO 81, .44 caliber, with 9" octagon to round barrel. Manufactured in 1847, with a total production of about 1,100, the Walker is the greatest prize of any Colt collection, according to *Flayderman's Guide to Antique American Firearms*. Slightly more than 10% of the original total made survive today in collections. The revolver weighs a massive 4 lbs 9 oz. Serial numbering is in five companies, A, B, C, D, and E, beginning with the number 1 in each grouping. The revolvers armed Dragoons of the U.S. Armed Forces engaged in the war with Mexico....................**$74,750**

James D. Julia, Inc.

Cased Colt Model 1851 London Navy Percussion Revolver, SN 35232, .36-caliber, circa 1855, 7-1/2" octagon barrel, one-piece varnished walnut grip. Entire revolver including cylinder, rammer and handle, wedge, hammer, trigger guard and backstrap are damascened with vines and flowerettes in heavy gold and dark brownish metal background. Includes original English mahogany casing.............................**$34,500**

James D. Julia, Inc.

Colt Model 1849 Wells Fargo Revolver, SN 48234, .31 caliber, five-shot cylinder with stagecoach holdup roll scene, 3" inch octagon barrel with brass pin front sight. Only about 4,000 of the so-called "Wells Fargo" model revolvers were manufactured; all without the loading lever. Varnished walnut grips.......**$29,900**

London Colt Model 1849 Pocket Revolver, SN 8364, .31 caliber, blue and color case hardened with 5" octagon barrel. More Model 1849 revolvers were produced than any other Colt percussion firearm. Production began in 1850 and continued through 1873. The total of the Hartford-made series was about 340,000. The London Model 1849 totaled about 11,000 from 1853-1857, during the height of British colonialism throughout Asia, Africa, and the Middle East............**$8,050**

James D. Julia, Inc.

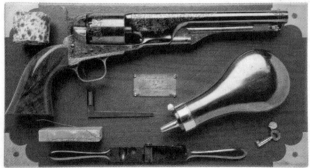

Colt Model 1861 New Model Navy Revolver, SN 19928/E, .36 caliber, six-shot cylinder, was presented by the Colt Co. to E.W. Parsons, of Adams Express Co., Hartford, Connecticut. The E.W. Parsons Navy ranks among the finest and most historic of Colt percussion revolvers. It is a prime example of the appearance of a rare Colt set, as it left the Colt factory destined for presentation. **$805,000**

Heritage Auctions

Colt Model 1862 Police Revolver, SN 10679, .36 caliber, blue and color case hardened with 5-1/2" round barrel, brass pin front sight and one-line New-York U.S. America address. Many collectors consider the Model 1862, made from 1861-1873, as the ultimate in streamlined design by Colt's factory in the percussion period. These revolvers were produced in limited quantities during the Civil War and became very popular with the military. They remained in service well into the 1870s before being supplanted by the advent of the self-contained cartridge revolvers. **$18,400**

James D. Julia, Inc.

Colt Single Action Army Revolver (Pinched Frame), SN 2., .45 Colt, has the rare pinched frame with nickel finish. Barrel reduced (from 7-1/2" to 5-1/2") and has carved raised ox-head, one-piece ivory grip. Manufactured before mid-July 1873, the revolver has seen hard service. **$63,250**

James D. Julia, Inc.

◀ Colt Cavalry Single Action Army Revolver, SN 137537, .45 Colt, martially marked, blue and color case hardened with 7-1/2" barrel. Accompanied by a Colt factory letter that states gun delivered to the U.S. Government inspector at the Colt plant on Jan. 20, 1891. All military marked Colts should be authenticated before purchase because many fakes have been discovered. **$23,000**

James D. Julia, Inc.

▶ Colt Civilian/Military Single Action Army Revolver, SN 41706, .45 Colt, blue and color case hardened with 7-1/2" barrel, full front sight and backwards or left hand 1-line block letter address, mounted with one-piece walnut grip. Accompanied by a letter from renowned Colt author and historian John Kopec, who authenticates this revolver as being completely original and one of very few known civilian/military revolvers... **$19,550**

James D. Julia, Inc.

Nimschke-engraved Colt Single Action Army Revolver, SN 105747, .45 Colt, nickel finish with 5-1/2" barrel, mounted with two-piece pearl grips with raised carved spread-winged eagle on right side. Revolver engraved in about "C" coverage by L.D. Nimschke. Colt factory letter identifies revolver was shipped to Hartley and Graham, New York, New York, on Aug. 21, 1884. ....**$25,875**

James D. Julia, Inc.

Colt Single Action Army Revolver Sheriff's Model, SN 122399, .45 Colt, nickel finish, 4" barrel. Colt Peacemaker Encyclopedia speculates that there were fewer than 1,000 Sheriff's model revolvers manufactured throughout the entire production. **$57,500**

James D. Julia, Inc.

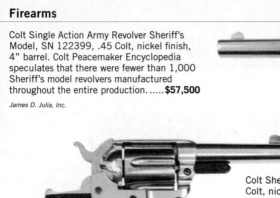

Colt Sheriff's Model D.A. Revolver, SN 1389, .38 Colt, nickel finish with 3-1/2" barrel, full front sight and 2-line address with etched panel on left side "COLT D.A. 38," mounted with one-piece checkered walnut grip. Colt factory letter states revolver shipped to George E. Pond, address unknown, on June 14, 1877...**$11,500**

Colt Cavalry Single-Action Army Revolver, SN 19536, .45 Colt, martially marked, usual configuration with 7-1/2" barrel. Gun was issued to Cavalry units participating in the Indian wars. No original finish remains except traces of blue under ejector housing; overall dark plum brown patina. **$7,475**

James D. Julia, Inc.

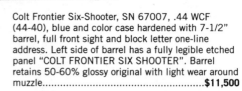

Colt Frontier Six-Shooter, SN 67007, .44 WCF (44-40), blue and color case hardened with 7-1/2" barrel, full front sight and block letter one-line address. Left side of barrel has a fully legible etched panel "COLT FRONTIER SIX SHOOTER". Barrel retains 50-60% glossy original with light wear around muzzle...**$11,500**

James D. Julia, Inc.

Rare example of Model 1911 A1 Pistol manufactured by the Singer Manufacturing Co. during World War II. There were only 500 pistols produced by Singer under the U. S. Army, Ordnance Educational Order No. W-ORD-396, with almost all of them issued to the U.S. Army Air Corps.....................................**$69,000**

Rock Island Auction Co.

One of an estimated 2,000 Remington Model 1890 Single Action Army Revolvers manufactured from 1891-1896. This scarce model revolver is one of the most sought after of all Remington produced handguns. Top of the barrel is marked "REMINGTON ARMS CO. ILION, N.Y." and "44 C.F.W." on the left side of the frame just below the cylinder. **$25,875**

Rock Island Auction Co.

Boxed pair Colt Third Model "Thuer" Deringer, SN 4563 and 12739, .41 RF, nickel finish, 2-1/2" barrels, tiny half moon front sights, marked "COLT" on tops. Made from 1870-1912, the Third Model, or Thuer Deringer, outsold by nearly three times its No. 1 and No. 2 companions. Both mounted with two-piece, smooth, birdhead pearl grips. Accompanied by rare two-piece dark burgundy cardboard box with pink top label..**$11,500**

James D. Julia, Inc.

Colt Model 1905 Semi-Auto Pistol, SN 3209, .45 caliber, blue finish and 5" barrel. Only about 6,100 of these rare pistols were produced from 1905-1911, according to Flayderman's Guide to Antique American Firearms. Slide has standard markings on both sides with rampant Colt in a circle at left rear end, mounted with diamond checkered walnut grips................................**$14,375**

James D. Julia, Inc.

Colt Model 1902 Military Pistol, SN 35560, .38 caliber with blue finish, 6" barrel. About 18,000 were produced from 1902-1929, remaining in service well into the 1950s with target shooters due to their reliability and accuracy, mounted with two-piece factory ivory grips with deep left and right Colt medallions. **$8,050**

James D. Julia, Inc.

Colt "Pony" Double-Action Revolver, SN 354658, .38 caliber, all blue finish with 6" unmarked, tapered round barrel, mounted with deep silver medallion diamond checkered walnut grips. Revolver appears in The Book of Colt Firearms, which states gun was "made to renew the registration of the 'Pony' name for Colt's exclusive use. ... The Pony model was patented Jan. 22, 1945. To date no commercially available Colt arms have used the Pony designation."..**$5,460**

James D. Julia, Inc.

Colt Model 1877 "Thunderer" Double-Action Revolver, SN 6751, .41 Colt, nickel finish with 6" barrel. The Model 1877 was Colt's first attempt at manufacturing a double-action revolver. More than 166,000 were produced from 1877-1909. They saw hard service on the American frontier with infrequent or no maintenance. History records numerous individuals on both sides of the law carrying this model of revolver, including Billy the Kid and others. **$43,125**

James D. Julia, Inc.

Remington Model 1875 Single Action Army revolver, SN 1296, .44 WCF (44-40), nickel finished with 7-1/2" barrel. Only about 25,000-30,000 Model 1875s were produced from 1875-1889. Remington revolvers were popular with their users but they arrived late on the market. Given Colt's head start with their Model 1873 and government contracts, along with Colt's advanced distribution system, Remingtons were never plentiful on the frontier. Mounted with smooth two-piece ivory grips. **$17,250**

James D. Julia, Inc.

Remington Beals Army Percussion Revolver, SN 1173, .44 caliber, 8" octagon barrel, dovetailed German silver cone front sight with grooved top strap rear sight. Few Beals Army revolvers remain today with only about 1,900 produced from 1861-1862. They were all issued to Union troops and saw continuous service throughout the Civil War and later on the American frontier, usually under harsh and adverse conditions with limited or no maintenance. **$20,700**

James D. Julia, Inc.

Smith & Wesson No. 3 Second Model American Single Action Revolver (dubbed the "American"), .44 revolver with 8" barrel, first such gun adopted by U.S. military. About 20,700 guns were made from 1872-1874. The interlocking hammer and latch and a bump in the bottom of the frame just above the trigger identify it.......**$23,000**

Rock Island Auction Co.

RIFLES

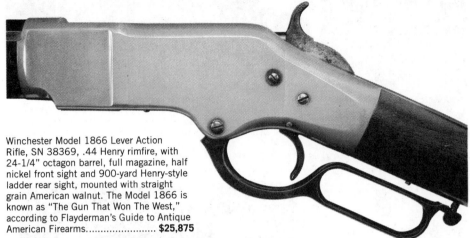

Winchester Model 1866 Lever Action Rifle, SN 38369, .44 Henry rimfire, with 24-1/4" octagon barrel, full magazine, half nickel front sight and 900-yard Henry-style ladder rear sight, mounted with straight grain American walnut. The Model 1866 is known as "The Gun That Won The West," according to Flayderman's Guide to Antique American Firearms........................ **$25,875**

James D. Julia, Inc.

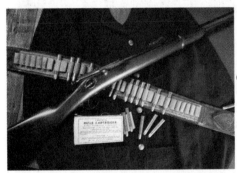

Rare U.S. Department of Indian Affairs Saddle Ring Carbine, SN 16214, .45-70 caliber, Winchester-Hotchkiss Second Model Bolt Action with 24" barrel with standard sights, single barrel band and marked near breech: Co. D. Varnished walnut stock, left side marked: USDIA [U.S. Department of Indian Affairs]. One of 4396 manufactured. **$2,760**

Heritage Auctions

Model 1928A1 Thompson Submachine gun, Savage Arms Corp., used by FBI, law enforcement agencies, and military in late 1920s, throughout World War II, Korea, and into Vietnam. Retains earlier and desirable features such as the short 10-1/2" finned barrel with Auto Ordnance Cutts compensator, detachable butt stock, and adjustable Lyman tangent rear sight with ear protectors........................**$25,875**

Rock Island Auction Co.

Deluxe Winchester 1st Model 1873 Lever Action Rifle, SN16140, special order rifle with 24-1/4" round barrel. Winchester Museum factory records are virtually complete for the rifle, making it a model collectors can specialize in. This rifle was received in the warehouse April 19, 1876..**$57,500**

James D. Julia, Inc.

FIREARMS

Browning Superposed Grade IV-W.410, SN P83RN1064, 26-1/2" barrels with raised, ventilated rib, choked IC and modified. Pheasants and quail engraved on left sideplate; four ducks in marsh on right; flying quail on bottom of action; and dog's head on trigger guard bow. Each sideplate is signed by engraver, "J. Lewanczyk." 6 lbs., 9 oz. **$29,900**

James D. Julia, Inc.

Model 1900 Colt Gatling Gun, SN 1093, 30-40 Krag, with original shipping crate. Usual open barrel configuration with 10 32" round to octagon barrels with brass housing and original iron rails. Top of housing has usual markings "GATLING GUN PATENTED / HARTFORD, CONN. U.S.A." in an elliptical shape surrounding "Manufactured By / Colt's Pt. F. A. Mfg. Co." Below that is marked "Model 1900 / Cal. 30 / No. 1093" and inspector initials "O.C.H." (Capt. Odus C. Horney). Mechanics are fine, strong bright bores. **$103,500**

James D. Julia, Inc.

Winchester Model 20 Junior Trap Shooting Outfit, SN 9945, .410 with 26" barrel with full choke, small bore shotgun offered 1920-1924. Black leatherette case (30"x 8-3/4" x 6") contains a Winchester midget hand trap and steel two-piece cleaning rod; two ounce tube of Winchester gun grease in green box; Winchester gun oil; Winchester rust remover; and a case of 100 midget-sized clay targets...............**$12,075**

James D. Julia, Inc.

Rare first Winchester Model 1894 Saddle Ring Carbine, SN 46, .38-45 caliber carbine with 20" barrel. The Model 1894 Winchester was first manufactured circa 1894 and evolved into the company's most successful selling centerfire rifle. Mounted with slab sawed American walnut with straight stock and carbine buttplate...**$63,250**

James D. Julia, Inc.

All-original transferable Colt Auto Ordnance Thompson 1921/1928 U.S. Navy over-stamp submachine gun originally produced in the 1921 configuration, later overstamped with "U.S. NAVY MODEL OF 1928." This weapon, SN 8689, has traditional and distinctive features found on early 1921/28 models............ **$37,375**

Rock Island Auction Co.

Folk Art

Folk art generally refers to handmade items found anywhere and everywhere people live. The term applies to objects ranging from crude drawings by children to academically trained artists' paintings of common people and scenery, with many varied forms from wood carvings to metal weathervanes. Some experts want to confine folk art to non-academic, handmade objects, but others are willing to include manufactured items.

The accepted timeframe for folk art runs from its earliest origins up to the mid-20th century.

Scrimshaw whale's tooth, circa 1840s, decorated with fashionably dressed lady, red pigment, base chip, 6-1/2" h. **$1,440**

Skinner, Inc., www.skinnerinc.com

Gilt molded copper and cast zinc pig weathervane, America, late 19th century, molded sheet copper flattened full-body figure with cast zinc head and curled tail, head with applied sheet copper ears, mounted on copper rod, weathered gilt surface with verdigris, metal stand, minor imperfections, overall 20-1/2" h., 35-1/2" l. **$36,000**

Skinner, Inc., www.skinnerinc.com

Scrimshaw paint-decorated whale earbone, late 19th/early 20th century, one side painted with profile of mustachioed gent, mounted on diamond-shaped bronze base, 4-3/4" h. **$246**

Skinner, Inc., www.skinnerinc.com

Two small souvenir albums with collections of seaweed, possibly Jamaica, late 19th century, albums each containing six pages with varieties of dried and pressed seaweed with ink-stamped identifications, album covers (according to inscription on last page) are made "from the vertebrae of the whale killed in Montego Bay, and buried in the ground and used as side walk for over 25 years," approximately 5" x 6". ... **$390**

Skinner, Inc., www.skinnerinc.com

Framed Scherenschnitte cut paper picture, "DONE ON BOARD THE MONARCH ON HER VOYAGE FROM JAMAICA JULY 14, 1809," detailed cut paper picture depicting oval reserve with Adam and Eve flanking fruit tree with encircling serpent above indistinct inscription "PARADISE," two angels blowing trumpets, man and woman linked with hearts and floral garland, flanked by allegorical figures of Hope and Charity, surrounded by flowering vines and geometric borders, minor losses, toning, stains, 9-3/4" x 7-3/4".. **$2,280**

Skinner, Inc., www.skinnerinc.com

Scrimshaw whale's tooth with engraved ship, 19th century, depicting a ship-of-the-line flying American flag flanked by floral borders, red, green, and blue, with initials "LS" near the base, 3-3/8" w. x 6-1/2" l.. **$4,500**

Skinner, Inc., www.skinnerinc.com

Jeanne Davies (American, b. 1936), oil on canvas portrait of boy, signed lower right, 24" x 20". **$533**

Pook & Pook, Inc.

Small scrimshaw ivory and bone yarn swift, 19th century, bird finial on slender shaft with expanding bone slats with carved open mouth, dog-head clamp, closed fist on threaded screw, billing birds on one end of head, loose slat segments, repair on lower shaft, 12-3/4" h. **$2,520**

Skinner, Inc., www.skinnerinc.com

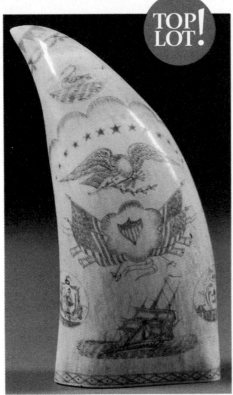

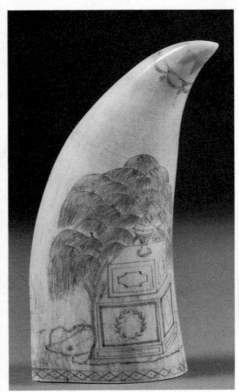

Scrimshaw whale's tooth, 19th century, obverse decorated with swan in circular reserve over patriotic motifs of 13 stars above spreadwing eagle and American shield in cloud-like reserve flanked by furled flags and panoply, red and blue pigments over ship-of-the-line at sea, flanked by two small round reserves depicting Seal of Massachusetts, anchor floating above sea with distant vessel, reverse depicting urn-topped monument beside weeping willow, sawtooth and swag and tassel borders at top and geometric border around base, 5-1/8" h..**$16,800**

Skinner, Inc., www.skinnerinc.com

Sailor's woolwork "wooly" ship picture, England or America, 19th century, executed with wool yarns and silk and metallic threads depicting a ship-of-the-line flying British naval white ensign off stern, distant lighthouse, border with flowers and trees in foreground, period mitered wood frame, toning, losses, 14" x 19". **$677**

Skinner, Inc., www.skinnerinc.com

John Scholl (Pennsylvania, 1827-1916), carved and painted geometric snowflake, 31" dia. **$17,775**

Pook & Pook, Inc.

FOLK ART

Relief-carved and painted walking stick, America, late 19th century, elaborate polychrome-painted, high relief-carved shaft depicting bird's talons, acorns, roses, grapes, lady's arm with bracelet, turtle, and serpent, imperfections, 33-1/4" l. **$4,613**

Skinner, Inc., www.skinnerinc.com

Southeastern Pennsylvania watercolor fraktur of rooster, signed verso, Samuel Flickinger, 1821, 4" x 4-3/4".......... **$1,422**

Pook & Pook, Inc.

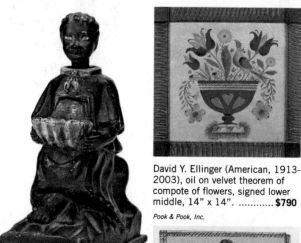

David Y. Ellinger (American, 1913-2003), oil on velvet theorem of compote of flowers, signed lower middle, 14" x 14". **$790**

Pook & Pook, Inc.

Folk art African-American nodding bank, robed figure with composite shell-shaped coin on wood base, old paint, late 19th/early 20th century, 13-3/4" x 8" x 5". . **$500**

Rago Arts and Auction Center

Southeastern Pennsylvania ink and watercolor fraktur bookplate, circa 1810, stylized flowers, 5" x 3-1/2". **$296**

Pook & Pook, Inc.

Continental carved and painted ship's figurehead, 19th century, 56-3/4" h. **$2,370**

Pook & Pook, Inc.

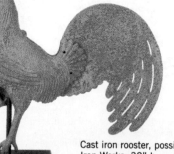

Cast iron rooster, possibly Rochester Iron Works, 32" h. **$1,896**

Pook & Pook, Inc.

Rupert P. Kreider (American, 1897-1983), carved pine plaque of houses in the woods, signed lower right, 9-3/4" x 31"..**$2,015**

Pook & Pook, Inc.

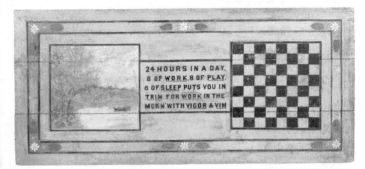

Unusual painted folk art games table, late 19th century, with folding legs, top decorated with landscape and checkerboard, 29" h. x 64" w. x 29-1/2" d. ..**$2,015**

Pook & Pook, Inc.

Scrimshaw engraved whalebone busk, 19th century, engraved with column of designs including five-point star, urn of flowers and vines, heart, plinth with central diamond flanked with leafy vines, and flowering plant, sawtooth border, 13-1/4" x 1-7/8". **$1,920**

Bucks County, Pennsylvania ink and watercolor fraktur bookplate, circa 1810, central robed figure surrounded by potted tulip, flowers, etc., 5-1/2" x 3-1/2" **$3,081**

Pook & Pook, Inc.

Painted tramp art model of a church, circa 1900, fitted with miniature pews and reliquaries, 43-1/2" h. **$119**

Pook & Pook, Inc.

English oil on canvas portrait of gentleman in military dress, circa 1800, 30" x 25"............ **$2,607**

Pook & Pook, Inc.

Wooden folk art magazine rack with applied motifs depicting rifle, canoe and paddle, ax, saw, fish, and ladder, American, circa 1920s-1930s, 18-1/2" h. x 24" w. x 8" d............................**$132**

Cowan's Auctions, Inc.

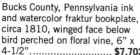

Bucks County, Pennsylvania ink and watercolor fraktur bookplate, circa 1810, winged face below bird perched on floral vine, 6" x 4-1/2"............................ **$7,703**

Pook & Pook, Inc.

Two carved and painted birds, 19th century, bark and fungus mounts, 8" h. **$356**

Pook & Pook, Inc.

Large carved and gilded pilot house eagle, mid-19th century, 42" h. x 66" w. **$9,113**

Pook & Pook, Inc.

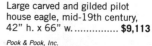

Wilhelm Schimmel (Cumberland Valley, Pennsylvania, 1817-1890), carved and painted spaniel, original red/brown surface, 2-1/2" h. x 4-1/4" w........**$13,035**

Pook & Pook, Inc.

Carved and painted beaver trade sign with plaque inscribed "Furs," 31" h. x 40" w. **$3,318**

Pook & Pook, Inc.

Jeanne Davies (American, b.1936), oil on canvas winter town scene, signed lower right, 20" x 24".
.... **$608**

Pook & Pook, Inc.

Carved and painted lion, inscribed "Karl Stoltz York PA, 1892," 10-1/4" h. x 10-3/4" l................ **$1,659**

Pook & Pook, Inc.

Jeanne Davies (American, b. 1936), oil on canvas street scene, signed lower left, 20" x 24". **$273**

Pook & Pook, Inc.

English watercolor coaching scene, signed "W. Ward Leviport 1804," 11" x 16"............................. **$182**

Pook & Pook, Inc.

Jeanne Davies (American, b. 1936), oil on canvas landscape with flower shop, signed lower right, 20" x 24".. **$425**

Pook & Pook, Inc.

Pair of tin folk art fishing signs, largest 9-1/2" h. x 19-3/4" w... **$125**

Kaminski Auctions

Furniture

Furniture collecting has been a major part of the world of collecting for more than 100 years. It is interesting to note how this marketplace has evolved.

In past decades, 18th century and early 19th century furniture was the mainstay of the American furniture market, but in recent years there has been a growing demand for furniture manufactured since the 1920s. Factory-made furniture from the 1920s and 1930s, often featuring Colonial Revival style, has seen a growing appreciation among collectors. It is well made and features solid wood and fine veneers rather than the cheap compressed wood materials often used since the 1960s. Also much in demand in recent years is furniture in the Modernistic and Mid-Century taste, ranging from Art Deco through quality designer furniture of the 1950s through the 1970s (see "Modern Furniture" later in this section).

These latest trends have offered even the less well-heeled buyer the opportunity to purchase fine furniture at often reasonable prices. Buying antique and collectible furniture is no longer the domain of millionaires and museums.

Today more furniture is showing up on Internet sites, and sometimes good buys can be made. However, it is important to deal with honest, well-informed sellers and have a good knowledge of what you want to purchase.

As in the past, it makes sense to purchase the best pieces you can find, whatever the style or era of production. Condition is still very important if you want your example to continue to appreciate in value in the coming years. For 18th century and early 19th century pieces, the original finish and hardware are especially important as it is with good furniture of the early 20th century Arts & Crafts era. These features are

Mid-Atlantic Hepplewhite mahogany Pembroke table, circa 1800, with single drawer and line inlaid square tapering legs, 28-1/2" h. x 20-1/4" w. x 30-1/2" d. **$2,370**

Pook & Pook, Inc.

not quite as important for most manufactured furniture of the Victorian era and furniture from the 1920s and later. However, it is good to be aware that a good finish and original hardware will mean a stronger market when the pieces are resold. Of course, whatever style of furniture you buy, you are better off with examples that have not had major repairs or replacements. On really early furniture, repairs and replacements will definitely have an impact on the sale value, but they will also be a factor on newer designs from the 20th century.

As with all types of antiques and collectibles, there is often a regional preference for certain furniture types. Although the American market is much more homogenous than it was in past decades, there still tends to be a preference for 18th century and early 19th century furniture along the Eastern Seaboard, whereas Victorian designs tend to have a larger market in the Midwest and South. In the West, country furniture and "western" designs definitely have the edge except in major cities along the West Coast.

Whatever your favorite furniture style, there are still fine examples to be found. Just study the history of your favorites and the important points of their construction before you invest heavily. A wise shopper will be a happy shopper and have a collection certain to continue to appreciate as time marches along.

For more information on furniture, see *Antique Trader Furniture Price Guide* by Kyle Husfloen.

ANTIQUE

Red-painted pine and cherry kitchen table, probably Pennsylvania, late 18th century, removable top above two thumb-molded drawers on block-turned legs joined by side and medial stretchers, old wooden pulls, original surface, minor imperfections, 28-1/2" h. x top 59-1/2" w. x 31-1/4" d. **$3,120**

Skinner, Inc., www.skinnerinc.com

Small cherry drop-leaf table, probably Connecticut, late 18th century, rectangular drop-leaf top over straight apron joining square legs with inside chamfering, square cross-stretchers, original surface, 28" h. x top 31" w. x 35-1/4" d. **$5,700**

Skinner, Inc., www.skinnerinc.com

Queen Anne figured maple drop-leaf dining table, probably Massachusetts, circa 1740-1760, circular top with rolled shaped apron, refinished, minor restoration, 28" h. x 41-1/2" dia. **$840**

Skinner, Inc., www.skinnerinc.com

John Linsly Queen Anne cherry and beech slant-lid desk, North Branford, Connecticut, area, circa 1730-1750, interior with valanced compartments with drawers and covered well, engraved brasses appear to be original, old surface, repairs, 42-1/4" h. x 36" w. x 18-1/2" d. Note: Accompanied by the last will and testament of John Linsly, dated 1775. The will refers to a writing desk, which may be this one. **$4,500**

Skinner, Inc., www.skinnerinc.com

Federal inlaid mahogany sideboard, probably Baltimore, Maryland, circa 1795-1800, central drawer above arch and flanking square tapering legs inlaid with stringing and flowers, hinged doors centering circular patera bordered by stringing and geometric banding, replaced brass pulls, refinished, restoration, 37-3/4" h. x 62-1/2" w. x 23" d. . **$4,800**

Skinner, Inc., www.skinnerinc.com

Paint-decorated pine six-board chest, probably New England, early 19th century, freehand-painted with central tree design, 23-3/4" h. x 55-3/4" w. x 24-3/4" d. **$1,320**

Skinner, Inc., www.skinnerinc.com

Cherry and hickory high chair, Pennsylvania, last half 18th century, old refinish, minor imperfections, 38-1/2" h. x seat 20-1/2" h. **$1,800**

Skinner, Inc., www.skinnerinc.com

Windsor comb-back armchair, in Philadelphia style, serpentine cresting and scroll-carved terminals above shaped arms with knuckle handholds, vase- and ring-turned supports on carved saddle seat and conformingly turned splayed legs ending in swelled feet, painted white, 46-1/2" h. x seat 18-1/2" h. **$960**

Skinner, Inc., www.skinnerinc.com

Green-painted Windsor braced bow-back chair, probably New York City, circa 1780-1800, with scratch-beaded bow, carved saddle seat, and bulbous turnings, old green paint, minor repair, 36-3/4" h. x seat 17" h. **$660**

Skinner, Inc., www.skinnerinc.com

Miniature painted three-slat ladder-back side chair, late 18th century, old red over blue surface, 19-1/2" h. **$563**

Pook & Pook, Inc.

Maple and ash fan-back Windsor side chair, probably James Mansfield, Gloucester, Massachusetts, circa 1790, marked on underside of seat "J. MANSFIELD," refinished, minor imperfections, 36-1/2" h. x seat 17-1/2" h. **$960**

Skinner, Inc., www.skinnerinc.com

Apple green-painted freehand and stencil-decorated arrow-back side chair, probably Pennsylvania, early 19th century, crest painted with flowers and leaves, original surface, paint wear, 33" h. x seat 18" h. **$240**

Skinner, Inc., www.skinnerinc.com

Chippendale carved figured maple tall chest of drawers, southeastern New England, late 18th century, case with six thumb-molded graduated drawers, topmost with three-drawer facade centering a carved fan, replaced brasses, refinished, 51-1/2" h. x 36" w. x 18" d.. **$1,680**

Skinner, Inc., www.skinnerinc.com

Chippendale tiger maple slant-lid desk, New England, late 18th century, interior of eight valanced compartments and nine drawers above case of four thumb-molded graduated drawers on bracket feet, replaced brasses, refinished, repairs, 42" h. x 36" w. x 18" d.. **$3,000**

Skinner, Inc., www.skinnerinc.com

Chippendale carved cherry chest of drawers, Connecticut, late 18th century, rectangular top with molded edge above cockbeaded case of four graduated drawers on gadrooned carved ogee bracket base, replaced brasses, refinished, imperfections, 37-1/2" h. x 36-1/2" w. x 17" d. **$1,320**

Skinner, Inc., www.skinnerinc.com

Federal string-inlaid mahogany butler's desk, Middle Atlantic states, circa 1810-1815, case of four drawers, topmost with two-drawer facade and fold-down writing surface, opening to central prospect door flanked by drawers and valanced compartments, replaced brasses, refinished, imperfections, 41-1/4" h. x 40" w. x 19-1/4" d................................... **$461**

Skinner, Inc., www.skinnerinc.com

FURNITURE

Turned ash slat-back armchair, New England, early 18th century, old black paint, seat re-rushed, some height loss, 43" h. x seat 15-1/2" h. **$840**

Skinner, Inc., www.skinnerinc.com

Windsor armchair, New England, late 18th century, serpentine cresting with shaped saddle seat and vase- and ring-turnings, old refinish, imperfections, 40" h. x seat 16-1/2" h. **$1,169**

Skinner, Inc., www.skinnerinc.com

Chippendale mahogany carved side chair, Boston, late 18th century, cresting with foliate carving above pierced diamond splat, 37" h. x seat 17" h....................... **$5,400**

Skinner, Inc., www.skinnerinc.com

Queen Anne cherry roundabout chair, New England, mid-18th century, old surface, minor imperfections, 30-1/2" h. x seat 17-1/2" h. **$1,080**

Skinner, Inc., www.skinnerinc.com

Chippendale cherry and maple carved scroll-top chest-on-chest, possibly Connecticut River Valley, late 18th century, crest with pinwheel-carved terminals and flame finials, top section with central pinwheel-carved drawer and flanking fluted pilasters, original brasses, old refinish, minor imperfections, 87" h. x lower case 38-3/4" w. x 20-1/2" d.................................... **$7,200**

Skinner, Inc., www.skinnerinc.com

Pennsylvania painted oak child's hutch, late 19th century, original blue surface, 49-1/2" h. x 23-1/4" w. **$652**

Pook & Pook, Inc.

Walnut rococo revival table, possibly John Henry Belter, New York, circa 1860, old surface, imperfections, 30" h. x 42" w. x 29-1/2" d. **$1,320**

Skinner, Inc., www.skinnerinc.com

Classical mahogany and mahogany veneer secretaire à abattant, probably Boston, circa 1820-1825, rectangular top with hidden drawer above a spring-loaded drop-front revealing compartments and five drawers, cupboard section below opening to a shelf, all flanked by freestanding columns continuing to turned feet, minor imperfections, 58-1/4" h. x top 39-1/2" w. x 20-1/2" d. **$2,040**

Skinner, Inc., www.skinnerinc.com

Diminutive Federal mahogany and tiger maple inlaid sideboard, probably Massachusetts, circa 1800-1810, central hinged door centering inlaid carnations flanked by two short drawers and one drawer with two-drawer facade, all with borders of stringing, crossbanding, and cockbeading, conformingly inlaid square double-tapering legs, old brass pulls, refinished, minor imperfections, 39-1/2" h. x 47-3/4" w. x 22" d. **$7,200**

Skinner, Inc., www.skinnerinc.com

Federal mahogany and bird's-eye maple inlaid tambour desk, New England, circa 1800, tambour doors open to interior of four drawers, flanking valanced compartments, old brass pulls, refinished, minor imperfections, 45-1/4" h. x 39" w. x 19" d.... **$1,560**

Skinner, Inc., www.skinnerinc.com

Red-painted single-tier cupboard, possibly New England, early 19th century, two hinged doors opening to shelved interior, valanced cutout base, old red paint, imperfections, 43-1/4" h. x case 54" w. x 18-1/2" d. **$4,500**

Skinner, Inc., www.skinnerinc.com

Pennsylvania painted pine dower chest, circa 1800, decorated by David Y. Ellinger (American 1913-2003), signed on lid, 33" h. x 47" w. **$4,029**

Pook & Pook, Inc.

FURNITURE

Classical mahogany and mahogany veneer desk bookcase, probably Massachusetts, circa 1830, top section with deep cove-molded cornice above arched frieze, two hinged doors with fluted paneling and flanking applied scrolls, three exterior drawers below, on projecting base of fold-out writing surface, drawer with ogee facade above two drawers, with flanking scrolled brackets continuing to legs, old wooden pulls, refinished, imperfections, 75" h. x 41-1/2" w. x 20" d............................ **$923**

Skinner, Inc., www.skinnerinc.com

Spanish-brown-painted maple tea table, probably New England, early 18th century, oval top on bulbous vase- and ring-turned splayed legs continuing to turned feet, joined by a straight apron and square stretchers, old surface, restored, 22-1/2" h. x top 28" w. x 21" d...... **$3,360**

Skinner, Inc., www.skinnerinc.com

Queen Anne cherry oval-top tea table, New England, mid-18th century, block-turned tapering legs, pad feet, old refinish, minor imperfections, 26-1/2" h. x 25" w. x 35" d........................... **$1,560**

Skinner, Inc., www.skinnerinc.com

Federal carved mahogany and mahogany veneer card table, coastal Massachusetts, circa 1795, skirt with central inlaid oval in mitered frame on waterleaf-carved, ring-turned, reeded legs, old surface, minor imperfections, 29-3/4" h. x 36" w. x 17-3/4" d. **$2,040**

Skinner, Inc., www.skinnerinc.com

White-painted and freehand seashell and leaf-decorated dressing table, New England, circa 1830, scrolled backboard above two short drawers with projecting top and long drawer below, vase- and ring-turned legs, replaced brass pulls, old surface, minor imperfections, 38-1/2" h. (not including backboard) x 35" w. x 18-1/2" d. **$960**

Skinner, Inc., www.skinnerinc.com

Federal mahogany and bird's-eye maple veneer work table, New England, early 19th century, octagonal top on conforming base with diagonally placed, square, tapering legs with compartmented drawer and bag drawer below, refinished, 28-1/4" h. x 20-1/2" w. x 15-1/4" d.................... **$960**

Skinner, Inc., www.skinnerinc.com

Red-painted pine doctor's wall cabinet, probably New England, early 19th century, hinged top opens to interior fitted for medicine bottles, projecting hinged lid above four compartments, curved brackets below, original surface, 32" h. x 24-1/2" w. x 10" d. **$1,107**

Skinner, Inc., www.skinnerinc.com

Green-painted pine chest over drawer ("mule" chest), New England, circa 1800, with thumb-molded drawer and arched bracket base, old green paint, replaced brasses, minor paint wear, 33-1/2" h. x 42" w. x 20" d. **$600**

Skinner, Inc., www.skinnerinc.com

▲ New Jersey Queen Anne cherry and gumwood slant front desk, circa 1760, 41-1/2" h. x 36" w....... **$948**

Pook & Pook, Inc.

Paint-decorated pine blanket chest, Pennsylvania, circa 1800, original surface, imperfections, 24" h. x case 49-1/2" w. x 22" d.................................. **$360**

Skinner, Inc., www.skinnerinc.com

Chippendale inlaid cherry chest of four drawers, Connecticut River Valley, top with string-inlaid edge on four cockbeaded graduated drawers, flanked by quarter columns, all on ogee bracket feet, replaced brasses, refinished, imperfections, 35-1/2" h. x case 41-1/2" w. x 19-1/2" d. **$2,214**

Skinner, Inc., www.skinnerinc.com

Federal cherry and mahogany veneer inlaid bowfront chest of drawers, southeastern New England, circa 1810, four cockbeaded drawers on cutout base inlaid with tiger maple banding, brasses appear original, refinished, 37" h. x 39-1/2" w. x 22-1/4" d. **$780**

Skinner, Inc., www.skinnerinc.com

Olive green-painted pine chest over drawer (mule chest), New England, late 18th century, molded hinged top above thumb-molded drawer, cutout ends, old surface of green paint over earlier blue, lacks hardware, imperfections, 37" h. x 42" w. x 18" d. **$570**

Skinner, Inc., www.skinnerinc.com

Painted cherry and tin pie safe, possibly Pennsylvania or Ohio, mid-19th century, old surface of worn green paint over red stain, interior opens to four shelves with drawer below, 55" h. x 39" w. x 17" d. **$1,320**

Skinner, Inc., www.skinnerinc.com

Classical mahogany carved tilt-top candlestand, New York, circa 1820, shaped top with elliptical sides, vase- and ring-turned post and four acanthus-carved and reeded tapering legs ending in brass cap casters, refinished, 26-3/4" h. x 17-1/2" w. x 24" d. **$1,200**

Skinner, Inc., www.skinnerinc.com

Federal carved and inlaid mahogany shield-back side chair, probably Baltimore, circa 1790-1800, center splat inlaid with bellflowers, old surface, imperfections, 37-1/2" h. x seat 17" h. **$615**

Skinner, Inc., www.skinnerinc.com

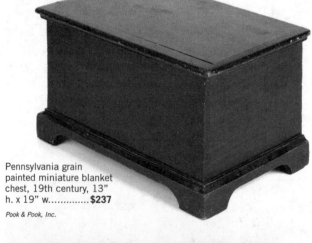

Pennsylvania grain painted miniature blanket chest, 19th century, 13" h. x 19" w. **$237**

Pook & Pook, Inc.

Pennsylvania Queen Anne walnut candlestand, circa 1765, dish top and suppressed ball standard, old dark surface, 27-1/2" h. x 16-1/2" w. **$3,555**

Pook & Pook, Inc.

Berks County, Pennsylvania Sheraton pine and poplar harvest table with backsplash, single leaf, and two drawers, 32" h. x 65-3/4" w. x 19-1/4" d. **$948**

Pook & Pook, Inc.

Pennsylvania Chippendale walnut table top desk, circa 1790, line inlaid slant front and drawer supported by bracket feet, old dry surface, 17" h. x 15-1/4" w. **$3,081**

Pook & Pook, Inc.

Pennsylvania walnut two-part Dutch cupboard, circa 1810, 85" h. x 59-1/2" w. **$5,688**

Pook & Pook, Inc.

Chippendale mahogany drop-leaf dining table, circa 1770, with carved knees and cabriole legs terminating in ball and claw feet, 29" h. x 16" w. x 45" d. **$2,370**

Pook & Pook, Inc.

Paint-decorated pine chest of drawers, New England, early 19th century, scrolled backboard above a case of four drawers on cutout feet, old surface of salmon and cream paint, replaced wooden pulls, imperfections, 38-1/4" h. x 40-1/2" w. x 19" d. **$360**

Skinner, Inc., www.skinnerinc.com

Pennsylvania Chippendale walnut tall chest in two parts, circa 1770, carved fishtail skirt and ball and claw feet, 72-1/2" h. x 40-1/2" w. **$5,451**

Pook & Pook, Inc.

FURNITURE

Lancaster County, Pennsylvania cherry architectural schrank, circa 1760, bold cornice overhanging case with tombstone panel doors flanked by fluted pilasters, resting on a base with five drawers, 89" h. x 78" w. **$65,175**

Pook & Pook, Inc.

Pennsylvania or New York Federal mahogany breakfast table, circa 1815, single drawer, carved base, and brass animal paw casters, 28-1/4" h. x 24-1/4" w. x 42" d...**$356**

Pook & Pook, Inc.

Mid-Atlantic Chippendale walnut slant front desk, late 18th century, 42-1/4" h. x 44" w..................**$1,304**

Pook & Pook, Inc.

Pennsylvania Chippendale walnut chest of drawers, circa 1770, 33-1/2" h. x 37-1/2" w. **$4,503**

Pook & Pook, Inc.

Lebanon County, Pennsylvania painted dower chest, circa 1800, original ochre sponge decoration with diamond border, 24" h. x 50" w....................**$3,555**

Pook & Pook, Inc.

Massive New England stained pine and maple harvest table, circa 1820, 28-1/2" h. x 142-1/2" l. x 44" d.**$4,503**

Pook & Pook, Inc.

Child's Federal cherry slant front desk, circa 1810, overall line inlay, 20" h. x 24" w....................$504

Pook & Pook, Inc.

New England Federal mahogany sideboard, circa 1800, with butler's desk interior and diamond and line inlaid legs, 40-1/2" h. x 61-1/2" w. x 24-1/4" d. $1,067

Pook & Pook, Inc.

Sheraton tiger maple bed, circa 1830, with palmette carved headboard, 60" h. x 57" w. x 83" d. $790

Pook & Pook, Inc.

Regency sofa table, exotic wood inlaid top with three drawers on bronze mounted feet, 19th century, 29" x 36-1/2" x 24"..$3,250

Rago Arts and Auction Center

New Hampshire Federal birch bowfront chest of drawers, circa 1805, line inlaid drawers and flame birch panel, 37-1/2" h. x 40" w.................$770

Pook & Pook, Inc.

Georgian server, mahogany, bowfront, line inlay on turned legs, early 19th century, 36" x 42" x 19"..........$1,125

Rago Arts and Auction Center

Pennsylvania Federal cherry two-part Dutch cupboard, circa 1820, 86" h. x 50" w................ **$3,792**

Pook & Pook, Inc.

Pennsylvania cherry and mahogany two-part corner cupboard, circa 1820, 86-1/2" h. x 47" w...**$2,252**

Pook & Pook, Inc.

Pennsylvania painted pine one-piece corner cupboard, circa 1810, scrubbed yellow surface, 90" h. x 56" w................ **$2,133**

Pook & Pook, Inc.

New England Queen Anne cherry high chest, circa 1760, probably Rhode Island, 65" h. x 35-1/2" w........................ **$3,792**

Pook & Pook, Inc.

Berks County, Pennsylvania hard pine one-piece architectural corner cupboard, circa 1770, stepped and blocked cornice with wall of troy molding above a scrolled keystone and two arched raised panel doors above similar lower doors flanked by fluted pilasters, original wrought iron H hinges and yellow interior, 94" h. x 58" w. **$3,318**

Pook & Pook, Inc.

Pennsylvania tiger maple blanket (mule) chest, late 19th century, 19" h. x 26-1/4" w............. **$770**

Pook & Pook, Inc.

English Eastlake Victorian hall rack, walnut, oval beveled mirror, brass hat and coat hooks, umbrella holder and marble shelf and drawer, circa 1880, 80" x 29-1/2" x 8". **$531**

Rago Arts and Auction Center

Stickley Brothers rare oval lamp table, Grand Rapids, Michigan, circa 1905, metal tag, partial paper label, 29-3/4" x 36" x 28". **$2,375**

Rago Arts and Auction Center

Gustav Stickley nine-drawer dresser, Eastwood, New York, circa 1908, black decal, 50" x 36" x 20". **$6,250**

Rago Arts and Auction Center

Windsor ash, pine, and maple sack-back chair, New England, late 18th century, old refinish, 40" h. x seat 17-1/2" h. **$1,800**

Skinner, Inc., www.skinnerinc.com

Gustav Stickley rare, early Thornden side chair, Eastwood, New York, circa 1901, red decal in box, 35" x 17-3/4" x 16". **$1,000**

Rago Arts and Auction Center

Renaissance Revival ebonized center table, circa 1855, original floral pietra dura marble top with Greek key edge tilting above a base with animal paw feet, 30-1/2" h. x 31" w. **$5,451**

Pook & Pook, Inc.

New York classical mahogany dressing table, circa 1820, 56" h. x 31-3/4" w. **$770**

Pook & Pook, Inc.

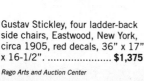

Gustav Stickley, four ladder-back side chairs, Eastwood, New York, circa 1905, red decals, 36" x 17" x 16-1/2". **$1,375**

Rago Arts and Auction Center

Pennsylvania Federal cherry two-part corner cupboard, early 19th century, 88" h. x 41-1/2" w............ **$1,185**

Pook & Pook, Inc.

Federal tiger maple Pembroke table, early 19th century, 27" h. x 19-1/2" w. x 31-1/2" d.... **$2,252**

Pook & Pook, Inc.

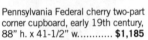

New England Federal birch and tiger maple end table, early 19th century, 29-1/2" h. x 19-1/4" w....................... **$1,541**

Pook & Pook, Inc.

TOP LOT!

Victorian Rococo revival rosewood étagère, circa 1865, 111-1/2" h. x 71" w. **$22,515**

Pook & Pook, Inc.

Renaissance Revival carved walnut stand, circa 1870, marble top and center shelf, carved dog and dog house, 34" h. x 12" w. **$2,133**

Pook & Pook, Inc.

New England Federal mahogany candlestand, early 19th century, 29-1/2" h. x 17-3/4" w. x 24" d. **$243**

Pook & Pook, Inc.

Pennsylvania architectural walnut two-part corner cupboard, circa 1780, with arched raised panel doors and interior with scalloped shelves, 93-1/2" h. x 49" w. **$2,607**

Pook & Pook, Inc.

Gustav Stickley large sideboard with plate rack, Eastwood, New York, circa 1905-1912, 48" x 66" x 24". **$2,875**

Rago Arts and Auction Center

Gustav Stickley rare diminutive crib settle, Eastwood, New York, circa 1909-1912, paper label, 41-1/2" x 72" x 25-1/4". **$2,750**

Rago Arts and Auction Center

Roycroft meditation chair, East Aurora, New York, circa 1905, carved orb and cross mark, 34-1/4" x 24" x 21-1/2". **$1,375**

Rago Arts and Auction Center

Shop of the Crafters unusual china cabinet, Cincinnati, Ohio, circa 1915, partial paper label, 64" x 43" x 15-1/2". **$875**

Rago Arts and Auction Center

Gustav Stickley Morris chair (no. 332), Eastwood, New York, circa 1912, burned-in mark, as shown 41" x 31" x 38-1/2". **$4,063**

Rago Arts and Auction Center

Gustav Stickley mahogany open-arm Morris chair, Eastwood, New York, circa 1904, unsigned, 41-1/2" x 30" x 32-1/2". **$938**

Rago Arts and Auction Center

Gustav Stickley single-door china cabinet (no. 820), Eastwood, New York, circa 1912, branded mark, 63" x 36" x 15".............. **$4,063**

Rago Arts and Auction Center

L. & J.G. Stickley double-door bookcase (no. 645), Fayetteville, New York, 1912-1916, unmarked, 55-1/4" x 52" x 12"........ **$4,063**

Rago Arts and Auction Center

Limbert cricket footstool, Grand Rapids, Michigan, circa 1905, oak, leather, brass, branded, 18" x 20" x 15". **$375**

Rago Arts and Auction Center

Roycroft rare oversized tall back slatted chair, East Aurora, New York, circa 1905, carved orb and cross mark, 47" x 29-1/2" x 26"..................... **$2,250**

Rago Arts and Auction Center

Aesthetic Movement ebonized corner cabinet, United States, 1870s, ebonized wood, glass, unmarked, 69-1/4" x 25-1/2" x 17", each side 18"............. **$625**

Rago Arts and Auction Center

L. & J.G. Stickley magazine stand, Fayetteville, New York, circa 1910, unsigned, 45" x 21" x 12". **$2,500**

Rago Arts and Auction Center

Stickley Brothers diminutive magazine stand, Grand Rapids, Michigan, circa 1905, unmarked, 31-1/4" x 16" x 12"........ **$1,188**

Rago Arts and Auction Center

Kimbel & Cabus drop-front desk, New York, 1870s, carved oak, brass, enamel, felt, unmarked, 54" x 36" x 20-1/2". Note: A similar example is in the Metropolitan Museum of Art, New York. **$1,500**

Rago Arts and Auction Center

Gustav Stickley book stand with V-trough, Eastwood, 1904-1907, unmarked, 30-1/4" x 32-1/2" x 10"..... **$1,000**

Rago Arts and Auction Center

Aesthetic Movement ebonized single-door bookcase, United States, 1870s, ebonized wood, glass, unmarked, 55" x 30" x 14"............... **$688**

Rago Arts and Auction Center

Aesthetic Movement sideboard with etched and painted decoration of fruiting branches, England, 1880s, unmarked, 49-1/2" x 60-1/2" x 22"................ **$2,625**

Rago Arts and Auction Center

American Hepplewhite chest of drawers, curly maple with four drawers on French feet, early 19th century, 35-1/2" x 39" x 21".................................... **$1,125**

Rago Arts and Auction Center

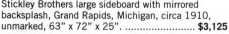

Stickley Brothers large sideboard with mirrored backsplash, Grand Rapids, Michigan, circa 1910, unmarked, 63" x 72" x 25". **$3,125**

Rago Arts and Auction Center

American Sheraton chest of drawers, cherry with bird's-eye maple drawer fronts, turned legs, 19th century, 38-1/2" x 42" x 20". **$813**

Rago Arts and Auction Center

English Regency chest, mahogany, two over three drawers on turned bun feet, early 19th century, 38" x 36-1/2" x 20"..................... **$625**

Rago Arts and Auction Center

William and Mary chest on chest, two-piece in burl walnut with stretcher base, 18th century, 62" x 40" x 20". **$1,063**

Rago Arts and Auction Center

American country schrank, pine, paneled doors over five drawers, circa 1800, 79-1/2" x 61-1/2" x 20"................................. **$2,750**

Rago Arts and Auction Center

Roycroft magazine stand, East Aurora, New York, circa 1905, some height loss, large orb and cross mark, 61-3/4" x 22" x 17-1/2"........................... **$3,125**

Rago Arts and Auction Center

English Arts & Crafts paneled hall bench carved with motto, "Cast Care and Labor Far Behind And Rest You Here A Spell," England, circa 1900, stamped 903, 66-1/2" x 52" x 24"........ **$4,688**

Rago Arts and Auction Center

Federal secretary desk, two-piece in mahogany with fitted interior, mullioned glass doors over four drawers, French feet, 19th century, 62" x 37-3/4" x 21". **$531**

Rago Arts and Auction Center

▶ American Sheraton sofa, mahogany frame, fluted legs and striped silk upholstery, early 19th century, 36-1/2" x 79" x 27"..............**$625**

Rago Arts and Auction Center

American Empire Revival sofa, mahogany frame carved with cornucopias, leather upholstery, 19th century, 35" x 79" x 29". **$1,125**

Rago Arts and Auction Center

Pair of Georgian side chairs, mahogany frames with flame-stitched upholstered seats, circa 1800, 38" x 19" x 18"..**$438**

Rago Arts and Auction Center

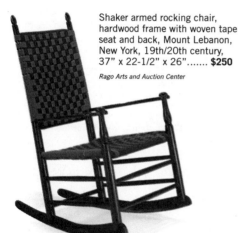

Shaker armed rocking chair, hardwood frame with woven tape seat and back, Mount Lebanon, New York, 19th/20th century, 37" x 22-1/2" x 26"....... **$250**

Rago Arts and Auction Center

Biedermeier settee, fruitwood inlaid frame, upholstered seat and back, mid-19th century, 38" x 55" x 25"... **$625**

Rago Arts and Auction Center

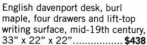

English davenport desk, burl maple, four drawers and lift-top writing surface, mid-19th century, 33" x 22" x 22".................. **$438**

Rago Arts and Auction Center

Pair of Art Nouveau side chairs, carved leaf design, black lacquer finish, circa 1900, 36" x 17" x 18". **$813**

Rago Arts and Auction Center

MODERN

Modern design is everywhere, evergreen and increasingly popular. Modernism has never gone out of style. Its reach into the present day is as deep as its roots in the past. Just as it can be seen and felt ubiquitously in the mass media of today – on film, television, in magazines and department stores – it can be traced to the mid-1800s post-Empire non-conformity of the Biedermeier Movement, the turn of the 20th century anti-Victorianism of the Vienna Secessionists, the radical reductionism of Frank Lloyd Wright and the revolutionary post-Depression thinking of Walter Gropius and the Bauhaus school in Germany.

"The Modernists really changed the way the world looked," said John Sollo, a partner in Sollo Rago Auction of Lambertville, New Jersey. Sollo's partner in business, and one of the most recognizable names in the field, David Rago, takes Sollo's idea a little further by saying that Modernism is actually more about the names behind the design than the design itself, at least as far as buying goes.

No discussion of Modern can be complete, however, without examining its genesis and enduring influence. Modernism is everywhere in today's pop culture. Austere Scandinavian furniture dominates the television commercials that hawk hotels and mutual funds. Post-war American design ranges across sitcom set dressings to movie sets patterned after Frank Lloyd Wright houses and Hollywood Modernist classics set high in the hills.

You have to look at the dorm rooms of college students and the apartments of young people whose living spaces are packed with the undeniably Modern mass-produced products of IKEA, Target, Design Within Reach and the like.

There can be no denying that the post-World War II manufacturing techniques and subsequent boom led to the widespread acceptance of plastic and bent plywood chairs along with low-sitting coffee tables, couches and recliners.

"The modern aesthetic grew out of a perfect storm of post-war optimism, innovative materials and an incredible crop of designers," said Lisanne Dickson, director of 1950s/Modern Design at Treadway-Toomey.

"I think that the people who designed the furniture were maybe ahead of society's ability to accept and understand what they were doing," Sollo said. "It's taken people another 30 to 40 years to catch up to it."

There are hundreds of great Modern designers, many of whom worked across categories – furniture, architecture, fine art, etc. – and many contributed to the work of other big names without ever seeking that glory for themselves.

For more information on Modernism, see *Warman's Modernism Furniture & Accessories Identification and Price Guide* by Noah Fleisher.

— *Noah Fleisher*

Pair of lounge chairs, United States, 1960s, stained and lacquered mahogany, leather, unmarked, designed by Maurice Bailey, manufactured By Monteverdi Young, 33" x 28" x 31".....................**$4,063**

Rago Arts and Auction Center

TOP LOT!

Cherry sideboard, Paoli, Pennsylvania, 1960, designed by Wharton Esherick (1887-1970), carved W.E. 1960, 36" x 139" x 21-3/4". Lot includes copies of correspondence between Esherick and client, copy of original drawing. **$118,750**

Rago Arts and Auction Center

Stool, Paoli, Pennsylvania, 1956, walnut, hickory, designed by Wharton Esherick (1887-1970), signed WE 1956, 19" x 12-1/2" x 10-1/2". **$5,938**

Rago Arts and Auction Center

Pair of lounge chairs, New York, 1950s, lacquered wood, leather, unmarked, designed by James Mont, manufactured by James Mont Design, 26-1/2" x 24" x 25". **$3,500**

Rago Arts and Auction Center

Large table lamp, New York, 1950s, carved, gilt and polychromed wood, painted shade, unmarked, designed by James Mont, manufactured by James Mont Design, body: 26-1/2" x 8" sq., overall: 43-1/2" x 20" dia. **$2,500**

Rago Arts and Auction Center

Pair of grass-seated chairs, New Hope, Pennsylvania, 1974, walnut, grass cord, unmarked, designed by George Nakashima, manufactured by Nakashima Studios, 27-1/2" x 22-3/4" x 19-1/2". **$2,750**

Rago Arts and Auction Center

Chan coffee table, New York, 1960s, etched, patinated and enameled bronze, pewter, designed by Philip and Kelvin LaVerne, raised signature, 18" x 42" dia...**$6,875**

Rago Arts and Auction Center

Tiered occasional table, New York, 1950s, lacquered wood, each stamped, designed by James Mont, manufactured by James Mont Design, 21-1/2" x 36" x 13" overall. **$875**

Rago Arts and Auction Center

Coffee table, New York, 1960s, etched, patinated, and enameled bronze, designed by Philip and Kelvin LaVerne, etched signature, 18-1/2" x 62-1/2" x 27". **$5,938**

Rago Arts and Auction Center

Cabinet, New York, 1950s, walnut, brass, branded, designed by Tommi Parzinger, manufactured by Parzinger Originals, overall: 84-1/2" x 90" x 18-1/4", lower cabinet: 33-1/2" h. **$6,250**

Rago Arts and Auction Center

Black walnut cutting board, Paoli, Pennsylvania, 1968, designed by Wharton Esherick (American, 1887-1970), signed and dated, 20" x 19"....**$2,250**

Rago Arts and Auction Center

Pair of open-back tufted lounge chairs, New York, 1950s, mahogany, silk, unmarked, designed by James Mont, manufactured by James Mont Design, 27" x 38" x 26"...**$1,875**

Rago Arts and Auction Center

Pair of new chairs, New Hope, Pennsylvania, 1967, walnut, hickory, designed by George Nakashima, manufactured by Nakashima Studios, signed with client's name, 36" x 19" x 21-1/2"............................ **$4,375**

Rago Arts and Auction Center

Floor lamp, United States, 1960s, enameled iron, brass, plastic, linen, designed by Tommi Parzinger, manufactured by Parzinger Originals, unmarked, 74" x 20" dia. **$2,250**

Rago Arts and Auction Center

Pair of four-drawer dressers, Boston, 1950s, bleached mahogany, tooled leather, brass, manufacturer's decals, designed by Tommi Parzinger, manufactured by Charak Modern, 34" x 44" x 18-1/2". **$5,938**

Rago Arts and Auction Center

Thin Edge full size bed (no. 5491), Zeeland, Michigan, 1950s, birch, cane, enameled steel, canvas, metal label, designed by George Nelson, manufactured by Herman Miller, 34" x 53-1/2" x 74-1/2". **$2,250**

Rago Arts and Auction Center

Lounge chair, one arm, New Hope, Pennsylvania, 1963, cherry, hickory, designed by George Nakashima, manufactured by Nakashima Studios, signed with client's name, 32-1/2" x 29-1/2" x 27". **$6,875**

Rago Arts and Auction Center

Pair of armchairs (NV-48), Denmark, 1948, teak, recycled leather, branded, designed by Finn Juhl, manufactured by Niels Vodder, 32" x 27" x 25". **$6,875**

Rago Arts and Auction Center

Tall-back armchair, New York, 1950s, bleached mahogany, patent leather, designed by Tommi Parzinger, manufactured by Parzinger Originals, unmarked, 41" x 26" x 27".............. **$2,625**

Rago Arts and Auction Center

Settee, Sweden, 1960s, teak, leather, unmarked, designed by Broderna Andersson Ekenassjon, 29" x 77-1/2" x 33"..............................**$3,250**

Rago Arts and Auction Center

Illuminated bar cabinet, Italy, 1960s, lacquered parchment and rosewood, gilt brass, glass, mirrored glass, unmarked, designed by Aldo Tura, 59" x 27-3/4" x 16-3/4"........... **$8,125**

Rago Arts and Auction Center

Three-seat sofa, Denmark, 1950s, teak, wool, brass, retailer's metal label, designed by Finn Juhl, manufactured by France and Sons, 29-1/2" x 73-3/4" x 28-1/2"..**$4,063**

Rago Arts and Auction Center

Cityscape executive desk, United States, 1970s, walnut, maple burl, patinated steel, designed by Paul Evans, manufactured by Directional, 29-1/2" x 84" x 36-3/4"...**$7,500**

Rago Arts and Auction Center

Cityscape dining table, United States, 1970s, chromed steel, plate glass, signed, designed by Paul Evans, manufactured by Directional, 29-1/4" x 96" x 48"... **$7,500**

Rago Arts and Auction Center

Origins full-size walnut headboard (model 292), Grand Rapids, Michigan, 1960s, branded, stenciled numbers, designed by George Nakashima, manufactured by Widdicomb, 44" x 63"........ **$1,750**

Rago Arts and Auction Center

Origins dresser and mirror, Grand Rapids, Michigan, 1960s, walnut, brass, mirrored glass, dresser is branded, designed by George Nakashima, manufactured by Widdicomb, mirror: 37" x 46" x 4-1/2", cabinet: 32" x 60" x 22". **$4,688**

Rago Arts and Auction Center

Four-drawer dresser, New Hope, Pennsylvania, before 1954, walnut, unmarked, designed by George Nakashima, manufactured by Nakashima Studios, 29-3/4" x 36" x 19", includes letter of authentication from Mira Nakashima. **$7,500**

Tall Origins dresser, Grand Rapids, Michigan, 1960s, walnut, brass, branded, designed by George Nakashima, manufactured by Widdicomb, 50" x 36" x 22". **$2,500**

Rago Arts and Auction Center

Dining table and four captain's chairs, New Hope, Pennsylvania, 1980, walnut, designed by George Nakashima, manufactured by Nakashima Studios, chairs marked with client's name, table: 28-3/4" x 41-1/2" dia., chairs: 28-1/2" x 23-3/4" x 20-1/2"..................................**$8,125**

Rago Arts and Auction Center

Lamp table, France, 1950s, beech, birch, bronze, unmarked, designed by Jacques Adnet, 65-1/2" x 24" x 33"........ **$5,313**

Rago Arts and Auction Center

Three amoeba-shaped three-legged walnut tables, New Hope, Pennsylvania, before 1954, unmarked, designed by George Nakashima, manufactured by Nakashima Studios, tallest: 21" x 16-1/2" x 18", includes letter of authentication from Mira Nakashima. **$5,625**

Rago Arts and Auction Center

Rectangular end table with shelf, New Hope, Pennsylvania, 1963, cherry, hickory, rosewood, designed by George Nakashima, manufactured by Nakashima Studios, signed with client's name, 21" x 27-3/4" x 17-3/4".. **$2,250**

Rago Arts and Auction Center

Oak cabinet, Denmark, 1960s, Danish Control label, designed by Ib Kofod-Larsen, manufactured by Faarup, 30-1/4" x 90-1/2" x 19-1/2".. **$5,625**

Rago Arts and Auction Center

Amoeba coffee table, New Hope, Pennsylvania, circa 1959, marble, walnut, unmarked, designed by Phil Powell, 16-1/2" x 46" x 29-1/2". **$4,063**

Rago Arts and Auction Center

Teak dining table, Denmark, 1950s, unmarked, designed by Finn Juhl, manufactured by Niels Vodder, open: 28-1/2" x 121-1/2" x 54-3/4", closed: 78", two leaves: 21-3/4". **$9,375**

Rago Arts and Auction Center

▶ Coffee table, Denmark, 1960s, rosewood, chromed steel, copper, unmarked, designed by Jens Quistgaard, manufactured by Richard Nissen, 18-1/2" x 30-3/4" sq. **$3,750**

Rago Arts and Auction Center

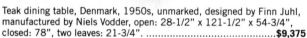

Hanging wall case, New Hope, Pennsylvania, 1974, walnut, designed by George Nakashima, manufactured by Nakashima Studios, signed with client's name, 14" x 65" x 13-1/2"..**$6,875**

Rago Arts and Auction Center

Adjustable floor lamp, United States, 1950s, enameled steel, enameled aluminum, brass, single socket, unmarked, designed by Greta Magnusson Grossman, manufactured by Ralph O. Smith, 49-3/4" x 14" x 14"........ **$9,375**

Rago Arts and Auction Center

Trestle table, Denmark, 1950s, bleached walnut, beech, additional table top, unmarked, designed by Finn Juhl, manufactured by Niels Vodder, 28-1/4" x 78-1/2" x 37-1/4...**$6,875**

Rago Arts and Auction Center

Pair of lounge chairs PK 22, Denmark, 2000s, woven wicker, matte-chromed steel, stamped and labeled, designed by Poul Kjaerholm, manufactured by Fritz Hansen, 27-1/2" x 25" x 26".................... **$4,375**

Rago Arts and Auction Center

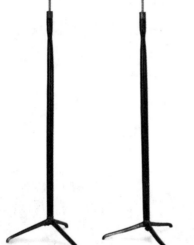

Settee PK 31/2, Denmark, 1950s, matte-chromed steel, leather, plastic, stamped signature, designed by Poul Kjaerholm, manufactured by E. Kold Christensen, 27-1/2" x 54" x 30"..............**$6,875**

Rago Arts and Auction Center

Pair of floor lamps, Austria, 1950s, stained and lacquered beech, bronze, linen, unmarked, designed by Carl Aubock, 64" x 20" dia. **$9,375**

Rago Arts and Auction Center

Coffee table, New Hope, Pennsylvania, circa 1959, laminated oak and walnut, unmarked, designed by Phil Powell, 16-1/2" x 52" x 18"........ **$6,875**

Rago Arts and Auction Center

Tiered sofa table, New Hope, Pennsylvania, circa 1959, walnut, cherry, slate, unmarked, designed by Phil Powell, 21" x 64" x 36"... **$2,625**

Rago Arts and Auction Center

Cabinet (no. 541), United States, 1950s, walnut, maple, chromed steel, fabric, manufacturer's label, designed by Florence Knoll, manufactured by Knoll Associates, 29" x 75-1/2" x 18". **$4,688**

Rago Arts and Auction Center

Set of three nesting tables, Denmark, 1960s, teak, pine, metal manufacturer's labels, designed by Edvard and Tove Kindt-Larsen, manufactured by Thorald Madsen, largest: 20-1/2" x 19-3/4" x 13-3/4". **$688**

Rago Arts and Auction Center

Set of six laminated walnut side chairs, Lawrence, Massachusetts, 1960s, all have manufacturer's labels, designed by Norman Cherner, manufactured by Plycraft, 31" x 17" x 21"................................**$3,125**

Rago Arts and Auction Center

Pair of lounge chairs, Danish, 1960s, chromed steel, leather, rosewood, unmarked, 28" x 24" x 33".........................**$2,125**

Rago Arts and Auction Center

Tambour-door cabinet, Denmark, 1960s, teak, birch, branded, designed by Arne Vodder, manufactured by Sibast Mobler, 49-1/2" x 48" x 19-1/2".. **$2,500**

Rago Arts and Auction Center

Eight conference chairs, Denmark, 1960s, mahogany, leather, manufacturer's paper labels, designed by Borge Mogensen, manufactured by Fredericia Stolefabrik, 28" x 24" x 20". **$5,313**

Rago Arts and Auction Center

Egg chair and ottoman, Denmark, late 1950s, vinyl, aluminum, plastic, unmarked, designed by Arne Jacobsen, manufactured by Fritz Hansen, 42" x 33" x 26", ottoman: 17" x 21" x 15". **$4,375**

Rago Arts and Auction Center

FURNITURE

Sofa, Denmark, circa 1962, teak, wool, unmarked, designed by Jorgen Christensen, 32-1/2" x 73" x 30"... **$3,500**

Rago Arts and Auction Center

Sofa, Denmark, 1960s, rosewood, upholstery, unmarked, designed by Ole Wanscher, manufactured by A.J. Iversen Snedkermester, 31" x 81-1/2" x 28-1/2".................................... **$4,375**

Rago Arts and Auction Center

Console table, Denmark, 1960s, rosewood, laminate, metal labels, designed by Arne Vodder, manufactured by Sibast Mobler, 29-1/2" x 51" x 21-3/4".... **$3,250**

Rago Arts and Auction Center

Cabinet, Denmark, 1950s, teak, white oak, brass, unmarked, designed by Hans Wegner, manufactured by Carl Hansen & Son, 49-3/4" x 66-1/4" x 17-1/2"....................................... **$8,750**

Rago Arts and Auction Center

Lounge chair PK 31/1, Denmark, 1950s, matte-chromed steel, leather, plastic, stamped signature, designed by Poul Kjaerholm, manufactured by E. Kold Christensen, 27-1/2" x 30" x 30". **$4,375**

Rago Arts and Auction Center

Two Time-Life chairs, Zeeland, Michigan, 1960s, leather, aluminum, plastic, paper and metal labels, designed by Charles and Ray Eames, manufactured by Herman Miller, 29-1/2" x 29" x 29-1/2". ... **$1,625**

Rago Arts and Auction Center

RAR chair, United States, 1950s, fiberglass-reinforced plastic, rope, enameled steel, birch, decal label, designed by Charles and Ray Eames, manufactured by Herman Miller, Zenith Plastics, 26-3/4" x 24-3/4" x 27"............................**$1,250**

Rago Arts and Auction Center

Walnut music stand, circa 1969, unmarked, designed by Sam Maloof (1916-2009), 52" x 37" x 25". **$8,125**

Rago Arts and Auction Center

Lounge chair and ottoman (no. 670-671), Zeeland, Michigan, 1980s, rosewood, leather, enameled aluminum, enameled steel, rubber, manufacturer's labels, designed by Charles and Ray Eames, manufactured by Herman Miller, chair: 33" x 32-1/2" x 35", ottoman: 17-1/2" x 26-1/2" x 22"..**$9,375**

Rago Arts and Auction Center

Cantilevered armchair, Finland, 1930s, beech, upholstery, stamped, metal tag, designed by Alvar Aalto, manufactured by Finmar, 36-1/2" x 24-1/2" x 34". **$1,625**

Rago Arts and Auction Center

Dining table and six Heart chairs, Denmark, 1960s, teak, beech, manufacturer's stamp to chairs, designed by Hans Wegner, manufactured by Fritz Hansen, table: 27-1/2" x 47" dia., chairs: 28-3/4" x 20" x 17-1/2". **$5,000**

Rago Arts and Auction Center

Lounge chair (no. 136), Denmark, 1950s, teak, leather, brass, manufacturer's brass label, designed by Finn Juhl, manufactured by France and Sons, 30" x 32" x 31"..............**$2,875**

Rago Arts and Auction Center

Three-seat sofa, 1950s, beech, upholstery, unmarked, style of Kerstin Horlin-Holmquist, 27-1/2" x 99" x 34". **$6,250**

Rago Arts and Auction Center

Pair of solid teak three-legged stools, Denmark, 1950s, paper labels, designed by Mogens Lassen, manufactured by K. Thomsen, 20" x 18-1/4" x 12"..... **$2,250**

Rago Arts and Auction Center

Pair of ebonized wood Crinolette chairs, Finland, 1960s, manufacturer's labels, designed by Ilmari Tapiovaara, manufactured by Asko, 29-1/4" x 27-1/4" x 26"..**$3,125**

Rago Arts and Auction Center

Set of six dining chairs, Denmark, 1960s, oak, vinyl, branded, designed by Hans Wegner, manufactured by C.M. Madsens Fabriker, 30" x 21-3/4" x 18-1/2"........**$2,500**

Rago Arts and Auction Center

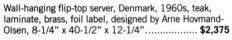

Ari lounge chair, Sweden, 1960s, leather, chromed steel, unmarked, designed by Arne Norell, manufactured by Aneby, 30" x 25-1/2" x 39". **$2,750**

Rago Arts and Auction Center

Wall-hanging flip-top server, Denmark, 1960s, teak, laminate, brass, foil label, designed by Arne Hovmand-Olsen, 8-1/4" x 40-1/2" x 12-1/4"................... **$2,375**

Rago Arts and Auction Center

Flip-top partner's desk, Denmark, 1960s, rosewood, brass, manufacturer's label, manufactured by Lovig, closed: 34" x 64" x 28-1/2", open: 38" wide. .. **$4,688**

Rago Arts and Auction Center

Flip-top partner's desk, Denmark, 1965, teak, brass, stenciled 1965 to underside of drawers, manufactured by Lovig, closed: 34" x 64" x 28-3/4", open: 38" wide. **$3,000**

Rago Arts and Auction Center

Coffee table, Italy, 1950s, Italian walnut, brass, glass, stamped Made in Italy, designed by Gio Ponti, manufactured by Singer and Sons, 15" x 39-1/2" dia. **$7,500**

Rago Arts and Auction Center

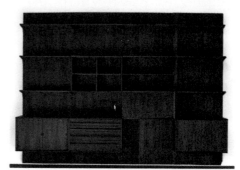

Four-bay teak shelving system, Denmark, 1950s, unmarked, designed by Paul Cadovius, manufactured by Cado, 93-1/2" x 127" x 18". **$5,000**

Rago Arts and Auction Center

Thin Edge dresser (no. 5723), Zeeland, Michigan, 1950s, Brazilian rosewood, aluminum, porcelain, foil label, designed by George Nelson, manufactured by Herman Miller, 33" x 67-1/4" x 18-1/2". **$9,375**

Rago Arts and Auction Center

Chair and ottoman, Mexico, 1970s, rosewood, leather, unmarked, designed by Don Shoemaker, manufactured by Senal, chair: 32" x 23" x 28", ottoman: 14-1/2" x 22-1/2" x 17-1/2". **$2,000**

Rago Arts and Auction Center

Desk and chair, France, 1940s, solid mahogany, unmarked, designed by Maxime Old, desk: 29-1/2" x 48" x 16", chair: 30-3/4" x 21" x 26"........**$8,750**

Rago Arts and Auction Center

Two cabinets, France, circa 1950, oak, dyed ash, enameled steel, unmarked, Escande, 36" x 35-1/4" x 13-3/4".. **$4,688**

Rago Arts and Auction Center

Campaign chair and ottoman, France, 1930s, blackened wrought iron, saddle leather, unmarked, French, 30-1/2" x 26" x 18", 19-1/2" x 23" x 16-1/2".. **$2,125**

Rago Arts and Auction Center

Pair of side chairs, France, 1960s, stitched leather, brass, enameled wood steel, unmarked, designed by Jacques Adnet, 32-1/2" x 20" x 25"..........**$6,250**

Rago Arts and Auction Center

Skyscraper cabinet, United States, 1920s, lacquered and silvered wood, polished aluminum, mirror, glass, unmarked, designed by Paul Frankl, manufactured by Frankl Galleries, 65-1/2" x 36" x 21-1/2". **$6,250**

Rago Arts and Auction Center

Lounge chair and illuminating ottoman, Italy, 1960s, chromed steel, hide, rubber, unmarked, Archizoom Associati, Poltrona, 30" x 29" x 51-1/2", 14" x 41" x 8"............................ **$3,250**

Rago Arts and Auction Center

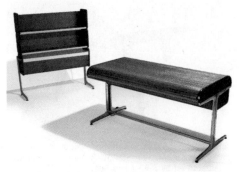

Action Office desk with tiered file cabinet, Zeeland, Michigan, 1960s, aluminum, lacquered wood, walnut, unmarked, designed by George Nelson, manufactured by Herman Miller, desk: 33-1/2" x 64-1/2" x 32", hanging cabinet (not pictured): 12" x 48" x 13-1/2", cabinet: 30" x 50" x 15-1/2". **$2,250**

Rago Arts and Auction Center

Pair of armchairs, France, 1940s, leather, enameled iron, unmarked, designed by Jacques Quinet, 31" x 22-1/2" x 22"..**$8,750**

Rago Arts and Auction Center

Cabinet, France, circa 1950, oak, dyed ash, enameled steel, unmarked, Escande, 35-3/4" x 35-1/2" x 13-1/2"...................................**$2,500**

Rago Arts and Auction Center

FURNITURE

Two cabinets, United States, 1940s, stained and lacquered mahogany, lacquered cork, brass, glass, stenciled numbers and branded, designed by Paul Frankl, manufactured by Johnson Furniture Co., each 84" x 42" x 22".......................................**$5,625**

Rago Arts and Auction Center

Skyscraper bookcase, United States, 1920s, lacquered and silvered wood, glass, unmarked, designed by Paul Frankl, manufactured by Frankl Galleries, 22-1/2" x 18" x 17-3/4" sq. **$3,750**

Rago Arts and Auction Center

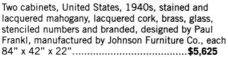

Wiggle chair, Canada/United States, 1970s, laminated cardboard, masonite, unmarked, designed by Frank Gehry, manufactured by Easy Edges, Inc., 33-1/2" x 14-1/2" x 24". . **$2,125**

Rago Arts and Auction Center

Pair of adjustable stools, United States/ Sweden, 1950s, enameled steel, vinyl, designed by Odelberg Olsen, manufactured by Knoll, fully extended: 24", fully dropped: 18" x 21" dia. **$2,125**

Rago Arts and Auction Center

Sculpture "Golden Dandelion," Pennsylvania, 1968, gilt metal wire, oak, paper label to base, Harry Bertoia, 25-1/2" x 3-1/2" sq............ **$5,938**

Rago Arts and Auction Center

Pair of butterfly chairs (no. 675), France/Netherlands, 1960s, stitched saddle leather, matte chrome steel, unmarked, designed by Pierre Paul, Indiana, manufactured by Artifort, 25" x 32" x 26"...**$5,313**

Rago Arts and Auction Center

Bedroom suite: pair of dressers (no. 3770), pair of nightstands (no. 3770), headboard (not pictured), Zeeland, Michigan, 1940s, Brazilian rosewood, mahogany, brass-plated metal, paper and foil labels, stenciled numbers, designed by Gilbert Rohde, manufactured by Herman Miller, dressers: 34" x 46" x 19", nightstands: 27-1/4" x 16" x 14-1/2", headboard: 31-1/2" x 57"..........................**$8,125**

Rago Arts and Auction Center

Tiered sofa table, Zeeland Michigan, 1940s, mahogany, chrome-plated steel, unmarked, designed by Gilbert Rohde, manufactured by Herman Miller, 29-1/4" x 48" x 13"...................................**$1,875**

Rago Arts and Auction Center

Pedestal dining table, United States, 1940s, stained wood, branded, designed by Eliel Saarinen, manufactured by Johnson Furniture Co., 30-1/2" x 52" dia., with six leaves: 78" dia...............**$3,000**

Rago Arts and Auction Center

▲ Triple band lounge chair, United States, circa 1934, chromed steel, leatherette, maple, unmarked, designed by K.E.M. Weber, manufactured by Lloyd Manufacturing Co., 34" x 28-1/2" x 41".....**$3,125**

Rago Arts and Auction Center

"Hokus" elephant doorstop, United States, 1930s, nickel-plated brass and lead, unmarked, designed by Russel Wright, Manufactured by Russel Wright, Inc., 11-3/4" x 5" dia.................**$7,500**

Rago Arts and Auction Center

Triple band sofa, United States, circa 1934, chromed steel, leatherette, maple, unmarked, designed by K.E.M. Weber, manufactured by Lloyd Manufacturing Co., 33" x 78-1/2" x 43"..**$4,000-$6,000**

Rago Arts and Auction Center

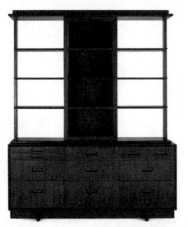

Breakfront (no. 2000), Morganton, North Carolina, 1950s, mahogany, glass, manufacturer's stamp, designed by Frank Lloyd Wright, manufactured by Heritage Henredon, lower cabinet: 28-1/4" x 61-1/2" x 20", upper cabinet: 49-1/2" x 60" x 15".... **$5,313**

Rago Arts and Auction Center

Sculpted walnut coffee table (no. 3304), Grand Rapids, Michigan, 1950s, stenciled numbers and manufacturer's label, designed by T.H. Robsjohn Gibbings, manufactured by Widdicomb, 16" x 73" x 19".. **$6,250**

Rago Arts and Auction Center

Coliseum console table (no. 3368), Grand Rapids, Michigan, 1950s, walnut, manufacturer's decal, stenciled numbers, designed by T.H. Robsjohn Gibbings, manufactured by Widdicomb, 30" x 54" x 18"...**$4,375**

Rago Arts and Auction Center

Pair of symmetric lounge chairs, Grand Rapids, Michigan, 1950s, walnut, upholstery, unmarked, designed by Paul McCobb, manufactured by Widdicomb, 33-1/2" x 29" x 28-1/2"............ **$2,000**

Rago Arts and Auction Center

Pair of tall dressers, Grand Rapids, Michigan, 1950s, bleach mahogany, brass, decal labels, designed by T.H. Robsjohn Gibbings, manufactured by Widdicomb, 45" x 34" x 21"........................ **$4,375**

Rago Arts and Auction Center

Two cabinets, Grand Rapids, Michigan, 1940s, bleached, stained and lacquered mahogany, brass, decal label, designed by T.H. Robsjohn Gibbings, manufactured by Widdicomb Modern, each 33" x 36" x 20-1/2"... **$3,625**

Rago Arts and Auction Center

Pair of lounge chairs, Grand Rapids, Michigan, 1950s, walnut, leather, unmarked, designed by T.H. Robsjohn Gibbings, manufactured by Widdicomb, 31" x 26-1/2" x 35"................................**$5,625**

Rago Arts and Auction Center

Pair of lounge chairs, Wilkes-Barre, Pennsylvania, 1960s, wool upholstery, unmarked, designed by Adrian Pearsall, manufactured by Craft Associates, 26" x 39-1/2" x 36"................ **$5,625**

Rago Arts and Auction Center

Lounge chair and ottoman, Berne, Indiana, 1960s, stained and lacquered ash, wool, signed, designed by Edward Wormley, manufactured by Dunbar, chair: 33-1/2" x 31-1/2" x 36", ottoman: 14" x 24-1/2" x 22-1/2"...................................... **$3,625**

Rago Arts and Auction Center

Lounge chair and ottoman (no. 670 and 671), United States, 1970s, rosewood, leather, enameled aluminum, enameled steel, rubber, manufacturer's labels, designed by Charles and Ray Eames, manufactured by Herman Miller, chair: 31-1/2" x 33" x 33", ottoman: 16-1/2" x 25-1/2" x 20". ...**$4,375**

Rago Arts and Auction Center

Three-seat sofa, United States, 1970s, gel-coated fiberglass, acrylic, leather, unmarked, Steelcase Furniture Co., 25" x 84" x 35".................**$2,125**

Rago Arts and Auction Center

Dining table and four chairs, United States, 1960s, ebonized wood, travertine, upholstery, unmarked, designed by Harvey Probber, manufactured by Harvey Probber, Inc., dining table: 25-1/2" x 50-1/2" sq., chairs: 29" x 26" x 25". **$2,125**

Rago Arts and Auction Center

FURNITURE

◀ Two LAX chairs, Gardenia, California, 1950s, fiberglass, rope, enameled steel, rubber, manufacturer's decals, designed by Charles and Ray Eames, manufactured by Herman Miller, Zenith Plastics, 25-1/2" x 25" x 25"................................ **$1,750**

Rago Arts and Auction Center

Coffee table (no. 6129), Berne, Indiana, 1960s, Carpathian elm, stained walnut, brass, manufacturer's labels, designed by Edward Wormley, manufactured by Dunbar, 14-1/4" x 33" x 33". **$2,125**

Rago Arts and Auction Center

Set of five nesting tables (no. 4785), Berne, Indiana, circa 1950, bleached mahogany, painted metal label, designed by Edward Wormley, manufactured by Dunbar, largest: 20-1/2" x 26-1/4" x 15-1/2".......... **$2,625**

Rago Arts and Auction Center

Magazine table, Berne, Indiana, 1940s, sap walnut, bleached mahogany, brass, painted metal label, designed by Edward Wormley, manufactured by Dunbar, 22" x 25" x 25-1/2". **$1,750**

Rago Arts and Auction Center

Small armchair with curved elements, Italy, 1960s, lacquered wood, unmarked, designed by Joe Colombo, manufactured by Kartell, 23" x 28" x 26-1/2"........ **$8,750**

Rago Arts and Auction Center

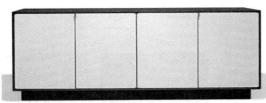

Custom cabinet, United States, 1950s, teak, lacquered wood, chromed steel, manufacturer's label, designed by Florence Knoll, manufactured by Knoll Associates, 23-1/2" x 64-1/2" x 19"...........................**$4,063**

Rago Arts and Auction Center

Set of four dining chairs (no. 175A), New York, 1950s, sculpted walnut, upholstery, unmarked, designed by Vladimir Kagan, manufactured by Kagan-Dreyfuss, 34-1/2" x 19" x 24", 34-1/2" x 25" x 24".......**$4,063**

Rago Arts and Auction Center

Set of three nesting tables, Italy, 1950s, exotic woods, brass, lacquered wood, unmarked, Erno Fabry Associates, largest: 20-1/2" x 26-1/2" x 27".................. **$5,000**

Rago Arts and Auction Center

Glass

BACCARAT

Baccarat glass has been made by Cristalleries de Baccarat, France, since 1765. The firm has produced various glassware of excellent quality as well as paperweights. Baccarat's Rose Tiente is often referred to as Baccarat's Amberina.

Pair of crystal three-light chandeliers with rare Art Deco cherubs, frosted clear to cranberry, 22" h. **$3,750**

Kaminski Auctions

Baccarat crystal Iceberg sculpture, Baccarat mark to base, very good condition, 7-1/2" h. **$70**

Manor Auctions

Two crystal paperweights, 20th century, eagle and lion, both signed with a stamp, eagle 7" h. x 4-7/8" w. x 3" d. **$325**

Crescent City Auction Gallery

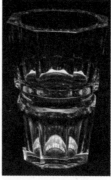

Crystal faceted vase with octagonal outer form with middle division, signed Baccarat on side with Baccarat mark on bottom, 11-5/8" h. x 8-1/4" dia. **$300**

Elite Decorative Arts

Two crystal obelisks, each with triangular form and Baccarat marks on bottom, taller one 18-1/8" h. **$400**

Elite Decorative Arts

BRIDE'S BASKETS

These berry or fruit bowls were popular late Victorian wedding gifts, hence the name. They were produced in a variety of quality art glass wares and sometimes were fitted in ornate silver plate holders.

Victorian air-trap bride's basket, glossy cased rose to pink with colorless rim, diamond air-traps and polished pontil mark, fitted in quadruple-plate frame marked for James W. Tufts and numbered 152, small sterling silver ladle in handle slot, fourth quarter 19th century, undamaged, stand heavily tarnished, 11-1/2" h. overall, 8-1/2" dia. overall. **$161**

Jeffrey S. Evans & Associates

Victorian decorated bride's basket, opal with light pink ground, floral and cartouche polychrome and gilt decoration, ruffled rim, polished pontil mark, fitted in a Forbes Silver Co. quadruple-plate frame, late 19th/early 20th century, excellent condition, interior of base with minor flake, minor normal wear to decorations, 11-1/4" h. overall, bowl 3-7/8" h. overall, 9-3/4" dia. rim. **$81**

Jeffrey S. Evans & Associates

New Martinsville salmon Muranese bride's bowl, crimped rim with moderate iridescence, fitted in unmarked silver-plate figural-stem frame depicting a cherub, New Martinsville Glass Co., first quarter 20th century, undamaged, frame with minor wear to finish, 13-1/4" h. overall, 11" dia. rim. **$127**

Jeffrey S. Evans & Associates

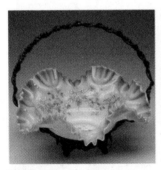

Victorian decorated cased bride's basket, shaded blue with polychrome enamel foliate decoration, pattern crimped and ruffled rim, ground pontil mark, fitted in a quadruple-plate frame marked for Wilcox Silver Plate Co. and numbered 7611, fourth quarter 19th century, undamaged with light wear to decoration, frame heavily tarnished, 8-1/2" h. overall, 9-3/4" dia. overall. **$127**

Jeffrey S. Evans & Associates

Victorian decorated bride's basket, cased dark rose to mustard yellow, polychrome floral decoration, interior with scalloped band of raised beading, ruffled rim, polished pontil mark, fitted in Wilcox quadruple-plate frame, late 19th/early 20th century, excellent condition, two beads with some minor roughness to points, otherwise undamaged, 11-3/8" h. overall, bowl 3-3/8" h. overall, 10-1/4" dia. rim. **$161**

Jeffrey S. Evans & Associates

Mt. Washington cameo bride's basket, blue and white heavily scalloped bowl with cameo design of phoenix on either side of crest, bowl supported by silver-plated ornate bride's basket, basket signed "Guaranteed Taunton MASS 1338," also marked "Poole Silver Co.," bowl in very good to excellent condition, basket has wear to silver plate, bowl 10" w., basket 12" x 12". **$690**

James D. Julia, Inc.

GLASS

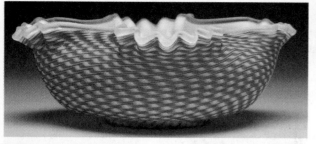

Victorian cased bride's bowl, white, yellow, russet and pink swirls around exterior, cased in interior with white, finished with applied frosted lip, very good to excellent condition, 10" dia. **$518**

James D. Julia, Inc.

Phoenix Knob Optic bride's bowl, cranberry opalescent, 20-row spot mold with exaggerated ruffled and crimped rim, polished pontil mark, Phoenix Glass Co., fourth quarter 19th century, undamaged, 5" h. overall, 9" dia. overall. **$161**

Jeffrey S. Evans & Associates

Victorian decorated bride's bowl on stand, green to opal bowl with heavy gilt and polychrome enamel decoration, fitted in tall quadruple-plate pedestal stand marked for Vanbergh S. P. Co., Rochester, New York, fourth quarter 19th century, undamaged, some wear to decoration in bottom of bowl, normal wear to plating, 12-1/2" h. overall, 11-3/4" dia. rim. **$196**

Jeffrey S. Evans & Associates

Victorian decorated opaline bride's basket, translucent blue with white enamel floral and gilt decoration, oblong bowl with silver-plate mount to foot, original quadruple-plate frame decorated with large flowers and leaves, marked for Meriden Silverplate Co., Meriden, Connecticut and numbered 1566, fourth quarter 19th century, bowl undamaged with some minor wear to gilding, frame with partial loss on one leaf, heavily tarnished, 11" h. overall, 8-1/4" x 12-3/4" dia. rim.... **$161**

Jeffrey S. Evans & Associates

Victorian decorated cased bride's basket, shaded rose with polychrome enamel and gilt decoration on interior and exterior, crimped and ruffled rim, ground pontil mark, fitted in a quadruple-plate frame marked for Wilcox Silver Plate Co. and numbered 7610, fourth quarter 19th century, bowl with loss, short crack to one rim point, light wear to gilding, frame with normal wear, 12" h. overall, 12" dia. overall. **$150**

Jeffrey S. Evans & Associates

Spatter bride's bowl, encased mica, ruby and opal flakes, light amber exterior casing, tightly crimped rim, base with lightly molded petals and polished pontil mark, probably Phoenix Glass Co., fourth quarter 19th century, undamaged, 3-5/8" h., 9-3/4" dia. overall. **$196**

Jeffrey S. Evans & Associates

New Martinsville pink Muranese bride's basket, scalloped rim with light iridescence, fitted in a Columbia quadruple-plate frame, New Martinsville Glass Co., first quarter 20th century, undamaged bowl, frame with some minor repairs and one detached arm, 3-3/4" h., 8-3/8" dia. rim. ..**$104**

Jeffrey S. Evans & Associates

Daisy and Fern bride's basket, blue opalescent, ruffled and crimped rim, fitted in unmarked silver-plate frame, late 19th/early 20th century, bowl undamaged, frame with loss to scrollwork at top of handle, 13" h. overall, 10-1/4" dia. overall. **$127**

Jeffrey S. Evans & Associates

BURMESE

Burmese is a single-layer glass that shades from pink to pale yellow. It was patented by Frederick S. Shirley and made by the Mt. Washington Glass Co. A license to produce the glass in England was granted to Thomas Webb & Sons, which called its articles Queen's Burmese. Gundersen Burmese was made briefly about the middle of the 20th century.

Hobnail pitcher, Mt. Washington Glass Co., unmarked, handle has been reattached, 10" h. **$70**

Quinn & Farmer Auctions

Verse pitcher, Mt. Washington Glass Co., bulbous form in pink satin glass at top gradating to cream at bottom, applied handle with gold trim on rim, handle and base, decorated with floral design on front and back, verse reads, "The cowslip is a country lass, The violet is a nun; But I will woo the dainty rose, The queen of every one. Thomas Hood"; very good condition with no breaks, chips or repairs, 5-3/4" h. **$2,655**

Fontaine's Auction Gallery

Art glass vase with swirled rib, hexagonal top, no chips, cracks or repairs, bubble on one rib, 4" h. **$102**

Dirk Soulis Auctions

Four-horn epergne and crimped bowl, Fenton Art Glass, 13-1/2" h. ... **$207**

ATM Antiques & Auctions, LLC

Tomato salt shaker, Mt. Washington Glass Co., deep rose over-fired Burmese, enameled white daisy decoration, original two-part lid, fourth quarter 19th century, undamaged, 1-3/4" h. **$288**

Jeffrey S. Evans & Associates

Cruet, Mt. Washington Glass Co., glossy finish, applied yellow handle and stopper, fourth quarter 19th century, undamaged, 6-5/8" h. overall. **$489**

Jeffrey S. Evans & Associates

Salt shaker, Thomas Webb & Sons, plush finish, butterfly and flower decoration, two-part silver-plate slide-on lid, England, fourth quarter 19th century, undamaged, 4" h. **$403**

Jeffrey S. Evans & Associates

GLASS

CAMBRIDGE

The Cambridge Glass Co. was founded in Ohio in 1901. Pieces are now sought, especially those designed by Arthur J. Bennett, including Crown Tuscan. Other productions included crystal animals, "Black Amethyst," "blanc opaque," and other types of colored glass. The firm was closed in 1954. It should not be confused with the New England Glass Co., Cambridge, Massachusetts.

Figural flower center, pink, #518, draped lady flower frog with patent number underneath, fitted in a #823 stand with four candle cups, second quarter 20th century, undamaged, stand with manufacturing bruise to interior base, 10" h. overall, 12-1/4" sq. **$172**

Jeffrey S. Evans & Associates

Colonial children's glass four-piece table set, green, covered butter dish, covered sugar bowl, creamer and spooner, late 19th/early 20th century, 2-1/8" to 3" h. overall. **$69**

Jeffrey S. Evans & Associates

Two children's glass four-piece table sets, green, Cambridge Fernland and Clear and Diamond Panels, each set comprised of covered butter dish, covered sugar bowl, creamer and spooner, late 19th/early 20th century, 2-3/8" to 3-1/2" h. overall. **$92**

Jeffrey S. Evans & Associates

Two children's glass four-piece table sets, blue, Cambridge Colonial and Stippled Vine and Beads, each set comprised of covered butter dish, covered sugar bowl, creamer and spooner, late 19th/early 20th century, 2-1/4" to 3" h. overall. **$207**

Jeffrey S. Evans & Associates

GLASS

CARNIVAL GLASS

Carnival glass is what is fondly called mass-produced iridescent glassware. The term "carnival glass" has evolved through the years as glass collectors have responded to the idea that much of this beautiful glassware was made as give-away glass at local carnivals and fairs. However, more of it was made and sold through the same channels as pattern glass and Depression glass. Some patterns were indeed giveaways, and others were used as advertising premiums, souvenirs, etc. Whatever the origin, the term "carnival glass" today encompasses glassware that is usually pattern molded and treated with metallic salts, creating that unique coloration that is so desirable to collectors.

Early names for iridescent glassware, which early 20th century consumers believed to have all come from foreign manufacturers, include Pompeiian Iridescent, Venetian Art, and Mexican Aurora. Another popular early name was "Nancy Glass," as some patterns were believed to have come from the Daum, Nancy, glassmaking area in France. This was at a time when the artistic cameo glass was enjoying great success. While the iridescent glassware being made by such European glassmakers as Loetz influenced the American market place, it was Louis Tiffany's Favrile glass that really caught the eye of glass consumers of the early 1900s. It seems an easy leap to transform Tiffany's shimmering glassware to something that could be mass produced, allowing what we call carnival glass today to become "poor man's Tiffany."

Carnival glass is iridized glassware that is created by pressing hot molten glass into molds, just as pattern glass had evolved. Some forms are hand finished, while others are completely formed by molds. To achieve the marvelous iridescent colors that carnival glass collectors seek, a process was developed where a liquid solution of metallic salts was put onto the still hot glass form after it was unmolded. As the liquid evaporated, a fine metallic surface was left which refracts light into wonderful colors. The name given to the iridescent spray by early glassmakers was "dope."

Many of the forms created by carnival glass manufacturers were accessories to the china American housewives so loved. By the early 1900s, consumers could find carnival glassware at such popular stores as F. W. Woolworth and McCrory's. To capitalize on the popular fancy for these colored wares, some other industries bought large quantities of carnival glass and turned them into "packers." This term reflects the practice where baking powder, mustard, or other household products were packed into a special piece of glass that could take on another life after the original product

Feathered Serpent bowl by Fenton, candy ribbon edge
....**$150**

Rococco vase, smoke, by Imperial.................. **$125**

was used. Lee Manufacturing Co. used iridized carnival glass as premiums for its baking powder and other products, causing some early carnival glass to be known by the generic term "Baking Powder Glass."

Classic carnival glass production began in the early 1900s and continued about twenty years, but no one really documented or researched production until the first collecting wave struck in 1960.

It is important to remember that carnival glasswares were sold in department stores as well as mass merchants rather than through the general store often associated with a young America. Glassware by this time was mass-produced and sold in large quantities by such enterprising companies as Butler Brothers. When the economics of the country soured in the 1920s, those interested in purchasing iridized glassware were not spared. Many of the leftover inventories of glasshouses that hoped to sell this mass-produced glassware found their way to wholesalers who in turn sold the wares to those who offered the glittering glass as prizes at carnivals, fairs, circuses, etc. Possibly because this was the last venue people associated the iridized glassware with, it became known as "carnival glass."

For more information on carnival glass, see *Warman's Carnival Glass Identification and Price Guide*, 2nd edition, by Ellen T. Schroy.

CARNIVAL GLASS COMPANIES

Much of vintage American carnival glassware was created in the Ohio valley, in the glasshouse-rich areas of Pennsylvania, Ohio, and West Virginia. The abundance of natural materials, good transportation, and skilled craftsmen that created the early American pattern glass manufacturing companies allowed many of them to add carnival glass to their production lines. Brief company histories of the major carnival glass manufacturers follow:

Cambridge Glass Co. (Cambridge)

Cambridge Glass was a rather minor player in the carnival glass marketplace. Founded in 1901 as a new factory in Cambridge, Ohio, it focused on producing fine crystal tablewares. What carnival glass it did produce was imitation cut-glass patterns.

Colors used by Cambridge include marigold, as well as few others. Forms found in carnival glass by Cambridge include tablewares and vases, some with its trademark "Near-Cut."

Diamond Glass Co. (Diamond)

This company was started as the Dugan brothers (see **Dugan Glass Co.**) departed the carnival glass-making scene in 1913. However, Alfred Dugan returned and became general manager until his death in 1928. After a disastrous fire in June of 1931, the factory closed.

Dugan Glass Co. (Dugan)

The history of the Dugan Glass Co. is closely related to Harry Northwood (see **Northwood Glass Co.**), whose cousin, Thomas Dugan, became plant manager at the Northwood Glass Co. in Indiana, Pennsylvania, in 1895. By 1904, Dugan and his partner W. G. Minnemayer bought the former Northwood factory from the now defunct National

Mary Ann three-handled vase by Dugan, amethyst.............................. **$800**

Glass conglomerate and opened as the Dugan Glass Co. Dugan's brother, Alfred, joined the company and stayed until it became the Diamond Glass Co. in 1913. At this time, Thomas Dugan moved to the Cambridge Glass Co., later Duncan and Miller and finally Hocking, Lancaster. Alfred left Diamond Glass, too, but later returned.

Understanding how the Northwood and Dugan families were connected helps collectors understand the linkage of these three companies. Their productions were similar; molds were swapped, retooled, etc.

Colors attributed to Dugan and Diamond include amethyst, marigold, peach opalescent, and white. The company developed deep amethyst shades, some almost black.

Forms made by both Dugan and Diamond mirrored what other glass companies were producing. The significant contribution by Dugan and later Diamond were feet – either ball or spatula shapes. They are also known for deeply crimped edges.

Vineyard water pitcher, peach opalescent, by Dugan....... **$1,600**

Fenton Art Glass Co. (Fenton)

Frank Leslie Fenton and his brothers, John W. Fenton and Charles H. Fenton, founded this truly American glassmaker in 1905 in Martins Ferry, Ohio. Early production was of blanks, which the brothers soon learned to decorate themselves. They moved to a larger factory in Williamstown, West Virginia.

By 1907, Fenton was experimenting with iridescent glass, developing patterns and the metallic salt formulas that it became so famous for. Production of carnival glass continued at Fenton until the early 1930s. In 1970, Fenton began to reissue carnival glass, creating new colors and forms as well as using traditional patterns.

Colors developed by Fenton are numerous. The company developed red and Celeste blue in the 1920s; a translucent pale blue, known as Persian blue, is also one of its more distinctive colors, as is a light yellow-green color known as vaseline. Fenton also produced delicate opalescent colors including amethyst opalescent and red opalescent. Because the Fenton brothers learned how to decorate their own blanks, they also promoted the addition of enamel decoration to some of their carnival glass patterns.

Forms made by Fenton are also numerous. What distinguishes Fenton from other glassmakers is its attention to detail and hand finishing processes. Edges are found scalloped, fluted, tightly crimped, frilled, or pinched into a candy ribbon edge, also referred to as 3-in-1 edge.

Imperial Glass Co. (Imperial)

Edward Muhleman and a syndicate founded the Imperial Glass Co. at Bellaire, Ohio, in 1901, with production beginning in 1904. It started with pressed glass tableware patterns as well as lighting fixtures. The company's marketing strategy included selling to important retailers of its day, such as F. W. Woolworth and McCrory and Kresge, to get glassware into the hands of American housewives. Imperial also became a major exporter of glassware, including its brilliant carnival patterns. During the Depression, it filed for bankruptcy in 1931, but was able to continue on. By 1962, it was again producing carnival glass patterns. By April 1985, the factory was closed and the molds sold.

Colors made by Imperial include typical carnival colors such as marigold. It added interesting shades of green, known as helios, a pale ginger ale shade known as clambroth, and a brownish smoke shade.

Forms created by Imperial tend to be functional, such as berry sets and table sets. Patterns vary from wonderful imitation cut glass patterns to detailed florals and naturalistic designs.

Millersburg Glass Co. (Millersburg)

John W. Fenton started the Millersburg Glass Co. in September 1908. Perhaps it was the factory's more obscure location or the lack of business experience by John Fenton, but the company failed by 1911.

The factory was bought by Samuel Fair and John Fenton, and renamed the Radium Glass Co., but it lasted only a year.

Colors produced by Millersburg are amethyst, green, and marigold. Shades such as blue and vaseline were added on rare occasions. The company is well known for its bright radium finishes.

Forms produced at Millersburg are mostly bowls and vases. Pattern designers at Millersburg often took one theme and developed several patterns from it. Millersburg often used one pattern for the interior and a different pattern for the exterior.

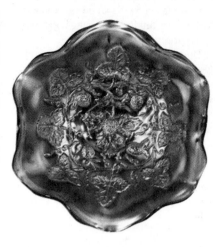

Blackberry Wreath large bowl by Millersburg, ruffled, purple. **$40**

Northwood Glass Co. (Northwood)

Englishman Harry Northwood founded the Northwood Glass Co. He developed his glass formulas for carnival glass, naming it "Golden Iris" in 1908. Northwood was one of the pioneers of the glass manufacturers who marked his wares. Marks range from a full script signature to a simple underscored capital N in a circle. However, not all Northwood glassware is marked.

Colors that Northwood created were many. Collectors prefer its pastels, such as ice blue, ice green, and white. It is also known for several stunning blue shades. The one color that Northwood did not develop was red.

Forms of Northwood patterns range from typical table sets, bowls, and water sets to whimsical novelties, such as a pattern known as Corn, which realistically depicts an ear of corn.

United States Glass Co. (U.S. Glass)

In 1891, a consortium of 15 American glass manufacturers joined together as the United States Glass Co. This company was successful in continuing pattern glass production, as well as developing new glass lines. By 1911, it had begun limited production of carnival glass lines, often using existing pattern glass tableware molds. By the time a tornado destroyed the last of its glass factories in Glassport in 1963, it was no longer producing glassware.

Colors associated with U.S. Glass are marigold, white, and a rich honey amber.

Forms tend to be table sets and functional forms.

Westmoreland Glass Co. (Westmoreland)

Started as the Westmoreland Specialty Co., Grapeville, Pennsylvania, in 1889, this company originally made novelties and glass packing containers, such as candy containers. Researchers have identified its patterns being advertised by Butler Brothers as early as 1908. Carnival glass production continued into the 1920s. In the 1970s, Westmoreland, too, begin to reissue carnival glass patterns and novelties. However, this ceased in February of 1996 when the factory burned.

Colors originally used by Westmoreland were typical carnival colors, such as blue and marigold.

Forms include tablewares and functional forms, containers, etc.

— Ellen T. Schroy

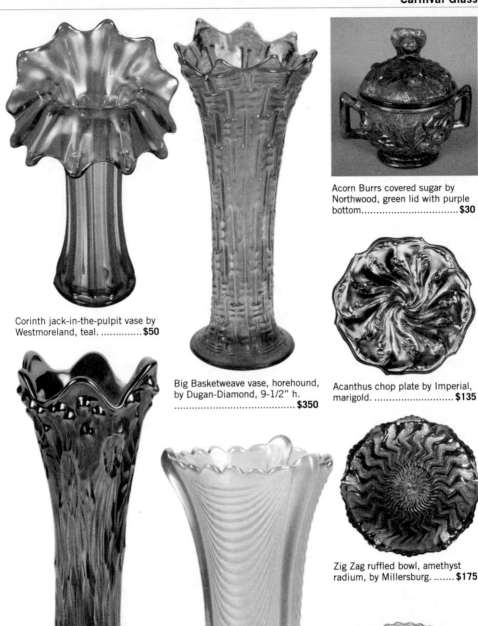

Corinth jack-in-the-pulpit vase by Westmoreland, teal. **$50**

Big Basketweave vase, horehound, by Dugan-Diamond, 9-1/2" h. **$350**

Acorn Burrs covered sugar by Northwood, green lid with purple bottom.................................. **$30**

Acanthus chop plate by Imperial, marigold. **$135**

Zig Zag ruffled bowl, amethyst radium, by Millersburg. **$175**

Bullseye and Beads vase by Fenton, blue, 11-1/4" h. **$350**

Drapery vase, ice blue, by Northwood, 7-1/4" h........... **$200**

Grapevine Lattice ruffled bowl, white, by Dugan, 7"............. **$30**

GLASS

Curved Star bowl with flower frog by U.S. Glass, marigold, 5-1/2" h. x 6-1/2" w. ....**$150-$200**

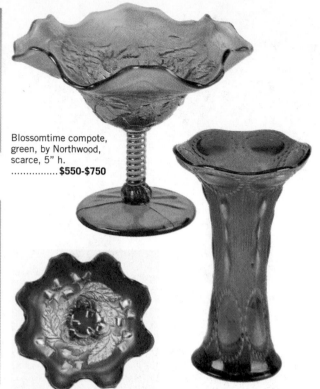

Blossomtime compote, green, by Northwood, scarce, 5" h. ....**$550-$750**

Blackberry Open Edge basket by Fenton, two sides up, red, 7". $250

Acorn bowl, ruffled, by Fenton, dark red, 6-1/2" dia............ **$400**

Beaded Bullseye vase, amber, by Imperial, scarce, 8-1/2" h. ....**$300-$400**

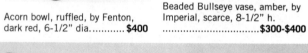

Checkerboard water pitcher and six tumblers by Westmoreland, amethyst. **$4,100**

Field Thistle vase by U.S. Glass, light marigold..................... **$325**

Inverted Feather cracker jar, green, by Cambridge........................ **$175**

Imperial Grape carafe by Imperial, purple, 9" h.............**$200-$400**

Floral and Grape ruffled-top pitcher, purple, by Dugan, 8-1/2" h. ....**$250-$400**

Grape and Cable fernery with crystal inset by Northwood, amethyst. .**$400**

Gothic Arches vase, smoke, by Imperial, 11" h., mouth 7-1/2" dia. ....**$1,100-$1,500**
Outstanding example **$2,500**

GLASS

Nippon ruffled bowl with basketweave exterior, purple with near-electric iridescence, by Northwood. **$475**

Hobnail spittoon, marigold, by Millersburg, radium iridescence. **$300**

Cosmos and Cane square bowl by U.S. Glass, honey amber. **$70**

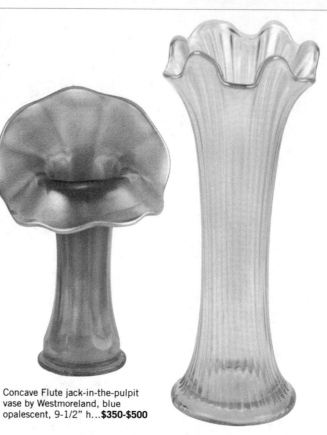

Concave Flute jack-in-the-pulpit vase by Westmoreland, blue opalescent, 9-1/2" h...**$350-$500**

Fine Rib vase by Northwood, ice green................................. **$450**

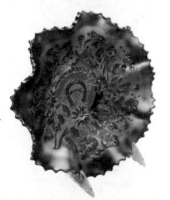

Good Luck ruffled bowl, electric blue, by Northwood, 8-1/2". ....**$300-$500**
Outstanding example **$900**

Hanging Cherries water pitcher by Millersburg, radium green...... **$900**

GLASS

Leaf and Beads nut bowl, aqua opalescent, by Northwood, footed, flared............................ **$1,500**

Lustre Rose tumbler, celeste blue, by Imperial. **$200**

Palm Beach vase, white, by U.S. Glass. **$250**

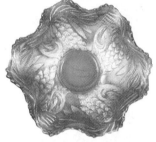

Pine Cone ruffled bowl, marigold, by Fenton, 7" dia. **$20**

Persian Medallion flat plate, black amethyst, by Fenton, 6-1/4" dia. ....**$250-$400**

Morning Glory, miniature vase, marigold, by Imperial, 3-1/2" h., shortest known. .... **$150-$250**

Rose Show plate, marigold over custard, by Northwood, extremely rare. **$11,000**

Inverted Thistle water pitcher and six tumblers, amethyst, by Cambridge. **$1,500**

GLASS

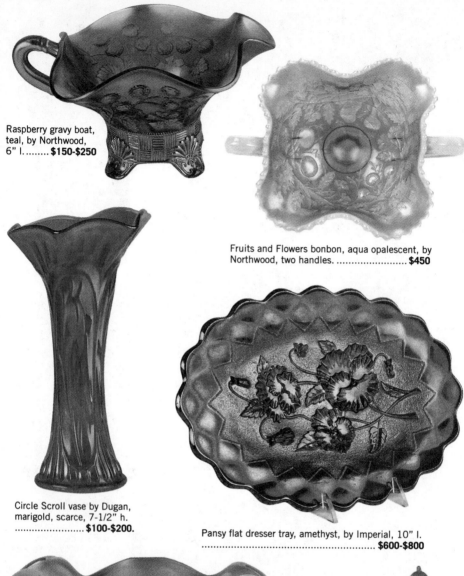

Raspberry gravy boat, teal, by Northwood, 6" l. .... **$150-$250**

Fruits and Flowers bonbon, aqua opalescent, by Northwood, two handles. **$450**

Circle Scroll vase by Dugan, marigold, scarce, 7-1/2" h. .... **$100-$200.**

Pansy flat dresser tray, amethyst, by Imperial, 10" l. .... **$600-$800**

Pearly Dots compote, blue opalescent, by Westmoreland, scarce, 4-1/2" dia. .... **$200-$350**

Leaf Tiers covered sugar and creamer, marigold, by Fenton. **$200**

Wreath of Roses punch bowl, base and two cups (not shown), Vintage interior, square, green, by Fenton. **$650**

Wisteria water pitcher and one tumbler, tankard, ice blue. **$10,000**

Wide Rib vase, peach opalescent, by Dugan/Diamond, 5" h. **$130**

Tree Trunk mid-size vase, green, by Northwood, 12" h. ..**$350-$650**

Roses and Ruffles lamp, Gone with the Wind, by Consolidated Glass, marigold. **$2,800**

Pulled Loop vase, purple with opalescent tips, by Dugan/Diamond, 8-1/2" h. **$550**

CENTRAL GLASS

From the 1890s until its closing in 1939, the Central Glass Co. of Wheeling, West Virginia, produced colorless and colored handmade glass in all the styles then popular. Decorations from etchings with acid to hand-painted enamels were used.

The popular "Depression" era colors of black, pink, green, light blue, ruby red and others were all produced. Two of its 1920s etchings are still familiar today, one named for the then-president of the United States and the other for the governor of West Virginia: Harding and Morgan patterns.

From high-end art glass to mass-produced plain barware tumblers, Central Glass Co. was a major glass producer throughout the period.

No. 796 / Rope and Thumbprint sugar shaker, blue, period lid, fourth quarter 19th century, undamaged, scattered light exterior wear, 5-1/4" h. overall. ...**$115**

Jeffrey S. Evans & Associates

Two U.S. Coin covered compotes, colorless with frosted coins and finial, each featuring nine quarters and six dimes, fourth quarter 19th century, 9" to 10" h. overall. **$184**

Jeffrey S. Evans & Associates

Columbian Coin Stand lamp, colorless with frosted coins, round paneled font, No. 1 Taplin-Brown collar, fitted with period No. 1 slip burner and chimney with beaded top, fourth quarter 19th century, 9-5/8" h. to top of collar, 5" dia. font, 4-1/2" dia. base. **$219**

Jeffrey S. Evans & Associates

U.S. Coin open compote, colorless with frosted coins, featuring nine quarters and six dimes, fourth quarter 19th century, 5-3/4" h., bowl 7-1/8" dia. **$288**

Jeffrey S. Evans & Associates

CONSOLIDATED GLASS

The Consolidated Lamp & Glass Co. of Coraopolis, Pennsylvania, was founded in 1894. For a number of years it was noted for its lighting wares but also produced popular lines of pressed and blown tableware. Highly collectible glass patterns of this early era include the Cone, Cosmos, Florette and Guttate lines.

Lamps and shades continued to be good sellers, but in 1926 a new "art" line of molded decorative wares was introduced. This "Martelè" line was developed as a direct imitation of the fine glassware being produced by Renè Lalique of France, and many Consolidated patterns resembled their French counterparts. Other popular lines produced during the 1920s and 1930s were Dancing Nymph, the delightfully Art Deco Ruba Rombic introduced in 1928, and the Catalonian line, which debuted in 1927 and imitated 17th-century Spanish glass.

Although the factory closed in 1933, it was reopened under new management in 1936 and prospered through the 1940s. It finally closed in 1967. Collectors should note that many later Consolidated patterns closely resemble wares of other competing firms, especially the Phoenix Glass Co. Careful study is needed to determine the maker of pieces from the 1920-1940 era.

A book that will be of help to collectors is *Phoenix & Consolidated Art Glass, 1926-1980*, by Jack D. Wilson (Antique Publications, 1989).

Blackberry umbrella vase, amber wash, factory ground rim, second quarter 20th century, undamaged, 18" h. ... **$150**

Jeffrey S. Evans & Associates

Nude Art Deco vase, creamy yellow background with dancing nudes with blue scarves, one satyr playing instrument, very good condition with one chip at fitter rim, 12" h. **$115**

James D. Julia, Inc.

Two Bulging Loops toothpick holders, opaque blue and opaque green, factory polished rims, fourth quarter 19th century, green example undamaged, other with rim flakes/roughness, 2-3/8" h. **$104**

Jeffrey S. Evans & Associates

Bulging Loops toothpick holder, cased pink, factory polished rim, fourth quarter 19th century, excellent condition with two minor rim flakes, body casing with two annealing lines, as made, 2-3/8" h. **$35**

Jeffrey S. Evans & Associates

Figural glass Santa Claus miniature lamp, opaque white, red suit, font consists of his boots standing on a mound of snow, period burner, fourth quarter 19th century, undamaged, 9-1/4" h. to top of shade, 3-1/4" dia. base... **$2,415**

Jeffrey S. Evans & Associates

Two Bulging Loops tumblers, pigeon blood red, factory polished rims, fourth quarter 19th century, undamaged, 3-3/4" h. **$138**

Jeffrey S. Evans & Associates

Bi-color on satin opal Nuthatch oblong bowl and blue wash Pine Cone vase, second quarter 20th century, bowl undamaged, vase with shallow chip to under edge of rim, 4-1/2" x 9-1/2", and 6-1/2" h. **$150**

Jeffrey S. Evans & Associates

GLASS

CRANBERRY GLASS

Gold was added to glass batches to give cranberry glass its color on reheating. It has been made by many glasshouses for years and is currently being reproduced. Both blown and molded articles were produced. A less expensive type of cranberry glass was made with the substitution of copper for gold.

Victorian decorated salt and pepper shakers, two pairs, cranberry/ruby, each with optic pattern, a pair with satin finish and Impasto Cameo floral decoration, and a pair with polychrome floral decoration, three with original two-part lid, fourth quarter 19th century, undamaged with some light wear, 2" and 2-1/2" h. overall...**$58**

Jeffrey S. Evans & Associates

Bohemian epergne, cranberry with gilded bronze floral scrolled framing, each flute painted with gilt design depicting flowers, 19th century, 22-1/2" h. x 15-1/2" w....... **$1,200**

Elite Decorative Arts

Spot Optic pickle caster, cranberry with full-round polychrome decoration, E. G. Webster & Bros. triple-plate stand with tongs, fourth quarter 19th century, very good overall condition, 9-1/8" h. overall, jar 4-5/8" h., 2-7/8" dia. base. **$460**

Jeffrey S. Evans & Associates

Spot Optic pickle caster, cranberry with polychrome bird and floral decoration, E. G. Webster & Son #67 quadruple-plate stand with applied pickles and leaves around base, dog finial cover and tongs, fourth quarter 19th century, excellent condition with minor flake to interior rim of jar, 9" h. overall. **$920**

Jeffrey S. Evans & Associates

Spot Optic pickle caster, cranberry with full-round polychrome decoration, silver-plate stand with tongs, base with souvenir presentation engraving, fourth quarter 19th century, undamaged, 12-3/4" h. overall, jar 4-1/2" h., 2-7/8" dia. base. **$403**

Jeffrey S. Evans & Associates

GLASS

◀ Hobbs No. 346 Optic Ribbed No. 5 jug/water pitcher, cased ruby/cranberry, colorless applied handle, polished pontil mark, Hobbs, Brockunier & Co., fourth quarter 19th century, undamaged, 9" h. overall.........................**$92**

Jeffrey S. Evans & Associates

▶ Ring Neck-Rib Optic sugar shaker, cranberry, period lid, Hobbs, Brockunier & Co. and Northwood Glass Co., fourth quarter 19th century, excellent condition with minor wear, 4-5/8" h. overall... **$92**

Jeffrey S. Evans & Associates

Two Leaf Mold salt shakers, frosted cranberry and vaseline (uranium), each with period lid, Northwood Glass Co., fourth quarter 19th century, undamaged, lids with wear, 2-1/2" h. overall............................... **$316**

Jeffrey S. Evans & Associates

Opaline Brocade/Spanish Lace water pitcher, cranberry opalescent, tri-corner crimped rim, colorless applied handle, late 19th/early 20th century, undamaged, 9-3/4" h. overall. **$431**

Jeffrey S. Evans & Associates

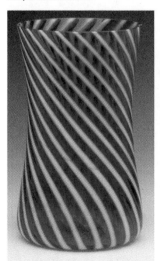

Hobbs No. 325/Opal Swirl celery vase, ruby opalescent/cranberry opalescent, Hobbs, Brockunier & Co., fourth quarter 19th century, undamaged, 6-1/2 h. **$173**

Jeffrey S. Evans & Associates

Ribbed Opal Lattice sugar shaker, cranberry with opalescence, period lid, late 19th/early 20th century, undamaged, lid with some light denting, 4-5/8" h. overall. **$138**

Jeffrey S. Evans & Associates

Daisy and Fern water pitcher and tumbler, cranberry opalescent, shoulder-mold pitcher with flared crimped rim, colorless applied reeded handle, late 19th/early 20th century, pitcher undamaged, tumbler with small faint rim bruise, pitcher 9-3/8" h. overall, tumbler 3-3/4" h. **$259**

Jeffrey S. Evans & Associates

GLASS

Coinspot five-piece water set, cranberry opalescent, ball-form water pitcher with square-form rim, colorless applied handle with pressed fan design to upper terminal, polished pontil mark, four tumblers, Beaumont Glass Co., early 20th century, very good condition, 8" h. overall, tumblers 3-3/4" h. **$288**

Jeffrey S. Evans & Associates

Hobbs Seaweed/Coral bulbous base syrup pitcher, cranberry opalescent, colorless applied handle, period lid, Hobbs, Brockunier & Co./Beaumont Glass Co., late 19th/early 20th century, undamaged with minor high-point wear, 6-3/8" h. overall. **$489**

Jeffrey S. Evans & Associates

Coinspot four-bottle condiment set, cranberry opalescent salt and pepper shakers with matching period lids, blue opalescent mustard jar with period lid, colorless opalescent oil bottle lacking stopper, fitted in Karanti nickel silver frame, late 19th/early 20th century, excellent condition, frame 8-1/4" h. overall, condiments 3-3/4" to 4-3/8" h. overall. **$150**

Jeffrey S. Evans & Associates

▲ Hobbs No. 325 Opal Swirl/Stripe pair of salt and pepper shakers, ruby opalescent/cranberry opalescent, cylinder form with ring neck, matching period lids, Hobbs, Brockunier & Co., fourth quarter 19th century, excellent condition, 6-3/8" h. overall....................**$115**

Jeffrey S. Evans & Associates

◄ Two Opaline Brocade/Spanish Lace tumblers, cranberry and bittersweet opalescent, factory polished rims, late 19th/early 20th century, undamaged, 3-7/8" h. **$403**

Jeffrey S. Evans & Associates

GLASS

CUSTARD GLASS

"Custard glass," as collectors call it today, came on the American scene in the 1890s, more than a decade after similar colors were made in Europe and England. The Sowerby firm of Gateshead-on-Tyne, England had marketed its patented "Queen's Ivory Ware" quite successfully in the late 1870s and early 1880s.

There were many glass tableware factories operating in Pennsylvania and Ohio in the 1890s and early 1900s, and the competition among them was keen. Each company sought to capture the public's favor with distinctive colors and, often, hand-painted decoration. That is when "custard glass" appeared on the American scene.

The opaque yellow color of this glass varies from a rich, vivid yellow to a lustrous light yellow. Regardless of intensity, the hue was originally called "ivory" by several glass manufacturers who also used superlative sounding terms such as "Ivorina Verde" and "Carnelian." Most custard glass contains uranium, so it will "glow" under a black light.

The most important producer of custard glass was certainly Harry Northwood, who first made it at his plants in Indiana, Pennsylvania, in the late 1890s and, later, in his Wheeling, West Virginia, factory. Northwood marked some of his most famous patterns, but much early custard is unmarked. Other key manufacturers include Heisey Glass Co., Newark, Ohio; Jefferson Glass Co., Steubenville, Ohio; Tarentum Glass Co., Tarentum, Pennsylvania; and Fenton Art Glass Co., Williamstown, West Virginia.

Custard glass fanciers are particular about condition and generally insist on pristine quality decorations free from fading or wear. Souvenir custard pieces with events, places, and dates on them usually bring the best prices in the areas commemorated on them rather than from the specialist collector. Also, collectors who specialize in pieces such as cruets, syrups, or salt and pepper shakers will often pay higher prices for these pieces than would a custard collector.

Key reference sources include William Heacock's *Custard Glass from A to Z,* published in 1976 but not out of print, and the book *Harry Northwood: The Early Years,* available from Glass Press. Heisey's custard glass is discussed in *Shirley Dunbar's Heisey Glass: The Early Years* (Krause Publications, 2000), and Coudersport's production is well-documented in Tulla Majot's book, *Coudersport's Glass 1900-1904* (Glass Press, 1999). The Custard Glass Society holds a yearly convention and maintains a web site: www.homestead.com/custardsociety.

— *James Measell*

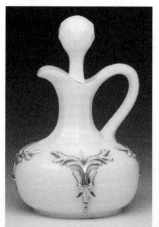

◄ Winged Scroll cruet, custard with gilt decoration, custard faceted stopper, A. H. Heisey & Co., late 19th/early 20th century, cruet undamaged, light wear to gilt decoration, stopper with light hairline, 5-3/4" h. overall. ... **$150**

Jeffrey S. Evans & Associates

► Argonaut Shell/Nautilus cruet, custard with gilt decoration, original shell-shaped stopper, Northwood Glass Co., late 19th/ early 20th century, undamaged, minor wear to gilt decoration, 6-3/4" h. overall................. **$184**

Jeffrey S. Evans & Associates

GLASS

Three various opaque tumblers, including custard Libbey Maize with blue decoration and custard Heisey Winged Scroll with gilt decoration, late 19th/early 20th century, undamaged except for minor flake under base of Heisey example, 3-1/2" to 4" h. **$92**

Jeffrey S. Evans & Associates

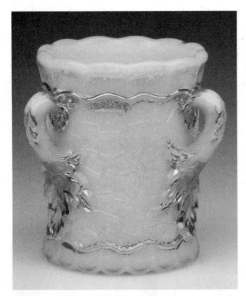

Wild Bouquet toothpick holder, custard with stained and gilt decoration, Northwood Glass Co., early 20th century, undamaged with expected light wear to decorations, 2-1/2" h. overall. **$259**

Jeffrey S. Evans & Associates

Maple Leaf toothpick holder, custard with green and gilt decoration, Northwood Glass Co., early 20th century, very good condition, 2-3/8" h. overall..............**$173**

Jeffrey S. Evans & Associates

CUT GLASS

Cut glass is made by grinding decorations into glass by means of abrasive-carrying metal or stone wheels. An ancient craft, it was revived in 1600 by Bohemians and spread through Europe to Great Britain and America.

American cut glass came of age at the Centennial Exposition in 1876 and the World Columbian Exposition in 1893. America's most significant output of high-quality glass occurred from 1880 to 1917, a period now known as the Brilliant Period. Glass from this period is the most eagerly sought glass by collectors.

Spirit decanter cut from cobalt to clear, fans and cross-cut diamonds on bulbous body with fluting on slender neck, 16-point ray cut in base, clear ball stopper cut with decorative nail heads, interior stain and minor usage nicks, 9-1/4" h. **$80**

Mark Mussio, Humler & Nolan

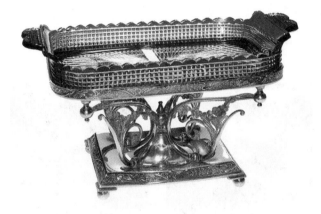

Ice cream tray, rectangular, cobalt cut to clear, fitted within Wilcox silver-plate stand, waffle pattern on sides and handles, crossed bars to center flanked by fans, excellent condition, 7-1/2" h., 1-5/8" x 14-1/4" x 8" across.. **$500**

Mark Mussio, Humler & Nolan

American brilliant cut glass cloverleaf bowl, colorless, triangular form, late 19th/early 20th century, very good condition with several minor flakes, rim with small bruise, 4-1/8" h. x 9-1/2" w. overall. **$288**

Jeffrey S. Evans & Associates

Two-piece American cut glass punch bowl with stand, circa 1900, bowl 12-3/8" h. x 14-1/4" dia., stand 5-7/8" h. x 9-1/2" dia. **$750**

Heritage Auctions

Cut glass vase, cobalt, 17" h. x 8" dia. **$50**

Kaminski Auctions

"Diamonds and Silver Threads" cut glass tray, colorless, rectangular form with central engraved hanging basket and different engraved flower in each shoulder reserve, not signed, H. P. Sinclaire & Co., Corning, New York, first quarter 20th century, undamaged with some light roughness wear to threads under base, 10" x 8". **$161**

Jeffrey S. Evans & Associates

Hawkes "St. Regis" brilliant cut glass set of five goblets, colorless, four examples signed on foot, late 19th/early 20th century, four examples undamaged, one with polished foot, 5-3/4" h. **$150**

Jeffrey S. Evans & Associates

Libbey "Empress" brilliant cut glass flower center vase, colorless, facet cut ring neck with signature, Libbey Glass Co., early 20th century, very good condition, 6-7/8" h. overall, 9-3/4" w. overall.................**$374**

Jeffrey S. Evans & Associates

Two brilliant cut glass lamps, 20th century, signed illegibly, 34-1/2" h. **$550**

Kaminski Auctions

Dorflinger brilliant cut glass cigar jar, cranberry cut to colorless, shoulder with band of cut punties over buttons and hobstars, fitted with marked Rothrock sterling silver cover, late 19th/early 20th century, very good condition, 9" h. overall, 5-7/8" dia. base.
......................................**$1,150**

Jeffrey S. Evans & Associates

Brilliant cut footed compote, 12" h. x 14-5/8" dia........... **$150**

Kaminski Auctions

J. Hoare & Co. "Elfin" brilliant cut glass flower center vase, colorless, late 19th/early 20th century, good condition, 7-1/2" h. overall, 10" w. overall. **$518**

Jeffrey S. Evans & Associates

CZECHOSLOVAKIAN GLASS

The country of Czechoslovakia, including the glassmaking region of Bohemia, was not founded as an independent republic until after the close of World War I in 1918. The new country soon developed a large export industry, including a wide range of brightly colored and hand-painted glasswares such as vases, tableware, and perfume bottles. Fine quality cut crystal or Bohemian-type etched wares were also produced for the American market. Some Bohemian glass carries faint acid-etched markings on the base.

With the breakup of Czechoslovakia into two republics, the wares produced between World War I and II should gain added collector appeal.

Glue-chipped glass vase, yellow with mottled polychrome spatter, pinched upper body, factory polished rim, acid "Czechoslovakia" stamp under base, first quarter 20th century, edge of base with shallow chip and two flakes, 8" h. **$150**

Jeffrey S. Evans & Associates

Two Art Deco glass snack sets, opaque black and orange with silver overlay decoration, two round trays and matching footed tumblers marked with circular acid stamp, first half 20th century, undamaged, trays 6-1/4" d., tumblers 3-1/2" h...**$81**

Jeffrey S. Evans & Associates

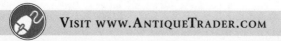

Bohemian glass pitcher, 19th
century, 11-7/8 x 6-1/2".. **$1,200**

Kaminski Auctions

Two art glass articles, basket with tortoise shell-type decoration and
acid stamped mark around polished pontil mark and green vase with
red paisley-style decoration and polished rim, first quarter 20th century,
undamaged, 6-1/2" and 6" h..**$219**

Jeffrey S. Evans & Associates

Loetz

Iridescent glass, some of it somewhat resembling that of
Tiffany and other contemporary glasshouses, was produced by
the Bohemian firm of J. Loetz Witwe of Klostermule and is
referred to as Loetz. Some cameo pieces were also made. Not
all pieces are marked.

Small Phanomen vase, Austria,
circa 1900, unmarked, 6-1/4" x
2-1/2".......................... **$1,750**

Rago Arts and Auction Center

Iridescent glass vase in floriform
pewter stand, Austria, circa 1900,
unmarked, 7-1/4" x 3-1/2".**$1,188**

Rago Arts and Auction Center

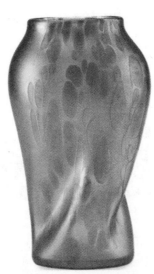

Asträa vase, Austria, circa 1900,
etched "Loetz Austria," 7" x 4".
.... **$3,500**

Rago Arts and Auction Center

Iridescent glass vase with blue
and green swirl decoration,
Austria, circa 1900, etched "Loetz
Austria," 6" x 5-1/2". **$1,875**

Rago Arts and Auction Center

Iridescent glass vase with ripple decoration in pink and orange, Austria, circa 1900, etched "Loetz Austria," 9-1/2" x 5". **$2,875**

Rago Arts and Auction Center

Federzeichnung glass ewer, cased chocolate brown with gilt tracery decoration, air-trap pearlized octopus pattern with connecting trails, base handwritten "Patent," fitted with silver-plate hinged lid and handle, fourth quarter 19th century, lower body with two light bruises, expected minor wear to gilt decoration, 8-3/4" h. overall, 2-3/4" dia. base. **$1,093**

Jeffrey S. Evans & Associates

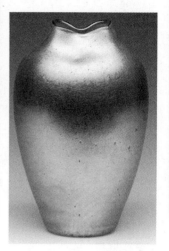

Bronce vase, gold iridescent, pinched square rim, polished pontil mark, late 19th/early 20th century, undamaged, 7-1/4" h. **$259**

Jeffrey S. Evans & Associates

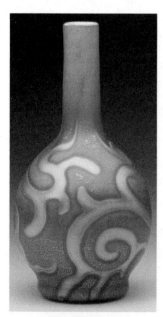

Federzeichnung glass vase, cased honey amber with gilt tracery decoration, air-trap pearlized octopus pattern with connecting trails, ball form, base handwritten "Pat 9159," fourth quarter 19th century, undamaged, some expected wear to gilt decoration, 10-1/8" h., 3-3/8" dia. base. **$978**

Jeffrey S. Evans & Associates

Diaspora vase, wavy textured gold cased over pearlized pink, body pinched in three areas, surface brightened with citron with blue at base, excellent condition, 7" h. **$1,200**

Mark Mussio, Humler & Nolan

Cret Rusticana vase, green iridescent, waisted form with flared rim and polished pontil mark, early 20th century, undamaged, 7" h. **$115**

Jeffrey S. Evans & Associates

GLASS

◀ Asträa pattern vase, honey balloon-shaped body finished in gold reflecting blue iridescence, surface spattered with "raindrops" all around, excellent condition, 8-1/4" h. x 7" w. **$325**

Mark Mussio, Humler & Nolan

▲ G Asträa silver overlay vase, gold iridescent finish with blue and platinum highlights and amber-colored oil spots, silver overlay in form of flowing flowers, stems and leaves surrounding body, very good to excellent condition, 4-1/2" h. **$2,300**

James D. Julia, Inc.

◀ Bulbous form vase, zipper pattern in blue iridescence with pink highlights, decorated around widest part of body with wave pattern in same blue iridescence against yellow background, very good to excellent condition, 3-1/2" h. **$1,093**

James D. Julia, Inc.

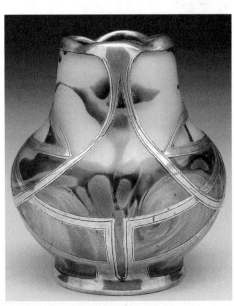

Creta Papillon vase with half twist body and free form clover leaf rim, attributed to Jutta Sika, designer of vases with distorted bodies, rainbow iridescence on surface, excellent condition, 4-3/4" h.
....**$250**

Mark Mussio, Humler & Nolan

Silver overlay vase decorated with mottled and swirled amber glass on bottom half, cream-colored frosted glass top half with splashes of forest green, overlaid with flowing lines of sterling silver, very good to excellent condition, 4" h. **$2,875**

James D. Julia, Inc.

Silver overlay vase, melon ribbed, blue iridescence with random threaded design, Art Nouveau silver overlay pattern on front three melon ribs, silver band encircling foot and lip, very good to excellent condition, 6-1/2" h....................................... **$4,600**

James D. Julia, Inc.

Phänomen vase, Genere 8100, attributed to Belgian artist Franz Hofstätter, unusual squashed form actualized from ruby red, surface arrayed with superimposed rhythmic patterns in blue Aurene with reddish and golden tones, engraved with crossed arrows and four stars within a circle and Austria in script on and near the polished pontil, excellent condition, 6-1/2" h. x 8-1/2" w. (Few examples created late in the 1890s have the company's crossed arrow mark.)...................................**$11,000**

Mark Mussio, Humler & Nolan

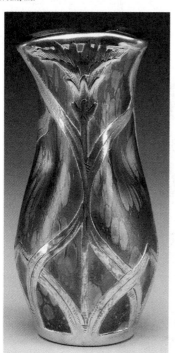

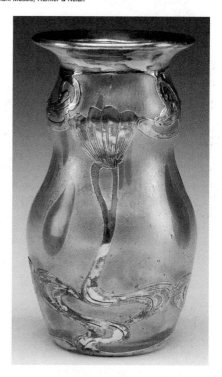

Silver overlay vase, blue iridescent oil spot design against transparent green background with light iridescence, pinched neck, overlaid with silver Art Nouveau floral design, silver marked "Patented B68" with Alvin Silver Co. trademark, very good to excellent condition, 5" h. **$2,875**

James D. Julia, Inc.

Asträa silver overlay vase, random large amber oil spots against clear glass background with light bluish iridescence, overlaid with sterling silver Art Nouveau floral design, very good to excellent condition, 4" h. **$1,150**

James D. Julia, Inc.

Moser

Ludwig Moser opened his first glass shop in 1857 in Karlsbad, Bohemia (now Karlovy Vary, Czechoslovakia). Here he engraved and decorated fine glasswares especially to appeal to rich visitors to the local health spa. Later other shops were opened in various cities. Throughout the 19th and early 20th centuries, lovely, colorful glasswares, many beautifully enameled, were produced by Moser's shops and reached a wide market in Europe and America. Moser died in 1916 and the firm continued under his sons. They were forced to merge with the Meyer's Nephews glass factory after World War I. The glassworks were sold out of the Moser family in 1933.

◄ Demitasse cup, cranberry glass decorated with white, green, blue and gold oak leaves with applied gold glass acorns and single enameled beetle, cup with applied glass handle in gold, very good to excellent condition with minor wear to gold, 2-3/4" h...................... **$345**

James D. Julia, Inc.

Cranberry glass pillow vase decorated with gold enameling and pink and blue flowers atop four applied curled glass feet, very good to excellent condition with wear to gold, 5" h. **$518**

James D. Julia, Inc.

Large amber paneled vase with applied blue glass accents and rigaree, applied bird, enameled insects, flowers and foliage, very good to excellent condition, 12-1/2" h. **$1,725**

James D. Julia, Inc.

Decorated pitcher, all over grapevines in gold on cranberry glass with applied and enameled bird and insects, thumbprint design and applied gold handle, numbered on bottom 8471, very good to excellent condition with minute wear to gold, 6" h. **$2,875**

James D. Julia, Inc.

Diamond-shaped vase decorated with enameled mallard ducks and intaglio cut marsh life with gold highlights on clear shaded to green glass, signed "Moser Karlsbad," very good to excellent condition with minor wear to underside, 7-1/2" h. x 6-1/4" w.
.... **$1,438**

James D. Julia, Inc.

Monumental cranberry vase enameled with design of heron by a stream, white, grey and brown bird with stream and foliage in earthen hues, two smaller birds on collar and one on reverse side of body, two applied glass handles with enameled foliage design, large circular foot with gold and white detailing, very good to excellent condition, 20" h.
.................................**$14,375**

James D. Julia, Inc.

Monumental applied decorated vase, three-dimensional bird design molded and enameled and finished with glass eye, enameled pattern of water lilies, lily pads and cattails at bottom against a clear to amethyst ground, top rim with gold gilding, unsigned, very good to excellent condition with minor wear to gold at rim, 16" h.
.... **$1,725**

James D. Julia, Inc.

Pair of aquatic life vases, blue bulbous crackle glass vases have applied fish with underwater flora, fish in green, orange and mauve with flowers enameled in pink, white and burgundy, gold highlighting, very good condition with repair to one fish head and minor wear to gold, 8" h.
....**$1,500-$2,000**

James D. Julia, Inc.

Monumental trumpet vase of topaz-colored glass decorated with yellow sunflowers with variegated green foliage and gold highlights throughout, very good to excellent condition, 31" h. **$2,990**

James D. Julia, Inc.

Decorated vase, applied and enameled decoration of bird on branch sitting amid blooms, amethyst bulbous form vase finished with gold bands and white dots, signed in script, very good to excellent condition, 10-1/2" h.
.... **$1,265**

James D. Julia, Inc.

Applied glass vase, applied glass hawk flies above marsh with three applied ducks, marsh enameled in gold with cattails and water lilies, body green to clear, very good to excellent condition, 10" h.
.... **$2,760**

James D. Julia, Inc.

Large topaz vase with blue applied glass foot, enameled decoration with blue bird resting amid flowers and foliage, flowers enameled in yellow, pink and blue, very good to excellent condition with minor wear to gold rim, 16-1/2" h.
.... **$3,163**

James D. Julia, Inc.

Pair of decorated vases, cranberry crackle glass enameled with grasshoppers, flowers and foliage, very good to excellent condition, 8-1/4" h. **$863**

James D. Julia, Inc.

Decorated clear to amethyst bulbous pillow vase with large scalloped rim, heavy enamel design of Art Nouveau poppies with applied bumblebees, very good to excellent condition with minor wear to gold at rim, 7-3/4" h. **$1,380**

James D. Julia, Inc.

Pair of floral decorated vases, amethyst receded to clear glass, flowers white to yellow to deep purple with green, gold highlights, gold rim, very good to excellent condition with minor wear to gold gilt, 15-1/2" h. **$748**

James D. Julia, Inc.

Pair of portrait cranberry pedestal vases decorated in gold, each with center medallion, one shows boy and girl at play, other shows boy and girl tending garden, very good to excellent condition with minor wear to gold, 14-1/2" h. **$3,163**

James D. Julia, Inc.

Pair of covered jars, each medium green glass with gold grapevines and applied glass bees, green lids with gold accents, jars signed in script, very good to excellent condition with minor wear to gold, 14-1/4" h. **$1,898**

James D. Julia, Inc.

DAUM NANCY

Daum Nancy fine glass, much of it cameo, was made by Auguste and Antonin Daum, who founded a factory in 1875 in Nancy, France. Most of their cameo and enameled glass was made from the 1890s into the early 20th century.

Cameo glass is made by carving into multiple layers of colored glass to create a design in relief. It is a process at least as old as the Romans.

◄ Vase with wheel-carved cameo decoration of orange and green flowers against frosted and marteled background, bulbous body and tall slender neck with martele decoration on shaded yellow, orange and green glass, signed on underside with engraved signature "Daum Nancy," very good to excellent condition, 9-1/2" h. **$23,000**

James D. Julia, Inc.

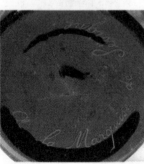

Mold blown vase with trees in high relief with church at mid ground, orange and yellow mottled background, signed "Daum Nancy" with Cross of Lorraine to underside, very good to excellent condition, 11-1/2" h........ **$9,200**

James D. Julia, Inc.

French cameo footed cup decorated with cameo and enameled columbine flowers with green stems and leaves and red columbine flowers set against acid-textured background of mottled brown shading to yellow, signed on side in cameo "Daum Nancy" and inscribed on underside in light brown "A La Marquise de Sevigne," very good to excellent condition, 4-1/2" h. **$2,588**

James D. Julia, Inc.

Cameo and enamel creamer, central flower with stems and clover-like leaves, flower is red shading to pink, stems and leaves enameled in gray with gold gilded highlights; backside of creamer decorated with same stems, leaves and single bud starting to blossom; lip decorated with gold band and cameo and enameled flowers, stems and leaves matching bottom decoration, applied frosted handle, textured opalescent background; front and back of creamer are flattened and pinched, signed on underside in gold "Daum Nancy" with Cross of Lorraine, very good to excellent condition with some touch-up to gold trim on top of lip, 3-1/2" h. **$1,495**

James D. Julia, Inc.

Wheel-carved vase with large autumnal leaves in dark cinnamon and sienna against orange and yellow mottled ground, bulbous shape with elongated neck and ends with flat lip, signed "Daum Nancy" with Cross of Lorraine to side of vase, very good to excellent condition, 11" h. **$8,625**

James D. Julia, Inc.

French cameo Thistle vase, cameo and enamel decoration of thistles with green thorn stems and leaves and red thistle flowers and buds set against acid-textured background of mottled yellow and green with faint swirling stripes of blue and red, signed on side in cameo "Daum Nancy" with Cross of Lorraine, very good to excellent condition, 8-1/2" h.......... **$2,760**

James D. Julia, Inc.

Mushroom vase, bulbous body with cameo decoration of various types and colors of mushrooms, underside of mushrooms are wheel-carved and enameled in brown, orange and green, mottled yellow shading to cream-colored background extends up long slender neck, top of neck decorated with cameo pinecones with pine needles falling down side of neck, neck finished with acid-textured background, signed on underside with engraved "Daum Nancy" with Cross of Lorraine, very good to excellent condition, 25" h.............**$17,250**

James D. Julia, Inc.

"Winter" vase, four sides with barren woodland and tire-tracked roadways, meadow covered with dusting of snow, orange to yellow sky, enameled "Daum Nancy" beneath, excellent condition, 4-1/2" h. **$2,000**

Mark Mussio, Humler & Nolan

◄ French cameo vase, snow scene with deciduous trees and snow-covered ground on yellow and orange mottled background, signed "Daum Nancy" with Cross of Lorraine to underside of base, very good to excellent condition, 4-1/2" h. **$2,185**

James D. Julia, Inc.

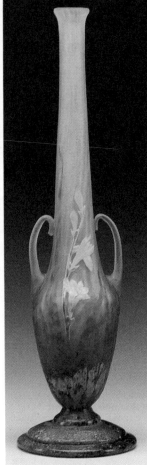

Rain scene vase, rare, swaying trees in dark earthen hues against pink, green and frost ground, rain depicted in clear glass against background, signed "Daum Nancy" with Cross of Lorraine to underside of vase, very good to excellent condition, 6" h. **$10,350**

James D. Julia, Inc.

French cameo pinecone vase, bulbous body and long, slender neck decorated with cameo and enamel pinecones descending from lip down to body enameled with gray trees along shoreline with areas of aquatic vegetation against mottled pink shading to yellow background, signed in cameo "Daum Nancy" with Cross of Lorraine, very good to excellent condition, 16-1/2" h. **$4,600**

James D. Julia, Inc.

French cameo vase, rare padded floral design in apricot against orange, yellow and ivory mottled ground, inverted saucer foot and two applied glass handles, very good to excellent condition, 13" h. **$8,050**

James D. Julia, Inc.

French cameo vase, brown cameo decoration of leaves and thorned stems with prickly seed pods against mottled green, yellow and white background, signed on side "Daum Nancy" with Cross of Lorraine "France," very good to excellent condition, 6" h. x 6" dia. **$1,150**

James D. Julia, Inc.

◄ Small cameo glass enamel-decorated bowl, circa 1905, etched Daum Nancy France, 2" x 4-1/4". **$1,250**

Rago Arts and Auction Center

DEPRESSION GLASS

Depression glass is the name of colorful glassware collectors generally associated with mass-produced glassware found in pink, yellow, crystal, or green in the years surrounding the Great Depression in America.

The housewives of the Depression-era were able to enjoy the wonderful colors offered in this new inexpensive glass dinnerware because they received pieces of their favorite patterns packed in boxes of soap, or as premiums given at "dish night" at the local movie theater. Merchandisers, such as Sears & Roebuck and F. W. Woolworth, enticed young brides with the colorful wares that they could afford even when economic times were harsh.

Because of advancements in glassware technology, Depression-era patterns were mass-produced and could be purchased for a fraction of what cut glass or lead crystal cost. As one manufacturer found a pattern that was pleasing to the buying public, other companies soon followed with their adaptation of a similar design. Patterns included several design motifs, such as florals, geometrics, and even patterns that looked back to Early American patterns like Sandwich glass.

As America emerged from the Great Depression and life became more leisure-oriented again, new glassware patterns were created to reflect the new tastes of this generation. More elegant shapes and forms were designed, leading to what is sometimes called "Elegant Glass." Today's collectors often include these more elegant patterns when they talk about Depression-era glassware.

Depression-era glassware is one of the best-researched collecting areas available to the American marketplace. This is due in large part to the careful research of several people, including Hazel Marie Weatherman, Gene Florence, Barbara Mauzy, Carl F. Luckey, and Kent Washburn. Their books are held in high regard by researchers and collectors today.

Regarding values for Depression glass, rarity does not always equate to a high dollar amount. Some more readily found items command lofty prices because of high demand or other factors, not because they are necessarily rare. As collectors' tastes range from the simple patterns to the more elaborate patterns, so does the ability of their budget to invest in inexpensive patterns to multi-hundreds of dollars per form patterns.

For more information on Depression glass, see *Warman's Depression Glass Identification and Price Guide*, 5th Edition, or *Warman's Depression Glass Field Guide*, 5th Edition, both by Ellen T. Schroy.

Thumbprint, green luncheon plate, Federal Glass Co. **$7**

Old Colony, pink 9-1/2" dia. bowl, ribbed, Hocking Glass Co. **$38**

GLASS

American Sweetheart, pink cup, MacBeth-Evans Glass Co.. .... **$18**

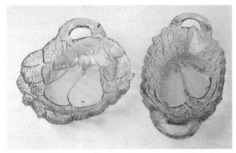

Avocado No. 601, green preserve bowl with handle, Indiana Glass Co.. **$32**
Bowl with two handles.................................... **$38**

Circle, green pitcher, 80 oz., Hocking Glass Co....**$30**

Adam, pink 10" oval bowl, Jeannette Glass Co....**$40**

Beaded Block, ice blue vase, Imperial Glass Co..**$85**
Crystal jelly, stemmed. **$25**

Cherryberry, crystal 7-1/2" dia. deep bowl, U.S. Glass Co..**$17.50**

Bubble, forest green sugar, Hocking Glass Co.. ....**$18.50**

Cameo, green vegetable bowl, Hocking Glass Co. **$35**

Cherry Blossom, Delphite 4-3/4" dia. berry bowls, Jeannette Glass Co.
....**$15 ea.**

Block Optic, green 4-3/4" cone-shaped footed tumbler, Hocking Glass Co. **$28**

Colonial, green 3-3/8" h. sherbet, Hocking Glass Co. **$14**

Constellation, amber water goblet, Indiana Glass Co........**$15**

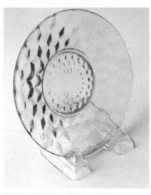

Cube, pink luncheon plate, Jeannette Glass Co. **$8.50**

Diana, crystal tumbler, Federal Glass Co.. ....**$18**

Florentine No. 2, green 7-1/2" footed cone pitcher, Hazel Atlas Glass Co.. ....**$40**

Homespun, pink 4" footed tumbler, Jeannette Glass Co. ...**$8**

Holiday, pink 9" dinner plate, Jeannette Glass Co..........................**$18**

Patrician, amber 5-1/4" footed tumbler, Federal Glass Co......**$40**

English Hobnail, crystal nappy with handle, Westmoreland Glass Co...**$22**

GLASS

Hex Optic, green 4-3/4" cone-shaped footed tumbler, Jeannette Glass Co. **$8**
5" flat tumbler. **$10**

Laurel, jade green dinner plate, McKee Glass Co..**$25**

Floral, green 9" oval vegetable bowl, Jeannette Glass Co. **$35**

Horseshoe, yellow cup, Indiana Glass Co......... **$10**

Diamond Quilted, green two-handled cream soup, Imperial Glass Co. **$12**

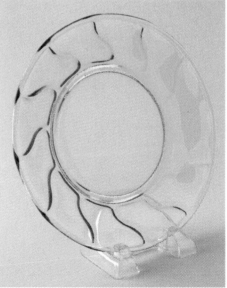

Forest Green, cup, Anchor Hocking Glass Co. **$7**
Saucer...**$3**

Jamestown, amber 8" plate, Fostoria Glass Co ... **$9.50**

GLASS

Old Café, pink candy jar with ruby cover, Hocking Glass Co.. .... **$32**

Oyster and Pearl, ruby sandwich plate, Anchor Hocking Glass Corp.. **$50**

Mayfair Open Rose, pink tumbler, 11 oz., Hocking Glass Co. **$225**
Pink satin-finish covered cookie jar.................. **$37**

Lincoln Inn, pink 8" plate, Fenton Art Glass Co...**$14**

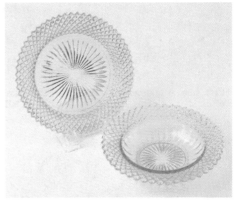

Miss America, green salad plate, Hocking Glass Co.
.... **$14**
Berry bowl.. **$30**

Normandie, iridescent dinner plate, Federal Glass Co.
.... **$25**

Moondrops, pink saucer, New Martinsville Glass Co. **$4**
Cup. **$12**

Princess, pink cup, Hocking Glass Co. **$12.50**

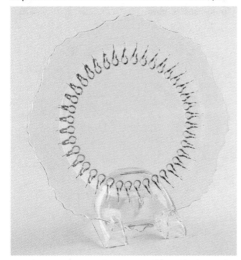

Radiance, ice blue plate, New Martinsville Glass Co. **$12**

Philbe, green creamer, Fire King. **$135**

Petalware, pink 5-1/4" cereal bowl, MacBeth-Evans Glass Co. **$12**

Patrick, yellow tray with caned center and two handles, Lancaster Glass Co. **$65**

Raindrops, green 4-1/2" dia. fruit bowl, Federal Glass Co. **$11**

Sandwich, crystal oval bowl, Hocking Glass Co....**$10**

Swirl, ultramarine 10-1/2" dinner plate, Jeannette Glass Co. **$30**
Closed-handled bowl. **$35**

Royal Ruby, Coolidge vase with original foil label, Anchor Hocking Glass Corp. **$20**

Rosemary, green platter, Federal Glass Co. **$24**

Ring, crystal sandwich server, Hocking Glass Co...**$15**

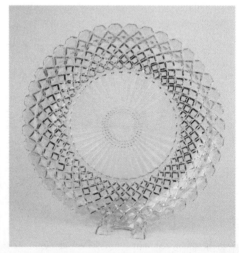

Waterford, crystal dinner plate, Hocking Glass Co.**$12**

Fire-King: King of Kitchenware

Fire-King dinnerware is a prime example of a vintage collectible that is affordable and usable. It is complementary when paired with more contemporary dinnerware patterns; pieces can easily be found in any number of styles from simple Restaurant Ware in plain, opaque white to fancy florals and bright geometrics.

Anchor Hocking Glass Corp. of Lancaster, Ohio, began producing low-cost, ovenproof, borosilicate low-expansion glass dinnerware marked "FIRE-KING" in 1942. Production ran through 1976, creating a plentiful supply of affordable table and ovenwares for households all over the country. It could be bought in sets or as single pieces; Fire-King items were often given away as grocery store premiums inside packages of pantry and cleaning supplies. Collectors often have fond memories of Fire-King from their youth, resulting in growing interest in the marketplace. Buyers are taking advantage of the ability to gather up affordable vintage pieces and use them to reconnect with a bit of the past.

GLASS

This vintage Fire-King Ovenglass advertisement guarantees better baking and two years against breakage.

Anchor Hocking

Fire-King is affordable both because there is a plentiful supply and because it's durable. It was produced around the clock for decades, so it can easily be found at estate and yard sales, as well as at auctions and online. Dealer Jay Hisle is a 30-plus year veteran of the trade and has been dealing exclusively in Fire-King for the last six years. He launched Grizzly-Wolf Fire-King on RubyLane.com after he decided to quit eBay. Hisle carries many rare pieces, but has noticed the most interest in Jade-ite and turquoise blue, especially D-handled mugs.

Jade-ite is very popular in Japan because jade is believed to bring good luck, health and prosperity, he said. Hisle does so much business with clients in Japan that his Fire-King descriptions are also listed in Japanese.

"Restaurant Ware is also a really good seller in Jade-ite and white; white is much more valuable because there was a lot less of it made," he said. Hisle reported instances of selling heavy Restaurant Ware C-handled mugs for $600 apiece, where a set of four mint-condition, C-handled Jade-ite mugs accompanied with their saucers is priced at $150.

A wide variety of advertising pieces, especially mugs, are available in the Fire-King brand. McDonald's "Good Morning" stacking mugs, originally given away with a specified breakfast purchase in 1976, can be found selling for less than $5 apiece; but a D-handled "Burger Queen" mug will set you back considerably more, perhaps as much as $40 or $50. Mugs advertising many local businesses are plentiful and have been selling in the $5 to $10 range online.

Hisle urges caution when buying advertising mugs because fakes abound. Some people are creating fantasy pieces by scanning in old logos from matchbooks with their computers and having them reprinted on old Fire-King mugs; they are being sold "for hundreds of dollars and buyers are being ripped off," he said. "It's hard to tell, but the graphics will be shinier. Older ones had a more matte finish."

Ron Cantrell has been collecting non-advertising Fire-King mugs for 15 to 20 years. He recalls his earliest interest stems from his father's favorite coffee mug: a plain ivory D-handled Fire-King mug. From that humble beginning, Cantrell and his family scoured estate sales and flea markets, searched online and ultimately expanded his collection to 560 different non-advertising Fire-King mugs.

Cantrell launched the informational website www.firekingmugs.com when he was exploring the possibility of writing his own book on Fire-King mugs. In lieu of a book, Cantrell decided to keep and maintain the website to provide collectors with as much "rock-solid information" as he could about collecting non-advertising Fire-King mugs, including identification and rarity details. His advice to collectors, beginning and advanced alike, is simple.

Five turquoise blue 6-5/8" Fire-King soup bowls in mint condition went to a new owner for $125 after eBay seller Tomkat Collectibles' listing ended Sept. 27, 2011. Tomkat specializes in selling Depression glass, elegant glass, Fire-King, Pyrex, pottery and dinnerware.

Tomkat Collectibles

"Buy the things you like and buy excellent condition," he said. "Beginners need to collect common, so they can get a feel for it."

Starting out by pursuing common pieces gives collectors much-needed experience for spotting cracks and flaws in authentic Fire-King, as well as what comes from the factory.

"Then they'll have better sense for spotting fakes," he said.

Unfortunately, the growing collector interest in Fire-King has blossomed into the burgeoning market of fakes, reproductions and fantasy pieces. Contemporary productions from Asia and Brazil are abundant in the marketplace; pieces marked "Fire-King Made in Japan" are new.

Buyers should educate themselves on shapes, sizes, patterns, and details. Take accurate measurements and compare them to trustworthy references to make sure you have the genuine article. If the measurements don't match, the piece may be a reproduction.

Fire-King's Red Baron mug with orange roof in very good condition earned $310 from a Nov. 27, 2011, eBay auction by seller "wisconsin-collectables." The mug is marked Copyright 1965 United Features Syndicate, Inc.

"wisconsin-collectables"

Authentic mugs have painted designs that are then fired on. Newer fakes and reproductions have a different, "softer" finish. Some of the fakes are even made by placing a super-sticky appliqué on a blank Fire-King mug. One example collectors should be aware of is the Disney Jiminy Cricket mug that is being reproduced with old Fire-King stock. Cantrell warns other Disney mugs are also out there that are just vinyl stick-ons; they don't come from the factory that way.

An example of rare mugs that to Cantrell's knowledge have not been reproduced and are still safe for collectors are children's "ABC" mugs; however, they are very hard to find and usually sell in the $400 to $500 range.

Cantrell has sold off most of his collection, keeping only 20 to 30 of the rarest examples, including a yellow-glass Philbe pattern mug that is extremely rare and one he suspects may be a "whimsy" piece. There are only one or two known to exist, and he turned down an offer of $500.

There are millions of pieces of Fire-King out there, so condition is key when collecting. It's important to check each piece of opaque glass very carefully because cracks and flaws are not as easy to spot as on clear glassware; try running your thumbnail around all edges to feel for chips and flea bites. Hisle advises if you are buying over the telephone or Internet, ask the seller as many questions about the condition as possible.

"A chipped mug, for example, nearly kills the value entirely, and you'd only want one chipped if it is both rare and needed to start or complete a set," he said.

Manufacturing flaws, such as minor roughness around mold lines, mold marks, dark specks found under the glaze and ripples, are common and shouldn't affect the value, Hisle said.

"Fire-King glassware at its best was an imperfect glassware," he said.

— *Karen Knapstien, Print Editor,* Antique Trader *magazine*

DUNCAN & MILLER

Duncan & Miller Glass Co., a successor firm to George A. Duncan & Sons Co., produced a wide range of pressed wares and novelty pieces during the late 19th century and into the early 20th century. During the Depression era and after, the company continued making a wide variety of more modern patterns, including mold-blown types, and also introduced a number of etched and engraved patterns. Many colors, including opalescent hues, were produced during this era, and especially popular today are the graceful swan dishes they produced in the Pall Mall and Sylvan patterns.

The numbers after the pattern name indicate the original factory pattern number. The Duncan factory was closed in 1955.

#42/Mardi Gras children's glass four-piece table set, colorless, covered butter dish, covered sugar bowl, creamer and spooner, fourth quarter 19th century, very good condition, 2-1/2" to 4-5/8" h. overall......**$115**

Jeffrey S. Evans & Associates

Two ruby-stained articles, colorless, #30 spooner and #45/Starred Loop butter dish, late 19th/early 20th century, spooner with pattern chip, butter cover undamaged, plate with crack, 4-1/4" and 5" h... **$69**

Jeffrey S. Evans & Associates

Eight various patterned children's glass items, colorless, each with slightly worn gilt decoration, #44/Button Panel table set and #42/Mardi Gras covered sugar, creamer, rose bowl and spooner, fourth quarter 19th century, early 20th century, very good overall condition, 2" to 4-1/2" h. overall. **$196**

Jeffrey S. Evans & Associates

GLASS

FENTON

The Fenton Art Glass Co. was founded in 1905 by Frank L. Fenton and his brother, John W., in Martins Ferry, Ohio. They initially sold hand-painted glass made by other manufacturers, but it wasn't long before they decided to produce their own glass. The new Fenton factory in Williamstown, W.V., opened on Jan. 2, 1907. From that point on, the company expanded by developing unusual colors and continued to decorate glassware in innovative ways.

Two more brothers, James and Robert, joined the firm. But despite the company's initial success, John W. left to establish the Millersburg Glass Co. of Millersburg, Ohio, in 1909. The first months of the new operation were devoted to the production of crystal glass only. Later iridized glass was called "Radium Glass." After only two years, Millersburg filed for bankruptcy.

Fenton's iridescent glass had a metallic luster over a colored, pressed pattern, and was sold in dime stores. It was only after the sales of this glass decreased and it was sold in bulk as carnival prizes that it came to be known as carnival glass.

Fenton became the top producer of carnival glass, with more than 150 patterns. The quality of the glass, and its popularity with the public, enabled the new company to be profitable through the late 1920s. As interest in carnival subsided, Fenton moved on to stretch glass and opalescent patterns. A line of colorful blown glass (called "off-hand" by Fenton) was also produced in the mid-1920s.

During the Great Depression, Fenton survived by producing functional colored glass tableware and other household items, including water sets, table sets, bowls, mugs, plates, perfume bottles and vases.

Restrictions on European imports during World War II ushered in the arrival of Fenton's opaque colored glass, and the lines of "Crest" pieces soon followed.

In the 1950s, production continued to diversify with a focus on milk glass, particularly in Hobnail patterns.

1905-1930

Drapery eight-piece water set, Blue Opalescent blown water pitcher with flared star-crimped rim and transparent blue applied handle and seven pressed tumblers, first quarter 20th century, excellent condition, pitcher with some minute high-point wear and shoulder flake, tumblers undamaged, pitcher 9-1/4" h., tumblers 3-3/4" h. **$184**

Jeffrey S. Evans & Associates

Topaz cut candlestick with notched profile, 1920s (?), 10-1/2" h. .... **$100+**

In the third quarter of Fenton's history, the company returned to themes that had proved popular to preceding generations, and began adding special lines, such as the Bicentennial series.

Innovations included the line of Colonial colors that debuted in 1963, including amber, blue, green, orange and ruby. Based on a special order for an Ohio museum, Fenton in 1969 revisited its early success with "Original Formula Carnival Glass." Fenton also started marking its glass in the molds for the first time.

The star of the 1970s was the yellow and blushing pink creation known as Burmese, which remains popular today. This was followed closely by a menagerie of animals, birds, and children.

In 1975, Robert Barber was hired by Fenton to begin an artist-in-residence program, producing a limited line of art-glass vases in a return to the off-hand, blown-glass creations of the mid-1920s.

Shopping at home via television was a recent phenomenon in the late 1980s when the "Birthstone Bears" became the first Fenton product to appear on QVC (established in 1986 by Joseph Segel, founder of The Franklin Mint).

In the latter part of the century, Fenton established a website—www.fentonartglass.com—as a user-friendly online experience where collectors could learn about catalog and gift shop sales, upcoming events and the history of the company.

In August 2007, Fenton discontinued all but a few of its more popular lines, and the company ceased production altogether in 2011.

For more information on Fenton Art Glass, see *Warman's Fenton Glass Identification and Price Guide, 2nd edition,* by Mark F. Moran.

Drapery three-piece water set, Green Opalescent, blown water pitcher with flared star-crimped rim and transparent green applied handle, and two pressed tumblers with polished bases, first quarter 20th century, excellent condition, pitcher with some high-point wear, tumblers undamaged, pitcher 9-3/8" h., tumblers 3-3/4" h.**$104**

Jeffrey S. Evans & Associates

Ruby flared vase with wheel-cut decoration, ribbed, late 1920s, 6" h................................... **$200+**

Persian Blue rose bowl, 1915, in Persian Medallion, with enamel decoration, 3-1/4" h. **$55**

Hanging Hearts and Vines off-hand footed bowl, mid-1920s, 10" d. .... **$2,800+**

Spiral Optic pair of vases, Crystal Opalescent/Colorless Opalescent, second quarter 20th century, undamaged, 7-1/4" h., 5-3/4" w. overall. **$35**

Jeffrey S. Evans & Associates

Mosaic off-hand candlestick, mid-1920s, 5" h.................... **$900+**

GLASS

FENTON CARNIVAL GLASS

The golden era of carnival glass was from about 1905 to the mid-1920s. It is believed that by 1906 the first cheap, iridized glass to rival the expensive Tiffany creations was in production. Carnival glass was originally made to bridge a gap in the market by providing ornamental wares for those who couldn't afford to buy the fashionable, iridized pieces popular at the height of the Art Nouveau era. It wasn't until much later that it acquired the name "carnival glass." When it fell from favor, it was sold off cheaply to carnivals and offered as prizes. Fenton made about 150 patterns of carnival glass.

Here are some of the basic colors:

Amethyst: A purple color ranging from quite light to quite dark

Aqua opalescent: Ice blue with a milky (white or colored) edge

Black amethyst: Very dark purple or black in color

Clam broth: Pale ginger ale color, sometimes milky

Cobalt blue (sometimes called royal blue): A dark, rich blue

Green: A true green, not pastel

Marigold: A soft, golden yellow

Pastel colors: A satin treatment in white, ice blue, ice green

Peach opalescent: Marigold with a milky (white or colored) edge

Red: A rich red, rare

Vaseline (Fenton called it topaz): Clear yellow/yellow-green glass

Green whimsy vase in Diamond and Rib, pinched in **$1,350**

Blue tankard in Floral and Grape Variant, candy-ribbon edge, 9-1/2" h............................. **$300-$500**
Outstanding example **$900**

Amethyst water pitcher in Butterfly and Berry......................... **$3,000**

Red ruffled bowl in Stag and Holly, spatula feet, 6-1/2" d. **$1,500**

Blue bowl with 3-in-1 edge, Ten Mums, 9-1/2" **$350**

Marigold cup and saucer in Kittens **$200**

1930-1955

Peach Crest vase, melon form, with Charleton decoration, mid-1950s, 8" h.......................**$90+**

Blue Opalescent jug and square-top goblet in Hobnail, part of a lemonade set that would have included six tumblers, 1950s; jug, 8" h.; goblet, 5-1/2" h...**$500+ for complete set**

Cranberry Opalescent 70-ounce jug in Coin Spot, mid-1930s, 8-1/2" h. ....**$200+**

Nymph in footed bowl in Green Transparent, 1930s, 7-1/2" h. ....**$275+**

▶ Topaz Opalescent basket in Coin Spot, 1930s, 12" h. .... **$300+**

French Opalescent three-horn epergne in Emerald Crest/Diamond Lace, 1949-55, 11" h. .... **$250+**

Rare experimental "Milady" vase in Kitchen Green, 1942, 11" h. ....**$500+**

No. 621 flared vase and stand, Mandarin Red and opaque black, base raised on five scrolled feet, 1932-1935, undamaged, 8-7/8" h. overall, 6-1/4" h. vase.....**$115**

Jeffrey S. Evans & Associates

Crystal Crest 70-ounce jug with original label, 9-1/2" h...... **$450+**

Ivy Overlay vase with applied Charleton Ivory Leaves and Needles decoration, early 1950s, 5" h. **$85**

◄ Black (Ebony) covered candy dish with flower finial, 1931, 6-1/2" h. ....**$250+**

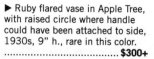

► Ruby flared vase in Apple Tree, with raised circle where handle could have been attached to side, 1930s, 9" h., rare in this color. ....**$300+**

1955-1990s

Two vases, Blue Iridescent, signed Favrene example with Coralene decoration, #170/850, 1994, and unsigned, undecorated example thought to be an experimental piece, fourth quarter 20th century, undamaged, 6-1/2" and 5-3/4" h. **$173**

Jeffrey S. Evans & Associates

Four vases, including a blue cased with Gold Iridescent interior example molded with swans and cattails, two signed, second half 20th century, undamaged, 6-1/4" to 7-1/2" h. **$115**

Jeffrey S. Evans & Associates

Rose Overlay pieces in Corn (also called Maize), made for L.G. Wright, 1960s:
jug, 9" h. .... **$300+**
sugar shaker, 5-1/2" h. ..... **$150+**

Cranberry Satin apothecary jar in Daisy and Fern, made for L.G. Wright, 1950s and 1960s, 8" h. .... **$350+**

Goldenrod condiment set (salt, pepper, mustard and stand) in Tear Drop, late 1950s, 7" h. with handle .... **$350+**

► Three vases, two cameo-type examples, both numbered limited editions, and an opaque black example signed by Louise Piper, fourth quarter 20th century, undamaged, 4-3/4" to 7" h. **$316**

Jeffrey S. Evans & Associates

▲ Aurene Jefferson comport, one of only 75 made as a test color before the Bicentennial colors were established, circa 1973, 10-1/2" h. .... **$300+**

◄ Ruby crimped bowl and platter in Pineapple, 1970s, each about 14" d. .... **$250+ pair**

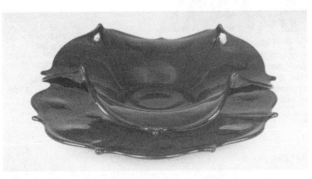

GLASS

FOSTORIA

The Fostoria Glass Co., founded in 1887, produced numerous types of fine glassware over the years. Its factory in Moundsville, West Virginia, closed in 1986.

Fostoria

Chanticleer rooster figure, unsigned, 10" x 8-1/2".......**$240**

Dirk Soulis Auctions

Atlanta/Square Lion covered compote, colorless, frosted finish to finial, pattern at bottom edge of bowl and edge of base, engraved floral decoration to bowl, late 19th/early 20th century, 9-7/8" h. overall, 6" dia. overall.........**$115**

Jeffrey S. Evans & Associates

Atlanta/Square Lion goblet, colorless, fourth quarter 19th century, 6" h........................**$69**

Jeffrey S. Evans & Associates

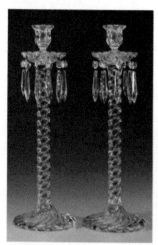

Queen Anne candlesticks, late 19th/early 20th century, each with single socket with finely threaded mounts hung with prisms over twisted stem and swirled base, 18-1/2"...........................**$350**

Brunk Auctions

Art glass bowl, 1977, heavy oval form with folded rim, opaque and transparent striations of orange, blue, green, yellow, and brown, inscribed Fostoria and dated 77 on base, 7-7/8"..................**$100**

Skinner, Inc., www.skinnerinc.com

George Sakier Art Deco vase, 7-1/2" h. x 6" w..................**$100**

Dirk Soulis Auctions

American low foot punch bowl with standard,
18"... **$800**

Mark Mattox Real Estate & Auctioneer

American punch bowl, 12" dia. x 7" h............. **$140**

Langston Auction Gallery

American square cake stand, 7-1/8" h............. **$120**

Mark Mattox Real Estate & Auctioneer

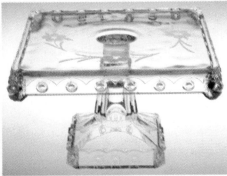

Atlanta/Square Lion cake stand, colorless, engraved
floral decoration, late 19th/early 20th century, 6" h.,
9" sq... **$115**

Jeffrey S. Evans & Associates

St. Bernard covered compote, colorless and frosted,
on high standard patterned stem, wafer construction,
late 19th/early 20th century, 8-1/2" h. overall,
6-1/4" dia..**$259**

Jeffrey S. Evans & Associates

Priscilla syrup pitcher, emerald green with traces of
gilt decoration, transparent emerald green applied
handle, hinged lid, late 19th/early 20th century,
undamaged, 6" h. overall. **$92**

Jeffrey S. Evans & Associates

American deep dish, 9" across, 3-1/2" deep.........................**$20**

Purcell Auction Gallery

Set of 14 American stems with amethyst glass stops, clear stems: six water goblets (one shown) and eight champagnes.................**$90**

A-1 Auction

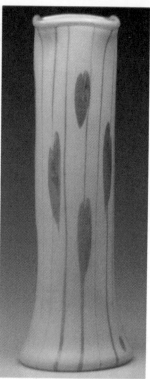

Glass Heirloom napkin fold bowl, green opalescent, circa 1950s/1960s, 2-1/2" h., 5-1/2" dia. **$15**

Premier Auction Galleries

Crown Hapsburg candy jar and lid, cobalt blue, 1961-1965, 10" h. **$25**

Hewlett's Auctions

Iris art glass vase, iridescent white with gold and green hanging hearts, gold iridescent interior, tall cylindrical form with square rim, ground pontil mark, circa 1910-1914, undamaged, 12-1/4" h., 3" sq. rim...............................**$863**

Jeffrey S. Evans & Associates

Wedding Bells – Maiden's Blush punch bowl, colorless, late 19th/early 20th century, 5-3/4" h. overall, 14-3/4" dia. overall. **$127**

Jeffrey S. Evans & Associates

Three Jenny Lind milk glass items, oval glove box, 10-1/2" x 4"; covered dresser box, 5-1/4" x 5-1/4"; and bottle 10-3/4" h., chip to bottom of stopper. **$81**

Vero Beach Auction

GALLÉ

Gallé glass was made in Nancy, France, by Emile Gallé, a founder of the Nancy School and a leader in the Art Nouveau movement in France. Much of his glass, both enameled and cameo, is decorated with naturalistic motifs. The finest pieces were made in the last two decades of the 19th century and the opening years of the 20th.

Pieces marked with a star preceding the name were made between 1904, the year of Gallé's death, and 1914.

Mold blown vase, red against butterscotch ground with flowers with trailing vines, signed Gallé on side, very good to excellent condition, 6-1/4" h.......... **$5,463**

James D. Julia, Inc.

Mold blown vase with clematis blooms and trailing foliage in blue and purple on cream and blue mottled ground, signed Gallé in cameo to side of vase, very good to excellent condition, 6-3/4" h. **$9,488**

James D. Julia, Inc.

Cameo vase with purple wisteria and foliage vine dangling from rim across frost and purple backdrop, signature of Gallé on front with falling blossom on back, excellent condition, 10-1/4" h.......... **$700**

Mark Mussio, Humler & Nolan

Cameo glass bowl acid-etched with fruiting branches, Nancy, France, circa 1900, signed Gallé to body, 3-1/2" x 8-1/2" dia................**$1,063**

Rago Arts and Auction Center

GLASS

Signed cameo cabinet vase, yellow green cut to shaded peach to colorless ground, suspended foliate decoration, polished base, France, first quarter 20th century, undamaged, 2-3/4" h. **$403**

Jeffrey S. Evans & Associates

Two cameo glass bud vases, one with landscape the other with vine and leaf decoration, late 19th/early 20th century, both signed Gallé France, taller vase 10-1/4"......................... **$2,000**

Rago Arts and Auction Center

Acid-etched and fire-polished bud vase with dragonfly and lily pads, Nancy, France, circa 1900, signed Gallé on body, 6-1/2" x 3-1/4"............................ **$2,000**

Rago Arts and Auction Center

Acid-etched vase with ferns, Nancy, France, circa 1900, signed Gallé on body, 7-1/2" x 2-3/4"............................ **$1,000**

Rago Arts and Auction Center

Floral marquetry vase with clear glass neck shading to purple at lip and amber on bulbous body decorated with green marquetry leaves with wheel-carved detail, thin brown marquetry stems lead up neck to wheel-carved applied and marquetry flowers, signed with engraved signature of Gallé, rests on clear glass foot, very good to excellent condition, 9" h...**$21,850**

James D. Julia, Inc.

French cameo mold blown vase decorated with fuchsia flowers, stems and leaves in red against background of frosted yellow shading to cream, finished with slight opalescence to interior of mouth, signed Gallé on side in cameo and stamped Made in France on underside, very good to excellent condition, 11-1/2" h. **$10,350**

James D. Julia, Inc.

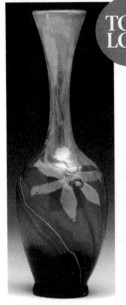

Marquetry floral vase with clear neck shading to green body and amber near foot, white marquetry flower with green marquetry stem extending up neck to cream-colored marquetry bud, flower petals have detailed wheel-carving; vase signed on side with engraved Oriental style signature of Gallé with remnants of what appears to be original paper label, most likely from retailer; very good to excellent condition, 10" h. **$27,050**

James D. Julia, Inc.

Cameo glass vase with lake scene, early 20th century, signed, 10-3/4" x 7". **$1,625**

Rago Arts and Auction Center

Marquetry vase, canoe-shaped, marquetry-carved leaves in amber, white, lavender, pink and tan against internally decorated cream and light orange background, further decorated with cameo lily pads and other aquatic vegetation enhancing background, signed on side with engraved Gallé, line of color on interior of glass near one end of canoe, very good to excellent condition, 6-1/2" l.. **$6,900**

James D. Julia, Inc.

Acid-etched and enamel-decorated toasting glass, "Bien l'amour," Nancy, France, 1890s, signed Gallé on body, 6-1/4" x 2-3/4". **$3,625**

Rago Arts and Auction Center

Mold blown vase decorated in hyacinth floral pattern in shades of purple with green foliage on muted yellow ground, signed Gallé in cameo to side of vase, very good to excellent condition, 12" h.. **$9,200**

James D. Julia, Inc.

GLASS

HEISEY

Numerous types of fine glass were made by A.H. Heisey & Co., Newark, Ohio, from 1895. The company's trademark, an H enclosed within a diamond, has become known to most glass collectors. The company's name and molds were acquired by Imperial Glass Co., Bellaire, Ohio, in 1958, and some pieces have been reissued. The glass listed below consists of miscellaneous pieces and types.

Five custard glass "Winged Scroll" items, cruet, butter dish, creamer, sugar and spooner........**$236**

Woody Auction, LLC

Prince of Wales Plumes five-piece water set, colorless with gilt decoration, water pitcher and four tumblers, first quarter 20th century, 4" to 8-3/4" h. overall. **$115**

Jeffrey S. Evans & Associates

Figural fish bookends, pair, colorless, each with polished base, mid-20th century, 6-1/2" h...... **$92**

Jeffrey S. Evans & Associates

Covered glass jar, enameled floral garland, gold trim, excellent condition, 10-1/4"....**$81**

Richard D. Hatch & Associates

Art Deco "Nimrod" charger with design by Hungarian artist Wilhelm Hunt Diederich, sand blasted with athletic man being pulled by two greyhounds, unmarked, excellent condition, 14-1/4" dia. ..**$225**

Mark Mussio, Humler & Nolan

IMPERIAL

From 1902 until 1984, Imperial Glass Co. of Bellaire, Ohio, produced hand-made glass. Early pressed glass production often imitated cut glass and may bear the raised "NUCUT" mark in the interior center. In the second decade of the 1900s, Imperial was one of the dominant manufacturers of iridescent or carnival glass. When glass collecting gained popularity in the 1970s, Imperial again produced carnival glass and a line of multicolored slag glass. Imperial purchased molds from closing glass houses and continued many lines popularized by others including Central, Heisey, and Cambridge. These reissues may cause confusion but they were often marked.

Iridescent glass vase with heart and vine pattern, 1920s, unmarked, 10" x 3-3/4"... **$1,000**

Rago Arts and Auction Center

Decorated free hand footed bowl, iridescent colorless with red drapes, short red stem, slight variation of catalog number FH 1, polished pontil mark, circa 1925, undamaged, 7" h., 8-3/4" dia. rim, 5-1/4" dia. foot. **$1,380**

Jeffrey S. Evans & Associates

Decorated free hand bowl, iridescent colorless with blue drapes, blue rim and applied slightly domed foot, shape as catalog number FH 162, polished pontil mark with original gold-foil label, circa 1925, undamaged, 4-1/2" h., 11" dia. rim, 5-1/8" dia. foot.......................... **$1,150**

Jeffrey S. Evans & Associates

Decorated lead lustre vase, glossy cobalt with opal hanging hearts, orange interior, shape 419, polished pontil mark, circa 1925, undamaged, 11-1/4" h. **$633**

Jeffrey S. Evans & Associates

Decorated free hand vase, shiny pale orange with blue drapes, blue rim and broad foot, catalog number FH 243, polished pontil mark, circa 1925, undamaged, 10-1/2" h. **$690**

Jeffrey S. Evans & Associates

Decorated free hand vase, iridescent colorless with green drapes, green rim, catalog number FH 168, polished pontil mark, circa 1925, undamaged, 11-1/2" h. **$1,093**

Jeffrey S. Evans & Associates

Decorated free hand vase, iridescent orange with blue hanging hearts, cut and folded out tri-part rim, catalog number FH 248, polished pontil mark, circa 1925, undamaged, 9-1/2" h. **$805**

Jeffrey S. Evans & Associates

Decorated free hand vase, colorless with blue drapes, applied cobalt blue handles, shape as catalog number FH 70, polished pontil mark, circa 1925, undamaged, 9-1/4" h. **$863**

Jeffrey S. Evans & Associates

Decorated free hand compote, iridescent colorless with opal hanging hearts, cobalt blue rim and tall stem, unlisted shape, polished pontil mark, circa 1925, undamaged, 9-7/8" h., 9-1/4" dia. rim, 5" dia. foot. **$3,738**

Jeffrey S. Evans & Associates

Decorated lead lustre vase, iridescent green with opal hanging hearts, orange interior with irregular color at rim, shape 655, polished pontil mark, circa 1925, undamaged, 10" h. **$863**

Jeffrey S. Evans & Associates

Decorated free hand ball vase, iridescent colorless with green drapes, green rim and applied broad foot, catalog number FH 218, polished pontil mark with original gold-foil label, circa 1925, undamaged, 6" h., 5-1/8" dia. foot. **$1,035**

Jeffrey S. Evans & Associates

Decorated free hand vase, glossy orange with blue drapes and rim, orange interior, raised on three applied loop-like feet, shape as catalog number FH 239, polished pontil mark, circa 1925, one foot with light hairline across upper terminal, wear to interior color, 6-1/2" h. **$575**

Jeffrey S. Evans & Associates

Decorated free hand vase, glossy iridescent light orange with blue drapes, applied deep cobalt open handles and broad foot, catalog number FH 241, polished pontil mark, circa 1925, undamaged, light scuff on one side, 9-5/8" h. **$1,150**

Jeffrey S. Evans & Associates

Decorated free hand vase, iridescent colorless with opal hanging hearts, cobalt blue rim, shape as catalog number FH 275, polished pontil mark, circa 1925, undamaged, 6" h. **$575**

Jeffrey S. Evans & Associates

Free hand vase, heavy iridescent marigold, applied blue-green upright open handles, drawn foot, shape as catalog number FH 10, polished pontil mark, circa 1925, undamaged, 8" h. **$2,300**

Jeffrey S. Evans & Associates

Decorated lead lustre vase, glossy deep cobalt with opal drapes, blue interior, shape 418, decoration 12, polished pontil mark with original oval label inscribed "418/12," circa 1925, undamaged, 11" h. **$633**

Jeffrey S. Evans & Associates

Decorated free hand vase, glossy deep cobalt with opal hanging hearts, opal rim, unlisted shape, polished pontil mark, circa 1925, undamaged, some interior residue, 6-1/4" h. **$460**

Jeffrey S. Evans & Associates

GLASS

LALIQUE

René Jules Lalique was born on April 6,1860, in the village of Ay, in the Champagne region of France. In 1862, his family moved to the suburbs of Paris.

In 1872, Lalique began attending College Turgot where he began studying drawing with Justin-Marie Lequien. After the death of his father in 1876, Lalique began working as an apprentice to Louis Aucoc, who was a prominent jeweler and goldsmith in Paris.

Lalique moved to London in 1878 to continue his studies. He spent two years attending Sydenham College, developing his graphic design skills. He returned to Paris in 1880 and worked as an illustrator of jewelry, creating designs for Cartier, among others. In 1884, Lalique's drawings were displayed at the National Exhibition of Industrial Arts, organized at the Louvre.

At the end of 1885, Lalique took over Jules Destapes' jewelry workshop. Lalique's design began to incorporate translucent enamels, semiprecious stones, ivory, and hard stones. In 1889, at the Universal Exhibition in Paris, the jewelry firms of Vever and Boucheron included collaborative works by Lalique in their displays.

In the early 1890s, Lalique began to incorporate glass into his jewelry, and in 1893 he took part in a competition organized by the Union Centrale des Arts Decoratifs to design a drinking vessel. He won second prize.

Lalique opened his first Paris retail shop in 1905, near the perfume business of François Coty. Coty commissioned Lalique to design his perfume labels in 1907, and he also created his first perfume bottles for Coty.

In the first decade of the 20th century, Lalique continued to experiment with glass manufacturing techniques, and mounted his first show devoted entirely to glass in 1911.

During World War I, Lalique's first factory was forced to close, but the construction of a new factory was soon begun in Wingen-sur-Moder, in the Alsace region. It was completed in 1921, and still produces Lalique crystal today.

In 1925, Lalique designed the first "car mascot" (hood ornament) for Citroën, the French automobile company. For the next six years, Lalique would design 29 models for companies such as Bentley, Bugatti, Delage, Hispano-Suiza, Rolls Royce, and Voisin.

Lalique's second boutique opened in 1931, and this location continues to serve as the main Lalique showroom today.

"Irene" ashtray in bright green glass, stenciled R. LALIQUE FRANCE (M p. 276, No. 304). .... **$1,200-$1,500**

"Fleur" bowl, circa 1912, in clear and frosted glass with sepia patina and black enamel, molded R. LALIQUE, 4-1/2" dia. (M p. 727, No. 3100). .... **$650-$750**

"Muguet" shallow dish, circa 1931, in opalescent glass, stenciled R. LALIQUE FRANCE, 11-7/8" dia. (M p. 302, No. 416). .... **$1,800-$2,000**

René Lalique died on May 5, 1945, at the age of 85. His son, Marc, took over the business at that time, and when Marc died in 1977, his daughter, Marie-Claude Lalique Dedouvre, assumed control of the company. She sold her interest in the firm and retired in 1994.

For more information on Lalique, see *Warman's Lalique Identification and Price Guide* by Mark F. Moran.

(In some of the descriptions of Lalique pieces that follow, you will find notations like this: "M p. 478, No. 1100." This refers to the page and serial numbers found in *René Lalique, maître-verrier, 1860-1945: Analyse de L'oeuvre et Catalogue Raisonné*, by Félix Marcilhac, published in 1989 and revised in 1994. Printed entirely in French, this book of more than 1,000 pages is the definitive guide to Lalique's work, and listings from auction catalogs typically cite the Marcilhac guide as a reference. A used copy can cost more than $500. Copies in any condition are extremely difficult to find, but collectors consider Marcilhac's guide to be the bible for Lalique.)

◀ "Dans" figure in clear and frosted glass, 20th century, signed, 9-1/4"
.... **$469**

Rago Arts and Auction Center

▶ "Hirondelle" car mascot (hood ornament), circa 1928, in clear and frosted glass, molded R. LALIQUE FRANCE, 6" h. (M p. 501, No. 1143).
........**$1,500-$2,000**

Rare "Koudour" vase, France, circa 1926, etched and raised signature R. Lalique France, 7" x 6-1/4" (M p. 432, No. 968).
.... **$4,375**

Rago Arts and Auction Center

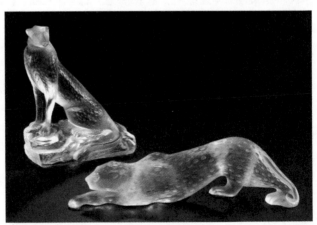

Two panthers, late 20th century, marks: Lalique ® France, 14" l., 10" h. (sitting)..**$2,750**

Heritage Auctions

GLASS

Rare "Picardie" vase of opalescent glass, France, 1927, etched R. LALIQUE, 9-1/2" x 10" (M p. 440, No. 1006).......................$31,250

Rago Arts and Auction Center

Pair of sconces, Champs Elysees, Lalique, post-1945, marks: Lalique France, 10". $3,500

Heritage Auctions

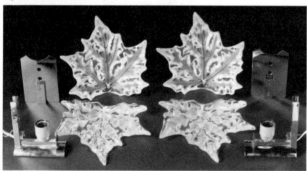

Two vases, "Hiboux" and "Spiral," post-1945, marks: Lalique France, 5-7/8" h. (Spiral)... $406

Heritage Auctions

Clear and frosted "Homage" vase, circa 1995, engraved: Lalique, France, inscribed to front: 1995 Homage à Rene Lalique, 11" h. $1,875

Heritage Auctions

"Formose" vase, circa 1924, marks raised: R. LALIQUE, 6-5/8" h. $2,375

Heritage Auctions

"Coeur Joie" perfume bottle for Nina Ricci, circa 1955, in clear and frosted glass, engraved Lalique France, 6" h...$400-$500

LIBBEY GLASS

In 1878, William L. Libbey obtained a lease on the New England Glass Co. of Cambridge, Massachusetts, changing the name to the New England Glass Works, W.L. Libbey and Son, Proprietors. After his death in 1883, his son, Edward D. Libbey, continued to operate the company at Cambridge until 1888, when the factory was closed. Edward Libbey moved to Toledo, Ohio, and set up the company subsequently known as Libbey Glass Co. During the 1880s, the firm's master technician, Joseph Locke, developed the now much desired colored art glass lines of Agata, Amberina, Peach Blow, and Pomona. Renowned for its cut glass of the Brilliant Period, the company continues in operation today as Libbey Glassware, a division of Owens-Illinois, Inc.

Empress brilliant cut glass flower center vase, colorless, facet cut ring neck with signature, early 20th century, very good condition, less than normal expected minor pattern flakes, base with several small chips and flakes, 6-7/8" h. overall, 9-3/4" w. overall. **$374**

Jeffrey S. Evans & Associates

Signed No. 211 Cherry Blossom cut glass bowl, colorless, circular signature in base, early 20th century, excellent condition, interior rim with two minor flakes, 3-7/8" h. overall, 8" dia. **$150**

Jeffrey S. Evans & Associates

Amberina Inverted Thumbprint pitcher, square rim, amber applied reeded handle, polished pontil mark, W.L. Libbey & Sons and others, late 19th/early 20th century, 6-1/4" h. overall, 5" dia. overall. **$126**

Jeffrey S. Evans & Associates

Two Nash Morning Frost tumblers, white opalescent, juice glass and tall tumbler, each with etched signature on base, second quarter 20th century, undamaged, 3-3/8" and 5-1/8" h..................**$138**

Jeffrey S. Evans & Associates

Amberina compote, fuchsia rim, polished pontil mark with acid etched "Amberina / Libbey," fourth quarter 19th century, undamaged, 4-7/8" h., 4-7/8" dia. rim. **$288**

Jeffrey S. Evans & Associates

Signed Libbey American brilliant cut glass loving cup, green cut to clear, engraved floral and rococo design, clear applied handles, sabre mark, 6-3/4". **$1,062**

Woody Auction

Maize celery vase, colorless with light amber iridescence and blue stained leaves, fourth quarter 19th century, excellent condition, rim with minor flake and exterior edge with some normal roughness, 6-1/2" h. **$127**

Jeffrey S. Evans & Associates

Amberina Diamond-Optic celery vase, square scalloped rim and rough pontil mark, late 19th/early 20th century, 6" h., 3-1/8" sq. rim. **$138**

Jeffrey S. Evans & Associates

Amberina scent bottle, lightly ribbed body with shading, finished with Amberina dauber stopper, signed on underside "Libbey Amberina," 8-3/8" h. **$1,380**

James D. Julia, Inc.

Art Deco wine glasses, long conical bowls with cut leaf and berry pattern, blue spherical knob at base of stem, round foot, signed on pontil "Libbey," perfect condition with no scratches, chips, cracks or breaks, 8-1/2" h. ... **$207**

Fontaine's Auction Gallery

MARY GREGORY

Glass enameled in white with silhouette-type figures, primarily of children, is now termed "Mary Gregory" and was attributed to the Boston and Sandwich Glass Co. However, recent research has proven conclusively that this was not decorated by Mary Gregory, nor was it made at the Sandwich plant. Miss Gregory was employed by Boston and Sandwich Glass Co. as a decorator; however, records show her assignment was the painting of naturalistic landscape scenes on larger items such as lamps and shades, but never the charming children for which her name has become synonymous. Further, in the inspection of fragments from the factory site, no paintings of children were found.

It is now known that all wares collectors call "Mary Gregory" originated in Bohemia beginning in the late 19th century and were extensively exported to England and the United States well into this century.

For further information, see *The Glass Industry in Sandwich*, Volume #4 by Raymond E. Barlow and Joan E. Kaiser, and the book *Mary Gregory Glassware, 1880-1900* by R. & D. Truitt.

Two dresser boxes, cranberry with separate lid and amberina with hinged lid, each with white enamel decoration depicting a child, late 19th/early 20th century, glass elements undamaged, brass mount with separation at hinge, 2" h. x 2-1/2" dia. and 2-1/2" h. x 3" dia..**$115**

Jeffrey S. Evans & Associates

Two dresser boxes, circular blue example and amber octagonal example, each with hinged lid and white enamel decoration depicting a child, late 19th/early 20th century, blue example undamaged, crack in amber lid, 3" h. x 4" dia. and 3-1/2" h. x 3-1/4" dia. **$173**

Jeffrey S. Evans & Associates

Four vases, cranberry, cobalt blue and amberina, three optic molded, each with white enamel decoration depicting child/young adult, late 19th/early 20th century and mid-20th century, cranberry example with two minor inner-rim flakes, remainder undamaged, 7-1/4" to 10-1/2" h. **$207**

Jeffrey S. Evans & Associates

Four cabinet vases, green and peach, one with gilt-brass base mount, each optic molded with white enamel decoration depicting child/young adult, late 19th/early 20th century, stick example with minute rim nick, remainder undamaged, 2-3/4" to 6-1/4" h. **$161**

Jeffrey S. Evans & Associates

MILK GLASS

Though invented in Venice in the 1500s, the opaque glass commonly known as milk glass was most popular at the end of the 19th century. American manufacturers such as Westmoreland, Fenton, Imperial, Indiana, and Anchor Hocking produced it as an economical substitute for pricey European glass and china.

After World War I, the popularity of milk glass waned, but production continued. Milk glass made during the 1930s and 1940s is often considered of lower quality than other periods because of the economic Depression and wartime manufacturing difficulties.

Milk glass has proven to be an "evergreen" collectible. When asked about milk glass, *Warman's Depression Glass* author and expert Ellen Schroy said, "Milk glass is great. I'm seeing a new interest in it."

"Milk glass" is a general term for opaque colored glass. Though the name would lead you to believe it, white wasn't the only color produced.

"Colored milk glasses, such as opaque black, green, or pink usually command higher prices," Schroy advises. "Beware of reproductions in green and pink. Always question a milk glass pattern found in cobalt blue. (Swirled colors are a whole other topic and very desirable.)"

Brownie salt shaker, opaque pastel green, square with different Palmer Cox Brownie in each panel, period lid, late 19th century, undamaged, lid with split and denting, 2-1/4" h. **$184**

Jeffrey S. Evans & Associates

The number of patterns, forms, and objects made is only limited by the imagination. Commonly found milk glass items include dishes – especially the ever-popular animals on "nests" – vases, dresser sets, figurines, lanterns, boxes, and perfume bottles.

"The milk glass made by Westmoreland, Kemple, Fenton, etc., was designed to be used as dinnerware," Schroy explains. "Much of the milk glass we see at flea markets, antique shows, and shops now is coming out of homes and estates where these 1940-1950s era brides are disposing of their settings." Schroy follows up with some practical advice: "Care should be taken when purchasing, transporting, and using this era of milk glass as it is very intolerant of temperature changes. Don't buy a piece outside at the flea market unless you can protect it well for its trip to your home. And when you get it home, leave it sit for several hours so its temperature evens out to what your normal home temperature is. It's almost a given if you take a piece of cold glass and submerge it into a nice warm bath, it's going to crack. And never, ever expose it to the high temps of a modern dishwasher."

So how do you tell the old from the new? Schroy says many times, getting your hands on it is the only way to tell: "Milk glass should have a wonderful silky texture. Any piece that is grainy is probably new." She further reveals, "The best test is to look for 'the ring of fire,' which will be easy to see in the sunlight: Hold the piece of milk glass up to a good light source (I prefer natural light) and see if there is a halo of iridescent colors right around the edge, look for reds, blues and golds. This ring was caused by the addition of iridized salts into the milk glass formula. If this ring is present, it's probably an old piece." She does caution, however, that 1950s-era milk glass does not have this tell-tale ring.

Old milk glass should also carry appropriate marks and signs, such as the "ring of fire"; appropriate patterns for specific makers are also something to watch for, such as Fenton's hobnail pattern. Collectors should always check for condition issues such as damage and discoloration. According to Schroy, there is no remedy for discolored glass, and cracked and chipped pieces should be avoided, as they are prone to further damage.

— *Karen Knapstein, Print Editor,* Antique Trader *magazine*

GLASS

Challinor and Taylor Jenny Lind pattern (aka Columbia) compote, 7-1/2" x 8-1/2"..................... **$30**

Woody Auction

Biscuit jar with floral décor, silverplate lid and bail, 8-1/2".......**$35**

Woody Auction

ONLINE RESOURCES:

Milkglass.org is an informational website. It includes historical and identification details, in addition to a collection of categorized links to milk glass items for sale on the Internet (primarily eBay).

The National Westmoreland Glass Collectors Club's mission is to promote the appreciation for the artistry and craftsmanship of Westmoreland glass and to continue the preservation of this important part of American history. (westmorelandglassclub.org)

▶ Little Shrimp sugar shaker, opaque white with polychrome floral decoration, satin finish, period lid, Dithridge Glass Co., fourth quarter 19th century, undamaged, 2-5/8" h. overall. **$115**

Jeffrey S. Evans & Associates

Three historical milk glass covered dishes, very good condition, no chips, cracks, repairs or heavy wear, 4-1/4" x 6-3/4" and 3-1/2" x 4-1/4". **$181**

Dirk Soulis Auctions

Pair of decorated milk glass lustres, large bowls with irregular cut rims, decorated on front and back with painted panels of figural cupids in clouds, green and white painted background with blue and white floral embellishments and hanging prisms, good overall condition, few chips to prisms, 14-1/4" h. **$826**

Fontaine's Auction Gallery

GLASS

MT. WASHINGTON

A wide diversity of glass was made by the Mt. Washington Glass Co. of New Bedford, Massachusetts, between 1869 and 1900. It was succeeded in 1900 by the Pairpoint Manufacturing Co. Throughout its history, the Mt. Washington Glass Co. made different types of glass including pressed, blown, art, lava, Napoli, cameo, cut, Albertine, Peachblow, Burmese, Crown Milano, Royal Flemish, and Verona.

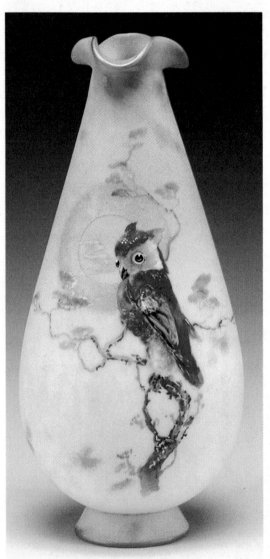

Acid Burmese condiment set, 3-1/2" barrel mustard pot with silver-plated hinged cover and pair of 4" salt and pepper shakers in 5-1/2" gold wash triangular holder, impressed EPNS, 690 beneath, excellent condition. **$275**

Mark Mussio, Humler & Nolan

Burmese decorated vase, bulbous form decorated with rare owl pattern on front and back, full moon, cream to pink ground, exhibition item sticker from Mt. Washington Art Glass Society, very good to excellent condition, 13-3/4" h..................... **$27,600**

James D. Julia, Inc.

Burmese lily vase with glossy finish, yellow and pink, rim tinged in yellow, excellent condition, 8-1/8" h. **$150**

Mark Mussio, Humler & Nolan

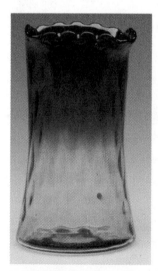

Amberina Diamond Optic celery vase with square, scalloped rim and polished pontil mark, probably Mt. Washington Glass Co., fourth quarter 19th century, edge of base with minor flake, 6-3/4" h., 3-1/4" sq. rim................................. **$81**

Jeffrey S. Evans & Associates

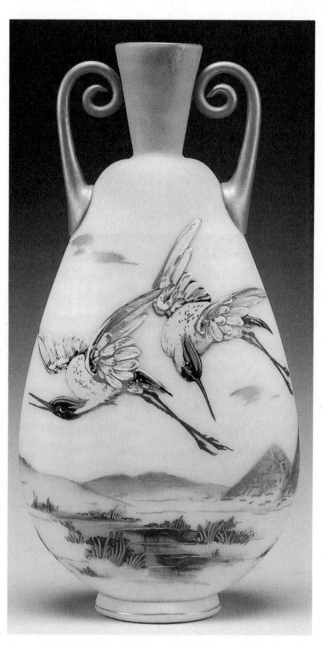

Burmese decorated vase, two large storks in flight, enameled with gold highlights, two applied glass handles in gold, label on underside says, "Exhibition item, Mt. Washington Art Glass Society" and "3074-Naeeej-Bonnie-91," very good to excellent condition, 11" h. **$12,650**

James D. Julia, Inc.

GLASS

!

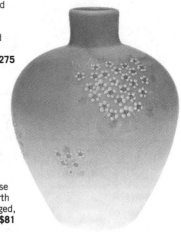

▶ Acid Burmese vase enameled with several bouquets of blue forget-me-nots scattered over surface, surrounded by painted foliage and pale pink flowers, excellent condition, 7" h. **$275**

Mark Mussio, Humler & Nolan

◀ Burmese celery vase, plush finish, scalloped rim, bulge base with polished pontil mark, fourth quarter 19th century, undamaged, 6-1/2" h. overall.................**$81**

Jeffrey S. Evans & Associates

TOP **!** LOT

Burmese monkey vase, bulbous form with applied glass foot and scalloped lip, decorated with realistically enameled monkey on either side, gold gilt bamboo shoots, cream and pink, very good to excellent condition, 13-1/4" h. **$28,750**

James D. Julia, Inc.

GLASS

Ostrich egg muffineer with factory top, body decorated with clumps of daisies arranged front and back, pink coloring at base, 4-3/8" h.
.... **$100**

Mark Mussio, Humler & Nolan

Egg sugar shaker, opal with fired-on Burmese-colored ground and polychrome Shasta daisy decoration, satin finish, period lid, fourth quarter 19th century, undamaged, minor wear to decorations and top with losses to ground, 4-1/4" h. overall. **$138**

Jeffrey S. Evans & Associates

Egg sugar shaker, custard with fired-on Burmese-colored ground and polychrome Shasta daisy decoration, satin finish, period lid, fourth quarter 19th century, undamaged, 4-1/4" h. overall.
.... **$161**

Jeffrey S. Evans & Associates

Egg sugar shaker, opal with soft blue shading and polychrome floral decoration, satin finish, period lid, fourth quarter 19th century, undamaged, lid with light denting, 4-1/4" h. overall. **$184**

Jeffrey S. Evans & Associates

▶ Egg sugar shaker, opaque custard with shaded yellow ground and polychrome forget-me-not decoration, satin finish, period lid, fourth quarter 19th century, undamaged, 4-1/4" h. overall.
.... **$230**

Jeffrey S. Evans & Associates

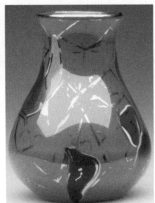

Lava/Sicilian glass vase, shiny opaque black with multicolor inclusions and gilt decoration, bulbous body with waisted neck and foot, polished pontil mark, 1878-1880, undamaged with only minor wear, 6-3/4" h., 3-1/4" dia. rim. **$2,760**

Jeffrey S. Evans & Associates

Lava/Sicilian glass vase, shiny deep amethyst/black with multicolor inclusions, classical urn form with two applied reeded scroll handles, polished pontil mark, 1878-1880, excellent condition, body with some minor high-point wear, several inclusions with open bubbles, as made, 5-3/4" h., 3-1/8" dia. rim. **$1,725**

Jeffrey S. Evans & Associates

Lava/Sicilian glass vase, rare shiny raspberry with multicolor inclusions and gilt decoration, bulbous-base form, polished pontil mark, 1878-1880, undamaged, only minute wear to gilt decoration, 4" h., 1-7/8" dia. rim. **$5,463**

Jeffrey S. Evans & Associates

◀ Lava/Sicilian glass vase, shiny opaque black with multicolor inclusions and gilt decoration, classical urn form with two applied reeded scroll handles, polished pontil mark, 1878-1880, undamaged, two light open bubbles, as made, minor wear to gilt decoration, 3-7/8" h., 2-3/4" dia. rim. **$2,300**

Jeffrey S. Evans & Associates

◀ Lava/Sicilian glass vase, shiny opaque black amethyst with multicolor inclusions, square rim, polished pontil mark, 1878-1880, undamaged, interior base with broken bubble, 3-3/8" h., 3" sq. rim. **$748**

Jeffrey S. Evans & Associates

Lava/Sicilian glass standard stand lamp, shiny opaque black with multicolor inclusions, colorless font with frosted finish and cut stars pattern, black-painted iron square base, brass connector, period No. 2 collar with shoulder plate, fitted with period set-up comprising a No. 2 slip burner and chimney, 1878-1880, undamaged, standard with two open bubbles, as made, 13-1/2" h. to top of collar, 5-3/4" sq. base. **$863**

Jeffrey S. Evans & Associates

Crown Milano sweetmeat jar, biscuit-color diamond-quilted surface with holly and red glass berries on tan coils, marked with CM logo and crown hand-applied in purple within pontil, silver-plated cover with twig finial and impressed M.W., 526 within, excellent condition, 5-1/4".
.... **$200**

Mark Mussio, Humler & Nolan

Swirled and Ribbed toothpick holder, opaque white with blue shading, polychrome floral decoration and tiny beading to top of rim, satin finish, fourth quarter 19th century, undamaged, 2" h.
.... **$345**

Jeffrey S. Evans & Associates

Peachblow tri-corner rim toothpick holder, satin finish, polished base, possibly Mt. Washington Glass Co., fourth quarter 19th century, undamaged, 2" h. overall.
.... **$1,610**

Jeffrey S. Evans & Associates

Mushroom form flower arranger, pink and white forget-me-nots on crown and stem in pale blue, excellent condition, 3" h. x 5" w. **$110**

Mark Mussio, Humler & Nolan

Crown Milano sachet jar or sugar shaker, satin finish, gold-traced polychrome floral decoration on shaded blue ground, original removable quadruple-plate two-part closing top perforated with eight holes and decorated with birds and flowers, not marked, fourth quarter 19th century, undamaged, rim of top with a small dent, 4-1/2" h. overall.
.................................**$460**

Jeffrey S. Evans & Associates

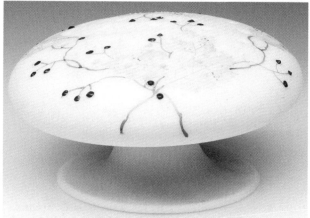

No. 535 mushroom flower arranger, opal with cream ground and polychrome fall leaf and berry decoration, late 19th century, undamaged, slightly tilted, 3" h., 5-1/4" dia. overall.................... **$219**

Jeffrey S. Evans & Associates

◄ Enamel-decorated pitcher, colorless with polychrome and gilt decoration of fish and undersea vegetation on each side, additional leaves on applied handle, polished pontil mark, Mt. Washington Glass Co./The Pairpoint Corp., late 19th/early 20th century, undamaged, 5" h., 3-1/2" dia. rim. $489

Jeffrey S. Evans & Associates

Crown Milano pickle caster, opal with pink shading and full-round polychrome floral decoration, embossed overall star-hobnail pattern, appropriate Pairpoint Mfg. Co., # 664 quadruple-plate stand, cover lettered to match stand, with tongs, fourth quarter 19th century, undamaged, decorations with minor wear, 9-7/8" h. overall, jar 4-1/8" h., 2-3/4" dia. base. **$633**

Jeffrey S. Evans & Associates

Napoli decorated pitcher, clear glass with twisted thumbprint pattern, enameled and gold decorated thistle and vine pattern on front and reverse, twisted and decorated handle with thorns on either side, signed on underside Napoli 848, very good to excellent condition with minor wear to gold gilt, 13-3/4" h. ....**$3,000-$4,000**

James D. Julia, Inc.

Van Dyke humidor, opal, nautical and windmill polychrome decoration on hinged lid and body, underside marked 2679/90 VAN DYKE, gilded mountings marked Pairpoint on base, interior of lid with perforated screen for sponge, Mt. Washington Glass Co./Pairpoint Manufacturing Co., late 19th century, 7-1/4" h., 5-1/4" dia. **$207**

Jeffrey S. Evans & Associates

Bark surface toothpick holder, opaque white with shaded mustard yellow rim with tiny bead decoration, polychrome pinecone decoration, satin finish, fourth quarter 19th century, undamaged, 2-1/2" h. **$316**

Jeffrey S. Evans & Associates

Brownie toothpick holder, opal with cream shading, transfer of brownie on front and reverse with perched owl and moon, fourth quarter 19th century, undamaged, expected minute wear to decoration, 2-1/4" h. **$431**

Jeffrey S. Evans & Associates

Crown Milano swirl cruet, opal with cream ground, light pink staining and gilt decoration, matching decorated applied reeded handle and stopper, polished pontil mark, fourth quarter 19th century, cruet body undamaged with minute wear to decoration, stopper reattached at stem, 8-1/8" h. overall. **$1,725**

Jeffrey S. Evans & Associates

World's Fair Peachblow miniature rose bowl, plush finish, 12 ribs and eight-petal rim, "World's Fair/1893" in gold script, rough pontil mark, probably Libbey Glass Co./New England Glass Co., or Mt. Washington Glass Works, circa 1893, undamaged, minor surface imperfection, as made, 2-3/4" h., 3" dia. overall.........**$288**

Jeffrey S. Evans & Associates

World's Fair Peachblow creamer, plush finish, body with 12 pronounced ribs and applied handle, "World's Fair/1893" in gold script, rough pontil mark, probably Libbey Glass Co./New England Glass Co., or Mt. Washington Glass Works, circa 1893, undamaged, 3" h. **$288**

Jeffrey S. Evans & Associates

World's Fair creamer and sugar, translucent powder blue with plush finish, each body with 12 pronounced ribs, applied handle(s), "World's Fair/1893" in gold script, rough pontil mark, probably Libbey Glass Co./ New England Glass Co., or Mt. Washington Glass Works, circa 1893, sugar undamaged, creamer handle with minute crack to upper terminal, 2-1/2" h..**$150**

Jeffrey S. Evans & Associates

Victorian Sugar Shakers

One of the most interesting aspects of collecting Victorian art glass shakers and condiment sets is that you can collect just about all types of Victorian art glass and display it in a small area.

These types of items include salt, pepper, and sugar shakers as well as mustard jars, small cruet bottles, and toothpick holders.

Some manufacturers who made these items are Mt. Washington, New England Glass, Consolidated Glass, Hobbs Brockunier, Challinor Taylor, Northwood and others. They made the shakers from cased glass, decorated opalware and many other forms of enameled glass. Shakers can be found in Amberina, Burmese, Peachblow, Findlay onyx, opalescent, chocolate glass, and many other colors and combinations.

Victorian era shakers can have either a two-piece or a one-piece cap. Two-piece caps contain a collar that is cemented to the shaker using plaster. This collar contains the threads that the top screws onto. The glass itself does not contain any threads.

A one-piece cap doesn't have a plaster collar, as the shaker's glass top has molded threads and the top screws on like modern-day tops. You will notice a very thin rough top edge on most shakers that use a one-piece cap. This rough, chipped edge is a telltale sign the shaker is an old one, but there are exceptions.

There are some reproductions out there; most reproductions will have a ground or smooth top edge and may be made of heavier glass. Not all old shakers have rough, chipped edges on the top; experience will give you the skills to differentiate old from new.

Every shaker and mustard had a cap of some sort. They were made of many types of

Ring neck-shaped sugar shaker with opalescent Coinspot pattern in an unusual amethyst color. Probably made by Hobbs Brockunier Co. of Wheeling, West Virginia, circa 1880s-1900.

Northwood's Leaf Umbrella pattern in a sugar shaker in cased mauve glass, circa 1880s-1900.

materials – typically brass, nickel, pewter and silver – and are either plain or embossed with designs and flowers. Specialty tops were reserved for certain shakers made by Mt. Washington and Monroe's Wavecrest line, to name two. For example, Mt. Washington made some shakers in the forms of tomatoes, eggs, and figs, and specific caps that served as part of the form's design.

When buying a Victorian era shaker, should it not have a cap, don't let this discourage you. Unless it's a shaker with a specific cap that is part of the identity of the shaker, you can always find a replacement. Most shaker collectors have a box of old caps for just this reason. Mustard jars are a natural to go along with a shaker collection. They come in all the same patterns and glass types. Mustards are harder to find in most cases, as there was only one mustard for every two shakers made. Other "go-withs" are toothpick holders, small oil bottles, and larger cruets. And, if you are lucky enough, you may run across a silver-plate holder of the period that will hold the pieces. The holders can be very ornate and enhance the shakers they hold.

Some of my favorite pieces are odd or non-production colors, slag glass shakers, as well as old carnival glass shakers, none of which are found very often. Enameled shakers can be miniature works of art representing flowers, designs, Mary Gregory-type figures, and even flying insects such as butterflies. Also, figural shakers, such as owls, chickens, and people, can be most interesting but hard to come by.

Shakers come in all price ranges. There are many very nice, pretty shakers that can be bought for less than $50. At the other end of the spectrum, high-end collectors can spend several thousand dollars for some very rare, unique pieces. In my opinion, most of the better pieces fall between $75 and $300 each.

The Antique Glass Salt and Sugar Shaker Club unites many collectors from around the United States and Canada. The club produces a quarterly newsletter and has an ongoing shaker identification project as well as an annual convention. Visit www.antiquesaltshakers.com for more club information.

— *Scott Beale*

Game Bird made by the Mt. Washington Glass Co. of New Bedford, Massachusetts, made in a cased vaseline glass, circa 1880s-1900.

Very rare circa 1880s-1900 pinched-in bulb shaker, made by Stevens & Williams of England, in decorated undeveloped Burmese glass that glows under a black light.

NEW MARTINSVILLE

The New Martinsville Glass Mfg. Co. opened in New Martinsville, West Virginia, in 1901, and during its first period of production came out with a number of colored opaque pressed glass patterns. The company also developed an art glass line named "Muranese," which collectors refer to as "New Martinsville Peach Blow." The factory burned in 1907 but reopened later that year and began focusing on productions of various clear pressed glass patterns, many of which were then decorated with gold or ruby staining or enameled decoration. After going through receivership in 1937, the factory again changed the focus of its production to more contemporary glass lines and figural animals. The firm was purchased in 1944 by The Viking Glass Co. (later Dalzell-Viking).

Two Muranese lamp shades, salmon and pink, hint of iridescence and gilt decorated rims, ribbed pattern, fitted on brass electric table lamp, first quarter 20th century, shades undamaged with normal minute flakes/roughness to fitters, lamp with repair to lower stem, shades 4-1/4" h., 2-1/4" dia. fitter, lamp 18-1/2" h. overall.............. **$374**

Jeffrey S. Evans & Associates

Three Muranese bowls, salmon, sunglow and opal, one with heavy and two with light iridescence to crimped rims, one example with folded-up rim, first quarter 20th century, undamaged, various sizes. **$92**

Jeffrey S. Evans & Associates

Opal Muranese bowl, scalloped rim with light iridescence to rim, fitted in Pairpoint No. 4970 figural silver-plated frame depicting cherub, weighted base, first quarter 20th century, undamaged, bowl interior with minor manufacturing flaw, 7-1/4" h. overall, 5-1/8" dia. rim.... **$161**

Jeffrey S. Evans & Associates

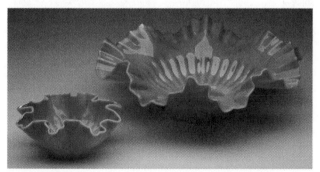

Two pink Muranese bowls, each with light iridescent crimped rim, master fruit bowl and individual bowl, first quarter 20th century, undamaged, 3-3/4" h. overall x 10-3/4" dia. rim and 2-1/8" h. overall x 5-1/4" dia. rim.. **$46**

Jeffrey S. Evans & Associates

NORTHWOOD GLASS CO.

Northwood Glass Co. was founded by Harry Northwood, son of prominent English glassmaker John Northwood, who was famous for his expertise in cameo glass.

Harry emigrated to America in 1881 and, after working at various glass manufacturers, formed the Northwood Glass Co. in 1896 in Indiana, Pennsylvania. In 1902 he created H. Northwood and Co. in Wheeling, West Virginia. After Northwood died in 1919, H. Northwood and Co. began to falter and eventually closed in 1925.

Northwood produced a wide variety of opalescent, decorated, and special effect glasses, and colors like iridescent blue and green, which were not widely seen at the time.

Chrysanthemum Sprig/Pagoda four-piece table set, opaque blue with gilt decoration, covered butter dish, covered sugar bowl, creamer, and spooner, each base signed "Northwood," early 20th century, excellent overall condition, various sizes. **$431**

Jeffrey S. Evans & Associates

Blown Twist wide-waist sugar shaker, vaseline (uranium) opalescent, period lid, late 19th/early 20th century, undamaged, 4-1/2" h. overall................. **$184**

Jeffrey S. Evans & Associates

Chrysanthemum Swirl sugar shaker, cranberry opalescent, period lid, late 19th/early 20th century, very good condition, 4-3/4" h. overall................. **$196**

Jeffrey S. Evans & Associates

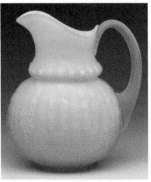

No. 263/Leaf Umbrella water pitcher, cased light lemon yellow, satin finish, colorless applied handle, fourth quarter 19th century, undamaged, satin finish with some expected minor wear, 9" h. overall....................... **$259**

Jeffrey S. Evans & Associates

Daffodils tumbler, blue opalescent, factory polished rim, early 20th century, exterior of rim with flake and interior with broken bubble, as made, 3-7/8" h. **$150**

Jeffrey S. Evans & Associates

Chrysanthemum Sprig/Pagoda four-piece condiment set, custard with green, pink and gilt decoration, cruet with correct faceted stopper, pair of salt and pepper shakers with matching period lids, each fitted on circular footed tray with base signed "Northwood," early 20th century, very good overall condition, 3-1/4" to 6-3/4" h. overall, tray 6-3/8" d. **$184**

Jeffrey S. Evans & Associates

Chrysanthemum Sprig/Pagoda four-piece condiment set, opaque blue with gilt decoration, cruet with correct faceted stopper, pair of salt and pepper shakers with matching period lids, each fitted on circular footed tray with base signed "Northwood," early 20th century, excellent condition, 3-1/4" to 7" h. overall, tray 6-3/8" d. **$460**

Jeffrey S. Evans & Associates

Quilted Phlox sugar shaker, transparent apple green with traces of gilt decoration, period lid, late 19th/early 20th century, undamaged, lid with some minor rust, 4-3/4" h. overall. **$92**

Jeffrey S. Evans & Associates

No. 263/Leaf Umbrella sugar shaker, ruby/cranberry, period lid, fourth quarter 19th century, very good condition, 4-1/2" h. overall. **$127**

Jeffrey S. Evans & Associates

Daisy and Fern wide-waist sugar shaker, blue opalescent, period lid, Northwood Glass Co. or Buckeye Glass Co., late 19th/early 20th century, undamaged, lid with light denting and a short split, 4-5/8" h. **$104**

Jeffrey S. Evans & Associates

Chrysanthemum Sprig/Pagoda toothpick holder, opaque blue with gilt decoration, signed on base "Northwood," early 20th century, undamaged with some expected minute wear to gilt decoration, 2-5/8" h. **$161**

Jeffrey S. Evans & Associates

◀ Quilted Phlox sugar shaker, opaque blue, period lid, late 19th/early 20th century, undamaged, 4-5/8" h. overall. **$92**

Jeffrey S. Evans & Associates

Poinsettia tankard pitcher and tumbler, green opalescent, ring tapered mold pitcher with transparent green applied handle, early 20th century, tankard undamaged with several manufacturing flaws, tumbler rim with several flakes, 13" h., tumbler 4" h. **$460**

Jeffrey S. Evans & Associates

Inverted Fan and Feather tumbler, light pink slag, Northwood Glass Co./ Dugan Glass Co., first quarter 20th century, undamaged.4" h. **$207**

Jeffrey S. Evans & Associates

Daisy and Fern–Northwood Swirl mold sugar shaker, cranberry opalescent, period lid, late 19th/ early 20th century, very good condition, 4-3/8" h. overall. **$104**

Jeffrey S. Evans & Associates

Chrysanthemum Sprig/Pagoda celery vase, opaque blue with gilt decoration, signed on base "Northwood," early 20th century, undamaged, some minute wear to gilt decoration, 6-5/8" h. overall, 5-1/8" dia. base. **$259**

Jeffrey S. Evans & Associates

Chrysanthemum Sprig/Pagoda (OMN) five-piece water set, opaque blue with gilt decoration, water pitcher with base signed "Northwood" and four tumblers with factory polished bases, early 20th century, excellent condition with expected minor wear to gilt decoration, pitcher and three tumblers undamaged, one tumbler with minute flake to base edge, pitcher 8-1/4" h. overall, tumblers 3-3/4" h................................ **$403**

Jeffrey S. Evans & Associates

Chrysanthemum Sprig/ Pagoda four-piece condiment set, custard with green, pink and gilt decoration, pair of salt and pepper shakers with matching period lids and a toothpick, each fitted on circular footed tray, last two articles with base signed "Northwood," early 20th century, very good overall condition, 2-3/4" to 3-1/4" h. overall, tray 6-3/8" d. **$196**

Jeffrey S. Evans & Associates

OPALESCENT GLASS

Opalescent glass is one of the most popular areas of glass collecting. The opalescent effect was attained by adding bone ash chemicals to areas of an item while still hot and refiring the object at tremendous heat. Both pressed and mold-blown patterns are available to collectors. *Opalescent Glass from A to Z* by the late William Heacock is the definitive reference book for collectors.

Daffodil water pitcher, blue opalescent, circular crimped rim, transparent blue applied handle, H. Northwood Co., early 20th century, undamaged, pitcher 9-1/2" h. overall.............................. **$690**

Jeffrey S. Evans & Associates

Coinspot ring neck syrup pitcher, blue opalescent, blue applied handle, period lid, fourth quarter 19th century, undamaged, 6-3/4" h. overall........... **$104**

Jeffrey S. Evans & Associates

Stripe ring neck syrup pitcher, blue opalescent, blue applied handle with lightly pressed feather design to upper terminal, period lid, late 19th/early 20th century, excellent condition, body with minute flake and some minute high-point wear, 7" h. overall.
.... **$115**

Jeffrey S. Evans & Associates

Herringbone water pitcher, blue opalescent, translucent blue applied handle, outstanding color depth and opalescence, fourth quarter 19th century, undamaged, 9" h. **$1,495**

Jeffrey S. Evans & Associates

▶ Coinspot ring neck sugar shaker, blue opalescent, period lid, late 19th/early 20th century, excellent condition, some light high-point wear, lid with denting, 4-3/4" h. overall. **$92**

Jeffrey S. Evans & Associates

▶ Two patterned sugar shakers, colorless opalescent, Reverse Swirl and Ribbed Opal Lattice, period lids, late 19th/early 20th century, Ribbed Opal Lattice with light high-point wear, other with light interior residue, one lid with light denting, 4-1/2" and 4-5/8" h. **$104**

Jeffrey S. Evans & Associates

Hobbs No. 323 Dew Drop/Hobbs Hobnail cruet, canary opalescent/vaseline (uranium) opalescent, colorless cut-facet stopper, canary/vaseline applied handle, polished pontil mark, Hobbs, Brockunier & Co., fourth quarter 19th century, bottom row of hobnails with some manufacturing imperfections and several with small losses, stopper with several minute flakes, 7" h. overall. **$184**

Jeffrey S. Evans & Associates

Buttons and Braids seven-piece water set, green opalescent, water pitcher with hexagonal-form crimped rim, transparent green applied handle, six tapered tumblers, Jefferson Glass Co., first quarter 20th century, very good condition, pitcher with some high-point wear, one tumbler undamaged, two tumblers each with a small rim chip and remaining with rim imperfections, pitcher 9-5/8" h. overall, tumblers 4" h. **$374**

Jeffrey S. Evans & Associates

Chrysanthemum Swirl celery vase, blue/green opalescent, Northwood Glass Co./Buckeye Glass Co., late 19th/early 20th century, excellent condition with some minute high-point wear to lower body, interior of rim with several normal minor flakes, 6-1/2" h. **$104**

Jeffrey S. Evans & Associates

Fern sugar shaker, blue opalescent, period lid, late 19th/early 20th century, undamaged, 5" h. overall. **$316**

Jeffrey S. Evans & Associates

Coinspot nine-panel mold sugar shaker, green opalescent, period lid, late 19th/early 20th century, excellent condition, some minor high-point wear, lid with some minute denting, 4-5/8" h. overall. **$92**

Jeffrey S. Evans & Associates

Coinspot nine-panel mold syrup pitcher, green opalescent, transparent green applied handle, period lid, probably Northwood Glass Co., early 20th century, undamaged, lid with some light rust, 6" h. overall. **$115**

Jeffrey S. Evans & Associates

◀ Reverse Swirl four-bottle condiment set, blue opalescent and vaseline (uranium) opalescent salt and pepper shakers with matching period lids, cranberry opalescent mustard jar with period lid, and colorless opalescent oil bottle lacking stopper, fitted in English metal holder, late 19th/early 20th century, excellent condition, vaseline opalescent shaker with moderate wear, remaining condiments and holder undamaged, shaker lids with imperfections, frame 6-1/4" h. overall, condiments 3-1/4" to 4" h. overall. **$150**

Jeffrey S. Evans & Associates

GLASS

◀ Diamond Optic opalescent glass water pitcher, shaded pink opalescent, ball-form with pinched sides, square-form rim, colorless applied reeded handle, polished pontil mark, probably Phoenix Glass Co., late 19th/early 20th century, excellent condition with some minor high-point wear, very minute body flake below lower terminal, 7-5/8" h. **$104**

Jeffrey S. Evans & Associates

Double Greek key spooner, blue opalescent, Nickel Plate Glass Co., late 19th/early 20th century, excellent condition with light interior wear and minor pattern flake, 6" h. **$196**

Jeffrey S. Evans & Associates

Two opalescent glass sugar shakers, colorless opalescent, Daisy and Fern wide waist mold and Coinspot tapered mold, one period lid and one non-period lid, late 19th/early 20th century, undamaged, Coinspot with several manufacturing flaws, period lid with light denting, 4-5/8" h. overall. **$104**

Jeffrey S. Evans & Associates

Diamond Optic opalescent glass apothecary/straw jar base, shaded dark to light rose, factory polished rim, late 19th/early 20th century, undamaged, 11-1/4" h., 4-1/2" dia. base............................ **$259**

Jeffrey S. Evans & Associates

Coinspot and Swirl syrup pitchers, dark blue opalescent and light blue opalescent, each with blue applied handle, period lid including one with patent information, late 19th/early 20th century, undamaged, one lid with light dent, 5-3/4" and 6-5/8" h. overall. **$230**

Jeffrey S. Evans & Associates

◀ Findlay Floradine toothpick holder, ruby with opalescent flowers, satin finish, Dalzell, Gilmore & Leighton Co., Findlay, Ohio, circa 1889, undamaged, 2-1/2" h. **$1,725**

Jeffrey S. Evans & Associates

Findlay Floradine tumbler, ruby with opalescent flowers, satin finish, barrel form, Dalzell, Gilmore & Leighton Co., Findlay, Ohio, circa 1889, undamaged, interior of rim with some minor losses to casing, as made, 3-5/8" h. **$1,610**

Jeffrey S. Evans & Associates

Findlay Onyx individual berry bowl, ivory onyx with ruby flowers, Dalzell, Gilmore & Leighton Co., Findlay, Ohio, circa 1889, excellent condition, interior with some minor wear and single shallow flake to exterior of rim, 1-5/8" h., 4" dia. rim. **$805**

Jeffrey S. Evans & Associates

Findlay Floradine mustard jar, ruby with opalescent flowers, satin finish, period lid, Dalzell, Gilmore & Leighton Co., Findlay, Ohio, circa 1889, undamaged, lid with light split and some minute denting, 3-5/8" h. overall, 1-5/8" dia. base......................... **$1,093**

Jeffrey S. Evans & Associates

Findlay Floradine covered butter dish, ruby with opalescent flowers, satin finish, Dalzell, Gilmore & Leighton Co., Findlay, Ohio, circa 1889, excellent condition, interior base rim with minor flake, cover rim with some minor roughness, 5-1/4" h. overall, 6" dia........................**$1,955**

Jeffrey S. Evans & Associates

GLASS

Findlay Onyx creamer, ivory onyx with light purple flowers, colorless applied handle, Dalzell, Gilmore & Leighton Co., Findlay, Ohio, circa 1889, undamaged with several minute rim flakes, probably as made, 4-1/2" h., 2-5/8" dia. base.
.... **$1,610**

Jeffrey S. Evans & Associates

Findlay Onyx creamer, butterscotch/amber onyx with iridescent dark amber flowers, colorless applied handle, Dalzell, Gilmore & Leighton Co., Findlay, Ohio, circa 1889, rim with flakes/roughness, primarily to spout, 4-1/2" h., 2-1/2" dia. base.
.... **$2,300**

Jeffrey S. Evans & Associates

Findlay Onyx celery vase, butterscotch onyx with amber flowers, Dalzell, Gilmore & Leighton Co., Findlay, Ohio, circa 1889, restoration to crack encircling base, 6-3/8" h., 3-1/4" dia. base......................... **$1,035**

Jeffrey S. Evans & Associates

Findlay Onyx water pitcher, ivory onyx with platinum flowers, ivory opalescent applied handle, Dalzell, Gilmore & Leighton Co., Findlay, Ohio, circa 1889, excellent condition, spout with small shallow exterior chip, 7-7/8" h. overall. **$489**

Jeffrey S. Evans & Associates

Findlay Onyx tumbler, ivory onyx with amber flowers, barrel form, Dalzell, Gilmore & Leighton Co., Findlay, Ohio, circa 1889, base with approximate 3" horizontal crack, 3-3/4" h., 2-1/4" dia. base.
.... **$690**

Jeffrey S. Evans & Associates

Findlay Onyx sugar bowl base, butterscotch onyx with amber flowers, Dalzell, Gilmore & Leighton Co., Findlay, Ohio, circa 1889, rim with polishing and reduction, body undamaged, 3-1/2" h., 2-1/2" dia. base.
.... **$1,265**

Jeffrey S. Evans & Associates

▶ Findlay Onyx individual berry bowl, ivory onyx with bronze and slightly iridescent flowers, Dalzell, Gilmore & Leighton Co., Findlay, Ohio, circa 1889, polished and reduced rim, interior with several striations to casing, as made, 1-7/8" h., 4-3/8" dia. base. **$460**

Jeffrey S. Evans & Associates

PAIRPOINT

Originally organized in New Bedford, Massachusetts, in 1880 as the Pairpoint Manufacturing Co. on land adjacent to the famed Mount Washington Glass Co., Pairpoint first manufactured silver and plated wares. In 1894, the two famous factories merged as the Pairpoint Corp. and enjoyed great success for more than 40 years. The company was sold in 1939 to a group of local businessmen and eventually bought out by one of the group, who turned the management over to Robert M. Gundersen. Subsequently, it operated as the Gundersen Glass Works until 1952 when, after Gundersen's death, the name was changed to Gundersen-Pairpoint. The factory closed in 1956. Subsequently, Robert Bryden took charge of this glassworks, at first producing glass for Pairpoint abroad and eventually, in 1970, beginning glass production in Sagamore, Massachusetts. Today the Pairpoint Crystal Glass Co. is owned by Robert and June Bancroft. They continue to manufacture fine quality blown and pressed glass.

No. 1059/"Pauline" pattern brilliant cut glass vase, colorless, shoulder form with flared rim and horizontal step-cutting to neck, featuring hobstars, buttons, and fans, early 20th century, very good condition, 11-1/2" h........... **$431**

Jeffrey S. Evans & Associates

Crystal "orange size" marmalade jar, surface wheel carved with wreath of flowers and leaves, cover embossed with flowers with "P" in diamond logo and numbered 665, 5" h. **$100**

Mark Mussio, Humler & Nolan

Unusual cracker container in hexagonal form, raised on four shell feet, three pink morning glories, cover with "P" in diamond mark and numbered 3953, also appearing below container, serpentine handle, 7". **$100**

Mark Mussio, Humler & Nolan

"Wickham" pattern pair of covered compotes, colorless, each with bubble-ball stem and cover finial, rayed base, first quarter 20th century, excellent condition, one lid with some minor high-point roughness, otherwise undamaged, 12" h. overall, 6-1/8" w. **$518**

Jeffrey S. Evans & Associates

"Adelaide" pattern cut overlay vase, rose to colorless, shape #B-1485, controlled bubble-ball stem, polished pontil mark, second quarter 20th century, foot edge with area of polishing that slightly disfigures profile, 12-3/4" h.. **$374**

Jeffrey S. Evans & Associates

Twin vases in ruby with clear spools, connectors and spears, some internal bubbles, mineral stains encircle interior of both vases, 11-1/2" h. **$225**

Mark Mussio, Humler & Nolan

PATTERN GLASS

Though it has never been ascertained whether glass was first pressed in the United States or abroad, the development of the glass-pressing machine revolutionized the glass industry in the United States, and this country receives the credit for improving the method to make this process feasible. The first wares pressed were probably small flat plates of the type now referred to as "lacy," the intricacy of the design concealing flaws.

In 1827, both the New England Glass Co., Cambridge, Massachusetts, and Bakewell & Co., Pittsburgh, took out patents for pressing glass furniture knobs; soon other pieces followed. This early pressed glass contained red lead, which made it clear and resonant when tapped (flint). Made primarily in clear, it is rarer in blue, amethyst, olive green, and yellow.

By the 1840s, early simple patterns such as Ashburton, Argus, and Excelsior appeared. Ribbed Bellflower seems to have been one of the earliest patterns to have had complete sets. By the 1860s, a wide range of patterns was available.

In 1864, William Leighton of Hobbs, Brockunier & Co., Wheeling, West Virginia, developed a formula for "soda lime" glass that did not require the expensive red lead for clarity. Although "soda lime" glass did not have the brilliance of the earlier flint glass, the formula came into widespread use because glass could be produced cheaply.

Two flint spooners, opaque white, comprising Groove and Diamond Point and Sandwich Loop/Hairpin, third quarter 19th century, excellent overall condition, Groove and Diamond spooner with small pattern flakes, 5-1/2" to 5-3/4" h. **$58**

Jeffrey S. Evans & Associates

U.S. Coin goblet, colorless with frosted coins, dimes surrounding lower bowl, fourth quarter 19th century, undamaged, 6-1/4" h. **$374**

Jeffrey S. Evans & Associates

Polar Bear goblet, colorless and frosted, flared rim, fourth quarter 19th century, undamaged, 6-1/8" h. **$259**

Jeffrey S. Evans & Associates

Valentine goblet, colorless, fourth quarter 19th century, undamaged, 5-3/4" h. **$161**

Jeffrey S. Evans & Associates

Greentown No. 102/Teardrop and Tassel seven-piece water set, cobalt blue, water pitcher and six tumblers, Indiana Tumbler & Goblet Co., circa 1900-1903, pitcher with flakes/small chips to rim, foot with chips, two tumblers with flakes, remaining articles undamaged, 3-3/4" to 8-7/8" h.........**$431**

Jeffrey S. Evans & Associates

Greentown No. 450/Holly Amber jelly compote, Golden Agate, base with beaded rim, Indiana Tumbler & Goblet Co., circa 1903, undamaged, 4-3/4" dia. rim. ... **$1,150**

Jeffrey S. Evans & Associates

Greentown No. 450/Holly Amber covered sugar bowl, Golden Agate, Indiana Tumbler & Goblet Co., circa 1903, undamaged, cover with minute separation near edge, as made, 6-5/8" h. overall, 3-1/4" dia. base. ... **$3,335**

Jeffrey S. Evans & Associates

Three figural pattern celery vases, colorless, two frosted, Cabbage Leaf, Classic with frosted panels, and Cupid and Venus, fourth quarter 19th century, Cupid and Venus undamaged, remaining articles with minor foot flakes, Classic with annealing line to one panel, as made, 8-1/8" to 8-1/2" h. **$81**

Jeffrey S. Evans & Associates

Greentown No. 102/Teardrop and Tassel relish, Nile green, deep oval form, Indiana Tumbler & Goblet Co., circa 1900-1903, rim flakes causing the loss of three beads, 1-1/2" h., 4-1/2" x 7" rim.........**$230**

Jeffrey S. Evans & Associates

Greentown No. 200/Austrian children's glass two-piece table set, vaseline (uranium), creamer and sugar bowl, circa 1900, sugar with minute flakes to foot, creamer undamaged, 2-3/4" to 2-7/8" h. overall. **$92**

Jeffrey S. Evans & Associates

Nursery Rhyme children's glass seven-piece punch set, opaque white, footed punch bowl and six cups, early 20th century, very good condition overall, 1-1/4" to 3-3/8" h. overall. **$92**

Jeffrey S. Evans & Associates

Liberty Bell children's glass four-piece table set, colorless, butter dish, covered sugar bowl, creamer and spooner, sugar cover embossed "PAT SEPT 23 1875" on outer edge below bell, Gillinder & Sons, fourth quarter 19th century, excellent overall condition, 2-1/4" to 3-1/2" h. overall. **$288**

Jeffrey S. Evans & Associates

Deer and Doe With Lily-of-the-Valley goblet, colorless, embossed "PAT APPLIED FOR" under foot, fourth quarter 19th century, undamaged, 5-7/8" h. **$207**

Jeffrey S. Evans & Associates

Daisy and Button celery vase, colorless, fitted in quadruple plate Webster & Son frame, fourth quarter 19th century, undamaged, 9-1/2" h. overall................. **$196**

Jeffrey S. Evans & Associates

TOP! LOT!

Pattern-molded and engraved sugar bowl and cover, colorless, compressed globular bowl with 12 basal flutes, gallery rim, and classic Daisy and Single Leaf copper-wheel engraved medial band, raised on applied button stem and thick circular foot with rough pontil mark, domed cover with folded rim, engraved vine and pinched button-like finial with polished pontil mark, attributed to Bakewell, Page & Bakewell or successors, Pittsburgh, 1820-1835, exceptional undamaged condition, 7-1/4" h. overall, 5-1/2" h. rim, 4-3/8" dia. rim, 3-7/8" dia. foot. **$8,625**

Jeffrey S. Evans & Associates

Greentown No. 102/Teardrop and Tassel cordial, colorless, Indiana Tumbler & Goblet Co., circa 1900-1903, undamaged, 3" h. **$374**

Jeffrey S. Evans & Associates

Three Face Medallion goblet, colorless, fourth quarter 19th century, undamaged, 6-1/8" h....................................... **$127**

Jeffrey S. Evans & Associates

Corn sugar shaker, colorless, period lid, probably Dithridge Glass Co., late 19th/early 20th century, undamaged, 4-5/8" h. overall. **$92**

Jeffrey S. Evans & Associates

PHOENIX GLASS

Phoenix Glass Co., Beaver, Pennsylvania, was established in 1880. Known primarily for commercial glassware, the firm also produced a molded, sculptured, cameo-type line from the 1930s until the 1950s.

Spot Optic Spatter seven-piece water set, colorless with green and opal flakes, eight-lobe water pitcher with star-form crimped rim, colorless applied handle, polished pontil mark, six tumblers, fourth quarter 19th century, undamaged except for some minute wear to one tumbler, rims with normal minute flakes, as made, pitcher 8-7/8" h., tumblers 3-3/4" h. . **$230**

Jeffrey S. Evans & Associates

Spot Optic Spatter water pitcher and tumbler, cased reverse rubina with opal flakes and silver mica flakes, eight-lobe pitcher with star-form crimped rim, colorless applied handle, polished pontil mark, fourth quarter 19th century, undamaged, tumbler with normal rim roughness, pitcher 8-3/4" h., tumbler 3-3/4" h. **$230**

Jeffrey S. Evans & Associates

No. 335/Venetian Thread five-piece water set, colorless with opal loops, satin finish, tall tankard with green tint and nine groups of opal loops, colorless applied handle with pressed ribs to upper terminal, polished pontil mark, circular rim, four tumblers, each with four groups of opal loops, fourth quarter 19th century, pitcher undamaged with some minute wear to satin finish, tumblers with minor to moderate rim flakes, tankard 11-1/2" h., tumblers 5-3/8" to 5-1/2" h... **$374**

Jeffrey S. Evans & Associates

Spot Optic Spatter four-piece water set, colorless with cranberry and opal flakes, eight-lobe water pitcher with colorless applied handle and star-form crimped rim, polished pontil mark, three tumblers with factory polished rims, fourth quarter 19th century, excellent condition, pitcher 8-7/8" h., tumblers 3-7/8" h... **$230**

Jeffrey S. Evans & Associates

GLASS

Zig-Zag air-trap mother-of-pearl satin celery vase, cased dark to light rose, square form with eight lobes, satin finish, polished pontil mark, fourth quarter 19th century, undamaged, satin finish with some minute wear, 6-3/4" h......... **$230**

Jeffrey S. Evans & Associates

Fine Rib water pitcher, colorless with dark to light bronze shading, satin finish, flared triangular-form crimped rim, colorless applied reeded handle, polished pontil mark, fourth quarter 19th century, undamaged, 8-7/8" h. overall..................................... **$115**

Jeffrey S. Evans & Associates

Amberina Zig-Zag Optic water pitcher, square form with eight alternating large and small lobes, amber applied handle, polished pontil mark, fourth quarter 19th century, body with some high-point wear, 8-3/4" h. **$161**

Jeffrey S. Evans & Associates

Spot Optic Spatter water pitcher, colorless with blue/green and opal flakes, New England shape with square-form rim, colorless applied reeded handle, polished pontil mark, fourth quarter 19th century, excellent condition, some areas of minute high-point wear, 7-3/8" h. **$259**

Jeffrey S. Evans & Associates

Spot Optic Spatter four-piece water set, colorless with maroon and opal flakes, eight-lobe water pitcher with star-form crimped rim, colorless applied handle, polished pontil mark, three tumblers, fourth quarter 19th century, very good condition, pitcher 8-7/8" h., tumblers 3-3/4" h. . **$207**

Jeffrey S. Evans & Associates

Spot Optic air-trap mother-of-pearl water pitcher, cased apricot to opal, satin finish, ball form with pinched sides, triangular-form rim, colorless applied high loop handle, polished pontil mark, fourth quarter 19th century, excellent condition with some minor high-point wear, 10-3/8" h. overall.... **$345**

Jeffrey S. Evans & Associates

GLASS

QUEZAL

In 1901, Martin Bach and Thomas Johnson, who had worked for Louis Tiffany, opened a competing glassworks in Brooklyn, New York, called the Quezal Art Glass and Decorating Co. Named for the quetzal, a bird with brilliantly colored features, Quezal produced wares closely resembling those of Tiffany until the plant closed in 1925. In general, Quezal pieces are more defined than Tiffany glass, and the decorations are more visible and brighter.

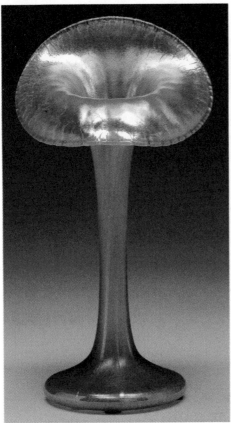

Quezal

Jack in the Pulpit vase decorated with green pulled feather pattern with gold and platinum highlights, face is gold with stretched iridescent finish, signed "Quezal N.Y," very good to excellent condition, 9" h. x 4-3/4" w. across face. **$2,588**

James D. Julia, Inc.

Silver overlay vase, bulbous form with elongated neck, flared lip, decorated with silver overlay Art Nouveau floral and ribbon pattern, signed "Quezal" to underside of vase, very good condition with minor scratches to iridescent finish, 8" h. **$1,725**

James D. Julia, Inc.

GLASS

Amber shade decorated with white feathers pulled from 2-1/4" fitter and edged in green, surface ensconced with amber threading, slightly scalloped rim, signed "Quezal" on fitter, very good condition, 5" h.................. **$140**

Mark Mussio, Humler & Nolan

Simplistic shaped vase, marigold color with blush of magenta at mid-section and near base, engraved "Quezal" within pontil, 7-7/8" h. **$275**

Mark Mussio, Humler & Nolan

Vase with green pulled feather decoration and gold iridescent leaves at foot, interior finished in bright gold iridescence with red highlights, signed in polished pontil "QUEZAL 870," bottom also has what appears to be a museum inventory number, very good to excellent condition, 4-1/2" h.................................... **$1,495**

James D. Julia, Inc.

Trumpet-shaped vase with wide ruffled opening, exterior decorated with green pulled feather design having platinum feather accents on ivory ground with gold interior, signed "Quezal 2317" to underside, very good to excellent condition, 6-1/2" h. x 5-1/4" w. **$1,035**

James D. Julia, Inc.

Pulled feather lamp shade, iridescent opal with gold interior, green and gold decoration, signed around fitter rim, on a brass electric table lamp, first quarter 20th century, shade undamaged, lamp with minor split to top of stem, 19-1/2" h. overall, shade 6" dia. overall. **$316**

Jeffrey S. Evans & Associates

Applied glass decorated vase with green pulled feather design extending from foot to lip, each pulled feather outlined in gold iridescence, tendrils in gold iridescence, interior of lip has gold iridescence, signed in polished pontil with engraved signature "Quezal K629," signature and number highlighted in gold, very good to excellent condition, 5-3/4" h. **$3,738**

James D. Julia, Inc.

SANDWICH GLASS

Numerous types of glass were produced at the Boston & Sandwich Glass Co. in Sandwich, Massachusetts, on Cape Cod, from 1826 to 1888. Founded by Deming Jarves, the company produced a wide variety of wares in differing levels of quality. The factory used free-blown, blown three-mold, and pressed glass manufacturing techniques. Both clear and colored glass were used.

Jarves served as general manager from 1826-1858, and after he left, emphasis was placed on mass production. The development of a lime glass (non-flint) led to lower costs for pressed glass. Some free-blown and blown-and-molded pieces were made. By the 1880s the company was operating at a loss, and the factory closed on Jan. 1, 1888.

Pair of blue and clambroth pressed Acanthus Leaf pattern glass candlesticks, 1840-1865, 9-3/8" h. **$600**

Skinner, Inc.

Pair of pressed Petal and Loop candlesticks, electric blue, each six-petal socket with hexagonal extension, raised on hexagonal knop and seven-loop circular base with rough pontil mark, wafer construction, Boston & Sandwich Glass Co. and possibly others, 1840-1860, 7" h., 4-3/8" dia. base. **$1,840**

Jeffrey S. Evans & Associates

GLASS

▶ Cut frosted and bright beaded top creamer, colorless with applied ruby rim insert, original Meriden Britannia Co. #376 quadruple-plated silver stand, both insert and stand with matching "33" number, 1870-1887, 4-3/4" h. overall, 2-3/4" dia. insert rim.
.... **$115**

Jeffrey S. Evans & Associates

Pressed Star and Punty spoon holder/spill, yellow (uranium), hexagonal bowl raised on low circular foot with polished pontil mark, Boston & Sandwich Glass Co. and probably others, 1850-1870, 4-3/4" h., 3-3/4" dia. overall. **$345**

Jeffrey S. Evans & Associates

Morning Glory egg cup, colorless lead glass, three leaves on top of foot, third quarter 19th century, 3-7/8" h., 2-1/2" dia. rim. .. **$173**

Jeffrey S. Evans & Associates

Pressed four-printie block vase, cobalt blue, deep conical bowl with gauffered six-petal rim and hexagonal-knop extension, raised on a hexagonal knop and flared base, wafer construction, 1840-1860, 11-3/4" h., 4-1/2" dia. rim, 5-1/4" dia. foot. **$1,495**

Jeffrey S. Evans & Associates

Large covered dish, Princess Feather Medallion and Basket of Flowers patterns, 1830 to 1845, dish 10-1/2" x 9-3/4", with lid 5-1/2" h. **$977**

James D. Julia, Inc.

Pair of colorless octagonal pressed glass dishes with eagle and shield, circa 1840, plates centered with spreadwing eagle with arrows and olive branch surrounded by 13 stars, curved panel sides with shield and floral motifs, scalloped rims, mold underfill on rims of both dishes in the making, minor rim chips, 1-3/8" h., 6-1/2" dia..**$123**

Skinner, Inc., www.skinnerinc.com

Pressed open-work dish on low foot, apple green, flared 22-scallop rim surrounding acid-roughed center with worn original silver floral decoration, polished table ring, 1860-1870, 2-1/4" h., 5-7/8" dia. rim, 3" dia. foot.
.... **$1,955**

Jeffrey S. Evans & Associates

STEUBEN

Frederick Carder, an Englishman, and Thomas G. Hawkes of Corning, New York, established the Steuben Glass Works in 1903 in Steuben County, New York. In 1918, the Corning Glass Co. purchased the Steuben company. Carder remained with the firm and designed many of the pieces bearing the Steuben mark. Probably the most widely recognized wares are Aurene, Verre De Soie, and Rosaline, but many other types were produced. The firm operated until 2011.

Creamer and sugar, selenium red, shape 6139 without optic molding, each with polished pontil mark and stamped acid fleur-de-lis mark, first half 20th century, undamaged, 5-3/8" and 5-5/8" h. overall. **$1,093**

Jeffrey S. Evans & Associates

"Stump" vase in gold Aurene, base engraved "Aurene" with shape number 2744, tallest prong 6-1/2" h. **$650**

Mark Mussio, Humler & Nolan

◀ Three-part vase, ivory, shape 7321, four spaced two-line pillars on each section, waffle-like pontil mark, not signed, first half 20th century, undamaged, 11-1/2" h., 4-3/4" dia. foot. **$1,840**

Jeffrey S. Evans & Associates

Candlesticks with topaz ribbed and flanged holders and raised ribbed bases connected by slender rope crystal stems, Steuben fleur-de-lis logo acid stamped into both bases, excellent condition, 12" h. **$400**

Mark Mussio, Humler & Nolan

Green jade and alabaster candlesticks with half twist stems, excellent condition, 9-7/8" and 10-1/4" h.
.... **$600**

Mark Mussio, Humler & Nolan

▶ Gold Aurene compote with flaring hexagonal rim, engraved "Steuben Aurene, 6241" on bottom, gold bowl with magenta reflecting on foot, excellent condition, 3-3/4" h. x 7" w.
....**$350**

Mark Mussio, Humler & Nolan

Two green jade covered jars finished with alabaster finials and applied glass inverted saucer feet, very good to excellent condition, 10-1/2" h. and 11" h.
.... **$920**

James D. Julia, Inc.

Cut crystal pelican figure, signed, 6-1/4" h. x 6-1/2" w. x 3" d.. **$275**

Crescent City Auction Gallery

Amethyst goblet, amethyst glass bowl cut in pattern with flowers, leaves and stems, blown hollow stem with applied crystal foot, signed on underside with acid-etched "Steuben" fleur de lis, very good to excellent condition, 8-1/4" h.......................................**$201**

James D. Julia, Inc.

Plum jade lamp acid cut with Pagoda pattern on four sides, layered with glossy black surface, matte finish backdrop, excellent condition, body 12" h., original decorative factory mounts 26" to finial. **$1,200**

Mark Mussio, Humler & Nolan

Covered jar, amethyst glass finished with clear glass finial, signed "Steuben" and "F. Carder," very good to excellent condition, 13-3/4" h. **$1,062**

James D. Julia, Inc.

Aurene lamp shade, iridescent green, intarsia border of green and white abstract waves on gold ground, not signed, first quarter 20th century, undamaged, 5" h., 7-1/2" dia. overall, 2-1/4" dia. fitter. ..**$1,955**

Jeffrey S. Evans & Associates

Gold Aurene candlesticks with candle cups, twisted stems on inverted saucer feet, signed "Aurene" and numbered, very good to excellent condition, 8" h...**$690**

James D. Julia, Inc.

Gold aurene cauldron-shaped open salt, signed "Aurene 2668," very good to excellent condition, 1" h. x 1-3/4" w. **$259**

James D. Julia, Inc.

Blue Aurene vase with wide ruffled rim, engraved "Aurene" with 723 shape number, minor surface scratches, 9" h. x 8-1/2" w. **$700**

Mark Mussio, Humler & Nolan

Oriental jade stem with jade cup with opalescent twisted stem on circular foot, very good to excellent condition, 6" h. **$690**

James D. Julia, Inc.

Ivory vase with ribbed body and scalloped rim, excellent condition, 5" h. **$150**

Mark Mussio, Humler & Nolan

▼ Ivorene vase, large bulbous form with rolled lip and two applied glass "M" handles, very good condition with minute rubbing to iridescent finish, 11-1/2" h. **$345**

James D. Julia, Inc.

Green jade vase in rectangular form with swirl pattern on surface, excellent condition, 9-1/4" h. **$160**

Mark Mussio, Humler & Nolan

Aurene glass vase with peacock feathers, circa 1905, etched "Aurene 273," 12-1/2" x 4-1/2". **$6,875**

Rago Arts and Auction Center

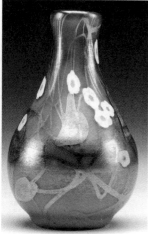

Millefiori decorated vase, bulbous form with elongated neck with green ground, decorated with platinum heart and vine pattern with white millefiori, signed "Aurene 575," very good to excellent condition, 3-7/8" h.
.... **$2,990**

James D. Julia, Inc.

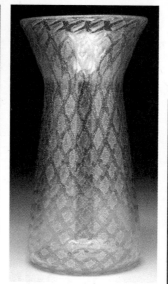

Silverina vase, large diamond quilted clear vase with flared neck decorated with Silverina finish, unsigned, very good to excellent condition, 12" h................. **$797**

James D. Julia, Inc.

TOP LOT!

Oriental floral design vase, acid cut back in Rosaline cut to alabaster, drilled at bottom, very good to excellent condition, 10" h.
.... **$575**

James D. Julia, Inc.

Gold Aurene vase of cylinder form with vertical ribbing and scalloped lip, signed "Aurene 355," very good to excellent condition, 10" h.
.... **$345**

James D. Julia, Inc.

Gold Aurene vase with brown Aurene pulled feather design descending from lip extending approximately halfway down body, gold iridescence on body has pink and blue highlights, gold iridescence on interior of mouth shows purple and pink highlights, signed on underside "Aurene 266," very good to excellent condition, 11-1/2" h........ **$8,050**

James D. Julia, Inc.

TIFFANY

Tiffany & Co. was founded by Charles Lewis Tiffany (1812-1902) and Teddy Young in New York City in 1837 as a "stationery and fancy goods emporium." The store initially sold a wide variety of stationery items, and operated as Tiffany, Young and Ellis in lower Manhattan. The name was shortened to Tiffany & Co. in 1853, and the firm's emphasis on jewelry was established.

The first Tiffany catalog, known as the "Blue Book," was published in 1845. It is still being published today.

In 1862 Tiffany & Co. supplied the Union Army with swords, flags and surgical implements.

Charles' son, Louis Comfort Tiffany (1848-1933), was an American artist and designer who worked in the decorative arts and is best known for his work in stained glass. Louis established Tiffany Glass Co. in 1885, and in 1902 it became known as Tiffany Studios. America's outstanding glass designer of the Art Nouveau period produced glass from the last quarter of the 19th century until the early 1930s. Tiffany revived early techniques and devised many new ones.

Tall gold Favrile glass trumpet vase with heart and vine pattern, New York, 1918, 1536-606M L.C. Tiffany Favrile, 15" x 8"... **$2,000**

Rago Arts and Auction Center

Inkwell cast in Spanish pattern with large gargoyles on each side with wings spread, inkwell finished in gold patina with light red highlights, retains original glass insert, very good to excellent condition, 5-3/4" w. x 4" h... **$4,500-$5,500**

James D. Julia, Inc.

Venetian pattern letter rack, bronze, highlighted with black enamel background, signed on underside Tiffany Studios NEW YORK 1644, very good to excellent condition, 6" h. x 10" w.
.... **$700-$1,000**

James D. Julia, Inc.

Flower form sherbet with clear body and pastel lavender interior, ruffled rim with interior ribs of white opalescence, opalescent exterior or rim, all supported by clear saucer foot with white opalescent edge, signed on underside LC TIFFANY FAVRILE 1938, very good to excellent condition, 5-1/4" h.......... **$1,380**

James D. Julia, Inc.

Rare gold Favrile glass low bowl with reticulated edges, New York, 1915, 5538J/L.C. Tiffany – Favrile, 2" x 6-3/4". **$750**

Rago Arts and Auction Center

Bronze pen tray cast in Venetian pattern with band of otters around edge, finished in gold patina and highlighted with green enamel background, marked on underside Tiffany Studios NEW YORK 1642, very good to excellent condition, 3-3/4" x 10".............................. **$460**

James D. Julia, Inc.

Pair of open salts, iridescent gold finish on amber glass with eight swirls, signed on underside L.C.T., very good to excellent condition, 1-7/8" dia... **$518**

James D. Julia, Inc.

Tiffany Furnaces, Inc. enameled dish, bronze, decorated with four blue enameled flowers, each with yellow and green centers, signed Louis C. Tiffany Furnaces Inc, plus Furnaces logo, Favrile 328, very good to excellent condition with minor wear, 4-1/2" w. **$489**

James D. Julia, Inc.

Pen tray cast in Spanish pattern with gold patina, brown enamel background, light red enamel highlights, marked on underside Tiffany Studios NEW YORK 1882, very good to excellent condition, 9-7/8" x 3-3/4"..**$500-$700**

James D. Julia, Inc.

Miniature Favrile glass cabinet vase with prunts, New York, 1906, L.C.T. 6082A, 2-1/4" x 1-3/4". **$1,375**

Rago Arts and Auction Center

Squat blue Favrile glass vase in feather pattern, New York, 1901, etched 06787, 2-3/4" x 4". **$3,125**

Rago Arts and Auction Center

Squat Favrile glass vase with gold pulled-feather decoration on emerald green ground, New York, 1921 2727P L.C. Tiffany Favrile, 3-1/2" x 5-1/2"............... **$1,625**

Rago Arts and Auction Center

Handkerchief box, etched metal gold grapevine pattern atop gold striated glass panels, four bun feet, signed Tiffany Studios New York 824, very good condition with minor wear, hinge is loose, 8" x 8" x 2-1/2". **$1,035**

James D. Julia, Inc.

GLASS

Pony (miniature) Wisteria table lamp, shade impressed TIFFANY STUDIOS NEW YORK, base impressed TIFFANY STUDIOS NEW YORK 249, 15-1/2" h., shade 10" dia. Provenance: The Garden Museum Collection, Matsue, Japan.............**$106,200**

Michaan's Auctions

Bulbous Favrile glass vase with gold and emerald pulled-feather decoration, New York, 1901, L.C.T. O4483, 4-1/2" x 4"......... **$1,750**

Rago Arts and Auction Center

Gold Favrile glass ruffled shade, circa 1910, etched L.C.T., 3-1/2" x 7-1/2"......... **$625**

Rago Arts and Auction Center

Humidor, oak with brass handles and fittings, custom silver-plated interior and monogrammed top, early 20th century, stamped Tiffany & Company Union Square, 5-3/4" x 12-3/8" x 11"....... **$938**

Rago Arts and Auction Center

Spanish blotter ends finished in gold patina with brown enamel background, signed on backside Tiffany Studios New York 1880, very good to excellent condition, 19-3/8" l. **$575**

James D. Julia, Inc.

Set of two "Zodiac" bronze items, inkwell and blotter rocker, both medium doré patina and both stamped "Tiffany Studios New York" with rocker shape number 909 and inkwell shape number 1072, both in excellent condition, inkwell has original glass well and is 3-1/2" h. . **$650**

Mark Mussio, Humler & Nolan

Three Favrile glass tiles, New York, two with raised Pat. Appld For, 4" sq., 3" sq. **$1,063**

Rago Arts and Auction Center

Patinated bronze-clad Favrile pottery vase with fuchsias, New York, circa 1910, stamped LCT, marked B.P. 288/ LC Tiffany-Favrile Bronze Pottery, 10" x 3-1/2". **$4,375**

Rago Arts and Auction Center

Monumental peacock vase, classic form with green background decorated with peacock feathers in platinum, eyes of feathers in hues of platinum, sapphire blue, and medium blue, signed L.C.T. F1976, overall good condition with stable spider hairline to interior layer of glass, which does not extend to exterior, 19-1/2" h............**$8,625**

James D. Julia, Inc.

Tall Favrile glass vase with gold sprigs on opalescent ground, New York, 1907, acid-etched L.C.T. 3909B, 13-1/2" x 4-1/2".. **$3,500**

Rago Arts and Auction Center

Favrile iridescent floriform bud vase, 20th century, signed LC Tiffany Favrile, HL189, 6". **$750**

Rago Arts and Auction Center

Byzantine spindle, rare pattern with ornate gold doré bronze work, accented with four coral cabochons, signed on underside Tiffany Studios New York 963, very good to excellent condition, 7-1/2" h. x 3-3/4" across............**$500-$700**

James D. Julia, Inc.

Small glazed ceramic vase with lily of the valley, Old Ivory glaze, New York, circa 1905, incised LCT, 6" x 2-3/4"......... **$1,875**

Rago Arts and Auction Center

Small Favrile pottery bisque-fired vase with maple pods, New York, circa 1905, incised LCT, 5-1/2" x 2-1/2"... **$1,000**

Rago Arts and Auction Center

Bisque-fired Favrile pottery vase with wisteria, New York, circa 1905, incised LCT, penciled P1429/ LCT Pottery, 10-1/4" x 4-1/2".............. **$1,500**

Rago Arts and Auction Center

TOP LOT!

Table lamp, part of both the Venetian and Ninth Century desk set patterns, base adorned with bands of circular glass cabochons, shade impressed TIFFANY STUDIOS NEW YORK 515-6, base of gilt bronze, enameled and gem-set, impressed TIFFANY STUDIOS NEW YORK 515, 20" h., shade 13-1/8" dia. Provenance: The Garden Museum Collection, Matsue, Japan. **$112,100**

Michaan's Auctions

Dragonfly table lamp, shade mounted on one of the most sought after, rare bases decorated with three dragonflies in heavy relief bronze with inlay of iridescent mosaic Favrile glass tiles that continue up shaft of base, shade of fractured (confetti) Favrile glass forming wings of blue-bodied dragonflies, shade impressed TIFFANY STUDIOS NEW YORK NY 1585, base impressed TIFFANY STUDIOS NEW YORK 356, 20" h., shade 14" dia. Provenance: The Garden Museum Collection, Matsue, Japan. **$141,600**

Michaan's Auctions

Cigarette box with rare medallion pattern finished with enameling in blue and green on gold finish, inside of box is complete with wood for storage of tobacco products, signed Tiffany Studios New York 2029, very good to excellent condition with minimal wear, 2" h. x 3-1/2" x 4-1/2". **$575**

James D. Julia, Inc.

Pine needle picture frame, etched metal design of pine needles in patina finish resting against green striated glass panels, signed Tiffany Studios New York 941, very good to excellent condition, 4" x 6" outside, 2-1/4" x 3" inside. **$1,093**

James D. Julia, Inc.

TIFFIN

A wide variety of fine glasswares were produced by the Tiffin Glass Co. of Tiffin, Ohio. Beginning as a part of the large U.S. Glass Co. early in the 20th century, the Tiffin factory continued making a wide range of wares until its final closing in 1984. One popular line is now called "Black Satin" and included various vases with raised floral designs. Many other acid-etched and hand-cut patterns were also produced over the years and are very collectible today. The three *Tiffin Glassmasters* books by Fred Bickenheuser are the standard references for Tiffin collectors.

Cockatoo evening lamp on black glass base with Bryant light socket, orange and green bird perched on brown branch, electrical cord appears original and has old style "on-off" capsule switch, comes with yellow cellophane-wrapped lightbulb, excellent original condition, 12-1/2" h., 13-1/2" h. overall. **$225**

Mark Mussio, Humler & Nolan

Parrot glass novelty lamp, frosted shade with polychrome decoration, opaque black base, U.S. Glass Co., Pittsburgh, circa 1925, rim of shade with glued chip is hidden when shade is in place, otherwise undamaged, 13" h. **$316**

Jeffrey S. Evans & Associates

Pair of candlesticks (one shown), one-light, floral cut decoration, Royal Blue. **$160**

Flower console glass novelty lamp, shiny puffy floral shade with polychrome decoration, fitted onto opaque black base, U.S. Glass Co., Pittsburgh, circa 1925, 9" h. overall, 8" dia. base............ **$431**

Jeffrey S. Evans & Associates

Candleholder, three-light, Art Deco style Pattern 308, Sky Blue, 7-1/4" w. x 6-3/8" h. **$65**

Flower basket glass novelty lamp, frosted puffy floral shade with polychrome decoration, opaque black base, U.S. Glass Co., Pittsburgh, circa 1925, undamaged, shallow chip to interior rim of shade as made, 7-1/2" h. overall................. **$230**

Jeffrey S. Evans & Associates

Candy jar, covered, plum, mold-blown, No. 6106, diamond optic ovoid body tapering to slender stem and foot, domed cover with pointed finial..................... **$125**

Colonial dame/crinoline girl glass novelty lamp, frosted shade with polychrome decoration, opaque black base, U.S. Glass Co., Pittsburgh, circa 1925, undamaged except for minor flake to hair and back of one arm, 9-1/2" h. **$218**

Jeffrey S. Evans & Associates

Pair of Black Satin glass vases with silver overlay irises, Tiffin Glass Co., slight damage to silver on one, 11" h..................... **$600**

Kaminski Auctions

Figural glass novelty perfume lamp, frosted puffy floral shade with interior polychrome decoration, opaque black base, U.S. Glass Co., Pittsburgh, circa 1926, undamaged, 5" h. **$488**

Jeffrey S. Evans & Associates

Candy jar, covered, Pattern No. 179, footed, widely flaring base and wide pagoda-style cover with Gold Ship decoration, Black Satin, 6-1/2" dia., 7-1/2" h. **$95**

GLASS

WAVE CREST

Now much sought after, Wave Crest was produced by the C.F. Monroe Co., Meriden, Connecticut, in the late 19th and early 20th centuries from opaque white glass blown into molds. It was then hand decorated in enamels, and metal trim was often added. Boudoir accessories such as jewel boxes, hair receivers, etc., predominated.

Cameo box depicting young man on country road with trees in full foliage, earthen hues set against peach and blue ground, tight hinge and clasp, very good to excellent condition with remnants of silk lining in bottom of box and minor wear to metal fittings, 3" h. x 8" w. **$1,610**

James D. Julia, Inc.

Open tray, cobalt blue with polychrome floral reserve on each side, gilt-metal rim and handles, two-line Wave Crest mark under base, late 19th/early 20th century, undamaged with light wear, 1-1/2" h., 3-1/2" dia. rim, 5-5/8" w......................**$69**

Jeffrey S. Evans & Associates

Two Erie Twist salt shakers, opal with cream ground and other with light blue ground, each with polychrome floral decoration, satin finishes, matching two-part period lids, late 19th/early 20th century, undamaged, lids with minor wear to finish, 2-1/4" h. overall. **$92**

Jeffrey S. Evans & Associates

Covered cracker jar painted with large blue and pink Shasta daisies and foliage front and back, twist rope handle, excellent condition, 8" h. **$160**

Mark Mussio, Humler & Nolan

"Collars and cuffs" box containing antique Van Heusen collars and decorative starched cuffs, box lid and one side decorated with lily of the valley and yellow flowers within a molded surround of scrolling, ormolu feet, stamped with red Wave Crest shield on bottom box, excellent condition, 7" h., 7-1/4" dia. **$200**

Mark Mussio, Humler & Nolan

▶ Dresser box with Helmschmied Swirl and large two-tone yellow mum flower heads and crescent-shaped area of blue violets, lilac enameling, pewter color feet, metal plate in bottom, unusual double decoration, excellent condition, 6" h. x 7" w........ **$475**

Mark Mussio, Humler & Nolan

Dresser box, pink rosebuds over Helmschmied Swirl cover and base, excellent condition, 4-3/4" h. x 6" w............................. **$170**

Mark Mussio, Humler & Nolan

No. 285 cracker jar, opal with rose ground and floral transfer decoration, silver-plated mountings and cover with bail handle, interior of cover impressed "1512," late 19th/early 20th century, excellent condition with minor high-point wear, metal mountings with some minute imperfections, 8" h. overall, 5-1/4" dia. base...... **$115**

Jeffrey S. Evans & Associates

▶ Candlestick with blue floral bouquets front and back with pink around base, bright and mat gold ormolu mounts, minor gilt loss due to handling, otherwise excellent original condition, 7" h. **$325**

Mark Mussio, Humler & Nolan

Match holder, cream ground with polychrome floral and gilt decoration, top of rim with tiny beading, mounted on gilt-metal pedestal base, early 20th century, undamaged with minor wear to decoration, 2-7/8" h. **$138**

Jeffrey S. Evans & Associates

Hooked Rugs

Beginning about a century-and-a-half ago, men and women created hooked rugs to warm their hearths and homes. These folk art floor coverings, which were originally made to cover dirt floors, were fashioned out of ingenuity and frugality and are now highly valued in collectors' and decorators' markets.

Wool rug hooking is thought to have begun in Canada's easternmost provinces and in the Northeast United States. Fabric scraps no longer suitable for clothing were cut into strips and hooked by varying techniques into a burlap ground in patterns. The end result – whether simple or complex, geometric, floral or pictorial – was only limited by the artisan's skill and imagination.

The earliest hooked rugs date from the early-to-mid-19th century; these early rugs are most often found in museums and historical societies.

Laura Fisher, proprietor of the Fisher Heritage gallery in New York, has several hundred vintage and antique quilts in her inventory, ranging from the mid-19th century through the 1950s. When asked about what hooked rug collectors gravitate toward, Fisher said

Old Dutch cleanser oval hooked rug, mid-20th century, 20" x 36".. **$200**

Northeast Auction

some people prefer early rugs with animals, which can fetch high prices at auction.

"The earlier and folksier, the more valuable," she said. "Other people love early 19th century florals that were popular in Maine and Canada. The flowers are raised, clipped and sheared so the rug has a three-dimensional quality." These rugs often have a center bouquet set within a scrollwork border.

Wool hooked rugs became widely popular in the third quarter of the 19th century. Some entrepreneurs saw the growing interest in this home activity and recognized that there would be a demand for pre-designed rug patterns, especially for rug hookers who were unsatisfied with their own artistic skills.

Edward Sands Frost of Biddeford, Maine, Ralph Burnham of Ipswitch, Massachusetts, and Ebenezer Ross of Toledo, Ohio, were three such entrepreneurs. Frost (1843-1894) was one of the earliest commercial hooked rug pattern makers. By creating pre-stamped patterns on burlap with sheet metal stencils, he expanded and transformed the homemade rug hooking industry, making rug hooking a viable cottage industry – an industry that helped fishing communities survive harsh Atlantic winters.

Probably the most noteworthy cottage industry name in the Atlantic region – and therefore some of the most prized hooked mats and rugs by collectors – is Grenfell Industries, which produced thousands of high-quality mats and rugs, many with regional themes such as wintertime, polar bears, fishermen and nautical; geometric designs were also created, but they are more rare.

Shortly after the turn of the 20th century, an English missionary, Dr. Wilfred T. Grenfell, saw the need for struggling communities in Canada to supplement the local fishing industry in the off-season. Recognizing the locals' extraordinary needlework skills (settlers brought mat hooking from England and Scotland), he established a mission based in St. Anthony, Newfoundland, Canada, to generate revenue for Labrador and northern Newfoundland residents: Material kits and patterns were distributed to home workers who then created mats, rugs and other textile products. Those products were then sold through stores and catalogs.

The original Grenfell Industries mats are distinctive because they were made using dyed silk stockings instead of wool; the artisans were so skilled that they were able to use every hole in the backing, sometimes achieving 200 stitches per square inch. Each finished piece was inspected to assure quality and workmanship standards were met.

Grenfell Mission octagonal mat, late 19th/early 20th century, unusual geometric pattern in blue, brown, and green, original label, very good condition, 12-1/2" x 12-1/2"......................................**$850**

Pook & Pook, Inc.

After peaking in the 1920s, the Great Depression hit Grenfell Industries hard. Sales and donations lagged and supplies were depleted. World War II caused supply and transportation challenges, as well as rising costs. After the war, silk stockings were no longer available.

Mat hooking continues today in St. Anthony by the independently owned Grenfell Handicrafts, which produces contemporary mats from original, copyrighted Grenfell patterns.

Other traditional designs manufactured a century ago also are still available and popular with contemporary rug hookers. Because hooked wool rugs were made in the home for personal use, seldom can they be traced back to the original maker or pinned down to an exact date; rarely do antique hooked rugs come with such detailed provenance. There are clues to a rug's age and value, however.

Hooked rugs generally fall into three different age categories. The first is antique: 100 years old or more. These rugs can command anywhere from a few hundred to thousands of dollars, depending upon the design, age, condition, provenance and other factors.

"Collectible" or "vintage" hooked rugs – rugs that are typically 25 to 75 years old – are often priced at less than $100 and come in an unlimited variety of styles and designs. One can pick up a collectible hooked rug for a fraction of what a true "antique" rug would cost.

Falling into the collectible rug category, "Hutchinson rugs are highly desirable and collectible," Fisher says. James and Mercedes Hutchinson designed their own rugs from the 1920s-1940s to sell to the public at auction. They are often humorous, with funny observations about relationships, poems and epigrams. Hutchinson rugs are one example of vintage rugs bringing sometimes extraordinary prices.

Pearl McGown rugs from the 1950s are also coveted by collectors. "Like Grenfell," Fisher says, "McGown rugs are extremely fine and beautiful." McGown, who was from West Amesbury, Massachusetts, wrote many books, taught people how to dye their own rag strips, and created the reverse lock stitch, making the back of a rug look as wonderful as the front. Fisher says McGown produced hundreds of patterns and trained women as rug hooking educators to share her techniques with a wider audience. McGown's granddaughter is involved with organizing contemporary rug hooking events.

Contemporary hooked rugs are newer than 25 years old. However, just because a contemporary hooked wool rug doesn't have a significant amount of age, doesn't mean it's not valuable. Each rug is still a handmade, unique work of art. Like collecting any contemporary art, the price paid for a piece will be as appreciation and recognition of the skill and design of the rug artist.

Fisher cautions that there are hooked rugs being made in China and India today, made by

HOOKED RUGS

companies capitalizing on the interest in old, folk-art type rugs. How do you tell the difference?

"There's a different technique of manufacturing," Fisher said. "Most international imports are hooked on monk's cloth cotton weave backing rather than burlap. Burlap is the foundation of choice for the majority of hooked rugs that are antique and vintage, either American or Canadian." Fisher continues, "Rug hookers today use monk's cloth cotton because it doesn't crack and dry like burlap."

Also, a lot of Eastern import rugs have a thick latex backing. They feel and handle differently than vintage or antique rugs. Fisher elaborates: "They have a heavy feel that old rugs don't have. New England rug restorers in the 1950s used a different kind of latex."

American figural wool hooked rug with Scottish terrier, mid-20th century, rectangular rug centered with standing gray and black dog, variegated red, light blue, and green background, red and black borders with yellow-outlined red trefoils in corners, 19" x 32-1/4". **$300**

Skinner, Inc.

Another detail that will help in determining if a hooked rug is old or new: Old rugs were made with rag strips; new imported rugs are usually made with wool yarn. And if they happen to be made with rag strips, it's cotton knit rather than wool. Old rugs were made with scrap fabric; there's a variation in color. Wear, use, air and environment all affect the color.

"Variegation in color and age patina give antique rugs a visual liveliness that so far no one has been able to match in manufacturing," Fisher explains. "A new-made rug has a flatter appearance … There's no substitution for age."

Jessie Turbayne, author of *The Complete Guide to Collecting Hooked Rugs: Unrolling the Secrets*, as well as seven other books on hooked rugs, has been buying, selling, collecting, and restoring hooked rugs for nearly 40 years. She recommends focusing on a particular type or age of hooked rug when starting a collection, "Buying just for the sake of buying is unwise and costly."

A respected authority on rug values and care, Turbayne teaches rug hooking and restores anywhere from 200 to 400 hooked rugs per year for museums, collectors and antiques dealers in her Massachusetts workshop. She estimates about 90 percent of the restoration work is hand stitching, sometimes using fine surgical needles.

American pictorial hooked rug depicting cottage and trees, wide border, first quarter 20th century, very good condition with expected fading, minor edge fray, 26-1/2" x 40". **$46**

Jeffrey S. Evans & Associates

Turbayne says people often don't know what they're buying. If they bring a rug to her for repair, she advises the potential client of the rug's value and its estimated restoration cost. Though she has executed restorations anywhere from $10 to $20,000, a typical restoration runs $100-$300.

The possibility of expenses incurred in restoring hooked rugs shouldn't dissuade collectors. As Turbayne says, "As functioning art, they are equally at home hung on walls as placed on floors." These hand-crafted works of folk art add color, texture and warmth to any décor.

— *Karen Knapstein, Print Editor,* Antique Trader *magazine*

American hooked rug, early 20th century, with running horse, 21-1/2" h. x 38" w. **$972**

Pook & Pook Inc.

American hooked rug with dog, circa 1900, 22" x 36"..**$889**

Pook & Pook. Inc.

American hooked rug, dated 1902, initialed SG, with galloping horse flanked by chickens, large tear to left chicken and other tears, large patch to chicken, some fading, 24" x 66". **$3,200**

Pook & Pook, Inc.

American hooked rug with horses, early 20th century, 28" x 39"...**$830**

Pook & Pook, Inc.

Hooked rug of steamboat Ticonderoga on Lake Champlain, depicted within scrollwork on red ground, 34-1/2" x 49"..................**$2,000-$3,000**

Northeast Auction

Hooked rug depicting dog seated on colorful diamond-patterned rug within oval foliate surround, 28" x 46"..**$472**

Northeast Auction

American hooked rug, inscribed Arthur Jr. 1932, 32" x 46". **$1,126**

Pook & Pook, Inc.

Framed American hooked rug, with date 1904 flanked by two American flags, 37" x 57". ...**$1,541**

Pook & Pook, Inc.

Raveled hooked rug with owl, paired birds, and cats; southeastern Pennsylvania, circa 1840-1860, wool yarns on fine linen, applied button eyes, fabric beaks, and silk ribbon edging, 23" x 36", stretched and mounted. .... **$8,000-$12,000**

Northeast Auction

American figural wool hooked rug with recumbent spaniel, late 19th/early 20th century, rectangular rug centered with spotted spaniel resting on plinth with scroll border, mounted on wooden stretcher, minor fading and toning, 28-3/4" x 42-1/2" overall. **$390**

Skinner, Inc.

Early American hooked rug of cat sitting at a window surrounded by flowers and butterflies within a multicolor border, mounted on stretcher, 25-1/2" x 36". **$450**

Northeast Auction

Grenfell Labrador Industries mat depicting two-masted schooner with red sails and black hull sailing on blue sea, original label, circa 1920, very good condition, 10-1/4" dia. **$70**

Louis J. Dianni, LLC

American folk art hooked rug depicting a family of ducks and ducklings, worked on a background of blues and greens with tan and black border, mounted on a frame, 24" x 33-3/4". **$400**

Northeast Auction

Early American hooked rug of trotting horse with red rose and scalloped border, mounted on stretcher, 23" x 39". **$1,062**

Northeast Auction

Grenfell mat depicting Inuit, dogsled, ship, snowshoes, etc., with original Grenfell Labrador Industries label, one small tear right center edge, 27-1/2" x 20-7/8".....................................**$1,700**

Kaminski Auctions

Early American hooked rug with flowerpot and red roses, mounted on stretcher, 36-1/2" x 34-3/4"............ **$550**

Northeast Auction

American large hooked rug with geometric border, circa 1900, wool, 87" x 73". ....**$1,200-$1,800**

Northeast Auction

American wool floral hooked rug, early 20th century, rectangular, central oval reserve with assortment of blossoms and leaves in gray-blue rectangle with more blossoms on either end, on a field of multicolored rectangular tile-shaped segments, repairs, 39" x 60"... **$360**

Skinner, Inc., www.skinnerinc.com

Set of six scenic hooked rugs, 9" h. x 22" w. (image), 13-3/4" x 27-1/4" (framed)............................**$600**

Kaminski Auctions

Illustration Art

Few new collecting categories appear in the world of fine art and collectibles. Illustration art is relatively new and values are going up every year. Although illustration or commercial art had been offered at auction for some time, it was generally lumped under American fine art auctions and only offered if the artist was a "somebody" such as Norman Rockwell or Maxfield

"The Beam of the Lighthouse," *The New Yorker* cover, June 23, 1973, watercolor, ink, and pencil on board, Charles Samuel Addams (American, 1912-1988), 21" x 15".......................................**$15,000**

Parrish. That all changed in 2009. That's when Heritage Auctions began offering selections from the estate of Charles Martignette, a voracious collector of original commercial art by generally obscure artists. The collection has launched an entirely new collecting category and is racking up world record prices in its wake.

"We really feel that since offering the Martignette estate starting in 2009, we've been building on that market ever since," said Todd Hignite, Vice President of Heritage Auctions. "With every auction we see a lot of new collectors coming in from other fields. No other major auction house took an interest in this area, and it really wasn't until 2009 that collectors were able to see these rare items. And people are holding huge amounts of it."

More than 5,000 pieces of the Martignette collection have been auctioned, including works by Joseph Christian Leyendecker and Arthur Saron Sarnoff and even pin-up art from giants such as Gil Elvgrin and Alberto Vargas. As expected, the most iconic images routinely bring six figures at auction. This has encouraged collectors all across the country to look at this artwork as true works of art. Most illustration art is sold at prices ranging from $1,000 to $10,000, although this amount creeps up each year.

For example, Patrick Nagel's early 1980s artworks are increasing exponentially. Nagel's painting titled "Covering Up" set a record for the artist when it sold for $56,250 in 2012. That record was shattered when a second painting, "Her Seductive Look," was sold in April 2013 for $158,500.

"Prices for these works have, in two years, gone through the roof," Hignite said. "It's an interesting situation in that people don't think of art from the 1980s as classic illustration art. The reason this took so long for prices to go up is that you had to get far enough away from that time period to see Nagel's work as a representation of that time period. For the longest time, people felt it was too new – too recent. Now that we're far enough away from that time period we see Nagel's work as an iconic representation of the 1980s.

"With ever high-profile auctions," Hignite added, "I fully expect to see records set and see new collectors get involved in the market."

All images courtesy Heritage Auctions

ILLUSTRATION ART

TOP LOT!

!

"Goldilocks and the Three Bears," Swift's Premium Soap Products calendar illustration, 1916, conte crayon and watercolor on board, Jessie Willcox Smith (American, 1863-1935), 25-1/4" x 16-1/4"..**$134,500**

"Thanksgiving," gouache on board, American artist (20th century), from the estate of Charles Martignette, 24" x 25". **$593**

"The Tarot Secrets of the Gypsy Card," *Fate Magazine* cover, February 1955, oil on canvas, American artist, not signed, 15-1/2" x 11". **$1,875**

"The Undefeated," paperback cover, 1974, acrylic on board, John Conrad Berkey (American, 1932-2008), signed lower right, created for cover for paperback *The Undefeated* by Keith Laumer (Dell books #9285, 1974),14-1/2" x 9".. **$937**

"A Refreshing Break," beverage advertisement, oil on canvas, Arnold Armitage (American, 1899-1991), signed lower right, 21" x 45". **$4,687**

"Starts Without a Murmur," Esso Motor Oil advertisement, oil on canvas, American artist (20th century), not signed, 16" x 35-1/2". **$1,625**

"Peace on Earth," oil on canvas, Harold Anderson (American, 1894-1973), 38" x 28". **$17,500**

"Pink Elephants," *Bedtime Stories* pulp cover, August 1935, oil on canvas, Earle Bergey (American, 1901-1952), 30" x 21".. **$7,500**

"Meccanismo di Volo Improbabile," mixed media on canvas, Giampaolo Bianchi (Italian, b. 1947), 48-1/2" x 60"... **$4,687**

"They All Want Budweiser...Nothing Else," Anheuser Busch advertisement, oil on canvas, not signed, American artist (20th century), 13-1/2" x 33". **$2,250**

"All the World to Mother," *Judge* magazine cover, Oct. 9, 1915, oil on canvas, W. Smithson Broadhead (British, 1888-1955), 29" x 22"..................... **$3,000**

"North of Sinanju," *The American Magazine* story illustration, June 1951, oil on canvas, Walter Martin Baumhofer (American, 1904-1987), from the estate of Charles Martignette, 23" x 34". **$593**

"On Set," magazine story illustration, 1934, pencil and watercolor on board, Ronald Norman Mcleod (American, 1897-1977), from the estate of Charles Martignette, 18" x 7"............................ **$937**

"Prairie Drama," oil on canvas, Harvey T. Dunn (American, 1884-1952), 24" x 30"..**$8,125**

"Sunday Gardening," *The Saturday Evening Post* cover, July 1, 1961, oil on panel, John Philip Falter (American, 1910-1982), 24" x 21-3/4"........**$68,500**

"Quick Change," Brown & Bigelow calendar illustration, 1967, oil on canvas, Gil Elvgren (American, 1914-1980), from the estate of Charles Martignette, 30" x 24". **$110,500**

"Two Beauties," 1930, pen and ink on board, Dorothy Flack (American, 20th century), from the estate of Charles Martignette, 17-1/2" x 15-1/4". **$516**

"A Visit With Chef," Cream of Wheat advertisement, 1911, oil on board, Susan E. Arthurs (American, 20th century), from the estate of Charles Martignette, 27-1/4" x 23"... **$4,687**

"Nazi Warfare," *The Saturday Evening Post* story illustration, watercolor and gouache on board, Stevan Dohanos (American, 1907-1994), 10-3/4" x 34-1/2"...**$687**

Startling Stories digest cover, November 1955, gouache and tempera on board, Edmund (Emsh) Emshwiller (American, 1925-1990), from the Jerry Weist Collection, 12-1/2" x 16-1/2". **$1,625**

"Boarding the Flight," watercolor and gouache on board, Manning Devilleneuve Lee (American, 1894-1980), 17" x 16-1/4". **$1,375**

"Jet Pilot Who Survived Peru's No-Return Jungle," *For Men Only* pulp cover, October 1964, gouache on board, Mort Künstler (American, b. 1931), 12" x 15". **$2,250**

"Afternoon Tea," *Cosmopolitan* magazine cover, September 1925, watercolor on board, Harrison Fisher (American, 1875-1934), painting was published twice: first as the cover for *Cosmopolitan* and again as the cover for Nash's *Pall Mall* magazine, October 1925; both published versions were also reproduced on pages 163 and 189 in *The Complete Works of Harrison Fisher, Illustrator* by Naomi Welch, Images of the Past, 1999, 17-1/2" x 13-1/2". **$11,250**

Science Fiction Plus cover, March 1953, mixed media on board, Alex Schomburg (American, 1905-1998), from the Jerry Weist Collection, 16-1/2" x 12-1/2". ...**$11,875**

"The Stolen Bride of Glengarra Castle," paperback cover, 1990, gouache and tempera on board, Uldis Klavins (American, 20th century), from the estate of Charles Martignette, 37-1/2" x 25"................................. **$875**

"Pin-Up in Black," color silkscreen print, not editioned, Patrick Nagel (American, 1945-1984), 32-1/2" x 23-1/2". **$2,000**

"A Silent Comedy," probable magazine cover, 1927, oil on canvas, Leslie Thrasher (American, 1889-1936), 15" x 13"... **$5,312**

"They Climbed Upon the Golden Rod," Carlyle Emory's Twinkle Town Tales story illustration, 1928, watercolor on paper, Arthur Edward Henderson (British, 1870-1956), not signed, 16-3/4" x 12-3/4". **$468**

"Cowboy on Bucking Bronco," probable western pulp cover, oil on canvas laid on board, Gayle Porter Hoskins (American, 1887-1962), 36" x 24". **$6,875**

"Pin-Up in Sun Hat," watercolor on board, Alberto Vargas (American, 1896-1982), from the estate of Charles Martignette, 22" x 30-1/2".

.... **$6,875**

"Girl Feeding a Canary," *The American Weekly* magazine cover, Feb. 21, 1954, oil on board, Morgan Kane (American, b. 1916), 17-1/4" x 16"...... **$2,500**

"Fairies Playing Games with a Little Girl," 1926, pen and watercolor on paper, Harold Gaze (American, 1884-1963), 14" x 10-1/2"........................... **$1,187**

"White Cross Nurse," oil on canvas laid on board with emblem, Haddon Hubbard Sundblom (American, 1899-1976), formerly in the Collection of the American Red Cross, 33" x 24-3/4". **$8,750**

"Some Folks Frown on It, But It's a Lot of Fun," Pan American Coffee preliminary advertisement, Oct. 7, 1940, oil on canvas, Joseph Christian Leyendecker (American, 1874-1951), not signed, 8" x 11"... **$5,000**

"Winter Landscape with House," gouache and tempera on board, Arthur Saron Sarnoff (American, 1912-2000), from the estate of Charles Martignette, 12" x 16".. **$875**

"Gypsies Paused at a Clearing," oil on canvas, Bartow Van Voorhis Matteson (American, b. 1894), 25" x 34"... **$2,500**

Baseball advertisement, watercolor and gouache on board, Howard Scott (American, 1902-1983), 13" x 24"... **$531**

"The Gambler," pen on paper, Winsor Mccay (American, 1871-1934), 14" x 11"............. **$5,312**

"The Long Shadow of Lincoln," study for story illustration, *The Saturday Evening Post*, Feb. 10, 1945, oil on gelatin silver photograph, Norman Rockwell (American, 1894-1978), accompanied by inscribed card, 13-1/4" x 10-1/4". **$46,875**

ILLUSTRATION ART

"Turmoil on the Ship," paperback cover, mixed media on board, Uldis Klavins (American, 20th century), from the estate of Charles Martignette, 24" x 18"................................. **$406**

"Varga Girl," circa 1940s-1950s, watercolor and pencil on board, Alberto Vargas (American, 1896-1982), from the estate of Charles Martignette, 14-3/4" x 21"..**$30,000**

"Chester Cricket's New Home," page 41 illustration, 1983, pen on paper, Garth Williams (American, 1912-1996), from the estate of Garth Williams, 14-1/2" x 11-3/4". **$406**

"Rockets and Men," interior story illustration, pen and ink on board, Frank R. Paul (American, 1884-1963), from the Jerry Weist Collection, 16-1/4" x 10-1/4". **$4,687**

"Fisherman on Pier," *Life Magazine* cover, Aug. 25, 1921, oil over engraver's proof on board, Maxfield Parrish (American, 1870-1966), 15" x 12"...........**$53,125**

"Rider on Horseback in Snow Storm," pencil, pen, and watercolor on paper, Alberto Vargas (American, 1896-1982), 4-1/2" x 6"...................... **$1,062**

"The Golden Journey #2," *The Saturday Evening Post* story illustration, oil on board, Stanley M. Zuckerberg (American, 1919-1995), 15-1/2" x 22"...... **$5,000**

Ballantine Beer advertisement, circa late 1950s, gouache and tempera on board, Mike Ludlow (American, b. 1921), from the estate of Charles Martignette, 19-3/4" x 16-1/4"........... **$1,625**

Indian Artifacts

Our interest in Native American material cultural artifacts has been long-lived, as was the Indian's interest in many of our material cultural items from an early period.

During recent years, it has become commonplace to have major sales of these artifacts by at least four major auction houses, in addition to the private trading, local auctions, and Internet sales of these items.

The majority of these valuable items are in repositories of museums, universities, and colleges, but many items that were traded to private citizens are now being sold to collectors of Native American material culture.

Native American artifacts are now acquired by collectors in the same fashion as any material cultural item. Individuals interested in antiques and collectibles find items at farm auction sales (an especially good place for farm family collections to be dispersed), yard sales, estate sales, specialized auctions, and from private collectors trading or selling items. There is no shortage of possibilities in finding items; it is merely deciding where to place one's energy and investment in adding to one's collection.

Native American artifacts are much more difficult to locate for a variety of reasons including the following: scarcity of items; legal protection of items being traded; more vigorous collecting of artifacts by numerous international, national, state, regional, and local museums and historical societies; frailties of the items themselves, as most were made of organic materials; and a more limited distribution network through legitimate secondary sales.

However, it is still possible to find some types of Native American items through the traditional sources of online auctions, auction houses in local communities, antique stores and malls, flea markets, trading meetings, estate sales, and similar venues. The most likely items to find in the above ways would be

Great Lakes beaded cloth bandolier pouch, circa third quarter 19th century, red trade cloth with ribbon appliqué, multicolored abstract floral designs and loom-woven American flag panel with 31 stars, mounted on cloth panel, 14-1/2" x 9". **$4,800**

Skinner, Inc.

items made of stone, chert, flint, obsidian, and copper. Most organic materials will not have survived the rigors of a marketplace unless they were recently released from some estate or collection and their value was unknown to the previous owner.

For more information on Native American collectibles, see *Warman's North American Indian Artifacts Identification and Price Guide* by Russell E. Lewis.

Plains hairpipe bandolier, circa late 19th century, strung with brass beads and a cluster of deer hooves and silk ribbon, traces of red ochre on the hooves, 39" l. **$1,020**

Skinner, Inc., www.skinnerinc.com, www.skinnerinc.com

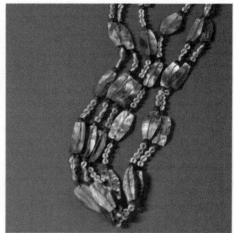

Northern California abalone and clamshell bead necklace, circa late 19th century (?), with Russian faceted blue trade beads, on three strands of twisted fiber. **$720**

Skinner, Inc., www.skinnerinc.com

Pair of Assiniboine fully beaded hide infant's moccasins, circa late 19th century, tops with crosses on green background, bottoms in white, 4-1/2" l. ... **$923**

Skinner, Inc., www.skinnerinc.com

Pair of Lakota child's fully beaded hide moccasins, circa late 19th century, yellow border lanes and bottle green "buffalo tracks," 5-1/4" l. **$840**

Skinner, Inc., www.skinnerinc.com

Cheyenne beaded hide moccasins, circa first quarter 20th century, fully beaded uppers and bifurcated tongues, multicolored geometric designs on light blue background, 10" l. **$800**

Skinner, Inc., www.skinnerinc.com

Pair of Delaware beaded hide moccasins, circa 1900, vamps with multicolored concentric designs, silk appliqué cuffs, 8-1/2" l. **$615**

Skinner, Inc., www.skinnerinc.com

Lakota beaded hide woman's leggings, circa last quarter 19th century, multicolored track design and vertical rows of small crosses on white background, custom mounts, 18" h. **$1,920**

Skinner, Inc., www.skinnerinc.com

Pair of Plateau beaded cloth girls' leggings, circa late 19th century, multicolored abstract floral designs on green trade cloth, edged with red cloth and small brads, fading to cloth, 13-3/4" h. **$984**

Skinner, Inc., www.skinnerinc.com

Central Plains beaded and quilled hide pipebag, circa last quarter 19th century, central panel with multicolored hourglass and box-and-border design, quill-wrapped rawhide slats with tin cone danglers, 18" l. **$984**

Skinner, Inc., www.skinnerinc.com

Dakota three-sided beaded hide tobacco bag, circa late 19th century, stained yellow, fringed edges and partially beaded with floral designs using small cut and uncut beads, 11" l. **$3,240**

Skinner, Inc., www.skinnerinc.com

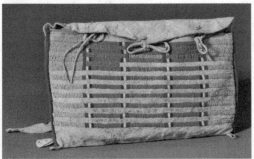

◄ Crow beaded hide possible bag, circa last quarter 19th century, buffalo hide with red trade cloth edging, front with multicolored striped design, hide strap, 13" x 9"....**$1,200**

Skinner, Inc., www.skinnerinc.com

Chippewa beaded cloth bandolier bag, circa late 19th century, multicolored foliate designs on white background, beaded tassels along bottom, 40" h. x 13-3/4" w.......................**$1,200**

Skinner, Inc., www.skinnerinc.com

Winnebego beaded cloth bandolier bag, circa late 19th century, loom-beaded with multicolored geometric designs on white background, tabs with wool tufts and large glass bead, 30" l. x 9-1/2" w. ... **$3,120**

Skinner, Inc., www.skinnerinc.com

Apache beaded hide pouch, circa last quarter 19th century, beaded on front and flap with multicolored stepped design, row of tin cone danglers across the bottom, bead loss, 6-1/2" l. **$1,020**

Skinner, Inc., www.skinnerinc.com

Eastern Sioux beaded hide bag, circa late 19th century, U-shaped form fringed at edge and partially beaded with abstract animal track (?) and floral devices, 13" l....**$461**

Skinner, Inc., www.skinnerinc.com

Miniature Kiowa cradle, circa first quarter 20th century, painted boards with pinhead decoration, multicolored geometric designs done in gourd stitch, commercial celluloid doll, 7-1/4" h. **$1,800**

Skinner, Inc., www.skinnerinc.com

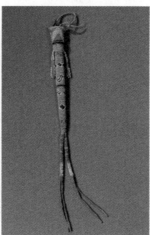

Comanche beaded hide awl case, circa last quarter 19th century, multicolored geometric designs on yellow background, tapered body done in brick stitch, small rocker-engraved German silver button on strap, 16" l. including fringe. **$2,214**

Skinner, Inc., www.skinnerinc.com

Plains beaded hide umbilical fetish, circa 1870s-1880s, in form of a lizard, with tin cone and horsehair danglers, 8" l.... **$1,230**

Skinner, Inc., www.skinnerinc.com

Acoma polychrome pottery jar, circa first quarter 20th century, decorated with a curvilinear design including hachuring, abstract feather, and foliate devices, 9-1/4" h., 10-1/2" dia......**$2,460**

Skinner, Inc., www.skinnerinc.com

Three Taos painted drums with typical polychrome designs, one with rain cloud design on one head, includes single beater, largest 19-1/2" h., 13-1/4" dia......**$1,722**

Skinner, Inc., www.skinnerinc.com

Mojave painted effigy jar, circa 1900, with human head below a handle and four spouts, body decorated with geometric and spotted motifs, repair to neck and handle, 8" h. **$492**

Skinner, Inc., www.skinnerinc.com

Two Woodlands carved wood ladles, circa mid-19th century, undecorated burl form and maple form with abstract bird finial, the second with custom stand, 14-3/4" and 9" l............... **$1,680**

Skinner, Inc., www.skinnerinc.com

Large polychrome pottery bowl, black and white repeat bear paw design on inside, restoration, 6-3/4" h., 12-1/2" dia............................. **$960**

Skinner, Inc., www.skinnerinc.com

Apache burden basket, circa early 20th century, multicolored banded design and hide fringe and bottom, red cloth trim at bottom, 12-1/2" h., 13-1/2" dia.....**$1,722**

Skinner, Inc., www.skinnerinc.com

Cochiti painted pottery canteen, circa late 19th century, two lugs and spout and painted with a bold banded design in black on cream slip, red stripe at bottom, 8-1/2" h. x 9-1/2" w....................**$1,169**

Skinner, Inc., www.skinnerinc.com

Santo Domingo painted pottery jar, circa 1900, flared rim and decorated with black repeat geometric and foliate devices on cream slip, clay loss, 7-3/4" h., 8-1/2" dia..........................**$584**

Skinner, Inc., www.skinnerinc.com

Apache coiled basketry bowl, banded geometric design, 3-1/2" h., 10-1/4" dia. **$400**

Skinner, Inc., www.skinnerinc.com

Northern California polychrome twined basketry hat, circa early 20th century, typical geometric designs on brown background, damage, 3-3/4" h., 7" dia. **$510**

Skinner, Inc., www.skinnerinc.com

Pima coiled basketry bowl, circa first quarter 20th century, double-banded scroll design, 5-1/2" h., 16-3/4" dia.....................**$1,320**

Skinner, Inc., www.skinnerinc.com

Nampeyo and Maria pottery, three items, early 20th century: Fannie Nampeyo Hopi pot, Maria and Santana San Ildefonso blackware pot, and unsigned double-handled canteen with stylized bird decoration, canteen 6-1/2" x 7-1/2"..**$1,750**

Rago Arts and Auction Center

Anasazi pottery, seven vessels, southwestern United States, circa 1100 AD: two bowls with geometric designs, two salado bowls and two ollas, tallest 4-1/2". **$1,125**

Rago Arts and Auction Center

Pacific Northwest Haida feast bowl, seal form with shell inlay, early 20th century, 3-1/2" x 16" x 7".
.... **$2,250**

Rago Arts and Auction Center

Anasazi pottery, five vessels with polychrome decoration, southwestern United States, circa 1100 AD: two ollas, canteen and two pitchers, tallest 5-1/4".
.... **$1,375**

Rago Arts and Auction Center

Inuit soapstone sculptures, four, mid-20th century: hunter skinning animal, woman eating from basket of fish, seal, and grotesque face of a woman, two with Canada Eskimo Art paper labels and serial numbers, tallest 10". **$1,875**

Rago Arts and Auction Center

Santa Clara blackware, four items, including: Angela Baca lobed bowl, Stella Chevarria carved bowl, Frances Salazar miniature vase, 20th century, most signed, tallest 5-1/2"................................... **$688**

Rago Arts and Auction Center

Zuni silver bracelet, cast and wrought silver with nine natural turquoise stones by Della Casa Appa, 20th century, 5", 2.8 OT. **$938**

Rago Arts and Auction Center

Navajo silver squash blossom necklace, turquoise stones, mid-20th century, 22". **$531**

Rago Arts and Auction Center

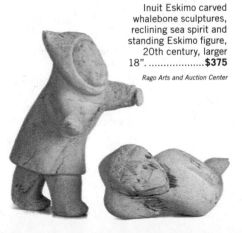

Inuit Eskimo carved whalebone sculptures, reclining sea spirit and standing Eskimo figure, 20th century, larger 18". **$375**

Rago Arts and Auction Center

Navajo silver cuff with turquoise stones, mid-20th century, marked Chee within a thunderbird, 6" interior, 1/4" at widest point, 4.23 OT. **$2,125**

Rago Arts and Auction Center

TOP LOT!

San Ildefonso etched redware jar by Tony Da, circa 1965, decorated on shoulder with etched band enclosing a pair of confronting avanyus, inset with three turquoise stones, heishi shell accents and fish and bear paw motifs, 5-3/4" h. **$32,500**

Sioux beaded hide bowcase and quiver, circa 1880, sinew sewn and lane-stitched in green, blue, white-heart red and yellow glass seed beads, each end decorated with concentric rectangles and hide fringe, trimmed with red wool trade cloth, wood bow and four arrows, 40" l. **$20,000**

Sioux beaded hide war shirt, circa 1900, overlaid across the shoulders and down the arms with beaded strips, sinew sewn and lane stitched classic bead colors, 63" l. **$20,000**

Potawatomie beaded cloth bandolier, circa 1890, composed of black velvet panels, overlaid with loom-beadwork in various shades of glass seed beads, trimmed with tab pendants, each with geometric motifs, black wool yarn tassels, 38" l. **$2,750**

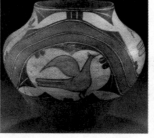

Zia polychrome jar, circa 1910, painted in yellow, orange, and black over creamy white slip, undulating band supporting and enclosing four birds, orange underbody, 11" dia. **$4,375**

Sioux pictographic painted hide shield, circa 1890, painted in black and red pigments enclosing a combat scene of three mounted Sioux, one with lance and shield opposing Crow man with bow and arrow, another wearing typical Sioux-style leggings, 18" dia. **$18,750**

All photos on this page courtesy Heritage Auctions

Letters describing the plight of Native Americans in Wild West Shows, 1891-1892. The first from June 3, 1891 from Herbert Welsh, corresponding secretary of the Philadelphia-based Indian Rights Association to Major James McLaughlin at Standing Rock Agency. Welsh asks McLaughlin to comment on the accuracy of charges leveled by Welsh in a letter to the *New York Evening Post* regarding the propriety of allowing reservation Indians to contract for performance in Buffalo Bill's Wild West show. The second is a retained copy of a June 21, 1892, typed letter to Welsh from Bishop M. Marty regarding the life of Indians in Dakota. He writes, "Travelling (Wild West) shows is not the best means to educate anyone, but the present condition of the Indians, and especially of the young men & women coming out of the schools, is such that they are better off anywhere else than at home." The third letter was written to McLaughlin by Welsh the next day, asking his opinion on the Bishop's comments. **$1,075**

Navajo regional rug, Eastern Reservation, circa 1900, woven of native handspun wool in natural ivory and brown against an aniline red ground, central column enclosing geometric elements, each end with arrow-like projections, stepped and hooked motifs along sides. **$1,250**

Navajo regional rug, Ganado, circa 1920, woven of natural and aniline shades of ivory, brown and red, central column of serrated diamonds, innermost enclosing whirling log motifs, flanked on either side by serrated wedges, border of whirling logs, 52" w. x 113" l. **$2,375**

Navajo regional rug, Teec Nos Pos, circa 1920, woven of native handspun wool, in natural and aniline shades of ivory, brown, tan, black, and green against a carded ground, pair of geometric elements surrounded by smaller motifs, enclosed within a serrated border, 45-1/2" w. x 78" l. **$1,750**

All photos on this page courtesy Heritage Auctions

Apache coiled bowl, circa 1900, woven of willow and devil's claw, seven-petaled rosette in basin, enclosed by concentric rosette, surmounted by stepped band and checkered band encircling beneath darkened rim, 20" dia...**$2,062**

Two Eskimo twined baleen baskets, circa 1960, each with fitted lid topped with carved ivory finial, one in shape of whale fluke, the other with polar bear, 3-1/4" x 3-3/4" dia. **$1,062**

Eskimo etched walrus tusk, circa 1910, decorated on one side with scene depicting walruses, whales and polar bears, 24-1/2" l.....**$1,375**

Pair of Comanche woman's beaded and fringed hide boot moccasins, circa 1900, painted overall in yellow ochre pigment with narrow lanes of small geometric motifs, stitched in various shades of glass seed beads, trimmed with small silver buttons and twisted hide fringe, rawhide soles, 19" h. **$6,250**

Papago pictorial coiled plaque, 14-3/4" dia........................**$218**

Micmac/Maliseet beaded cloth pouch, 3-1/2" h. **$56**

Huron moose hair embroidered box, 3-1/2" l.... **$325**

Plains hair roach, circa 1930, composed of red-dyed fiber enclosing a crest of porcupine hair, stitched to a cloth base, metal stand, 13" l................... **$1,187**

Iroquois cornhusk mask, 17" h. **$643**

Northern California twined maiden's cap, 6-3/4" dia.
.... **$275**

Cree duck decoy, 7-1/2" l............................**$187**

Northwest Coast carved wood bowl, 8-3/4" dia...**$200**

Plains stone head club, 23-1/4" l. **$375**

Jewelry

There's no question about the timeless appeal of jewelry. Even people who don't see themselves as bona fide collectors likely have a stash of jewelry they have either purchased, inherited, or received as gifts. Time passes, and suddenly it's "vintage." Some people sell it once they realize the value, others pass it on to family members, and a few become true collectors, adding to the pieces they have already accumulated over the years.

From precious metals and gemstones to trinkets of yesteryear purchased at dime stores, every piece of jewelry has a place in a collection somewhere, and each collection is as unique as the individual who puts it together. The pieces gathered together express the past in a unique way, since popular movies, celebrities and historical events are reflected in these unique adornments. From antique suffragette jewelry to pieces inspired by "Gone with the Wind" to sterling items made during World War II when metals were rationed, and even peace sign pendants dating to the 1960s, popular culture has always been reflected in jewelry worn around the world.

Georgian topaz brooch, 18th century, designed as floral and foliate motifs and set throughout with faceted foil-back topaz, silver mount, 3-1/4" w. **$3,851**

Skinner, Inc., www.skinnerinc.com

But why the buzz and interest in antique, vintage, and collectible jewelry today? Believe it or not, pop culture is still influencing the way women accessorize and, now more than ever, what individuals are inspired to collect.

"Antique" jewelry, defined as 100 years old or older by the United States Customs Service, encompasses many eras collectors find appealing. From before the Civil War, moving into the Victorian era, and during the decades when automobiles, electricity and telephones were just coming about, jewelry with great romanticism and symbolic meaning was lovingly worn. Whether a family heirloom or treasure found at a flea market, these older pieces take their new owners back in time. Even the recent Steampunk movement, which combines steam-age fashion with the age-old tendency to rebel against the norm, has a new generation learning about Victorian adornment.

Fans of the "Downton Abbey" television series have admired jewelry on the show, which ranges from Victorian to Edwardian and Art Deco styles, and they're inspired to own similar looks. Movies like "The Great Gatsby" and shows like "Boardwalk Empire" also have revived style elements of vintage jewelry. "Mad Men" spawned an interest in 1960s culture that carried over from clothing to jewelry. Even multi-strand "granny" beads once considered common and undesirable were being worn by the young and fashionable set quite recently.

But when it comes right down to it, the timetable for defining vintage is based on a sliding scale that changes as we move from one decade to the next. It's loosely deemed newer than antique and older than collectible, and defined by many as Edwardian through the 1980s as of now. However, because Edwardian is more akin to Victorian in style than the Deco and "flapper" looks of the 1920s, that era is sometimes referenced as antique jewelry (and within a few short years it will, indeed, become antique without question). Some people even define jewelry from the early 1990s as vintage when there is great demand for it, as with costume pieces made by the House of Chanel and other couturiers that are still sought by both collectors and fashionistas, often prompted by what celebrities are wearing.

Collectible jewelry also has its fans and shouldn't be overlooked in terms of desirability and value. Even though it's not necessarily old – generally dating from the mid-1990s through today – it has a place in most jewelry collections especially in the instance of "revival" pieces. These are inspired by older looks, and some of them even use old components but are newly made and offered for sale in boutiques and sometimes department stores or through individual reps.

For a vintage jewelry lover to take notice, newer pieces should be finely made of quality components and most often made in limited quantities, whether machine fabricated or artisan crafted. That rules out most mass imports and low quality discount store pieces in the costume jewelry realm, although who knows how many of those items will be considered collectible 20, 50 or 100 years from now? After all, no one would have ever suspected that cheap Bakelite figural brooches purchased at the local 5 & 10 in the 1930s would be so highly valued today, with celebrities Whoopi Goldberg and Lily Tomlin being rumored to collect them.

As long as we have art imitating life through pop culture, the response will be life imitating art. We may not know what the next trendsetting movie, television program or historical event will bestow on us, or what collecting whim will create a flux of demand. What we do know is that it will inevitably come, and collectors will respond – along with the general populace – by wearing and collecting jewelry.

For more information on jewelry, see *Warman's Jewelry Identification and Price Guide*, 5th edition, by Christie Romero.   — *Pamela Y. Wiggins*

LATE GEORGIAN

Two rare rose gold and hair bands: one size 7, 6 mm wide, rose gold with gold initialed rectangle frame and coin edges; one size 9 with pearls, 6.5 mm w... **$167**

Heritage Auctions

Unsigned miniature portrait on ivory of John Quincy Adams, pin with unusual black-and-white image of youthful Adams around 1820s, housed in mid-Victorian case that does not appear to be original, miniature attached to probably original cloth backing that has deteriorated around perimeter, included is oval cardboard insert, probably from a previous mounting, on which is written in vintage ink, "John Quincy Adams 1825-29"; painting is 1-7/8" x 2-3/8"..**$478**

Heritage Auctions

Late Georgian gold and garnet ring, circa 1810-1820, cushion-cut garnet within foil-back ribbed collet, flanked by fancy-cut diamonds set in silver, size 6. ....**$3,081**

Skinner, Inc., www.skinnerinc.com

Georgian topaz clip set with faceted foil-back topaz, gilt-silver mount, later clip back, 1-1/2". **$4,444**

Skinner, Inc., www.skinnerinc.com

Georgian purple paste girandole pendant-brooch, 18th century, set with faceted purple pastes and suspending drops, silver mount, 2-1/2" l. **$2,726**

Skinner, Inc., www.skinnerinc.com

Georgian rose-cut diamond and enamel star and moon brooch, star set with circular rose-cut diamond approximately 8.50 mm, joined to crescent moon with oval and circular rose-cut diamonds, blue enamel ground, silver mount with gold pinstem, 1-1/8" l. **$1,659**

Skinner, Inc., www.skinnerinc.com

Rare Georgian gold, diamond, emerald and porcelain pendant/locket, 78 mm from top diamond and emerald set hook/bale to bottom of frame, 47 mm across, filigree gold frame (tests 15k gold) with uncut diamonds in 12 ball form mounts, central hinged paste set silver bezel and interior-mounted painted porcelain portrait (porcelain is loose from setting on inner flange of bezel rim), hinged back oval door with a glass crystal. **$875**

Heritage Auctions

Diamond and silver-topped gold earrings designed for pierced ears, each earring, designed with a floral motif, has a mine-cut diamond 5.50 x 5.00 mm with rose-, mine-, and single-cut diamonds, set in silver-topped 14k gold, 2-11/16" x 3/4". **$3,346**

Heritage Auctions

Memorial portrait watch chatelaine and key, circa 1820, composed of upper 1-1/2" wide blue and white enamel bar and gilt back hook, four suspended unmarked rose-colored links, central oval braided hair memorial bordered by gold and blue enamel, color portrait locket with enamel frame, swivel ends, one holding a black enamel and gold winding key, 7-1/2" top to bottom........................ **$1,015**

Heritage Auctions

TOP
LOT!

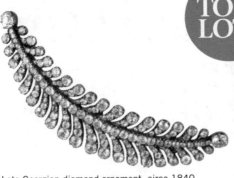

Late Georgian diamond ornament, circa 1840, designed as a feather and set throughout with 140 old mine-cut diamonds, approximate total weight 12 carats, silver-topped gold mount, 3-3/4" l. **$18,960**

Skinner, Inc., www.skinnerinc.com

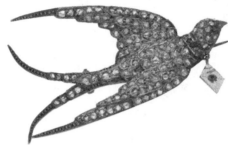

Diamond, ruby and silver-topped gold brooch designed as a swallow, rose-cut diamonds weighing approximately 1.55 carats, round-shaped rubies weighing approximately 0.10 carat, set in silver-topped 10k gold, pinstem and "C" clasp, 2" x 1-1/8"..**$1,500**

Heritage Auctions

Gold ring with topaz stone, 14k yellow gold, late Georgian, circa 1830-1840, topaz set in multi-rounded prong mount, topaz is oval mixed cut, approximately 15.5 x 12.2 x 7.9 mm for approximate weight of 11.10 carats, shank 5 mm w. with all-bright polish, size 5. The ring was given by statesman and politician Sam Houston to his wife; inside shank is engraved in script "Sam Houston to Marga...L (?)..."; due to heavy wear it is not possible to determine final lettering of engraving, but Houston's wife's name was Margaret Moffette Lea. **$49,500**

Heritage Auctions

Emerald, diamond, pearl and silver-topped gold necklace, French, rectangle-shaped emerald 14.50 x 12 mm and weighing approximately 10 carats, emerald-shaped emeralds weighing approximately 10 carats, rose-cut diamonds weighing approximately 0.65 carat, and button-shaped pearls measuring 5.10 x 5.40 mm, set in silver-topped 18k gold, French hallmarks; total emerald weight is approximately 20.00 carats; necklace accompanied by original fitted box; 16" l... **$6,273**

Heritage Auctions

JEWELRY

EARLY VICTORIAN

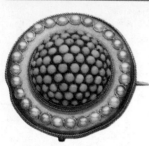

Turquoise and pearl gold brooch, circa 1858, unmarked yellow gold tests 18k, 12.7 grams, 31 mm across, 14 mm h., accented with small pearls and turquoise, lightly engraved on back, "June 28. 1858," dent on one side front and back, repair where pin is attached on back. **$275**

Heritage Auctions

Gold and aquamarine brooch, upper section 57 mm across, fine repoussé gold work with faceted aquamarines, tests 15k, 14.1 grams, 3-3/4" top to bottom.**$657**

Heritage Auctions

Onyx pearl, gold and black onyx hard stone memorial cameo, unmarked gold, 58 mm x 32 mm, seed pearls set around cameo on onyx, cameo needs cleaning, small chip on bottom of onyx, back set with gold bezel and glass oval frame. **$286**

Heritage Auctions

Rose-cut diamond and gold earrings, unmarked gold, tests 10k, 3.6 grams, 18 mm top to bottom, center setting approximately .09 mm across, both rose-cut diamonds with edge chips, approximately 4 mm x 5 mm in triangle shape, lever backs for pierced ears. **$275**

Heritage Auctions

Gilt metal necklace with enameled center piece under glass, alternating rose-gold links with pieced panel links, 55 mm x 34 mm shield pendant, raised glass crystal, blue high relief bird motif, 57.1 grams, 16-1/2" l. **$310**

Heritage Auctions

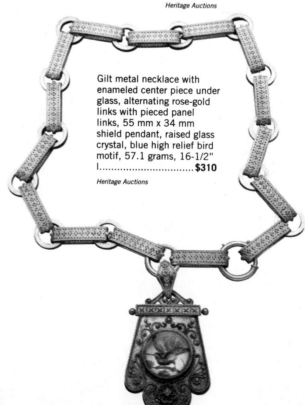

Gold pin with diamonds, ruby and sapphire, 15k gold, hallmarked, 49 mm, 7.6 grams.............**$227**

Heritage Auctions

Early Victorian Revival vermeil (gilt over sterling silver) necklace, 66.3 grams, necklace 19" with 2-1/2" drop, accented with small garnets.......**$406**

Heritage Auctions

Portrait pin, unmarked gold, tests 14k, 7.1 grams, 30 mm x 34 mm, two chips on the top right sides on edges, portrait has some wear. **$131**

Heritage Auctions

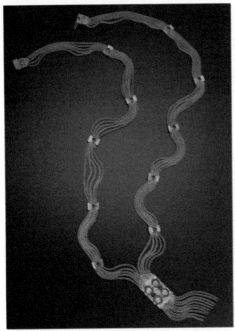

Diamond, ruby and enamel ring, set in unmarked rose gold, size 6-3/4, ring 35 mm end to end, mine cut diamonds, rubies, one emerald, blue and red enameled accents, 7.9 grams. **$203**

Heritage Auctions

Two gold pins, total weight is 8.3 grams, one 14k griffin pin, 29 mm with pearl and emerald eye, one unmarked early Victorian gold pin with amethyst (small side chip), 32 mm. **$286**

Heritage Auctions

Coral and gold necklace, clasp and chain 14k yellow gold, 156.3 grams, chain is 10", coral piece is 3" x 5-1/2"...**$250**

Heritage Auctions

Coral cameo gold pin/pendant, 14k yellow gold, 7.6 grams, 32 mm x 27 mm, with bale..........**$300**

Heritage Auctions

Early coral and gold cameo, 14k gold, 8 grams, 38 mm top to bottom....................................**$118**

Heritage Auctions

Scottish opal and gold hardstone brooch, unmarked gold tests 14k, 12.3 grams, 27 mm x 24 mm, one stone has two scratches.................................... **$325**

Heritage Auctions

Rose gold and diamond pin, mine cut diamonds, leaf motif, 54 mm, 7.4 grams........................**$262**

Heritage Auctions

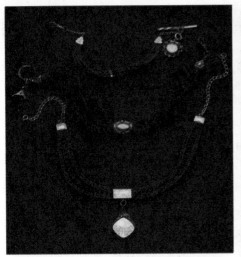

Three hair chains: 6" with gold-filled chain and fob and three small seed pearls; 10" chain with center gold-filled locket; 10-1/2" chain. **$100**

Heritage Auctions

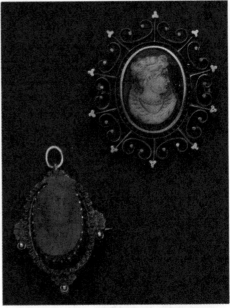

Two cameo pins, one 30 x 21 mm high relief coral cameo with gold frame, one 36 x 30 mm early Victorian hardstone cameo in very fine unmarked rose gold fancy frame, 16.3 grams total................**$334**

Heritage Auctions

Coral cameo and gold pendant, carved coral cameo depicting Victorian lady's profile, 18k gold bail, gross weight 31.70 grams, 2-1/8" x 1-7/8"............**$448**

Heritage Auctions

Diamond, enamel and gold mourning hinged locket, European-cut diamonds weighing approximately 0.85 carat, black enameled star applied on 14k gold, locket opens to reveal a lock of hair and is personalized on reverse, 1-1/4" x-7/8". **$875**

Heritage Auctions

MID-VICTORIAN

Victorian 14k gold bangle with a scarab and double ram's head design, weight 9.20 grams, 5-3/4". **$516**

Heritage Auctions

Gold bracelet, unmarked gold tests 10k, 66.4 grams, with seed pearls and black enamel, bracelet is circular link weave pattern at 25 mm wide, buckle is 32 mm wide, accented by tassels, double slide clasp opens to 7-1/2" and slides to make bracelet smaller to any size under 7-1/2". **$1,673**

Heritage Auctions

Pair of Victorian 14k gold bracelets, each hinged bangle with black tracery enamel and engraved ornament, 6-1/4" interior circumference. **$948**

Skinner, Inc., www.skinnerinc.com

Victorian 14k bicolor gold bangle, ornate cuff with braided ropetwists and leaf accents, centering a seed pearl, 6-1/4" interior circumference. **$1,185**

Skinner, Inc., www.skinnerinc.com

Gold hinged bangle, 14k gold, gross weight 44.30 grams, 6-1/2" x 1-1/8". **$1,314**

Heritage Auctions

Victorian 14k gold and enamel bracelet, woven with slide and terminal in black tracery enamel, foxtail fringe, adjustable length. **$652**

Skinner, Inc., www.skinnerinc.com

Coral cameo and gold brooch, carved coral cameo depicting an angel, 10k gold pinstem with "C" catch on reverse, gross weight 20 grams, 2-1/2" x 1-3/4".
....**$478**

Heritage Auctions

Three cameo rings: one hardstone with pearls in rose gold, size 7-1/4; one in 14k white filigree mount with pearl border, size 6; one 26 mm round shell in rose mount, size 4, gross weight is 23.5 grams. **$657**

Heritage Auctions

Shell cameo and gold brooch, rectangular-shaped shell cameo depicting bouquet of flowers, 39 x 46 mm, set in 14k gold, pinstem and "C" catch on reverse, gross weight 11.30 grams, 1-1/2" x 1-7/8".
.... **$187**

Heritage Auctions

Shell cameo and gold brooch, oval-shaped shell cameo depicting mythological scene, resting within 9k yellow gold frame, safety chain, gross weight 15.90 grams, 1-3/4" x 1-1/2".............**$298**

Heritage Auctions

Gold brooch crafted of 18k gold, pinstem and "C" catch on reverse, gross weight 23.27 grams, 2-1/8" x 1-3/4"...**$1,075**

Heritage Auctions

Jet cameo pendant-brooch, Bacchanalian theme depicting god of wine with rams and grapes, dangling flowers, carved in jet, pendant bail, pinstem and "C" catch on reverse, gross weight 23.80 grams, 1-3/4" x 1-7/8". **$298**

Heritage Auctions

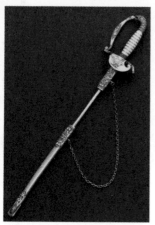

Rare Victorian gold and enamel sword pin, unmarked, 18k gold, finely detailed with white enamel, eagle motifs, 13.4 grams, 5-3/4" l..**$750**

Heritage Auctions

Gold and black enamel memorial locket, unmarked gold tests 14k, 11.4 grams, 27 mm x 21 mm, memorial inscription on inside of locket with dates of "June 17, 1856, April 18, 1879 & November 28, 1879" with names for each date, both sides of locket contain memorial hair, light surface scratches on both sides of locket. **$375**

Heritage Auctions

Victorian smoky quartz pendant, designed as a fly resting on faceted oval berry capped by carved leaves, white metal mounts, 2-1/4" l. **$563**

Skinner, Inc., www.skinnerinc.com

Lava cameo and silver brooch, oval-shaped lava cameo 30 x 26 mm, depicting gentleman's profile, set in silver, pinstem and "C" catch, gross weight 12.10 grams, 1-1/2" x 1-3/4"..................**$418**

Heritage Auctions

Hardstone cameo, cultured pearl, gold pendant-brooch, oval-shaped banded onyx cameo 34 x 25 mm, depicting lady's profile in high relief, cultured half-pearls, set in 10k rose gold, retractable bail and pinstem and "C" catch on reverse, gross weight 19.40 grams, 2-1/4" x 1-3/4". **$717**

Heritage Auctions

Shell cameo gold pendant-brooch, shell cameo 54 x 41 mm, depicting lady's profile, set in textured 14k gold frame, bail, pinstem and "C" catch on reverse, gross weight 25.45 grams, 2-5/8" x 2". **$896**

Heritage Auctions

Coral and gold cameo brooch, oval-shaped, 28 x 20 mm, depicting lady's profile, resting in decorative 14k yellow gold frame, pinstem and catch mechanism, gross weight 11.60 grams, 1-7/16" x 1-1/8"...............**$537**

Heritage Auctions

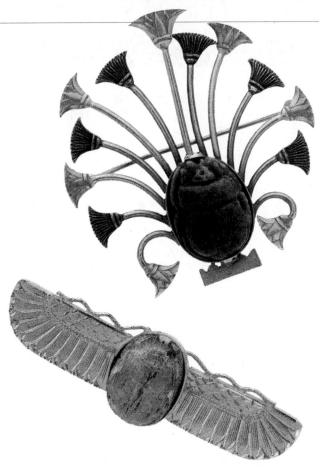

Hardstone cameo, seed pearl and gold pendant-brooch, carved banded onyx cameo approximately 26 mm x 26 mm, depicting woman's profile, encircled by seed pearls, set in openwork 14k yellow gold frame, retractable pendant bail, pinstem and catch on reverse, gross weight 8.80 grams, 1-3/8" x 1-3/8". **$597**

Heritage Auctions

Two Etruscan Revival gold brooches: carved scarab with 18k gold lotus blossom frame, signed Blanchard, Cairo, 1-3/4" x 1-7/8"; real dung beetle in 22k gold winged frame, 2" x 1/2". **$956**

Heritage Auctions

Shell cameo and gold brooch, oval-shaped shell cameo 47 x 40 mm depicting mother Mary and a praying child, set in openwork design frame of 18k gold, pinstem and catch on reverse, gross weight 22.10 grams, 2-1/8" x 2-1/2". **$717**

Heritage Auctions

Micromosaic and gold hinged bangle depicting Greek scene with cherubs, set in 22k gold, gross weight 20.60 grams, 6-1/2" x 7/8". **$1,375**

Heritage Auctions

LATE VICTORIAN

Victorian diamond, multi-stone, seed pearl, gold and silver brooch, circa 1880, designed as butterfly, round-cut rubies, sapphires, emeralds and opal set in 14k yellow gold, seed pearls and rose-cut diamonds set in silver, 1-3/4" x 1". **$597**

Heritage Auctions

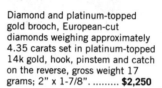

Diamond and platinum-topped gold brooch, European-cut diamonds weighing approximately 4.35 carats set in platinum-topped 14k gold, hook, pinstem and catch on the reverse, gross weight 17 grams; 2" x 1-7/8". **$2,250**

Heritage Auctions

Victorian 18k gold and garnet memorial brooch, 18k yellow gold, 9.4 grams, 36 mm x 29 mm, front side is ornate set with garnet approximately 12 mm x 7 mm, back side is memorial picture of a lady, some damage to gold on back side bottom and one side, piece also has a bale that can be used as a pendant for front side... **$437**

Heritage Auctions

Diamond, enamel and gold locket-pendant-necklace, pear-shaped diamond 7.20 x 4.40 x 3.50 mm and weighing approximately 0.55 carat, European-, mine- and rose-cut diamonds weighing approximately 6 carats, black enamel applied on 18k gold, 14k gold chain, 10k gold clasp, gross weight 23.20 grams; locket 1-5/8" x 1-1/8"; chain 20" l. **$2,390**

Heritage Auctions

Sapphire, diamond and platinum-topped gold ring, cushion-cut sapphire 9 x 9 x 4.15 mm and weighing approximately 2.65 carats, European-cut diamonds weighing approximately 1.65 carats set in platinum-topped 14k gold, Austrian hallmarks, gross weight 4 grams, size 6-1/2 (sizeable). **$2,151**

Heritage Auctions

Diamond and silver-topped gold ring, rose-cut diamond 6.50 x 6 mm, rose-cut diamonds set in silver-topped 14k gold, gross weight 3.90 grams, size 6-3/4 (sizeable). $1,912

Heritage Auctions

Seed pearl, enamel and gold mourning pendant/ locket, hinged, seed pearls, black enamel applied on 14k gold, black cord, gold spacers with black and white enamel, locket opens to reveal two photo panes, gross weight 25.00 grams, locket 2" x 1", cord 22" l..............$537

Heritage Auctions

Victorian seed pearl, enamel and gold longchain, circa 1880, 14k yellow gold fancy link longchain necklace with shield-shaped slide highlighted by seed pearls, applied black enamel accents, 14k yellow gold swivel hook, 54" l........$310

Heritage Auctions

Victorian 14k gold tassel necklace, longchain of fine circular links with engraved slide set with split pearls and black tracery enamel, foxtail fringe ending in a tassel, 27.0 dwt, 43-1/2" l............................$1,680

Skinner, Inc., www.skinnerinc.com

ART DECO

Art Deco 14k gold, onyx, dyed green chalcedony bracelet, links of alternating onyx pyramids and chalcedony rings, 14.3 dwt, 7-1/4" long.
............................**$1,020**

Skinner, Inc., www.skinnerinc.com

Six-strand cultured pearl bracelet with Art Deco platinum and diamond clasp, pearls approximately 3.8 to 3.6 mm, 32 old European-cut diamonds approximately 1.50 carats, clasp circa 1920, 6-3/8" l. **$1,625**

Doyle New York

Art Deco platinum and diamond bow brooch/hair clip, diminutive form bead-set with full-cut diamond melee, with element for hair-clip conversion, 1-3/8" l.
.... **$1,080**

Art Deco platinum, blue zircon, and diamond brooch, bezel-set with circular-cut blue zircon approximately 11.80 x 8.50 mm, old European- and single-cut diamonds, millegrain accents, 1-3/8" l............................ **$1,599**

Skinner, Inc., www.skinnerinc.com

Art Deco gentleman's diamond, frosted rock crystal quartz, platinum and gold dress set, includes pair of double-sided cufflinks featuring cut-cornered square-shaped frosted rock crystal quartz tablets 12.40 x 12.60 x 3.70 mm, rose-cut diamonds weighing approximately 0.16 carat, set in platinum, 14k gold findings, with four matching shirt studs, cuff links 5/8" x 5/8"; shirt studs 5/8" x 5/8"...**$1,434**

Heritage Auctions

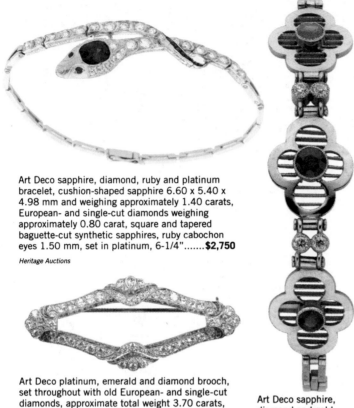

Art Deco sapphire, diamond, ruby and platinum bracelet, cushion-shaped sapphire 6.60 x 5.40 x 4.98 mm and weighing approximately 1.40 carats, European- and single-cut diamonds weighing approximately 0.80 carat, square and tapered baguette-cut synthetic sapphires, ruby cabochon eyes 1.50 mm, set in platinum, 6-1/4".......**$2,750**

Heritage Auctions

Art Deco platinum, emerald and diamond brooch, set throughout with old European- and single-cut diamonds, approximate total weight 3.70 carats, fancy-cut emerald accents, millegrain details, 2-3/4" l. $1,800

Skinner, Inc., www.skinnerinc.com

Art Deco sapphire, diamond and gold bracelet, round-cut sapphires set in 18k yellow gold, European-cut diamonds set in 18k white gold, openwork 18k pink gold links, 7" x-1/2". **$567**

Heritage Auctions

Art Deco cultured pearl, diamond and platinum necklace, Mikimoto, composed of cultured pearls ranging in size from 3.70-4 mm to 5.75-5.85 mm, forming a graduated single knotted strand, platinum clasp with full-cut diamonds weighing approximately 0.20 carat, maker's mark "M" for Mikimoto, 20" l..............**$1,075**

Heritage Auctions

Art Deco chalcedony, coral, marcasite and onyx earpendants, Theodore Fahrner, each designed as shaped blue chalcedony tablet suspended from marcasite pagoda form with coral bead accents, cabochon onyx tops, silver mounts, hallmark, 3" l. **$1,200**

Skinner, Inc., www.skinnerinc.com

Two Art Deco clasps, 14k gold, enamel, gem-set, one with carved lapis, other with chalcedony, enamel frames, joined to matching beads, each 7-3/8" l..............**$2,829**

Skinner, Inc., www.skinnerinc.com

Art Deco platinum and diamond cuff links, France, each double link set with old European-cut diamond weighing approximately 0.50 carat, single-cut diamond melee accents, approximate total diamond weight 2.40 carats, millegrain details. **$2,400**

Skinner, Inc., www.skinnerinc.com

Art Deco amethyst cameo cuvee brooch depicting lady in profile, framed by onyx and old single-cut diamonds, platinum and 14k gold mount, 1-1/4" l. **$1,320**

Skinner, Inc., www.skinnerinc.com

Art Deco rock crystal quartz, ruby, diamond and white gold ring, cut-cornered rectangle-shaped rock crystal quartz base supporting carved rubies, single-cut diamonds weighing approximately 0.35 carat, set in 10k white gold, size 6-3/4 (sizeable). **$2,500**

Heritage Auctions

Art Deco diamond, platinum pendant-necklace, teardrop-shaped, features European-, full-, single-, and rose-cut diamonds weighing approximately 1.50 carats, set in platinum, handmade platinum fancy link chain, European- and single-cut diamond accents, total diamond weight for pendant-necklace is approximately 1.90 carats, pendant 1-9/16" x 13/16"; chain 15" l. **$2,629**

Heritage Auctions

Art Deco platinum, enamel, jadeite, and diamond earpendants, each designed as carved jadeite drop suspended from old European-cut diamonds, joined by black and white enamel lattice motifs, 2-1/4" l. **$2,400**

Skinner, Inc., www.skinnerinc.com

Art Deco moonstone, sapphire, diamond and platinum-topped gold necklace, moonstone cabochon, French-cut sapphires, single-cut diamonds, set in platinum-topped 18k gold, stationed by a fancy link platinum chain, gross weight 6.40 grams, 16-1/2" l............**$896**

Heritage Auctions

Art Deco diamond and platinum lorgnette, hinge and spring loaded, opens to reveal round-shaped spectacles; handle features European-cut diamonds weighing approximately 0.55 carat, single-cut diamonds weighing approximately 0.45 carat, set in platinum, 3-3/4" x 2-1/4"... **$1,250**

Heritage Auctions

Art Deco amethyst, rock crystal quartz bead necklace, circa 1920, faceted rock crystal quartz rondelles, faceted amethyst beads, graduating in size, forming single knotted strand, yellow metal clasp, 38" l......... **$1,885**

Heritage Auctions

ART NOUVEAU

Art Nouveau gold, pearl and diamond watch pin, 27 mm across, 14k matte finished gold, pearls and gypsy set diamond, 5.6 grams........................... **$203**

Heritage Auctions

Art Nouveau 14k gold and enamel stickpin depicting maiden in profile with diamond and gem-set bandeau, seed pearl border, 5/8" dia. **$385**

Skinner, Inc., www.skinnerinc.com

Two Art Nouveau gold and enamel pins, one in 10k gold with green center stone, one in 14k gold with baroque pearl, enamel and half pearl accents, one with watch pin loop on the back, both pin backs. **$239**

Heritage Auctions

Art Nouveau fire opal owl stickpin, rose-cut diamond eyes, perched on gold branch, 3/4" l. **$1,067**

Skinner, Inc., www.skinnerinc.com

Art Nouveau 18k gold brooch, Wiese, designed as finely pierced gold scrollwork, replaced pinstem, no French marks, only signed WIESE, 7/8" dia. **$889**

Skinner, Inc., www.skinnerinc.com

Art Nouveau gold bracelet, 14k, 29.19 grams, 6-1/4" x 9/16". **$1,187**

Heritage Auctions

Art Nouveau 14k gold and demantoid garnet cufflinks, each lion's head with demantoid garnet eyes, 5/8".......................... **$1,440**

Skinner, Inc., www.skinnerinc.com

Three gold and enamel Art Nouveau pins, one cloverleaf motif with watch loop on back, one acorn motif with pearls, one crescent (later added pin back). **$244**

Heritage Auctions

Art Nouveau pin and pendant set with amethysts and pearls, 14k pin 1.7", 18k drop is 2-1/3" top to bottom........................... **$388**

Heritage Auctions

Art Nouveau 18k gold locket-brooch depicting elegant lady with high collar and wearing elaborate floral hat, rose-cut diamond accents, opening to compartment, signed Holy Frs, 1-1/4" l. **$652**

Skinner, Inc., www.skinnerinc.com

Art Nouveau 14k gold and diamond locket, Pierrot figure set with old mine-cut diamond melee, reverse monogrammed, 1" dia. **$563**

Skinner, Inc., www.skinnerinc.com

Art Nouveau diamond pendant/ brooch, France, set with pear and old mine-cut diamonds, rose-cut diamond accents, maker's mark and guarantee stamp, 1-1/2" l. **$563**

Skinner, Inc., www.skinnerinc.com

▶ Art Nouveau gold, pearl and enamel drop, 64 mm top to bottom, three hinged pearl drops, unmarked gold, test 14k, enameled central leaf (some restoration to the top right area), 9.7 grams. **$286**

Heritage Auctions

Art Nouveau 14k gold cuff links, each double link depicting buds, maker's mark for Sloan & Co.. **$563**

Skinner, Inc., www.skinnerinc.com

Gold and pearl Art Nouveau ring, 31 mm end to end, set in unmarked gold, two baroque pearls, one round (later with nacre loss), size 3-3/4. ....**$79**

Heritage Auctions

Art Nouveau pearl and enamel gold pendant and neck chain, 14k gold drop 46 mm top to bottom, enamel, seed pearls and large Baroque pearls, chain is 14k gold and 18"......................................**$418**

Heritage Auctions

Art Nouveau 18k gold and diamond ring, designed as lion's head with old European-cut diamond in mouth, size 7-1/4. ....**$1,778**

Skinner, Inc., www.skinnerinc.com

Art Nouveau sterling silver lorgnette, Krementz & Co., mask and tiger lily motifs, maker's mark, suspended from later chain, 7" l. **$356**

Skinner, Inc., www.skinnerinc.com

Art Nouveau 14k gold lorgnette, Krementz & Co., with flower and scroll border, trace link chain, 32.3 dwt, 4-1/8" l. **$1,440**

Skinner, Inc., www.skinnerinc.com

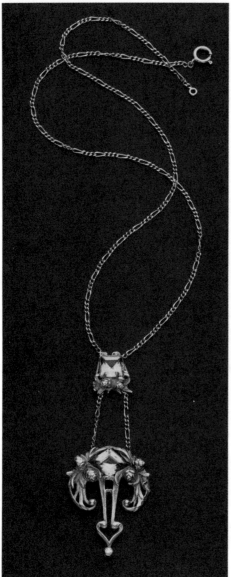

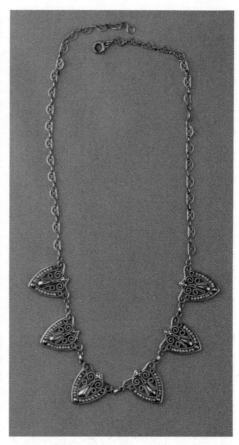

Art Nouveau 18k gold and seed pearl necklace, designed as shield-shape fringe with seed pearls and urn motifs, filigree links, 15-3/4" l................ **$1,422**

Skinner, Inc., www.skinnerinc.com

Art Nouveau plique à jour enamel pendant, France, set with white resin Madonna within plique à jour enamel frame, rose-cut diamond accents, maker's mark and guarantee stamp, 1-1/2"................. **$444**

Skinner, Inc., www.skinnerinc.com

Art Nouveau peridot and diamond necklace, 14k yellow gold, 10.8 grams, peridot stones 6 mm x 6 mm, 8 mm x 11 mm, accented with small diamond, chain 7-1/4", small peridot drop 13 mm x 12 mm, second chain drop 20 mm, large pendant 33 mm x 25 mm, total length 19"..............................**$627**

Heritage Auctions

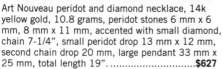

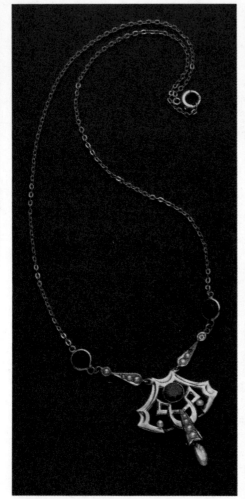

Art Nouveau pearl and amethyst necklace, 10k gold, 22 mm across main frame, 14" chain. **$262**

Heritage Auctions

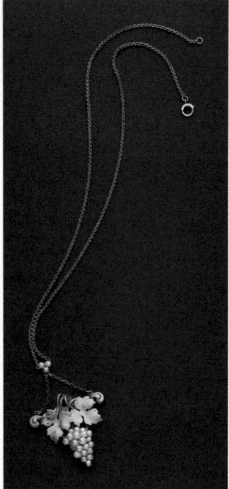

Art Nouveau enamel and gold pearl necklace, gold 14k enameled leaf and pearl pendant, 14k 15" chain, 30 mm across top frame........................ **$448**

Heritage Auctions

◄ Art Nouveau Mesoamerican-style 14k gold, opal, and diamond brooch, designed as figure with outstretched arms, centering cabochon opal, old European-cut diamond melee accents, reverse inscribed "Julie from Spencer 3-28-1900," 1-1/4". **$711**

Skinner, Inc., www.skinnerinc.com

ARTS & CRAFTS

Arts & Crafts ivory brooch, carved to depict bouquet of flowers, gold frame with scroll and foliate devices, with box from The Society of Arts and Crafts, 9 Park St., Boston; 1-3/4" l. **$296**

Skinner, Inc., www.skinnerinc.com

Arts & Crafts carved ivory brooch depicting exotic dragon among scrolling foliage, braided gold frame, with pouch from The Society of Arts & Crafts, 32 Newbury St., Boston; 1-5/8" l. **$237**

Skinner, Inc., www.skinnerinc.com

Arts & Crafts moonstone ring, Edward Oakes, circa 1930s-1940s, set with high-domed cabochon moonstone, foliate shoulders and scrolling tendrils, full-cut diamond and circular-cut sapphire accents, gold and platinum mount, unmarked, size 4-1/2. ..... **$2,489**

Skinner, Inc., www.skinnerinc.com

Arts & Crafts 18k gold and purple sapphire ring, bezel-set with a sapphire approximately 11.50 x 8.50 x 6.50 mm, framed by foliate devices and seed pearls, size 8-1/2......................................**$2,370**

Skinner, Inc., www.skinnerinc.com

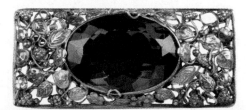

◄ Arts & Crafts 14k gold and amethyst brooch, set with cushion-cut amethyst measuring approximately 29 x 20 x 13.10 mm, in a plaque of grapevine motifs, 2-3/8" long. **$1,200**

Skinner, Inc., www.skinnerinc.com

Arts & Crafts moonstone and amethyst necklace, pendant set with oval and circular moonstone cabochons with amethyst center among scrolling floral and foliate devices, conforming chain, pendant 1-3/4" l., necklace 17" l... **$1,353**

Skinner, Inc., www.skinnerinc.com

Arts & Crafts gold nugget and hardstone cufflinks, each oval cabochon framed by gold nuggets, reverse marked "Native Gold Nuggets." **$948**

Skinner, Inc., www.skinnerinc.com

Arts & Crafts silver and blister pearl pin, Josephine Hartwell and Frederick Shaw, set with two blister pearls and cabochon sapphire, signed J&F Shaw, 7/8"...**$1,541**

Skinner, Inc., www.skinnerinc.com

Arts & Crafts 18k gold cufflinks, Tiffany & Co., each double link of cushion form with scroll and bead borders, 13.4 dwt, letter date M for 1907-1947, directorship of John C. Moore II, signed Tiffany & Co., Makers... **$2,760**

Skinner, Inc., www.skinnerinc.com

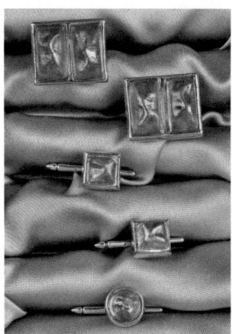

Arts & Crafts 14k gold and Favrile glass dress set, Potter Mellen, comprising a pair of cufflinks and three shirt studs each set with molded glass, maker's mark. **$1,080**

Skinner, Inc., www.skinnerinc.com

Arts & Crafts black opal and gold brooch, oval-shaped black opal cabochon measuring 20.88 x 11.32 x 3.28 mm and weighing approximately 3.80 carats, set in 14k gold, pinstem and catch, 1-1/4" x 7/8"...... **$2,000**

Heritage Auctions

Arts & Crafts gold and amethyst brooch, circa 1900, 14k one cushion-shaped amethyst, approximately 40 carats, amethyst is deep purple with deep lavender hues, several minor scratches and nicks not visible to eye, 1-1/16" x 1-5/8"..**$875**

Doyle New York

Arts & Crafts chrysoprase ring, attributed to Edward Oakes, set with cabochon chrysoprase with gold leaf form shoulders, old mine-cut diamond accents, silver mount, unsigned, size 5-1/2............ **$948**

Arts & Crafts 14k gold, sapphire and diamond ring, centering old European-cut cognac diamond, further set with four old European-cut diamonds, sapphire melee, foliate mount, indistinct maker's mark, size 5-1/4. .... **$2,133**

Skinner, Inc., www.skinnerinc.com

Arts & Crafts 14k gold, citrine and diamond ring, attributed to Edward Oakes, set with emerald-cut citrine approximately 16.45 x 12.40 x 7.40 mm, shoulders with bezel-set old European-cut diamonds and floral and foliate motifs, size 6, unsigned. **$2,607**

Skinner, Inc., www.skinnerinc.com

EDWARDIAN

Edwardian 18k gold, demantoid garnet and diamond bracelet composed of thick square links set with demantoid garnets and rose-cut diamonds, 23.6 dwt, 7-1/4" l. **$3,600**

Skinner, Inc., www.skinnerinc.com

Edwardian opal and diamond brooch, bezel-set with three cabochon opals, further set with old mine-cut diamonds, approximate total diamond weight 1.20 carats, platinum-topped gold mount, millegrain accents, 1-7/8" l. **$1,440**

Skinner, Inc., www.skinnerinc.com

Edwardian diamond and platinum brooch, European-cut diamonds weighing approximately 2.70 carats, set in openwork platinum, pendant bail, pinstem and catch on reverse, gross weight 7.90 grams, 1-3/8" x 1-1/4"... **$2,151**

Heritage Auctions

Edwardian brooch, diamond, seed pearl and platinum-topped gold, European-cut diamonds weighing approximately 0.40 carat, native-cut diamonds and seed pearls, set in platinum-topped 18k gold, pinstem and catch on reverse, gross weight 4.10 grams, 1-3/8" x 3/4". **$500**

Heritage Auctions

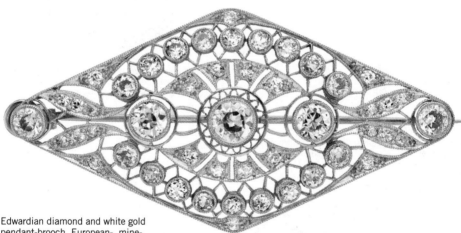

Edwardian diamond and white gold pendant-brooch, European-, mine-, and single-cut diamonds weighing approximately 2.50 carats, set in openwork 14k white gold, retractable bail, pinstem, and catch on reverse, gross weight 11.20 grams, 2-1/4" x 1-1/8". **$836**

Heritage Auctions

Edwardian amethyst, pearl and diamond brooch, navette form, set with fancy-cut amethyst approximately 30 x 19.30 x 11.20 mm, old European- and old single-cut diamonds, framed by seed pearls, platinum and 18k gold mount, 1-3/4" l. **$2,040**

Skinner, Inc., www.skinnerinc.com

Edwardian bar brooch, diamond, cultured pearl and platinum-topped gold, cultured pearl 4.80 x 5 mm, enhanced by European-cut diamonds weighing approximately 0.85 carat, set in platinum-topped 18k gold, pinstem and "C" catch on reverse, gross weight 7.0 grams, 2-1/4" x 3/8". **$625**

Heritage Auctions

Edwardian 18k gold, enamel, and diamond brooch designed as silver and rose-cut diamond trophy on blue guilloche enamel ground, French import stamps, 1" dia.. **$480**

Skinner, Inc., www.skinnerinc.com

Edwardian freshwater pearl and diamond brooch-pendant set with pear-, old mine-, and rose-cut diamonds suspending a freshwater pearl, platinum-topped 18k gold mount, 2" l. **$1,920**

Skinner, Inc., www.skinnerinc.com

Edwardian diamond and platinum brooch, European, Swiss and single-cut diamonds weighing approximately 3.25 carats, accented by blue stones, set in platinum, pinstem and catch on reverse, gross weight 12.91 grams, 3" x 1-1/4". **$1,971**

Heritage Auctions

Edwardian diamond, sapphire and platinum brooch, European- and single-cut diamonds weighing approximately 3.60 carats, pear and square-shaped sapphires weighing approximately 1.65 carats, set in platinum, pinstem and catch on reverse, gross weight 11.65 grams, 1" x 2-1/4"............................ **$2,390**
Heritage Auctions

Edwardian sapphire, diamond, seed pearl and platinum brooch, one oval-shaped sapphire 8.50 x 6.50 x 2.90 mm and weighing approximately 1.30 carats, European, Swiss and single-cut diamonds weighing approximately 0.85 carat, seed pearls 2-2.50 mm, set in platinum, gross weight 7.50 grams, 2" x 7/8".............................. **$2,151**
Heritage Auctions

Edwardian diamond and platinum bar brooch, European-cut diamonds weighing approximately 3 carats, set in platinum, pinstem and catch on reverse, gross weight 7.75 grams, 2-3/4" x 5/8". **$1,135**
Heritage Auctions

Edwardian diamond and white gold ring, European-cut diamond measuring 6.50-6.45 x 4.10 mm and weighing approximately 1 carat, European- and single-cut diamonds weighing approximately 0.50 carat, set in 14k white gold, total diamond weight is approximately 1.50 carats, gross weight 4.50 grams, size 3 (sizeable)......................**$2,031**

Heritage Auctions

Edwardian platinum, aquamarine, seed pearl and diamond brooch, bezel-set with cushion-cut aquamarine approximately 19.50 x 13.90 x 8.95 mm, framed by seed pearls and old European-cut diamonds, engraved gallery, 1-1/8" l.
.........................**$1,680**

Skinner, Inc., www.skinnerinc.com

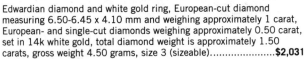

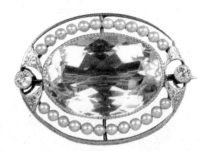

Edwardian stickpin, diamond and platinum-topped gold, mine-cut diamonds weighing approximately 0.50 carat, set in openwork platinum-topped 14k yellow gold, gross weight 3.40 grams, 2-5/8" x 7/16".................................**$262**

Heritage Auctions

Edwardian pendant-brooch, diamond, ruby and white gold, European-, mine-, and single-cut diamonds weighing approximately 3.50 carats, enhanced by marquise and fancy-cut rubies, set in openwork 14k white gold, retractable bail, pinstem, and catch on reverse, gross weight 12.20 grams, 2-9/16" x 1-1/16". **$2,390**

Heritage Auctions

Edwardian moonstone and diamond crown brooch set with five cabochon moonstones and old mine-cut diamonds, approximate total diamond weight 3 carats, platinum-topped 14k gold mount, 2-1/8" l. **$1,020**

Skinner, Inc., www.skinnerinc.com

Edwardian platinum, emerald and diamond bar pin and white gold and diamond filigree pin; diamond pin has one old European-cut diamond weighing approximately .40 carat and 44 old European-cut diamonds weighing approximately 2.20 carats; bar pin, circa 1915, is approximately 13.9 grams. **$2,375**

Doyle New York

Edwardian diamond and
platinum lorgnette, French,
hinged and spring loaded, opens
to reveal two circular-shaped
spectacles, handle features single-,
European-, rose-, and native-cut
diamonds, set in platinum, French
hallmarks, gross weight 23.80 grams,
5-1/4" x 3-3/4" (open); 3-7/8" x
1-5/8" (closed)................... **$836**

Heritage Auctions

Edwardian diamond, cultured pearl and platinum
ring, two European-cut diamonds weighing
approximately 1.50 carats, cultured pearl
5.95 x 6.20, European-cut diamonds weighing
approximately 0.50 carat, set in platinum, total
diamond weight approximately 2 carats, gross weight
7.92 grams, size 7-1/4 (sizeable)...............**$2,750**

Heritage Auctions

Edwardian diamond and platinum ring, mine-cut diamonds weighing approximately 3.55 carats, single-cut diamonds, set in platinum, total diamond weight is approximately 3.60 carats, gross weight 4.50 grams, size 6-1/4 (sizeable)....................................... **$2,750**

Heritage Auctions

Edwardian diamond and platinum ring, mine- and rose-cut diamonds weighing approximately 2.30 carats, set in platinum, gross weight 6.40 grams, size 6-3/4 (sizeable).................. **$2,750**

Heritage Auctions

Edwardian ruby, diamond, and platinum-topped gold necklace, pear-shaped ruby 8.40 x 6.10 x 3.80 mm and weighing approximately 1.55 carats, European- and rose-cut diamonds weighing approximately 0.85 carat, set in platinum-topped 18k gold, platinum chain, gross weight 6.18 grams, pendant 1-3/8" x 1/2"; chain 16" l............................... **$2,987**

Heritage Auctions

KITCHENWARE

Kitchenware

VINTAGE

Everyone knows that the kitchen is the hub of the home. So when the wildly successful "Downton Abbey" series streamed across television screens earlier this year, the show's Edwardian kitchen became a visual primer on class and comfort in our increasingly uncertain times.

That vision not only riveted viewers to each "Downton Abbey" installment, but the show's anti-snobbery theme created a new market niche for antique kitchen collectibles.

When stoic butler Mr. Carson chides housekeeper Mrs. Hughes about a new-fangled electric toaster, antique dealers nationwide said vintage toasters flew off the shelves.

"We simply could not believe how much interest 'Downton Abbey' has sparked in antique kitchen utensils," said Rege Woodley, a retired antique dealer in Washington, Pennsylvania. "I sold one of my antique rolling pins to my neighbor for $100 because it looked like the one used by Mrs. Patmore, the cook in 'Downton Abbey.'"

Pat Greene, owner of Nothing New Antiques, said she is excited about all the "Downton Abbey" fuss and hopes her antique kitchenwares fetch some lasting prices, too. "My rolling pins usually go for $5 to $10, but I'm seeing a big rush on my cookie cutters," said Greene of Pittsburgh.

Mary Kirk of New Alexandria, Pennsylvania, said she collects old antique cookbooks and was especially interested in trying to prepare some of the food served in the "Downton Abbey" show. "I am extremely interested in trying to prepare the eggs poached with spinach – a dish that poor young kitchen maid Daisy had to prepare during one show scene," said Kirk, a retired librarian. Because of the show's lengthy shooting schedule, producers have reported that most of the food served during production consists of light salads.

Pennsylvania tin wrigglework coffeepot, 19th century, bird and tulip decoration, 11-1/2" h. **$1,541**

Pook & Pook, Inc.

Jimmy Roark of Nashville, Tennessee, said he has not seen as large a rush for his kitchen collectibles as a result of the show. "What I see is a more gradual demand for these items," said Roark, who operates a small antique collectible shop in his garage. "I sell a lot of my cookie cutters, antique wooden bowls, and vintage mixer beaters during the holidays."

Still, the "Downton Abbey" magic continues to seed interest in a broad swath of antique kitchen utensils and artifacts from Bennington mixing bowls to turn-of-the-century tiger wood rolling pins.

Stephen White of White &White Antiques & Interiors of Skaneateles, New York, said interest in vintage antique kitchenware remains steady. At the ninth annual Antique Show at Oakmont Country Club March 9-10, 2013, near Pittsburgh, kitchenwares were front and center with collectors. The show, a benefit for the Kerr Memorial Museum, sports a broad mix of antiques for all ages.

White was quick to feature his rare whale ivory crested Nantucket rolling pin valued at $425. "I have unusual kitchen antiques from hand food choppers to copper pots," said White.

Other dealers at the Oakmont show featured kitchen antiques

from old historical companies instrumental in the economic growth of western Pennsylvania.

"When you think of Pittsburgh, you can't escape the long history that the H.J. Heinz Co. has here," said Toni Bahnak of Candlewood Antiques in Ardara, Pennsylvania. "We have rare old vinegar bottles and ketchup bottles that denote an era when the Heinz Co. made its own glass," said Bahnak.

And industry experts say ketchup and pickle collectibles will continue to soar in value because of the recent business deal that saw the H.J. Heinz Co. announce a $23.3 billion deal to be purchased by Warren Buffett's Berkshire Hathaway and 3G Capital, which was co-founded by Jorge Lemann, one of Brazil's richest men.

Pennsylvania wrought iron trivet, dated 1843, punched star decoration, 1-3/4" h., 4-3/4" dia.
.... **$1,896**

Pook & Pook, Inc.

Even before the blockbuster deal was announced, some Heinz memorabilia collectors reported that their antique bottles and jars were fetching higher prices than normal.

"I had one of my antique vinegar bottles sell for about $225 and I think I could have gotten more for it," said Ruth Oslet, an antique collector from Waynesburg, Pennsylvania. She sold it to a marketing executive who collects business memorabilia.

Tom Purdue, a long-time collector of food company antiques, said history and nostalgia play an important role in what people remember and want to save for their modern kitchens. "I can remember the distinct smell of my grandmother's old pickle jars and Heinz horseradish in her musty old kitchen where she used a hand pump to wash dishes," said Purdue, an 89-year-old former blacksmith from Wheeling, West Virginia.

The ever-expanding business reaches back to 1869 when Henry John Heinz and neighbor L. Clarence Noble began selling grated horseradish, bottled in clear glass to showcase its purity. It wasn't until 1876 that the company introduced its flagship product, marketing the country's first commercial ketchup.

Not all history, though, is tied to corporate America. Family memories still stoke the embers of home cooking although many young people today find fast food the fuel of the future.

"I still have my family's old cornbread recipe and I use it all the time," said Elizabeth Schwan, gallery director for Aspire Auctions in Pittsburgh.

Schwan, who scans the country for antiques, admits she has a soft spot for old kitchen utensils. "Flower-sifters, antique copper mixing bowls, and rolling pins were all part of my heritage because my family grew up on a Kentucky farm," Schwan said. "I can still smell the homemade bread and jams."

And like most farm families, the kitchen served as a meeting place and refuge from a long day's work. "Between verbal debates about what to plant on the south flats, we would help our parents churn butter and chop wood for the old country stove," said Myrtle Bench, 91, of Washington, Pennsylvania.

But as a young America turned from the agricultural frontier in the late 1890s and began to embrace a manufacturing economy, automation replaced handcrafts, and the kitchen became a new testing ground for a variety of modern gizmos like the automatic dishwasher.

The automatic dishwasher was a toy for the rich when an electric model was introduced on 1913 by Willard and Forrest Walker, two Syracuse, New York brothers who ran a hardware store when they were not tinkering with kitchen machines. The new dishwasher sold for $120 (the equivalent of $1,429 in today's dollars), a hefty premium over the $20 the Walkers charged for their popular hand-cranked model and also more expensive than a gasoline-powered washer the brothers put on the market in 1911.

"You can still find some of the old hand-crank washers, but I like to spend my time finding kitchen utensils that reflect how people prepared their food," said Dirk Hayes, a freelance cook from Uniontown, Pennsylvania. "I love watching 'Downton Abbey' because the kitchen scenes really give you a flavor of how the food was prepared. I never had that kind of staff, but it's fun to dream," said Hayes, who collects rolling pins and antique carving knives.

– Chriss Swaney

Two Pennsylvania carved butterprints, 19th century, decorated with lovebirds and an eagle, 3-3/4" dia. and 4-3/8" dia............... **$1,185**

Pook & Pook, Inc.

Seven Pennsylvania carved butterprints, 19th century, philphlot, tulip, and star-decorated examples...**$4,029**

Pook & Pook, Inc.

Seven Pennsylvania carved butterprints, 19th century, tulip and star examples, together with three paddles. **$2,370**

Pook & Pook, Inc.

Turned burl bowl, American, early 19th century, with turnings around collar and base, base crack, 4" h., 11-3/4" dia. **$2,040**

Skinner, Inc.

Copper and brass inlayed flesh fork, early 19th century, 19-1/2" l.
.... **$1,541**

Pook & Pook, Inc.

Three Pennsylvania wrought iron and brass utensils, 19th century, including taster with three brass bands and wrigglework decoration, small fork with brass inlay, spatula with decorated handle and blade, longest 10-1/8"..**$3,081**

Pook & Pook, Inc.

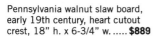

Pennsylvania walnut slaw board, early 19th century, heart cutout crest, 18" h. x 6-3/4" w. **$889**

Pook & Pook, Inc.

Six Pennsylvania inlaid wrought iron utensils, 19th century, including whitesmithed flesh fork inscribed IPHT 1808............................**$1,067**

Pook & Pook, Inc.

Collection of Pennsylvania tin, 19th century, including two strainers, large dipper, funnel, fat lamp on stand, pie pan, and match holder. **$770**

Pook & Pook, Inc.

Pennsylvania wrought iron flesh fork, 19th century, heart cutout terminal, together with two spatulas. **$3,081**

Pook & Pook, Inc.

Pennsylvania wrought iron spatula, 19th century, extensive punched star decoration, 18-1/2" l. **$1,126**

Pook & Pook, Inc.

Pennsylvania wrought iron flesh fork and spatula, circa 1830, with brass and copper inlaid bands and wrigglework decoration, 19-1/8" h..**$1,304**

Pook & Pook, Inc.

Pennsylvania wrought iron and copper straining ladle, circa 1830, with a brass inlaid handle with copper rivets, 22" h. **$356**

Pook & Pook, Inc.

Oversized Pennsylvania wrought iron spatula with elaborate inlaid brass decoration and the initials IB 1826, 21" h. The size and proportion of this piece suggest it may have been made as a wedding gift. **$5,346**

Pook & Pook, Inc

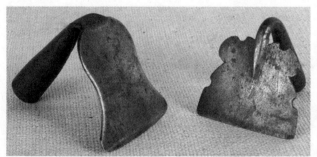

Two Pennsylvania wrought iron dough scrapers, 19th century, one engraved SR, 3-1/4" l. and 4-1/2" l. **$1,304**

Pook & Pook, Inc.

Pennsylvania wrought iron dough scraper, circa 1830, heart cutout, 2-3/4" h. x 3-1/4" w. **$1,422**

Pook & Pook, Inc.

Pennsylvania wrigglework coffeepot, 19th century, heart and floral decoration, 10" h. **$533**

Pook & Pook, Inc.

Tin sheet iron cookie cutter of a monkey on an elephant, 7-3/4" h. x 7-3/4" w. **$415**

Pook & Pook, Inc.

Three tin sheet iron cookie cutters, 19th century, depicting a horse-drawn sleigh, 5-1/8" h. x 8-3/4" w., and two figures on horseback. **$790**

Pook & Pook, Inc.

Tin sheet iron cookie cutter of a soldier playing a bugle, 19th century, 10-3/8" h. **$304**

Pook & Pook, Inc.

Five tin sheet iron cookie cutters, 19th century, including a gentleman in top hat, chimney sweep, etc., tallest 8-3/4" h. **$304**

Pook & Pook, Inc.

Pennsylvania painted tape loom, dated 1826, possibly western Pennsylvania, initialed NL, heart cutouts and lovebird decoration on red ground, yellow border, 15" h. x 13-3/4" w. x 6-3/4" d.
.... **$9,480**

Pook & Pook, Inc.

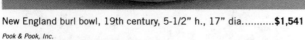

New England burl bowl, 19th century, 5-1/2" h., 17" dia...........**$1,541**

Pook & Pook, Inc.

Copper kettle, early 19th century, stamped W. Wolf, 11-1/2" h.
.... **$533**

Pook & Pook, Inc.

Four Birmingham silver nutmeg graters, 19th century.................**$4,131**

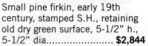

Pook & Pook, Inc.

Small pine firkin, early 19th century, stamped S.H., retaining old dry green surface, 5-1/2" h., 5-1/2" dia........................ **$2,844**

Pook & Pook, Inc.

York, Pennsylvania copper kettle, circa 1800, stamped John W. Schlosser, 11-1/2" h........... **$504**

Pook & Pook, Inc.

Dovetailed copper kettle, 19th century, stamped on handle Brandt, 7" h. **$273**

Pook & Pook, Inc.

Pennsylvania hatchel, dated 1804, original painted cover with date and initial HS, 8-3/4" h. x 17" w. **$4,266**

Pook & Pook, Inc.

French hammered copper roasting pan and lidded Dutch oven, early 20th century, roasting pan 6" h. x 16-1/2" w. x 12" d. **$450**

Cowan's Auctions, Inc.

Early hand-hewn wooden trencher with original red paint with notched ends and thin walls, 19th century, 5-1/4" x 32" x 11-1/2". **$120**

Cowan's Auctions, Inc.

Set of nine Victorian English pewter measures with brass rims, circa 1840. .... **$600**

Kaminski Auctions

Two York, Pennsylvania walnut coffee grinders, early 19th century, stamped J. Fisher Warranted, together with another grinder with gilt bowl..**$415**

Pook & Pook, Inc.

MODERN

The diverse area of kitchenware/household objects offers a world of collecting opportunities. Your interests may lead you to antique rarities more than 100 years old or to items of more recent manufacture. Any and all territory should be considered fair game. As with other collectibles, your primary motivation should be your individual likes and preferences.

There is a great deal of interest in kitchenware and related items from 35 to 60 years old; these objects rekindle old memories and represent a different, less-complicated era for many.

The items here represent a broad spectrum of kitchen items and cooking activities. These include just about every task you would want to try to master in your kitchen of yesteryear. There are gadgets of all types and all sorts of accessories, sets, holders, and miscellaneous gizmos. Most of the items are non-electrical and small in scale.

For more information on kitchen collectibles, see *Spiffy Kitchen Collectibles* or *Warman's Kitschy Kitchen Collectibles Field Guide*, both by Brian S. Alexander.

Nutbrown Chipper & French Fry Cutter, metal with wooden handles, simple to operate, "The finest of all chippers!," boxed, 1940s, Thos. M. Nutbrown Ltd., Blackpool, England. .... **$25-$28**

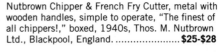

Big Top Peanut Butter, W.T. Young Foods, division of Proctor & Gamble, sealed large water goblet. ....**$30-$35**
Small dessert dish with lid ....**$15-$20**

Eggcups, two-part plastic with hand-painted design, 1950s.
................................**$12-$15 pr.**

Ekco/Mary Ann Cooking and Measuring Set, four pieces, aluminum, boxed, 1940s-1950s, Ekco Products Co., Chicago. ....**$18-$22**

Mirro cake pan, aluminum, "The pan that makes all 3 perfectly, Chiffon, Sponge Cake, Angel Food," with label, 1950s, Mirro Aluminum.........**$18-$20**

Mirro 4-Tier Cake Pan Set, aluminum, for "Parties...holidays, for every gala occasion," boxed, 1950s, Mirro Aluminum, Manitowoc, Wisconsin. ....**$18-$22**

Griswold Corn Cake Pan, early American quality cast iron, "There's nothing like iron to cook in," with cardboard sleeve, 1950s, Griswold Mfg. Co., Sidney, Ohio..................**$45-$50**

Eggbeater with yellow Bakelite handle, 1940s, A&J High Speed, Ekco Products Co. ...**$20-$22**

Mix Matic Food Mixer, "Mixes, beats, whips, blends," boxed, 1950s-1960s, E-Z-Por Corp., Chicago. .... **$22-$25**

Ekco batter whip, 1940s. ....**$12-$15**

Metal ricer and press with stand and wood wedging element, 1930s-1940s. .... **$15-$18**

Mechanical Cookie Cutter, metal, "Cuts dozens of cookies in seconds, No more one at a time!," boxed, 1940s-1950s, Syndicate Sales, Minneapolis. ....**$20-$22**

Androck flour sifter, three screens, "Hand-I-Sift," mom and kids in the kitchen design, 1950s. ....**$35-$65**

◄ Knapp's Safety Veg-E-Grater, metal, boxed, 1930s, Knapp Monarch Co., Belleville, Illinois. ....**$18-$22**

Ice crusher, chromed metal top with black plastic ice cup, adjusts for fine, medium, or coarse ice, boxed, 1940s................ **$35-$45**

4-Piece Tier Cake Set, boxed 1950s, Bake King, Chicago Metallic Mfg. Co., Chicago. ....**$20-$25**

► Rubbermaid plate rack, large size, "Keeps cupboards neat–Conserves space and provides handy access," 1940s-1950s. ....**$18-$22**

▼ Krispy Krust rolling pin, chrome, with catalin plastic handles and ball bearings, 1940s, Buffalo Toy and Tool Works, Buffalo, New York. ....**$40-$45**

◄ Miniature Revere Ware Utensils, copper clad stainless steel with plastic handles, "Just like mom's," boxed, 1950s, Revere Copper and Brass Inc., Rome Mfg. Div., Rome, New York. ....**$200-$225**

◀ Plas-tex cream and sugar set, styrene with hand-painted design, 1950s. Art-Deco in appearance, this set was made in the 1950s, and is usually found without decoration. The sugar bowl is missing its lid. .... **$15-$18**

▲ Juice-O-Mat, metal with chrome and plastic top, 1940s, full-size unit, Rival Mfg. Co., Kansas City, Missouri .... **$28-$30**
Junior model .... **$25-$28**

Tupperware canister set with decoration, 1970s. Also available in lime green, yellow and orange .... **$18-$22**

Egg beaters, Blend-R-Mix, stainless steel blades, adjustable handle for right- or left-hand use. 1940s, Dazey Corp., metal handle .... **$22-$25**
1950s, plastic handle .... **$18-$22**

Geared Swing-A-Way Can and Bottle Opener, metal with plastic knob, geared, "Swings flat against the wall," boxed, 1940s, Steel Products Mfg. Co. ....**$15-$18**

▶ Ice Box Cookie Moulds, "A favorite at parties and teas," boxed 1930s, Edward Katzinger Co. ....**$30-$35**

Lighting Devices

Lighting devices have been around for thousands of years, and antique examples range from old lanterns used on the farm to high-end Tiffany lamps. The earliest known type of lamp was the oil lamp, which was patented by Aimé Argand in 1784 and mass-produced starting in the 19th century. Around 1850 kerosene became a popular lamp-burning fluid, replacing whale oil and other fluids. In 1879, Thomas A. Edison invented the electric light, causing fluid lamps to lose favor and creating a new field for lamp manufacturers. Decorative table and floor lamps with ornate glass lampshades reached their height of popularity from 1900-1920, due to the success of Tiffany and other Arts & Crafts lamp makers, such as Handel.

Brass cold blast tubular signal marine lanterns, polished, ring handle, thread screws for elevation of band that secures top of globe and allows for removal, wire guard to top and bottom, underside with two hooks, one example with glass base, colorless 360-degree fresnal lens with one embossed PERKINS 17 MLD NO 2 ANCHOR FIG 61, fourth quarter 19th century, very good condition, 25-3/4" h. overall, 11-1/4" dia. base................... **$2,185 pr.**

Jeffrey S. Evans & Associates

New England Glass Co. "WRR" pierced sheet iron whale oil lantern, bail handle, fixed colorless globe embossed "WRR," removable base with spring mechanism and fitted with a 10-panel colorless glass font secured by plaster, underside marked "N.E. GLASS CO./PATENTED OCT. 24, 1854," No. 1 fine line collar, fitted with brass and tin double-tube burner, third quarter 19th century, excellent condition, 14-7/8" h. overall, 18-7/8" h. to top of cap, 6-1/4" dia. base................................. **$1,380**

Jeffrey S. Evans & Associates

EARLY LIGHTING

Pair of gilt-bronze Argand lamps, manufactured by and marked JOHN B. JONES BOSTON, second quarter 19th century, each with urn-form fonts on baluster shaft supporting a single arm with burner, on a round beaded and weighted base, accompanied by frosted colorless wheel-cut glass shades in looping and punty-cut pattern, with brass manufacturer's tag, 14" h., dia. to 10-1/4"...............................**$3,240**

Skinner, Inc., www.skinnerinc.com

Swirled marbrie loop stand lamp, ruby with opal pulled and swirling loops, stamped brass stem and single-step marble base, No. 1 fine line collar, fitted with period set-up comprising an E. F. Jones No. 1 lip burner, thumbwheel marked E. F. JONES, BOSTON/ PATENT MAY 4. 1858, translucent pale lavender lip chimney, third quarter 19th century, lamp undamaged, 9-1/8" h. to top of collar, 3-3/4" sq. base. **$2,760**

Jeffrey S. Evans & Associates

Free-blown saucer-base whale oil lamp, colorless globular font raised on applied colorless medial-button stem and cobalt blue conical saucer-edge base with folded rim and rough pontil mark, Boston & Sandwich Glass Co. and others, 1825-1830, 6-1/4" h., 3-1/4" dia. font, 4-5/8" dia. base..... **$6,325**

Jeffrey S. Evans & Associates

Samuel Yellin (1885-1940) Arts & Crafts wrought-iron candleholder, open-spiral shaft raised on circular pan-like base and three five-toed pad feet, stamped SAMUEL YELLIN under base, Samuel Yellin Studios, Philadelphia, first half 20th century, good as-found condition, 9" h., 5-3/4" dia. base. **$4,600**

Jeffrey S. Evans & Associates

Lantern with four colorless pressed lacy glass panes with steamboat and thistle, panels manufactured by J. & C. Ritchie, Wheeling, West Virginia, circa 1833, square green-painted wooden lantern with shaped edges, each side mounted with pane of glass centered with steamboat with plaque reading "J&C RITCHIE" over large thistle flanked by vases of flowers resting on cornucopia-shaped devices, with stippled background, one pane with small chip to lower right corner, 10" h. x 6-1/4" w............. **$5,700**

Skinner, Inc., www.skinnerinc.com

York, Pennsylvania brass fire lantern, inscribed Voted to Frank P. Spangler at Laurel Festival Aug. 22, 1874, with cobalt and clear globe, etched Union 3 within a wreath, with a placard inscribed Wm. Porter's Sons, 13" h. **$2,252**

Pook & Pook, Inc.

Wood and glass candle lantern, square soft-wood frame with worn red paint, three full glass panels with wire guards, remaining side with hinged door fitted with small glass window and guards, single socket, sheet iron top with central vent over three cupolas with pierced decoration and ring hanger, 19th century, good condition, 15-1/2" h. overall, 13" to top of vent, 5-1/4" sq... **$3,335**

Jeffrey S. Evans & Associates

Hobbs Snowflake miniature lamp, sapphire opalescent/blue opalescent, matching patterned crown shade, period collar and burner, Hobbs, Brockunier & Co., fourth quarter 19th century, undamaged, 6-7/8" h. to top of shade, 4" h. to top of collar, 2-3/4" dia. base. **$1,265**

Jeffrey S. Evans & Associates

Opalescent swirl miniature lamp, cranberry opalescent, matching patterned umbrella form shade, period burner. L. G. Wright Glass Co., 20th century, undamaged, 7-1/2" h. to top of shade, 3" dia. base. **$184**

Jeffrey S. Evans & Associates

Swirled Beads & Ribs miniature lamp, cranberry, matching patterned chimney-shade, period No. 1 Taplin-Brown collar, period burner, late 19th/ early 20th century, font undamaged, top of chimney-shade with a small light bruise, 8-3/8" h. to top of chimney-shade, 2-7/8" dia. base. **$92**

Jeffrey S. Evans & Associates

Junior banquet lamp, heavily embossed brass-plated pot metal base with drop in font, P & A Victor burner, reverse frosted ball shade with torch and wreath design, shade very good to excellent condition, 15-1/4" h. **$173**

James D. Julia, Inc.

Figural mini lamp, porcelain owl base with inset yellow and black eyes, yellow cased half shade, shade in excellent condition, 10" h. **$403**

James D. Julia, Inc.

Junior banquet lamp, painted pink metal font on tripod-style stem and foot, white milk glass ball shade with multicolored floral décor, P & A Victor burner, good condition, 15-1/4" h. **$201**

James D. Julia, Inc.

Hobbs Snowflake miniature lamp font, ruby opalescent/cranberry opalescent, period collar and burner, Hobbs, Brockunier & Co., fourth quarter 19th century, undamaged, 4" h. to top of collar, 2-3/4" dia. base. **$219**

Jeffrey S. Evans & Associates

Wrought iron rush holder with candle socket, circa 1770-1800, approximately 12" h. **$275**

Jeremy B. Teel Auction

Hobbs hand-stem stand lamp, colorless, drip edge embossed PATD SEPT 29TH 1863 JAN 9TH 1877, No. 1 Taplin-Brown collar with patent information, Hobbs, Brockunier & Co., fourth quarter 19th century, undamaged, 9-3/4" h. to top of collar, 4-5/8" dia. base. **$978**

Jeffrey S. Evans & Associates

Embossed satin glass miniature lamp, opal cased mottled pink with satin finish, matching patterned umbrella shade, period burner, late 19th/early 20th century, undamaged, 8-1/2" h. overall, 2-7/8" dia. base. **$489**

Jeffrey S. Evans & Associates

Sheldon swirl stand lamp, bubbly pink and opal spatter reverse swirl font, colorless base, No. 1 Taplin-Brown collar with patent information, fitted with period set-up comprising a slip burner and chimney with serrated scalloped top, fourth quarter 19th century, undamaged, 8-3/8" h. to top of collar, 4-5/8" dia. base. **$288**

Jeffrey S. Evans & Associates

Continental wrought iron fat lamp on stand, early 19th century, 16-1/2" h. **$304**

Pook & Pook, Inc.

Mini lamp, Delft decoration on white milk glass ball shade and porcelain base, foreign burner, very good to excellent condition, 6-1/4" h. **$316**

James D. Julia, Inc.

Pair of Bohemian cut cameo overlay lustres with prisms, 10-1/4 x 5". **$325**

Kaminski Auctions

Mini lamp, End of Day glass shade and base with applied crystal feet, 1/16" V-chip in fitter edge of shade, manufacturing bubble near top edge of shade, 8" h.... **$1,093**

James D. Julia, Inc.

Quezal candle lamp, art glass shade with ivory ground, green hooked feather pattern, gold border, shade finished with orange interior, brass base with single wick, shade signed Quezal to exterior border, base unsigned, very good to excellent condition, 11" h. **$633**

James D. Julia, Inc.

Skater's lamp, brass frame with amber globe, minor denting in brass cap, otherwise excellent condition, 7" h. **$1,150**

James D. Julia, Inc.

Tiffany Studios blown glass candelabra, six bronze arms supporting candle cups with green blown glass inserts, each cup finished with a bobeche, single Art Nouveau center stem that hides candle snuffer, green/brown patina finish with hints of red, signed Tiffany Studios New York 164, very good to excellent condition, 15" h. x 21" w. **$4,600**

James D. Julia, Inc.

Mini lamp, optic paneled green glass, shade and base with applied crystal shell feet, Nutmeg burner, 1/8" flake, 1/2" long smoothed area on top outside edge of shade, 8-1/2" h. **$230**

James D. Julia, Inc.

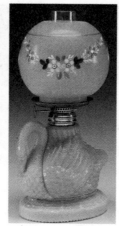

Figural mini lamp, white milk glass reclining elephant with original shade highlighted with gold paint, Nutmeg burner, very good condition, paint well worn, 7-1/2" h. **$230**

James D. Julia, Inc.

Swan mini lamp, pink milk glass swan base with replacement ball shade, shade has pink ground with blue, white, green and yellow floral décor, very good condition, 7-1/2" h. **$345**

Mini brass double student lamp with pink painted milk glass shades, glass good to excellent condition, 8-1/2" h. ....**$4,500-$5,500**

James D. Julia, Inc.

Spider Web/Pansy miniature lamp, colorless with red enamel and gilt decoration, frosted finish, matching patterned and decorated ball shade, period burner, Fostoria Glass Co., first quarter 20th century, undamaged, 8-1/4" h. to top of shade, 3-1/2" dia. base. **$81**

Jeffrey S. Evans & Associates

Opalescent mini lamp, pale green opalescent shade and base with matching chimney, shade and base have narrow and wide paneling pattern, base with clear green applied shell feet, very good to excellent condition, 10" h. to top of shade, 11-1/4" h. to top of chimney. **$460**

James D. Julia, Inc.

Pair of matching crystal table lamps in Pineapple & Fan pattern, sometimes referred to as the Shepherd's Plaid, glass good to excellent overall condition, 17" h... **$748**

James D. Julia, Inc.

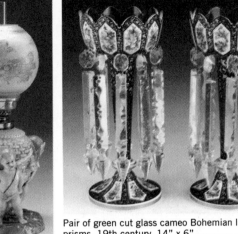

Pair of green cut glass cameo Bohemian lustres with prisms, 19th century, 14" x 6". **$1,900**

Kaminski Auctions

English sterling candlesticks and snuffers hallmarked Daniel Smith and Robert Sharp 1785-1786 with modern wick trimmers marked sterling, 4-1/4" h. x 6-1/4" w. across handle, approximately 22 troy oz. total weight. **$850**

Kaminski Auctions

Satin glass mini lamp, yellow shading to white mother of pearl satin finish, diamond pattern, applied frosted shell feet on square base, foreign burner, three of shell feet have roughness at tips, shade matches base but may not be original, 10" h. **$518**

James D. Julia, Inc.

Dresden mini lamp, basket font with applied flowers and leaves supported by three winged cupids standing on round footed base, acid etched cupid shade trimmed with gold and green, Gaudard burner, almost no damage to applied floral decoration or wing tips, 14-1/4" h. **$920**

James D. Julia, Inc.

Mini lamp, Royal Worcester style base, cream colored with multicolored floral décor, reverse swirl dark shading to light pink satin glass shade, foreign burner, shade in very good condition, 13" h. **$115**

James D. Julia, Inc.

Single log student lamp, brass with old 6" milk glass shade, glass good to excellent condition, 15" h. **$288**

James D. Julia, Inc.

Embossed satin glass miniature lamp, red with satin finish, font with embossed lion heads, appropriate petal and lightly beaded shade, period burner, late 19th/ early 20th century, very good condition, 8-5/8" h. to top of shade, 3 1/8" dia. base overall. **$104**

Jeffrey S. Evans & Associates

Impasto cameo fairy lamp, satin ruby/ cranberry, off-white enamel floral decoration, unmarked colorless base, lacking candle insert, probably Phoenix Glass Co., fourth quarter 19th century, few nicks to shade, 5-1/2" h., 3-1/2" dia. base. **$150**

Jeffrey S. Evans & Associates

Miniature sleigh student lamp with yellow painted milk glass shade, lamp stamped OCT.28 79, good to excellent condition, 6" h. **$805**

James D. Julia, Inc.

Mini lamp, honey amber color with white spatter, very good to excellent condition, 6" h. **$633**

James D. Julia, Inc.

Swan mini lamp, white milk glass with heavily embossed shade, Nutmeg burner, top edge of shade has 1/4" repair; bottom edge of shade has two flakes, 8" h. **$518**

James D. Julia, Inc.

Hobbs dot finger lamp, blue, applied transparent blue handle, No. 1 Taplin-Brown collar, Hobbs, Brockunier & Co., late 19th/early 20th century, excellent condition, 2-7/8" h. to top of collar, 3-1/2" dia. base... **$161**

Jeffrey S. Evans & Associates

Mini student lamp, brass single student lamp with floral decorated green milk glass slant side shade, very good condition, 10-1/2" h. to top of finger ring..... **$403**

James D. Julia, Inc.

Miniature double brass student lamp with Nutmeg burners, marked "Nutmeg England," powder blue umbrella style glass shades, very good to excellent condition, 13-1/2" h................ **$518**

James D. Julia, Inc.

Figural mini lamp, porcelain owl in colors of tan and white with inset yellow and black eyes, white umbrella style shade, base marked William Whiteley, China manufactured in France, foreign burner, very good to excellent condition, 13-1/2" h. **$920**

James D. Julia, Inc.

Mini florette lamp, green cased glass with heavily embossed pattern, Nutmeg burner, very good to excellent condition, 7" h........................... **$259**

James D. Julia, Inc.

Kerosene stem lamp, pear-shaped crystal font mounted on brass stem and marble foot, P&A Victor burner and shade ring, cut and frosted shade, very good to excellent condition, 8-1/4" to top of collar, overall to top of shade is 16-1/4"................**$144**

James D. Julia, Inc.

White milk glass mini lamp, painted floral décor, very good to excellent condition, 5-3/4" h. **$288**

James D. Julia, Inc.

Mini lamp, amber glass in Honeycomb pattern, very good to excellent condition, 7" h.......**$403**

James D. Julia, Inc.

Junior banquet lamp, copper font shell mounted on metal stem and cast metal foot painted black, drop in lamp font with Victor burner, 6" dark maroon cased ball shade lined in white, good to excellent condition, 15" to top of shade. **$230**

James D. Julia, Inc.

Mini lamp, white milk glass eagle with all-over yellow and blue paint highlighted with gold, Acorn burner, very good to excellent condition, 7-1/2" h. **$173**

James D. Julia, Inc.

Mini lamp, cranberry opalescent snowflake encased in silver filigree, Nutmeg burner, hairline crack from top to bottom of glass shade, covered by silver filigree, 7" h. ..**$201**

James D. Julia, Inc.

Junior size lamp, Delft decorated porcelain base mounted on cast brass footed base, white milk glass ball shade with blue angel décor, foreign burner marked "Kosmos," very good condition, 12-1/4" h.......**$144**

James D. Julia, Inc.

Cranberry mini lamp, heavily paneled cranberry glass in both base and umbrella shade, good to excellent condition, 7-1/2" h. **$374**

James D. Julia, Inc.

LIGHTING DEVICES

An American Art Form: Exploring the Emergence of Leaded Glass Lamps

Unlike other members of the decorative arts, the common stained or leaded glass lamp has a history that sets it apart in the fields of glass art and interior decorative elements. In its short lifespan of not quite 150 years, what we generically and incorrectly refer to as the Tiffany lamp (Tiffany is a brand name and not an art form or discipline in itself) has enjoyed an interesting existence.

On one hand, the finest examples are considered some of the most valuable, beautiful and desirable objects on earth, fetching fine art prices in private dealings and at auction. On the other, the leaded glass lamp has been commercialized to the point of absurdity, where the most insignificant examples can be found in home improvement stores, flea markets, home shopping programs, and junk shops. Despite this drastic polarity, the leaded glass lamp at its finest remains a young, vibrant medium worthy of its continuing and future popularity.

The leaded glass lamp is unique for two important reasons. First, prior to the late 19th century, it has no European heritage or historical precedent. No ancient artifacts resembling a leaded lamp have been dug up. No medieval, renaissance or baroque masters delegated their designs to dimensional glass design as they did to stained glass window fabrication, and no one has, as yet, unearthed any information or evidence identifying the originator, or originators, of the form. Many names are associated with the earliest examples of leaded glass lamp art and craft, but none of them can, or have claimed, authorship. This distinguishes the leaded glass lamp as an artistic and craft-based oddity of sorts, as it popped up almost full blown in both its production and image at some time during the late 19th century.

Furthermore, its development cannot be traced to any one discipline. True, the lamp has obvious links to the stained glass arts and related crafts, given its basis of pieces of colored glass fit together by means of a metal matrix; and also to the art of mosaics, despite the difference in method of construction. Mosaic glass is set into a bed of cement or a similar bonding material while the leaded glass lamp's glass pieces are surrounded by a metal foil (copper). But the specific product consisting of pieces of colored glass fit together using a flexible matrix to create a representational design onto a three-dimensional form and then set upon a standard support as a finished source of light is exclusively a late 19th century phenomenon whose real source and periods of development remain a mystery.

Second, it is an entirely American invention. Just like the lightbulb, cotton gin, abstract expressionism, rock 'n' roll, Mickey Mouse, and Elvis, the leaded glass lamp is all American. In its relatively short history as a decorative

Bigelow and Kennard table lamp, Boston, shade with foliate band on faceted base, leaded slag glass, patinated bronze, two sockets, shade stamped Bigelow, Kennard & Co. Boston, base unmarked, 20" x 14" **$3,500**

Rago Arts and Auction Center

art, and despite the fact that the entire field has been dominated by the works of one firm, the leaded glass lamp has become an icon of domestic lighting with exclusive American roots.

To further understand its cloudy emergence in the decorative arts and crafts, it is helpful to consider the developments and conditions that were contemporary to the period. What kind of cultural environment provided the requisite dynamics for such an invention to come to being? The economic and industrial landscape of the period was marked by an unrivalled surge of manufacturing innovation and invention; one of the results being the emergence of what we have come to describe as the industrial arts, an apropos category for the fledgling leaded glass lamp.

If we accept the time period when the leaded glass lamp first made its appearance, circa 1897, we can also identify an almost perfect storm of economic and manufacture-related conditions that would provide the requisite opportunities for the new leaded glass lamp to flourish. Add to this the introduction of electric incandescent lighting, and the groundwork for the leaded lamp was firmly in place.

The earliest of leaded glass lamps were no doubt fuel lamps illuminated by a gas burner and flame, and in this category, Tiffany Studios held the reigns. Aided by its involvement with the Bray Patent for gas burners, and up until its expiration in 1903, Tiffany Studios was able to secure the market and name recognition necessary to establish its lighting products and develop design and production techniques far in advance of any competitors.

Add to this the introduction of the "copper foil" technique of framing and joining the individual pieces of stained glass into a lamp form – another of Tiffany's seemingly "signature" innovations (though no claim or patent for the technique has ever been attributed to the firm, nor to anyone else for that matter) – and you have the makings of the new decorative art form known as the leaded glass lamp.

The popular legend that the leaded glass lamp was inspired by the need to make use of excess glass left from stained glass window construction has no real basis or logic. For one thing, the types of glasses required for stained glass window production differ from those preferred for lamps. The former relies on glass that easily transmits light to the point of translucence and transparence, while lamps require glass that is more opaque. Additionally, the design, tooling and production processes inherent in lamp creation are in no way the result of spontaneity or any "off the cuff, end of the day" effort. The process is a sophisticated and perfectly integrated combination of artistic vision, three-dimensional design, precision tooling, glassworking technique, and component metal (brass, copper and bronze) additives.

For a good part of the early 20th century, several American manufacturers such as Tiffany, Handel, Bigelow and Kennard, Duffner & Kimberly, Seuss and a host of others adopted the leaded glass lamp as their own, providing a body of work that remains unique, substantial, rich in invention and timeless beauty, and a testament to the innovative spirit of the era.

— Joseph Porcelli

Contemporary Porcelli Studios geometric leaded glass table lamp by Joseph Porcelli, overlapping half circles of square geometric panels in yellow and cream glass, shade bordered on top and bottom with single row of butterscotch iridescent glass tiles, shade signed on inside with initials JP etched into top border tile, Art Nouveau-style spelter base with brown patina and overall green highlights, bronze riser supporting four-light cluster and contemporary Tiffany-style heat cap, very good to excellent condition, shade 20" dia., lamp 26" h. **$6,900**

James D. Julia, Inc.

Joseph Porcelli has been a professional glass artist and craftsperson since 1979. He is the former publisher of Glass Craftsman Magazine, the producer and publisher of the GCTV line of glass instructional videos, and the author of The Lamp Making Handbook and Stained Glass, Jewels of Light. He is currently a full-time glass artist whose original lamps and bronze bases have fetched record auction prices for contemporary leaded glass. www.josephporcellistudio.com

ELECTRIC LIGHTING

Art Deco figural lamp, circa 1925, patinated brass and white metal depicting nude female seated below a lantern, numbered 520 on base reverse, excellent working condition, 14" h.....**$230**

Jeffrey S. Evans & Associates

Frankart lamp, $10 model, circa 1925, 10-1/4" h. x 6-1/4" w. x 5" d. **$400**

Kaminski Auctions

Arts & Crafts four-arm brass and slag glass hanging fixture, circa 1920, 16" x 21".......................**$2,000**

Rago Arts and Auction Center

Frankart lamp, African-American woman, 14-3/4" h. x 6" w. x 6" d. **$450**

Kaminski Auctions

Roseart lamp, circa 1930, 12-1/2" h. x 10" w. x 8" d................**$250**

Kaminski Auctions

Gothic-style gilt bronze pricket lamp, Continental, mounted as floor lamp, of architectural form, tripartite base, 63-1/2" h. x 8-1/2" w..........**$300**

Cowan's Auctions, Inc.

Josephine Baker, pair of lamp bases, ceramic, circa 1930s/1940s, 16" h. x 9" w.................**$175**

Kaminski Auctions

Arts & Crafts-style table lamp, 20th century, 18" umbrella shade of leaded slag sections and wide border of green scrolls and red jewels, patinated bronze base............**$150**

Kaminski Auctions

Art Deco/Machine Age tubular wall lamp, glass and aluminum, circa 1935, 16" l. x 3-1/2" dia. **$175**

Kaminski Auctions

Handel, chandelier, Meriden, Connecticut, 1910s, faceted shade with applied geometric overlay on pierced cluster, caramel slag glass, patinated metal, enamel, three sockets, unmarked, shade 9" x 22", approximately 42" h. **$5,625**

Rago Arts and Auction Center

Handel, floor lamp with harp and geometric shade, Meriden, Connecticut, 1920s, leaded glass, patinated metal, single socket, cloth label to base, 57" x 13-3/4". **$1,375**

Rago Arts and Auction Center

Dore bronze and crystal chandelier, 20th century, six arms with prisms and glass globe and smoke bell, electrified, 30" x 31"................................... **$3,125**

Rago Arts and Auction Center

Handel, adjustable floor lamp with brown obverse-painted Mosserine shade, Meriden, Connecticut, 1910s, acid-etched glass, patinated metal, single socket, cloth label to base, 58" x 10-1/2"...... **$2,000**

Rago Arts and Auction Center

Lucite spiral lamp, missing harp and finial, 17" h. x 14" w. **$175**

Kaminski Auctions

Art Nouveau-style cast resin pair of boudoir lamps, 21st century, gold and blue with frosted glass panel, each signed D. Tupton on back, excellent working condition, 13" h. **$316**

Jeffrey S. Evans & Associates

Quezal eight-light lily lamp with cast bronze base with openwork near foot and eight arching arms, each supporting a lily shade, ribbed shades have green pulled feather design against creamy white background with gold iridescent trim around leaves, interior of each shade is finished in gold iridescence; six shades signed Quezal on fitter rim, two unsigned shades have a more yellowish background than six signed shades; very good to excellent condition, 25-1/2" h. **$5,750**

James D. Julia, Inc.

Le Verre Français cameo glass table lamp, signed on base with blue, white, and red candy cane, Roses Savage or Wild Rose pattern, 16-1/4" h., shade 9-3/4" dia. **$2,000**

Kaminski Auctions

Pairpoint puffy-shade table lamp, circa 1915, reverse-painted shade with butterflies and roses, gilt tracery on exterior, raised on bronze-patinated metal base with two electric sockets, signed PAIRPOINT / P in diamond / C3066 under base, shade with inner rim chip, base with minor wear to finish, 21-1/2" h. overall, 14" dia. shade. **$1,610**

Jeffrey S. Evans & Associates

Roseart lamp, model R102, circa 1930, small as-made casting imperfection, 13-1/4" h. x 7" w. x 6-1/2" d. **$250**

Kaminski Auctions

Handel, adjustable desk lamp, Meriden, Connecticut, circa 1915, patinated metal, leaded slag glass, single socket, base stamped Handel, 14" x 10", shade 6" x 5-3/4". **$750**

Rago Arts and Auction Center

Machine Age aircraft lamp, glass and chrome, circa 1930s/1940s, 7" h. x 13-1/2" w. x 12" l. **$700**

Kaminski Auctions

Swirled opalescent glass shades, pair, cranberry opalescent, fitted on a brass electric table lamp, 20th century, shades undamaged, 6-1/4" h., 2-1/8" dia. fitter, lamp 24" h. overall. **$374**

Jeffrey S. Evans & Associates

Table lamp with leaded glass shade in honeycomb pattern on classical patinated base, United States, 1920s, leaded slag glass, patinated metal, two sockets, unmarked, 24-1/2" x 19". **$1,000**

Rago Arts and Auction Center

Table lamp, California, circa 1920, hammered copper, mica shade, two sockets, unmarked, 21-1/2" x 16"..... **$2,375**

Rago Arts and Auction Center

Tiffany Studios adjustable desk lamp with Damascene shade, New York, patinated bronze, Favrile glass, single socket, base stamped TIFFANY STUDIOS NEW YORK 419, shade etched L.C.T. Tiffany – Favrile, 13-1/2" x 9" x 7". **$6,250**

Rago Arts and Auction Center

Handel, table lamp on fluted base, Meriden, Connecticut, 1920s, shade reverse- and obverse-painted with pine trees, chipped glass, patinated metal, two sockets, shade signed Handel 5345 with U.S. patent and stamps to collar, 21-3/4" x 16". **$4,375**

Rago Arts and Auction Center

Handel, adjustable desk lamp with tulip shade, Meriden, Connecticut, circa 1915, patinated metal, slag glass, single socket, base stamped Handel, approximately 17" x 9-1/2", shade 5-1/4" x 7-3/4" sq............... **$1,625**

Rago Arts and Auction Center

Charles Schneider bronze pheasant leaded lamp with segmented glass body of yellow, amber, and red with long tail feathers, Charles Schneider in script located on side of base, excellent condition, 16-1/2" h. x 22-1/2" l. **$2,000**

Mark Mussio, Humler & Nolan

Handel table lamp, Meriden, Connecticut, 1910s, shade reverse- and obverse-painted with Glasgow roses, organic base, acid-etched glass, patinated metal, two sockets, base unmarked, shade signed Patent Applied and Handel 5463, 20" x 14"..................... **$4,063**

Rago Arts and Auction Center

Moe Bridges table lamp, 1920s, shade reverse-painted with lake scene at dusk on Aesthetic Movement-style bronze base, chipped glass, bronze, patinated metal, two sockets, shade signed, 23" x 18".......... **$2,500**

Rago Arts and Auction Center

Pair of Pairpoint lamps with nautical shades, circa 1915, base impressed D 3076, 22-1/2" h. x 15-3/4" dia. **$6,875**

Heritage Auctions

TOP! LOT!

Tiffany Studios pair of large turtleback glass wall sconces, New York, circa 1900, patinated bronze, glass, single socket, unmarked, 16-1/2" x 11" x 8"... **$38,750**

Rago Arts and Auction Center

Tiffany Studios early and large electrolier, New York, circa 1900, glass gems, gilt metal, four sockets, unmarked, to top of post: 70" x 22" dia. **$38,750**

Rago Arts and Auction Center

Handel table lamp, Meriden, Connecticut, 1920s, rare four-sided shade with leaf pattern on a fine curled base, leaded yellow slag glass, patinated metal, three sockets, shade and base stamped Handel, 28" x 18" sq. **$8,125**

Rago Arts and Auction Center

Handel table lamp with reverse-painted shade with landscape of trees in autumn colors and earth tones, chipped ice finish, signed and numbered 6957 on inner rim, also signed on interlocking ring, base of bronzed metal, acorn pulls, three Bryant sockets, signed on cloth base covering, two areas of paint loss near edge of shade, finish wear and loss to base, shade 17-7/8" dia., base 23-1/4" h.......................... **$2,100**

Kaminski Auctions

Table lamp with Nordic landscape overlay, United States, 1910s, patinated metal, slag glass, two sockets, unmarked, 23-1/2" x 18"........**$688**

Rago Arts and Auction Center

Peter Tereszczuk Loetz figural table lamp, Austria, circa 1900, patinated bronze, iridescent glass shade, single socket, base signed P. Tereszczuk, 14-1/2" x 7"........**$3,750**

Rago Arts and Auction Center

Tiffany Studios zodiac desk lamp with fully leaded slag panel shade in yellow and orange, two socket gold dore zodiac lamp base with zodiac top cap, shade signed TIFFANY STUDIOS 1587, base signed Tiffany Studios New York 587, very good to excellent condition, shade 11" dia., lamp 15" h......... **$2,875**

James D. Julia, Inc.

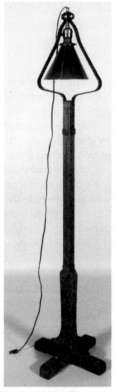

Gustav Stickley floor lamp #500, adjustable hammered copper frame supported by oak pedestal base, period correct antique green and white cased glass shade, unsigned, some chipping to wood of base, cleaned original finish, original patina on copper; silk, wire and brass framed shade with damage, 58-1/4" h. x 14" sq. base...........**$850**

Kaminski Auctions

Victorian decorated parlor lamp, late 19th/early 20th century, opaque white with pink shading and polychrome floral and foliage decoration, later ball shade hand-painted to match base, cast-metal base embossed 246 to underside, font with metal lining and brass drop-in font with embossed scroll pattern, No. 3 collar, period central draft burner components, non-period slip chimney, electrified, very good condition, 29-1/2" h. overall, lamp 17" h. to top of collar, 7-1/4" sq. base.....**$150**

Jeffrey S. Evans & Associates

Tiffany Studios harp desk lamp with vertically ribbed foot and brown patina, base holds art glass shade with gold iridescent wave design against cream-colored background, shade may or may not be Tiffany, very good to excellent condition, shade 7" dia., base 13-1/2" h. **$1,093**

James D. Julia, Inc.

Mid-century brass floor lamp of flower form with tripod base, eight small bulbs and one standard spun fiberglass shade, 63" h., shade 18" dia. ...**$475**

Kaminski Auctions

1960s table lamp, spun acrylic shades, 34-1/2" h..........................**$150**

Kaminski Auctions

Magic & Illusion

Magic is an ancient art with a rich history. The earliest reported magic trick—the ball and cups trick—began thousands of years ago, around 1700 B.C. Books on magic began to be published in the 16th century, and the first magic theater opened in London in 1873.

Magic or stage magic, as it is technically called, is a performing art that entertains audiences by staging tricks, effects, or illusions of seemingly impossible feats using natural means. The person who performs these illusions or tricks is called a magician or illusionist, prestidigitator, conjuror, mentalist, or escape artist.

No discussion of magic is complete without mentioning Harry Houdini, the great escape artist who performed in the early 1900s and is considered to be one of the most famous magicians in history, or the fictional boy wizard, Harry Potter, who made magic a household word in today's culture.

Collectors are interested in the history of magic as a performing art and the magicians who performed it. They collect books, posters, tokens, apparatus, printed ephemera (programs, tickets, broadsides, etc.) about magic as well as photos, letters, and other memorabilia about past and present performers.

The most well known club for collectors of magic is the Magic Collectors' Association, founded in 1949 in New York City by several prominent collectors of that era. It has members throughout North America, England, Europe, and Australia.

Hotsie Totsie Bathing Beauty, Colon, Michigan, Blackstone Magic Co., 1928, hand painted and sewn, with original cape but lacking suit, scarce, 15" x 23-1/2". Painting on cloth of a seaside "bathing beauty" is shown, cloth is folded in half, and magician reaches into painting and removes the bather's cape, then swimsuit. When the painting is unfolded it has transformed – the tide has come in, covering the bather's body and protecting her dignity in the process.. **$550**

Owned and operated by Percy Abbott and Harry Blackstone, Sr., The Blackstone Magic Co. was a short-lived enterprise, operating for only 18 months. A serious disagreement between the partners shuttered the business permanently. Consequently, everything the company produced is scarce or rare, including printed instructions, correspondence, and in particular the apparatus it produced – in any condition.

Potter & Potter Auctions

Card spider, Los Angeles, F.G. Thayer, circa 1940; very good condition, 16" x 16". Selected card visibly appears in the legs of the spider when its web is spun...**$400**

Potter & Potter Auctions

Douglas Blackburn, *Thought-Reading or Modern Mysteries Explained*, London: Field & Turner, circa 1884. Printed wrappers, 12mo, wrappers chipped and binding fragile. **$1,200**

Potter & Potter Auctions

Floating lightbulb, American, circa 1935, with gimmicked art deco table lamp and special bulb, lamp 16" h. Lit glass lightbulb is removed from table lamp and floats around theater. **$650**

Potter & Potter Auctions

Herman Pinetti, *Second Sight Secrets and Mechanical Magic*, Bridgeport: The Dunham Press, 1905. Dark grey pictorial wraps, illustrated, 12mo, good condition. Secrets of table tipping, levitation, and second sight codes are explained. **$225**

Potter & Potter Auctions

Penetrating glass, Boston, Val Evans, circa 1945, good condition, tray 14-1/2" x 10". A glass is covered with a handkerchief and a plate is set on top of both. A tube is then balanced on the plate. The glass then slowly and visibly penetrates the cloth and plate, and is removed from the tube. Ingenious mechanical gimmick built into tray..................................... **$850**

Potter & Potter Auctions

Talking skull with instructions, Los Angeles, Thayer Mfg. Co., circa 1925, minor chips and repairs at jaw. Realistic composition skull that answers questions by clicking its jaw, once for "yes" and twice for "no." **$1,300**

Potter & Potter Auctions

Eclipse vanishing lamp, Los Angeles, F.G. Thayer, circa 1920, table 32" h., felt top and decorative ornaments on table show visible wear, uncommon. A lit lamp is wrapped in paper, which is then crushed between the magician's hands. The lamp has vanished. **$2,200**

Potter & Potter Auctions

Billiard ball stand, Sweden, Harries Magic, circa 1950, some paint wear to shells, 19-1/4" h. Mechanical stand facilitates the production of seven billiard balls from thin air........................**$900**

Potter & Potter Auctions

Flower production, American, circa 1920; mechanical pedestal in good working condition, feather flowers and finish worn; overall 33" h. Empty pot is shown and set on a high wooden pedestal. The bowl is covered with a paper cornucopia, and when this is lifted, a bouquet of flowers appears. **$800**

Potter & Potter Auctions

Portrait of magician Harry Kellar (Henrich Keller), Columbus, Ohio, Baker's Art Gallery, circa 1900, half-length portrait of American magician in cabinet card format on a mount 4-1/4" x 6-1/2", accompanied by two clipped Kellar program fragments; mount chipped and worn on verso; good condition. **$850**

Potter & Potter Auctions

MAGIC & ILLUSION

!

Three items, including a sepia-toned photo of Harry Houdini, verso stamped "Houdini Collection"; Houdini letter-gram bearing two portraits of the magician, signed in pencil; and a small brass key owned by Houdini......... **$2,000**

Potter & Potter Auctions

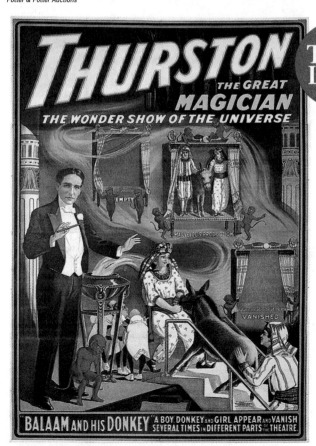

TOP! LOT!

Howard Thurston, Thurston the Great Magician, Balaam and his Donkey, Cincinnati, Strobridge Litho., circa 1910, eight-sheet (74" x 107") color lithographed billboard advertising a transposition illusion from Thurston's show, which included a boy, girl, and donkey vanishing and reappearing in several parts of the theater; minor restoration and over-coloring, fewer than six examples known. **$6,000**

Potter & Potter Auctions

Harry Houdini advertising brochure, London, circa 1905, four-page brochure shows a young Houdini posed with the famous Mirror Cuffs, advertises his appearance at the Holborn Empire; 4to, minor wear in corners, old repair in gutter, otherwise good condition. **$1,300**

Potter & Potter Auctions

Harry Blackstone, Blackstone, Big Combination, Long Island City, National Printing and Engraving, circa 1929, one sheet (28-1/2" x 41") three-color poster depicting vignettes from Blackstone's illusion show, cartoons drawn by staff artist of Montgomery Advertiser, minor over-coloring in margins. **$1,300**

Potter & Potter Auctions

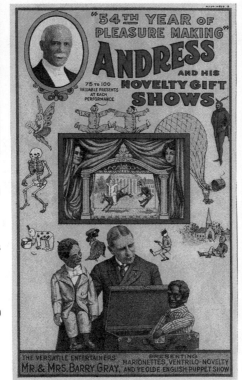

Charles Andress, 54th Year of Pleasure Making, Andress and his Novelty Gift Shows, Cincinnati, Strobridge Litho. Co., circa 1917, small panel (8-3/4" x 15-1/4") color lithograph heralding the performance of this circus owner, magician, and ventriloquist, folds visible. **$2,600**

Potter & Potter Auctions

Charles Carter, Carter the Great, Do the Dead Materialize? The Absorbing Question of All Time. Cleveland, Otis, Litho., circa 1926, color lithographed panel poster (12-1/4" x 39-1/2") depicting the spirit cabinet routine and the all-seeing Priestess of Delphi; framed and glazed; one closed tear and three folds visible; not examined out of frame....**$750**

Potter & Potter Auctions

Thomas Denton advertising token, Lambeth, 1796, copper. **$175**

Potter & Potter Auctions

Arthur Lloyd, Arthur Lloyd, The Elite Entertainer in Magic, Stockton on Tees, John Harrison, circa 1920, half-sheet (20" x 30") color lithograph bearing a full-length portrait of the "human card index," expert over-coloring in margins, scarce. **$950**

Potter & Potter Auctions

Alexander (Claude Alexander Conlin), Alexander the Man Who Knows, Bombay, Av Yaga, circa 1915, one-sheet (28" x 40") color lithograph poster depicting Alexander's turbaned head on a red field. **$325**

Potter & Potter Auctions

Brass cups and balls, European, circa 1890; well worn from professional use, 4-1/4" high, mouth 3-1/2" dia. Large set of three spun brass cups for the perennial magic feat.............**$475**

Potter & Potter Auctions

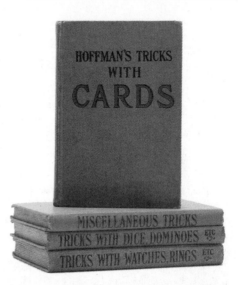

Professor Hoffmann, four Professor Hoffmann magic books, including *Tricks with Cards, Tricks with Dice, Dominoes, etc.*, *Miscellaneous Tricks*, and *Tricks with Watches, Rings, etc.*, Philadelphia: David McKay, circa 1910. Uniformly bound in green cloth stamped in red and black, illustrated, 8vo, one page damaged in final title, otherwise good condition. **$225**

Potter & Potter Auctions

Professor Hoffmann, *Modern Magic*, London: George Routledge and Sons, 1876. First edition, first state (black hat, gold cone), red cloth stamped in black and gold, engraved frontispiece, 318 illustrations, thick 8vo, rebacked, cloth significantly worn, new endpapers, contents sound. Toole-Stott 386...**$550**

An unabashed literary success, this, the first printing of Modern Magic, sold out – to the great surprise of the author and his publisher – some six weeks after its initial publication. The substantial success of this book (and the nature of its content, as it was the first book to reveal "professional" secrets of a type) ushered in a new era in conjuring literature that flourished for over a century. Only 2,000 copies of the first edition were printed, and few have survived.

Potter & Potter Auctions

Tony Andruzzi (Tom Palmer), *The Grimoire of the Mages*, Chicago: Author, 1978. Number 171 from a limited, numbered edition of 250 copies. Publisher's pictorial silk-screened brown cloth. 8vo. Each book handmade; all text silk screened by hand, numerous hand-tipped colored photographs, advertising material and advertisements laid in, very good condition. **$550**

Potter & Potter Auctions

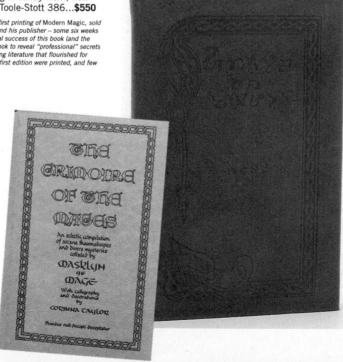

Illustrated Harry Houdini Christmas card, large-format greeting from Houdini filled with cartoons of great escape artist by artist McBride, central fold, otherwise good condition,12-3/4" x 9-1/2". **$375**

Potter & Potter Auctions

Photograph of Harry Houdini and fellow magicians Charles Carter and Allan Shaw, Australia, circa 1910, posed in front of a three-sheet Houdini poster; two corners clipped, 7" x 5"................................. **$300**

Potter & Potter Auctions

H.C. (Herman) Weber oval souvenir pocket mirror, American, circa 1909, oval souvenir mirror bearing portrait of Weber, devils on either side of him, three known examples, 71mm x 45mm, rare. **$1,000**

Potter & Potter Auctions

Harry Houdini signed bank draft dated May 12, 1914 and completed in Houdini's hand, check for one guinea payable to Magicians Club of London, a fraternal organization of which Houdini was the president; verso endorsed by well-known British magician Stanley Collins, secretary of the club; boldly signed "Harry Houdini." **$1,300**

Potter & Potter Auctions

Magician A.H. Zano advertising token, American, circa 1920, rare. **$800**

Potter & Potter Auctions

John Mulholland advertising token, American, 1925, Mulholland's rabbit-in-hat logo on obverse, plain reverse, aluminum variant. **$200**

Potter & Potter Auctions

Maps & Globes

Map collecting is slowly growing in visibility thanks to recent discoveries and sales of historically important maps. In 2010 a rare copy of George Washington's own map of Yorktown sold for more than $1.1 million, while a pair of terrestrial and celestial globes sold for $37,000 in 2012, and a copy of a unique map of the Battle of Gettysburg realized $5,400 in 2013.

Top of the market aside, map collecting remains a surprisingly affordable hobby when one considers most made in the early 19th century are hand-colored and represent the cutting edge scientific knowledge at the time. In fact, as more mainstream media tout the possible profitability and entertainment value of collecting, maps are often among the collecting interests listed for best potential rate of return. In a June 2013 article titled "Five Collectibles to Stash for Big Cash Later," Fox News Business included maps as one of the five categories of collectibles to invest in now. Most examples from the last 400 years are available for less than $500, and engravings depicting America or its states may be owned for less than $150. Larger maps are usually worth more to collectors.

◀ Rare, large terrestrial globe, circa 1909, rotates on original stand, includes makers' mark AnD, manufactured by W. And A.K. Johnston, a Scottish-based publisher of educational resources, 44" h. x 38" w. **$8,500**

J. Garrett Auctions

Hand-colored, copper-engraved map of Northeastern Canada, 1756, including Nova Scotia, Labrador and Newfoundland, format is vertical, which results in St. Lawrence River appearing to run nearly north-south, includes both European and Indian names for places along coastlines and rivers, scene with ships on bottom right corner, collection of characters resembling Native American chiefs, explorers, mapmakers, fisherman and wildlife on top left corner, 22-3/4" x 19-1/2". **$500**

PBA Auctions

Terrestrial and celestial globes, each with brass hour disc on bottom, hand-colored paper ring, mounted on mahogany tripod stand with twist carving, splay legs joined by rotund compass featuring wooden compass case and paper compass card, some scratching on globes and breaking in legs, globes 15" dia. and 40" h. **$37,000**

CRN Auctions

Joslin's terrestrial globe displayed on a special mount that allows people to visualize motion of earth revolving around sun, circa 1853, cast iron in good shape with no signs of breaks, lithography on base in good working order with some minor losses and some staining, mechanical gears all work properly, globe 6". **$3,750**

Grogan & Co.

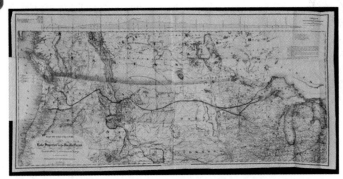

Hand-colored lithographed map, dated 1867, illustrating area of United States from Detroit west to Pacific Ocean, into Canada and south to Great Salt Lake, Utah; includes Pony Express route, overland mail routes, Fremont's exploration routes and dates, proposed and existing railroads, wagon roads, and forts; accompanied report submitted to U.S. Senate regarding Northern Pacific Railroad's plans, 9" x 5-3/4". **$3,000**

PBA Auctions

"United States of America" folding engraved map, dated 1829, one of the largest early maps of America, hand-colored in outline, 60 sections backed onto linen and edged with blue silk ribbon, marbled boards, gilt-lettered spine, engraved by H.S. Tanner, with vignette cartouche of deer in bucolic setting. **$8,000**

Heritage Auctions

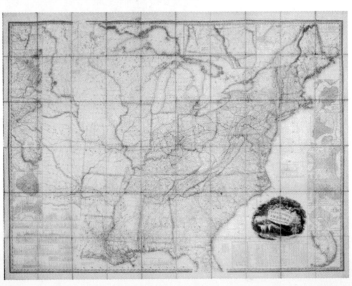

Earliest known existing map to include and identify America, woodcut, circa 1507, produced in Vienna, also referred to as "Tipus Orbis Universalis iuxta Ptloemei Cosmographi," a few short tears, some minor spotting and marginal staining, 11-1/4" x 16-1/4". **$25,000**

PBA Auctions

Antique French globe on wood stand with frame, globe 14" h., stand 11-1/2". **$400**

Bill Hood & Sons Art & Auction

H. Jaillot engraved world map, shows California as an island, 19" x 24". **$2,309**

Pook & Pook

▶ *Johnson's New Illustrated Family Atlas*, circa 1863, embossed green cloth cover with gilt on title, leather spine and corners, marbled fore-edges and end papers, with hand colored maps. **$475**

Forsythes' Auctions, LLC

"A New and Correct Map of the World," hand-colored engraving with some discoloration, laid down according to newest observations and discoveries including trade winds, monsoons, variation of compass, illustrated with celestial planisphere, created by Godson W., published by George Willdey, 1702, 36" x 49"......... **$3,250**

Material Culture

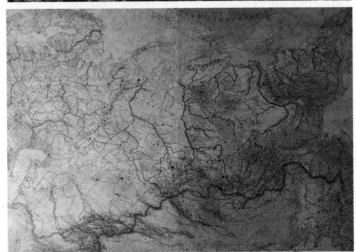

Large map of Communist Russia, dated 1955, slight fading due to age, some fold creasing, 50" x 75". **$950**

Nico Auctions

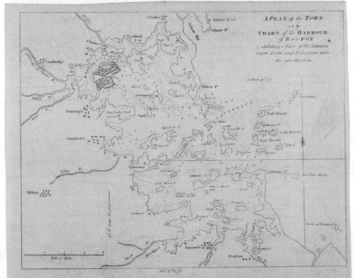

Copper-engraved map/chart of Boston Harbor prior to American Revolution, dated Feb. 1, 1775, includes view of forts and entrances into harbor, some light offset to map, 10-1/2" x 13".....................**$160**

PBA Auctions

Oddities

These collectibles fall in the "weird and wonderful" category of unusual items.

Two felt pen wipes featuring three cats, inscribed Anna on one and three mice on the other, both 19th century, 4-1/2" dia. and 3-3/4" dia. **$593**

Pook and Pook, Inc.

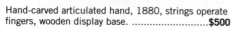

Hand-carved articulated hand, 1880, strings operate fingers, wooden display base. **$500**

Red Baron Antiques

Carved and painted watch hutch, 8-1/2" h., together with Pennsylvania walnut slide lid box, 2-3/4" h. x 5-3/4" w. x 3-1/2" d. **$237**

Pook and Pook, Inc.

Jailhouse Carvers, early 20th century, elaborately carved and painted tavern scene in glass case, 11" h. x 18-3/4" w. x 19" d...............................**$3,555**

Pook and Pook, Inc.

Wood, tin, and iron squirrel cage, late 19th century, four carved mechanical figures, 24" h. x 30" w. **$593**

Pook and Pook, Inc.

Victorian set of 12 fruit knives displayed in fan shape in silver-plate frame with horse and rider jumping through center, base with raised flowers and grasshopper, handles of knives decorated with flowering vines and insects, 4-1/2" dia. base, 9-1/2" w. at knives x 12-1/2" h. **$800**

Omaha Auction Center

Wire coat hanger sculpture of a horse, 20th century, can be dismantled, approximately 10' h. **$2,500**

Red Baron Antiques

◄ Cast iron parlor fan, 19th century, leaf and vine framework and louvered vent in front over a series of metal blades, cast iron and nickel tripod base, plaque on back reads "Luminaire – the Cincinnati Victor Co," cloth covered cord, 57" h. **$472**

James D. Julia, Inc.

Softwood articulated artist's mannequin, 19th century, brown casein paint, still flexible, 29" h. **$6,900**

Thomaston Place Auction Galleries

Continental wrought iron fat lamp on stand, early 19th century, 16-1/2" h. **$304**

Pook and Pook, Inc.

Rare spool silk or thread display in glass globe with wood pedestal, made by American Thread Co., Holyoke, Massachusetts; display used at Colombian Exposition in 1893.............................. **$2,300**

Rich Penn Auctions

ODDITIES

!

Underwood Elliot Fisher railroad timetable typewriter with extra wide carriage, 1910, often used on trains and ships, 9-1/4" h. x 39-1/2" w. x 11-3/4" d. **$600**

Red Baron Antiques

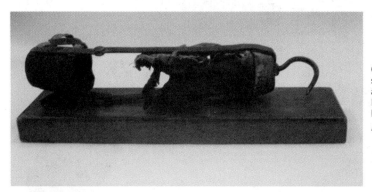

Original "Captain Hook" said to replace a pirate's arm, 1855, made from leather and canvas with hand rivets.......... **$800**

Red Baron Antiques

TOP LOT!

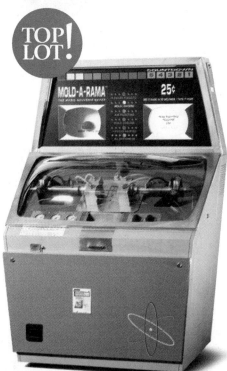

Burglar alarm, 20th century, part of Terry Wesner collection of patent models, incorporates a series of weights, pulleys, cranks, bells, and wires in its operation. **$3,000-5,000**

James D. Julia, Inc.

Mold machine featuring microcars, fully operational, 54" x 42" x 60"; popular in the mid-1960s, these machines could produce a blow-molded plastic souvenir in under 30 seconds. **$14,375**

RM Auctions

Bronze bear bench, 19th century...................**$1,000**

Red Baron Antiques

Oak English jockey scale on wheels, rare, early 19th century, 32" x 41" x 24"......................................**$1,250**

Red Baron Antiques

Benjamin Franklin's lightning rod house, tin toy demonstration model, hand painted, designed by Charles Chevalier, 1860. ....**$2,340**

Auction Team Breker

Hollow pinecone form mounted on wood wall plaque, label reads "Formacone, The Formaldehyde, Disinfector Deodorizer, The Formacone Co., 12-16 John Street, New York," 11" h. **$100**

Omaha Auction Center

Early Ethiopian throne, bronze, with figures of people serving as back and pedestal, 51" h. x 24" w. x 21" d. ....**$5,000-$9,000**

Red Baron Antiques

Vampire killing kit, 19th century, with holy water, bible, stake, rosary, gun for silver bullets, axe, and candles, housed in wooden box. **$5,500**

Red Baron Antiques

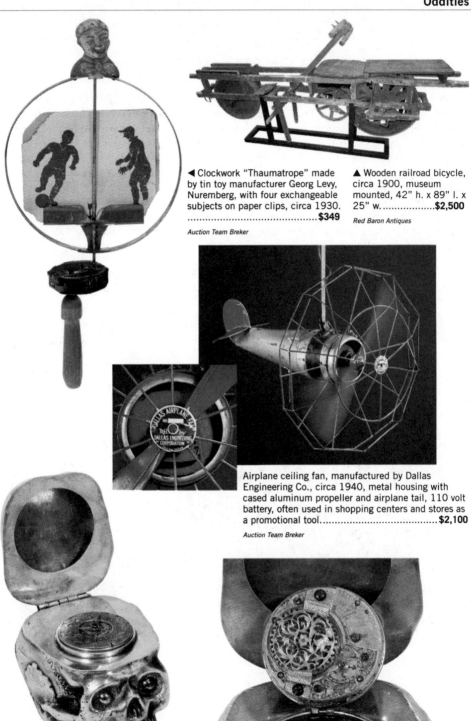

◄ Clockwork "Thaumatrope" made by tin toy manufacturer Georg Levy, Nuremberg, with four exchangeable subjects on paper clips, circa 1930. ....**$349**

Auction Team Breker

▲ Wooden railroad bicycle, circa 1900, museum mounted, 42" h. x 89" l. x 25" w. **$2,500**

Red Baron Antiques

Airplane ceiling fan, manufactured by Dallas Engineering Co., circa 1940, metal housing with cased aluminum propeller and airplane tail, 110 volt battery, often used in shopping centers and stores as a promotional tool..**$2,100**

Auction Team Breker

Silver skull clock, 1770, clock housed in large heavy silver case, verge and chain movement, signed "Markham, London 19922," in working condition, includes operating key. **$3,640**

Auction Team Breker

Paperweights

Although paperweights had their origin in ancient Egypt, it was in the mid-19th century that this art form reached its zenith. The finest paperweights were produced between 1834 and 1855 in France by the Clichy, Baccarat, and St. Louis factories. Other weights made in England, Italy, and Bohemia during this period rarely match the quality of the French weights.

In the early 1850s, the New England Glass Co. in Cambridge, Massachusetts, and the Boston and Sandwich Glass Co. in Sandwich, Massachusetts, became the first American factories to make paperweights.

Popularity peaked during the classic period (1845-1855) and faded toward the end of the 19th century. Paperweight production was rediscovered nearly a century later in the mid-1900s. Baccarat, St. Louis, Perthshire, and many studio craftsmen in the United States and Europe still make contemporary paperweights.

Bob Banford floral paperweight, yellow and black bumblebee hovers over branch with yellow blossoms and buds on powder blue ground, six side facets, one top facet, signed with "B" signature cane, very good to excellent condition, 3" dia. x 2" h..........................**$144**

James D. Julia, Inc.

Tony De Palma crimp rose paperweight, 15 petaled burgundy rose with four green leaves, four side facets and one top facet, signed in script "A De Palma 1985," very good to excellent condition, 2-3/4" h. x 3-3/8" dia. **$173**

James D. Julia, Inc.

Jim D'Onofrio frog paperweight, green frog perched atop three lily pads and amethyst pond lily blossom, entire design rests on green ground, signed in script "Jim D'Onofrio 97," very good to excellent condition, 3-1/4" dia. x 2-3/4" h. **$546**

James D. Julia, Inc.

Bob Banford dahlia paperweight, single flower blossom with yellow stamen surrounded by five tiers of purple petals and green leaves, signed on underside with "B" signature cane, very good to excellent condition, 2-7/8" dia. x 2-3/4" h.....**$403**

James D. Julia, Inc.

Bob Banford pansy bouquet paperweight, three purple and yellow pansy blossoms, one bud and green leaves, signed with "B" signature cane, very good to excellent condition, 2-7/8" dia. x 2-1/4" h. **$403**

James D. Julia, Inc.

Chris Buzzini floral bouquet paperweight, brown stems with purple flowers and three white blossoms, signed on side of paperweight in script "Buzzini '89 BPL 14/75," very good to excellent condition, 3-1/8" dia. x 2-1/4" h. **$633**

James D. Julia, Inc.

Baccarat close pack millefiori paperweight, complex canes including several zodiac silhouette canes and "1967" date cane, signed on underside with acid etched Baccarat insignia, multifaceted on sides with one top facet, 3" dia. x 2" h. Provenance: Barry Schultheiss Collection...................................**$345**

James D. Julia, Inc.

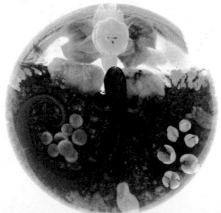

◀ Rick Ayotte salamander paperweight, red, perched along water's edge overlooking a white pond lily, surrounded by mushrooms, yellow flowers and rocks with moss, signed in script "Ayotte Ed/50 '90," very good to excellent condition, 3-1/2" dia. x 2-1/4" h..............**$1,093**

James D. Julia, Inc.

Caithness Partridge in a Pear Tree paperweight, yellow and brown partridge sits on brown branch with green leaves and one pink flower blossom, entire design surrounded by pink and white millefiori canes on white snow ground, six side facets and one top face, signed in script on underside and numbered "319/500," very good to excellent condition, 3" dia. x 2-1/4" h. **$115**

James D. Julia, Inc.

Randall Grubb bouquet paperweight, one large red flower blossom, two white calla lilies and two orange blossoms, translucent green ground, signed in script "Randall Grubb '87," very good to excellent condition, 3" dia. x 2-3/8" h. **$345**

James D. Julia, Inc.

Memorial Hall oval paperweight, frosted except for top surface, pressed intaglio building with dates "1776 1876" above and title below, probably Gillinder & Sons, circa 1876, undamaged, 1-1/8" h., 4" x 5-3/8" base... **$81**

Jeffrey S. Evans & Associates

Caithness fire lizard paperweight, iridescent blue lizard has gold aventurine highlights with spotted orange head on green and brown rock ground among three lampworked flowers, one ladybug rests on a flower, signed on underside and "86/100," very good to excellent condition, 2-7/8" dia. x 2-1/2" h... **$460**

James D. Julia, Inc.

Boston & Sandwich Glass Co. or New England Glass Co. paperweights, third quarter 19th century, one with blue poinsettia with millefiore center with five lampwork leaves set on white latticinio cushion, and a fruit group with four red and yellow pears and leaves and three cherries on white latticinio ground, light scratches, base edge chips, 1-5/8" h., 2-3/8" dia., 2-1/2" h., 2-5/8" dia. .... **$185 pr.**

Skinner, Inc., www.skinnerinc.com

Randall Grubb floral paperweight, single pink flower blossom with four tiers of petals, green leaves and stems on clear ground, signed in script "Randall Grubb 87," very good to excellent condition, 3" dia. x 2-1/4" h.. **$345**

James D. Julia, Inc.

Charles Kaziun pansy paperweight, two large purple petals and three smaller blue and white petals with green leaves, stem and single bud, entire design rests on opaque yellow ground, signed on underside with gold "K," two minor surface blemishes, very good to excellent condition, 2-1/4" dia. x 1-3/4" h........ **$575**

Rookwood frog paperweight, cast in 1912, mat green glaze, impressed Rookwood logo, date and shape 1233, no crazing, chips to corners and edges of plinth, 3-1/4" h. x 3-7/8" w............................. **$350**

Mark Mussio, Humler & Nolan

St. Louis honeycomb paperweight, large central Clichy-type yellow rose surrounded by red and white honeycomb tiers, applied crystal pedestal foot, signed on underside with "SL 1977" signature/date cane, retains original paper label, very good to excellent condition, 3-7/8" dia. x 5" h. **$748**

James D. Julia, Inc.

William Manson butterfly paperweight, compound paperweight consisting of three butterflies hovering over pink and white flower blossom surrounded by pink and white millefiori canes, signed on underside with "WM 81" signature/date cane, very good to excellent condition, 2-7/8" dia. x 2-1/2" h........ **$230**

James D. Julia, Inc.

Victor Trabucco rose bouquet paperweight, large central yellow rose surrounded by blue and white flower blossoms, yellow buds and green leaves on cobalt blue ground, signed in script "Trabucco 1987" and "VT" signature cane underneath one leaf, very good to excellent condition, 3" dia. x 2-3/4" h. **$403**

James D. Julia, Inc.

St. Louis upright bouquet paperweight, white, red, blue and yellow blossoms with green leaves, six side facets and one top facet on red over white double overlay, signed with "SL 1970" signature/date cane, very good to excellent condition, 2-7/8" dia. x 2" h. **$575**

James D. Julia, Inc.

Lotton Studio glass paperweight, double clematis with variegated foliage on colorless ground, signed "Lotton 1986," fourth quarter 20th century, undamaged, 2-3/4" dia. **$207**

Jeffrey S. Evans & Associates

Charles Kaziun millefiori paperweight, central silhouette cane of rabbit surrounded by seven cane clusters in blue, white and green, entire design rests on gold aventurine blue ground surrounded by pink and white twist torsade, signed on underside with gold "K," clear crystal pedestal foot, very good to excellent condition, 2-3/4" h. **$403**

James D. Julia, Inc.

Rookwood cocker spaniel paperweight, cast in 1954, Wine Madder glaze, impressed with Rookwood logo, date and shape 7024, without crazing, excellent original condition, 4-1/8" h. ... **$180**

Mark Mussio, Humler & Nolan

TOP LOT!

Rookwood mouse paperweight, designed by Shirayamadani, cast in 1937, Coromandel glaze, impressed with Rookwood symbol, date and shape 6618, without crazing, excellent condition, 3-1/4" h. **$3,100**

Mark Mussio, Humler & Nolan

Whitefriars cylindrical paperweight, concentric millefiori canes in red, white and blue encased in crystal with seven side flutes, one large top facet and seven edge facets on top and bottom, signed with Whitefriars signature cane and dated "1976," very good to excellent condition, 2-3/4" dia. x 2-5/8" h. **$201**

James D. Julia, Inc.

Perfume Bottles

Although the human sense of smell isn't nearly as acute as that of many other mammals, we have long been affected by the odors in the world around us. Science has shown that scents or smells can directly affect our mood or behavior.

No one knows for certain when humans first rubbed themselves with some plant or herb to improve their appeal to other humans, usually of the opposite sex. However, it is clear that the use of unguents and scented materials was widely practiced as far back as Ancient Egypt.

Some of the first objects made of glass, in fact, were small cast vials used for storing such mixtures. By the age of the Roman Empire, scented waters and other mixtures were even more important and were widely available in small glass flasks or bottles. Since that time glass has been the material of choice for storing scented concoctions, and during the past 200 years some of the most exquisite glass objects produced were designed for that purpose.

It wasn't until around the middle of the 19th century that specialized bottles and vials were produced to hold commercially manufactured scents. Some aromatic mixtures were worn on special occasions, while many others were splashed on to help mask body odor. For centuries it had been common practice for "sophisticated" people to carry on their person a scented pouch or similar accoutrement, since daily bathing was unheard of and laundering methods were primitive.

Commercially produced and brand name perfumes and colognes have really only been common since the late 19th and early 20th centuries. The French started the ball rolling during the first half of the 19th century when D'Orsay and Guerlain began producing special scents. The first American entrepreneur to step into this field was Richard Hudnut, whose firm was established in 1880. During the second half of the 19th century most scents carried simple labels and were sold in simple, fairly generic glass bottles. Only in the early 20th century did parfumeurs introduce specially designed labels and bottles to hold their most popular perfumes. Coty, founded in 1904, was one of the first to do this, and they turned to Rene Lalique for a special bottle design around 1908. Other French firms, such as Bourjois (1903), Caron (1903), and D'Orsay (1904) were soon following this trend.

People collect two kinds of perfume bottles—decorative and commercial. Decorative bottles include any bottles sold empty and meant to be filled with your choice of scent. Commercial bottles are any that were sold filled with scent and usually have the label of the perfume company.

The rules of value for perfume bottles are the same as for any other kind of glass—rarity, condition, age, and quality of glass.

The record price for perfume bottle at auction is something over $200,000, and those little sample bottles of scent that we used to get for free at perfume counters in the 1960s can now bring as much as $300 or $400.

For more information on perfume bottles, see *Antique Trader Perfume Bottles Price Guide* by Kyle Husfloen.

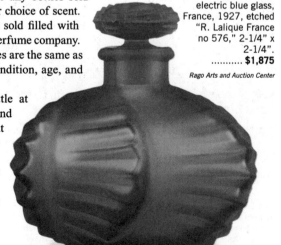

Camille perfume bottle in frosted electric blue glass, France, 1927, etched "R. Lalique France no 576," 2-1/4" x 2-1/4".
.... **$1,875**

Rago Arts and Auction Center

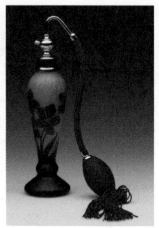

Imperial decorated free hand/ DeVilbiss atomizer, deep blue/ black with opal hanging hearts, original gilt-metal mount, replaced bulb, signed "DeVilbiss" in gold script under base; Imperial Glass Co., circa 1925, undamaged, light wear to gilding, 10-1/4" h. overall. **$1,725**

Jeffrey S. Evans & Associates

Signed Daum Nancy cameo dresser bottle, blue cut to mottled ground, multi-bloom floral decoration, fitted with modern metal collar and screw-in atomizer, France, first quarter 20th century, undamaged, 6" h. to collar, 8-1/2" h. overall. **$489**

Jeffrey S. Evans & Associates

Hawkes engraved cologne bottle, Verre-de-Soie, original numbered stopper with sterling silver top and long dauber, polished pontil mark with Hawkes acid stamp; bottle possibly by Steuben Glass Works, first half 20th century, undamaged, 5-1/2" h. **$196**

Jeffrey S. Evans & Associates

Webb laydown scent bottle, white fronds deeply cut against citron ground, trademark Webb butterfly, sterling silver marks at collar, glass inner stopper, several minute chips to ends of foliate pattern, end of bottle has professional grind, 10-1/2" l. **$1,438**

James D. Julia, Inc.

Two Gorham silver overlay perfumes and one scent bottle, two bulbous bottles with stoppers in Art Nouveau style, each with a different monogram to top of stopper, both marked on silver "Gorham Mfg. Co S1819 999/1000 FINE," small square clear glass bottle with silver overlay of roses, vines and leaves and metal screw-on top, marked on underside "Sterling .925." All three have tarnish to silver overlay and mineral deposits to interiors, 3" to 4-1/4" t. **$230**

James D. Julia, Inc.

St. Louis cased glass perfume bottle with stopper, circa 1987, marked SL 1987 (signature cane), original blue hinged display box and shipping box (not shown), 6-1/4" h. x 2-5/8" dia......... **$813**

Heritage Auctions

Baccarat swirl cologne bottle, Rose Tinte, original stopper numbered to match bottle, first quarter 20th century, undamaged, 7-1/2" h. (5-3/4" h. bottle)..................**$81**

Jeffrey S. Evans & Associates

English cameo tapered scent bottle, white cut to blue, differing floral decoration on each side, two-part sterling silver screw cap marked for Theodore B. Starr; probably Thomas Webb and Sons, England, fourth quarter 19th century, undamaged, cap with edge dent, 6-3/4" l.............**$978**

Jeffrey S. Evans & Associates

Mary Gregory-style atomizer, cranberry, panel optic, white enamel decoration featuring young girl, metal mount, replaced fabric and bulb, late 19th/early 20th century, undamaged, 5" h. ..**$173**

Jeffrey S. Evans & Associates

Webb decorated Burmese tapered scent bottle, plush finish, butterfly and floral decoration, two-part silver screw cap hallmarked for Birmingham; Thomas Webb and Sons, England, fourth quarter 19th century, undamaged with no wear, cap with scattered minute dents, 5" l. **$805**

Jeffrey S. Evans & Associates

Steuben art glass cologne bottle, Rosaline and Alabaster, tapered form, polished pontil mark, appropriate stopper that sits slightly high, not signed; Steuben Glass Works, first half 20th century, undamaged, 8" h. ..**$288**

Jeffrey S. Evans & Associates

Mary Gregory-style atomizer, cranberry, satin finish, white enamel decoration featuring boy riding grasshopper, metal mount, replaced fabric and bulb, late 19th/early 20th century, undamaged, 5-1/2" h. ..**$92**

Jeffrey S. Evans & Associates

Daum Nancy French cameo laydown scent bottle, frosted ground, decorated with transparent green cameo glass leaves with gold highlights, decorative silver finished top, engraved "Josephine," signed on underside "Daum Nancy" with cross of Lorraine, overall very good condition, missing inner glass stopper, 6-1/2" l.............**$1,380**

James D. Julia, Inc.

Steuben Aurene cologne bottle and atomizer, gold iridescent, each shape 6136 with matching gilt-metal mounts, cologne with original stopper and dauber, signed "aurene," atomizer with original bulb, not signed; Steuben Glass Works, first half 20th century, undamaged, atomizer with loss to fabric, 6-1/2" and 7" h. **$575**

Jeffrey S. Evans & Associates

Steuben decorated Aurene atomizer, gold iridescent, shape 6407, engraved floral decoration around base, polished pontil mark, not signed, fitted with a later incorrect top and bulb apparatus; Steuben Glass Works, first half 20th century, undamaged, annealing check at pontil mark as made, 8-1/2" h. **$316**

Jeffrey S. Evans & Associates

Imperial decorated free hand/DeVilbiss atomizer, iridescent orange with blue hanging hearts, original gilt-metal mount, signed "DeVilbiss" in gold script under base; Imperial Glass Co., circa 1925, undamaged, short horizontal scratch at base, lacking bulb attachment, 10" h. overall. **$863**

Jeffrey S. Evans & Associates

Baccarat Ming Toy figural perfume bottle, colorless with enamel and gold decoration, inscribed "FOREST PARIS" on lower edge of reverse, Baccarat acid stamp under base, non-original stopper, France, circa 1923, undamaged, minor losses to gold, 3-3/4" h. **$518**

Jeffrey S. Evans & Associates

Moser chatelaine scent bottle, cobalt blue with Victorian floral and leaf pattern with original metal hardware, chatelaine and finger ring, missing inner stopper, very good to excellent condition, 2-1/4" t **$633**

James D. Julia, Inc.

R. Lalique Worth scent bottle, Art Deco shaped, emerald green, original presentation, front of stand marked "WORTH," underside marked "Paris France," bottle marked "R. Lalique France," very good to excellent condition with loss at one corner of wooden stand, 6-1/4" h. overall. **$1,150**

James D. Julia, Inc.

Petroliana

Petroliana covers a broad range of gas station collectibles from containers and globes to signs and pumps and everything in between.

As with all advertising items, factors such as brand name, intricacy of design, color, age, condition, and rarity drastically affect value.

Beware of reproduction and fantasy pieces. For collectors of vintage gas and oil items, the only way to avoid reproductions is experience: making mistakes and learning from them; talking with other collectors and dealers; finding reputable resources (including books and websites), and learning to invest wisely, buying the best examples one can afford.

Marks can be deceiving, paper labels and tags are often missing, and those that remain may be spurious. Adding to the confusion are "fantasy" pieces, globes that have no vintage counterpart, and that are often made more for visual impact than deception.

How does one know whether a given piece is authentic? Does it look old, and to what degree can age be simulated? What is the difference between high-quality vintage advertising and modern mass-produced examples? Even experts are fooled when trying to assess qualities that have subtle distinctions.

There is another important factor to consider. A contemporary maker may create a "reproduction" sign or gas globe in tribute to the original, and sell it for what it is: a legitimate copy. Many of these are dated and signed by the artist or manufacturer, and these legitimate copies are highly collectible today. Such items are not intended to be frauds.

But a contemporary piece may pass through many hands between the time it leaves the maker and winds up in a collection. When profit is the only motive of a reseller, details about origin, ownership, and age can become a slippery slope of guesses, attribution, and, unfortunately, fabrication.

As the collector's eye sharpens, and the approach to inspecting and assessing petroliana improves, it will become easier to buy with confidence. And a knowledgeable collecting public should be the goal of all sellers, if for no other reason than the willingness to invest in quality.

For more information about petroliana, consult *Warman's Gas Station Collectibles* by Mark Moran and *An Illustrated Guide to Gas Pumps* by Jack Sim.

Lion Oil Naturalube motor oil display and 12 assorted one-quart motor oil cans in various conditions, stand in good condition, Naturalube sign shows some slight fading, 19" x 32" x 13-1/2"..........................**$805**

RM Auctions

Texaco Marine Motor Oil cans, circa 1950s, metal one-quart round shape, various boat images as graphics, some wear, scratching, and rusting..... **$190**

Matthews Auctions

Oil cans from various farm equipment companies including International Harvester, McCormick-Deering, Ford, and others, circa 1940s, with names marked on exterior. **$60**

McLaren Auction Services

Gulfpride and Cold-Proof, Heat-Proof motor oil signs, metal, two-sided with glossy finish and bright colors, each with some scratches and minor shelf rub, Cold-Proof sign 12" x 17", Gulfpride 12" x 18". **$430**

RM Auctions

Marx service station island display with clock face gas pump, air meter, oil bottle display, tin litho, light wear and scratches, 5-1/2" x 9" x 4". **$60**

Matthews Auctions

Smith Miller GMC Mobiloil tanker truck, circa 1960s, die cast cab and pressed steel body, good condition with some wear and scratches, 22" l. **$180**

Matthews Auctions

Texaco metal oil cans, circa 1930s, including one-eighth gallon flat metal can and medium motor oil can with swing spout at top, both with heavy wear and holes. **$125**

Matthews Auctions

Bay Gas glass globes, 15". **$140**

Maring Auction Co.

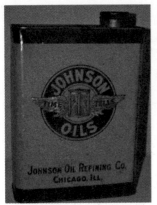

Cities Service Oils porcelain signs with a different image on each side, 1947, some scratching, chipping, and color discoloration but no significant surface flaws. **$690**

RM Auctions

Johnson Motor Oils flat metal oil can with official "Time Tells" logo on front, one gallon, fair to good condition with light wear and scratches. **$190**

Matthews Auctions

Ventura Motor Oil can, early 20th century, manufactured by CALPET, California Petroleum Corp.... **$650**

Hamilton Antiques Auction Gallery

Group of Sinclair collectibles including tin oil cans, radiator flush, 1965 car care guide, maps with stand, vintage key chains, lighter, vintage cash radio, popular Sinclair Dino toy, brake fluid. **$690**

RM Auctions

Various signal motor oil canisters, including signal dust cloth, gear lubricant and motor oil.................... **$403**

RM Auctions

Texaco Sky Chief gas globe insert with glass surround, 13-1/2" dia.......................... **$450**

Maring Auction Co.

Skelly Regular gas globe insert with glass surround, some wear on frame, circa 1960s. **$350**

Maring Auction Co.

Golden West Oil Company (formed in 1929) sign with early logo of blue mountains graphics, great color and gloss, small chips at mounting holes, 10" dia... **$2,700**

Matthews Auctions

Leonard Diesel Fuel globe representing a Michigan-based fuel company in operation from 1936 to 1970, globe with all original components, very good condition. **$225**

Harris Brothers Auctions

Crown Gold gas globe, glass lenses on glass screw base, display side has wear and stained spots on gold, reverse has more staining, 13-1/2" dia......................... **$450**

Matthews Auctions

Fisk tire clock, lights up when in operation, features message "Time to Re-Tire Get a FISK" with a little boy holding a tire on face, 28" dia., framed by tire, 6" x 16". ... **$5,500**

Matthews Auctions

Assortment of petroliana accessories, including gas cans, water can, 30 one-quart oil cans from various manufacturers, some dating back to 1940s, grease tubes, toolbox..................... **$460**

RM Auctions

Shell clam-style milk glass gas globe, circa 1940s, glass and body in good condition. **$600**

Matthews Auctions

Penn-Empire milk glass globe, body in good condition, display paint has some wear, reverse has more paint wear. Penn-Empire is a nod to one of the first oil wells ever drilled, the "Empire" oil well on Funk Farm in Pennsylvania in 1861.............................. **$2,500**

Matthews Auctions

Safety Richlube Motor Oil five-gallon metal bucket manufactured by Richfield Oil Corp. (1936-1966), good color with a few scratches in field, reverse has more scratches. **$120**

Matthews Auctions

Amoco Gill lenses in Gill glass body, lens in good condition, reverse a bit weak around perimeter, 15" dia. **$425**

Matthews Auctions

Shell double-sided porcelain sign, finish and color are glossy and bright, minimal chipping, weathering, and scratching, 46" x 47". $1,150

RM Auctions

Metal oil drum with Socony Motor Oil sign attached, finish and color on sign is glossy and bright, moderate chipping, drum in good condition, entire piece 19" x 29". Socony (Standard Oil Co. of New York) was founded in 1920 and merged with Vacuum Oil in 1931........................ **$230**

RM Auctions

Twenty-two glass oil bottles with metal spouts in metal carrying cases, bottles manufactured by Master Manufacturing Co., holders branded HR Hood & Sons, circa 1930s. **$575**

RM Auctions

Trio of gallon indicators from a Wayne 10-gallon visible gas pump...... **$60**

Kaptain Kirk's Auction & Appraisals

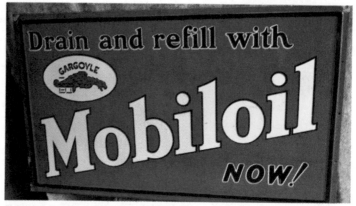

Mobiloil metal sign, self-framed, strong color and high gloss, a few small chips and wear, Gargoyle logo and message to "Drain and refill with Mobiloil NOW!" **$2,700**

Matthews Auctions

Pint glass oil bottle produced by McColl-Frontenac Oil Co., Marvelube pour spout with a few dents, detailed Indian logo graphics, minor surfaces scratches. **$300**

Matthews Auctions

Assortment of oil cans from Sinclair and Pennsylvania's Mobiline Motor Oil, varying condition from near pristine to well used, some contain original motor oil....... **$575**

RM Auctions

Gamages Motor Oil five-gallon metal can, circa 1930s, printed tinplate featuring car, plane, and boat racing scenes on alternating panels, usual wear and signs of rust, 22" x 11". **$600**

Matthews Auctions

Opaline Motor Oil metal gas can, circa 1940s, open-wheel race car graphics, predecessor to current Sinclair dinosaur logo image, both sides with good color, reverse with more wear. **$600**

Matthews Auctions

Duplex Motor Oil five-gallon square metal can, wear on top and bottom, including some rusting. This oil was manufactured specifically for Pierce-Arrow cars and trucks; company was in operation from 1901 to 1938................. **$1,000**

Matthews Auctions

Sears Motor Oil one gallon squatty-shaped metal can, circa early 1900s, with image of Sears Motor Buggy, wear and light scratches. Sears Motor Buggy, with a two-cylinder, air cooled motor, was manufactured from 1909 to 1911. .... **$1,200**

Matthews Auctions

Pennzip Gasoline globe, yellow ethyl burst logo including name of company that produced Pennzip, Ethyl Gasoline Corp., minor paint chips around outside edge, 14". **$675**

Matthews Auctions

White Rose gasoline globe produced by The National Refining Co. (1882-1950), featuring the company's most recognized trademark, a little boy with a slate that reads EN-AR-CO, clean lenses, very light scratching and small chips at notches, 13-1/2". White Rose was one of the first premium automobile gasolines made available to the public.......... **$550**

Matthews Auctions

Champion Spark Plug display and plug tester pair, faux wooden display unit, manufacturer's guide and vintage gas pump nozzle, metal spark plug testing unit with some rust, faded colors. **$2,875**

RM Auctions

Postcards

In the first half of the 20th century, postcards were cheap, often one cent and rarely more than five cents on the racks. Worldwide exchanges were common, making it possible to gain huge variety without being rich.

Those days are gone forever, but collectors today are just as avid about their acquisitions. What postcards are bestsellers today? The people most likely to have the pulse of the hobby are dealers who offer thousands of cards to the public every year.

Ron Millard, longtime owner of Cherryland Auctions, and Mary L. Martin, known for running the largest store in the country devoted exclusively to postcards, have offered some insights into the current state of the market. Both dealers have taken a son into their business, a sure sign of the confidence they have in the future of postcard collecting.

Real photo postcards of the early 1900s are highly rated by both dealers. Martin, who sells at shows as well as through her store, reports that interest in rare real photos is "increasing faster than they can be bought."

Early pre-sinking "S.S. Titanic" postcard, # 25960, color, divided back, very fine condition...... **$250**

Cherryland Auctions

Millard, whose Cherryland Auctions feature 1,800 lots closing every five weeks, indicates that real photos seem to be "holding steady with prices actually rising among the lower-end real photos as some people shy from paying the huge prices they have been bringing ... Children with toys and dolls have been increasing and also unidentified but interesting U.S. views."

Cherryland bidders have also been focused on "advertising cards, high-end art cards, Halloween, early political and baseball postcards." Movie stars, other famous people and transportation, especially autos and zeppelins, also do very well. Lower-priced cards with great potential for rising in value include linen restaurant advertising, "middle range" holidays, and World War I propaganda.

Millard also cites vintage chromes, especially advertising, is "really starting to take off with many now bringing $10 to $15. These were $1 cards a few years ago."

At one time, foreign cards were largely ignored by collectors, but online sales have broadened the international market. In Millard's experience, "The sky is the limit on any China related." A few months ago Cherryland had a huge influx of new bidders from Australia, and the number from Asia is also increasing.

Advertising Falstaff Bottled Beer, St. Louis, Missouri, real photo, very fine condition. **$8**

Cherryland Auctions

Martin sees hometown views as the most popular category, with real photo social history, dressed animals, and Halloween also in high demand. She reports: "We see a lot of interest in military right now, and I don't believe it has really peaked yet." Social history from the 1950s and '60s also does well. She's encouraged by the number of new and younger collectors at postcard shows.

Will anyone want your postcards when you're ready to sell? It's a valid question, and our two experts have good advice for anyone with a sizeable accumulation, say 500 or more postcards.

Auctions are one good option, both for direct purchases and consignments. Millard is always looking for quality postcards to offer collectors worldwide. His firm can handle collections of any size from small specialized to giant accumulations, and is willing to travel for large consignments. Active buying is a necessity for dealers to keep their customers supplied, which should reassure collectors that their cards will have a ready market. Contact Millard at CherrylandAuctions@charter.net or www.Cherrylandauctions.com.

Martin suggests that collectors go back to some of the dealers who sold them cards when they're ready to sell. Her firm is always willing to buy back good quality cards. She also sees reputable auction houses as a good avenue, and strongly suggests, "They should never be sold as a very large group if they can be broken down into different subject matter or topics." Martin can be contacted at marymartinpostcards@gmail.com.

Both experts agree there's an active demand for quality collections. That would exclude postcards in poor condition, a caution for collectors expanding their holdings. Look for the best and pass up damaged and dirty cards.

Billions of postcards were produced in the last century on practically every topic imaginable. As collections become more specialized, new subjects are sure to attract attention. Many outstanding collections were put together with moderate expense by people who were among the first to recognize the value of a new collecting area.

As an example of an area yet to be fully explored, the photographers who made postcards possible haven't been widely collected in their own right. Many were anonymous, but some, like Bob Petley, famous for Western views as well as comic humor, have attracted collectors' attention. The Tucson Post Card Exchange Club has made a specialty of gathering and listing the output of its "favorite son." No doubt there are fresh, new specialties just waiting to be discovered.

Postcard collectors love history, appreciate fine art, enjoy humor, and above all, are imaginative. There's every indication that today's favorite topics will be joined by new and exciting ones in the future.

— *Barbara Andrews*

Chesterfield cigarettes, with soldier, divided back, minor corner wear, near very fine condition.......... **$65**
Cherryland Auctions

Real photo, "Harry Six, Champion High Diver of the World, Carnival at Bryan, O July 08," used, minor corner crease, fine to very fine condition. **$85**
Cherryland Auctions

Advertising Fox's Jail House Restaurant, Indianapolis, real photo, "Eat, Drink, Music... in a Cell," very fine condition................................ **$125**

Cherryland Auctions

Advertising Sleepy Eye flour, "Sleepy Eye Monument," undivided back, minor corner album marks and minor corner crease, fine to very fine condition. **$45**

Cherryland Auctions

Artist signed Nini Hager, early French publisher, Art Nouveau, including frog, undivided back, very fine condition. **$100**

Cherryland Auctions

KKK tonic, real photo, medicine salesman, message identifies as Iowa, used with 1909 Des Moines RPO (Railway Post Office) cancel, very fine condition. **$350**

Cherryland Auctions

Art by Eva Daniell, early Raphael Tuck publisher, French series 176, undivided back, very fine condition... **$150**

Cherryland Auctions

POSTCARDS

Four-card Japanese art series, artist signed with hand color, undivided back, very fine condition. $22

Cherryland Auctions

Art by Philip Boileau, Russian publisher, series No. 5, rings on fingers, divided back, minor edge wear, fine to very fine condition. .$8

Cherryland Auctions

Art Nouveau, R. Tuck publisher, #3569, undivided back, minor corner wear, near very fine condition..............................$60

Cherryland Auctions

Artist signed E. Colombo, Italian publisher, series 961/6, divided back, minor corner wear, near very fine condition. $5

Cherryland Auctions

Artist signed Dwig, series #55, Fortune Teller series, divided back, embossed, very fine condition. .$15

Cherryland Auctions

Advertising Fox Visible Typewriter, Grand Rapids, Michigan, divided back, very fine condition..........$5

Cherryland Auctions

▶ 1900 Paris Exposition, advertising Remington Typewriter, black and white, undivided back, corner wear, near fine to very fine condition. $8

Cherryland Auctions

Artist signed Philip Boileau, Reinthal & Newman publisher, watercolor series No. 379, "Lullabye," divided back, near very fine condition. $6

Cherryland Auctions

Artist signed Philip Boileau, Reinthal & Newman publisher, series No. 109, "True as the Blue Above," divided back, near very fine condition. $6

Cherryland Auctions

Art by Samuel Schmucker, Detroit Pub. Co., Fantasy Pipe Smoke series, "Molly," used 1907, divided back, writing on face and few minor edge tone spots, fine to very fine condition. $10

Cherryland Auctions

Snow White and the Seven Dwarfs French postcard set (Superlux, 1938), set of 25, color illustrations and captions in French, excellent condition, 3-1/2" x 5-1/2". $221

Heritage Auctions

Artist signed Harrison Fisher, Reinthal & Newman publisher, *Cosmopolitan Magazine* No. 977, "My Hero," divided back, fine to very fine condition. $20

Cherryland Auctions

POSTCARDS

Real photo, person in costume on roller skates advertising Edward's Ringer & Co., Bristol, England, Red Bell Tobacco, divided back, near very fine condition. **$150**

Cherryland Auctions

Little People boxing match, printed photo, "Prince" vs "King," New York publisher, divided back, corner wear and edge crease, fine condition. **$4**

Cherryland Auctions

Fantasy Metamorphic, ladies in skull, "All is Vanity," quality sepia printed Gibson postcard, divided back, minor edge stain, near fine to very fine condition...............**$5**

Cherryland Auctions

1912 poster advertising Rose Festival, Portland, Oregon, Northbank Road Railroad, used May 23, 1912, divided back, corner crease, near very fine condition. **$20**

Cherryland Auctions

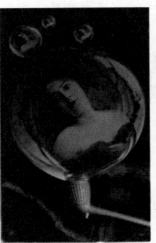

Fantasy tinted photo, NPG (Neue Photographische Gesellschaft AG, Berlin, Germany) publisher, series 464/11, woman in pipe bubble, divided back, near very fine condition. **$13**

Cherryland Auctions

1915 poster advertising Pan. Pac. International Exposition, San Francisco, Edward H. Mitchell Co. publisher, pre-fair Admission Day 1910 Festival, divided back, corner wear, fine to very fine condition. **$45**

Cherryland Auctions

Dionne Quintuplets with Dr. Dafoe, Callander, Canada, printed photo, copyright 1937, very fine condition. **$4**

Cherryland Auctions

Artist signed A. Bertiglia, Italian publisher, series 2053-1, woman and Cupid, minor corner crease, very fine condition. **$5**

Cherryland Auctions

Halloween, John Winsch, copyright 1914, witch in space, sepia tone series, divided back, embossed, one minor corner crease, very fine condition...... **$37**

Cherryland Auctions

Josephine Baker, real photo, #249, near very fine condition....................**$100**

Cherryland Auctions

Fantasy Exaggeration, real photo with DOPS postcard back by Conard, #27, copyright 1936, "Haulin em Out," minor corner wear, near very fine condition. **$20**

Cherryland Auctions

Jean Harlow, real photo, PC-136, very fine condition.**$25**

Cherryland Auctions

1939 San Francisco World's Fair, advertising Chicago & North Western Railway Exhibit, minor corner crease, very fine condition. **$5**

Cherryland Auctions

Fantasy Metamorphic, "Diabolo," real photo of art, nudes make face, divided back, corner crease and minor edge wear, fine condition........................ **$5**

Cherryland Auctions

Artist signed HBG (H.B. Griggs), Lubrie & Elkins publisher, series # 2273, Thanksgiving, divided back, embossed minor corner wear, near very fine condition. **$12**

Cherryland Auctions

Artist signed Ellen Clapsaddle, International Art Pub. Co., series 4440, Thanksgiving, with color beads, divided back, embossed, very fine condition. **$4**

Cherryland Auctions

Halloween, John Winsch, copyright 1911, art by Samuel Schmucker, with green goblins, used, divided back, embossed, near very fine condition. $50

Cherryland Auctions

Halloween, Stecher Lithographic Co. publisher, series 248 F, used 1916, divided back, embossed, one minor corner wear, near very fine condition. $16

Cherryland Auctions

Raphael Tuck publisher, Halloween series No. 160, divided back, embossed, minor corner wear and some back stains, fine condition. $17

Cherryland Auctions

Halloween, Whitney publisher, divided back, embossed very fine condition. $13

Cherryland Auctions

Artist signed Ellen Clapsaddle, International Art Pub. Co., series 1311, Thanksgiving, divided back, embossed, fine to very fine condition. $4

Cherryland Auctions

Artist signed Ellen Clapsaddle, International Art Pub. Co., series 2940, Christmas, used 1912, divided back, embossed, edge tear and minor corner wear, near fine to very fine condition.............$10

Cherryland Auctions

Hold to the light, die-cut brown-suited Santa, used 1910, divided back, minor edge crease, very fine condition. **$300**

Cherryland Auctions

Red-suited Santa with novelty red silk suit, copyright 1906 P. Sanders, used 1907, divided back, embossed, minor corner crease, fine to very fine condition. **$15**

Cherryland Auctions

Blue-suited Santa, Erika publisher, #4174, used 1909 but missing stamp, divided back, embossed, very fine condition. **$50**

Cherryland Auctions

Black-suited Santa, tinted printed photo, #2041.2, used 1910, gel finish, divided back, near very fine condition. **$12**

Cherryland Auctions

Red-suited Santa driving double-decker motorbus, John Winsch, copyright 1913, divided back, embossed, near very fine condition. **$22**

Cherryland Auctions

Red-suited Santa in automobile, series # 540, divided back, very fine condition. **$10**

Cherryland Auctions

Red-suited Santa, John Winsch, copyright 1914, divided back, embossed, minor corner crease, fine to very fine condition. **$4**

Cherryland Auctions

Small brown-suited Jack-in-the-box Santa, Stecher Lithographic Co. publisher, Christmas series 338 E, divided back, embossed, minor corner crease, fine to very fine condition. **$3**

Cherryland Auctions

Easter, John Winsch, copyright 1911, art by Samuel Schmucker, divided back, embossed, near very fine condition. **$3**

Cherryland Auctions

Woven silk, early French publisher, undivided back, minor writing on face and few minor tone spots, very fine condition. **$80**

Cherryland Auctions

Hold to the light transparency, Japanese publisher, with fantasy fox, reveals woman's reflection, undivided back, near very fine condition. **$150**

Cherryland Auctions

St. Patrick's Day, art by HBG (H.B. Griggs), Lubrie & Elkins publisher, series 2259, used 1910, divided back, embossed minor cancel on face, near very fine condition. ..**$4**

Cherryland Auctions

St. Patrick's Day, John Winsch, copyright 1912, art by Samuel Schmucker, divided back, embossed, near very fine condition. **$5**

Cherryland Auctions

Hold to the light transparency, Japanese publisher, reveals fantasy genie, divided back, very fine condition. **$15**

Cherryland Auctions

Real photo, "Fat Annie Largest Engine Ever Built Crestline," Pennsylvania Lines, used Crestline, Ohio 1910, very fine condition. **$50**

Cherryland Auctions

Wright biplane at Maple Avenue, Claremont, New Hampshire, real photo by Powers, used 1911, edge tear, fine to very fine condition. **$200**

Cherryland Auctions

Fourth of July, Raphael Tuck publisher, series No. 159, "Call To Arms – American Revolution," divided back, embossed, very fine condition. **$5**

Cherryland Auctions

Horse-drawn wagon advertising Borden's Condensed Milk Co., real photo with Velox postcard back, owner identifies as Chicago, minor corner wear and edge crease, fine to very fine condition. **$225**

Cherryland Auctions

◀ Easter, Raphael Tuck publisher, series 2814, including chicks and frog, unusual, divided back, embossed, near very fine condition. **$10**

Cherryland Auctions

10 Things You Didn't Know About **Vintage Postcards**

1 The origin of postcards is steeped in a bit of controversy, with Austria, Germany and the United States each staking claim to a piece of the historical postcard pie. The first postcard patent in the United States was submitted by John P. Charlton in 1861, and then sold to Hymen Lipman. However, this early postcard did not feature images. There are also reports of the first souvenir picture postcard showing up in Austria in 1869, followed by the first advertising postcard making its premiere in Britain in 1870.

2 German-born artist Rudolph Dirks' rascally comic strip characters "Hans and Fritz" inspired a game-changing series of postcards in the early 20th century, which featured the troublemaking young boys. In keeping with the devious behavior the duo was known for, the postcards had to be held to a heat source to reveal the joke on the postcard.

3 Two long-running magazines serving the postcard collecting community are *Barr's Post Card News*, based in Vinton, Iowa, which offers both a print and digital subscription at www.barrspcn.com, and *Picture Postcard Monthly*, based in Nottingham, England, which also offers a print and digital subscription at www.postcardcollecting.co.uk/subscribe.php.

4 Hundreds of postcard collectors gather regularly on PostcardCollector.org to talk postcards and enjoy superb postcard galleries.

5 Postcards were among the first items used by charities to share news of their efforts and raise much-needed funds. During World War I, The Salvation Army released a series of postcards that featured images of "doughnut girls" dishing out homemade doughnuts – fried right in the field – to soldiers stationed overseas, while also offering them a healthy dose of appreciation and encouragement from home.

6 The popularity of postcards is celebrated in a few spectacular museums. Next time you're in the Windy City, be sure to stop by the Chicago Postcard Museum, and while you're in the state of Illinois, check out Libertyville's Curt Teich Postcard Archives – featuring more than 365,000 postcards. Plus, the Museum of Fine Arts in Boston includes a number of impressive postcards among its various collections, as does The Metropolitan Museum of Art in New York.

7 An age-old debate between deltiologists (postcard collectors) and artists is the use of postcards to create art. As collage art started to take hold in the early 20th century, artists including Pablo Picasso used bits of newspaper, wallpaper, and postcards to create pieces of art.

8 Postcrossing is a modern postcard exchange program. Participants open a free account on Postcrossing.com, receive the name and address of another member, mail a postcard to that person, wait to receive a return postcard, and register it in the system. In the eight years this project has been active, more than 400,000 people from 217 countries have participated, and 16,758,199 postcards have been registered.

9 Postcardy.com is a popular virtual postcard hub filled with tips and advice about collecting postcards, links to sites for connecting with fellow deltiologists and viewing postcard collections.

10 Basic methods for preserving postcards include: storing them in photo albums; placing them in non-acidic plastic wallets, which offer a way to preserve and present postcards; and framing them (using archival-quality materials) for display out of bright sunlight.

Compiled by Antoinette Rahn. Sources: *Postcard Collector* by Barbara Andrews, Smithsonian Libraries, Picture Postcard Monthly, Barr's Post Card News, PostcardCollector.org, Postcardy.com, The Salvation Army (www.uss.salvationarmy.org), Lake County Forest Preserves (www.lcfpd.org), Postcrossing.com.

Posters

A poster is a large, usually printed placard, bill, or announcement, often illustrated, that is posted to advertise or publicize something. It can also be an artistic work, often a reproduction of an original painting or photograph, printed on a large sheet of paper.

Vintage posters are usually between 20 and 50 years old and must be original and not copies or newer reproductions.

The value of a vintage poster is determined by condition, popularity of the subject matter, rarity, artistic rendering, and the message it conveys.

"Byrd-North Pole Plane Tour" poster issued by Vacuum Oil Co., good to very good condition, some wear to fold lines, sight size 35-1/2" x 21-5/8". ...**$150**

Mosby & Co. Auctions

"Tompkins' Real Wild West" with image of cowboys roping, riding and trick shooting, printed by Donaldson Litho, excellent/near mint condition, some minor wear to center fold line and some edge tears, 32" x 22"...........**$825**

Mosby & Co. Auctions

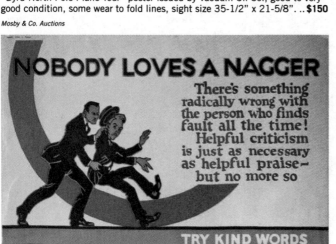

1923 Mather work incentive poster from Mather's first year of production, titled "Nobody Loves a Nagger," poster uses Mather's typical humor-inspired art, very fine/excellent condition, missing small piece of upper right corner, a couple of small right edge tears. **$210**

Mosby & Co. Auctions

World War I Food Administration colorful linen mounted poster of fruits and vegetables, artwork by Hendee, printed by Edwards & Deutsch, mint condition...........**$80**

Mosby & Co. Auctions

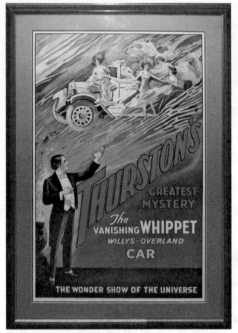

Framed Thurston Vanishing Wippet poster, one-sheet with image of Thurston's famous vanishing car act, near mint/mint condition, slight wear to center fold line, sight size 37-1/2" x 23-5/8". **$1,300**

Mosby & Co. Auctions

1893 Red Star Line steamship poster, archively mounted and framed, artwork by C. Saltzmann, depiction of Steamship Westernland, which also has masts for sail power; background of image shows Brooklyn Bridge at bow and large Statue of Liberty at stern; bottom reads, "Entre Anvers et New York, Philadelphie." Excellent plus condition, minor restoration to edges, borders a bit trimmed, sight size 36" x 26", matte and framed size 42-1/4" x 33-1/2". **$3,500**

Mosby & Co. Auctions

Raymond the Magician six sheet poster, linen, mounted, French poster, 1910, central image of Raymond surrounded by women, only known example of this poster, lithographed by Moody Frères, very fine/excellent condition, scattered light restoration. **$1,800**

Mosby & Co. Auctions

Mounted linen World War I poster with Santa, dated 1918, promoting Christmas shopping during World War I and has unusual juxtaposition of Santa Claus with soldiers and military hardware, excellent condition, minor restoration to left edge.........**$360**

Mosby & Co. Auctions

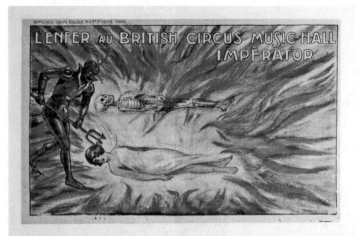

Inman Bros. Flying Circus poster, tri-motor plane, great color, attached paper includes writing with "Sept 28-29-30 Moberly Airport," 38" x 25". **$400**

Matthews Auctions

British circus musical poster, linen mounted, circa 1920s, Lucifer with floating woman and skeleton magic act, printed by Louis Galice, Paris, excellent condition, couple repaired edge tears. **$280**

Mosby & Co. Auctions

English Queen's Guard colorful linen mounted poster with image of regular-sized Queen's Guardsman next to giant Queen's Guardsman with giant gun, printed by Creber Lithograph, Plymouth, excellent condition, minor restoration to fold lines. **$300**

Mosby & Co. Auctions

Abbott and Costello Meet Captain Kid, 1953, starring Bud Abbott, Lou Costello, Charles Laughton, Hillary Brooke, Fran Warren, Bill Shirley, Leif Erickson, Joe Kirk, and Rex Lease, directed by Charles Lamont, folded, very fine condition, unrestored with bright color and clean overall appearance, 27" x 41". **$209**

Heritage Auctions

Passage to Marseille, 1944, unmounted one sheet, starring Humphrey Bogart, very fine condition, minor wear to fold lines, 41" x 27". **$450**

Mosby & Co. Auctions

Ohio poster, undated, probably 1960s, published by Ohio Development and Publicity Commission, fine condition, some scattered surface creasing. **$100**

Mosby & Co. Auctions

Laubenheimer beer advertising poster, unmounted, French, artwork by G. Ripart, printed by Bacholet, Paris, very good/fine condition, some edge wear with minor tears to borders, 47" x 31-1/2". **$300**

Mosby & Co. Auctions

1930s travel poster for Versailles mounted on board, image of palace and fountains in back, artwork by Maurice Toussaint, printed by Cornille and Serre, very fine/excellent condition, minor surface and edge wear. **$175**

Mosby & Co. Auctions

Chinese anti-discrimination propaganda poster, 1963, rare and vibrant, unmounted, with images of African American men, promoting "Oppose Racial Discrimination" in six different languages, lower left corner features image of U.S. capitol, fine/very fine condition with some damage and wrinkling to left edge and some wrinkling to right border, 42" x 30-1/2".....................$170

Mosby & Co. Auctions

Casablanca, post-war, Belgian, romantic painting, one of the most sought after of all foreign posters, original, very fine condition on linen.....**$1,792**
Heritage Auctions

American Graffiti, 1973, starring Richard Dreyfuss, Ronny Howard, Paul Le Mat, Charlie Martin Smith, Candy Clark, Mackenzie Phillips, Cindy Williams, Wolfman Jack, Bo Hopkins, Manuel Padilla Jr., Harrison Ford, Kathleen Quinlan, Johnny Weissmuller Jr., Joe Spano, Debralee Scott, Suzanne Somers, directed by George Lucas, artwork by Mort Drucker, folded, near mint condition, lightly used, unrestored, 27" x 41".........**$209**

Heritage Auctions

World War I era linen mounted Red Cross poster featuring baby girl with doll and toy, artwork by A.M. Upjohn, near mint/mint condition, 31-1/2" x 21-1/2". **$275**

Mosby & Co. Auctions

Babes in Arms starring Mickey Rooney and Judy Garland, rare Style B one sheet, linen backed with minimal touch-up to address large chips and surface paper loss, very good condition. **$836**

Heritage Auctions

Superman cartoon stock, one sheet, 27" x 41", 1941, Paramount, blank imprint area where individual cartoon titles could be written or printed, fine/very fine condition, slight fold separation at top of vertical fold with separation along bottom quarter of vertical fold, reinforced on verso with archival tape, tiny hole with paper loss at lower center point and in Superman's foot, both areas with small bits of paper added, colored and reinforced with tape on verso, some tape reinforcement of other center points, one of the most sought after posters in the hobby..**$23,900**

Heritage Auctions

Andy Warhol exhibition poster, 1971, British, advertising artist's exhibit at Tate Gallery from Feb. 17 to March 28, 1971, poster features Warhol's famous silk-screen image of Marilyn Monroe from the early 1960s, rolled, near mint/mint condition, unused, un-restored, 20" x 30". **$740**

Heritage Auctions

"Jesus Christ Superstar" record store poster, artwork by Byrd promotes Decca Records release, copyright MCA, 1971, fine condition, some old tape to top and bottom edges and some light creases. **$60**

Mosby & Co. Auctions

Terry-Toon Cartoons, 20th Century Fox, 1941, one sheet, "The Baby Seal," fine/very fine condition, fold and cross fold separation with small paper loss and tape on verso, edge wear with tears, and pinholes in corners, 27" x 41". Paul Terry, the founder of Terry-Toons animation house, had little artistic ambition and no interest in innovating the medium. The key to surviving Disney's dominance was to keep costs low, and by aiming for the bargain basement, he hit upon a mode of production – cel animation – that not only offered a cheap alternative, but also allowed animators to use more richly textured backgrounds. This rare one sheet for the Terry-Toons short "The Baby Seal" is packed with characters from the series in vivid color. **$102**

Heritage Auctions

Dumbo the Flying Elephant, Disneyland Park ride, plus two other rides, Mad Tea Party and King Arthur's Carousel, both original opening day rides, fine/very fine condition, rolled, set of staple holes in each of the upper corners, creases in each of the lower corners with a tiny chip off lower left, minor crimps within image area, 36" x 54". **$1,553**

Heritage Auctions

Michelin motorcycle tire poster with bibendum, mounted on linen, 1959, marked Verga-Milano, 32" x 25". **$325**

Matthews Auctions

Les Miserables lobby cards, 1935, starring Fredric March, Charles Laughton, Rochelle Hudson, Cedric Hardwicke, Florence Eldridge, John Beal, and Frances Drake, directed by Richard Boleslawski, very fine condition, unrestored with clean overall appearance, 11" x 14". **$107**

Heritage Auctions

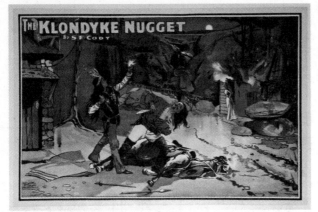

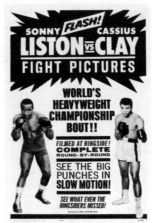

"The Klondyke Nugget" playbill poster, linen mounted, circa 1898, printed by David Allen and Sons, Ltd., Belfast, mint condition, 28-1/2" x 19". Play was created and produced by S.F. Cody, an early Buffalo Bill imitator. The cast of the play was mostly filled by Cody's family members. S.F. Cody's real last name was Cowdery. Originally from America, he used the profits from this successful play to experiment with aviation, building his own plane in England around 1908, about the same time he became a British citizen. **$260**

Mosby & Co. Auctions

Liston vs. Clay poster for theater-released, filmed replay of fight between Sonny Liston and Cassius Clay, won by Clay, fine/very fine condition, faint tape residue under "Fight Pictures," horizontal crease in top section, 27" x 41". ...**$896**

Heritage Auctions

The Razor's Edge starring Tyrone Power, Gene Tierney, and Anne Baxter, extremely rare Style B one sheet with artwork by Norman Rockwell, fine condition, restoration to bottom left corner chip, top left corner bend, and pinholes in borders, fold wear visible, 27" x 41"............ **$4,481**

Heritage Auctions

Loving You, 1957, starring Elvis Presley, Lizabeth Scott, Wendell Corey, Dolores Hart, and James Gleason, directed by Hal Kanter, folded, fine plus condition, unrestored with overall presentable appearance, 27" x 41".................................. **$418**

Heritage Auctions

Snoopy, Come Home!, 1972, starring the voices of Bill Melendez, Stephen Shea, Chad Webber, David Carey, Christopher de Faria, and Robin Kohn, directed by Bill Melendez, three sheets, artwork by Charles Shultz, very fine/near mint condition, unrestored poster appears unused, 41" x 76-1/2." **$50**

Heritage Auctions

POSTERS

!

Tarzan the Ape Man, MGM, 1932, one sheet, very fine condition, a few pinholes in corners and in center of upper border and just below those in artwork, small hole between the R and Z of title, 3-1/4" clean tear in lower border that extends into background art, small tear in right border, some minor center point separation, slight stain in Neil Hamilton's credit, 27" x 41". The rarest Tarzan one sheet known and the most coveted poster for the entire series, this is only the second example to surface. It is also the most sought after and important as it is from the first film in the series to star famous swimmer and Olympic medalist Johnny Weissmuller as Lord of the Apes...**$65,725**

Heritage Auctions

Tim McCoy Wild West door insert, two-sheet on linen, printed by Tooker-Moore Litho, excellent/near mint condition, a couple of minor spots of discoloration on bottom edge from old tape...............**$220**

Mosby & Co. Auctions

Cleopatra, 20th Century Fox, 1963, British quad, very fine/near mint condition, few crimps and dings, 30" x 40". Elizabeth Taylor was the logical choice to play the queen of Egypt as she had become one of the greatest actresses in Hollywood. In the film, and as Cleopatra, she conquered Rome, not by her armies but by her charm. **$120**

Heritage Auctions

Quilts

Each generation made quilts, comforters and coverlets, all intended to be used. Many were used into oblivion and rest in quilt heaven, but for myriad reasons, some have survived. Many of them remain because they were not used but stored, often forgotten, in trunks and linen cabinets.

A quilt is made up of three layers: the top, which can be a solid piece of fabric, appliquéd, pieced, or a combination; the back, which can be another solid piece of fabric or pieced; and the batting, which is the center layer, which can be cotton, wool, polyester, a blend of poly and cotton, or even silk. Many vintage quilts are batted with an old blanket or even another old, worn quilt.

The fabrics are usually cotton or wool, or fine fancy fabrics like silk, velvet, satin, and taffeta. The layers of a true quilt are held together by the stitching, or quilting, that goes through all three layers and is usually worked in a design or pattern that enhances the piece overall.

Quilts made from a seemingly single solid piece of fabric are known as wholecloth quilts, or if they are white, as whitework quilts. Usually such quilts are constructed from two or more pieces of the same fabric joined to make up the necessary width. They are often quilted quite elaborately, and the seams virtually disappear within the decorative stitching. Most wholecloth quilts are solid-colored, but prints were also used. Whitework quilts were often made as bridal quilts and many were kept for "best," which means that they have survived in reasonable numbers.

Wholecloth quilts were among the earliest type of quilted bedcovers made in Britain, and the colonists brought examples with them according to inventory lists that exist from colonial times. American quiltmakers used the patterns early in the nation's history, and some were carried with settlers moving west across the Appalachians.

Appliqué quilts are made from shapes cut from fabric and applied, or appliquéd, to a background, usually solid-colored on vintage quilts, to make a design. Early appliqué quilts dating back to the 18th century were often worked in a technique called broderie perse, or Persian embroidery, in which printed motifs were cut from a piece of fabric, such as costly chintz, and applied to a plain, less expensive background cloth.

Appliqué was popular in the 1800s, and there are thousands of examples, from exquisite, brightly colored Baltimore Album quilts made in and around Baltimore between circa 1840 and 1860, to elegant four-block quilts made later in the century. Many appliqué quilts are pictorial with floral designs the predominant motif. In the 20th century, appliqué again enjoyed an upswing, especially during the Colonial Revival period, and thousands were made from patterns or appliqué kits that were marketed and sold from 1900 through the 1950s.

Pieced or patchwork quilts are made by cutting fabric into shapes and sewing them together to

Three Pennsylvania pieced and appliqué privy bags, one dated 1869.............................. **$1,126**

Pook & Pook, Inc.

Pieced and trapunto poinsettia variant quilt, dated 1844, inscribed "Emeline Talbott Montgomery County, Maryland Oct. 10th 1844," 96" x 96".... **$1,778**

Pook & Pook, Inc.

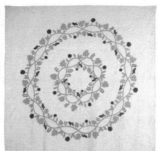

Appliqué quilt with birds on a floral wreath, circa 1870, 87" x 87"................................ **$4,266**

Pook & Pook, Inc.

Appliqué eagle quilt, late 19th century, 76" x 76". **$1,185**

Pook & Pook, Inc.

make a larger piece of cloth. The patterns are usually geometric, and their effectiveness depends heavily on the contrast of not just the colors themselves, but of color value as well. Patchwork became popular in the United States in the early 1800s.

Colonial clothing was almost always made using cloth cut into squares or rectangles, but after the Revolutionary War, when fabric became more widely available, shaped garments were made, and these garments left scraps. Frugal housewives, especially among the westward-bound pioneers, began to use these cutoffs to put together blocks that could then be made into quilts. Patchwork quilts are by far the most numerous of all vintage-quilt categories, and the diversity of style, construction and effect that can be found is a study all its own.

Dating a quilt is a tricky business unless the maker included the date on the finished item, and unfortunately for historians and collectors, few did. The value of a particular example is affected by its age, of course, and educating yourself about dating methods is invaluable. There are several aspects that can offer guidelines for establishing a date. These include fabrics; patterns; technique; borders; binding; batting; backing; quilting method; and colors and dyes.

For more information on quilts, see *Warman's Vintage Quilts Identification and Price Guide* by Maggi McCormick Gordon.

Quilt Care Tips

The National Quilt Museum is not only a place you can visit to bask in the beauty and stunning handiwork of quilters from the past and present; among other things, it's a source for valuable information about preserving and displaying quilts. Below are a few tips and hints the museum has for caring for all types of quilts, especially vintage and antique quilts.

1. Be careful not to subject quilts to direct sunlight, as sunlight is known to cause irreversible damage to textiles. Exposure of quilts to other light sources should be kept at a minimum.
2. Avoid placing quilts in unpainted wooden chests or using unpainted wooden poles to display a quilt. The acids produced by raw wood are damaging to textiles. Use acid-free, non-buffered tissue paper and an acid-free box to properly store a quilt.
3. When handling a quilt, use clean cotton gloves.
4. Do not wash or dry clean a quilt. Visit your local quilt shop or fabric store to inquire about methods for vacuuming quilts.
5. Skip the plastic bags when looking for materials to store your quilts in. It can do more harm than good and compromise the condition of a quilt.
6. Be sure to store quilts in an area where the temperature and humidity are consistent throughout the year – attics and basements are not good choices.

Source: The National Quilt Museum (www.quiltmuseum.org)

Two Pennsylvania floral appliqué pillow shams, 19th century, 19-1/2" x 36-1/2" and 19" x 33". **$652**

Pook & Pook, Inc.

Pennsylvania pieced and appliqué quilt, late 19th century, with philphlot, heart, and star decoration, 94" x 94".. **$729**

Pook & Pook, Inc.

New England linsey woolsey quilt, circa 1800, with eight-point Ohio star, 78" x 94".................... **$2,307**

Pook & Pook, Inc.

Pair of Pennsylvania pieced pillow shams, 19th century, with flying goose border, 18-1/2" x 26-1/2".. **$1,126**

Pook & Pook, Inc.

Appliqué sampler quilt, late 19th century, 86" x 88"... **$3,081**

Pook & Pook, Inc.

Baltimore appliqué album quilt, dated 1855, signed Mary Jane Magry, with ruched flowers, 80" x 80".. **$1,659**

Pook & Pook, Inc.

Baltimore trapunto and appliqué album quilt, circa 1860, with floral and acorn blocks within a grapevine border, 97" x 102".............................. **$2,370**

Pook & Pook, Inc.

Pieced and trapunto quilt of political interest with vignettes of George Washington, Henry Clay, and Zachary Taylor, quilted flag of the Union, 77" x 77"....... **$1,499**

Pook & Pook, Inc.

Appliqué crossed tulip quilt, late 19th century, with a swag border, 87" x 87"........................ **$1,778**

Pook & Pook, Inc.

Chintz pieced and appliqué quilt, early 19th century, with center star of Bethlehem and floral basket appliqués, 180" x 111"............................**$8,888**

Pook & Pook, Inc.

Baltimore album quilt, circa 1850, with 25 floral blocks, trapunto and ruching within a swag border, 115" x 122"...**$2,607**

Pook & Pook, Inc.

Pieced lone star and eagle quilt, late 19th century, 85" x 87"...**$3,555**

Pook & Pook, Inc.

Pieced feather star quilt, late 19th century, 86" x 86"..**$1,541**

Pook & Pook, Inc.

Appliqué cockscomb variant quilt, late 19th century, 71" x 73"..**$1,304**

Pook & Pook, Inc.

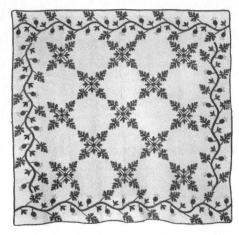

Appliqué and trapunto oak leaf quilt, circa 1860, 83" x 85"..**$2,133**

Pook & Pook, Inc.

Important Philadelphia Broderie Perse quilt, inscribed, "The work of my Mother Ruth McConnell & her cousins Hannah & Mary Parry in year 1793 previous to my birth (September of that year) during yellow fever - Julia M. Miles May 14th 1849," the quilt features a large central basket with floral vines surrounded by smaller bouquets and cornucopia corners within a chintz border, in a remarkable state of preservation for a quilt of its age, 103" x 111". **$28,440**

Pook & Pook, Inc.

Broderie Perse crib quilt, circa 1830, 38" x 42". **$2,844**

Pook & Pook, Inc.

Outstanding Baltimore album quilt, mid-19th century, with 25 appliqué and trapunto squares depicting the capital of the United States, American sailing ship, house, monument with American flags, elaborate baskets of flowers, cornucopia and garlands, 101-1/2" x 101-1/2"................................. **$28,440**

Pook & Pook, Inc.

Pieced Mennonite block pattern quilt, early 20th century, 78" x 81"....................**$207**

Pook & Pook, Inc.

Appliqué president's wreath quilt, circa 1870, 96" x 96".. .**$1,304**

Pook & Pook, Inc.

Appliqué whig rose quilt, late 19th century, with swag border, 81" x 81". **$948**

Pook & Pook, Inc.

Records

A lot has happened in the 140-odd years since the first functional phonograph debuted. In the 1870s, early recordings were made on tin foil cylinders and played back on phonographs. American inventor Thomas Edison improved the technology when he patented wax-coated cylinders in 1886. By 1908, Edison's cylinders faced increasing competition from the now-familiar flat discs we call records.

Record sizes and playback speeds varied: 7", 10", 12" records all were available, and speeds typically ranged from 74 to 82 revolutions per minute. To make a recording, performers would gather around a large acoustic horn. The sound energy from the performance was channeled through the horn, and the signal was inscribed on a master cylinder. This technique was known as acoustical recording.

By 1925, the advent of microphones and amplifiers made electrical recording methods a reality. Records were louder and clearer. As electric-powered record players and amplifiers became the norm, a playback rate of 78 RPM was chosen as the industry standard — a speed that worked with electrical infrastructure in place both in the United States (110 volts/60 Hz) and abroad (220 volts/50 Hz). Ironically, 78 RPM records weren't actually referred to as 78s until much later, when the term was used to help distinguish among 78, 45, 33-1/3 and 16-2/3 RPM records.

Early records were fashioned from hard rubber. By 1898, mass production began for records containing shellac, a resin secreted by beetles. Shellac records were incredibly brittle; dropping one was pretty much a death sentence for the disc. In 1904, the first "unbreakable" records hit the market. Made of cardboard core discs coated with celluloid, an early form of unbreakable plastic, these records suffered from a lot of surface noise during playback. They didn't catch on with consumers.

RCA introduced the first commercially available vinyl records in 1930: 12", 33-1/3 RPM

Astronauts, "Surfin' With the Astronauts," LP, mono, 1963. RCA Victor LPM-2760. .... **$60**
Stereo LP, RCA Victor LSP-2760........................ **$80**

The Beach Boys, "Heroes and Villains"/"You're Welcome," 45 RPM single, 1967, Brother 1001.**$12**
With picture sleeve **$100**

The Bell Hops, "For the Rest of
My Life"/"It Would Take a Million
Years," 45 RPM promo single,
1951, Decca 48208 .... **$100**

ABBA, "Happy New Year" (mono/stereo), 45 RPM
promo single, 1980, Atlantic PR 380 .... **$15**

"program transcription" discs. These records boasted less surface noise and greater strength than shellac records, but the format, which was introduced in the middle of the Great Depression, was a commercial failure.

After World War II, 7" 45s and 12" LPs challenged the 78's dominance. Both of these formats used narrower grooves, sometimes referred to as microgrooves, and a smaller stylus for playback. Columbia's 33-1/3 LP made its debut in 1948; it boasted up to 30 minutes of playback time.

RCA rolled out 45 RPM records in 1949. Made of polystyrene or vinyl, each 45 had a large hole to accommodate its placement on a record changer. This allowed listeners to stack up several 45s on top of a changer, where discs could then drop and be played one at a time. (The little record with the big hole also was perfect for jukeboxes.) Many music lovers had to buy spindle-size adapters or snap-in inserts, sometimes called "spiders," in order to play 45s on their record players.

By the late 1950s, 45 RPM records were outselling 78s. Most U.S. record labels stopped pressing popular music on 78s by the early 1960s, although the format hung on for a few more years abroad and in select uses, including children's records. As the new industry standard for shorter-duration recordings, 45s were either singles, which offered one song per side, or extended-play records that could contain up to three songs per side.

Even though stereo recording technology had been around since its invention by EMI's Alan Blumlein in 1931, it didn't become a key factor in playback until much later. In 1958, the first two-channel records were issued by Audio Fidelity and Pye in the United States and the United Kingdom, respectively. For a while, records were offered in both monaural and stereo formats, because stereo records couldn't be played on monophonic systems. But most record companies abandoned mono recordings by the close of the 1960s. Although stereo eventually became the industry standard, many collectors prefer mono records, and labels recently have reissued classic albums in mono format due to consumer demand.

Post-World War II Americans wanted to be able to take their music with them, and automakers paid attention. In 1956, Chrysler, DeSoto, Dodge, and Plymouth offered optional in-car phonographs made by Columbia that could play 45s and 7", 16-2/3 RPM records. These systems had a lot of drawbacks, not the least of which included bumpy roads that made records skip during playback. Inspired by radio station technology that used cartridge tapes, inventors came out with magnetic tape recording technology known as the Lear Jet Stereo 8, or 8-track, in the early 1960s. By the 1966 model year, Ford offered 8-track tape players as an option available on select models of its cars.

If two is better than one, four must be better than two, right? That was the philosophy behind the four-track quadraphonic playback system, which arrived in 1971 with the promise of providing an incredible listening experience. But the technology, which was the forerunner to Surround Sound, never took off. Quadraphonic records typically cost at least $1 more than their stereo counterparts. Quadraphonic recordings also required a custom audio system for playback. The record labels were divided on the quadraphonic technology that was in use, so listeners who bought a quadraphonic sound system were very limited as to which label's recordings were compatible.

> **CAPITOL STEREO ALBUM**
> **THE BEATLES—MEET THE BEATLES**
> IT WON'T BE LONG · THIS BOY · ALL MY LOVING
> DON'T BOTHER ME · ALL I'VE GOT TO DO
> I WANNA BE YOUR MAN
> ——— S E E B U R G ———

The Beatles, "Meet The Beatles," 33-1/3 compact EP (with small hole), stereo jukebox edition, 1964, features "It Won't Be Long"/"This Boy"/"All My Loving" backed with "Don't Bother Me"/"All I've Got to Do"/"I Wanna Be Your Man," Capitol SXA-2047.
.... **$400**
With picture sleeve **$479**
With picture sleeve and all jukebox title strips intact
.... **$700**

In the 1970s and 1980s, recording companies experimented with different ways of producing records, including new mastering techniques that promised even better sound, and portability continued to be a driving force for music lovers. Cassette tapes, which emerged around the same time as 8-tracks, grew in popularity during the 1970s and reached their peak in the 1980s, thanks to boom boxes, in-car tape decks, and Sony's Walkman individual portable cassette players.

By the 1990s, 8-track tapes and vinyl records had basically been phased out, and cassette tapes were facing the same threat in the United States that 78s and cylinders had before them: obsolescence. The new technology known as the compact disc was gaining ground, thanks to its ability to fit the contents of a 12", two-sided vinyl record on a single-sided polycarbonate disc that measured just 4-3/4 inches in diameter.

Sound recordings managed to get even smaller with the advent of digital music players, the best known of which is Apple's iPod. Introduced in 2001, the player was touted by Apple CEO Steve Jobs as a way to put "1,000 songs in your pocket," thanks to the cassette-tape-sized player's hard drive that stored downloadable MP3 music files, and later video and other multimedia files. The iPod and other MP3 players literally sounded the death knell for the Sony Walkman. The company halted production and sales in Japan of the portable cassette players in spring 2010 after 30 years and more than 200 million units sold. Chinese makers continued to manufacture Sony Walkmans for sale in Asia and the Middle East. Production also is continuing — for now — on Sony's Discman portable CD player.

If you look to car stereos, it's clear what automakers see as the future of music. CD players are basically standard equipment along with AM/FM radios, and most new cars come with at least the option for an MP3 port, if not with a digital music system in place. Sales of digital recordings have exploded to the tune of 1.41 billion digital singles and albums sold in 2011 vs. 248 million vinyl and CD singles and albums, according to RIAA statistics.

But don't count vinyl records out just yet. Sales of vinyl singles, EPs, and LPs began to bounce back in 2008 as a new generation of music lovers and collectors discovered the format. That year, sales hit 2.9 million units shipped — the most that the format had seen since 1998. Just three years later, vinyl record sales had nearly doubled to reach 5.9 million units sold. Longtime fans tout the "warmth" of the sound that vinyl provides, and many credit the format's less-compressed audio as providing a listening experience superior to that of CDs or MP3s.

— *Susan Sliwicki, Editor,* Goldmine *magazine, www.goldminemag.com*

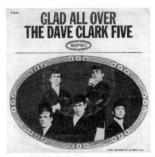

Dave Clark Five, "Glad All Over"/"I Know You," 45 RPM single, 1964, Epic 5-9656. ....**$15**
With picture sleeve **$20**

Bobby Darin, "That's All," LP, mono, 1959, Atco 33-102, with yellow "harp" label. **$40**
Atco SD 33-104 (stereo) **$120**
Atco 33-104, 1962 pressing with gold and dark blue label... **$20**
Atco SD-33-104, 1962 stereo pressing with purple and brown label.................................... **$25**

Diana Ross with Michael Jackson, "Ease on Down the Road," 6:02, same on both sides, 12" single, 1978, MCA, L33-1801.........**$60**

The Who, "Who's Next," LP, 1973, MCA 2023.................**$12**
1977 pressing, MCA 3024....**$10**
1979 pressing, MCA 5220......**$8**

Cadillacs, "Gloria"/"I Wonder Why" 45 RPM single, 1954, Josie 765, with original with "Joz" logo at top. **$700**
Pressing with 1960s label **$25**

Commodores, "Brick House," 6:11, same on both sides, 12" single, 1977, Motown M000007D1.........................**$15**

Big Maybelle, "What More Can a Woman Do," LP, mono, 1962, Brunswick BL 54107............**$50**
Stereo version, Brunswick BL 754107...............................**$70**

The Doors, "Strange Days," LP, 1967, Elektra, EKL-4014, mono. There are two different covers for this; some copies have mono numbers on two covers and stereo number on spine, while others have mono number on spine and stereo number on front and back covers...................................**$600**

Carpenters, "Offering," LP, 1969, A&M SP-4205. ....**$80**
1970 reissue with same catalog number, new cover, retitled "Ticket to Ride"...**$12**

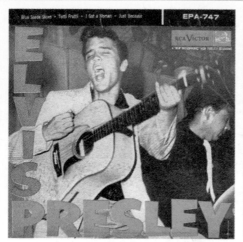

Elvis Presley, "Blue Suede Shoes"/"Tutti Frutti" backed with "I Got a Woman"/"Just Because," 45 RPM EP, 1956, RCA Victor, EPA-747, with horizontal line on label................................. **$50**
1956 pressing with incorrect label on Side 1 that lists "I'm Gonna Sit Right Down and Cry (Over You)" as the third song, which does not appear on this record. Known copies of this version do not have horizontal line on label. **$200**
1956 pressing, without horizontal line on label... **$50**
1956 pressing with horizontal line on label, no dog...**$200**
1965 pressing with black label featuring dog on left **$30**
1969 pressing with orange label **$80**
1956 pressing titled "Elvis Presley" with picture sleeve (five different back covers exist, all with titles on front cover, all of equal value) **$50**
1956 picture sleeve pressing with temporary envelope sleeve with dark blue print, "Blue Suede Shoes by Elvis Presley" in big letters **$1,000**
1956 picture sleeve pressing with temporary envelope sleeve with black print, "Blue Suede Shoes by Elvis Presley" in big letters **$600**
1965 picture sleeve pressing with no titles at top of front cover.. **$30**

Led Zeppelin, "Physical Graffiti," double LP with gatefold cover, 1975, Swan Song, SS-2-200... **$20**

Oscar Peterson, "Oscar Peterson Plays Count Basie," LP, 1957, Verve Clef Series, mono, MGV-8092, reissue of Clef 708. .... **$40**

Lawrence Welk, "My Golden Favorites," LP, 1961, mono, Coral CRL 57353. .... **$12**

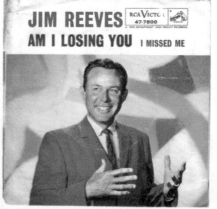

Jim Reeves, "Am I Losing You"/"I Missed Me," 45 RPM single, 1960, RCA Victor, 47-7800... **$12**
With picture sleeve **$20**

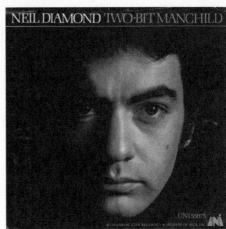

Mahavishnu Orchestra, "Between Nothingness and Eternity," LP, 1973, Columbia KC 32766....... **$15**
Columbia CQ 32766 (quadraphonic pressing) . **$40**
Columbia PC 32766 (later reissue with new prefix, with or without bar code on cover).................... **$8**

Neil Diamond, "Two-Bit Manchild"/"Broad Old Woman," 45 RPM single, 1968, Uni 55075..... **$8**
With picture sleeve **$25**
Promo version pressed on red vinyl, with "Two-Bit Manchild" on both sides, 1968 .... **$80**

Frankie Avalon, "What a Little Girl"/"I'll Wait For You," 45 RPM single, 1958, Chancellor 1026.. **$15**
With picture sleeve **$40**

The Rolling Stones, "Out of Our Heads," LP, 1965, London LL 3429, red or maroon label with "London" boxed at top... **$25**
Maroon label with "London" unboxed at top........ **$40**
Maroon label with "London/ffrr" in box at top **$200**

◄ Patsy Cline, "Walkin' After Midnight"/"A Poor Man's Roses (or A Rich Man's Gold)," 45 RPM single, 1957, Decca 9-30221, black label with star under "Decca" or black label with lines on either side of "Decca." **$30**
With picture sleeve ... **$80**

Fats Domino, "Fats Domino Rock and Rollin'," LP, 1956, Imperial LP 9009, mono, with maroon label. $150
1958 mono pressing featuring black label with stars on top...$80
1964 mono pressing featuring black and pink label $25
1967 mono pressing with black and green label...$20

What's the Scoop on Promotional Records?

For years, dire warnings plastered on promotional recordings prompted collectors to steer clear of them altogether (or at least check over their shoulders if they did indulge). But while those "not for sale" warnings on test pressings and deejay copies have a lot of bark, they lack legal bite, according to a 388-page ruling by the U.S. Ninth Circuit Court of Appeals.

Long story short: Troy Augusto was buying promos from thrift stores and record shops, then reselling them via eBay. Universal Music Group found out, objected and tried to stop the auctions. Augusto invoked the century-old First Sale Doctrine, which, among other things, clarifies the difference between owning a copyright and owning a physical copy. Per the doctrine, the record label's choice to give away a copy constituted the "first sale" of that item. So, unless you mugged the publicist hauling copies to the post office, pulled a "Mission Impossible" or otherwise broke the law to obtain promo recordings, they are fair game for the free market.

So, why do promotional recordings appeal to collectors?

1. SUPPLY AND DEMAND: Promos are often pressed in very limited numbers, as is the case with The Rolling Stones' 1969 eponymous promotional LP. It is believed that only 400 copies of the 14-track record were pressed on the London Records label (RSD-1). The records were shipped to influential radio programmers

in advance of the band's "Let It Bleed" album. These days, copies of that promo LP sell for $4,550 and up in online auctions, as reported in Goldmine magazine's Market Watch column.

2. VARIATIONS: Sometimes, promo records are markedly different from their stock siblings. They may be pressed on colored or special high-quality vinyl; follow a special promo-only numbering series; follow a different playback order; or, perhaps most desirable, feature alternate versions, remixes or tracks not available on the stock copy or feature a cover design that was altered or abandoned altogether for the final release. Sometimes, though, the only difference is that the record label turned someone loose with a roll of stickers, an ink stamp and a maybe box cutter to morph a stack of stock releases into "promo" copies.

3. RARITY AND POPULARITY: If an album or single hit it big, the value of the promo version may well exceed that of a comparable stock copy, as fans seek to collect variations or less-beat-up versions. A release that only saw the light of day via promo may automatically get a boost in its value on both fronts. However, if the music on said release "lacks an audience" (or, in more direct terms, "stinks on ice"), all bets are off.

4. QUALITY: Back in the 1980s, some record labels pressed promo discs only on Quiex II vinyl, which was considered to be more like audiophile-quality vinyl than what was used for the stock copies that followed. We're seeing Quiex II pressings from that period gaining favor with collectors. But buyers, beware: Just because there's a sticker on the cover that claims the record was pressed on Quiex II vinyl doesn't mean the disc inside actually was. Want to find out? Provided the LP was pressed on standard black vinyl, simply hold it up to a bright light source. If you can see through it, it's Quiex II.

5. CONDITION: Some collectors view promo pressings as inherently inferior because the covers, sleeves and labels bear intentional markings and damage. Others are attracted to promos for their history. But before you dismiss a promo based on the outer package, take a good look at the vinyl. Why? Unless you're looking at a copy that disc jockeys regularly used on the air, the promo record may have been played only once or twice (if at all). Copies sent to record label executives, artists and magazine reviewers have been known to go

Goldmine's Record Grading Guide

Before you can figure out what a record is worth, you need to grade its vinyl, sleeves and labels. Play grading can be a definite advantage for a record that looks much worse than it sounds. When you're visually grading records, use a direct light, such as a 100-watt desk lamp, as less direct lighting can hide defects.

Think like the buyer as you set your grades. If you're on the fence, go with the more conservative grade under consideration. Records and covers always seem to look better when you're grading them to sell to someone else than when you're on the other side of the table, inspecting a record for purchase. And, if you have a Still Sealed record, subject it to these same grading standards, short of breaking the seal.

MINT (M): Perfect in every way. Often rumored but rarely seen, mint should never be used as a grade unless more than one person agrees the item truly is in this condition. There is no hard-and-fast percentage of the near mint value a mint record can bring; it is best negotiated between buyer and seller.
- **Overall Appearance:** Looks as if it just came off the manufacturing line.
- **Record:** No scuffs or scratches.
- **Labels:** No writing, stickers or spindle marks. Labels are perfectly placed.
- **Cover/Sleeve:** No blotches, stains, discoloration, stickers, ring wear, dinged corners, sleeve splits or writing.

NEAR MINT (NM) OR MINT MINUS (M-): It's estimated that no more than 2 to 4 percent of all records remaining from the 1950s and 1960s are truly near mint. Many dealers won't use a grade higher than this, implying that no record or sleeve is ever truly perfect.
- **Overall Appearance:** Looks as if it were opened for the first time. Includes all original pieces (inner sleeve, lyric sheets, inserts, cover, record, etc.).
- **Record:** Shiny surface, free of visible defects. No surface noise at playback. Records can retain NM condition after many plays provided the record has been played on a properly equipped turntable and has been cared for properly.
- **Labels:** Properly pressed and centered on the record. Free of writing, stickers, spindle marks, blemishes or other markings.
- **Cover/Sleeve:** Free of creases, ring wear and seam splits. Cut-out markings are unacceptable. Picture sleeves look as if no record was ever housed inside. Hint: If you remove a 45 from its picture sleeve and store it separately, you will reduce the potential for damage to the sleeve.

VERY GOOD PLUS (VG+) OR EXCELLENT (E): Except for a few minor condition issues, these records would be near mint. Most collectors who want to play their records will be happy with a VG+ record, especially if it is toward the high end of the grade, sometimes called VG++ or E+.
- **Overall Appearance:** Shows slight signs of wear.
- **Record:** May have light scuffs or very light scratches that don't affect the listening experience, or slight warps that don't affect the sound. Expect minor signs of handling, such as telltale marks around the center hole (but the hole is not misshapen). Light ring wear or discoloration may be present, but barely noticeable.
- **Labels:** Free of writing, stickers or major blemishes.
- **Cover/Sleeve:** Outer cover may show some minor seam wear or a split less than one inch long along the bottom, which is the most vulnerable location. A cut-out marking may be present.

untouched for decades, until someone finally cleans out the climate-controlled offices and vaults where they have languished. And those same copies have been known to turn up in harder-to-find audio formats, such as mono, stereo or quadraphonic, depending on the era of the record's initial release.

What you can expect to pay for a promo record may vary, especially when you're dealing with in-demand artists like The Beatles, The Rolling Stones and Elvis Presley. Cover, vinyl or track variations also can boost prices; values for such differences can be quite fluid from one sale to the next. But if all other things are equal – same cover, vinyl color and quality, packaging, catalog number, release year, song order, number of (and versions of) songs – expect value of a promo pressing to mirror that of a similar-condition stock pressing.

— *Susan Sliwicki, editor, Goldmine magazine*

Picture sleeves may show some slight creasing where it is obvious the record once resided (or still does reside). May show minor seam wear or a split less than 1" long along the bottom.

VERY GOOD (VG): VG records have more obvious flaws than records in better condition. VG records – which usually sell for no more than 25 percent of their NM counterparts – are among the biggest bargains in record collecting, because most of the "big money" goes for more perfect copies. For many listeners, a VG record or sleeve will be worth the money. Many collectors who have jukeboxes will use VG records in them and not think twice. They remain a fine listening experience, just not the same as if it were in better shape.

- **Overall Appearance:** Shows signs of wear and handling, including visible groove wear, audible scratches and surface noise, ring wear and seam splits.
- **Record:** Lacks the original glossy finish. Groove wear is evident on sight, and light scratches are deep enough to feel with a fingernail. When played, a VG record has surface noise, and some scratches may be audible, especially during a song's intro and ending, but the noise won't overpower the music otherwise.
- **Labels:** May have minor writing, tape or a sticker.
- **Cover/Sleeve:** Expect obvious signs of human handling and normal wear. Ring wear is expected in the middle or along the edges of the cover where the labels or edges of a record would rest. Seam splits may appear on all three sides, but they won't be obvious. Writing or a price tag may be present. The cover may be dull or discolored, have bent corners, stains or other problems. If the record has more than two of these problems, reduce its grade.

VERY GOOD MINUS (VG–), GOOD PLUS (G+) OR GOOD (G): Good does not necessarily mean bad! A true G to VG- record still plays through without skipping, so it can serve as filler until something better comes along. If the record is common, you may want to pass it up in this condition. If you've sought for a long time, get it cheap and upgrade later. And sellers? Don't expect big profits for records in these grades: They bring 10 to 15 percent of the near mint value at most.

- **Overall Appearance:** Shows considerable signs of handling, including groove wear, ring wear, seam splits and damaged labels or covers.
- **Record:** The surface sheen is almost gone, but the record plays through without skipping. Significant surface noise and groove wear.
- **Labels:** Worn, possible stains, heavy writing, or obvious damage caused by someone trying to remove tape or stickers and failing.
- **Cover/Sleeve:** Shows ring wear to the point of distraction, has obvious seam splits and may have even heavier writing, such as huge radio station letters (or the former owner's name) written across the front to deter theft. Expect dinged and dog-eared edges.

FAIR (F) OR POOR (P): These records go for 0 to 5 percent of the near mint value, if they go at all. More likely, these records will end up going in the trash, or having their covers, labels or discs turned into kitschy craft items like clocks, journals, purses, jewelry, bowls or coasters.

- **Overall Appearance:** Beat, trashed and dull. Records may lack sleeves or covers (or vice versa).
- **Record:** Expect the vinyl to be cracked, horrifically scratched and/or impossibly warped. The record will skip and repeat when you attempt to play it.
- **Labels:** Stains, tears, stickers and damage are the least of your problems; the label may be missing some sections altogether.
- **Cover/Sleeve:** Heavily damaged. Only the most outrageously rare items ever sell for more than a few cents in this condition – again, if they sell at all.

Salesman Samples

Sometimes mistaken as toys, salesman samples are miniature versions of full-size goods that were carried by door-to-door salesmen. The high quality and elaborate details of these working scale models made them look exactly like the full-size products, tempting would-be buyers to purchase. Only large items that could not easily be toted along on the salesman's route were reproduced in miniature.

Hay rake, wooden with two large spoke wheels, between which is a wooden crossbar and brass saddle seat above a series of curved tines to rake hay, tines are raised and lowered by two foot pedals located beneath seat, crossbar pinstriped and marked "Wiard Plow Co, Batavia, NY," very good condition, missing one wooden fork tine at rear, 13" w. x 6-1/2" h...............**$4,542**

James D. Julia, Inc.

Hay press with original box, attributed to Eli, wood and nickel with four spoked wheels with spring loaded mechanism that compresses hay from top hopper by rotating the front tongue, pushing tamper, and completed bale down a tapered chute, accompanied by original wood and canvas-lined carrying case with original label indicating "Wilkins Trunk Mfg. Co." of Dallas, very good to excellent condition with some dulling and light scratches to nickel, case is good to very good condition, missing handle and metal components show light surface rust and oxidation; 19-1/2" l. x 4-1/2" w..........**$5,750**

James D. Julia, Inc.

Coffee bar, nickel and black painted metal display bottle consisting of three round covered receptacles and two floor cooler receptacles with rectangular lids marked "Prosper" in script, top has three turn handles of unknown purpose (one handle missing), round receptacles have screened windows on front and two dummy grinder levers each with drawers beneath to catch grounds, six drawers that can open from either side, original carrying case with slide top and flip-down sides, very good to excellent condition with some light wear to nickel and various paint chips to black, base is 14-1/2" l. x 5" w. x 6" h. **$1,725**

James D. Julia, Inc.

Carved and painted model of a house, early 20th century, found in Meyerstown, Pennsylvania, 21" h. x 20" w. **$889**

Pook & Pook, Inc.

Oliver walk-behind plow with long wooden body with large brass plow, stabilizing wheel and hitch, hand-painted in red and black with "Oliver's Patent" across top and on both handles and "Oliver's Combination Plow" on either side, overall very good condition with scattered paint chips and alligatoring to paint, 22-1/2" l. x 8-1/4" h. Provenance: Descended through the Oliver family that invented it. **$10,925**

James D. Julia, Inc.

Disc harrow, miniature farm implement with three rows of nine round discs and one row of perforated discs within a brass framework, perched above this unit is a formed saddle seat and a lever that raises and lowers the drag of the rear tines. Very good to excellent overall condition with a few discs having minor fleabites and one perforated disc with a few broken teeth, 14" l. x 13-1/2" w. x 6-1/4" h.. **$5,175**

James D. Julia, Inc.

Adriance Buckeye sickle bar mower, brass with marked gear box and stamped "140," raised, pierced saddle seat and long working sickle bar, spring loaded levers for idle switch and bar adjustment, very good condition with worn surfaces, traces of original paint, 18" w. x 14" l. x 7-3/4" h. **$5,175**

James D. Julia, Inc.

Grain separator, hand crank unit operates internal paddle mechanism to churn grain as it passes over mesh screen to gather finished product in drawer below, good condition, some paddle blades need to be reattached and hand crank reset with cotter pin, 16-1/2" l. x 11" w. x 13" t.................. **$1,840**

James D. Julia, Inc.

Seeder, manual gear-driven push machine consisting of long wooden hopper between two spoked steel wheels, when pushed along interior rod moves side to side distributing seed evenly, marked "L.R. Forney, Pat. June 6, 1876," very good condition with wear to wood, possibly replaced connection piece, 22" l. **$920**

James D. Julia, Inc.

Hay tender with original carrying case, triangular metal framework in red with green spoke wheels, one set for traction, gear driven, lever at two wheels adjusts height, turning gear by hand sets fingers into motion to fluff hay, appears to be missing piece or pieces of linkage mechanism to fully function properly, affixed with plaque reading "Dr. J.H. Goodell & Son, Model Makers Marseilles, Ill," original lined carrying case, very good condition with scattered paint chips, 17" l. x 15" w. **$6,325**

James D. Julia, Inc.

Harvester in brass and wood, formed saddle seat rests above large spoked wheel that, by means of chain drive, rotates series of rake arms that sweep wheat past sickle bar and into large receptacle, two levers adjust height of mower and wheels, gear/tool box stenciled "Leader," with wooden carrying case bottom, good to very good condition, one rake detached but present with some parts missing and some parts appearing to be replaced, case bottom is in good condition with a few missing slivers, 39" l. x 21" w. **$7,475**

James D. Julia, Inc.

Hay loader, wood frame and cast iron wheels, pulled behind a team of horses. When activated, tines rake the hay, which is then transported via a chain drive "elevator" that pulls the hay into a waiting wagon. Affixed with a metal plaque reading "Pat Ap'ld For," some areas need resoldering, otherwise generally very good condition, 11" w. x 12" h. x 12" d. ...**$11,500**

James D. Julia, Inc.

Casket, shaped pine box covered in fabric with aluminum carrying handles, braided pinstripe at head and foot, viewing window and hinged lid that open to reveal silk and muslin padded interior, embossed metal plaque stating "Portland Casket Co., Portland, Oregon," overall very good to near excellent condition, some fading to fabric and slight discoloration to and around aluminum handles, 8" l. x 3" h. x 3" d. **$826**

James D. Julia, Inc.

Railroad car/frame, large walnut frame base of railroad car with large wooden flange wheels with brass, steel and tin hardware, believed to be showing a railroad brake mechanism with tubes running to bellows and wheel brakes on underside, overall very good condition with some nicks and scratches, 35" l. x 11-1/2" w. x 5" h. **$1,207**

James D. Julia, Inc.

SALESMAN SAMPLES

Victorian door with etched glass panel, late 19th century, oak door with acid-etched glass panel depicting woman seated in a garden with a cherub at her feet, original finish to wood, original silvered plaque stating "R.C. Kuhn Sash & Door Co., LaCrosse, WIS.," etched into lower portion of glass panel is maker's name, overall very fine original condition, 26" h. x 11" w. **$1,725**

James D. Julia, Inc.

Coin-op toilet seat cover dispenser, cased display houses germ-free protective paper toilet seat covers for a nickel, distributed by St. George Paper Co. of New York City, very good to excellent condition, appears to be unused, 18-1/2" w. x 16" d. x 4-1/2" h............. **$920**

James D. Julia, Inc.

Scale model of Autocar military transport vehicle built by Autocar Co. in 1915 in Ardmore, Pennsylvania, one of two sales samples for a commercial vehicle show in New York City. Quarter-scale, closed-cab dump truck model with original olive drab paint and factory lettering, made of steel, brass, aluminum, iron, hardwood, leather, rubber, and canvas, precise replica of company's standard two-ton truck known as "the Mule" in World War I in Europe. Carbide-type headlamps, leather driver's seat cushions, cab-mounted klaxon horn, grease fittings, fully finned radiator core, 12-lug artillery spoke wheels and hard tires, functional gear shifts and brake levers, full leaf suspension, electric motor-driven shaft to lift two-section dump bed, roll-down side and front curtains, clutch, brake, and accelerator pedals mounted on diamond-plate cab floor, treated canvas fabric covers "C" cab frame assembled from tongue-in-groove hardwood slats over operator's compartment, bronze tow hooks mounted on chassis corners, engine crank at base of radiator shell, cast mounting steps on both sides of cab. Very good original condition with uniform wear and paint chips, 51" l. x 21" w. x 25" h. **$57,500**

James D. Julia, Inc.

Wooden wagon in red with black and yellow pinstripes and steel hardware, spoke wagon wheels reinforced with metal strips, generally good condition, overall minor paint chipping with slightly heavier chipping to front right hub, missing one hub ring, 30-1/2" l. x 7-1/2" h......**$1,437**

James D. Julia, Inc.

Two-wheel plow, nickel-plated brass model with two offset spoke wheels and heavy disc wheel at back, each is adjustable by its own hand lever, formed saddle seat with footrests over large plow blade with secondary blade above, very good to excellent condition with wear and dulling to finish, 12" l. x 8-1/2" w. **$4,025**

James D. Julia, Inc.

Seeder, nickel and wood with two large spoke wheels supporting formed saddle seat and wooden hinge top hopper leading to four curved, spring-loaded spikes that cut through soil, depositing seed through funneled tubes, two hand levers that adjust depth of spikes, very good condition with wear and chipping to painted wheels, one hand lever is missing handle, other has small split, 12" w. x 12" h. **$4,600**

James D. Julia, Inc.

Gale Chilled plow from Albion, Michigan company in old red paint with yellow and black highlights, hand-painted with patent dates from 1874 to 1876, below is a large, heavy steel blade with secondary blade above, decorated with fancy scrollwork and steel guiding wheel at front, good to very good condition, right handle has old repair and turned cross-piece between handles is a replacement, 26" l. x 11" h. **$8,625**

James D. Julia, Inc.

Animal trap, nickel spring-loaded device with custom wooden case that appears to have been made from an "Our Fairy" soapbox, very good to excellent condition, 8-1/2" l. **$690**

James D. Julia, Inc.

Wooden slat farm gate within wooden framework with steel hardware and latch mechanism, stenciled "Patented" on both sides, base swivels out for better stability, a few chips and scratches to paint, but structurally very good condition, 34" l. x 16" h. **$862**

James D. Julia, Inc.

Glider rocker garden seat, slat back, seat, foot rest, fully adjustable back rests, natural weathered finish on original base in worn red paint, overall very good to excellent condition, missing a couple of small pieces from base, 18" l. x 10" w. **$1,207**

James D. Julia, Inc.

Plow, all steel model in green with yellow spoke wheels with raised saddle seat and dual hand levers to adjust wheel height, third lever raises and lowers plow blade in conjunction with foot pedal, back turning wheel tied to front wheel, accompanied by two brass horses with leather trappings mounted to wooden bases, missing one cotter pin, otherwise very good overall condition, 22" l. x 16" w. x 9-1/2" h. Horses: 16" l. x 13" h. **$4,887**

James D. Julia, Inc.

Grinding station, brass model mounted to wood base consisting of three levels of flywheels presumably to be attached to belt drives, front of model allows for adjustment left to right and front to back against central grinding wheel, finished with a copper flash, very good to excellent condition, back legs don't appear to match shape and finish of front legs, 13" h. x 6-1/2" w. x 7-1/4" d....................................**$1,265**

James D. Julia, Inc.

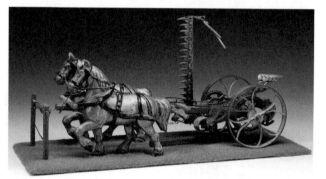

Sickle bar mower, cast brass model with curved spoke wheels and formed saddle seat and lever to raise and lower blades, gear box marked "Young Eagle," affixed to base with two cast iron work horses as a static display, tongue replaced to accommodate horses, original tongue is present, some paint touch-up and replaced flag at tip of sickle bar, 23" l. x 9" w..**$4,312**

James D. Julia, Inc.

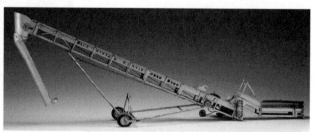

Ride-on plow, large steel plow blade between two large spoke wheels affixed with cast iron frame and wood post on which is mounted pierced formed saddle seat, unit has two levers, one adjusts height of right wheel, while other lever moves blade forward and back, some wear and scuffs to paint, overall very good to excellent condition, 15-1/2" l. x 7" w. x 10-1/2" h. **$575**

James D. Julia, Inc.

Hay bale or grain elevator, electric miniature machine consisting of a long conveyor belt leading to adjustable incline and adjustable chute mounted to wheeled base with rubber tires for transport, marked "Blue Master Bantam Seed Buro" on side, good condition, wheels show some flattening and loosening from hubs, electrics untested, 66" l. x 11" w. **$2,587**

James D. Julia, Inc.

Miniature steam station on cobblestone-type base on raised platform, three-unit plant consists of large boiler drum with steam gauge and piston leading to central drum leading to brass turbine with exhaust pipe, surrounded by nickel-plated fence, brass plaque reads "DeLaval Steam Turbine With Gravity Boiler Reduction Gear Box and High Speed Water Pump Circa 1930," very good to excellent condition, 22" l. x 13-1/2" d. x 12-1/2" h.............................. **$2,300**

James D. Julia, Inc.

Columbia washer, cubical wood model stenciled with patent dates of "Dec 3, 1895" on sides and "Manuf'd by Benbow Mfg. Co St. Louis, MO," interior line with corrugated metal and topped with gear mechanism that works agitating mechanism, underside fitted with pull-out drying rack, good condition with average wear and splits to wood, 12-1/2" w. x 11-1/2" d. x 19" h. **$920**

James D. Julia, Inc.

Seeder with ob, nickel plated piece with six spoked wheels supporting formed saddle seat and wooden hopper leading to six curved spring-loaded blades that cut through soil depositing seed through a conduit attached to rear of each blade, top of hopper has plaque that reads "E.A. Havens, Maker, Peoria, Illinois," original cloth-covered, felt-lined wooden carrying case, very good to excellent condition, case cover is deteriorating but still structurally sound, 18" l. x 11-1/2" w. x 11-1/2" h.........................**$7,475**

James D. Julia, Inc.

Horse-drawn yard roller consisting of wooden plank and tow tongue, below which are five heavy cast iron wheels, hand lever moves rollers back and forth for additional coverage, generally very good condition with a few replaced screws, 10" w. x 10-1/2" l. **$460**

James D. Julia, Inc.

Cebco coin-operated hot nut dispenser and leather case, glass globes intact with decals and red faceted jewel between coin slots that would light up, indicating machine was heating the nuts; on left side is cylindrical glass tube with aluminum base, which held paper cups, plus nickel plated steel tube; machine constructed of polished aluminum and overall condition is very fine to near mint with only minor loss to decals, case: 16-1/2" w. x 20" h., machine: 11-1/2" w. x 18" h.....................**$1,150**

James D. Julia, Inc.

Samplers & Needlework

Samplers: The name says it all. Avid seamstresses of the 1400s had no pattern books to turn to. Instead, when running across a unique stitch or pattern, the custom was to sew a small example of the new find on a piece of fabric: in other words, a "sampler."

The term is drawn from the Latin exemplum ("an example to be followed"). Over the years, these samplers, their designs quickly and randomly worked in the cloth, served as treasured three-dimensional reference guides. The conscientious needleworker used them to perfect her skill, while at the same time continuing to bolster her sampler collection.

The 1500s gave rise to "band samplers." Fabric was costly, and these very narrow cloth bands of six to nine inches were closely covered with stitchery, incorporating numerous styles and types of ornamentation, such as the use of metallic and multicolored threads. "Spot samplers" were popular in the 1600s. In this version, stitched motifs on silk were made to be cut out and used as ornamentation.

Since the first pattern book appeared in 1523, samplers had progressed past the point of serving as a means of sharing and preserving new patterns. Instead, the creation of a sampler became an art form in itself, an enduring exhibition of sewing expertise.

Early samplers were the province of skilled adult seamstresses. However, by the 1700s, the ability to successfully embroider a sampler was considered the mark of a girl's growing maturity. The pattern was no longer random. Instead, a variety of nature images (trees, fruits,

Italian needlepoint on silk, probably 19th century, some loose threads, 12-1/2" x 20". **$375**

Kaminski Auctions

flowers, birds, and animals) were now worked into a carefully planned overall picture. In its new incarnation, the sampler was viewed as an excellent learning tool. That educational aim is evidenced by the array of alphabet samplers, number samplers, almanac samplers, and even map samplers brought into being by their youthful embroiderers.

By the 1800s, the needle art was often accompanied by a stitched verse. Those verses drew heavily on the sort of Biblical quotations, moral platitudes, and uplifting poetry considered suitable for impressionable young minds. Personalization also played an important role, with the name of the maker and the date often stitched into the design, and even at times incorporated into the verse.

With the growing availability of printed pattern books, the sampler format became increasingly more regimented; full designs proved easy to emulate, with only slight variations. Originality took the form of new themes suited to the locale. In the United States, patriotic and homespun images (eagles, farm scenes, and liberty bells) proved favorites. Church sewing circles specialized in Biblical figurals.

Collectors of samplers focus on such measurable factors as age of the work; overall design; skill of execution; and use of color. Signed samplers are in high demand, with signed-and-dated samplers among the most desirable. Condition also plays an important role, particularly if the sampler is intended for display. However, if the sampler is a unique one, any age-related damage can be outweighed by its rarity. For a vintage sampler with damage, only professional restoration is recommended, and only if absolutely necessary; incompetent work will decrease the sampler's value.

Small framed crewelwork panel, dated 1787, stitched with silk threads on twilled wool ground depicting a stylized basket issuing several flowers on curving stems, over stitched monogram "PC" over a "2" and the year "1787," period molded wood frame, toning to background fabric, sight size 6-1/2" x 6-1/2". **$1,599**

Skinner, Inc., www.skinnerinc.com

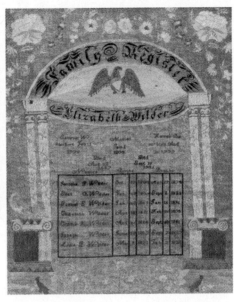

Needlework family register executed by Elizabeth Wilder (1811-1873), Lancaster, Massachusetts, circa 1822, stitched with silk threads on linen ground depicting vital statistics of Sawyer Wilder (1779-1837), Hannah Bailey (1777-1846), and their seven children, under arch inscribed "Family Register" over eagle, American shield, and "Elizabeth Wilder" in large letters, flanked by columns on plinths encircled with flowering vines, one plinth set with cornucopia and two birds, minor toning and fading, sight size 21" x 17". **$3,360**

Skinner, Inc., www.skinnerinc.com

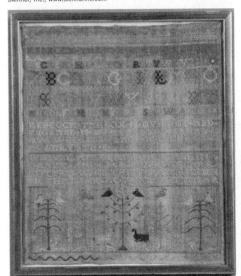

Needlework sampler, "REBECCA TARBOX BORN SEPTEMBER THE 30 1739," Wenham, Massachusetts, stitched with silk threads on linen ground, Rebecca's signature and birth date above alphabets and verses, "REBECCA TARBOX IS MY NAME AND ENGLAND IS MY NATION/WENHAM IS MY DWELLING PLACE AND CHRIST IS MY SALVATION" and "WHEN I AM DEAD AND LADE IN GRAVE AND ALL MY BONES ARE ROTTEN/WHEN THIS YOU SEE REMEMBE[R] ME THAT I BE NOT FORGOTTEN," and a panel depicting scene with sheep, birds perched in trees, top and bottom with undulating line borders, later molded giltwood frame, fading, toning, losses, 13-1/2" x 11-1/2". **$584**

Skinner, Inc., www.skinnerinc.com

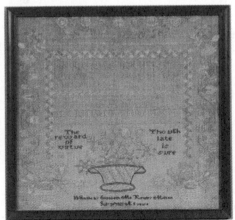

Needlework sampler "Wrought by Elizabeth McKendry Milton/July 20th 1821 AE 11 years," Massachusetts, stitched with silk threads on linen ground, depicting central reserve with rows of alphabets over basket of flowers flanked by a pious verse, potted flowering plants forming border on three sides, later molded wood frame, fading, toning, 16-3/4" x 17-3/4". **$510**

Skinner, Inc., www.skinnerinc.com

Needlework sampler executed by Sarah (Sally) Weston, Dilworthtown, Chester County, Pennsylvania, circa 1800, worked in silk threads on linen ground, depicting rows of alphabets over names of Sarah's parents and six siblings above a scene with yellow house, pine tree, flowering tree, bird, rose bush, and strawberries, molded tiger maple frame, scattered background losses, fading, toning, light staining, 16-1/4" x 14".. **$720**

Skinner, Inc., www.skinnerinc.com

Early sampler from Franklin, Warren County, Ohio, 1827, with floral border, rows of alphabets and numbers, symmetrical building at bottom, surrounded by trees on either side, inscribed "Sally T. Schencks. Franklin. W.C.O. / Through all the changeing scenes of life / in trouble or in joy / oh may the praises of my God / my heart and tongue imploy," discolored, light stain at right margin, 15-1/2" x 19" (sight), 20-1/2" x 24" (frame)..**$11,400**

Cowan's Auctions, Inc.

Pennsylvania silk on linen sampler, circa 1820, wrought by Sarah Jenkins Weaver, 16-1/2" x 17" **$889**

Pook & Pook, Inc.

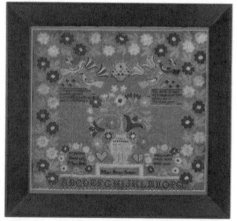

Pennsylvania wool needlework, dated 1847 and wrought by Mary Beyer, 19" x 21". **$851**

Pook & Pook, Inc.

English 18th century needlework of a lady surrounded by animals and birds, 8-1/4" x 10-1/4" (sight), 12-1/2" x 14-1/2" (frame). **$1,200**

Kaminski Auctions

SAMPLERS & NEEDLEWORK

Rare set of three Massachusetts silk on linen samplers, wrought by sisters Mary Jane, Deborah, and Sarah Allen, daughters of Captain Rufus and Deborah Allen, in 1832, 1829, and 1827, 16-1/2" x 17"..... **$5,925**

Pook & Pook, Inc.

Rare important early stump work (embroidery where stitched figures are raised from surface of work to form three-dimensional effect), 18th century, gold thread and seed pearls, decorated with a queen surrounded by animals, insects and flowers, 15" h. x 16-3/4" (sight), 19-3/4" (frame). **$1,500**

Kaminski Auctions

Science and Technology

Science and technology shows bright promise for collectors and investors. The reasons are many: It is not limited to a production year and the oldest examples become more appealing as contemporary technology improves. Auction houses are creating new departments in these categories and are now holding biannual sales. Although science and technology are combined in this section, they generally represent two distinct collecting categories.

Vintage Technology

Strictly speaking, the earliest development of human technology would involve crude tools for getting things done more quickly. The most famous technological advancement is, of course, the wheel, invented in the 4th millennium B.C. Early scientific objects that show some foreshadowing of future technological breakthroughs are highly desirable. Astrolabes were first used by astronomers, navigators and even astrologers to locate the positions of the sun, moon, planets and stars. Surviving examples developed in the Persian Empire as early as the 10th or 11th centuries have brought as much as $50,000 to $190,000 at auction.

Generally speaking, most collectors of science and technology focus on objects that were developed or mass-produced during the Industrial Revolution (steam engines, bicycles, interchangeable parts) through the present day (telephones, spacecraft, computing). Oddball examples (or outright failures) remain the most desirable of all scientific objects because they are unique and offer a "missing link" in mankind's pursuit to bigger and better technological advancements.

One of the first books devoted to collecting vintage technology was published in 2001. *Miller's: Collecting Science & Technology* by Lindsay Stirling and George Glastris is the first true guide to the subject. *Eccentric Contraptions and Amazing Gadgets, Gizmos and Thingamabobs* by Maurice Collins, published by David & Charles in 2005, focused on an object's form and function rather than its value and dimensions.

Since then, a number of websites devoted to technology collectors have been launched to cover a broad and always-growing hobby. There are websites devoted to 20th century technological collectibles such as old computers, handheld computers or personal digital assistants, televisions, robots, cell phones, calculators, video game consoles and even calculators. More sites exist for vintage scientific instrument collectors and even those devoted to the grandfather of the modern word processor: the typewriter. There is even a small but growing group of young collectors eagerly scooping up items relating to the history of the Internet, which was first envisioned as early as 1934 by Belgian lawyer and librarian Paul Otlet. The Internet has fundamentally altered how humans communicate, do business and solve problems, and it was only a matter of time before nostalgia sparked a race to accumulate items relating to its cultural impact.

Science and Natural History

A science or natural history collector refers to one who pursues natural objects. These were the first collectors – historically speaking – who became financially secure enough to amass a group of curious objects that piqued their interest. These collections formed the basis of the wunderkammer or "cabinet of curiosities," which eventually evolved into the modern museum in the 1500s. Minerals, meteorites and natural history, among others, all fall within this area,

and all of them are enjoying a renaissance among wealthy collectors.

American auction houses have found a new market in offering fossils, fine minerals and meteorites at auction. Prices realized range from a few hundred dollars for a specimen of azurite to as much as $2.7 million, which was paid in 2011 for two complete allosaurus and stegosaurus skeletons.

As fascinating as the science and natural history hobby is, it largely operates behind closed doors. The leading event for this hobby remains the Tucson Gem & Mineral Show, held annually in Tucson, Arizona. China offered a credible challenge to the event's dominance in the hobby by hosting the first China (Changsha) International Mineral & Gem Show in 2013. Heritage Auctions seeks further still to redefine the auction market for fine minerals with The Hoppel Collection, considered the most significant private fine mineral collection ever to be auctioned.

"We expect The Hoppel Collection to redefine the mineral collecting hobby in two ways," says James Walker, Director of Fine Minerals for Heritage. "First, it holds items that are rarely seen outside of museums or institutions. Second, for the first time, the collection will create a body of publicly available information, including prices, which collectors can use to estimate comparable values for similar objects. It stands to move the hobby away from ambiguous, covert pricing toward an open, market-driven approach, basically redefining the entire mineral collecting arena."

Thanks to the effort to bring transparency to the science category and a young demographic fascinated by vintage tech, the collecting categories for both science and technology are dynamic and stand to grow in the near future. As values rise, it just might be time to blow the dust off your old rock collection and your vintage Texas Instruments calculator.

J & W Cary George III terrestrial globe, J & W Cary, London, England, circa 1815, marks: Cary's New Terrestrial Globe with ring listing months and constellations, set in satinwood tripod base with ebonized details supporting compass, 46" h. x 29" w. **$21,250**

Heritage Auctions

SCIENCE & TECHNOLOGY

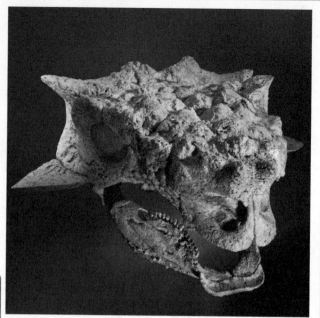

Dinosaur skull, Saichania chulsanensis, Cretaceous, Campanian stage, Central Asia, complete skull, raised over stained oak base, 14" l. x 21" w. x 17-1/2" h. overall, including base. **$62,500**

Heritage Auctions

TOP LOT!

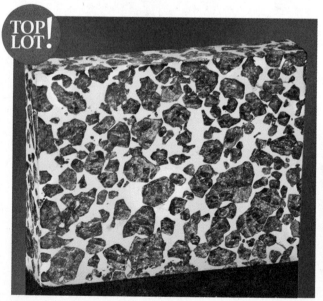

Meteorite, pallasite – PAL, Fukang, Xinjiang Uyghur Autonomous Region (44° 26' N, 87° 38' E), sculpture fashioned from legendary Fukang meteorite recovered in China's Gobi Desert, comprised of approximately 50% olivine and peridot crystals suspended in 50% nickel-iron, pallasitic meteorites originated from mantle-core boundary of large planetary body between Mars and Jupiter that broke apart during formation of solar system, Keith Jenkerson, 8-1/2" x 6" x 2".
....**$112,900**

Heritage Auctions

Cobaltoan calcite with malachite, katanga copper crescent, katanga (shaba), Democratic Republic of Congo (Zaïre), custom labeled base, 4"x 3"x 2". **$86,500**

Heritage Auctions

Quartz "Herkimer Diamond," Ace of Diamonds Mine, Middleville, Town of Newport, Herkimer County, New York; Herkimer "diamonds" are a brilliant and limpid form of quartz found in environs of Herkimer; excellent condition, custom labeled acrylic base, 3" x 2-1/2" x 1-1/2".
....**$18,750**

Heritage Auctions

Dolomite and calcite, unusual bicolored Franklin fluorescent, Sterling Hill, Sussex County, New Jersey, such specimens are found in both Franklin proper and at Sterling Hill, the source of this example, 5-1/2" x 3-1/2" x 2-1/2". **$212**

Heritage Auctions

SCIENCE & TECHNOLOGY

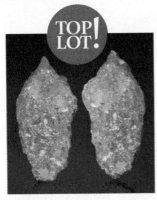

Fossil, Diplomystus dentatus, Knightia eocaena, Eocene, Green River Formation, Lincoln County, Wyoming, rare instance of giant Diplomystus that choked to death eating a Knightia, gray-cream limestone matrix, 16" x 30-7/8"...**$6,875**

Heritage Auctions

Lunar breccia – LUN, Libya (27° 22' 30" N, 16° 11' 4" E), fourth largest portion of moon available for private acquisition, DaG 1058 is a lunar highland breccia from far side of moon with single largest surface area to mass ratio of any of largest lunar meteorites. **$330,000**

Heritage Auctions

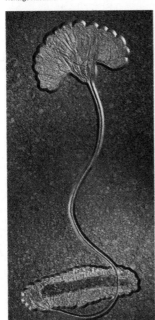

Fossil, Troodontidae: Jinfengopteryx elegans, Cretaceous, Central Asia; Troodontidae were small to medium-sized theropod raptors that flourished at end of dinosaurs' reign, 28" l. x 17-1/2" h...........**$32,000**

Heritage Auctions

Fossil, Seirocrinus subangularis, Lower Jurassic, Posidonienschiefer Formation, Holzmaden, Baden-Württemburg, Germany; Crinoid, known also as the Sea Lily or Feather Star, is one of the world's so-called "living fossils" with species still to be found in today's oceans from Indonesia to Caribbean, 84-3/8" x 44-1/4". **$40,625**

Heritage Auctions

Industrial glass-top painted iron console, 29-1/2" h. x 51" w. x 29" d. **$1,188**

Doyle New York

SCIENCE & TECHNOLOGY

Altazimuth theodolite, 18th century, rare, glazed brass, cased with brass geometric instruments, pens and rules; wooden case original with heavy protective brass fittings, lid crudely engraved "1767" with initials "G.H."; instrument is probably earlier than owner's mark on case, lined with combed paste paper, alidade signed "HD," maker unknown. **$5,313**

Doyle New York

TOP LOT!

Apple 1 personal computer, Apple Computer Co., 1976, working, rare, one of 200 units produced; of 43 known surviving examples, only six are in working order, hand-built by Steve Wozniak, retaining original period peripherals – transformer, Panasonic 2102 cassette recorder, Sony monitor and Datanetics ASCII keyboard – in addition to reprints of original manual and schematic diagram signed by " Wozniak." Wozniak's friend, Steve Jobs, had the idea of selling the computer..**$640,000**

Auction Team Breker

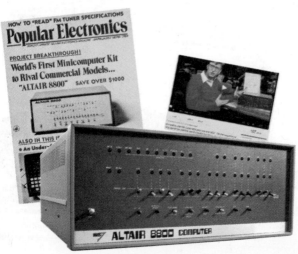

◀ MITS Altair 8800 personal computer, 1975, considered to be first documented "microcomputer kit"; the success of the Altair 8800 inspired inventors Steve Wozniak and Steve Jobs to create the Apple 1, as well as inspiring inventor Bill Gates and Paul Allen to produce a BASIC Interpreter for the system, leading to establishment of Microsoft, Inc. in April 1975. Advertised on front cover of January issue of *Popular Electronics*.....................**$16,000**

Auction Team Breker

Ross, London, binocular microscope No. 5115, England, made of lacquered brass, eyepieces with rackwork adjustment, coarse focus, prism mounted above dual nosepiece with objectives marked C Zeiss, circular stage, X and Y adjustments, and plano/concave mirror on swing arm, V-base marked ROSS, LONDON 5115, bull's-eye condenser on stand and two brass objective cases. **$1,680**

Skinner, Inc., www.skinnerinc.com

Astrolabe, brass, Persian, circa 19th century, engraved, with four plates, 7". **$910**

Auction Team Breker

Fuller calculator, W.F. Stanley & Co., London, model no. 1, with 6-1/2" paper label cylinder mounted on spiral logarithmic calculating scale, metal indexing arm with scale .02-.98, housed in finger-jointed mahogany box with paper label, instruction manual, and arm attachment, 17" l..**$780**

Skinner, Inc., www.skinnerinc.com

Binocular, Zeiss, stainless steel, WWII 12X60 spotting binocular, circa 1940, 2-1/4" dia. optics, individually adjusting eyepieces with angle-mounted prism, left eyepiece having a lever for interpupillary adjusting, flip-up adjustable headpiece, mounted center plaque stating Jumelle 12 x 60, mounted on original adjustable tripod, 51" h... **$4,500**

Skinner, Inc., www.skinnerinc.com

Single-cylinder steam engine model, brass, iron and steel, four-pillar model, double-action cylinder, two water taps, slide valve control, strong feed pump, working governor and flywheel with belt pulley, circa 1850, 34-3/4" overall h. Provenance: From the French Naval Academy. **$5,370**

Auction Team Breker

Meteorite, iron, fine octahedrite – IVA, Great Nama Land, Namibia. Provenance: Includes a loan to American Museum of Natural History in New York City.
....**$46,875**

Heritage Auctions

Transit, W. & L.E. Gurley, Troy, New York, 11" brass telescope, 6" silvered compass dial signed by maker, needle dial calibrated 0-90 in four quadrants, blued steel hand, dual spirit levels, vernier read out, brass leveling screws for tripod attachment, mounted on a board, approximately 12-1/2" l.
....**$615**

Skinner, Inc., www.skinnerinc.com

▶ Exhibition surgical set, George Tiemann and Co., 67 Chatham Street, New York, 1876, ruby-set mother-of-pearl-handled implements including large and small bone saw, four surgical knives, capillary hook, nippers and tweezers-forceps, fitted compartments with tourniquet, needles, wire sutures, and lidded container with eight additional rubies, all in felt-lined, silver-bound, rosewood carrying case with original gilt leather maker's tag. **$85,200**

Skinner, Inc., www.skinnerinc.com

Mahogany traveling apothecary cabinet, circa 1900, hinged lid opening to circular divided compartments housing colorless glass and porcelain jars, mixing bowls, associated lids, seven test tubes, lower drawer with small pewter mixing bowl, group of W.T. & Co. filter papers and other related medical items, 10-3/4" l. x 7" h. x 7-1/2" w. **$720**

Skinner, Inc., www.skinnerinc.com

▲ Steam engine, demonstration model to drive beams, working, manufactured by Eugène Bourdon, circa 1850, France. **$57,600**

Auction Team Breker

Stereoscope, Brewster-pattern, green marbleized, circa 1855, wedge-shaped body with ground glass for illuminating tissue or glass views, pair of lenses at rear, 6-3/4" h. x 8" w. x 4-1/2" d.
....**$480**

Skinner, Inc., www.skinnerinc.com

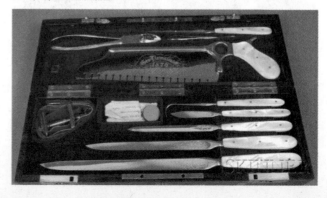

Swiss miniature phonograph manufactured by Casimir Sivan, Geneva, December 1892, originally a trial run for what he would call the "Talking Pocket Watch," a spring-driven phonograph with a disc that announced the time. Sivan was a watchmaker and would become the first Swiss motion-picture maker. **$14,300**

Auction Team Breker

Pinwheel calculator, Odhner Arithmometer, circa 1886, model considered first Russian calculator as developed by W.T. Odhner, a Swedish immigrant. **$8,450**

Auction Team Breker

Thatcher calculator, patented by Edwin Thatcher, November 1881, Keuffel & Esser, New York, model 4012, no. 2134, with inner cylinder and outer scales, on mahogany base in finger-jointed mahogany box, 22-1/2" w. **$1,020**

Skinner, Inc., www.skinnerinc.com

Cipher machine, three-rotor Enigma Ciphering Machine, circa 1943, three rotors, working, used by British code-breakers at Bletchley Park to break German-produced codes and contributing to end of World War II, accompanied by scarce metal carrying case. **$56,000**

Auction Team Breker

Spiral apparatus, brass, steel, cast iron, mid-19th century, black-painted cast iron base, graduating brass gear wheels, all housed in a compartmentalized mahogany case with hinged lid, bail handles, 24" l. x 16" w. x 4-1/2" h....... **$2,520**

Skinner, Inc., www.skinnerinc.com

Lathe, Holtzapffel & Co. Rose Engine Lathe No. 1636 and Cabinet of Accessories, London, 1838, mahogany bench with 6" center lathe and complete assortment of accoutrements, including chuck and other components, 76" h. x 37-1/2" w. x 18-1/2" d........................**$228,000**

Skinner, Inc., www.skinnerinc.com

10 Things You Didn't Know About Collectible Telephones

1   On March 7, 1876, Alexander Graham Bell filed a patent for the telephone. It's reported that Bell filed his patent just two hours ahead of a request for a similar device, filed by Elisha Gray, working with inventor Thomas A. Edison. Ownership of the invention of the telephone is steeped in controversy and was the focus of extensive legal battles. In the end, the courts recognized Bell as the official inventor of the telephone.

2   A Charles Williams Coffin telephone, circa 1878, mounted on a display board with a Samson glass battery and other related items, sold for $12,000, while a Ericsson wooden candlestick telephone, circa 1895, sold for $9,000, to claim the top two spots in a Feb. 24-25, 2012 sale at Morphy Auctions. The two phones, which were among 141 vintage telephones sold, fetched more than double their low estimates.

Measuring 12" x 12-1/2", this Ericsson wooden candlestick telephone, circa 1895, earned $9,000 – exceeding the presale estimate of $4,000-$8,000 – during a sale in February 2012.

Morphy Auctions

3   The current Guinness World Record for the largest collection of telephones is 1,135, held by Mike and Mary Phillips of Zebulon, Georgia.

4   While the number of museums and exhibits dedicated to more niche collecting areas, like telephones, have declined, there are no less than 10 active telephone museums in the United States today, including the Georgia Rural Telephone Museum, which is said to house the world's largest collection of telephones and related memorabilia.

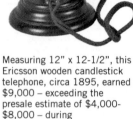

5   One of the very first songs with a telephone theme was "Hello! Ma Baby" released in 1899, written by Andrew B. Sterling and published on the legendary Tin Pan Alley in New York.

6   Two of the largest active telephone collector clubs include the Antique Telephone Collectors Association (www.atcaoline.com) formed in 1971 and the Telephone Collectors International (TCI) organization (www.telephoncollectors .org) formed in 1986.

This rare grouping, which sold for $12,000, includes a Charles Williams Coffin telephone, circa 1878, wooden Butterstamp receiver, reproduction Blake transmitter, copy of 1878 New Haven directory, Samson glass battery, and street sign.

Morphy Auctions

7   Vintage phones – especially the Western Electric 203 model designed by Henry Dreyfuss – are finding favor among interior designers as the demand for classic retro décor is on the rise.

8   Telephone companies were among the first types of businesses, along with oil companies, to use porcelain signs in the early 1900s to advertise their services. Today those signs are among the most highly sought-after advertising signs.

9   In addition to Western Electric, some of the big names in telephones are Kellogg Switchboard and Telephone Co., Stromberg-Carlsen Telephone Manufacturing Co., and Automatic Electric Co.

10 A lot has changed in the 137 years since Bell made that first call to Watson, who was just down the hall from him. Today Bell could call Watson and enjoy a crystal clear connection whether he was down the hall or across the globe – and he'd have the option to use video chat if he wanted to.

Compiled by Antoinette Rahn. Sources: History.com; Antique Telephone Collectors Association (www.atcaoline.com); Telephone Collectors International (www.telephoncollectors .org); Georgia Rural Telephone Museum (www.grtm.com); www.antiquetelephonehistory.com; Guinness World Records; Songwriters Hall of Fame; Morphy Auctions (www.morphyauctions.com); Modern Home Today (www.modernhometoday.com); Porcelain Signs (www.porcelainsigns.com); Antique Telephone History Website (www.antiquetelephonehistory.com)

SILVER

Silver

Sterling silver (standard silver) is an alloy made of silver and copper and is harder than pure silver. It is used in the creation of sterling silver flatware (silverware) as well as tea services, trays, salvers, goblets, water and wine pitchers, candlesticks and centerpieces. Coin silver is slightly less pure than sterling.

The value of silver has seen steady growth since the first indications of the Great Recession in late 2008. From a low of $8.92 in November 2008, silver prices topped out at $48.48 in May 2011 and hit a plateau between $25 and $35 in late 2012 and early 2013. Silver prices are so high that in some cases the auction value of an antique or collectible silver object is nearly identical to the prices paid for scrap silver. This presents a quandary for newly inherited silver and a looming threat for unique works produced by craftsmen: High melt prices threaten objects whose designs enhance its value among collectors or institutions.

Silversmithing in America goes back to the early 17th century in Boston and New York and the early 18th century in Philadelphia. Boston artisans were influenced by English styles, New Yorkers by Dutch. American manufacturers began to switch to the sterling standard about the time of the U.S. Civil War.

"For those of us dedicated to the world of antiques and art, the idea of scrapping is difficult to take, but we know that it is an option for people looking to generate income from unwanted objects," said Skinner Auctioneers, Inc. CEO Karen Keane on the Skinner blog. "But with all things being equal, before making that decision, we encourage investigating selling your silver at auction rather than melting it down."

Take, for example, the American Gorham silver martelé vase #1838. Although highly decorative, the vase looks similar to many silver vases produced at the turn of the 20th century. In the hands of a novice, the 34.6 troy oz. piece would have been scrapped out for about $835 based on early 2013 spot silver prices. According to the Gorham archives, production of vase #1838 began on March 29, 1899 and required 38 hours to produce, plus an additional 34 hours of chasing. That's nearly a full two weeks of labor for one vase. Martelé is softer and purer (950/1000 parts of silver than sterling's 925/1000 parts) in order to make the silver more malleable and easier to work by hand. Each martelé object begins as a flat piece of silver, raised with hammering to the desired shape before being passed on to the chaser. The finished pieces show hammer marks because they were not buffed. Rather than fall victim to the smelter, this martelé silver vase (shown at right) brought $22,500 at Heritage Auctions in 2013.

This is but one reason why it's important to take a piece of silver to an auction house for inspection before you consider a dealer or scrap metal buyer. A seller should know both the spot silver price as well as the historical or decorative price in order to make the best decisions. Some dealers do not deal in silver weight and couldn't care less about current spot silver prices.

American, vase, Gorham, martelé silver, circa 1899, marks: (lion-anchor-g under eagle), 950-1000 fine, 1838, (sickle), 13-1/4" h., 34.6 troy oz. **$22,500**

SILVER

!

In addition to relatively high silver melt values, older silver objects suffer another threat. American dealers often lament that young buyers are turned off by the thought of owning silver. It's seen as a high-maintenance object. What they may not know is that fine silver of some quality actually improves in value if it's used rather than stored.

What silver objects are likely to increase in value? High quality silver objects from American name-brand makers, such as Gorham, Tiffany, Towle, Stieff, and Reed & Barton, remain desirable and represent a solid purchase. Functional pieces will survive longer than those that are purely decorative.

There exist a number of excellent resources on the topic of sterling silver. The most famous continues to be *Discovering Hallmarks on English Silver* by John Bly. This 1968 book was recently re-released in 2008 by Shire Publishing and remains the mainstay for English hallmarks. Flatware is well covered in *Warman's Sterling Silver Flatware*, 2nd edition, by Phil Dreis. However, a 21st century generation of resources is available on tablets and tablet personal computers: Dealer Steve Freeman developed a free app for iPad users offering a free library of hundreds of images of English silver makers' marks. The SilverMakers app was released in March 2012 and offers an easy way to find marks based on the object's intended use, marks, and even silver content.

TOP LOT!

English, caviar server, G.J. Dennis, Elizabeth II, 2002, marks: (lion passant), (leopard's head), (jubilee mark), ee, c, 925, 33-1/2" l., originally commissioned by the Silver Fund, London, England, 1,196 troy oz. **$68,500**

Heritage Auctions

American, sandwich tray, Tiffany & Co., circa 1892-1902, pattern no. 11145, shell form, decorated with chased and repoussé rocaille motifs and pierced border, irregular rim, bun feet, 16" l., approximately 34 oz..................................**$4,063**

Doyle New York

American, tea service, Spaulding-Gorham, Inc., Art Deco, circa 1929, kettle on stand, teapot, creamer, two-handled covered sugar bowl, waste bowl, each with paneled sides and shoulders, 10-3/4" h., approximately 84 oz..................................**$2,500**

Doyle New York

American, coffee pot and creamer, Alphonse La Paglaia (American, 1907-1953), for International Silver Co., after 1952, marks: International Sterling, La Paglaia designed, 9 cups, 4, 13901; 13904, 10" h. 100.1 oz. (gross). **$2,500**

Heritage Auctions

American, cigar box, Smith & Smith, accented with 9 karat gold and tiger's eye, circa 1950, marks: Smith & Smith, Sterling, 16, 1-7/8" h. x 9" l. x 6-1/2" w. (not including figures), 25.43 troy oz. silver; .36 troy oz. **$1,875**

Heritage Auctions

American, creamer and covered sugar bowl, Peter Muller-Munk Studio, New York, circa 1930, marks: Peter Müller-Munk, (p inside circle), hand-wrought sterling silver, 925 (over) 1000, 5-1/4" h. 21.4 oz. (gross). **$31,250**

Heritage Auctions

French, tea service, Puiforcat, ivory, teapot, hot water kettle on stand, two-handled covered sugar bowl, creamer, waste bowl, two-handled shaped rectangular tray, each with paneled sides, kettle on stand: 17-1/2" h., tray: 27-1/2" l., total approximately 336 oz. **$11,250**

Doyle New York

Austro-Hungarian, smoking set, Art Deco, tray, cigarette box, matchbook holder with ashtray, two graduated holders, match holder and five individual ashtrays, tray: 17" l., total approximately 58 oz. **$1,750**

Doyle New York

▼ English, tea and coffee service, Walter Morrisse, London, England, circa 1849-1850, Victorian, marks to tea and coffee pots, creamer and sugar bowl: (lion passant), (leopard's head), (duty mark), James and William Marshall, 13-3/4" h. 155.4 oz. (gross). **$6,250**

Heritage Auctions

Mexican, centerpiece, circa 1940, maker unknown, marks: Sterling 925 plata, 7-1/4" h. 16.7 troy oz...**$1,625**

Heritage Auctions

Austrian, wine ewers, circa 1870, baluster form ewer with etched glass set in silver mounts with winged griffin finial holding shield, marks: WC, (Diana's head with 3 and A), 14-1/8" h............. **$5,312**

Heritage Auctions

American, bowl, Gorham, with handles, 6-1/2", approximately 14 oz. **$875**

Doyle New York

American, flask, Tiffany & Co., New York, NY, circa 1892-1902, motoring scene, marks: Tiffany & Co., 7076 makers 5289, sterling silver 925-1000, t, 1-3/4" gills, 5-3/4" h., 7.3 oz. (gross). .. **$3,250**

Heritage Auctions

Portuguese, candy dish, Rococo-style .833, post-1938, marked on top of dish, tripartite form with engraved stylized floral and foliate designs on textured ground, large cast handle in form of winged cherub seated on abstract mass of scrolling leaves or waves, with three small cherubs applied to outside of dish, 5-1/4" h. x 6" w., approximately 17.8 troy oz. . **$738**

Skinner, Inc., www.skinnerinc.com

Israeli, menorah, modernist .935, circa mid-late 20th century, attributed to Gumbel, u-shaped candle arms with conical sconces on spade-shaped base pierced with scriptural quote in stylized Hebrew lettering, marks: Handmade Israel 935, 13-1/2" h., approximately 15 troy oz. **$1,422**

Skinner, Inc., www.skinnerinc.com

American, centerpiece, Empire style, tapering circular form, paneled sides, domed octagonal base ending in pierced rose decorated scrolling feet, cobalt molded glass insert, 17" h., 8-5/8" dia...................... **$1,375**

Doyle New York

American, coffee and tea service with tray, Gorham, designed by Donald Colflesh, circa 1970, marks: (lion-anchor-g), Gorham, Sterling, 7, 1461, 1 pint; 1462, 2-3/4 pint; 1463; 1464, 3/4 pint; 1468, 26-1/2" dia., 252.3 oz. (gross)................ **$30,000**

Heritage Auctions

Mexican, tea and coffee service, hot water kettle on stand, coffee pot, teapot, creamer, covered two-handled sugar bowl, waste bowl, oval two-handled tray, each vessel with gadrooned sides and acanthus leaf decorated rims, kettle: 15-1/4" h., tray: 27-1/4", approximately 280 oz................................... **$7,500**

Doyle New York

India, picture frame, maker unknown, 1913, patterned with flora and fauna and capped by Maharaja crest, 25" h. x 17-1/2" w. **$46,875**

Heritage Auctions

Italian, compote, shallow circular bowl on twisted twig-form standard continuing to bacchanalian satyr and nymph, bowl with grape clusters, leaves and vines, on gilt domed stepped circular foot, 9-3/8" h., 10" dia., approximately 52 oz....................... **$2,125**

Doyle New York

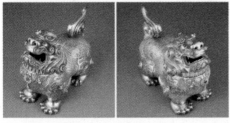

Mongolian, censers, pair, lion-form, removable heads raised with open mouths, gilded detailing and inset turquoise and coral beading, 9-1/2" l. **$3,750**

Doyle New York

French, table box, Schroth, enamel and mahogany, 20th century, plaque signed: Belliard, 3" d. x 14" l. x 9-3/4" w.. **$1,625**

Heritage Auctions

Mexico, center bowl, Tiffany & Co., makers, New York, large, marked on base rim: Sterling, Mexico, Tane, numbers not decipherable, Eagle with 71 lunt 49, 3-3/4" h., 9-1/2" dia., total wt. 27 troy oz. **$7,200**

Skinner, Inc., www.skinnerinc.com

American, candleholder, hand-wrought by Henry Petzal, silversmith (1906-2002), La Jolla, California, and Lenox, Massachusetts, 1968, cylindrical candle cup within three tiers of petaled leaves with veining, marks: Sterling Silver, handwrought, on base, 3-3/4" h. x 10-1/2" w., approximately 43 troy oz. **$4,800**

Skinner, Inc., www.skinnerinc.com

American, ladle with stand, Henry Petzal silversmith (1906-2002) hand wrought sterling silver, La Jolla, California, and Lenox, Massachusetts, 1966, deep bowl with side spout on long handle with shaped terminus, marks with artist's initials: handwrought, sterling, 1979 over 2 in a circle, 16" dia., 5-5/8" w., 15 troy oz., lg... **$2,760**

Skinner, Inc., www.skinnerinc.com

American, charger, Mary Catherine Knight (American, 1876-1956), handicraft shop, circa 1902-1911, rim decorated with repeating tooled floral motifs, center monogrammed KCW, stamped with maker's mark, handicraft shop stamp and Sterling, bearing museum accession number in red paint, 12-3/4" dia., 31 troy oz. **$3,240**

Skinner, Inc., www.skinnerinc.com

German, five musician figures, Art Nouveau, circa 1900, playing French horn, oboe, flute and two violins, all in period dress raised on decorated domed base, marks 925, with German hallmarks and maker's mark for Ludwig Neresheiemer and Co. Hanau, 6" h., approximately 45 troy oz. total weight. **$3,600**

Skinner, Inc., www.skinnerinc.com

American, punch bowl, Tiffany & Co., New York, commemorating the opening of F.W. Woolworth building in New York City in 1913; round footed bowl with notched rim over band with raised inscribed in gold, over border of alternating large and small pendant trefoils intercepted with shield-shaped reserve with raised gold monogram, bowl interior centered with chased depiction of F.W. Woolworth building, supported on round molded base, impressed maker's marks on base, 9-5/8" h. 17" dia., approximately 222 troy oz....................**$42,000**

Skinner, Inc., www.skinnerinc.com

Italian, watering can, circa 20th century, hinged lid with waisted finial, cylindrical body with gadrooned shoulders, molded bands, applied flower spray, tapered angular spout, wood handle, 9-3/4" h., approximately 24.2 troy oz. **$900**

Skinner, Inc., www.skinnerinc.com

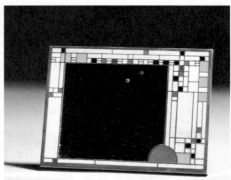

American, frame, Frank Lloyd Wright/Tiffany & Co., enamel and silver, circa 20th century, rectangular form with green, orange, and black enamel accents within silver grid, after FLW iconic window design, hinged stand, marks: Tiffany & Co. Sterling 925, FLW, sight: 3-3/8" h. x 3-5/8" w., 4-5/16" h. overall......... **$2,400**

Skinner, Inc., www.skinnerinc.com

Russian, tea service, Nemirov-Kolodkin, circa 1896-1908, teapot, two-handled covered sugar bowl, teacup, oval basket with swing handle, each engraved with a reserve containing monogram, teapot: 5-3/4" h., basket: 9" l., total approximately 57 oz..... **$2,813**

Doyle New York

Israeli or Italian, Kiddush cups, set of two, one in original box, circa 1860, marks: 13, 3-3/8" h., 5.01 troy oz. **$300**

Heritage Auctions

Scottish, curling trophy, Edinburgh, circa 19th century, possible maker's mark for Hamilton & Inches, hinged circular form, chased band to center and stylized curling handle finial that opens to reveal gold-washed interior top with glass container for inkwell, raised on crossed broomsticks with four feet, 3" h., approximately 6.55 troy oz.................. **$1,800**

Skinner, Inc., www.skinnerinc.com

English, tea service, International "Wedgwood," teapot, creamer, two-handled open sugar, waste bowl, each piece decorated with band of medallions and scrollwork to waist, all but waste bowl with foliate handles, teapot with foliate spout and finial and resin heat stops, 10-1/2" h., approximately 43.5 troy oz. **$1,440**

Skinner, Inc., www.skinnerinc.com

TIFFANY CIRCUS FIGURINES

Tiffany Circus is a set of sterling silver and enamel circus players designed by Tiffany's window dresser, Gene Moore (American, 1910-Nov. 23, 1998). The set was sold at Tiffany's flagship stores as well as other fine retailers nationwide. The whimsical set has grown in popularity in recent years and, due to the craftsmanship and limited edition production run, it's expected a complete set will appreciate in value.

Italian, circus performer under umbrella, Tiffany & Co. New York, circa 1990, Gene Moore for Tiffany (American, 1910-1998), marks: Tiffany & Co. sterling ©, Made in Italy, cushion with holes to base to accommodate pegs on other figures in series, 4-7/8" h., 3.3 oz. (gross). **$937**

Italian, female circus acrobat, Tiffany & Co. New York, circa 1990, Gene Moore for Tiffany (American, 1910-1998), marks: Tiffany & Co. sterling 925 ©, 4" h., 8.5 oz. (gross). **$3,250**

Italian, bear on roller skates, Tiffany & Co. New York, circa 1990, Gene Moore for Tiffany (American, 1910-1998), marks: Tiffany & Co. sterling ©, Made in Italy, 4-5/8" h., 10.1 oz. (gross). **$2,375**

Italian, acrobat figure group, Tiffany & Co., New York, circa 1990, Gene Moore for Tiffany (American, 1910-1998), marks: Tiffany & Co. sterling 925 ©, Made in Italy, 5-3/8" h., 10.4 oz. (gross). **$3,250**

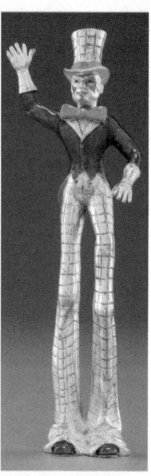

Italian, tall man circus figure, Tiffany & Co. New York, circa 1990, Gene Moore for Tiffany (American, 1910-1998), marks: Tiffany & Co. sterling ©, Made in Italy, 5-3/4" h., 6.8 oz. (gross). **$10,650**

Sports

People have been saving sports-related equipment since the inception of sports. Some of it was passed down from generation to generation for reuse; the rest was stored in dark spaces in closets, attics, and basements.

Two key trends brought collectors' attention to sports collectibles. First, decorators began using old sports items, especially in restaurant décor. Second, collectors began to discover the thrill of owning the "real" thing.

There are collectible items representing nearly every sport, but baseball memorabilia is probably the most well-known segment. The "national pastime" has millions of fans, with enthusiastic collectors seeking out items associated with players such as Babe Ruth, Lou Gehrig, and others who became legends in their own lifetimes. Although baseball cards, issued as advertising premiums for bubble gum and other products, seem to dominate the field, there are numerous other items available.

Sports collectibles are more accessible than ever before because of online auctions and several auction houses that dedicate themselves to that segment of the hobby. Provenance is extremely important when investing in high-ticket sports collectibles. Being able to know the history of the object may greatly enhance the value, with a premium paid for items secured from the player or directly from their estate.

1914-1916 photo of Babe Ruth as a member of the Boston Red Sox, mid-tier condition..... **$9,560**

Heritage Auctions, Inc.

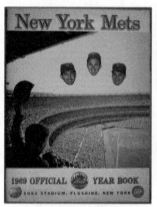

1969 New York Mets Official Year Book celebrating the Amazin' Mets' World Series run. **$100**

1939 baseball centennial Coca-Cola advertising poster, 20" x 27"....................... **$3,200**

Robert Edward Auctions

NASCAR die-cast, signed, circa 1998................................... **$50**

Sealed packs of Mattel mini records featuring "replays" of famous plays by superstars on the court, 1971. .... **$10 ea.**

1930s plastic bank with New York Yankees Lou Gehrig and Bill Dickey facsimile signatures. **$75**

SPORTS

!

Edward's Big League Table Baseball Game from 1915, showcasing the "advancing technology" of the times. **$10,755**

Heritage Auctions

TOP LOT!

Pair of boxing gloves worn by Cassius Clay in his 1964 bout against Sonny Liston; gloves came from his trainer, Angelo Dundee. ... **$385,848**

Note: Another pair of gloves worn by Muhammad Ali against Joe Frazier in 1971 brought an identical amount.

SCP Auctions

TOP LOT!

Bloody sock worn by Boston Red Sox pitcher Curt Schilling during the 2004 World Series in which the Red Sox won, breaking the fabled "curse" for trading away Babe Ruth in 1919......................**$92,613**

Heritage Auctions

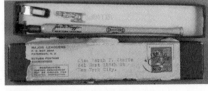

Wooden bat fountain pen reads "World's Champions 1941" on the center brand and "Joe DiMaggio New York Yankees" on the barrel. **$50**

1950s Willie Mays Day booster pin. **$2,000**

Robert Edward Auctions

Key to the city of Boston presented to Boston Celtics player Bill Russell in 1956. .... **$9,500**

Heritage Auctions

1960-1961 promotional Green Bay Packers nodder, 14" h. **$11,980**

Heritage Auctions

Louisville Slugger relied on Jimmie Foxx and Connie Mack to pitch its bats from the early 1930s, 9" x 12-1/2". **$388**

Legendary Auctions

Harlem Globetrotters broadside advertising a game against the Seneca Indians in the 1940s, 12" x 18". **$1,673**

Legendary Auctions

Container providing the retail display for a Wilson (then known as "Wilson-Western") Red Grange football, 13-1/4" x 6-1/4" x 3". Boxes in which sports products were sold is a niche collecting category. **$550**

Legendary Auctions

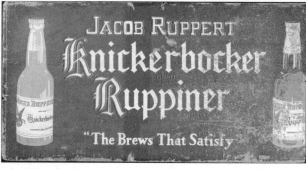

Advertising sign featuring beer no longer produced and a connection to the New York Yankees, as Jacob Ruppert was an owner of the club, now a member of the Baseball Hall of Fame. **$70**

Collect Auctions

Al Capone and Babe Ruth signed baseball, courtesy of the family of Hall of Famer Herb Pennock. **$61,863**

Mile High Card Co.

Hockey gear owned by 1980 U.S. Olympic Hockey Team Captain Mike Eruzione, including this jersey worn during the historic "Miracle on Ice" match in which Eruzione scored the winning goal against the Soviet Union ... **$657,250**

Heritage Auctions

TOP LOT!

1952 Jackie Robinson salesman's sample calendar, 8" x 13-1/4" **$200**

Willie Parker Bent Neck Putter from the 1920s. **$75**

The Golf Auction

Hockey stick from the Miracle on Ice hockey match between the United States and the Soviet Union in the 1980 Winter Olympics in Lake Placid, New York; used by Mike Eruzione to score the winning goal against the Soviets **$262,900**

TOP LOT!

Gartland statue, Luis Aparicio version. **$88**

Collect Auctions

Superballs from Chemtoy with images of Boston Red Sox players inside, complete set, 1970. . **$88**

Collect Auctions

Yogi Berra Hartland statue, 1958-1962, with box and tags. **$350**

Republican Party presidential hopeful Mitt Romney signed baseball. **$300**

1944 World Championship program, New York Giants and Green Bay Packers. **$700**

Wilson "Rajah" Hornsby Champion Batsman Model 972 glove with original box. **$350**

1865 Brooklyn Atlantics CDV found in a photo album at a flea market; one of two known to exist. **$80,000**

Saco River Auction

Ball commemorating the All American Girls Professional Baseball League, used for only one year – 1948, with box. **$593**

Robert Edward Auctions

Stickers from 1974's Rumble in the Jungle in Zaire featuring George Foreman/Muhammad Ali, rectangular sticker 6-1/4" x 3-1/2", circular sticker 4" dia. **$1,778**

Robert Edward Auctions

Celluloid mirrors showcasing female catchers, produced before there was a professional baseball league for women; turn-of-the-century photos also served as vanity mirrors on reverse, 2-1/4" dia. **$270**

Legendary Auctions

Muhammad Ali doll by Effanbee, 17" h. **$75**

Kareem Abdul-Jabbar signed biography. **$25**

Hardcover, 600-page *The American Boy's Book of Sports and Games*, first book to feature a color plate relating to baseball, devotes 10 pages to "Base-Ball." **$593**

Robert Edward Auctions

1938 30-pin lapel set, called Our National Game, showcasing the best ballplayers of the day, including Joe DiMaggio, Lou Gehrig and Jimmie Foxx....... **$400**

Four Wonder "Sports Club" bread labels featuring four different hockey players: Bobby Hull, Dave Keon, Gordie Howe, and "Rocket" Richard, 2-3/4" x 2-3/4"... **$239**

Legendary Auctions

Baseball ticket from the June 12, 1970 game between the Pittsburgh Pirates and San Diego Padres in which Doc Ellis pitched a no-hitter while under the influence of LSD.. **$533**

Robert Edward Auctions

Old team stock certificate issued by the Salt Lake City Baseball Corp. for the Salt Lake City Bees of the Pacific Coast League in 1958. .... **$25**

Love of the Game Auctions

Calendar made by Ballantine Beer featuring 1961 schedule for the Washington Senators, 13-1/2" x 18"... **$50**

Commemorative stein featuring all-time baseball hit king Pete Rose, reads "Major League Record - 4192 Hits," signed........... **$35**

1948 Babe Ruth wristwatch in original plastic, "baseball" case. **$475**

Robert Edward Auctions

Badge from 1934 Augusta National Invitational (later dubbed The Masters), considered the toughest of all Masters badges. . **$18,000**

The Golf Auction

1904 "Husky Hans" sheet music honoring Honus Wagner. **$260**

Love of the Game Auctions

Book titled *Par Golf in Eight Steps*, 1950s
.... **$38**

The Golf Auction

Protective head gear worn by Oscar Robertson, 1960s. **$3,300**

SCP Auctions

TOP LOT!

Baseball Hall of Famer Ozzie Smith's entire run of Gold Glove Awards..... **$519,203**

SCP Auctions

1913 *Baseball Magazine* with Hall of Famer Frank Chance on the cover. **$150**

Love of the Game Auctions

Minneapolis Lakers basketball player George Mikan version Wheaties box with accompanying ad, 1950s. **$100**

Legendary Auctions

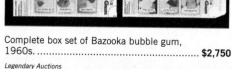

Complete box set of Bazooka bubble gum, 1960s. **$2,750**

Legendary Auctions

Stamps

1957 4c 48-Star Flag..................**$.40 unused; $.20 used**

1939 3c Baseball Centenary, violet .. **$3.75 unused; $.30 used**

Stamp collecting, called philately, is generally accepted as the world's oldest hobby, dating to the introduction of prepaid adhesive stamps to indicate the payment of mailing fees in Great Britain in 1840. The Universal Postal Union, an international postal watchdog and clearinghouse, estimates that 30 million people around the world collect stamps today, and retail sales in the hobby total $10 billion annually.

It is safe to say no two collections are alike. An entire library of books on the hobby would be needed to cover all its nuances.

The first government postage stamps in the United States were authorized to take effect July 1, 1847. In Great Britain, where stamps originated seven years earlier, the first issues featured a portrait of the long-sitting Queen Victoria. But in America, Congress decided to bypass the president, James K. Polk, in favor of two giants of the nation's founding, President George Washington, whose image graced the 10-cent stamp (designated by a Roman "X"), and statesman Benjamin Franklin, who also happened to be the United States' first postmaster, on the 5-cent stamp.

The subjects on U.S. stamps represent famous people, places and events of our nation's past or, in many issues of recent years, popular culture. Call it nostalgia, appreciation or education, history plays a major role in many collections.

From the fine engraving of early intaglio stamps to the full-color gravure of today, the printer's art is on display in stamps. From tiny "secret marks" used to distinguish some early stamps to almost microscopic nicks and spots to "hidden images" that can be seen only with special lenses, stamps carry an array of attractions for the technophile.

Some stamp subjects, such as scenes from our national parks, are original art, created especially for the medium of the postage stamp. Others are exquisitely detailed, tiny reproductions of larger originals. Artists themselves have been commemorated on stamps. A collector could concentrate entirely on this aspect, but visually every stamp collection is essentially an artistic display of its owner's creation.

For more information on U.S. stamps, see *Warman's U.S. Stamps Field Guide*, 2nd edition, by Maurice D. Wozniak.

1863-1866 2c Jackson.
.... **$300 unused; $40 used**

1851-1857 12c Washington,
black... **$4,000 unused; $375 used**

1857-1861 5c Jefferson, brick
red.. **$25,000 unused; $2,300 used**

1890-1893 90c Perry, orange.
.... **$800 unused; $140 used**

1897-1903 4c Lincoln, rose-
brown ...... **$40 unused; $2.50 used**

1949 3c Edgar Allan Poe.
.... **$.60 unused; $.20 used**

Second Bureau Issue $2 James
Madison, dark blue.
.... **$1,500 unused; $225 used**

1904 Louisiana Purchase
Exposition 3c James Monroe,
violet........ **$125 unused; $58 used**

2006 39c DC Comics Super Heroes, pane of 20 .... **$28 unused**

1869 15c Landing of Columbus,
Type II, brown and blue.
.... **$3,000 unused; $275 used**

1869 24c Declaration of
Independence, green and violet.
.... **$5,000 unused; $750 used**

1918 $5 Franklin, deep green
and black, unwatermarked paper,
Perforation 11.
.... **$425 unused; $53 used**

1976 Declaration of Independence, strip of 4... **$6.95 unused; $.70 used**

1879 15c Webster, red-orange,
American Bank Note Co. printing
on soft, porous paper.
.... **$350 unused; $25 used**

2005 37c The Art of Disney, block of four............. **$5 unused; $.20 used**

1940 3c Emancipation.
.... **$.75 unused; $.20 used**

STAMPS

1922-1926 8c Ulysses S. Grant, olive-green.
.... **$65 unused; $1.30 used**

1922-1926 14c American Indian, blue .... **$9 unused; $2 used**

1922-1926 12c Grover Cleveland, brown-violet.
................**$15 unused; $.50 used**

1c Yosemite, green, Trans-Mississippi Philatelic Exposition souvenir sheet.
.................**$3.50 unused; $2 used**

5c Yellowstone, blue, imperforate.
.... **$4.25 unused; $2.50 used**

1935 3c Boulder Dam, purple, perforation 11.
................**$.50 unused; $.20 used**

1902-1903 8c Martha Washington (first woman on a definitive U.S. stamp), violet-black.
....................**$55 unused; $3 used**

1898 1c Marquette on the Mississippi, green.... **$45 unused; $6.25 used**

◀ 1936 3c Susan B. Anthony, dark violet. **$.50 unused; $.20 used**

▲ 1992 29c Love. .... **$1.60 unused; $.20 used**

1888 30c Hamilton, orange-brown .... **$400 unused; $115 used**

◀ 1922-1926 5c Theodore Roosevelt, dark blue. .... **$33.50 unused; $.20 used**

1847 5c Franklin, red-brown. .... **$6,000 unused; $600 used**

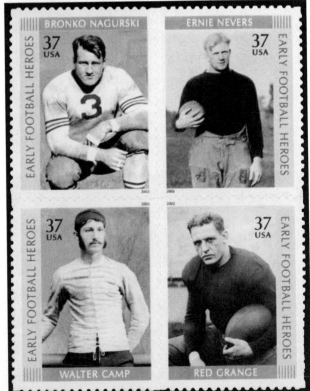

2003 37c Early Football Heroes, block of four...................... **$4 unused**

1983 20c Martin Luther. .... **$1.30 unused; $.20 used**

STAMPS

1982 20c Franklin D. Roosevelt.
.... **$1.20 unused; $.20 used**

Heiltsuk, Bella Bella
Indian Art USA 15c

Chilkat Tlingit
Indian Art USA 15c

Tlingit
Indian Art USA 15c

Bella Coola
Indian Art USA 15c

1980 American Folk Art Indian Masks, block of four.
.... **$5.50 unused; $.75 used**

1908-1909 10c Washington,
yellow...... **$90 unused; $2.50 used**

◀ 1980-1985
Great Americans
20c Harry S.
Truman, black.
...... **$.90 unused;
$.20 used**

3c Mothers of America, violet, imperforate.
.... **$1.85 unused; $1.50 used**

1958-1959 Lincoln Sesquicentennial 4c Statue of
Lincoln .... **$.50 unused; $.20 used**

1982 20c International Peace Garden.
.... **$1.10 unused; $.20 used**

Grosbeak & Owl, pair ....**$2 unused; $.30 used**

1984 20c Vietnam Veterans Memorial.
....**$2 unused; $.20 used**

1984 20c Christmas, Santa Claus.
....**$1.25 unused; $.20 used**

2c Grand Canyon, red, imperforate.
....**$.75 unused; $.50 used**

1952 3c Betsy Ross ....**$.50 unused; $.20 used**

1972 8c Mail Order Business... **$.60 unused; $.20 used**

1985 22c Christmas, Poinsettia.
....**$1 unused; $.20 used**

1968 6c Father Marquette ... **$1.20 unused; $.20 used**

Tools

Tool collecting is nearly as old as tools themselves. Certainly it was not long after Stone Age man used his first stone tool that he started watching for that special rock or piece of bone. Soon he would have been putting tools away just for the right time or project. The first tool collector was born!

Since earliest man started collecting tools just for the right time or project, many other reasons to collect have evolved. As man created one tool, he could then use that tool to make an even better tool.

Very quickly toolmakers became extremely skilled at their craft, and that created a new collecting area – collecting the works of the very best makers. In time toolmakers realized that tools were being purchased on the bases of the quality of workmanship alone. With this realization an even more advanced collector was born as toolmakers began making top-of-the-line tools from special materials with fine detailing and engraving. These exquisite tools were never intended for use but were to be enjoyed and collected. Many of the finest tools were of such quality that they are considered works of art.

So many tools exist in today's world that many tool collectors focus on one special category. Some of the most popular categories to collect fall into the general areas of: function, craft or trade, personal connection, company or brand, patents, and investments.

For more information on tools, see *Antique Trader Tools Price Guide* by Clarence Blanchard.

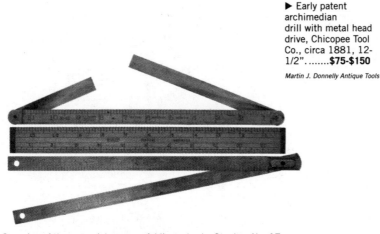

▶ Early patent archimedian drill with metal head drive, Chicopee Tool Co., circa 1881, 12-1/2". ....**$75-$150**

Martin J. Donnelly Antique Tools

Grouping of three special purpose folding rules by Stanley: No. 17 blacksmith's, No. 42 shipwright's bevel, No. 34-1/2 bench type, 12" total. ....**$80-$160**

Martin J. Donnelly Antique Tools

Furring plane, No. 340, Stanley, rare and unusual, circa early 20th century, new condition with original pasteboard box, 10" l. **$10,350**

Martin J. Donnelly Antique Tools

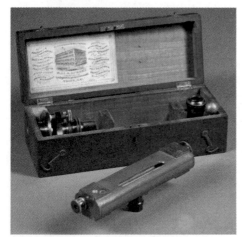

W. & L.E. Gurley drainage or farm level, circa 1883, green-painted body, four-screw leveling base, ball and socket joint with staff mount, wood adjusting bar, mahogany fitted case with label, level 8-1/2". **$123**

Skinner, Inc., www.skinnerinc.com

Plane, G.H. Thompson, patented, July 21, 1874, marked on top of iron, corrugated top and bottom, cutter adjustment is lever arm that engages teeth on back of blade, similar to Stanley No. 9 1/2 block planes and Bailey patent of Aug. 8, 1867, nickel plated, red paint on inside surfaces, frog brass, possible presentation piece, possibly unique, good condition. **$13,750**

Hand crank drill press, circa late 19th century, used in woodworking, metalworking and construction projects, 43" l... **$60**

North American Auction Co.

Drawknife with folding handles, marked Enders and Oak Leaf, used to shape wood by removing shavings. .... **$50-$100**

Scheerer McCullock Auctioneers

Treadle drive metal-working lathe, L.F. Grammes & Sons, Allentown, Pennsylvania, circa late 19th century, 40".. **$300-$600**

Martin J. Donnelly Antique Tools

◀ Group of three double iron molding planes, A. Mathieson & Son, Glasgow, Scotland, 9-1/2"..................$120-$240

Martin J. Donnelly Antique Tools

▶ Plow plane, Babson & Rapplier, Boston, Phillips improved model, much original finish on tote, black japanning 96% with most of red, blue, and gold highlights showing, fine condition..................**$3,300**

▼ Late 20th century patent marking gauge, A.A. Welsh, some staining on gauge, 7-1/2"..................**$60-$120**

Martin J. Donnelly Antique Tools

Cast iron book press, early 20th century, much of original decorative striping and early red and black paint remain, 17" w..................**$100-$200**

Martin J. Donnelly Antique Tools

Skew iron cornice molding plane, mid-18th century, yellow birch with double ogee profile, set at 60-degree angle, dark golden brown and smooth patina, excellent condition with some slivers that have separated from base, produced by Cesar Chelor, a slave of New England planemaker Francis Nicholson, who received land, tools and his freedom from Nicholson before he died..................**$28,600**

Martin J. Donnelly Antique Tools

Plow plane, Phillips patent, marked "M.C. Mayo's Improved Jan. 1, 1872," painted black with red, gold, and blue highlights, paint about 80%, perfect tote, good+ condition. **$990**

Scraper plane, Stanley No. 87, patent-applied-for type, unmarked but proper blade, japanning 100%, fine+ condition. **$1,980**

Bronze body scraper plane, circa 1855, Leonard Bailey & Co., horizontal rosewood front handle, adjustment mechanism screw secured with wedges, fitted with thick scraper iron that is not marked in any way, rear handle fashioned from rosewood with slot cut in front of base that slides onto raised boss cast in body. **$32,200**

Martin J. Donnelly Antique Tools

Bedrock smoothing plane, No. 604, Stanley, circa 1915, "Type 11" trademark, 85% of original finish remaining, 9" l. ....**$100-$200**

Martin J. Donnelly Antique Tools

Plow plane, I. Nicholson, 18th century, strong A2 mark, yellow birch, thumbscrew-locked arms and stop, good condition, 10-1/8". **$5,060**

Victor jack metallic plane, No. 5, L. Bailey & Co., late 19th century, screw lock cap, 14"............**$150-$300**

Martin J. Donnelly Antique Tools

Group of tools including Stanley No. 8 jointer plane, Stanley No. 45 molding plane with selection of blades, Record No. 20 compass plane, and assorted other planes, spoke shave, mortice gauge, and various chisels.............................. **$235**

Dreweatts Auctions Bloomsbury

TOP!
LOT!

Plow plane, Ohio Tool Co. No. 113, number mark only, ebony retains much original finish, six ivory tips, rosewood bridle, boxwood spindle, center wheel, handled, set of five Ohio Tool irons, longtime storage box, couple of minor chips, fine condition. **$34,100**

Plow plane, E.W. Carpenter, Lancaster, Pennsylvania, boxwood body, arms, and fence facing, rosewood adjuster nuts, rosewood handle supported top and bottom on brass arms, improved arms and handle, arms adjust and lock fence in plane, fine condition. **$10,120**

Plow plane, A. Howland & Co., New York, ebony, four ivory tips, handled, screw arm, boxwood arms, good+ condition. **$1,760**

Plow plane, Sandusky Tool Co., E.H. Morris patent, March 31, 1871, scissor mechanism keeps fence and skate parallel, japanning 65%, good+ condition. **$3,850**

Plow plane, Stanley No. 42, Miller patent, type 1, hook, oval trademark, gunmetal, one cutter, tote perfect, filletster bed missing slitter, japanning 99%, fine condition. **$22,550**

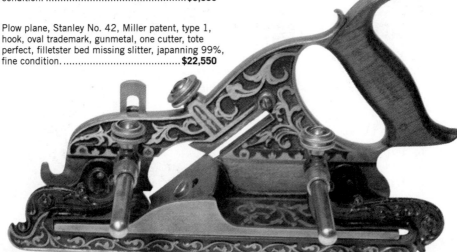

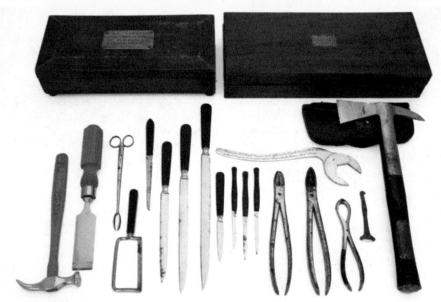

Collection of Victorian-era and later tools with presentation inscriptions from 1885, includes three commemorative tools related to events in India, including spanner commemorating railway link between Bezwada and Madras, ornamental hammer and chisel in presentation box awarded at Bombay dockyard in 1938, 15-piece set of surgeon's tools in wood case presented by Church of Scotland to William Peven for missionary services in Africa in 1885, together with British fireman's axe presented at retirement ceremony in 1919. From the collection of Malcolm S. Forbes. **$1,434**

Heritage Auctions

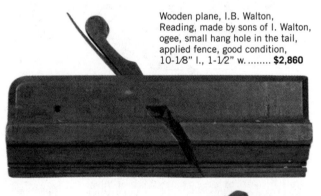

Wooden plane, I.B. Walton, Reading, made by sons of I. Walton, ogee, small hang hole in the tail, applied fence, good condition, 10-1⁄8" l., 1-1⁄2" w. **$2,860**

Brass and rosewood smoothing plane marked to blade support iron as Alex Mathieson and Glasgow, actual blade impressed GV & H Stormont, 9-1/8" along base. **$240**

Dickins Auctioneers

▶ Wooden plane, E. Clifford, sash, yellow birch, handled, flat chamfers, round-top wedge, offset tote, fine condition. **$3,080**

Toys

The American antique toy market remains one of the bright spots among collecting categories. Longtime collectors are deciding it's time to pass decades' worth of accumulation to a new generation, and those fine collections continue to lead the market. Wonderful objects are now available to own and collectors are digging deep for rare items.

As collectors are increasingly drawn to rarity, it means a slow-down in values among low-end and mid-range items. Some auction houses are starting to offer group lots like never before in an effort to sell lesser-quality items. Luckily, lots like these offer newcomers a chance to own an instant collection of toys without having to scour a dozen flea markets in the process. This trend shows no signs of slowing.

This serves as a lesson to toy collectors: Pay close attention to trends in pop culture and take note of your rarest items. If you are serious about building an investment-grade collection of antique toys, then research your next purchase, pass on the common stuff, and spend your money buying the best examples you can afford.

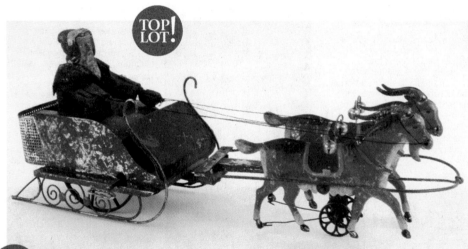

TOP LOT!

TOP LOT!

▲ Althof-Bergmann Santa sleigh, rare, one of two known original examples, excellent condition, paint losses to sleigh sides and basket, 20" l. **$84,000**

Noel Barrett Auctions

◀ Buddy L 11-piece outdoor railroad train set, near mint unplayed-with condition, track retains substantial amount of black paint on top of rails, two variant flat cars, including shorter version and rare ore car, original cardboard box present for cattle, other boxes missing. Engine and tender: 42" l.; caboose: 19" l.; small flat car: 19" l.; large flat car: 22" l.; hopper: 22" l.; gondola: 22" l.; ore: 21" l.; tank car: 17" l.; cattle car: 22" l.; box car: 22" l., approximate total 220". **$23,000**

James D. Julia, Inc.

VISIT WWW.ANTIQUETRADER.COM

TOYS

Martin bicycle rider, painted tin with flywheel drive on front wheel, good to very good condition, incorrect handle bars, some overpaint, 5-1/2" l............... **$650**

Noel Barrett Auctions

Murray Atomic Missile pedal car, 1958, rare chain drive, wing-shaped back painted brown with white highlights and decals of rockets and flame decals shooting out of bottom, steel wheels with rubber tires, faux rocket control levers, steel steering wheel, formed metal seat, secondary lever on side attached to interior flapper to adjust noise level while riding, very good condition, 44" l............**$460**

James D. Julia, Inc.

Bush kaleidoscope made of painted cardboard and brass, mounted on turned wooden base, elements on view are primarily hand-blown glass including glass ampules filled with colored liquid, very good to excellent condition, 13" h.................... **$425**

Noel Barrett Auctions

Frisbee Beam cast iron steam engine, original paint flourish decoration, walking beam engine mounted over boiler, marked on top of boiler "Frisbie - Patent 1871," very good to excellent condition, 9" h................... **$600**

Noel Barrett Auctions

◄ Distler Busy Lizzie tin lithographed sweeper toy showing Lizzie sweeping floor in realistic manner with original box bottom, overall very good plus condition with minor scratches and chipping, box bottom shows some creasing and minor tears, 7" h. ..**$633**

James D. Julia, Inc.

TOP LOT!

Ives Clockwork Hippodrome, tin chariot has two applied ormolu Roman-style figures on horseback, enameled in blue with yellow band and red pinstriping, wreathed floral decal, woman driving chariot is 8" h. and all original condition, her stamped brass face is mounted to wooden molded dowel, large fancy red cast iron wheels with smaller wheels at back to adjust for steering, tips of lances on ormolu figures missing, 14" l. When toy is wound and proceeds forward, an eccentric mechanism gives the effect of horses running. ... **$69,000**

James D. Julia, Inc.

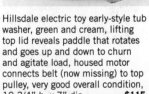
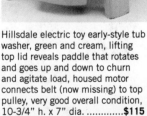

Hillsdale electric toy early-style tub washer, green and cream, lifting top lid reveals paddle that rotates and goes up and down to churn and agitate load, housed motor connects belt (now missing) to top pulley, very good overall condition, 10-3/4" h. x 7" dia. **$115**

James D. Julia, Inc.

▶ Seaworthy windup wooden boat carved from solid wood with brass rails and steel dash, set with powerful windup motor with on/off switch that powers single propeller, retains most of original decal on bow, accompanied by custom display stand, overall very good and working condition, approximately 20" l. **$431**

James D. Julia, Inc.

▶ Three Linemar windup Disney walkers, Pinocchio (nose missing), Jiminy Cricket, and Goofy with spinning tail, overall very good to near excellent and working condition, Goofy missing one ear, Jiminy has slight oxidation, largest is 5" h. **$345**

James D. Julia, Inc.

Lehmann autobus, lithographed in red with yellow and gold highlights, overall very good condition, 8" l. **$920**

James D. Julia, Inc.

▶ Lehmann Coco Climbing Native, scarce early version of rare Lehmann, native climbs tree and releases "coconut" ball, which causes him to descend; hooking ball back in treetop causes him to climb, ornately embossed tin circular base, fronds are stained tin, very good to excellent condition, 15" h. **$950**

Noel Barrett Auctions

Linemar Disney character toys with Mickey and Goofy riding wide-wheeled unicycles; when wound, feet simulate pedaling. Overall very good condition, both appear to have replaced pants, Goofy has darkened color, 5-1/2" h. **$403**

James D. Julia, Inc.

Buddy L steam shovel in as-found all original condition, paint vibrant and shiny, decal largely intact, very fine plus to near mint condition, 23" l. x 13" h. **$345**

James D. Julia, Inc.

Linemar Chevy friction car, orange/red body with yellow roof, lithographed striped front and back seats, chrome highlights and celluloid windshields, friction motor functional, very good plus original condition, 11" l. x 5" w. **$690**

James D. Julia, Inc.

Maggie & Jiggs German litho comic character windup toy depicting couple in duel, she with rolling pin and he with cane, 8" l..**$633**

James D. Julia, Inc.

Two Disney windup toys, Linemar Knitting Minnie Mouse and Marx Ferdinand the bull, both very good plus condition with minor wear, 6-3/4" h. and 6" l., respectively. **$431**

James D. Julia, Inc.

Marx Doughboy Tank, one of the earliest versions of famed Marx Sparkling Tank lithographed tin clockwork toy with colorful box, pop-up rifleman, excellent condition, 9" l........**$275**

Noel Barrett Auctions

▲ McLoughlin The Yacht Race Game with four-part folding board with inset spinner and image of New York harbor, eight lithographed cardboard yachts on lead bases, each with different names: Thistle, Puritan, Mayflower, Seafox, Volunteer, Galatea, Genesta, and Cinderella, plus instruction sheet, 8-1/5" x 16-1/2"....**$475**

Noel Barrett Auctions

Hand-painted German tin windup toy of American Indian with tomahawk in one hand and bow and arrow in other, painted feathers in hair, wearing Native American skirt; when wound, figure wobbles side to side at waist, lead feet stabilize it as it dances across surface. Overall very good all original condition, 7-1/2" h. **$403**

James D. Julia, Inc.

Lionel Mickey Mouse Hand Car, maroon, No. 1100 painted tin clockwork hand car with composition Mickey and Minnie, full circle of track in original illustrated box, minor chips to car, 7-1/2" l. **$950**

Noel Barrett Auctions

Steiff Mickey Mouse doll with original paper tag, velvet with felt ears and string whiskers, traditional red shorts, orange boots, retains original Steiff chest tag and original Steiff button, personalized by former owner with "Ruth" and "Bill" on each hand and "I love you" on Mickey's backside, on bottom of foot is written "Me Too," other foot is stamped "Walt Disney Mickey Mouse Design Patent New York," overall very good condition with some minor discoloration to white portion of face, tail is missing, 7" h. **$472**

James D. Julia, Inc.

Marx Honeymoon Express with original box, lithographed tin, clockwork, 9-1/2" dia. **$225**

Noel Barrett Auctions

TOP LOT!

Buck Rogers 25th Century Laboratory, Porter Chemical Co., Hagerstown, Maryland, extremely rare, damaged cover, remarkable unplayed-with condition, retains all original components including test tubes and wooden containers, all with Buck Rogers labels, Buck Rogers labeled telescope, original three instruction manuals enclosed in envelope with images of Buck, Wilma Deering, and Dr. Huer at work in a laboratory, also included is an original microscope not marked Buck Rogers, 31" x 17". **$5,000**

Noel Barrett Auctions

McCormick Farmall 400 pedal tractor, red with dual front wheels and knobby back tires, circa 1960s, generally good to very good condition, 39-1/2" l. x 28-1/2" h. x 18" w. **$633**

James D. Julia, Inc.

◄ Composition cat squeak toy and small Pennsylvania slide lid box, dated 1873, decoupage dog and cat decoration, toy 2-3/4" h., box 2-1/2" h. x 3-1/2" w. **$563**

Pook & Pook, Inc.

Lionel 400E locomotive, American steam profile electric engine with copper trim, needs some parts and cleaning for restoration, 19" l.....**$650**

Noel Barrett Auctions

Sheep on wheels pull toy, papier mâché, covered in white fleece with hide muzzle, glass eyes, white kid ears, 15" h. x 17" l. **$561**

James D. Julia, Inc.

Marx Popeye with Parrot Cages, lithographed tin with clockwork, well-above-average condition example of scarcer black shirt version, 8" h. **$250**

Noel Barrett Auctions

Roullet-Decamp windup poodle, circa 1920s, long-tailed white mohair fur with inset glass eyes; dog bounces around with pipe in mouth, hat on head, celluloid orange bouncing off floor while slapping at it with paddle. Overall very fine working order, approximately 10" h. **$403**

James D. Julia, Inc.

Marklin carousel, circa 1910, original cloth canopy, eight girls (two each in vis-a-vis chariots), four boys in sailor suits on hide-covered horses, 10 additional figures seated around central mirrored column. Action and musical accompaniment propelled by hand when large drive wheel with wooden crank is turned; drive wheel is grooved so power could be supplied by a steam engine, making this the most elaborate steam accessory toy ever made. Colorful decal decoration throughout, original colored glass balls simulate lighting, two lampposts on stair landing, scarce and original piece, excellent to near mint condition, 16" dia., 21" h. **$192,000**

Noel Barrett Auctions

Dimensional Red Riding Hood puzzle, circa 1905, depicting girl and wolf, painted ceramic material, over 70 pieces, bright colors, original cardboard frame (shown here in plywood frame), ex. Atlanta Toy Museum, excellent condition, frame 14" x 10". **$250**

Noel Barrett Auctions

Two Schoenhut Buster Brown roly polys, larger one with more pronounced Buster Brown style haircut than smaller version, smaller version has original cloth Schoenhut label with patent date of 1908, 9-1/2" and 6", respectively......**$345**

James D. Julia, Inc.

American tin prancing horse on sculpted and embossed wheeled platform, all original finish with fading of various black trappings, overall very good condition, approximately 6-1/2" l. **$575**

James D. Julia, Inc.

Boy and girl dancers on spinning platforms, cloth-dressed papier mâché and wood dancers mounted on gyroscopic top-type cast metal platforms that are spun by pulling a string, European manufacture, probably French origin, very good to excellent condition, boy missing hand, 9-1/2" h. **$650**

Noel Barrett Auctions

Sand-activated moving picture toy with painted and lithographed paper drummer figure, very good to excellent condition, 6" w. x 8" h. **$450**

Noel Barrett Auctions

Feeding cow on platform painted tin toy, clockwork action has cow bending head to eat from bowl, stands on green platform that appears to have had wheels, very good to excellent condition, 7" l. **$600**

Noel Barrett Auctions

World Syndicate animated picture machine, circa 1920, scarce miniature hand-crank mutoscope or "flicker" machine would utilize series of drawings to simulate motion within lithographed tin drum decorated with gold highlights, very good to near excellent condition, 5" h. **$649**

James D. Julia, Inc.

Transistor Radios

The most collectible and historic transistor radios were made in America from 1955 to 1960 and Japan from 1956 to 1963. An easy way to date a transistor radio of this period is to look for small triangles or circles between the 6 and 7 and the 12 and 16 on the dial. These are Civil Defense (CD) marks, which appeared on all radios manufactured or sold in the United States from 1953 to 1963.

At the height of the Russian Red Scare, the United States enacted the CONELRAD program, establishing two civil defense frequencies, 640 and 1240 kilohertz. During times of emergencies, all stations except the CONELRAD stations at 640 and 1240 AM would cease operations (note that some Japanese radios made by Sharp and Hitachi during the late 1950s left out the CD marks).

American companies were the first out of the solid-state-radio gate with the release of the Regency TR-1 in 1954 (it sold well into 1955 and 1956 as the redesigned TR-1G and TR-4). As a transistor radio collector I think it's important to have one example of this historic radio in your collection. Depending on color, they run between $300 and $1,000. Basic ivory and gray cabinets bring less money than the "mandarin" red and black models.

For a brief period the TR-1 was released in very attractive pearlescent pink and light blue colors as well as swirled, jade green, and mahogany. These later examples command

World's first commercially released transistor radio, Regency TR-1, 1954, U.S., "Mandarin red," used uncommon 22.5-volt battery; Texas Instruments supplied the radio's four transistors. ....**$200-$600**

top dollar on the secondary market. Early Zenith radios like the Royal 500 series are also worthy of having in a collection. The first Royal 500 was hand wired and had a metal chassis. The fifth generation Zenith 500 was the 500H. It has a large oval speaker and is considered to be the best sounding/performing portable transistor radio.

Other collectible American-made radios are from RCA, General Electric, Admiral, Motorola, Magnavox, Philco, Raytheon, Arvin, Sylvania, and Emerson. American radios tend to be slightly larger than their Japanese counterparts. Most U.S. radios are considered "coat pocket"-sized – too big for your shirt pocket. Many were also larger, leather-clad portable sets like the Zenith Royal 750 and Raytheon 8TP-1.

The Emerson 888 series is one of the most popular and attractive coat pocket radios. Emerson released several models in this series from 1958 to 1960, such as the Vanguard, Pioneer, Explorer, Satellite, and Atlas – all named after various U.S. space programs. These radios can be found in great numbers today, and are terrific looking and often reasonably priced (typically from $20 to $100, depending on condition).

The first Japanese transistor released was Sony's TR-55, an incredibly rare find today. But it was the Sony TR-63 that created the greatest stir. Released in 1957, it was considered the world's first truly pocket-sized radio and was the first to utilize all miniature components. It was also the first Japanese radio to be imported into the United States (several other early Sony radios were sold in Canada in 1956). Even examples with cracks or chips can fetch $400. Mint condition models are considerably more valuable.

Toshiba, Hitachi, Sharp, Standard, Sanyo, Matsushita (Panasonic), Mitsubishi, Aiwa, Realtone, Global, and Zephyr soon arrived on North American shores. Small, affordable and colorful, these radios were an immediate hit with the youth market. The simultaneous arrival of imported pocket radios and rock 'n' roll conspired to change the electronics industry forever.

By the late 1950s and early 1960s, many American companies had opted to have their radios made in Japan but retained their American brand names, such as Trancel, Penny's, Channel Master, and Bulova. Even giants like Zenith, RCA, Motorola, Philco, and G.E. had their radios made in Japan. They could no longer compete with the lower prices and more attractive designs coming from Asia.

One of the classic features of Japanese radios is reverse-painted plastic. Reverse (back) painting was a popular method of ornamenting transistor radios between 1958 and 1962. By painting all artwork on the inside of the clear plastic dial cover, there would be no wear or damage to the most attractive features of the radio. A smooth protective surface remained on the outer dial.

This process also gave the radio a three-dimensional appearance. The depth and palette of colors was breathtaking. Gold on white, black accents, bright red and powder blue along with geometric shapes like starbursts, chevrons, jet wings, diamonds and parallel lines make reverse-painted radios visually stunning and highly sought after by collectors. Makers like Toshiba and Crown were exceptional with their creative use of reverse painting.

Even Japanese radios without reverse painting are highly collectible. The Sony TR-610, with its sleek cabinet and round speaker grill, spawned a host of imitators like the Realtone TR-1088 "Comet." These radios can be found in abundance today and range in price from $50 to $150, depending on condition and color.

In your travels you may even encounter pocket radios called "Boy's Radios." Japanese firms were hit with both a domestic export tax and a North American import tax on any AM radio

Crown TR-555, Japan, circa 1959, top portion reverse-painted, uncommon find. Crown Radio Corp. was originally known as Asahi Radio Mfg. Co. Ltd. .....**$100-$200**

Crown TR-999, nine transistors, Japan, reverse-painted dial area, chrome speaker grille, rare. ....**$150-$200**

Comet 660, six transistors, Japan, early 1960s, reverse-painted dial, brass nameplate and badge at bottom left of speaker grille, hefty and solid......................**$40-$80**

having three or more transistors. To avoid the expense, Japanese manufacturers in the 1960s developed AM radios that operated on two transistors. They were marketed as "toys" rather than electronic devices, thus sidestepping the taxes.

These radios would either have Boy's Radio or Two Transistors prominently and proudly displayed on the cabinet. In many cases, the cabinets were identical to "real" radios with six transistors. Performance was less than stellar, but these radios could still pick up local stations. Teenagers were swayed by price and appearance; performance was low on their list. Today Boy's Radios often range in value from $25 to $70.

With any transistor radio from the 1950s or early 1960s, it seems the brighter the color the higher the price. Cool 1950s shades like robin's egg/powder blue, sea foam green and bright red or yellow command higher prices. Black and ivory cabinets are considered less attractive by some and may reduce a radio's value on the collector market.

Of course condition is key in valuing a radio as well. Finding a radio with its original box, leather case, earphones, owner's manual, and warranty card/sales slip will inflate worth. Be sure to examine the cabinet closely when making a purchase. Small hairline cracks or chips are often found in the corners.

Some collectors refuse to buy damaged radios. Others are not troubled by buying less than perfect examples. Restoring and repairing are an option. If you want to keep a radio historically accurate, I recommend not changing its electronic components.

During the 1970s radio design experienced a renaissance. Bright colors and cool shapes made a comeback (perhaps inspired by disco, mood rings and the excesses of the decade). Panasonic released several radios that are highly collectible today, such as the Panapet and Toot-A-Loop. They can be found at flea markets or online auctions ranging in price from $10 to $50. Be prepared to spend more if you find one in its original box.

— Michael Jack

Inflicted with the collecting disease, Michael Jack has more than 1,100 transistor radios in his collection. He owns everything from the world's first transistor radio, the Regency TR-1, to the extremely rare Sony TR-5 (a redesign of Sony's very first radio). Jack also has many classic "Made in the U.S.A." sets and the best of "Made in Japan" models. By day, Michael is a recording engineer and music producer (see www.recordandmix.ca.). To view more of his radios go to: http://www.flickr.com/people/transistor_radios/

All photos courtesy Michael Jack and Steve Locke

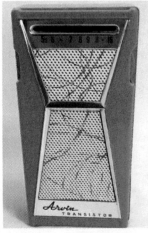

Commodore Super De Luxe, eight transistors, Japan, reverse painting.........................**$20-$40**

Arvin 9577, six transistor radio, U.S., 1957, hourglass speaker grille, chrome trim, slide rule dial, retailed for $59.97.......**$60-$100**

Constant 6T-180, six transistors, Japan, early 1960s, automotive-inspired dial looks like speedometer................**$50-$100**

Crown TR-800, eight transistors, Japan, circa 1958-1959, coat pocket radio, rounded corners, reverse-painted dial area on right, powder blue. ....**$150-$200**

Koyo Eureka KR-6TS35, Japan, 1958, reverse-painted dial, tapered, maroon plastic cabinet and angled brass nameplate. Radio can also be found as a Polyrad (same model number) and under Koyo name as model KTR-621; less often found as Electramatic with model number KR-6TS35. ....**$50-$80**

Emerson 888 Pioneer, eight transistors, U.S., circa 1959, coat pocket radio; many early Emerson radios were named after U.S. space programs/rockets: Vanguard, Explorer, Titan, Satellite and Atlas. ....**$30-$90**

Crown TR-777, Japan, stunning reverse-painted panels and uniquely designed, perforated speaker grille, gold chevron, half silver/half ivory checkered panels, uncommon find. ....**$150-$200**

Global GR-900, nine transistors, Japan, circa 1961. ....**$60-$90**

Hitachi TH-668, second radio made by Hitachi, Japan, circa 1957, thin, long coat pocket radio, rare..**$100-$200**

Kobe Kogyo KT-63, six transistors, Japan, circa 1959, shirt-pocket radio with powder-blue reverse paint, orange plastic, horizontal grille and chevron. ....**$60-$90**

Koyo KR-6TS1, six transistors, Japan, circa 1957, Koyo's first transistor radio, comet-shaped speaker grille; colors: maroon, black, ivory, light blue or gray cabinet. May encounter this model under the Weston or Peak brand name.. **$60-$90**

General Electric 678, U.S., 1955, G.E.'s first transistor radio, available in four cabinet colors with each color having a unique model number: black 675, ivory 676, red 677, and green 678; radio retailed for $49.95. .... **$40-$80**

Sony TR-6 green, Japan, 1956, sold mainly in Japan when Sony's corporate name was still Tokyo Tsushin Kogyo (Sony was the brand name for electronic products); rare – only a small number were manufactured and few have survived. .... **$900-$1,300**

Regency TR-4 ivory, U.S., circa 1957, redesign of TR-1 using a standard 9-volt battery. ....**$100-$200**

Japanese-made, six transistors, circa 1960; radio can be found under several brand names such as Harlie, Star Lite, Hi-Tone, Hollywood, HearEver, Gaiety (model TR-601), Valiant and Selfix; thin cabinets prone to chips and cracks. ....**$20-$30**

Sony TR-63, six transistors, Japan, first Sony radio imported into United States (1957), first shirt-pocket radio. ....**$300-$500**

Sony TR-610, six transistors, Japan, 1958, perhaps the most copied transistor radio of all time; colors: ivory, red, black and green; almost 500,000 radios sold worldwide. ....**$80-$120**

Sony TR-510, five-transistor version of Sony's famous 610, Japan, 1959. ....**$70-$100**

Summit S-900, nine transistors, Japan, shirt-pocket set with reverse-painted dial featuring gold starburst. ....**$80-$100**

Toshiba 5TR-221, rare find, Japan, little known about radio. ....**$500-$700**

Standard SR-F22, Japan, 1957, recessed tuning dial....... **$50-$90**

Toshiba 6TP-219, Japan, circa 1958, gold reverse-painted dial, angled speaker grille and inset tuning knob, considered by many collectors as one of the best looking Toshiba radios. ..**$80-$100**

Toshiba 7TP-303, nicknamed "Cat's Eye" by collectors, Japan. ....**$80-$100**

Toshiba 6TP-31A, six transistors, Japan, known as the "Bath Scale" because of its look......**$100-$200**

Zenith Royal 500, seven transistors, U.S., 1955, Zenith's first transistor radio; hand-wired metal chassis as opposed to printed circuit board; colors: black or maroon. The Royal 500 series was in production for 10 years and went through several electronic and cosmetic changes.............**$150-$220**

Sony TR-86, eight transistors, Japan, 1958, colors: red, ivory, black and green; one of a handful of Sony radios to utilize reverse painting; about 100,000 sold..**$100-$150**

Windsor 6T-220, Japan, bold reverse pain, target design below tuning window, made by Fuji High Radio Frequency Lab Co. Ltd......................**$40-$80**

Toshiba 6TR-186, six transistors, Japan, circa 1958, lace-covered speaker, rare. ....**$300-$500**

Sony TR-66, six transistors, Japan, 1957, cream/red cabinet, also available with two-tone blue or two-tone green cabinet; rare – seldom seen TR-66 was Tokyo Tsushin Kogyo's follow-up to the TR-6. ..**$900-$1,500**

Toshiba 6TR-186, six transistors, Japan, circa 1958, also found with lace-covered speaker cover, generally more sought after by collectors. ....**$200-$300**

TRANSISTOR RADIOS

Toshiba 6TP-309A, Japan, colors: ivory, gray and black. ..... **$60-$80**

Toshiba 6TP-304, six transistors, Japan, circa 1958, colors: red, gray and ivory/yellow; nicknamed the "coffin" because of shape. ....**$200-$300**

Toshiba 8TP-90, eight transistors, Japan, circa 1960, concentric speaker design reminiscent of Studebaker grille, gold-colored plating.......................**$200-$300**

Zenith 500H, U.S., circa 1959, fifth-generation Royal 500, considered one of the best sounding/performing portable radios of all time, retailed for $59, approximately 250,000 radios sold.............................**$80-$150**

Zenith Royal 500B pink, U.S., 1957, second-generation Zenith Royal 500 more commonly referred to as the "B" series; first of the 500s to utilize a printed circuit board and the only time the radio was offered in pink and tan.......................**$80-$100**

Yaou 6, six transistors, Japan, 1960, ivory plastic front covered by a horizontal grille, upper dial area reverse-painted, filled with checkerboard design and topped with silver chevron, shirt-pocket size. ....**$80-$100**

Zephyr AR-600, Japan, 1959, translucent/lavender cabinet. ....**$80-$100**

Vintage Fashion

Throughout history, women have adorned themselves with the likes of found objects to create a look or style that is unique to them. Carryall bags and footwear were made from the hides of last night's dinner. It was quickly discovered that the head needed to be protected from the elements, so a good fur pelt became the most ideal source for warmth. In the tropics, raffia or straw hats were fashioned to shield one from the sun.

It was only a matter of time before these utilitarian items would be artistically adapted by the individual wearer, and fashion had begun.

Fashion changes over the next couple millennia were insignificant compared to the past couple of centuries. People were generally clothed in full-length garb with little variation in accessorizing.

It wasn't until the industrial revolution that we had the ability to mass produce items that would affect the buying and selling of fashionable frills. The more a machine could crank out, the less pricey these items became.

Of course, the best hats and shoes continue to be those of the handmade variety, but these goods are justifiably costly and may not be affordable to all. Mass production allows the manufacturer to lower the cost of their goods to the consumer since there is an unlimited supply.

Mink collar with pearls sewn on gold knitted base, 1950s. ... **$58**

Men and women alike utilize the availability of accessories to express their individuality. A businessman carefully chooses his tie so as not to offend his clients, whereas a salesman might choose a loud, showy one to attract customers. A woman of this same status might have a chic designer handbag on her arm or perhaps drape a graceful scarf around her neck.

The history of fashion is a mirror to the future. Nearly every style has already been done in some form and is reproduced with variations today. The popularity and demand for vintage pieces is growing because clothing and accessories are great collectibles that are also a good investment.

Many factors come into play when assessing value. When shopping vintage, keep the following in mind:

Popularity: How well known the designer is affects the price.

Condition: Collectors tend to want the original design and condition with no modifications or repairs.

Relevance: The piece should be a meaningful representation of a designer's work.

When you're hot you're hot: As a trend develops, it is shown in fashion magazines, and the original vintage pieces go up in value (and plummet when it goes out of favor).

Location: Prices fluctuate from one geographic region to another.

Value: The appeal of vintage items has greatly increased over the last few years. The rule of thumb is to buy quality.

For more information on vintage fashion, see *Warman's Handbags Field Guide* by Abigail Rutherford, *Vintage Fashion Accessories* by Stacy LoAlbo, and *Warman's Shoes Field Guide* by Caroline Ashleigh.

HANDBAGS

Belgian navy blue beaded evening bag with lighter blue bead design, flap front, snap closure, maker unknown, 20th century, 7-1/2" w. x 5-1/2" h............................**$54**

Heritage Auctions

Silver repoussé purse, maker unknown, circa 1950, marks: 925, 9.93 troy ounces, 3-3/8" x 5-5/8" not including handle. **$478**

Heritage Auctions

Rhinestone and yellow metal evening bag with rhinestones in red, black, and silver, set in yellow metal mesh bag, snap closure, French hallmarks, circa 1920, gross weight 184.10 grams, 6" x 4-5/8", purse suspends by yellow metal chain measuring 13"....................**$155**

Heritage Auctions

Designer lizard skin clutch bag, cream with various cylindrical-form stones inset into gold tone clasp, optional chain shoulder strap, label to interior, Judith Leiber, 20th century, 9" l. x 5" h. **$86**

Heritage Auctions

Gucci 1970s classic monogram multi-compartment change clutch, good condition, 9" w. x 6" h. x 1" d..**$161**

Heritage Auctions

Judith Leiber bright pink lizard long wallet in French purse style, frame clasp change purse, interior in pink with two slide compartments, six card compartments, change compartment; pristine condition, 7-1/2" w. x 3-1/2" h. x 1" d. **$100**

Heritage Auctions

Brown alligator clutch bag with a baby alligator to front flap, loop handle to top, maker unknown, 20th century, 11-1/2" w. x 8" h...............................**$54**

Heritage Auctions

Judith Leiber lilac velvet evening bag with enamel and crystal frame, interior in lilac satin, finished with neutral color enamel and crystal bow frame closure, hideable silver shoulder strap, excellent to pristine condition, comes in Judith Leiber box, 7" w. x 5" h. x 2" d.....................**$500**

Heritage Auctions

CLOTHING

Judith Leiber full-bead red, white and blue crystal minaudiere evening bag, interior in gold metallic leather, includes gold shoulder chain, excellent condition, 3" w. x 2-1/2" h. x 2-1/2" d.............. **$875**

Heritage Auctions

Vintage 1890s ladies silk blouse, lace cuffs and beadwork along lapel, decorative collar intact and matches insert.. **$10**

Heritage Auctions

Judith Leiber magenta satin and multicolor crystal top handle evening bag with shoulder strap, excellent condition, 6" w. x 5" h. x 3" d........................... **$406**

Heritage Auctions

Beaded clutch evening bag in dark green with paisley pattern made of pale green, black and gold beads, Dorian, 20th century, 12" w. x 5" h....................... **$77**

Heritage Auctions

Vintage black silk taffeta ladies blouse with tatting attached to collar for decoration, silk has some small tears through back and around seams................ **$39**

Heritage Auctions

Vintage two-piece dress and jacket, yellow silk with geometric design, blue and brown designs, dress is sleeveless with V-neck, applied flower and bow, pleated bottom, back zip, below knee length, jacket long sleeved, notch collar, open front and same length as dress, size small.............**$58**

iGavel Auctions

Vintage 1890s silk and brocade dress with bustle, white lace collar may have been a later addition to this ensemble, very fine condition. **$39**

Heritage Auctions

Vintage Adele Simpson silk one-shoulder gown, retailed by Sara Fredericks, labeled, navy blue and gray silk in star and polka dot pattern with hand-sewn silver beading accents, bust approximately 36, size large, 56"..............**$184**

Skinner, Inc., www.skinnerinc.com

Two vintage G.J.M./Goods silk dressing gowns, Newbury Street, Boston, one with matching nightgown, size medium.....................................**$98**

Skinner, Inc., www.skinnerinc.com

Farrah Fawcett tennis dress with shoes and sunglasses set: size 6 white tennis dress by A.J. Bari, size 9B beige shoes designed by Stuart Weitzman, pair of Steriflex sunglasses with rose-tinted lenses; all in excellent condition and accompanied by certificates of authenticity from Robert Johnson Memorabilia Collection....................................**$537**

Heritage Auctions

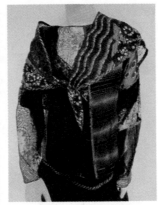

Four-piece vintage 1980s Koos Van Den Akker outfit by Koos Van Den Akker Couture; black cotton velvet two-tiered ruffled knee-length skirt with gold accents and side zipper, waist 28"; black brocade camisole with elastic waist and black lace trim, size medium; black sheer patchwork long-sleeve scoop neck blouse with black lace and geometric gold pattern panels, size medium; black and gold lace and Lurex patchwork shawl. **$58**

iGavel Auctions

Vicky Tiel couture cocktail dress, fitted short style constructed of various iridescent silk fabrics gathered throughout dress, fabric flowers at shoulders, size 4.... **$330**

Skinner, Inc., www.skinnerinc.com

Vintage black and white beaded caftan by Thea Porter, London, hook and eye front closure, beaded and sequined stripes, gold lurex ribbon accents, black piping trim, braided interior belt with belt holes at waist and black cord tassels on sides. **$2,256**

iGavel Auctions

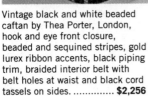

Silk taffeta vintage 1890s ladies blouse with lace embroidered decoration through bodice and around cuffs, all buttons are matching, little damage.........**$39**

Heritage Auctions

Vintage blue silk jersey knit dress and coat with multicolor floral and gemstone pattern by Leonard-Paris, dress has elbow-length tie puff sleeves, V-neck and hand sewn back zipper (size S-M), 50" tie belt included, matching jacket has long sleeves, open front and pleated shoulders. **$330**

iGavel Auctions

Velvet floral printed dress by Nanette Lepore, black and apple green floral print velvet dress on cream ground, dress has straight line fitted bodice, removable velvet straps, back zip closure and is knee length, size 10. ....**$90**

iGavel Auctions

Nolan Miller ruby red beaded chiffon gown and matching silk evening coat with Russian sable collar, and Bruno Magli shoes dyed to match for Barbara Stanwyck, worn at 1981 Academy Awards when she received an honorary Oscar. Dress: chiffon, silk twill, satin, bugle and rocaille beads, sequins; coat: silk twill, satin taffeta; dress and coat label: Nolan Miller. Shoe label: Bruno Magli made in Italy. Dress size: 6/8; shoe size: 8-1/2........ **$1,553**

Heritage Auctions

Reversible leopard print raincoat, black nylon and gray black and white cotton blend, no label, coat is knee length with front slip pockets, hidden snap front closure, size large. **$58**

iGavel Auctions

Vintage multicolor multi-pattern striped cotton blend quilted jacket by Mary McFadden, from Bergdorf Goodman, jacket has long sleeves, gold piping, size 12. .... **$174**

iGavel Auctions

Vintage ivory cotton-blend jersey knit sweater with multicolor stripes by Emanuel Ungaro Parallele Paris from Bergdorf Goodman, long sleeves, front patch pockets and open front, size large. **$58**

iGavel Auctions

Vintage ivory chiffon gown attributed to Madame Grès, unlabeled. **$237**

Skinner, Inc., www.skinnerinc.com

MEN'S ACCESSORIES

Three pairs of Gucci shoes, 1960s-1970s: brown suede loafers with gold metal detail on top, size 45; brown leather ankle boots with side buckle closure; cordovan leather loafers with gold metal detail on top. All marked "Gucci" either on inside or on sole, all with evident wear...................................**$1,255**

Heritage Auctions

Two pairs of dress shoes, 1960s-1970s: black leather oxfords, inside stamp reads "Wing by Bally of Switzerland," size 10-1/2 D; black leather loafers, inside stamps reads "Carroll & Co. Beverly Hills," size 11; both with evident wear. **$1,195**

Heritage Auctions

Victorian beaver top hat, Boston, circa 1880s, by Aborn, Washington & Boston, inside silk lining mostly missing, leather band intact with small cracks, 6" h. x 8-1/2" w. **$49**

Heritage Auctions

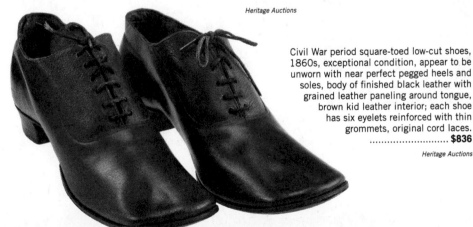

Civil War period square-toed low-cut shoes, 1860s, exceptional condition, appear to be unworn with near perfect pegged heels and soles, body of finished black leather with grained leather paneling around tongue, brown kid leather interior; each shoe has six eyelets reinforced with thin grommets, original cord laces. **$836**

Heritage Auctions

Watches

Collecting timepieces is not a new fad, but one enjoyed by men and women, the young and old alike. Essentially, there is something for everyone. Whether you collect by maker, by style or by the type of movement, you can find things for any budget.

Most everyone has a watch. They were given as graduation gifts from high school or college, something that was handed down to you from a family member, or potentially a gift received from a company you work for. By collecting watches, not only do you have a fun collectible, but it also has function.

Over the last 100+ years, millions of watches have been produced. Some were made for the masses, others made in very small quantities for a select few. There are dealers who specialize in watches, but they can also be found at flea markets, garage sales, auctions, on the Internet and at antique shops. Collecting creates an opportunity for you to have a watch for every occasion. You can have a watch to wear to work, one when out on the town, another one to use while participating in sports, and finally, an everyday watch.

The values placed on the watches illustrated in this section are market value, representing what they have recently sold for privately or at auction. Values can fluctuate due to many variables. How a watch is sold, where it is sold, and the condition all play a big role in the value.

The Internet has helped collectors identify watches worn by their favorite celebrity, worn on the moon, in a car race, in their favorite action film, etc.

One of the not-so-positive aspects of Internet collecting is the sheer volume of reproductions out there posing as authentic watches. They turn up everywhere, with links to professionally designed websites offering the best of the best for a discount, or up for bid on an Internet auction. You must keep in mind the old saying, "If it looks to good to be true, it probably is."

For more information on watches, see *Warman's Watches Field Guide* by Reyne Haines.

Elgin Father Time, 21-jewel pocket watch with wind indicator, open face, circa 1914, size 16....**$1,050**

Woody Auction

18k yellow gold men's Presidential Rolex watch, automatic, day, date, white gold dial and bezel, round dial and baguette-cut diamonds, bezel with round diamonds, approximately 8 ctw., 86.5 dwt.............**$10,800**

Morphy Auctions

Jaeger-LeCoultre Snowdrop
wristwatch. **$1,700**
Cordier Auctions

Limited edition Vacheron Constantin wristwatch, 250th anniversary
timepiece, circa 2005, 18k white gold case, automatic with 27 jewel
movement, adjusts to five positions, silver engine-turned dial with
applied baton markers and Roman numerals, two subsidiary dials for
day and date, fan form selector for power reserve, circular case, leather
strap, fitted stock case with paperwork....................................**$15,000**

John Moran Auctioneers

Original Rolex "Oyster Perpetual"
men's wristwatch, date adjust
chronometer, rare Roman
numerals, 31 jewels......... **$1,000**
Woody Auction

Swiss movement wristwatch offered by BMW dealers, automatic
operation with calendar and stylized speedometer, leather strap, original
case. **$575**

RM Auctions

◀ French sterling case pocket
watch, porcelain open face, circa
1820-1860, size 12. .... **$200**
Woody Auction

▶Tag Heuer Carrera automatic
men's watch, automatic movement,
stainless steel case, silver dial and
stainless steel strap. **$600**
Woody Auction

Men's Hublot "Big Bang" chronograph watch, 18k brushed rose gold bezel and case, model 301W S/N 643189 with original rubber band and 18k rose gold buckle, sapphire crystal, clear back and "H" style screws on bezel, Arabic numerals, chronograph stopwatch functions include red central seconds counter with "H" logo counterweight, approximately 6.5 oz...**$11,000**

Kaminski Auctions

Hamilton "Pacer" electric men's wristwatch, 10k gold-filled case, black leather band..............**$500**

Woody Auction

◄ Waltham 14k tri-color gold ladies pocket watch, engraved dust cover, fancy dial, hunter case, circa 1908, size "O." **$450**

Woody Auction

Girard Perregaux Sea Hawk men's wristwatch. **$250**

Woody Auction

Steinhausen "Flying Tourbillon" men's wristwatch, brown leather band...................................**$300**

Woody Auction

Swiss Lucien Piccard, 14k gold ladies wristwatch and band with diamond bezel....................**$450**

Woody Auction

TOP
LOT!

M.J. Tobias Liverpool 18k gold captain's watch with independent seconds, circa 1860s, engine turned front and back, gold chain and "spyglass" form winding key with inner photo of Bunker Hill Monument, Charleston, signed on cuvette, 118 grams.................................**$5,625**

Heritage Auctions

Patek Philippe 18k yellow gold annual calendar wristwatch with center seconds, moon phases and power reserve indication, circa 2008, Arabic numerals, outer minute track with luminous dots, subsidiary guilloche dials for days of week and months, brown band featuring 18k gold deployant clasp, all elements signed Patek Philippe Geneve. **$27,500**

Heritage Auctions

Swiss Patek Philippe, 18k gold ellipses men's wristwatch, black leather band, 18k gold buckle......................**$2,500**

Woody Auction

▶ American Waltham #645 pocket watch, 21 jewel, railroad grade with chain and attached pocket knife, circa 1968. ....**$300**

Woody Auction

▶ Moilliet Geneva enamel and gold pendant watch, circa 1860, 18k yellow gold, signed gold cuvette with champlevé polychrome enameled flowers and leaves, white enamel dial with Roman numerals and gold moon hands, signed Moilliet Geneva on cuvette. **$875**

Heritage Auctions

▼ Krigner rare early 18th century solar watch, oval gilt brass case, top chased and engraved, inner top engraved with latitudes for 30 Polish cities, movable silver hour ring adjusted for latitude, 3-1/4" x 2-1/4"................................**$4,062**

Heritage Auctions

Swiss Rose 14k gold retro watch, square-cut rubies and round single-cut diamonds, 17 jewels in all, manual wind, 30 mm x 15 mm. **$1,250**

Heritage Auctions

Bulova Accutron Spaceview men's wristwatch, circa 1961-1967, brown leather band. **$225**

Woody Auction

▶ E Vacheron & Constantin enamel and silver gold padlock form watch, circa 1908, hinged silver back with crystal over movement, front with gold screws, gold bezel and hinges, black inlaid enamel with swirls, blue Arabic numerals on raised white porcelain beads, dial and movement signed Vacheron & Constantin, signed Black Starr & Frost, 47 mm x 32 mm...... **$4,375**

Heritage Auctions

Wild West

Western Americana, or Wild West memorabilia and collectibles, generally refers to items that romanticize the settling of the American frontier. The term applies to a host of objects, ranging from wanted posters, knives, photographs, cowpoke items, railroad equipment, and so on. The most popular subjects include American Indians, cowboys, gold rush mementos, and ephemera from Wild West Shows, such as those performed by Annie Oakley or Wild Bill Hickok. Some collectors prefer to classify true Wild West memorabilia as authentic items used by the historical figures themselves, while others include factory-made items created to honor the history and folklore of this uniquely American collectible. The generally accepted timeframe for Wild West or Old West runs from about 1812 to a heavier emphasis on the years 1850-1900.

Sheet music, Buffalo Bill Wild West, the first: "Buffalo Bill Polka" composed by May Ostlere to commemorate the Wild West show's appearance in England as part of Queen Victoria's Golden Jubilee in 1887, four-color lithograph portrait, 13-1/4" x 9-7/8"; the second: "The Two Bills March Two-Step" composed by William Sweeney for the Wild West Cowboy Band, two-color lithograph cover with portraits of Buffalo Bill and Pawnee Bill, 13-3/4" x 10-3/4", published in New York in 1912; the third: "Special Song Book" published for Buffalo Bill and Pawnee Bill in Chicago in 1912. .... **$687**

Relic brooch, oval brooch, T-bar pin, holding one of the first gold flakes discovered at Sutter's Mill in Coloma, California, on Jan. 24, 1848 by James Wilson Marshall, housed under glass and surrounded by mother-of-pearl, 1-1/4" x 1". **$35,850**

Cane, mechanical folk art carved, Indian Wars, belonging to a member of 12th Infantry Regiment, U.S. Army, features head of a trooper, carved whale tooth or walrus tooth, separate cigar moves in and out of the trooper's mouth, band of copper or rose gold engraved: "B/12" (for Company B, 12th Regiment), shaft of snake wood, with copper tip, 35" l...................................... **$4,481**

Map, J[acob] De Cordova, Texas, "Compiled from the records of the General Land Office of the State, by Robert Creuzbaur, Revised & Corrected by Charles W. Pressler." New York: J. H. Colton & Co., 1857. Next to the title is printed, "Without my signature all copies of this map have been fraudulently obtained," followed by De Cordova's facsimile signature. Large format lithograph map, 33-1/2" x 36-1/4", colored by hand, showing counties, cities and towns, roads, rivers, and Indian villages. **$44,812**

Booklets, Buffalo Bill Wild West Courier Souvenir, set of two, 16 pages, illustrated, buffalo head courier, published in 1898...**$537**

Carte de visite, James Butler "Wild Bill" Hickok, period ink title "Wild Bill" below image, rare. Provenance: From the estate collection of E. F. Mueller. **$5,975**

Poster, Buffalo Bill's Wild West, "White Eagle Poster," in reference to Cody's nickname "The White Eagle," 1893, stone lithograph with nine-color printing and metallic gold by A. Hoen & Co., Baltimore, 22-1/4" x 27-1/4", rare. ...**$14,340**

Pipe belonging to Oglala Sioux Chief Little Wound, underside inscribed in period black ink: "Sioux Pipe from Little Wound Pine Ridge Agency Dakota Chiefs 'Little Wound' and 'Man Afraid of his Horse,'" high relief horned armorial heads, overall length including catlinite bowl 26". Little Wound took part in the 1873 Battle of Massacre Canyon in Nebraska between the Sioux and Pawnee, the last large-scale battle between Plains tribes (detail image at right).....**$3,883**

Photograph, George Armstrong Custer, half-plate ambrotype, leather case, original from-life photograph taken in or around September 1863 by William Frank Browne, only existing photograph from this session outside the collection of the National Gallery, Smithsonian Institution, 4-1/8" x 5-3/8".
.... **$83,650**

Cabinet photograph, Younger Gang: Cole, Jim, and Bob Younger with their sister Henrietta, taken at Stillwater Prison in 1889, rare. **$5,975**

World War II Collectibles

In the 68 years since the end of World War II, veterans, collectors, and history buffs have eagerly bought, sold and traded the "spoils of war." Actually, souvenir collecting began as soon as troops set foot on foreign soil. Soldiers from every nation involved in the greatest armed conflict mankind has known eagerly sought items that would remind them of their time in the service, validate their presence during the making of history, and potentially generate income when they returned home. Such items might also be bartered with fellow soldiers for highly prized or scarce goods. Helmets, medals, Lugers, field gear, daggers, and other pieces of war material filled parcels, which were mailed home or stuffed into the duffel bags of soldiers who gathered them.

As soon as hostilities ended in 1945, the populations of the defeated nations quickly realized that they could make money by selling souvenirs to their former enemies. This was particularly true in Germany and Japan, which hosted large contingents of occupying U.S. soldiers and troops from other Allied nations. The flow of war material increased. Values became well established. For instance, a Luger was worth several packs of cigarettes, a helmet, just one. A Japanese sword was worth two boxes of K-rations, and an Arisaka bayonet was worth a chocolate Hershey bar.

Over the years, these values have remained proportionally consistent. Today, that "two-pack" Luger might be worth $4,000 and that one-pack helmet $1,000. The Japanese sword might fetch $1,200 and the Arisaka bayonet $85. Though values have increased dramatically, demand has not slackened. In fact, World War II collecting is the largest segment of the militaria hobby.

The value of military items resides in variation. Whether it is a difference in manufacturing technique, material or markings, the nuances of an item will determine its true value. Do not expect 20 minutes on the Internet—or even glancing through this section—to teach these nuances. Collectors are a devoted group. They have spent years and hundreds, if not thousands, of dollars to establish the critical knowledge base that enables them to navigate through the hobby. This basic information may be used to assist in acquiring the necessary foundation of price negotiations.

U.S. Army Air Force banner, 13th Air Force unit, circa 1945, cloth, 13th insignia painted in middle, surrounded by female South Sea islander, palm tree, four aircraft, shark, 16 patches, medals, tie pins and badges, include names of locations the unit was in, cloth framed and glazed, 20" x 20"............ **$3,750**

Bonhams

Whether an individual is hoping to sell military items or to buy, chances are there is a military collector living in close proximity. Check your local classifieds. Advanced collectors will often run "Military Items Wanted" ads in local newspapers and classified ad websites. Even those hoping to buy items may call these people and initiate a conversation that will lead to subsequent deals.

Militaria shows take place throughout the U.S., Europe, and Japan. Ranging from just a dozen dealers to more than 2,000, these shows are still the best source of fresh material for the devoted collector.

For more information on World War II collectibles, see *Warman's World War II Collectibles Identification and Price Guide* by Michael E. Haskew.

Collection of nine Essex Class aircraft carrier shipyard launching ashtrays, made from aluminum, featuring U.S.S. Ticonderoga, U.S.S. Philippine Sea, U.S.S. Tarawa, U.S.S. Randolf, U.S.S. Bennington, U.S.S. Leyete, U.S.S. Valley Forge, together with circular ashtray for U.S.S. Ranger and model deck gun not shown, largest item 13" l. **$1,062**

Bonhams

Mahogany hat and glove box and items, box inlaid with image of submarine on hinged top, inside box are two white Navy visor caps, both with name of owner, a Naval lieutenant, on inside; olive drab cloth rain cover for visor cap, pair of grey suede dress gloves, and two flat wool campaign hats, one black and one grey. **$1,550**

Bonhams

B-17 Recognition Spotter Model Cruver, marked B-17 US July 42 British Fortress 2 on underside, small mold line imperfection on one wing, 17-1/4" x 12-1/2". **$175**

Noel Barrett Auctions

TOP! LOT!

Bronze edition of Arlington Marine Corps Memorial maquette, one of only seven to 10 examples cast from plaster original, circa 1948-1954, created by American decorative artist Felix de Weldon, part of a lot that included eight period photographs of bronze during time of presentation, featured in "Reporting the War" exhibit at National Portrait Gallery of Smithsonian Institution in 1944, 22" x 24" x 14" without flag. **$56,250**

Bonhams

World War II Japanese Naval bridge/conning tower "Big Eye" binoculars, circa 1943, includes objective lenses, folding sights, adjustable eye-piece with individual focusing, trunnion mounts with radial quadrant and handle, finished in original grey paint, fitted wooden box with lid inscribed The Superintendent/Admiralty Research Laboratory,/Teddington,/Middlesex./Via. S.N.S.O. at Ports concerned./Case No. E.C. 4624/155/from Capt., R. O-B. H.M.S. Euryalus, binoculars 9-3/4" x 22-1/4" x 16". Captured by a specialist in the Navy, the soldier, who was in charge of experimental mine sweeping during the war, submitted them to the Admiralty for examination, which in turn returned the binoculars to him after deeming they had no use for them. **$7,761**

Charles Miller Ltd.

U.S. military swivel bale helmet, green finish with tan netting, liner, web straps and chin strap, 11" x 9-1/4" x 7-1/4".. **$150**

Cordier Auctions

Eisenhower jacket worn by technical sergeant in 101st Airborne, insignia includes 101st division patch with Airborne tab, pair of Technical Sgt. stripes, nine months service stripes, overseas stripes, ruptured duck discharge patch, in addition to ribbons and badges such as jump wings, combat infantryman badge, European/Italy/North African campaign medal with battle stars, American Defense ribbon, Victory medal, Unit Commendation ribbon. **$375**

Cordier Auctions

U.S.M.C. backpack with trenching shovel with camo carrier, one box of unopened 12 gauge shells, 12 gauge wooden cleaning rod and brushes, poncho and shelter half, assembled pack 16" h. x 12" w. x 6" d.....**$210**

Cordier Auctions

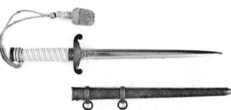

Nazi Army dagger with scabbard and Porte Pee, on underside of handle is medieval style helmet, opposite side decorated with Nazi eagle and symbol, 14-3/4" overall. **$375**

Cordier Auctions

German battle uniform including mannequin, side cap, long sleeve pullover undershirt, NCO combat tunic, combat gloves, pants with suspenders, marching boots with hobnail NCO rank, leather belt and Y straps, decorated with General's assault badge, iron cross 1st class, bronze wound badge, bronze 50-day close order combat class, gold cloth German cross and tank destruction badge, plus unopened pack of German cigarettes and French tobacco with smoking utensils in pocket. **$1,500**

Cordier Auctions

Hamilton Model 4992B United States Army Air Force navigation master pocket watch, stem wound, black 24-hour dial with white number markings, marked "G.C.T." for Greenwich Civil Time, used by navigator and pilot as airplane's master time source during World War II and after, 2" dia. **$450**

Cordier Auctions

U.S. Army Air Force reflex sight, manufactured by W. L. Maxson Corp., 17". Reflex sights came into use in military aircraft and firearms in World War II, although they were originally used by the military in the early 20th century... **$650**

Grogan Co.

Sixty-five mission decorated A-2 flight jacket belonging to Joseph W. Gould, sleeve length approximately 25". Gould served as a captain in the Air Force from 1942-1945; he flew in 65 successful missions over northern Italy and southern Germany, which is represented by 65 bomb patches on the right front of the jacket. Due to a head cold, he was grounded from joining his squadron on its 66th mission, from which the group never returned........................... **$1,200**

Cordier Auctions

Japanese type 14 leather holster, designed for type 14 Nambu pistol, wear consistent with age, 9-1/2" x 7-1/2" x 2-1/2"....................... **$250**

Cordier Auctions

Original ship's bell from HMS Activity, escort carrier of British Royal Navy during World War II, launched in 1942, period mounting with four brass supports, dolphin bases and crown surmount on octagonal wood table stand, 60". **$11,250**

Heritage Auctions, Inc.

Nazi unit police dress dagger, marked "CARL EICKHORN SOLIGEN" surrounding image of sitting squirrel with "C.E." stamped below it, left side of hilt stamped "P. Hi. 198," bird's head pommel with stag grip panels with two connecting rivets, police insignia, 19" overall. **$600**

Cordier Auction

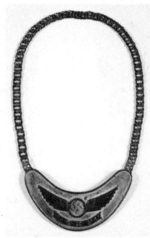

Nazi air traffic controller's gorget with link chain and "REICHS-LUFT-AUFSICHT" label under Nazi symbol, 6-1/4" x 3-1/2.".......**$950**

Cordier Auctions

U.S.M.C. jungle pack with 18" jungle machete and sheath, trenching shovel with canvas carrier, and jungle hammock. **$300**

Cordier Auctions

Three Hitler youth ornaments: Hitler Youth Air Raid helper's sleeve diamond backed with German newspaper, Hitler Youth arm band, and Hitler Youth shoulder board. **$100**

Cordier Auctions

Barr and Stroud Field Rangefinder, circa 1945, 80 cm base, used to measure distances from 500 to 20,000 yards, standard equipment in most of Europe's armies before World War I, 36" l. x 2-1/4" d. **$170**

Cordier Auctions

Japanese signed officer's samurai sword, Army brown cord-wrapped white rayskin grip with gilt cherry blossom menuki, typical gilt brass floral decorated tsuba, 37" overall... **$800**

Cordier Auctions

Japanese officer's uniform and related items, cap with chin strap and Imperial star, tunic, combat pants, officer's highcut pigskin boots, white cotton gloves, NCO leather utility belt, leather sword belt hanger, leather ammo pouch, artillery range finder, map case with strap, eyeglasses and case compass with leather pouch, 9x24mm binoculars with carrying case, canteen with carrying strap, raincoat, and officer's leather backpack with bound ledger written in Japanese. **$1,000**

Cordier Auctions

U.S.A.A.F. Major General Ike jacket attributed to Claire Lee Chennault, commander of famous Flying Tigers; on inside right breast pocket is a laundry tag ink-stamped with "CHENNAULT" and number "49837" in black ink, plus Major General screwback stars, clutch back officer U.S. insignia on lapels, embroidered 14th Air Force patch, service ribbons including Distinguished Service Medal, Outstanding Unit Award with oak cluster, American Defense Medal and Legion of Merit, U.S. Army service cap in size 7 with Flight Ace label, sweatband stamped "CLC" (Claire L. Chennault) in gold and ink stamped "M-837." Chennault entered the U.S. Army in 1917, retired from Army Air Corps in 1937, went to China and became the director of the Chinese Air Force Flight School, then became the leader of an international air force (American Volunteer Group) that flew P-40 fighters painted with shark faces, and went on to become one of the most recognized fighter squadrons of World War II. Chennault later commanded the 14th Air Force and served as president of the Civil Air Transports from 1946-1950... **$2,250**

Rock Island Auction Co.

Nazi Panzer collar tabs with metal skulls mounted on black felt bordered in silver/gray cord, 2-1/4" x 1-5/8"... **$110**

Cordier Auctions

Rare Lange & Söhne German Air Force watch, circa 1942, matte gray, anti-corrosion nickel, snap back, body engraved FL 23883 on rim, 55 mm, concave lugs, large winding crown, frosted gilt finish, band in tan leather with steel buckle, triple signed A. Lange & Söhne...**$10,625**

Heritage Auctions

Special Contributors and Advisors

The following collectors, dealers, sellers, and researchers have supported the *Antique Trader Antiques & Collectibles Price Guide* with their pricing and contacts for nearly 30 years. Many continue to serve as a valuable resource to the entire collecting hobby, while others have passed away. We honor all contributors past and present as their hard work and passion lives on through this book.

Andre Ammelounx

Mannie Banner

Ellen Bercovici

Sandra Bondhus

James R. and Carol S. Boshears

Bobbie Zucker Bryson

Emmett Butler

Dana Cain

Linda D. Carannante

David Chartier

Les and Irene Cohen

Amphora Collectors International

Marion Cohen

Neva Colbert

Marie Compton

Susan N. Cox

Caroline Torem-Craig

Leonard Davis

Bev Dieringer

Janice Dodson

Del E. Domke

Debby DuBay

Susan Eberman

Joan M. George

Roselyn Gerson

William A. and Donna J. Gray

Pam Green

Linda Guffey

Carl Heck

Alma Hillman

K. Robert and Bonne L. Hohl

Ellen R. Hill

Joan Hull

Hull Pottery Association

Louise Irvine

Helen and Bob Jones

Mary Ann Johnston

Donald-Brian Johnson

Dorothy Kamm

Edwin E. Kellogg

Madeleine Kirsh

Vivian Kromer

Curt Leiser

Gene Loveland

Mary McCaslin

Pat Moore

Reg G. Morris

Craig Nissen

Joan C. Oates

Margaret Payne

Gail Peck

John Petzold

Dr. Leslie Piña

Joseph Porcelli

Arlene Rabin

John Rader, Sr.

Betty June Wymer

LuAnn Riggs

Tim and Jamie Saloff

Federico Santi

Peggy Sebek

Steve Stone

Phillip Sullivan

Mark and Ellen Supnick

Tim Trapani

Jim Trautman

Elaine Westover

Kathryn Wiese

Laurie Williams

Nancy Wolfe

Contributors by Subject

Advertising Items: Donald-Brian Johnson/
              Antoinette Rahn
Barbie: Steve Evans/Antoinette Rahn
Books: Karen Knapstein/Mary Sieber
Bottles: Michael Polak
Clocks: Antoinette Rahn/Donald-Brian Johnson
Cloisonné: Arlene Rabin
Compacts & Vanity Cases: Roselyn Gerson
Country Store: Donald-Brian Johnson/Eric Bradley
Disney Collectibles: Eric Bradley/Antoinette Rahn
Hooked Rugs: Karen Knapstein
Jewelry (Costume): Kathy Flood
Kitchenwares (vintage): Chriss Swaney/
              Karen Knapstein
Lady Head vases: Donald-Brian Johnson
Electric Lighting: Joseph Porcelli
Early Lighting: Donald-Brian Johnson
Moss Lamps: Donald-Brian Johnson
Nativity Sets: Donald-Brian Johnson
Plant Waterers: Bobbie Zucker Bryson
Pop Culture Collectibles: Dana Cain and
              Emmett Butler
Ribbon Dolls: Bobbie Zucker Bryson
Salesman Samples: Karen Knapstein
Samplers: Donald-Brian Johnson/Karen Knapstein
Sports: Tom Bartsch
Steins: Andre Ammelounx
Vintage Clothing: Nancy Wolfe and Madeleine Kirsh
Watches: Antoinette Rahn
World War II: Antoinette Rahn

CERAMICS

Abingdon: Elaine Westover
American Painted Porcelain: Dorothy Kamm
Amphora-Teplitz: Les and Irene Cohen
Bauer Pottery: James Elliott-Bishop
Belleek (American): Peggy Sebek
Belleek (Irish): Del Domke
Blue & White Pottery: Steve Stone
Blue Ridge Dinnerwares: Marie Compton
              and Susan N. Cox
Brayton Laguna Pottery: Susan N. Cox
Buffalo Pottery: Phillip Sullivan
Caliente Pottery: Susan N. Cox
Catalina Island Pottery: James Elliott-Bishop
Ceramic Arts Studio of Madison: Donald-Brian
              Johnson
Clarice Cliff Designs: Laurie Williams
Cleminson Clay: Susan N. Cox
deLee Art: Susan N. Cox
Doulton/Royal Doulton: Reg Morris, Louise Irvine
              and Ed Pascoe
East Liverpool Potteries: William and Donna J. Gray
Fine Art: Antoinette Rahn
Flow Blue: K. Robert and Bonne L. Hohl
Franciscan Ware: James Elliott-Bishop/Eric Bradley
Frankoma Pottery: Susan N. Cox

Fulper Pottery: Eric Bradley
Gonder Pottery: James R. and Carol S. Boshears
Gouda: Antoinette Rahn
Haeger: Donald-Brian Johnson
Hall China: Marty Kennedy
Haviland: Eric Bradley
Hedi Schoop: Donald-Brian Johnson
Harker: William A. and Donna J. Gray
Hull: Joan Hull
Ironstone: General - Bev Dieringer; Tea Leaf -
              The Tea Leaf Club International
Limoges: Eric Bradley
Majolica: Michael Strawser
McCoy: Craig Nissen
Mettlach: Andre Ammelounx
Noritake: Tim Trapani
Old Ivory: Alma Hillman
Overbeck: Karen Knapstein
Pacific Clay Products: Susan N. Cox
Phoenix Bird & Flying Turkey: Joan Collett Oates
Pierce (Howard) Porcelains: Susan N. Cox
Quimper: Sandra Bondhus
Red Wing: Gail Peck
Royal Bayreuth: Mary McCaslin
Rozart Pottery: Susan N. Cox
R.S. Prussia: Mary McCaslin
Russel Wright Designs: Kathryn Wiese
Satsuma: Melody Amsel-Arieli
Schoop (Hedi) Art Creations: Susan N. Cox
Shawnee: Linda Guffey
Shelley China: Mannie Banner; David Chartier;
              Bryand Goodlad; Edwin E. Kellogg;
              Gene Loveland and Curt Leiser
Stoneware and Spongeware: Bruce and Vicki Waasdorp
Sumida Gawa: Karen Knapstein
Vernon Kilns: Pam Green
Warwick China: John Rader, Sr.
Zeisel (Eva) Designs: Kathryn Wiese
Zsolnay: Federico Santi/ John Gacher

GLASS

Animals: Helen and Bob Jones
Carnival Glass: Jim and Jan Seeck, Ellen T. Schroy
Crackle Glass: Donald-Brian Johnson
Custard Glass: James Measall
Depression Glass: Ellen T. Schroy
Fenton: Helen and Bob Jones; Mark F. Moran
Fire-King: Karen Knapstein
Higgins Glass: Donald-Brian Johnson
Milk Glass: Karen Knapstein
New Martinsville: Helen and Bob Jones
Opalescent Glass: James Measell
Paden City: Helen and Bob Jones
Phoenix Glass: Helen and Bob Jones
Schneider Glass: Donald-Brian Johnson
Sugar Shakers: Scott Beale
Wall Pocket Vases: Bobbie Zucker Bryson

SPECIAL CONTRIBUTORS

Pricing, Identifications, and Images Provided By:

Live Auction Providers

AuctionZip
113 West Pitt St., Suite C
Bedford, PA 15522
(814) 623-5059
www.auctionzip.com

Artfact, LLC.
38 Everett St.
Suite 101
Allston, MA 02134
(617) 746-9800
www.artfact.com

LiveAuctioneers LLC
2nd Floor
220 12th Ave.
New York, NY 10001
www.liveauctioneers.com

Auction Houses

A-1 Auction
2042 N Rio Grande Ave., Suite E
Orlando, FL 32804
(407) 839-0004
a-1auction@cfl.rr.com
http://www.a-1auction.net/

Allard Auctions, Inc.
P.O. Box 1030
St. Ignatius, MT 59865
(406) 745-0500
(800) 314-0343
www.allardauctions.com

American Bottle Auctions
2523 J St., Suite 203
Sacramento, CA 95816
(800) 806-7722
americanbottle.com

American Pottery Auction
Vicki and Bruce Waasdorp
P.O. Box 434
Clarence, NY 14031
(716) 759-2361
www.antiques-stoneware.com

Antique Helper Auction House
2764 East 55th Pl.
Indianapolis, IN 46220
(317) 251-5635
www.antiquehelper.com

Apple Tree Auction Center
1616 West Church St.
Newark, OH 43055-1540
(740) 344-4282
www.appletreeauction.com

Artingstall & Hind Auctioneers
9312 Civic Center Dr. # 104
Beverly Hills, CA 90210
(310) 424 5288
www.artingstall.com

Arus Auctions
www.arusauctions.com
arusauctions@gmail.com
(617) 669-6170

ATM Antiques & Auctions, LLC
811 SE US Hwy. 19
Crystal River, FL 34429
(352) 795-2061
(800) 542-3877
www.charliefudge.com

Auction Team Breker
Otto-Hahn-Str. 10
50997 Köln (Godorf), Germany
02236 384340
www.breker.com

Bertoia Auctions
2141 DeMarco Dr.
Vineland, NJ 08360
(856) 692-1881
www.bertoiaauctions.com

Bonhams
7601 W. Sunset Blvd.
Los Angeles CA 90046
323-850-7500
www.bonhams.com

Brunk Auctions
P.O. Box 2135
Asheville, NC 28802
(828) 254-6846
www.brunkauctions.com

Charles Miller Ltd.
Suite 6 Imperial Studios
3/11 Imperial Rd.
London, England
SW6 2AG
+44 (0) (207) 806-5530
www.charlesmillerltd.com

Charlton Hall Auctioneers
912 Gervais St.
Columbia, SC 29201
www.charltonhallauctions.com

Cherryland Postcard Auctions
Ronald & Alec Millard
P.O. Box 427
Frankfort, MI 49635
231-352-9758
CherrylandPostcards.com

Christie's New York
20 Rockefeller Plaza
New York, NY 10020
www.christies.com

Cincinnati Art Galleries
225 East Sixth St.
Cincinnati, OH 45202
www.cincinnatiartgalleries.com

Clars Auction Gallery
5644 Telegraph Ave.
Oakland, CA 94609
(510) 428-0100
www.clars.com

The Coeur d'Alene Art Auction
8836 North Hess St., Suite B
Hayden, ID 83835
(208) 772-9009
www.cdaartauction.com

John W. Coker, Ltd.
1511 W. Hwy. 11E
New Market, TN 37820
(865) 475-5163
john@antiquesonline.com
www.antiquesonline.com

Collect Auctions
(888) 463-3063
collectauctions.com

Conestoga Auction Co.
768 Graystone Rd.
Manheim, PA 17545
(717) 898-7284
www.conestogaauction.com

Cordier Auctions
1500 Paxton St.
Harrisburg, PA 17104
(717) 731-8662
www.cordierantiques.com

Cowan's Auctions
6270 Este Ave.
Cincinnati, OH 45232
(513) 871-1670
www.cowanauctions.com

CRN Auctions, Inc.
57 Bay State Rd.
Cambridge, MA 02138
(617) 661-9582
www.crnauctions.com

Dargate Auction Galleries
326 Munson Ave.
McKees Rocks, PA 15136
(412) 771-8700
Fax (412) 771-8779
www.dargate.com

DGW Auctioneers & Appraisers
760 Kifer Rd.
Sunnyvale, CA 94086
www.dgwauctioneers.com

Dickins Auctioneers Ltd.
Calvert Rd.
Middle Claydon
Buckingham, England
MK18 2EZ
+44 (129) 671-4434
www.dickinsauctioneers.com

Doyle New York
175 E. 87th St.
New York, NY 10128
(212) 427-2730
www.doylenewyork.com

Dreweatts Auctions Bloomsbury
24 Maddox St.
London, England W1S 1PP
+44 (207) 495-9494
www.dnfa.com

Elite Decorative Arts
1034 Gateway Blvd. #108
Boynton Beach, FL 33426
(561) 200-0893
www.eliteauction.com

Frasher's Doll Auction
2323 S. Mecklin Sch. Rd.
Oak Grove, MO 64075
(816) 625-3786

Fontaines Auction Gallery
1485 W. Housatonic St.
Pittsfield, MA 01210
www.fontainesauction.net

Forsythes' Auctions LLC
P.O. Box 188
Russellville, OH 45168
(937) 377-3700
www.forsythesauctions.com

Fox Auctions
P.O. Box 4069
Vallejo, CA 94590
(631) 553-3841
Fax (707) 643-3000
foxauctions@yahoo.com
www.foxauctionsonline.com

J. Garrett Auctioneers, Ltd.
1411 Slocum St.
Dallas, TX 75207
(214) 683-6855
www.jgarrettauctioneers.com

Garth's Arts & Antiques
P.O. Box 369
Delaware, OH 43015
(740) 362-4771
www.garths.com

Glass Works Auctions
Box 180
East Greenville, PA 18041
(215) 679-5849
www.glswrk-auction.com

The Golf Auction
209 State St.
Oldsmar, FL 34677
(813) 340-6179
thegolfauction.com

Great Gatsby's Antiques and Auctions
5180 Peachtree Industrial Blvd.
Atlanta, GA 30341
(770) 457-1903
www.greatgatsbys.com

Grogan & Co.
22 Harris St.
Dedham, MA 02026
(781) 461-9500
www.groganco.com

Guyette, Schmidt & Deeter
24718 Beverly Rd.
St. Michaels, MD 21663
(410) 745-0485
Fax (410) 745-0487
decoys@guyetteandschmidt.com
www.guyetteandschmidt.com

GWS Auctions, LLC
41841 Beacon Hill # E
Palm Desert, CA 92211
(760) 610-4175
www.gwsauctions.com

Ken Farmer Auctions and Appraisals
105 Harrison St.
Radford, VA 24141
(540) 639-0939
www.kfauctions.com

Hake's Americana & Collectibles
P.O. Box 12001
York, PA 17402
(717) 434-1600
www.hakes.com

Hamilton's Antique & Estate Auctions, Inc.
505 Puyallup Ave.
Tacoma, WA 98421
(253) 534-4445
www.joe-frank.com

Norman Heckler & Co.
79 Bradford Corner Rd.
Woodstock Valley, CT 06282
www.hecklerauction.com

Heritage Auctions
3500 Maple Ave.
Dallas, TX 75219-3941
(800) 872-6467
www.ha.com

Hess Fine Auctions
1131 4th St. N.
St. Petersburg, FL 33701
(727) 896-0622
www.hessfineauctions.com

Hewlett's Antique Auctions
PO Box 87
13286 Jefferson St.
Le Grand, CA 95333
(209) 389-4542
Fax (209) 389-0730
hewlettsdirect@sbcglobal.net
http://www.hewlettsauctions.com/

**Bill Hood & Sons Art
& Antique Auctions**
2925 S. Federal Hwy
Delray Beach, FL 33483
(561) 278-8996
www.hoodauction.com

Humler & Nolan
The Auctions at Rookwood
225 E. Sixth Street, 4th Floor
Cincinnati, OH 45202
(513) 381-2041
fax (513) 381-2038
info@humlernolan.com
www.humlernolan.com

iGavel Auctions
229 E. 120th St.
New York, NY 10035
(212) 289-5588
www.igavelauctions.com

Ivey-Selkirk Auctioneers
7447 Forsyth Blvd.
Saint Louis, MO 63105
(314) 726-5515
www.iveyselkirk.com

Ivy Auctions
22391 Hwy. 76 E
Laurens, SC 29360
(864) 682-2750
www.ivyauctions.com

**Jackson's International
Auctioneers & Appraisers**
2229 Lincoln St.
Cedar Falls, IA 50613
jacksonsauction.com

James D. Julia, Inc.
P.O. Box 830
203 Skowhegan Rd.
Fairfield, ME 04937
(207) 453-7125
jamesdjulia.com

Jeffrey S. Evans & Associates
2177 Green Valley Ln.
Mount Crawford, VA 22841
(540) 434-3939
www.jeffreysevans.com

John Moran Auctioneers
735 West Woodbury Rd.
Altadena, CA 91001
(626) 793-1833
www.johnmoran.com

Julien's Auctions
9665 Wilshire Blvd. Suite 150
Beverly Hills, CA 90210
(310) 836-1818
www.juliensauctions.com

Kaminski Auctions
564 Cabot St.
Beverly, MA 01915
(978) 927-2223
fax (978) 927-2228
http://www.kaminskiauctions.com/

Kennedy Auctions Service
160 West Court Ave.
Selmer, TN 38375
(731) 645-5001
www.kennedysauction.com

Legend Numismatics
P.O. Box 9
Lincroft, NJ 07738
(800) 743-2646
www.legendcoin.com

Legendary Auctions
17542 Chicago Ave.
Lansing, IL 60438
(708) 889-9380
www.legendaryauctions.com

Los Angeles Modern Auctions
16145 Hart St.
Van Nuys, CA 91406
(323) 904-1950
www.lamodern.com

Leslie Hindman Auctioneers
1338 West Lake St.
Chicago, IL 60607
(312) 280-1212
www.lesliehindman.com

**Louis J. Dianni, LLC Antiques
Auctions**
May 1-Oct. 15:
982 Main St., Suite 175
Fishkill, NY 12524
Oct. 20-April 15:
1304 SW 160th Ave., Suite 228A
Sunrise, FL 33326
https://louisjdianni.com

Love of the Game Auctions
P.O. Box 157
Great Meadows, NJ 07838
loveofthegameauctions.com

Manitou Auctions
205 Styer Dairy Rd.
Reidsville, NC 27320
(336) 349-6577
www.manitou-auctions.com

Manor Auctions
2415 N Monroe St.
Tallahassee, FL 32303
(850) 523-3787
Fax (850) 523-3786
www.manorauctions.com

**Mark Mattox Auctioneer & Real
Estate Broker, Inc.**
3740 Maysville Rd.
Carlisle, KY 40311
(859) 289-5720
http://mattoxauctions.com/auctions/

Martin J. Donnelly Antique Tools
5523 County Rd. 8
Avoca, NY 14809
(607) 566-2617
www.mjdtools.com

Matt Maring Auction Co.
P.O. Box 37
Kenyon, MN 55946
(507) 789-5227
www.maringauction.com

Material Culture
4700 Wissahickon Ave.
Philadelphia, PA 19144
(215) 849-8030
www.materialculture.com

Matthews Auctions
111 South Oak St.
Nokomis, IL 62075-1337
(215) 563-8880
www.matthewsauctions.com

McLaren Auction Service
21507 Highway 99E
Aurora, OR 97002
(503) 678-2441
www.mclarenauction.com

McMasters-Harris Auction Co.
P.O. Box 755
Cambridge, OH 43725
www.mcmastersharris.com

Michaan's Auctions
2751 Todd St.
Alameda, CA 94501
(510) 740-0220
www.michaans.com

Midwest Auction Galleries
925 North Lapeer Rd.
Oxford, MI 48371
(877) 236-8181 or (248) 236-8100
Fax (248) 236-8396
sales@midwestauctioninc.com
www.midwestauctioninc.com

Mile High Card Co.
7200 S. Alton Way, Suite A230
Centennial, CO 80112
(303) 840-2784
www.milehighcardco.com

Dan Morphy Auctions
2000 N. Reading Rd.
Denver, PA 17517
(717) 335-3435
morphyauctions.com

Mohawk Arms Inc.
P.O. Box 157 Bouckville, NY 13310
(315) 893-7888
www.militaryrelics.com

Mosby & Co. Auctions
5714-A Industry Ln.
Frederick, MD 21704
(240) 629-8139
www.mosbyauctions.com

Neal Auction Co.
4038 Magazine St.
New Orleans, LA 70115
(504) 899-5329
www.nealauctions.com

Nest Egg Auctions
30 Research Pkwy.
Meriden, CT 06450
(203) 630-1400
www.nesteggauctions.com

New Orleans Auction Gallery
1330 St. Charles Ave.
New Orleans, LA 70130
www.neworleansauction.com

Nico Auctions
4023 Kennett Pike, Suite 248
Greenville, DE 19807
(888) 390-0201
www.nicoauctions.com

**Noel Barrett Vintage Toys @
Auction**
P.O. Box 300
Carversville, PA 18913
(215) 297 5109
toys@noelbarrett.com
www.noelbarrett.com

North American Auction Co.
78 Wildcat Way
Bozeman, MT 59718
(800) 686-4216
northamericanauctioncompany.com

Northeast Auctions
93 Pleasant St.
Portsmouth, NH 03801
(603) 433-8400
Fax: (603) 433-0415
contact@northeastauctions.com
www.northeastauctions.com

**O'Gallerie: Fine Arts, Antiques
and Estate Auctions**
228 Northeast 7th Ave.
Portland, OR 97232-2909
(503) 238-0202
www.ogallerie.com

Omaha Auction Center
7531 Dodge St.
Omaha, NE 68114
(402) 397-9575
www.omahaauctioncenter.com

**Pacific Galleries Auction House
and Antique Mall**
241 South Lander St.
Seattle, WA 98134
(206) 441-9990
Fax (206) 448-9677
www.pacgal.com

Past Tyme Pleasures
39 California Ave., Suite 105
Pleasanton, CA 94566
www.pasttyme1.com

PBA Galleries
133 Kearny St., 4th Floor
San Francisco, CA 94108
(415) 989-2665
www.pbagalleries.com

Phoebus Auction Gallery
18 East Mellen St.
Hampton, VA 23663
(757) 722-9210
www.phoebusauction.com

Pioneer Auction Gallery
14650 SE Arista Dr.
Portland, OR 97267
(503) 496-0303
bidpioneer@aol.com
www.pioneerantiqueauction.com

Pook & Pook, Inc.
463 East Lancaster Ave.
Downingtown, PA 19335
(610) 269-4040
info@pookandpook.com
www.pookandpook.com

Potter & Potter Auctions
3759 N Ravenswood Ave #121
Chicago, IL 60613
(773) 472-1442
info@potterauctions.com
www.potterauctions.com

Premier Auction Galleries
12587 Chillicothe Rd.
Chesterland, OH 44026
(440) 688-4203
Fax (440) 688-4202
jessemathews@pag4u.com
http://www.pag4u.com

Don Presley Auction
1319 West Katella Ave.
Orange County, CA 92867
(714) 633-2437
www.donpresley.com

Preston Hall Gallery
2201 Main St. Suite #820
Dallas, TX 75201
(214) 718-8624
www.prestonhallgallery.com

Profiles in History
26901 Agoura Rd., Suite 150
Calabasas Hills, CA 91301
(310) 859-7701
www.profilesinhistory.com

Purcell Auction Gallery
2156 Husband Rd.
Paducah, KY 42003
(270) 444-7599
purcellauction@bellsouth.net
http://www.purcellauction.com/

Quinn's Auction Galleries
360 S. Washington St.
Falls Church, VA 22046
(703) 532-5632
www.quinnsauction.com

Rago Arts & Auction Center
333 N. Main St.
Lambertville, NJ 08530
(609) 397-9374
www.ragoarts.com

Red Baron's Antiques
8655 Roswell Rd.
Atlanta, GA 30350
(770) 640-4604
www.rbantiques.com

Richard Opfer Auctioneering, Inc.
1919 Greenspring Dr.
Lutherville-Timonium, MD 21093
(410) 252-5035
www.opferauction.com

Rich Penn Auctions
P.O. Box 1355
Waterloo, IA 50704
(319) 291-6688
www.richpennauctions.com

RM Auctions
One Classic Car Dr.
Blenheium, Ontario
N0P 1A0 Canada
+1 (519) 352-4575
www.rmauctions.com

Robert Edward Auctions
P.O. Box 7256
Watchung, NJ 07069
(908) 226-9900
www.robertedwardauctions.com

Rock Island Auction Co.
7819 42 St. West
Rock Island, IL 61201
(800) 238-8022
www.rockislandauction.com

RR Auction
5 Route 101A, Suite 5
Amherst, NH 03031
(603) 732-4280
www.rrauction.com

Saco River Auction Co.
2 Main Street
Biddeford, ME 04005
(207) 602-1504
www.sacoriverauction.com

Scheerer McCulloch Auctioneers
515 E Paulding Rd.
Fort Wayne, IN 46816
(260) 441-8636
www.smauctioneers.com

SCP Auctions, Inc.
32451 Golden Lantern, Suite 308
Laguna Niguel, CA 92677
(949) 831-3700
www.SCPauctions.com

Seeck Auction Co.
Jim and Jan Seeck
P.O. Box 377
Mason City, IA 50402
www.seeckauction.com

SeriousToyz
1 Baltic Pl.
Croton on Hudson, NY 10520
(866) 653-8699
www.serioustoyz.com

Showtime Auction Service
22619 Monterey Dr.
Woodhaven, MI 48183-2269
www.showtimeauctions.com

Skinner, Inc.
357 Main St.
Boston, MA 01740
617-350-5400
www.skinnerinc.com

**Sloans & Kenyon Auctioneers
and Appraisers**
7034 Wisconsin Ave.
Chevy Chase, MD 20815
(301) 634-2330
www.sloansandkenyon.com

Sotheby's New York
1334 York Ave.
New York, NY 10021
(212) 606-7000
www.sothebys.com

Specialists of the South, Inc.
544 E. Sixth St.
Panama City, FL 32401
(850) 785-2577
www.specialistsofthesouth.com

Stanley Gibbons
399 Strand
London, England
WC2R 0LX
+44 (0)207 836 8444
www.stanleygibbons.com

**Stefek's Auctioneers &
Appraisers**
18450 Mack Ave.
Grosse Pointe Farms, MI 48236
(313) 881-1800
www.stefeksltd.com

**Stephenson's Auctioneers &
Appraisers**
1005 Industrial Blvd.
Southampton, PA 18966
(215) 322-6182
www.stephensonsauction.com

Stevens Auction Co.
301 North Meridian St.
Aberdeen, MS 39730-2613
(662) 369-2200
www.stevensauction.com

Strawser Auction Group
200 N. Main St.
P.O. Box 332
Wolcottville, IN 46795
www.strawserauctions.com

Sullivan & Son Auction, LLC
1995 E. County Rd. 650
Carthage, IL 62321
(217) 743-5200
www.sullivanandsonauction.com

Swann Auction Galleries
104 E 25th St., # 6
New York, NY 10010-2999
(212) 254-4710
www.swanngalleries.com

Teel Auction Services
619 FM 2330
Montabla, TX 75853
(903) 724-4079
jteelenterprises@aol.com
www.teelauctionservices.com

Theriault's – The Doll Masters
P.O. Box 151
Annapolis, MD 21404
(800) 638-0422
www.theriaults.com

**Thomaston Place Auction
Galleries**
51 Atlantic Hwy.
Thomaston, ME 04861
(207) 354-8141
www.thomastonauction.com

John Toomey Gallery
818 North Blvd.
Oak Park, IL 60301

Tradewinds Antiques & Auctions
24 Magnolia Ave.
Manchester-by-the-Sea, MA 01944
(978) 526-4085
www.tradewindsantiques.com

Treadway Gallery, Inc.
2029 Madison Rd.
Cincinnati, OH 45208
www.treadwaygallery.com

Turkey Creek Auctions, Inc.
13939 N. Hwy. 441
Citra, FL 32113
(352) 622-4611
(800) 648-7523
www.antiqueauctionsfl.com

Vero Beach Auction
492 Old Dixie Hwy.
Vero Beach, FL 32962
(772) 978-5955
Fax (772) 978-5954
verobeachauction@bellsouth.net
www.verobeachauction.com

**Victorian Casino Antiques
Auction**
4520 Arville St. #1
Las Vegas, NV 89103
(702) 382-2466
www.vcaauction.com

Philip Weiss Auctions
74 Merrick Rd.
Lynbrook, NY 11563
(516) 594-0731
www.weissauctions.com

**William J. Jenack Estate
Appraisers & Auctioneers**
62 Kings Highway Bypass
Chester, NY 10918
(877) 282-8503
info@jenack.com
www.jenack.com

Witherell's Art & Antiques
300 20th St.
Sacramento, CA 95811
(916) 446-6490
witherells.com

Woodbury Auction, LLC
50 Main St. N.
Woodbury, CT 06798
(203) 266-0323
info@woodburyauction.com
www.woodburyauction.com

Woody Auction
317 S. Forrest St.
Douglass, KS 67039
(316) 747-2694
www.woodyauction.com

Wright
1440 W. Hubbard St.
Chicago, IL 60642
(312) 563-0020
www.wright20.com

Zurko Promotions
115 E. Division St.
Shawano, WI 54166
www.zurkopromotions.com

Additional Photographs and Research Provided By:

45cat.com, an online archive dedicated to the magic of the vinyl 7" single; Belleek Collectors International Society, www.belleek.ie/collectors-society; CAS Collectors, www.cascollectors.com and www.ceramicartstudio.com; International Perfume Bottle Association, www.perfumebottles.org; National Association of Warwick China & Pottery Collectors; popsike.com, Rare Records Auction Results; Red Wing Collectors Society, www.redwingcollectors.org; and Tea Leaf Club International, www.tealeafclub.com.

Index